ANDY STEVES'
EUROPE

CITY-HOPPING ON A BUDGET

CONTENTS

Modern travelers have the world at their fingertips thanks to mobile technology. Budget airlines and online resources have turned backpackers into shrewd precision travelers, city-hopping across Europe at the spur of the moment. We're visiting cities rather than countries, and packing incredible adventures into increasingly shorter time slots. This book leverages all the tools at your disposal today—tech, on-the-ground resources, and my many local friends—to help you maximize your time, money, and fun in Europe's top destinations.

MY TRAVEL PHILOSOPHY

Good travel is all about two things: bringing the right mindset to embrace the unexpected and sorting out the practical logistics. The second part of that equation is what the rest of this book is all about—the logistics of getting from A to B in the most time-efficient and cost-effective way, and having a blast while you're there. I'll be with you every step of the way!

But your mindset is just as important. We live in a complex world, with many different points of view swirling around us in more media formats and screens than ever before. Technology is accelerating progress around the globe, and world cultures and economies are changing at a rapid rate. It's never been more important to understand and connect with people from other cultures. The lower to the ground you travel, the more you embrace each fascinating destination and the more likely you are to have life-changing experiences.

Connect with the Culture

In all my years of travel, the most memorable experiences and my most fond memories are ones I've collected with the new friends and connections I've made on the road. If you've never traveled or studied outside the country, being somewhere completely different can be nerve-racking. People, food, language...even the laws will be different than what you're used to. The resulting anxiety can lead you to trap yourself inside your "Comfort Bubble."

The Comfort Bubble is that safe group of familiar friends you meet abroad. They listen to the same music as you do, eat the same food, take the same classes, and are easy to relate to. Don't get me wrong; I enjoy meeting compatriots while traveling. However, if at the end of your time abroad, the only new friends you made are English speakers, you may need to reevaluate why you're traveling in the first place.

Don't let the Comfort Bubble prevent you from experiencing Europe to the fullest. Break free and immerse yourself in something new. Dive into a local festival, sample strange food, flirt with that cute French guy (or girl). You'll make memories that will ultimately make you a better, more worldly human being.

Say Yes

In my experience, simply saying "yes" to things I haven't tried before is the most direct route to creating unforgettable memories. Of course, some lines should never be crossed, but in general, being a yes-man or yes-woman for the day (or night) can be really fun. You have a chance to catch a *fútbol* match in Madrid? Say yes! Never tried smoked herring? Gulp it down in Amsterdam. Do as the Berliners do and stay out till sunrise. Expose yourself to new experiences. You won't regret it.

Ask Questions

Take every opportunity to learn something new about each place you visit. Ask locals where *they* go on a Saturday night. Ask them about *their* political climate or discuss American politics. Ask them about their unique national holidays or about some other facet of their culture. They'll appreciate your interest, and they are sure to have questions for you as well—Lord knows we've got a lot to talk about.

When it comes to making conversation, don't ask where someone is from without a follow-up ready to go (without it the conversation will be short lived). Instead, have a lineup of compelling opening questions to ask those sitting next to you on the train or at the bar. Some suggestions:

- Where are you headed next? What is there to do there?
- Where else should I travel?
- I really like X. Where should I go to experience that?

Maintain Perspective

As this book was nearing completion, terrorism in Europe once again dominated the headlines. Terrorism has become an unavoidable fact of life. Though media coverage of these events makes it seem as though the world is rapidly going to hell in a handbasket, rest assured that Europe is a safe place for travelers (Western or otherwise). If you're anxious about terrorist attacks in Europe, take a deep breath and try to place the risk in perspective. The chances of your being affected directly are astronomically minuscule—you can look it up—and as every European understands, the best way to counter terrorism is by refusing to be terrorized.

Sustainable Travel

We travel to faraway cities because of their romantic and pristine charm. Adopt local habits and customs to preserve the fragile beauty that attracted you to Europe in the first place.

Europe has been quick to understand the threat of climate change, embracing ambitious initiatives to minimize cities' and people's carbon footprints. You can help. Use public transit or walk. Avoid waste. Remember that electricity and energy are closely monitored and optimized for your use. Support locally owned and operated businesses. Give back as much as you gain from your travel experience so that the local communities you visit can thrive.

ABOUT THIS BOOK
Who Is Andy Steves?

I grew up traveling with my father, travel guru Rick Steves—you may have read his books, seen his TV show, listened to his radio specials, or even taken one of his tours. From infancy through high school, I spent weeks each summer with my family in Europe learning the ins and outs of budget travel.

My approach to travel fuses my father's love of culture with all the tools available today thanks to modern technology. Through college, I worked as a tour guide for Rick Steves' Europe. While studying abroad in Rome in 2008, I started organizing trips for my friends each weekend, leading groups of 5-10 fellow students. By the end of the semester, these groups had swelled to more than 30 people, and that's when I recognized a need.

Upon returning home, I began formulating ideas for tips and trips designed specifically for budget travelers and students abroad in Europe. That led to **Weekend Student Adventures** (wsaeurope.com)—a business concept that won the University of Notre Dame's entrepreneurship competition in 2010 and led to an appearance on ABC's *Shark Tank* in 2014. WSA Europe now leads thousands of students and budget travelers on affordable, local tour experiences in thirteen cities over 3- to 12-day packages. The tours I designed and refined for my company provided the foundation for each city chapter in this book.

Andy Steves Travel Podcast

Check out my podcast, available in iTunes, for fun and easy on-the-go listening. I connect with international friends, travel entrepreneurs, and digital nomads to share a wide range of practical tips, interesting stories, and funny situations you can only encounter while on the road.

AndySteves.com & Social Media

Find my locally guided tours, DIY Detours, a travel store, additional travel recommendations, and more at AndySteves.com. Check it out and follow us on social media: @AndyStevesTravel.

How to Use this Book

Each of the book's chapters starts with important background information and recommendations for which sights and activities will need reservations ahead of time. Following this is a detailed three-day itinerary—one that groups your most popular sightseeing options in a way that makes geographical sense. Bolded points of interest are described in greater length later in the chapter. These itineraries are based on my extensive experience as a tour guide, but they are by no means the only way to see the city. Use the itineraries as a skeleton of sorts, seeing the places that sound interesting to you and replacing the ones that don't with any of the other recommended sights.

After the itinerary are descriptions of the top neighborhoods in each city. Then you'll find my recommendations for sights, food, nightlife, shopping (including markets), recreation (including parks), tours, and hostels. After that are transportation tips, then a section on day-trip destinations close to each city, and, finally, emergency information.

For brevity's sake, this book doesn't recommend everything you'll find to do in each city. An exhaustive list for any of these cities might run into multiple volumes, but there's enough in these pages to keep even the most ambitious traveler occupied for a week or more.

LET'S GET STARTED

Think of your trip as one big piece of artwork: Start with the outline, then fill in the finer shading and details. Your outline will consist of the following:

- **Where you want to go.** The longer this list, the less time you'll have in each city, so trim as much as possible off the top.
- **How much time you have.** It's worth asking yourself from the outset how much time you're willing to spend in transit.
- **What your budget—daily and total—will be.** Start with a budget of $1,200 for the flights to and from Europe.
- **What you want to do and see.** What are your priorities—sightseeing, music, culture, architecture, nightlife, or a mixture of all of the above?

Decide Where to Go

If you have three weeks or less and want to hit a wide range of European destinations (this is the starting point for most travelers), you'll have to decide which cities you'll visit and which you'll miss. Let's say that eight of the cities in this book sound like must-sees for you—eight cities in 21 days means you'll be in transit for more than a third of your trip. You'll barely have a chance to catch your breath before you're packing your bags again. For this reason, I recommend no more than six cities for a three-week European trip. You might want to group these cities geographically, or you

IF YOU LIKE...

Grand museums:
Paris, London, Berlin, Rome

Culture and live performances:
Dublin, Madrid, Edinburgh

Outdoor recreation:
Edinburgh, Barcelona

Art history:
Paris, Rome, Venice, Florence, Madrid

Cuisine:
Rome, Madrid, Venice

Festivals:
Budapest, Venice, Amsterdam

Cheap thrills:
Madrid, Budapest, Prague

GO TO...

Euro-trash techno discos:
Berlin, Barcelona, Rome

Pub life and beer:
Berlin, Prague, Dublin, London

Alternative scene:
Berlin, Budapest, Prague

Casual and social ambience:
Paris, Amsterdam, Prague

Old-world atmosphere:
Prague, Budapest

Late, late nights:
Berlin, Barcelona, Madrid

LGBT nightlife:
Amsterdam, Paris, London, Barcelona

might want to select based on the price of flights or accommodations.

Also consider the similarity of experiences in each city. For example, London, Dublin, and Edinburgh have a good deal in common, as do Barcelona and Madrid, Florence and Rome, and Budapest and Prague. For a varied and perspective-shifting experience of Europe, mix east and west, north and south, English-speaking and non-English-speaking destinations.

If you're studying abroad and will be taking multiple trips throughout your school semester, map out when to go based on each destination. Go to the beach cities (like Barcelona) when it's warmer, visit active or pedestrian cities (like Prague) before it gets too cold, and save "museum" cities (like Berlin) for the winter.

Plan Your Route

With a manageable list of cities, it's time to consider how to get from A to B to C. Trains, buses, and planes are generally your best (i.e., quickest and cheapest) options. If you're on a tight budget, book transportation ahead of time, as prices can climb the closer you get to your travel date. For tips on choosing the best mode of transit, along with step-by-step instructions on booking your transportation between cities, see page 400.

Links: Try Google Flights, skyscanner.com, kayak.com, cheapoair.com, momondo.com for flights; sbb.ch for train travel; eurolines.com, orangeways.com, berlin-linienbus.de, renfe.com, and studentagencybus.com for bus travel; carpooling.co.uk for ride sharing.

Apps: For a list of helpful transportation apps, see page 408.

Decide Where to Sleep

Travelers often ask me whether they should book all of their accommodations ahead of time. It's a question of what you prefer: do you want value or flexibility? You'll save money by booking early, but spontaneity will be impossible (or at least costly). For extremely tight budgets, book accommodations as far in advance as possible. For more tips on booking accommodations, see page 406.

If you do book in advance, go the extra mile and find out how to get to your hostel

before you leave for your trip. Nothing is worse than arriving in a foreign city with a heavy backpack and not knowing where to go. Have the location saved on your phone and keep the battery charged.

Hostels provide fun, social atmospheres and cheap prices for solo travelers, but quality sleep is harder to come by. Airbnb often offers great value for couples or groups of friends to stay in private apartments. If traveling in a group of friends, compare the total cost you'll pay at my recommended hostels with a private apartment nearby and make your decision from there. Note that "charming," "cozy," and "intimate" often mean "tiny."

A note on bedbugs: You can catch a bout of bedbugs anywhere, from a dank hostel to a five-star hotel. All it takes is a fellow traveler to pack a family in on their backpack. Hostels are more predisposed to bedbugs simply because they have a higher volume of individuals passing through. Hostels with wooden—as opposed to metal-framed—bunks are more susceptible to bedbug problems.

Links: Use hostelworld.com or airbnb.com and their respective apps.

Calibrate Your Budget

Know roughly how much your trip is going to cost before jumping in headfirst. How much for a meal? How much for a typical night out including drinks? How much for that famous museum? Each of the chapters starts with a number of budget-calibrating tips that will help you remove some of the budgeting guesswork.

Credit cards are widely accepted across Europe. Visa tends to be more common than Mastercard, and it's difficult to find anyone who takes American Express. The more secure chip-and-pin system is ubiquitous in Europe, but swipe cards will work just about everywhere. It's worth asking your bank to issue a chip-and-pin card ahead of time. **Cash** is often preferred in southern European countries like Italy and Spain. You may encounter minimums (around €10) set by merchants to use a card.

Warning: The **Dynamic Currency Conversion (DCC)** is a "service" offered at many European ATMs and payment

CITY-HOPPING

Group cities geographically so that you don't waste time and money zigzagging across the continent. Each of these itineraries can also be done in the opposite direction, and you can link them together for a longer trip—for example, Best of the North followed by Best of the British Isles (Amsterdam → Paris → London → Edinburgh → Dublin). Prices are approximate, and tend to be lower the farther in advance you book.

Best of the North
London → Paris → Amsterdam
In as little as one week, you can get a taste of three of Western Europe's major cultural capitals.
• From London's St. Pancras station, take the fast train to Paris (2.5 hours, from €50).
• From Paris, hop a train to Amsterdam (3.5 hours, around €75).

Best of Eastern Europe
Berlin → Prague → Budapest
Explore complex history by day and dive into an alternative nightlife at night. This itinerary is great for history buffs and architecture fiends.
• From Berlin, use studentagencybus.com or orangeways.com to book a bus to Prague (4.5 hours, €40).
• From Prague, consider a Czech Airlines flight to Budapest (1 hour, from €60), or take a train (7 hours, €75).

Best of Spain
Barcelona → Madrid
Whether you love nightlife, tapas, museums, or simply having a good time, Spain's two most important cities have got you covered.
• Fast trains connect Barcelona and Madrid (3 hours, from €50) several times daily. Buses are also an option. Book at renfe.com.

Best of Italy
Rome → Florence → Venice
This route is a no-brainer for pizza- and gelato-loving foodies. Add in robust art history and architecture, and you'll see why this trip has become a classic.
• From Rome, take a fast train (1.5 hours, from €25, reservations required) or a slow train (3.5 hours, from €20) to Florence. Avoid rush hour for cheaper prices.
• From Florence, take a fast train (2 hours, from €30, reservations required) or a slow train (7.5 hours, €15) to Venice. As with the previous leg of the journey, avoid rush hour for the best price.

Best of the British Isles
London → Edinburgh → Dublin
Head to the capital cities of the British Isles for pubs, live music, and the ease of connecting with friendly, English-speaking locals.
• From London, hop a cheap flight to Edinburgh (1 hour, €60), or take a train (4.5 hours, €110).
• From Edinburgh, numerous airlines run cheap flights to Dublin (1 hour, from €45) multiple times a day. For the best price, avoid rush hour. Many people commute between these cities for business.

terminals, which will give you the option of paying in your home currency (USD). At first blush, this may seem like a good idea, but don't be fooled. The exchange rate plummets and you're charged a commission of 3.5 percent. Your bank conversion rate is much fairer. Always decline and pay in the local currency. If you're not given an option to decline, cancel the transaction and have them run it again in the local currency.

Apps: Use the XE Currency app to keep track of fluctuating conversion rates and the Mint.com app to balance your budget.

Plan for Precision Sightseeing

Make a list of the top 3-5 things you want to see in each city, and make reservations online to save yourself hours in line. At the beginning of each chapter, you'll find a list of sights that you should reserve in advance. A word to the wise: see less rather than more. Immerse yourself in the history and culture rather than just snapping a quick selfie and moving on.

ON-THE-GROUND TRAVEL TIPS

Walking Tours

Multiple free English-speaking walking tours are offered every day in every major city in Europe. They act as feeders into the companies' paid, smaller group tours like Street Art Tours in Berlin or Red Light Walks

in Amsterdam. Payment for the free tours isn't mandatory, but in many cases the guide pays the operator a 3- to 5-euro commission per person and keeps whatever is left—if you stiff them, you are effectively making them pay to give you a free tour. Tip your guides generously!

If traveling with a group of friends, a private professional guide is nearly always a great investment. They can tailor their tour to your preferences, and they can often point you in the direction of local dining or nightlife hot spots. My favorite private tour operators are listed in each chapter.

Cycling

If you're a competent cyclist, renting a bike dramatically changes how accessible each city becomes. Biking in Europe is not the same as biking in the United States, so wait to rent a bike until you've got your bearings and have observed how traffic flows. You'll find recommended bike rental and tour options in each chapter. **Donkey Republic** is an international Airbnb-style bike rental option that, via an easy-to-use app, allows you to rent a local's bike for the duration of your stay. Check them out at donkey.bike.

Carry a Map

Getting lost in foreign cities can be fun, but it's always nice to know the way back home. Always carry a map, and take time

to look up from it every once in a while to orient yourself. When asking around for recommendations, having a map gives you a way to take notes and makes it easy for non-English speakers to point you in the right direction. I take my first morning in town to study up on my favorite sights and mark them on the map, planning a convenient route between them (this has been done for you in the three-day itineraries).

Flash Your Student ID

Some cities, such as Madrid, offer students with a valid student ID free or discounted admission to museums and other attractions. It's always worth checking when booking ahead or buying tickets.

Customize Your Experience

Whether it's sporting matches, concerts, or film festivals, it's worth researching what's going on in each city during your visit. I'm always on the lookout for concerts, sailing, and cycling races, so whenever I'm planning a trip, I check online to see what's happening in Europe during my stay. If I'm in France in July, I make a point to catch a stage of the Tour de France. The summer is concert festival time all over the continent, so I check the concert programs early. If I'm in town for the spring, I plan to take a friend sailing for an afternoon on one of the lakes outside of Berlin. Chase your passion all over the continent.

Ready to hit the road? Read on!
Bon voyage, buon viaggio, and *gute Fahrt!*

Andy Steves

LONDON

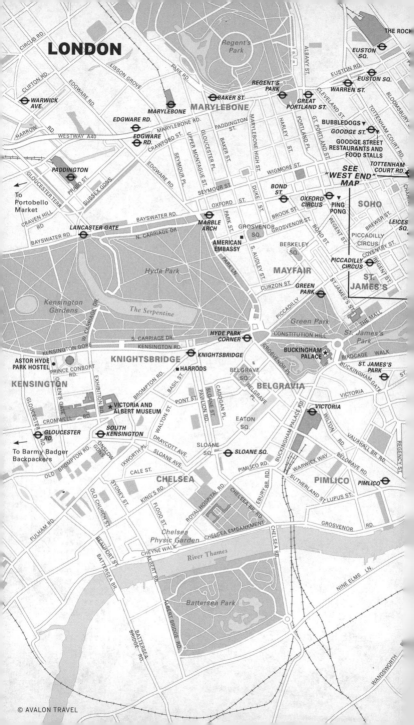

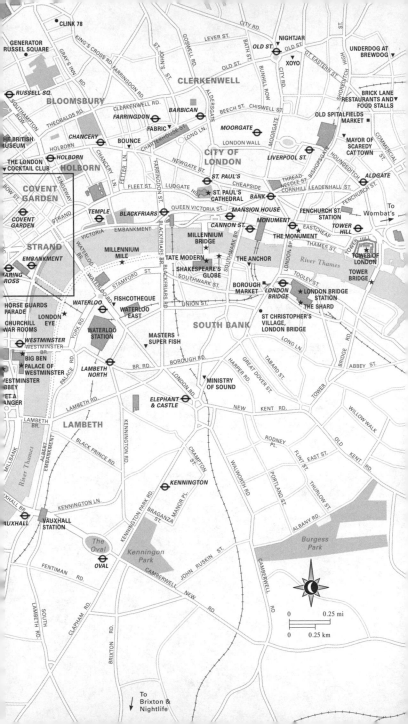

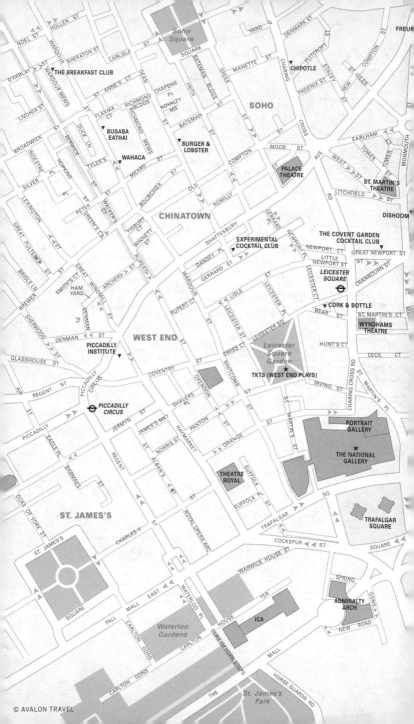

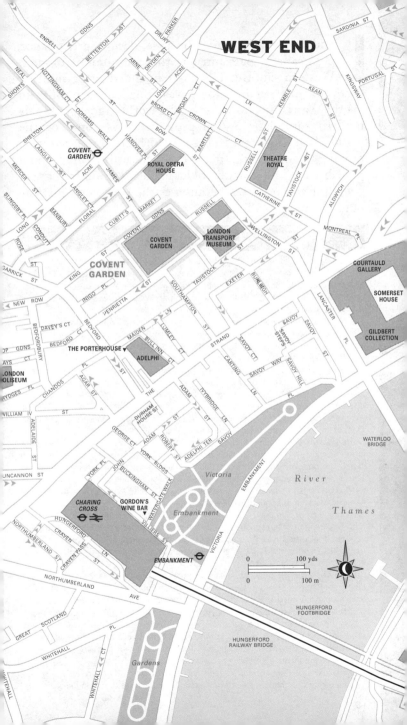

London, a world leader in style, design, art, finance, politics, and pageantry, is the epicenter of modern Western culture. Having rebounded after fighting tooth and nail against the devastating German Blitz in World War II, it's now one of the world's most strikingly modern capitals. London proudly offers some of the world's best museums (most of which are free!), nightlife ranging from classic pubs to trendsetting clubs, and probably the best chicken tikka masala outside India. Get ready for a good time, because, as the Clash so famously put it, London's calling.

LONDON 101

London was founded as a far-flung outpost of the Roman Empire nearly 2,000 years ago. Its strategic location on the River Thames put it squarely on the route leading from Britannia to Europe. The city grew in both size and importance, and by the end of the 11th century landmarks such as the Tower of London and Westminster Abbey were already part of the city's skyline.

By the Middle Ages, London had become a tangle of overcrowded, filthy streets. Disease spread quickly in the dense tenements. In 1348, the Black Death killed more than 40,000 Londoners, equal to one-quarter of the population. Disease and pestilence continued to plague the city for the next three centuries, culminating in the Great Plague of 1665-1666, which killed more than 100,000 Londoners (modern construction crews regularly turn up mass graves from this period when breaking ground). To add insult to injury, 80 percent of the city burned to the ground in the 1666 Great Fire of London, displacing 65,000 of those who had survived the plague. Numerous plans for rebuilding were submitted, but these were never fully realized. Even today, London's streets follow many of the same lines of the city's haphazard medieval layout.

The Industrial Revolution toward the end of the 18th century transformed London once more. Technologies like the telegraph and industries like the railway propelled explosive wealth and population growth in London—as did Britain's burgeoning global empire. British naval prowess extended the island's influence and turned the country into a global superpower with territories in the Americas, Africa, and Asia, concentrating riches never before seen in London. By 1800, London was home to one million inhabitants, becoming the first European city to cross that benchmark since ancient Rome.

In 1863, London began construction on the world's first underground railway, the Underground (aka the Tube). An idea many contemporary skeptics initially ridiculed now transports over one billion passengers a year, removing significant traffic from the congested streets.

These same tunnels provided shelter when the Germans bombed the city tirelessly during the Battle of Britain in World War II. Winston Churchill conducted the war effort from his own bunker just a few blocks from the Palace of Westminster. You can visit the Churchill War Rooms today and see them just as they were when the war ended in 1945.

After the war, the city grew, as rebuilding efforts focused on reducing density by encouraging residents to move to outlying communities. A massive labor shortage after World War II led to relaxed immigration policies with former British colonies, which helped transform London into the thriving and diverse metropolis it is today.

Any casual walk down London's streets reveals these layers of history and culture artfully coexisting with modern life, making it one of the top cities to visit in Europe.

PLAN AHEAD

RESERVATIONS

Reservations are recommended for the following sights (and just about any popular bar or restaurant—especially my recommended cocktail lounges):

Tower of London (hrp.org.uk/Tower OfLondon)
London Eye (londoneye.com)

LOCAL HAPPENINGS

Wireless Festival

This three-day music festival at Finsbury Park is held annually in early July, featuring headliners like Justin Timberlake, John Legend, Jay Z, and Rihanna. (wirelessfestival. co.uk)

Notting Hill Carnival

For more than 50 years, throbbing Afro-Caribbean beats and colorful parades have taken over Notting Hill for two days at the end of August. It's best to celebrate with the crowds while the sun's still up—after sundown, the party quickly veers into seedy territory. (thelondonnottinghillcarnival.com)

Bonfire Night

"Remember, remember! The fifth of November, the Gunpowder treason and plot." These words refer to Guy Fawkes, who infamously conspired to blow up the Houses of Parliament in 1605. His plan was thwarted just in time. Today, Brits celebrate the foiling of the Gunpowder Plot with pyrotechnics of their own, lighting up the sky with fireworks and bonfires. Battersea Park hosts the biggest of London's bonfires and light shows.

KNOW BEFORE YOU GO

KEY STATS & FIGURES

Currency:
British pound (£);
£1 = about 1.3 USD

Population:
8.6 million

Language:
English

Number of metro lines:
11

Amount of tea consumed daily in the United Kingdom:
120,000,000 cups

National dishes:
fish-and-chips, full English breakfast, chicken tikka masala, Sunday roast

The Queen's English:
bus = city bus, coach = private, Greyhound-style buses, lift = elevator, loo = toilet, cheers = thank you, quid = pound

CALIBRATE YOUR BUDGET

TYPICAL PRICES FOR:

Hostel dorm bed:
£22

Two-course dinner and drink:
£19

Pint of beer:
£5

Daily bicycle rental:
from £6

Single Tube ride:
£2.40 with Oyster Card, £4.90 without

Museums:
mostly free!

MOVIES TO WATCH
The King's Speech, Love Actually, A Clockwork Orange, V for Vendetta, Bridget Jones's Diary, London Has Fallen

THREE DAY ITINERARY

You'll be flanking the south side of the Thames on the first day, and the north side on the second day. Save your third day for markets and shopping—especially if it's Sunday.

DAY 1: WELCOME TO LONDON
MORNING
Spend your morning strolling along the South Bank, London's famous **Millennium Mile.** It's an enjoyable three-hour stroll, so fuel up with breakfast and coffee at **Borough Market,** the city's oldest food market. Continue on to see **Shakespeare's Globe** and the **Tate Modern,** featuring one of the world's best contemporary art collections. This walk will orient you and give you a sense of the layout of the city as it wraps around the Thames.

AFTERNOON
After a busy morning, it's time for some typical English fare. Drop south a couple blocks from the roundabout at Waterloo Station and grab lunch at the best fish-and-chips joint in the city, **Master's Superfish.**

Head back to the Millennium Mile for a ride in the **London Eye.** Afterward, cross Westminster Bridge to glimpse two of London's most recognizable landmarks: **Big Ben** and the **Palace of Westminster.**

Hop on the Circle Line at Westminster station and get off at Bayswater. Take the Royal London Bike Tour with **Fat Tire Bike Tours** (leaves daily at 15:00 May 15 through September). If you're outside the season, flip today's itinerary to catch Fat Tire's daily morning departure at 11:00. If you prefer a less active tour, take bus 11 (connecting Victoria and Liverpool Street stations) straight through the heart of the city.

EVENING
Get dinner in the eccentric Covent Garden neighborhood. Choose gastropub grub at **Porterhouse,** authentic southern Mexican at **Wahaca,** or spicy Thai at **Busaba Eathai.** The nightlife and bars around Covent Garden are sure to keep you busy. **Freud** is an excellent hidden little spot for a nightcap. Or, if wine is your thing, head to **Gordon's Wine Bar** right next to the Embankment stop for candlelit glasses within exposed-brick cellar walls.

LATE
Stay in the **West End** and explore the back streets toward **Soho** for the night. Consider catching a **West End show.** You can find last-minute discount tickets in **Leicester Square** at the **TKTS** booth.

DAY 2: CHECK OUT THE CITY
MORNING
Start your day at the **Tower of London** when it opens at 9am. Beeline straight for the Crown Jewels to save yourself hours in line. Double back to catch the enthralling Beefeater-guided tour (leaves every half hour from the main gate). Plan to spend at least a couple of hours here.

AFTERNOON

Next, head west on Eastcheap to reach the **Monument** (the tall stone column), which commemorates the Great Fire of London. Pay the £4.50 to climb to the top—the view is well worth the effort. Continue westward to the magnificent baroque **St. Paul's Cathedral.** Opt for the free and up-close view of St. Paul's dome and the surrounding area from the **One New Change** shopping center just behind the church. Take the lift up to the top floor for a sweet panorama.

Continue west beyond St. Paul's for a pit stop at **Ye Olde Cheshire Cheese.** (If you're getting thirsty for a brew, consider following my **London Ale Trail,** page 31.) Keep your eyes peeled for **17 Fleet Street,** one of the few buildings that predate the Great Fire of 1666. Just beyond, you'll see a dragon statue denoting the border between Westminster and the City of London.

As Fleet Street turns into the Strand, London's main boulevard, you'll pass a number of important landmarks, like **Trafalgar Square,** the **National Gallery,** and **Nelson's Column.** Angling left down Whitehall, you'll pass the mounted **Horse Guards** and **10 Downing Street.**

Wrap up your sightseeing at the impressively neo-Gothic **Palace of Westminster, Big Ben,** and **Westminster Abbey,** where you'll find all the VIPs of British history interred: royals, scientists, and writers like Chaucer and Charles Dickens.

EVENING

Rest up at your hostel, then head over to **Brick Lane** for the city's best chicken tikka masala. Soak in the hipster culture while you're in **Shoreditch,** one of London's trendiest neighborhoods. Check out the speakeasy-style **Nightjar** for a discreet subterranean cocktail bar that does some of the best old-fashioneds and gimlets around.

DAY 3: MUSEUMS & SHOPPING
MORNING

Spend the morning in the **British Museum** and immerse yourself in the extensive collection of art and artifacts from all over the world. Then find **Goodge Street** for an early lunch. Choices abound for nearly every type of cuisine. Continue up to **Oxford Street** and wander toward **Hyde Park** to enjoy London's main shopping district. Give yourself the "London look" with a stop in **Selfridges.**

Alternatively, if it's Sunday, spend your morning shopping at **Old Spitalfields Market** (open daily, but at its best on Sunday). Spend the rest of the day following my **Shoreditch Walk.** Along the way, you'll find endless vintage clothing shops, hipster goods galore, and delicious snacks and food stalls.

AFTERNOON

Wander south through **Soho** and explore the many music stores, market stands, adult shops, and cafés. The eccentric locals make this an ideal place to people-watch.

Make your way west past **Hyde Park** to **Harrods**—packed to the ceiling with curved-screen TVs, luxury toys, and haute couture. Just down the street is the **Victoria and Albert Museum,** the world's largest collection of decorative arts and design—a veritable treasure trove of beautiful historical artifacts.

EVENING

Head up to **Camden Market** to explore the punk alternative scene via the Piccadilly line, transferring to the Northern line. Get ready for an eclectic, bohemian scene with all sorts of curiosity shops and busy street-food stalls. The most popular stretch of bars and venues leads from the Camden Town Tube stop north along Chalk Farm Road to **Proud Camden.**

The Thames bisects London west to east, creating a useful navigational aid. The City of London, north of the river, is a mere square mile that was once enclosed within medieval walls. As it's known today, **the City** is where you'll find St. Paul's Cathedral and the Tower of London.

West of the City is London's **West End,** the entertainment destination. Its streets are lined with restaurants of every possible variety, bars and clubs to suit the most discerning tastes, and great shopping on Oxford Street. The West End includes undeniably hip **Soho,** the hub of London's LGBT community, as well as the theater district of **Leicester Square** (pronounced "Lester") and the neighborhood of **Covent Garden,** known for its tasty food and easygoing bars.

Westminster, just south of the West End, is the political, royal, and religious hub of England. This is where you'll find Buckingham Palace and Westminster Abbey.

South of the river lies **South Bank,** which includes famous sights like the London Eye, the Tate Modern, and Shakespeare's Globe—all of them conveniently linked via the Millennium Mile riverside path.

Bloomsbury, with the British Museum at its heart, offers a couple of convenient hostels and awesome budget food options on Goodge Street. **West London** is home to the Victoria and Albert Museum, along with famous Hyde Park.

Shoreditch (northeast of the City) and **Camden** (about 20 minutes north of the city center on the Tube) are great nightlife districts and magnets for the hipster crowd. If you really want to feel as though you're ahead of the trend, drop south to **Brixton** or head northeast to **Dalston,** two of London's hottest up-and-coming neighborhoods.

Shoreditch Walk

It's not the destination that's important, but the journey. With an open mind, you'll find eight or more hours of entertainment along this 1.5-mile walk through Shoreditch. Start any time after noon at the south side of **Brick Lane near Old Spitalfields Market.** Make your way north, heading toward the Old Street Roundabout. Veer off Brick Lane—now established and rather touristy—and into the surrounding areas. You'll soon be awash in trendy spots.

Fill the tank up at either **Poppie's Fish n Chips** (6-8 Hanbury St, +44 (0)20 7247 0892, poppiesfishandchips.co.uk), a block west of Brick Lane, or the farther-afield **Tayyab's** (83-89 Fieldgate St, +44 (0)20 7247 6400, tayyabs.co.uk), regarded as the area's best-value Bangladeshi restaurant.

If you don't feel like you blend in, duck into **Blitz** (55-59 Hanbury St, +44 (0)20 7377 8828, blitzlondon.co.uk), London's largest vintage clothing store. You're sure to find hipster camouflage—perhaps an '80s snapback or some vintage plaid or paisley. Store reps frequently distribute discount flyers on Brick Lane and Hanbury.

Continue north along Brick Lane toward the overpass by the Shoreditch High Street Overground station. Keep an eye out to the left for **Junkyard Golf Club** (Old Truman Brewery, 91 Brick Ln, junkyardgolfclub.co.uk), where you can putt your way through a boozy mini-golf course with several themes, including creepy clowns.

(Heads up: Find **original Banksy and Shepard Fairey art** behind Sunday Upmarket and down the alley from Junkyard Golf.)

On the weekends, the **Boiler House Food Hall** (Sat 11:00-18:00, Sun 10:00-17:00, 152 Brick Ln, +44 (0)20 7770 6028, boilerhouse-foodhall.co.uk) can't be missed for its oodles of diverse ethnic street food.

Themed cafés are taking over London. Just beyond Sclater Street, at **Cereal Killer** (139 Brick Ln, +44 (0)20 3601 9100, cerealkillercafe.co.uk), you can select from over 100 cereals and 24 flavors of milk. A block east of Brick Lane, **Lady Dinah's Cat Emporium** (152-154 Bethnal Green Rd, +44 (0)20 8616 9390, ladydinahs.com) allows cat-loving patrons, for the price of a tea, to make a new feline friend.

Those who take doughnuts seriously should pop into **Crosstown Doughnut & Coffee Bar** (157 Brick Ln, +44 (0)20 7729 3417, crosstowndoughnuts.com), where you can try one of 14 constantly cycling flavors—from chili-chocolate to lemon-thyme.

To experience another mainstay of the district, and to acknowledge the Jewish roots of the area, stop at **Beigel Bake** (24 hours, 159 Brick Ln, +44 (0)20 7729 0616) for a salt beef sandwich. Be sure to get the mustard *and* pickle. Expect gruff service.

For a taste of artisan beer, head to **Brewdog** (51-55 Bethnal Green Rd, +44 (0)20 7729 8476, brewdog.com), a passionate brewing collective with 10 beers on tap—at least 5 of which are local brews you probably won't find anywhere else. Successfully hydrated, continue west down Bethnal Green toward the Overground station. Stop at **Boxpark Shoreditch** (2-10 Bethnal Green Rd, boxpark.co.uk), an innovative shopping complex made from more than 60 stacked shipping containers, with a pop-up vendor occupying each one.

Turn north (right) onto Shoreditch High Street, passing **Pump** (168 Shoreditch High St, +44 7564 117 339) on your left, another street-food market occupying what used to be a gas station. Find two more original Banksy pieces by hanging

a left on Rivington Street. At the popular bar and club **Cargo** (83 Rivington St, +44 (0)20 7739 3440, cargo-london.com), the artworks are behind protective plexiglass. Cargo is open until 6am on the weekends, so you may want to return later.

Continue west on Rivington, then turn south (left) onto Curtain Road. A half block down, the cultural hub **Strongroom Bar & Kitchen** (120-124 Curtain Rd, +44 (0)20 7426 5103, strongroombar.com) is a creative space that houses one of the only taps of unfiltered and unpasteurized Pilsner Urquell in London. Strongroom offers oodles of other beers on tap, a bustling kitchen, and excellent wines. Head downstairs to while away some time playing board games.

Is it dinnertime already? Head back to Rivington and continue west until it intersects with Great Eastern Street. Jump into **Floripa's** (91-93 Great Eastern St, +44 (0)20 7739 3817, floripalondon.com) to kick off your evening with a Brazilian meal of plantains, meat, rice, and beans—and, of course, music and dancing. Or, if you're feeling a little more carnivorous, head a couple blocks northeast to **MEATMission** (15 Hoxton Market, +44 (0)20 7739 8212, meatliquor.com) for delectable burgers, ribs, barbecue pork, and succulent fried chicken sandwiches. Fair warning: A dinner here may put you into a blissful protein coma, leading to an earlier-than-expected bedtime.

Follow Great Eastern Road west to the roundabout, then turn north (right) onto City Road. Go for a speakeasy cocktail at **Nightjar** (129 City Rd, barnightjar.com), where aproned bartenders take their craft seriously. Sip your drink while admiring the art deco glamour. Continue the party at **The Magic Roundabout** (Old Street Roundabout, +44 7494 029 420, magic-roundabout.co), a social bar occupying possibly the world's trendiest traffic circle, located inside the Old Street Tube stop.

Still going strong? Cap off the night a block southeast at **XOYO** (32-37 Cowper St, +44 (0)20 7608 2878, xoyo.co.uk), famous for its techno and club nights.

Tower of London

Since the earliest foundations were laid in the 11th century, this castle on the banks of the Thames was under constant expansion, serving as both a defensive fortress and the palace of England's kings and queens right up until the Tudors in the 1500s. Besides its defensive and royal purposes, the Tower of London also served as a high-security prison with a long, bloody history of torture and public executions. The lively **Beefeater-guided tours** departing every 30 minutes cost nothing, but provide an enjoyable history of the complex. Inside the tower itself, an exhibit walks you through the 500-year history of royal armor, medieval architectural plans and relics, and full-size replicas of siege weaponry.

Your best bet to minimize standing in line is to beeline to the Crown Jewels (included with admission) upon first morning entry at 09:00. Taking a Beefeater tour, seeing the museum in the tower, and peeking at the Crown Jewels takes most people around three hours. As you leave, don't miss the unimpeded view of Tower Bridge.

£25 online, £26 in person, Tues-Sat 09:00-17:30, Sun-Mon 10:00-17:30, closes one hour earlier Nov-Feb, The City, +44 (0)20 3166 6000, hrp.org.uk/TowerOfLondon, Tube: Tower Hill

St. Paul's Cathedral

St. Paul's Cathedral, founded in 604, was rebuilt 1675-1710 after succumbing to the Great Fire of London in 1666. The rebuilding was carried out by London's most revered architect of the time, Sir Christopher Wren. He drew direct inspiration from St. Peter's Basilica in Rome and used all the formulas of the popular neo-Renaissance style to create what many consider to be the crown jewel of his architectural career.

St. Paul's Cathedral emerged unscathed from the Nazi blitzes of World War II, standing tall in the face of nightly bombing raids. Many took this as a sign that, even in the darkest of times, God was watching over the British. The proud dome was actually protected by a crew of brave blokes who lived in the church and ran water buckets up at the first sign of danger. Thanks to

good old-fashioned English perseverance, they emerged from the flames of war with their heads held high, and so did St. Paul's Cathedral. The cathedral became a symbol of British national identity and of the country's collective stiff upper lip.

You can take in beauty of overwhelming magnitude at this Anglican cathedral, if you can swallow the entry fee. With its white stone construction, St. Paul's is an imposing presence, dominating the skyline in the area. Inside, you'll discover gilded architectural accents and hundreds of intricate golden mosaics. Climb the 528 steps to the top of the dome for a beautiful panorama of downtown London. It's possible to visit for free if you stay for the length of the breathtaking service (Mon-Fri 17:00, Sat 15:00, Sun times vary).

£16 online, £18 in person, includes audio guide and crypt and cupola entry, Mon-Sat 08:30-16:00, Sun worshippers only, The City, +44 (0)20 7246 8350, stpauls.co.uk, Tube: St. Paul's

The Monument

The world's tallest freestanding stone column, known simply as the Monument, was erected to commemorate the Great Fire of London, which destroyed 80 percent of the city in 1666. Climb the 311 steps to the top and you're rewarded with a spectacular 360-degree view of London. Its location right downtown—only a couple of blocks from the Tower of London—and the £4.50 price of admission make this sight as convenient as it is cheap.

£4.50, Apr-Sept daily 09:30-18:00, Oct-Mar daily 09:30-17:30, Fish Street Hill, The City, +44 (0)20 7626 2717, themonument.info, Tube: Monument

Palace of Westminster & Big Ben

The Palace of Westminster we see today was designed and built during the 19th century, when Britain was in the midst of its colonial heyday. The sun, so it was said, never set on the British Empire. Strategically located just outside of England's capital city, the City of London, the Palace of Westminster is where the wealthy and powerful had to come to get their voices heard in government. Today, the neo-Gothic building that housed the parliament of the most powerful empire of the world is quite a sight to behold. While Britain's politics have played out in this governmental center since the palace's completion in 1870, England has been ruled from this neighborhood for even longer—numerous wooden-construction palaces have been lost to fire.

The Elizabeth Clock Tower—tourists refer to the tower itself as Big Ben, but that name actually refers to the 13-ton bell (which you can't see from the street)—stands at the north end of the Palace of Westminster. The best angle for selfies is from a few paces down Westminster Bridge. The clock face is a full 23 feet wide, and the minute hand moves six feet every

LONDON'S BEST VIEWPOINTS

Some of London's top sights also offer amazing panoramic city views:

St. Paul's Cathedral

Climb the 528 steps to the top of this architectural masterpiece to take in a beautiful panorama of the City and its surroundings.

One New Change

Take an elevator up to the top floor of the building also known as the "Stealth Bomber" to experience a panorama of downtown London and an up-close look at the dome of St. Paul's. The roof terrace has a bar and cocktail lounge.

Tate Modern

Head to the viewing platform above the museum's restaurant on the 10th floor for a nice (and free) view of the South Bank.

Millennium Bridge

Get a view of the Thames from this beautiful, modern, glass-and-steel pedestrian bridge, which spans the river from the Tate Modern to St. Paul's Cathedral.

The Shard

Pay to ride to the top of this London landmark or enjoy a posh cocktail on the 31st floor. The best views are seen from halfway up. Otherwise, your vantage point is too far removed and the buildings fade into the distance.

London Eye

Take in impressive views from this 450-foot-tall observation wheel. Go at dusk for shorter lines and beautiful sunset shots—but remember, the sun is gone by 4pm in the winter.

Tower of London/Tower Bridge

The best angle for a shot of one of the most iconic symbols of the city, the Tower Bridge, is to be found just towards the riverside of the Tower of London. Don't miss a selfie there!

Parliament Hill, Hampstead Heath

Need a break from the hustle and bustle? Head to the far north side of town for a distant view of the entire skyline of greater London.

five minutes. Big Ben has tolled the hours without fail since 1859.

While it is possible to visit inside the Houses of Parliament (for information, see parliament.uk/visiting), those on a three-day visit to London might be content with a view from the outside.

Free, open when Parliament is in session, Westminster, Tube: Westminster

Buckingham Palace

No self-respecting visitor can leave London without a selfie in front of Buckingham Palace. The grand and opulent residence of the royal family, and an enduring symbol of the English monarchy, is located about a 15-minute walk west of Westminster Abbey. William and Kate shared a kiss on the neoclassical balcony, as did Prince Charles and Lady Diana before them. Before snapping your picture and moving on, take a moment to admire the perfectly balanced facade, a classic example of Renaissance-style architectural harmony. Located at the edge of St. James's Park, Buckingham Palace contains a total of 775 rooms and has been the official home of British sovereigns since 1837 when Queen Victoria moved in. While today the palace functions as both a residence to the queen and an administrative building, it also is the setting for one of England's most popular tourist attractions: the changing of the guard.

From July through September, it's possible to tour the palace. In this half-mile experience that takes about two hours, you can check out the State Rooms (where the royal family entertains guests) and the Royal Mews (the stables). You'll also see dozens of priceless art pieces from greats like Rembrandt, Titian, and Van Dyck in the Queen's Gallery. To see the entirety of the palace, purchase the Royal Day Out package (from £20); otherwise, purchase tickets by individual attraction.

Changing of the guard 11:00 Mon, Wed, Fri, and Sun (weather dependent, confirm schedule on website), Westminster, +44 (0)20 7766 7300, check palace information and purchase tickets at royalcollection.org.uk, changing-the-guard.com/dates-times.html, Tube: Victoria

Westminster Abbey

London's premier Gothic church—complete with pointed arches, stained glass, and flying buttresses—has played host to the major life events of England's royal families and has been the site of nearly 1,000 years of coronations. This Anglican church is still quite active: It was the site of Princess Diana's funeral (1997) and Kate and William's wedding (2011). Many of the UK's most famous thinkers and national figures, including Darwin, Chaucer, and Newton, are entombed here, as are 13 kings and 16 queens of England. They are interred underneath sequoia-like pillars supporting breathtaking arches and elaborate structural ribbing.

£22, Mon–Fri 09:30-16:30, Wed until 19:00, Sat 09:30-14:30, Sun worshippers only, 20 Deans Yard, Westminster, +44 (0)20 7222 5152, westminster-abbey.org, Tube: Westminster

Churchill War Rooms

Can you imagine running a war effort in which millions of lives counted on you, coordinating movements of troops by pinning their positions on a wall in a damp, dark bunker deep in the earth? With the help of copious quantities of tobacco and whiskey, that's exactly what Winston Churchill and his military chiefs of staff did for nearly the entirety of World War II, all from a series of reinforced concrete rooms located deep beneath the Treasury Building.

Some of these war rooms have been frozen in time to create a museum. In each room you'll see maps, notepads, and communication systems, all left exactly as they were on VE Day in 1945.

£20 (audio guide included), daily 09:30-18:00, Clive Steps, King Charles St, Westminster, +44 (0)20 7930 6961, iwm.org.uk/visits/churchill-war-rooms, Tube: Westminster

Horse Guards on Whitehall

This graveled parade ground has served as an open space in the heart of the city for events, ceremonies, and practices of the British military and royal family. Today the changing and dismounting of the mounted guards make for fun, quick photo ops.

Free, guards change daily at 11:00 (10:00 Sun) and dismount at 16:00, Whitehall, Westminster, Tube: Charing Cross

Millennium Mile

Also known as the Queen's Walk, the Millennium Mile is an easy-to-stroll riverside path on the south side of the Thames. Anchored by the **London Bridge** and the **Shard** on one end, and **Big Ben** and the **London Eye** on the other, it's an extremely pleasant and convenient way to see a number of London's most famous sights. Between those major sights, you'll also pass by the **Borough Market, Shakespeare's Globe** theater, the **Tate Modern,** and the **Millennium Bridge.**

Free, always open, South Bank, Tube: London Bridge or Waterloo

The Shard

London's newest and most visible landmark is the Shard. Named for its distinctive glass design that seems to tear into the London sky, the skyscraper was completed in 2013. Take the elevator to the 32nd floor, about a third of the way up, where you can enjoy an affordable coffee in the posh restaurant **Oblix** (dress code enforced, reservations recommended for dinner). The best views are seen from here; otherwise your vantage point is too far removed and the buildings fade into the distance.

Viewing platform £26 in advance/£31 in person adults over 16, £21 in advance/£26 in person students with valid ID, Apr-Oct daily 10:00-22:00 (last entry 21:00), Nov-Mar Sun-Wed 10:00-19:00 (last entry 18:00), and Thurs-Sat 10:00-22:00 (last entry 21:00), 32 London Bridge St, South Bank, +44 3334 564 000, the-shard.com, Tube: London Bridge

Shakespeare's Globe

While the design of Shakespeare's original theater was innovative, it was not particularly firesafe. The theater burned down in 1613 after a malfunctioning prop cannon set the stage alight. This replica theater, designed to faithfully re-create the Globe as it would have looked before it burned down—complete with the trademark black timber-framed construction and intimate stage—was completed in 1997. Today, with capacity for about 1,000 seated nobles and 2,000 standing commoners, viewing a performance here is fascinating. Plays are performed much as they would have been in Shakespeare's day (with the addition of female actors), with no voice amplification

or artificial lighting. Check showtimes and book online (from £5 for standing tickets, £20 for seated).

It's also possible to **tour the theater** with an excellent guide who speaks about the original building, how plays work in this purpose-built space, and the function of the venue today. Just like Shakespeare's plays, this guided walk appeals to intellectuals as well as fans of potty humor. Tours leave every 30 minutes throughout the day, except in summer when they stop for the daily afternoon matinees.

Tour £16, daily 09:00-17:30, 21 New Globe Walk, South Bank, +44 (0)20 7902 1400, shakespearesglobe.com, Tube: London Bridge

Tate Modern

This imposing remodeled power plant on the South Bank was opened in 2000 to house London's premier modern art museum, which features one of the best collections of contemporary art in the world. With stark, dark brick construction and wide-open gallery spaces, the Tate is packed with works from an all-star roster of artists. You can seek out great and iconic modern works of art such as Andy Warhol's Marilyn Monroe diptych, Roy Lichtenstein's large-scale comics, and Donald Judd's installation sculptures of spatial explorations. Plan to spend about 90 minutes here, but, if you're a fan of modern art, block off an afternoon—the bookstore alone can keep art fans enraptured for hours. On the 10th floor toward the back of the building is a restaurant with a beautiful view of the city. While the restaurant is pricey, the view is free.

Free, Sun-Thurs 10:00-18:00, Fri-Sat 10:00-22:00, South Bank, +44 (0)20 7887 8888, tate.org.uk, Tube: Blackfriars

London Eye

Erected in 1999 to celebrate the millennium, this 450-foot observation wheel—not a Ferris wheel, as locals are quick to clarify—is the UK's most popular tourist attraction, with over 3.5 million riders each year. The 32 air-conditioned glass and steel pods, each holding up to 25 people, rotate around a wheel on a single, cantilevered arm that extends out over the Thames. The Eye moves evenly and slowly, completing its rotation in about 30 minutes. Guests hop in and out of the moving pods as they skim the boarding area at the bottom. Insider tip: Sunny days wash out all your pictures. Go at dusk for shorter lines and striking sunset shots.

£23.50 online, £26 in person, daily 10:00-sunset, Riverside Bldg, County Hall, Westminster Bridge Rd, South Bank, 0800 093 012, londoneye.com, Tube: Waterloo

British Museum

Opened in 1759, the British Museum was the first national public museum, and today it boasts one of the world's most extensive collections at some eight million pieces. Showcasing some of history's greatest treasures, like the Rosetta Stone, the Parthenon Sculptures (also known as the Elgin Marbles), and the world's finest examples of Assyrian reliefs, this well-appointed museum is dedicated to history, art, and culture. It takes about two hours to see the highlights—much longer if you want to inspect each room closely. The museum also offers free 40-minute walking tours in the section of your choice throughout the day. Find the relevant times on the free brochure when you walk in, or check the website.

Free, daily 10:00-17:30, Great Russell St, Bloomsbury, +44 (0)20 7323 8299, britishmuseum.org, Tube: Tottenham Court Road

National Gallery

The National Gallery's exhibits include artworks from the Dark Ages to the late 19th century. Enjoy the free entry, and drink in more than 2,000 canvases, including masterpieces from Renaissance bosses like Leonardo and Michelangelo to Baroque master Caravaggio and impressionist Van Gogh.

The National Gallery is right on Trafalgar Square, as is the **National Portrait Gallery** (npg.org.uk), another excellent free museum displaying thousands of pieces that bring you face-to-face with the great and not-so-great characters of history—a must for those who want a deeper understanding of the men and women who shaped

our world. From the steps of the gallery, you can see **Nelson's Column.** At the top of the column stands the one-armed Admiral Horatio Nelson, who was killed in the Battle of Trafalgar in 1805 while leading his navy to a crucial victory over Napoleon and the French.

Free, daily 10:00-18:00, Thurs-Fri until 21:00, Trafalgar Square, West End, nationalgallery.org.uk, +44 (0)20 7747 2885, Tube: Charing Cross

West End Shows

Well before the time of Shakespeare, theaters began popping up in London on the west side of town, or the West End. Today, the district is home to dozens of theaters large and small, and it's a popular place to catch a show while you're in town. Large-scale productions like Les Misérables and Mousetrap run constantly. Newer entries like Hamilton, Wicked, and The Lion King give theatergoers a chance to see popular Broadway musicals. Find the **TKTS** booth in Leicester Square, or visit the box offices for tickets up to half off in the hours and minutes before the show starts.

Theater locations, prices, and showtimes vary, West End, officiallondontheatre.com, Tube: Leicester Square, Covent Garden, or Piccadilly Circus

Victoria and Albert Museum

With a collection of more than 4.5 million design and decorative art pieces from all around the world, this massive museum can overwhelm any visitor in both quantity and quality of artifacts dating from the last five millennia. A stop at the information desk is key to organizing your time. Exhibits span religions, centuries, styles, materials, subjects, geography, and media. Beeline toward the subjects that interest you most, because it's easy to get lost in the 146 galleries, which make you feel like you're walking through a life-size encyclopedia. I like to geek out upstairs in the 20th-century design gallery.

Free, daily 10:00-17:45, Fri until 22:00, Cromwell Rd, West London, +44 (0)20 7942 2000, vam.ac.uk, Tube: South Kensington

TOP EATS

London has undergone a culinary renaissance in the last couple decades. People used to turn up their noses at the thought of British cuisine, but the English take this ribbing in stride. Incorporating foods from dozens of cultures that have left their mark on the city, London's culinary scene boasts a cornucopia of relatively affordable options. Heads up: Sit-down lunches can easily run £14 ($20), and dinners can cost over £20 ($30). My suggestions will help you either save or get the best bang for your buck when you do splurge. There is no need to tip at fast-food or takeaway shops. If you're sitting down for a meal, look over your bill and assess whether cover and service are already included. If not, feel free to round up 10 percent or so, based on the speed and quality of service.

As fish-and-chips is the national dish of England (sharing the title with chicken tikka masala), it would be a crime not to duck into one of the many local establishments that stake their reputation on their battered cod and haddock. If you see halibut on the menu, it's worth the upgrade. Try it at **Master's Superfish** on the South Bank walk or at **Poppie's Fish n Chips** in Shoreditch.

Master's Superfish

Take a short walk southeast from Waterloo station and get ready for London's best tempura goodness! When ordering, remember that you've come for the great fish-and-chips, not for the service. Don't let the gruff staff get to you. This is a no-frills bar that feels more like a homey cafeteria than a fast food joint. The food will more than make up for any hard feelings.

Takeaway £5.50, eat in from £9, Mon-Sat 04:30-22:30, 191 Waterloo Rd, South Bank, +44 (0)20 7928 6924, Tube: Waterloo

Timber Yard (TY)

Start your day with a caffeine buzz and a healthy meal at TY. The aproned and tatted staff here take their delicious pastries, hearty sandwiches, fresh salads, and artisan yogurts seriously. As you might expect, they are equally passionate about the coffee, which comes just about any way you want it: brewed, pressed, or as shots of espresso. Vegan and vegetarian options abound in this work/play/socialize space. Find more seating downstairs.

Coffee from £3, food from £4, Mon-Fri 08:00-19:00, Sat-Sun 10:00-18:00, 7 Upper St Martin's Ln, +44 (0)20 3217 2009, tyuk.com, Tube: Covent Garden

Ping Pong

Modern and fresh both in decor and food, Ping Pong is a stylish Asian fusion joint with delicious steamed dim sum (don't pass up the spring rolls or the beef dumplings). Reserve a table or at least call ahead, as they fill up with the post-work crowd. Prices climb apace with the restaurant's popularity, but Ping Pong often offers deals or combos that can save you some change. Show your student ID to save 15 percent.

Meals from £14, Mon-Fri 11:00-24:00, Sat 12:00-24:00, Sun 12:00-22:30, 45 Great Marlborough St, West End,

+44 (0)20 7851 6969, pingpongdimsum.com,
Tube: Oxford Circus

Dishoom

This is my favorite spot for Indian food in the center of London. You pay a little more for the casual-yet-refined atmosphere, but the quality of the naan (go for the garlic), the curries (especially the unique mahi tikka), and the grills (I love the lamb roti) is superb. Top it all off with a mango lassi for a meal to remember. I like the open interior, which has a modern-yet-authentic feel with brass accents, family photos, and large windows. You'll find three other locations throughout town. They don't take reservations, so you might wait up to an hour for your food. Head downstairs to their posh bar for a cocktail while you wait.

From £20, Mon-Thurs 08:00-23:00, Fri 08:00-24:00, Sat 09:00-24:00, Sun 09:00-23:00, 12 Upper St Martin's Ln, West End, +44 (0)20 7420 9320, dishoom.com, Tube: Covent Garden

The Breakfast Club

Famous for serving one of the best breakfasts in London, The Breakfast Club has lines that spill out of the door and onto the street year-round. Depending on the time of day, waiting for a table might be a two-hour affair. Whether you come for the delicious coffee or hot chocolate, the thick-sliced bacon, the pancakes, or the indulgent eggs Benedict, The Breakfast Club may have you coming back every morning of your stay. Slept in? Don't worry, The Breakfast Club serves breakfast all day, along with lunch and dinner options. With eight locations in town, you're never far from a face full of their cinnamon apple French toast.

Breakfast from £9, Mon-Sat 08:00-22:00, Sun 08:00-19:00, 33 D'Arblay St, West End, +44 (0)20 7434 2571, thebreakfastclubcafes.com, Tube: Oxford Circus or Tottenham Court Road

Burger & Lobster

These guys have built their brand around doing two things exceptionally well: burgers and lobster. Truth be told, they do more than this, and their seasonal drinks and desserts are every bit as good as their namesake dishes. Service is friendly, and the menu is simple: choose burger, lobster, or lobster and salad roll (basically a thickly sliced sandwich) and pick your size and spiciness. The restaurant offers daily specials, which will make the meal much more affordable than you might expect from a restaurant with "lobster" in the name. There are an additional 10 locations in town, if you're not in the West End.

From £14, Mon-Wed 12:00-22:30, Thurs-Sat 12:00-23:00, Sun 12:00-22:00, 36-38 Dean St, West End, +44 (0)20 7432 4800, burgerandlobster.com, Tube: Leicester Square or Tottenham Court Road

Busaba Eathai

Kick-ass curry and delicious pad thai make this one of my favorite places in London. All of Busaba's locations are done up in a mod, dark, Asian-fusion theme, with welcoming servers who are happy to make recommendations. Their tom yam goong (spicy and sour prawn soup) will make you think you're in Bangkok. The Songkhla-style red curry is my favorite. In addition to the Soho shop, you'll find many other locations across town.

From £8, Mon-Thurs 12:00-23:00, Fri-Sat 12:00-23:30, Sun 12:00-22:00, 106-110 Wardour St, West End, +44 (0)20 7255 8686, busaba.com, Tube: Piccadilly Circus

Wahaca

Wahaca offers some of the best tacos, burritos, grilled steak, and horchata (sweet cinnamon rice milk) I've had this side of the pond. The fresh ingredients and authentic Mexican dishes remind me of my travels south of the border. Expect colorful decorations, fast and cheerful service, and a casual, hospitable atmosphere. As a unique touch, orders are noted on your big paper tablecloth. There are many locations across town.

From £11, Mon-Sat 12:00-23:00, Sun 12:00-22:30, 80 Wardour St, West End, +44 (0)20 7734 0195, wahaca.co.uk, Tube: Piccadilly Circus

Pret a Manger

This chain, serving fresh-made sandwiches, healthy salads, and snacks, is a London staple, dotting the landscape like Starbucks in Seattle. You might stand in line between a businessperson and a backpacker—almost everybody seems to enjoy their wholesome, cheap lunches. Grab a sandwich from the display rack, order your coffee, and pay at the bar. The whole oper-

LONDON ALE TRAIL

For a mile-long stretch of London's best alehouses, look no further than my wee London Ale Trail. It wanders through the oldest streets in the City and into Westminster. Starting near Blackfriar's Bridge, and wrapping up not far from the action in **Soho,** this route is an excellent way to sip the afternoon away without too many steps in between.

The Blackfriar

I love this pub for its charm and beautiful interior. Its intricate mosaics and detailed woodwork make this building a work of art. You'll feel like you're stepping into a chapel that serves beer and fish-and-chips. 174 Queen Victoria St

Ye Olde Cheshire Cheese

You'll quickly know you're in one of London's most historic pubs as you descend into its cavernous subterranean barrooms. 145 Fleet St

The Old Bank of England

Power lunchers from the high courts come here, drawn by the sumptuous interior, so you may well see some big shots enjoying a snack and pint before heading back into their legal proceedings next door. 194 Fleet St

Seven Stars

If the mounted animals in the windows outside don't catch your eye, the hoppy laurels on the inside of this quaint, friendly, and intimate pub will. 53 Carey St

Cittie of Yorke

One of the most impressive interiors of any pub in London, with high ceilings and giant casks of port on the wall. 22 High Holborn

The Princess Louise

Customers have been knocking back the ales since 1891 in this renovated alehouse with dark wood Victorian interior. Don't miss a visit to the loo. 208 High Holborn

ation takes a matter of minutes, and you'll leave primed for your next adventure.

£3-6, Mon-Fri 07:30-21:00, Sat 08:00-20:00, Sun 12:00-18:00, 47 Great Peter St, Westminster, +44 (0)20 7932 5401, pret.com, Tube: Westminster or St. James's Park

Bubbledogs

Bubbledogs, one of Goodge Street's most popular eateries, is a novel experience. Get a gourmet hot dog served in a classic red plastic bowl, and wash it down with a glass of champagne. The high-rolling hipster vibe runs deep here, but the unusual combination is anything but ironic—the staff take their bubbles and their dogs seriously. Aproned servers happily suggest which champagne to pair with your dog. The Mac Daddy, a brat topped with piping hot mac-n-cheese, fried onions, and bacon bits, is a favorite of everyone except cardiologists. For a combination you might not have experienced since the third grade, add a side of tater tots.

For a step up, find **Kitchen Table,** the hidden Michelin-starred restaurant in the back, for an experimental culinary experience that will take both your taste buds and your wallet for a ride. Saddle up to the bar along with 18 other diners and enjoy the show for the next few hours. Try to keep your mouth from watering as you watch the chefs dish up unforgettable tasting menus (£125 per person). Find more information and make reservations at kitchentablelondon.co.uk.

Dogs from £7, Tues-Thurs 12:00-16:00 and 17:30-23:00, Fri-Sat 11:30-23:00, 70 Charlotte St, Bloomsbury, +44 (0)20 7637 7770, bubbledogs.co.uk, Tube: Goodge Street

Goodge Street Restaurants & Food Stalls

Goodge Street (linking Tottenham Court Road and Cleveland Street) and its surrounding streets are where you'll find the highest density of inexpensive, fresh, and fast-casual restaurants in all of London. At every lunch hour, this street fills with young professionals enjoying the range of choices that includes gourmet hot dogs at **Bubbledogs**, burritos at **Benito's Hat** (56 Goodge St), pad thai at **Thai Metro** (38 Charlotte St), Greek salads at **Andreas** (40 Charlotte St), and sushi at **Roka** (37 Charlotte St). You'll discover classic British tea at **Yumchaa** (9 Tottenham St), tapas at **Salt Yard** (54 Goodge St), and delicious pizza at **ICCo** (Italian Coffee Company, 46 Goodge St)—all in the space of just a few blocks. All places listed are casual with fast service.

Goodge St between Tottenham Court Rd and Cleveland St, Bloomsbury, Tube: Goodge Street

Brick Lane Restaurants & Food Stalls

Brick Lane between Whitechapel High Street and Buxton Street is home to many immigrants from the former British colonies, particularly those in South Asia. On this meandering street and in the surrounding district, you'll find some of the most authentic Indian food outside of India. It's a truly intercultural dining experience, from the moment you're approached by restaurant reps on the street to the moment you push yourself away from the table at the end of your meal. Do a lap up and down the lane and don't be afraid to barter with the reps—talk them down on price or ask them to throw in a free drink or dessert. Part of the fun of Brick Lane is

the step into the unknown. Have you chosen wisely? You won't know for sure until you've tucked in. I usually start my lap at **Brick Lane Clipper** (104 Brick Ln) and **Cinnamon** (134 Brick Ln). I avoid Saffron (53 Brick Ln) and Preem & Prithi (118-122 Brick Ln), where quality and service vary widely.

Brick Ln between Whitechapel High St and Buxton St, Shoreditch, Tube: Aldgate East

London's Greasy Spoons

As you wander the streets of London, it's easy to overlook the thousands of nondescript greasy-spoon breakfast joints sprinkled across the city. Without the flashing lights and LED menus that the big chains have, these independently run restaurants are also known as "workmen's restaurants," as they fill with police officers just getting off shift or early-morning contractors taking a coffee break. These spots offer a full English breakfast for around a fiver, as opposed to £12 (or more) at the touristy spots.

For a historic example, head to **Terry's Cafe** (158 Great Suffolk St, +44 (0)20 7407 9358, terryscafe.co.uk, Tube: Borough) in the South Bank. It's famous for The Works (their full English breakfast) and their Ploughman's Lunch. No matter how insatiable your appetite, you won't leave this place hungry. Take in the traditional atmosphere in this cozy spot just around the corner from the recommended St. Christopher's Inn Hostel.

TOP NIGHTLIFE

London sports one of the hottest nightlife scenes around, with bars, pubs, and clubs to suit just about any interest. When going out, keep some things in mind: While the Jubilee, Northern, and Piccadilly lines run 24 hours in central London, the other lines close at midnight. Some bars and most clubs stay open late, especially along these routes. Always bring valid **photo ID** (getting bounced at the door will put a damper on your night). You'd be well advised to make reservations ahead of time for any spots you're dying to visit. For up-to-the-minute information and party inspiration, look at latenightlondon. co.uk and designmynight.com.

NIGHTLIFE DISTRICTS

London is a massive city, so it's best to plan your nights out based on which neighborhoods you're most interested in. While I recommend some of my favorite spots below, hot new venues open constantly, so approach your night in these exciting districts with a flexible attitude and

keep your head on a swivel. Are you looking for bright, easy, central, touristy pubs and bars or posh cocktail lounges? Serious nightclubs or ultramodern watering holes? Whittling down your options will become easier once you decide what atmosphere best suits you.

LGBT LONDON

The gay scene in London is alive and well. The city is broadly LGBT friendly, but, for gay travelers, all you need to know is **Soho.** In this tangle of streets in central London you'll find hotels, shopping, bars, restaurants, cafés, dance bars, clubs, lounges, and theaters that cater to the gay community, especially along **Old Compton Street.** From Old Compton, most will stop at the pub **Halfway to Heaven** (between Charing Cross Station and Trafalgar Square), where you can find cabaret and karaoke downstairs almost every night of the week. Ramp up for an evening of dancing at **Heaven** (covers around £5, coat check £1, 11 The Arches, +44 (0)20 7930 2020), the go-to Soho nightclub for a gay old time. They've got a massive dance hall with three bars and a side room for hip-hop—and the drinks are strong! All are welcome for the show. You can find Heaven underneath Charing Cross Station. For more drinks and great music, try **G-A-Y** (30 Old Compton St, +44 20 7494 2756, g-a-y.co.uk) or **SheSoho** (23-25 Old Compton St, she-soho.com). Check their websites for events.

West End

The West End, London's premier entertainment district, is always happening on the weekends. Its nightlife joints span the spectrum from alehouses to throbbing discotheques. **Soho,** one of the West End's hippest neighborhoods, offers numerous live music venues, off-the-wall bars, and bohemian cafés. Soho is also London's LGBT hub, with countless gay-friendly bars and clubs.

West End, Tube: Tottenham Court Road, Piccadilly Circus, Leicester Square, or Covent Garden

Shoreditch

Full of hipsters, artists, and other interesting people, this neighborhood on the east side of town is one of London's coolest. The area's communal workspaces and open-plan offices are home to more than 32,000 startups, making the post-work and evening scenes wide-ranging and always exciting. I've spent unforgettable days wandering from one funky spot to the next—from **Nightjar,** a Prohibition-themed speakeasy, to **XOYO,** a famed clubbing destination. In Shoreditch, you should expect the unexpected. (See page 22 for a walking tour through Shoreditch.)

Shoreditch, Tube: Old Street

Camden Town

Camden is the heart of London's punk and bohemian scene. Revelers flock here for the underground music—you'll know you're in the right place when the hairdos start to get a little wilder and the tattoos and piercings begin to multiply. While it's been slowly (and reluctantly) sliding toward the mainstream, Camden Town is one of the best places to find cutting-edge music venues like **Proud Camden.**

Camden, Tube: Camden Town

Dalston

As Shoreditch gentrifies, London's trendsetters are migrating north to Dalston. Throwback lounge bars like **Little Nan's Rio Bar** (107 Kingsland High St) blend with curiosity shops like the **Last Tuesday Society** (11 Mare St)—technically outside Dalston, but nearby and worth a mention for delectable cocktails in an odd and erotic throwback to turn-of-the-20th-century Barnum and Bailey's. Tourists rarely venture as far north as Dalston, so it's a good taste of what Shoreditch probably felt like when it was still up-and-coming. The action centers along Kingsland High Street, stretching north and south from the Dalston Kingsland/Junction Overground stations. New edgy and alternative lounges, bars, and clubs are constantly opening.

Dalston, Overground: Dalston Junction

BARS & PUBS

Spend a few days in London and you'll notice the sheer quantity of pubs—one on nearly every corner. And they all have proud, bold signage featuring names that stretch your imagination, like **Shakespeare's Head** (29 Regent St), **Ye Olde Cheshire Cheese** (145 Fleet St), and the **Hung Drawn and Quartered** (26-27 Great Tower St). King Richard II declared in 1393 that pubs must have signs to mark them

CRAFT BEER WALKING TOUR

Serious hops aficionados will be pleased to learn that London is enjoying a craft brewery renaissance. The epicenter of this revolution is known as the **Bermondsey Beer Mile,** home to microbreweries that are tucked into the brick arches of an old elevated train line. These breweries open their doors on the weekends for tastings and a great time.

To get started, take your beer-loving butt down to the Bermondsey stop on the Jubilee line. Turn south down St. James's Road and then head west on Dockley Road to **Kernel Brewery** (Dockley Rd, thekernelbrewery.com). The team at Kernel is widely respected not only for their beers, but also for kicking off the brewery revolution here in Bermondsey.

From here, you've got a choice: **The southern version** (just over a mile) or **the northern version** (just under a mile). For the southern route, head southeast along Lucey Way to visit the taproom at **Partizan** (8 Almond Rd, partizanbrewing.co.uk), which is pet friendly and has outdoor seating. Next, jog south down St. James's Road, then cut east on Southwark Park Road. Take Raymond Road southeast to reach **Fourpure** (Rotherhithe New Rd, fourpure.com), where you'll find 16 taps at an industrial-chic bar.

The northern route heads in the opposite direction, northwest to **Brew by Numbers** (79 Enid St, brewbynumbers.com), which is just 0.1 miles northwest of Kernel. At this taproom, you can try out the brewery's newest beers before they land in stores.

Get to **UBREW** (24 Old Jamaica Rd, ubrew.cc), the next stop, by continuing up Enid Street, heading east under the elevated tracks on Abbey Street, then turning south on Old Jamaica Street. UBREW calls itself an open brewery, allowing members to create their own beer. But you can also drink their branded beers at this taproom.

To reach the next two stops, **BottleShop: Bermondsey** (128 Druid St, bottle-shop. co.uk) and adjacent **Anspach & Hobday** (118 Druid St, anspachandhobday.com), retrace your steps back to Abbey Street, then turn north onto Druid Street.

The last stop, **Southwark Brewing Company** (46 Druid St, southwarkbrewing. co.uk), is a bit farther northwest along Druid Street.

From here, it's another three-quarters of a mile to reach the London Bridge Underground station. If you're hungry, hang a left on Bermondsey Street just before the station for a crop of foodie-approved restaurants.

as such. Most of the signs also feature bright illustrations, as most pub patrons were illiterate at the time. Modern English pubs carry on the tradition with their unique names and colorful signage.

The Anchor Bankside

If you're looking for the classic London pub, check out this historic one, located on the banks of the Thames along the Millennium Mile between Borough Market and Shakespeare's Globe. They've been serving ale at this location for more than eight centuries (the name has changed, but the business model hasn't). Pint-sized exposed-brick rooms, complete with over-stuffed red leather chairs and benches and creaky wooden decor, make this a favorite pit stop for tourists, locals, and even tour guides.

Pints from £5, daily 11:00–23:00, 34 Park St, South Bank, +44 (0)20 7407 1577, greeneking-pubs.co.uk, Tube: London Bridge

The George Inn

One of the oldest pubs in London, the George Inn is your classic stereotypical English tavern with wooden floors, exposed beams, and old-fashioned, dark wood furniture. Charles Dickens and Shakespeare are both said to have cozied up to the George's fireplace—and Dickens even mentioned the pub by name in *Little Dorrit*. Currently owned and operated by the National Trust, the pub is a registered historic site. It's a humbling feeling to toss back a London Pride ale in an establishment that was founded in the Middle Ages.

Pints from £5, pub grub £7–15, daily 10:00–23:00, 77 Borough High Street, South Bank, +44 (0)20 7407 2056, george-southwark.co.uk, Tube: Borough

ACT LIKE A LOCAL

Be Trendy

Londoners take staying on trend seriously, from fashion and food to neighborhoods and living arrangements. Pick up a *Time Out* or gig-focused *NME* magazine to know what's making waves in the city. There is something going on every night of the week in London (you just have to know how to find it), which is what makes this town such a lively one for those adventurous enough to keep their ear to the ground and follow the rumble. Year after year, the trendiest set of Londoners are picking up stakes and moving to the next neighborhood (moving on as soon as the rest of the scenesters have caught up with them). The deeper you dig into London's underground, the richer the treasures you'll find. On the surface, London is pristine and cosmopolitan, and for many, this is just the way they like it, but there's another side to London that only a handful of visitors get to experience. Find it and you'll quickly see why it's such a closely guarded secret.

Freud

With a name like Freud, you might expect a bawdier crowd, but sometimes a bar is just a bar. This little basement spot is a favorite of the stylish hipster set. Come out for some "speed cocktails" (i.e., drinks that are made quickly, like rum and coke or vodka soda) and enjoy the welcoming scene.

Cocktails from £5.50, Mon–Wed 12:00–24:00, Thurs-Sat 12:00–01:00, Sun 12:00–11:00, 198 Shaftesbury Ave, West End, +44 (0)20 7240 1100, freud.eu, Tube: Tottenham Court Road

The Porterhouse

Brewing its own collection of beers, the Porterhouse is a dependable sports café and bar. Come out to catch just about any televised sport matches, or descend into the dark basement to enjoy your fresh brew in one of the many nooks and crannies in this creatively constructed pub. In good weather, the sunny patio packs out once the workday is done.

Pints from £4.50, Mon–Thurs 12:00–23:00, Fri 12:00–23:30, Sat 12:00–24:00, Sun 12:00–22:30, 21-22 Maiden Ln, West End, +44 (0)20 7379 7917, porterhouse.london, Tube: London Charing Cross, Leicester Square, or Covent Garden

Bounce

Ever spent a night out at a social Ping-Pong club? Europe's first and largest such establishment, Bounce features the finest tables and paddles around. The fun, almost childlike atmosphere will have you and your friends bouncing off the walls. There are plenty of tables to go around, and the pizza (available upstairs) is far better than I expected it to be. Call ahead and make reservations to ensure that you don't have to wait for a table.

Table tennis £15.50 (30 mins.), Mon–Wed 16:00–24:00, Thurs 16:00–01:00, Fri–Sat 12:00–01:00, Sun 12.00-23:00, 121 Holborn, The City, +44 (0)20 3657 6525, bouncepingpong.com, Tube: Chancery Lane

SPEAKEASIES

One of London's hottest trends is the Prohibition-style cocktail bar in a low-lit lounge setting. Sprinkled across town, they're hard to find (that's half the point), but if you know where to look, you'll experience some of the best hidden gems that London has to offer. To act the part of a true speakeasy denizen, order an old-fashioned or a gimlet.

Nightjar

Take a step back in time and into Nightjar. Look forward to live music, a cozy atmosphere, and excellent Prohibition-era cocktails in this trendy little bar. Due to its popularity and limited seating, it can be quite hard to get in. Dress the part to better your chances at the door.

Cocktails £10-14, Sun–Wed 18:00–01:00, Thurs 18:00–02:00, Fri–Sat 18:00–03:00, 129 City Rd, Shoreditch, +44 (0)20 7253 4101, barnightjar.com, Tube: Old Street

London Cocktail Club

For one helluva classy cocktail bar that expertly blends life's simple pleasures with high-society London, check out the London Cocktail Club. With innovative options like Jägerbombs from an oyster shell, martinis featuring fried bacon, and even a sexy love potion that comes complete with a condom (in a wrapper, of course), your mind is sure to be blown. While the unpretentious bartenders are experts at whipping up bizarre concoctions, they haven't forgotten their roots. They can stir up an old-fashioned or a mojito to rival any that you've tasted. The Covent Garden location (one of just several outposts around town) requires that guests sign up for a free membership 24 hours in advance of their visit.

Drinks along with the experience £11, membership free, but advance enrollment required, Mon-Thurs 16:30-23:30, Fri-Sat 16:30-24:00, 6-7 Great Newport St, West End, +44 (0)020 7580 1960, londoncocktailclub.co.uk, Tube: Leicester Square

Mayor of Scaredy Cat Town

In the rear of the Spitalfields location of The Breakfast Club is one of London's best-kept secrets, serving exquisite cocktails. Enter through the refrigerator door by giving the password ("I need to speak with the mayor"). There's exposed brick everywhere and porthole mirrors—every surface oozes nostalgia for a bygone era. Be sure to read and obey the house rules, which include "The town is Scaredy Cat Town, not Cool Cats Town. The Mayor demands the highest standard of self-deprecation."

Drinks from £10, Mon-Thurs 17:00-24:00, Fri 15:00-24:00, Sat 12:00-24:00, Sun 12:00-22:30, 12-16 Artillery Ln, Shoreditch, +44 (0)20 7078 9639, themayorofscaredycattown.com, Tube: Aldgate East

Experimental Cocktail Club

If you like classics with a twist, this dimly lit, Roaring '20s cocktail lounge is for you. Utilizing proprietary syrups and bitters and the freshest ingredients available, these guys have rejuvenated the art of the cocktail—this ain't your grandma's vodka tonic! Besides perfectly executed traditional cocktails and updates on the same, the ECC has an extensive list of new cocktails featuring exotic liquors, top-shelf spirits, and ingredients more at home in the kitchen than behind the bar (e.g., homemade ginger syrup and habanero bitters). For a tasty splurge, try the Watermelon Cooler. All drinks are served in the appropriate vessel, whether that's a lowball or martini glass, adding to the experience.

Innovative cocktails from £11, daily 18:00-03:00, easy-to-miss door at 13a Gerrard St, West End, no phone, chinatownecc.com, reservation@chinatownecc.com, Tube: Leicester Square

Extra Credit

Trailer Happiness (177 Portobello Rd, +44 (0)20 7041 9833, trailerh.com, Tube: Notting Hill Gate, Westbourne Park) is a cozy and kitschy island-themed throwback cocktail bar. **Escapologist** (35 Earlham St, +44 (0)20 7240 5142, escapologistbar.co.uk, Tube: Covent Garden) is a spacious Houdini-themed speakeasy serving flaming cocktails that lean heavily on their wide range of bitters. **Lounge Bohemia** (1e Great Eastern St, +44 7720 707 000, loungebohemia. com, Tube: Shoreditch High Street), just a sidestep from my Shoreditch walk (see page 22), delivers creative libations underneath low-slung concrete arches amid a warm bohemian vibe, complete with menus pasted into Czech literary classics.

WINE BARS

Gordon's Wine Bar

Dating back to the 1890s, this place, with its candlelit brick arches, feels like a trip back in time. If the sun is shining, grab a bottle and enjoy the shaded outdoor terrace. The food selection goes well with the wines—from finger food and tapas to meat dishes and Sunday roasts. Rest assured you can get both your drink on and your grub on at Gordon's.

Reasonable bottle prices from £22, daily 11:00-23:00, 47 Villiers St, West End, +44 (0)20 7930 1408, gordonswinebar.com, Tube: Embankment or London Charing Cross

Cork & Bottle

You may be surprised to find food and wine of this caliber in such a touristy district (just a block off Leicester Square), but the people at Cork & Bottle are aiming at a discerning class of wine drinkers. Count on a vast selection of international wines available by the glass or bottle, along with a slew of unforgettable finger foods and entrées like chili squid and an impressive ham-and-cheese pie. Cork & Bottle, with its sophisticated pretheater crowd and its emphasis on wines of every conceivable vintage, feels like a cozy little slice of France. The servers are happy to walk you through both the wine list and menu, and, if you have time, don't miss their wine tastings (find the schedule online).

Glasses from £6, sides and salads from £7, mains from £13, daily 11:00-24:00, 44-46 Cranbourn St, West End, +44 (0)20 7734 7807, thecorkandbottle.co.uk, Tube: Leicester Square

Vagabond

With drippy candles and beautiful bottles lining the walls, elegance defines Vagabond. You'll feel quite sophisticated as you use a prepaid card to sip some of the world's finest wines and cheeses one swipe at a time. Clientele are usually well dressed.

House wines from £4, Mon-Sat 11:00-23:00, Sun 11:00-22:00, 67 Brushfield St, Shoreditch, +44 (0)20 3674 5670, vagabondwines.co.uk, Tube: Liverpool Street

CLUBS
Fabric

After being shuttered for the latter half of 2016, one of London's most famous clubs is back with a vengeance. Fabric is famous for its resident DJs, multiple dance floors, and the "bodysonic" room, where 400 independent subwoofers will shake you to your core. You'll think that half of London is waiting in the queue with you to get in. Fortunately for you, if you stay at one of my suggested hostels, they can make a reservation for you—and they'll even cut the cover charge in half.

Tickets online from £10, Fri-Sun 23:00-05:30, sometimes open later, 77A Charterhouse St, The City, +44 (0)20 7336 8898, fabriclondon.com, Tube: Barbican

Piccadilly Institute

Explore this labyrinth of rooms, each decorated according to a theme that explores a different shade of insanity. I've had great experience with the service, and the music choices are always on point. The five bars and two clubs draw a young, chic crowd, so dress stylishly (nice shoes and a collared shirt will do the trick) and the bouncers will quickly wave you in.

£5 cover weekdays, £10 cover weekends, daily 17:00-late, cover charge after 21:00, 1 The London Pavilion, West End, +44 (0)20 7287 8008, piccadillyinstitute.com, Tube: Piccadilly Circus

XOYO

XOYO is an established London clubbing classic. Any big-time DJ coming through town is sure to schedule a gig here. Two floors and a top-of-the-line sound system mean you can dance the night (and part of the morning) away. Avoid the usually long lines by getting on the guest list online or by hitting the club up on a Monday or Tuesday. Music is of the indie electronic DJ variety.

Cover varies (up to £20), open daily, hours vary by event, 32-37 Cowper St, Shoreditch, +44 (0)20 7354 9993, xoyo.co.uk, Tube: Old Street

Ministry of Sound

The Ministry puts its commitment to music above all else. The club has long been a favorite of house and techno fans, and it provides something for every fan of electronic music. Each of its three independent dance rooms plays a different style of EDM. They're clearly onto something: The house has been packed every night without fail since the early '90s.

Cover varies (up to £26), Fri 22:30-06:00, Sat 23:00-06:00, 103 Gaunt St, South Bank, +44 (0)20 7740 8600, ministryofsound.com, Tube: Elephant & Castle

Proud Camden

What was formerly an equestrian hospital is now a massive multipurpose venue hosting everything from launch parties to drag shows and concerts. Former horse stables are now VIP booths with karaoke options, fitting up to 25 guests. The booths have all been renovated in a unique style, such as pinup tattoos, the Desert Orchid room, and the gold-bedazzled '70s Disco Room. When the sun's still up, Proud Camden is a great place for a meal or a beer in the garden out back. After sunset, the party heats up with live music—primarily indie rock bands, who quickly fill the large dance hall to capacity. Proud Camden truly is a microcosm of Camden in London, with all of its funkiness distilled into one venue.

Check the events listings online ahead of time to see what's going down. The crowd is young, hip, and professional: a well-dressed set that likes to let their hair down. Thursdays are student nights.

Show tickets from £10, drinks from £4, Wed 11:00-01:30, Thurs-Sat 11:00-02:30, The Horse Hospital,

The Stables Market, Chalk Farm Rd, Camden, +44 (0)20 7482 3867, proudcamden.com, Tube: Camden Town

PUB CRAWLS

Pub crawls offer guided parties that run nightly and can be a good choice if you're looking to sample a range of nightlife and meet fellow travelers. The savings you get from discounted drink deals and what you would have spent on club entry generally covers the ticket price.

1 Big Night Out

The biggest pub crawl in London, with 50-100 revelers nightly, kicks off with beer pong during the meeting time (19:30-21:30) near Piccadilly Circus. The tour includes five bars and five free shots in five hours. There are parallel Camden and Shoreditch options available.

£15 with this book, meets nightly at Riley's Sports Bar (80 Haymarket), +44 (0)20 7836 9995, 1bignightout.com, Tube: Leicester Square

Camden Pub Crawl

As the name suggests, this pub crawl operates in Camden. Pub crawls kick off 19:30 to 21:30.

£14 weekdays, £16 weekends, save £2 by booking online, meets nightly at Belushi's Camden (48-50 Camden High St), undiscoveredlondon.com, info@ undiscoveredlondon.com, Tube: Mornington Crescent

London Gone Wild

London Gone Wild is a pub crawl option that helps you navigate the trendy scene in Shoreditch.

£13.50, meets Thurs-Sat 20:00-21:00 at the Shoreditch (145 Shoreditch High St), +44 (0)20 7096 0371, nightsgonewild.com, Tube: Aldgate East

TOP SHOPPING & MARKETS

SHOPPING DISTRICTS
Oxford Street

If it's brand names you're after, mile-long Oxford Street is quite possibly London's single best shopping thoroughfare. You'll find all the major retailers, along with one of London's most famous top-end department stores, **Selfridges** (400 Oxford St, +44 113 369 8040, Tube: Bond Street). Be sure to venture southward off of Oxford down **Regent Street** to satisfy that shopping fix of yours.

West End, Tube: Oxford Circus

DEPARTMENT STORES
Harrods

Harrods is your one-stop shop for everything high-end. This cathedral to consumerism boasts everything from luxury chocolates to the latest technology, designer lingerie, larger-than-life stuffed Paddington Bears, and posh home furnishings, all spread across eight expansive floors. Harrods also houses more than 25 restaurants and cafés. It's a good idea to pick up a store guide to navigate this labyrinth—don't miss the famous Egyptian escalator deep in the belly of the store, which feels more like a ride through King Tut's tomb than a moving staircase in London.

Mon-Sat 10:00-20:00, Sun 11:30-18:00, 87-135 Brompton Rd, West London, +44 (0)20 7730 1234, Tube: Knightsbridge

MARKETS
Portobello Market

Every Saturday, one of the world's biggest antiques markets takes over the Notting Hill neighborhood, spreading its wares all up and down Portobello Road. If you're actually planning on buying the jewelry, vintage clothing, and other items on offer, bring cash (the ATMs often run out or have insane lines). Saturday mornings before 10:00 are best for avoiding the crowds. The market also runs Monday through Friday, featuring produce, secondhand clothing, and other goods. Stop into the famous **Hummingbird Bakery** (133 Portobello Rd, +44 (0)20 7851 1795, hummingbirdbakery. com) to fortify yourself with goodies.

Mon-Wed 09:00-18:00, Thurs 09:00-13:00, Fri-Sat 09:00-19:00, West London, Tube: Notting Hill Gate

Camden Market

London's original craft market dates back to the 1970s. Once a place for the quirkier side of the city to display itself, gentrification has subdued the bolder tones. This bustling street market sees tens of thousands of visitors each weekend. Explore

large open-air clothes vendors and thrift shop-type stalls, street food galore, and, my favorite, a large shopping complex in a repurposed barn. Save time for food, and stick around for the nightlife, as this is one of London's most eclectic neighborhoods and the center of the alternative fashion scene. The market, open daily, is busiest on weekends. Blow your mind at the multi-level neon rave shop **Cyberdog** (cyberdog. net), and pick up a well-made belt at the **M&M Leather Workshop** (mmleather-workshop.com).

Daily 10:00–19:00, individual shop hours may vary, +44 (0)20 3763 9900, camdenmarket.com, Camden, Tube: Camden Town

Borough Market

South of the river, this open-air food market is the place to challenge your taste buds, with loads of free samples ranging from wild boar to ostrich sandwiches. Conveniently located near the Millennium Mile, Borough Market has permanent shops, restaurants, and cafés built into the ironwork of the awnings, along with farm stalls that pop up daily to sell fresh goods. Those who just want to nibble can pick up cheeses and meats by the slice. Otherwise, dive into the delicious ethnic dishes, sandwiches, and smoothies available throughout the market.

Mon–Thurs 10:00–17:00, Fri 10:00–18:00, Sat 08:00–17:00, 8 Southwark St, South Bank, boroughmarket.org, Tube: London Bridge

Old Spitalfields Market

This grand covered arts-and-crafts market has been located here for the better part of 400 years. Today's wares include graphic tees, hipster shoulder bags, genuine leather belts, and handmade art pieces and frames. In the massive barn-like warehouse are both permanent retail stores and semipermanent stalls. The market makes for great window shopping and even better photos. Skip the overpriced restaurants inside and opt for food at the Brick Lane Market nearby.

Sun–Fri 10:00–17:00, Sat 11:00–17:00, individual shop hours may vary, 16 Horner Square, Shoreditch, oldspital-fieldsmarket.com, Tube: Liverpool Street

Brick Lane Market

Brick Lane Market is a collection of warehouses and streets where you can wander and discover untold pop-up shops, custom bike stores, and tons of bars and cafés. Sundays, when street performers and crowds create quite a buzz, are the best day to visit. If vintage is your thing, come here for heaven on earth. Find the **Boiler House** (Sat 11:00–18:00, Sun 10:00–17:00, 152 Brick Ln, +44 (0)20 7770 6028, boilerhouse-foodhall.co.uk) for an international street food extravaganza.

Permanent stores and shops open throughout the week, 91 Brick Ln, Shoreditch, +44 (0)20 7770 6028, bricklanemarket.com, Tube: Aldgate East

TOP PARKS & RECREATION

Hyde Park

This park is the largest in the city, covering more than 350 acres. Highlights include the Diana Memorial Fountain, the large Serpentine Lake, and the Speakers' Corner, a place where Londoners can come and speak their minds loudly and proudly on any subject they wish. Take paddleboats (£10/30 min., £12/1 hr.) out on the lake, or enjoy a drink at any one of the outdoor cafés that line its shores. Any time there are important sports matches going on, thousands flock to the park to watch on massive projector screens. It's also a popular year-round spot for concerts and festivals.

West London, Tube: Hyde Park Corner

Battersea Park

Well off the beaten track for most tourists, this is my favorite park in town. It's a calm oasis in the midst of the urban jungle. There are miles of running trails, waterfront views, and the unique and spectacular 100-foot-tall Buddhist Peace Pagoda monument, perfect for a moment's reflection. It's also the site of a huge bonfire and light show held every November 5 to commemorate the thwarting of the Gunpowder Plot—a failed terrorist plot to blow up the Houses of Parliament in 1605.

South Bank, Tube: Sloane Square

Football

Premier League football is a weekly ritual for many Londoners, and being a spectator for a match is a unique and unforgettable experience. Tickets to Chelsea (chelseafc.com) and Arsenal (arsenal.com) games can be incredibly expensive and hard to come by. Perhaps try West Ham United (whufc.com), which plays in the Olympic stadium, or Fulham (fulhamfc.com), which plays on London's oldest football pitch. Plan transportation well in advance at tlfg.uk, and purchase tickets directly at official club websites. On the day of the match, ticket touts (scalpers) may be outside the Tube stations nearby. Touts are not officially authorized to sell tickets, and you risk being denied entry to the stadium if you present unauthorized tickets. That said, I wouldn't pay more than £75 each, even for the best tickets, and make sure you have the physical tickets in your hands before you fork over the money.

TOP TOURS

Fat Tire Bike Tours

My favorite way to see the city! Take the Royal London Bike Tour and enjoy the musings of a great guide as you pedal through some of the city's most beautiful scenery. You'll learn a ton about London and its history as you cruise through Hyde Park, Kensington Gardens, and Green Park and then down the Mall, stopping at each interesting point and photo op along the way. This bike tour avoids the major thoroughfares, sticking to the parks for the most part.

£24 adults, £22 students, low season Mon and Thurs-Sun 11:00, shoulder season daily 11:00, high season daily 11:00 and 15:30, meets at Queensway Tube Station, West London, fattirebiketours.com, Tube: Queensway

Blue Badge Guides

Hire a Blue Badge Guide if you're seeking a serious authority on just about any topic. The group's easy-to-navigate website will connect you with a guide who is an expert in the subject you're searching for. No matter your niche (music, architecture, birds, or London's LGBT history), these guides have you covered—and they don't only operate in London. A quick call to their office can line up a tour within a day. Having passed rigorous qualification exams, Blue Badge Guides take their tours seriously. They can also be a great value when the cost is split among a group. Even if you end up footing the bill yourself, the premium gets you world-class professionalism, a customized itinerary, and the expertise of your guide.

£155 half day, £262 full day, +44 (0)20 7403 1115, britainsbestguides.org

London Walks

Offering a wide range of tours, times, and subjects, these walking tours are almost as varied as the city itself. London's longest-running walking tour company offers just about every itinerary you could imagine, each led by an expert in the subject. Archaeologists, architects, lawyers, and public servants guide these in-depth and entertaining walks, most of which run daily. From neighborhood street art walks to ghost tours, and even partial-day trips out to Hampstead Heath, it's easy to integrate one of these tours into your itinerary.

£10 for 2-hour walk, daily, meeting points vary depending on tour, +44 (0)20 7624 3978, londonwalks.com

TOP HOSTELS

Besides the hostels listed here, be sure to check out airbnb.com for affordable private apartment listings. Battersea, Chelsea, and Shoreditch make for affordable, well-connected neighborhoods where you can begin your search. Many universities (such as UL, UCL, Imperial College, and London Met) open up their empty dorms for affordable, self-service, short-stay private rooms over the summer months. Book directly on their websites.

Clink78 Hostel

If buildings could talk, this hostel would certainly have some stories to tell. Originally a courthouse, it's made up of dorms that used to be prison cells. What are now the Internet café and the movie room used to be courtrooms. In one of these rooms, the Clash went before a judge for avicide (two band members were busted for taking potshots at pigeons with an air rifle). They pled guilty and were fined 30 quid each. Today, you'll find a large hostel with comfortable beds and a very social atmosphere with an on-site Clash-themed bar where the iconic London band's music plays day and night. Some complain about the noise and sleep quality, but for those looking for a memorable time in London, Clink78 is calling.

From £17, £3 Wi-Fi, 24-hour reception, laundry, bar, free breakfast, 78 King's Cross Rd, Bloomsbury, +44 (0)20 7183 9400, clinkhostels.com, reservations@clinkhostels.com, Tube: Kings Cross St Pancras

St. Christopher's at the Village, London Bridge

One of London's top party hostels features a bar, DJs spinning on the weekends in the nightclub, and karaoke and cinema nights. Its rooms and bathrooms are clean, and it's located next to some great sights (Borough Market is only a few blocks away) and solid nightlife options. The hostel offers everything from 33-bed dorms to private rooms. Free breakfast is a perk if you book online. Four other St. Christopher's locations across the city offer similar social scenes and amenities.

From £20, free Wi-Fi, 24-hour reception, free lockers, 161-165 Borough High St, South Bank, +44 (0)20 7939 9710, st-christophers.co.uk, village@st-christophers.co.uk, Tube: London Bridge

Generator Russell Square

The Generator chain is well known for reliably clean rooms, affordable prices, and more amenities than you'll know what to do with. Aimed at the discerning backpacker set, this hostel has its own bar, game room with pool tables, and a lounge equipped with multiple flat-screens, and it offers free walking tours and daily events like karaoke night and drinking games. It's also just a five-minute walk from the Euston, St. Pancras, and King's Cross train and Tube stations.

From £27, free Wi-Fi, laundry, 24-hour reception, lockers, 37 Tavistock Plaza, Bloomsbury, +44 (0)20 7388 7666, generatorhostels.com, info@generatorhostels.com, Tube: Russell Square

Wombat's

Wombat's, one of Europe's well-known hostel chains, puts you right where you want to be for sightseeing by day and partying by night. It's a five-minute walk from the Tower of London and Tower Bridge, and ten minutes from the Brick Lane food scene and the nightlife in Shoreditch. Count on a welcoming and highly social atmosphere, a helpful staff that provides good recommendations, and delicious breakfast. It's done up in shabby-chic decor with a reception desk that's built from recycled lumber. You'll feel cool from check-in till you're downing drinks under brick arches at the on-site bar. Rooms are clean and bright, featuring electrical outlets and reading lamps at each bunk.

Beds from £24, 24-hour reception, on-site bar, hair dryers, adapters, and towels available, pool table, free Wi-Fi, breakfast extra, 7 Dock St, The City, +44 (0)20 7680 7600, wombats-hostels.com, booklondon@ wombats.eu, Tube: Tower Hill

Astor Hyde Park Hostel

The Astor chain is a great option for budget travelers. Set in a 19th-century mansion, this old building has been retrofitted to feature all the modern amenities without losing its authentic wooden soul. Its 180 beds are comfortable, the staff is extremely welcoming, and the location near Hyde Park is prime. Simple rooms range in everything from private doubles up to 12-bed mixed dorms. The Hyde Park branch is my favorite Astor location, but other options include Victoria, Queensway, and one near the British Museum.

Bunks from £21, free Wi-Fi, 24-hour reception with lockers, laundry, common room; £1 towels for rent, £1 donation for breakfast and hair dryers on deposit, 191 Queensgate, West London, +44 (0)20 7581 0103, astorhostels.com, hydepark@astorhostels.com, Tube: Gloucester Road, South Kensington

Barmy Badger Backpackers

This place, in the posh Earls Court district, feels a bit like your aunt's town house, complete with a large living room and a nice couch to sink into. Barmy's makes a point of including everything in your booking: Wi-Fi, continental breakfast, kitchen use, and travel advice are all included in the price of your bed. Get extras like towels and adapters for a refundable deposit. The owner's two dogs are friendly and affectionate. While the bunks are stacked three high in the six-bed dorms, each cubby sports a comfortable mattress, a personal light, and a charging port. If a solid night's sleep is your top priority, look no further.

Six-bed dorm £25, private rooms from £45, 24-hour reception, cable TV, free maps, laundry facilities, free Wi-Fi, outdoor terrace, breakfast included, towels with deposit, 17 Longridge Rd, West London, +44 (0)20 7370 5213, barmybadger.com, barmybadger@hotmail.com, Tube: Earls Court

TRANSPORTATION

GETTING THERE & AWAY

Although Great Britain is an island, international travel into London has never been easier thanks to the city's efficient infrastructure and extensive public transit system.

Plane

The city of London has five international airports. All have quick and inexpensive public transportation options into the center.

London City (LCY, londoncityairport. com) is the airport closest to downtown London. Hop on the commuter train DLR (dlrlondon.co.uk) and transfer onto the Tube at Canning Town to connect to the rest of London. Your journey from the airport to the center will cost £4.90.

From **Heathrow,** (LHR, heathrow.com) London's busiest airport, take the Piccadilly Tube line straight into the center (this takes about an hour, stopping at every station along the way) and connect to your accommodation's Tube stop from there. A single fare runs £6. I find the Heathrow Express to be overpriced at £26, even though it'll get you into the center in 15 minutes. It's better by far to save the money and spend the hour on the train planning your itinerary.

From **Gatwick** (LGW, gatwickairport. com) take the Southern Train (southernrailway.co.uk) service, which runs every 15 minutes, to Victoria station (45 minutes, single fare £15). You'll be tempted to spring for the Gatwick Express (30 minutes, single fares from £18, gatwickexpress.com), but the Southern Train saves you cash without sacrificing too much time.

Luton (LTN, london-luton.co.uk) has connections into London every 15 minutes via EasyBus (easybus.com, from £2); the 80-minute journey puts you at Victoria station. Or take a shuttle to Luton Airport Parkway (from £14), which offers different rail services that can get you into the center. For the cheapest fares, visit Trainline (thetrainline.com).

I avoid **Stansted Airport** (STN, stanstedairport.com) because of the longer transit times into the city center, and the airport itself isn't very comfortable. If you have to depart or arrive there, your best options are either the Stansted Express train (£22.50, runs every 15 min, 45-min journey, stanstedexpress.com), which will take you to Liverpool Street station, or National Express Buses (run every 20 min, 75-min journey, sometimes much longer), which will take you to Baker Street station. Buses can take three hours in rush hour, so be sure to factor that in!

Some budget airlines are also beginning to offer cheaper flights into regional airports well outside of London. As seductive as these ticket prices are, flying into these far-flung airports can add considerable time and costs to your travel plans. From London Southend Airport, for example, it takes at least 1.5 hours to get to the center.

Train

There are nine major train stations in London. All are connected to the Tube and the bus system. Rates from Paris—on fast trains taking just under 2.5 hours—range from about £42 (€50) and up, depending on student discount and how far in advance you book your ticket. Visit Eurostar.com for prices and routes.

Bus

There are bus options to London from the rest of the UK as well as from Paris, Amsterdam, and Brussels. While rates can be significantly cheaper than train options, hours spent on buses add up quickly. Check out routes and fares at Eurolines (eurolines.com), Megabus (uk.megabus.com), and Student Agency (studentagencybus.com).

Car

By car, London is 460 kilometers (about 6.5 hours) from Paris and 660 kilometers (about 8 hours) from Edinburgh.

GETTING AROUND

London is a massive but highly walkable city. A nonstop walk from Big Ben to the Tower of London takes about an hour. Walking is a great way to explore the city in detail, one historic block at a time. Keep an eye out for the helpful dark blue map signposts around the city and near bus stops. When you arrive at your lodgings, don't assume that you'll be able to find them again easily, especially if you're returning after sundown. Take in your surroundings and snap a picture of any landmarks that'll help you find your way back again.

Prepare to be amazed, and possibly intimidated, by London's **public transportation** system. Comprising 11 metro lines and over 700 bus routes, it's one of the best and most extensive public transport systems in the world. On day one, buy yourself an **Oyster Card** (£5 deposit) at Heathrow or London City Airport or at any Tube station to reduce the cost of your bus and Tube tickets by nearly half.

Underground/Tube

One of the world's most extensive underground networks runs 24 hours on Fridays and Saturdays, but only on the primary lines downtown (Central, Victoria, Jubilee, Northern, and Piccadilly). A single journey costs £4.90 or £2.40 with the Oyster Card. Download the TubeMap app (which will keep you advised of any delays or closures) or pick up a free metro map from the desk at any Tube station.

Bus

London's buses work like clockwork too. You must have an Oyster Card to ride, as bus drivers do not accept cash. If you ever find yourself lost or disoriented, every bus stop has a map that shows you where you are and which buses stop there. Do your homework before going out at night to see which night bus can take you home. Ask the driver when you should exit the bus if you are ever in doubt of your stop. A single journey costs £1.50. Map out your route beforehand with the Google Maps app.

Bus 11 between Liverpool Street station and Victoria is a great way to get oriented with the city. It takes you right through the middle of London, past Westminster, the city's main parks, and Buckingham Palace.

Taxi

You might be tempted to use Uber while in London. But taking a classic London black taxi is an experience in itself. The quirky, chatty drivers are always happy to help with your plans for the day, and the ride is a good deal (about £8.50/12-min. ride) if you're splitting between four or five friends. If you need to call for a taxi, use only a licensed Black Cab or a taxi service recommended by your hostel. If you're unable to hail a taxi from the street, call 087 1871 8710, which will give you access to hundreds of licensed taxis 24 hours a day. Cabbies evaporate when the bars let out, and they're nearly impossible to wave down.

Bicycles

Santander Cycles (tfl.gov.uk/modes/cycling/santander-cycles) runs London's public bike-rental system. For £2, you get access to the bikes for a full 24 hours. Each ride is free as long as you check it back into a Santander stand within 30 minutes. It's possible to check out another bike as soon as you've checked the previous one in for no additional fee (as long as the ride was less than 30 minutes). If you decide to keep the same bike longer, each subsequent half hour costs £2.

DAY TRIPS

Windsor Castle

This strikingly beautiful fortress is the largest castle in the world and the oldest continually inhabited one as well. This castle-turned-palace, just over 20 miles from downtown London, has housed the British royal family since the days of Henry I—that's an unbroken string of 39 English monarchs. Over nearly a millennium, many royals left their own mark on this ever-evolving palace, which rivals even Versailles in its opulence. Surrounded by well-manicured lawns, the castle draws more than a million visitors annually. Explore the royal halls, admiring furniture dripping in golden Baroque accents and the castle's many fine works of art (including a number of Rembrandts). Join the free 30-minute tour for the rundown on the history of the castle and a summary of the layout of the grounds. The tour ends with a visit to the lavish State Apartments. Allow three hours at the castle for a good visit.

Hop on the South West train (southwesttrains.co.uk) from London's Waterloo station and alight at the Windsor & Eton Riverside stop, only a short walk from the castle itself.

£22, daily 09:45-16:15, last entry 15:00, royalcollection.org.uk, +44 (0)20 7766 7304, rail station: Windsor & Eton Riverside

Stonehenge

This world-famous prehistoric rock formation is within reach of a day trip from London. The purpose, meaning, and construction methods of this monument—carbon dated to before 3000 BC—continue to evade experts. So we are left to use our own imaginations to try to figure out how and why such massive stones (weighing up to four tons each) were hoisted and placed in perfect alignment, all without machinery, modern engineering, or even nylon ropes.

An early-morning trip will get you out to Stonehenge in time to enjoy it for a bit. Go for one of the numerous day-trip options from London, which will get you there more quickly than public transportation (two hours, rather than three-plus). **London Toolkit** (£47, londontoolkit.com) offers a day trip with a stop in Bath. **Premium Tours** (from £35, premiumtours.co.uk) has a Stonehenge-only option. **Viator** (viator.com) has curated options available online.

I recommend booking Stonehenge with a tour that also takes you to Windsor Castle or **Bath,** an old Roman fort town named after the hot springs that bubble out of the ground in the area. Otherwise, no matter how impressive it is, it's quite a long time on the bus to see a stack of large rocks, no?

£16.50, £15 with valid student ID, daily 09:30–19:00, closes at 17:00 in winter, last admission two hours before closing time, +44 (0)0370 333 1181, english-heritage.org.uk

HELP!

Tourist Information Centers

Look for London's excellent tourist information centers at the major rail and Tube stations. All the information you'll need for your visit can be found online (cityoflondon.gov.uk and visitlondon.com). For many sights, you can even book tickets through these websites.

There are shops throughout London that purport to be unbiased tourist resources, but they keep the lights on by selling (often quite aggressively) overpriced tickets to West End shows or other tour options. Here's one that's independent and impartial:

City Information Centre, Mon-Sat 09:30-17:30, Sun 10:00-16:00, St Paul's Churchyard, +44 (0)20 7332 1456

Pickpockets & Scams

As in almost all major Western European cities, the crime rate in London is extremely low. Still, be alert for pickpockets in the larger touristy areas, in restaurants, and on metros, buses, and trains. Teams of thieves on bikes have been known to snatch phones right out of tourists' hands while they cruise by. If you need to call for a taxi, you should use only a licensed Black Cab or a taxi service recommended by your hostel. Most travelers who lose their phone, purse, or other valuables tend to do so when they are out late at night and are disoriented. If you're heading out, lock up your valuables or keep them safely tucked away on your person.

Emergencies

In an emergency, dial 999.

Pharmacies

Boots (boots.com) has dozens of locations throughout downtown London.

Hospital

St Thomas' Hospital (serious emergencies only) Westminster Bridge Rd, Lambeth, SE1 7EH +44 (0)20 7928 9292

US Embassy

Nine Elms Lane +44 (0)20 7499 9000

PARIS

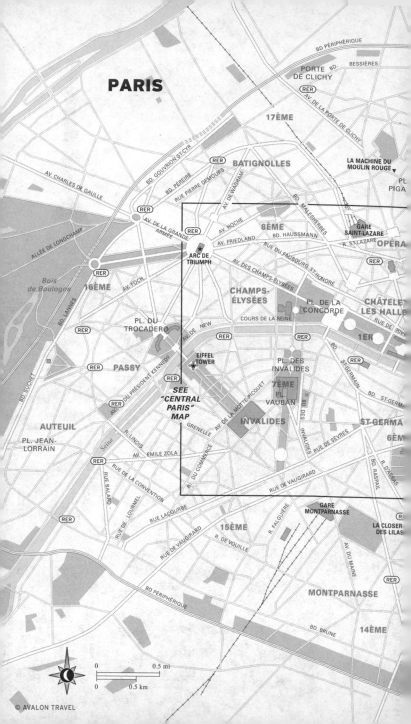

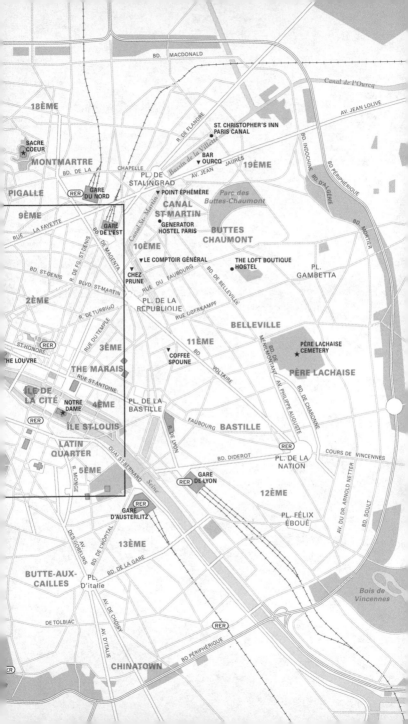

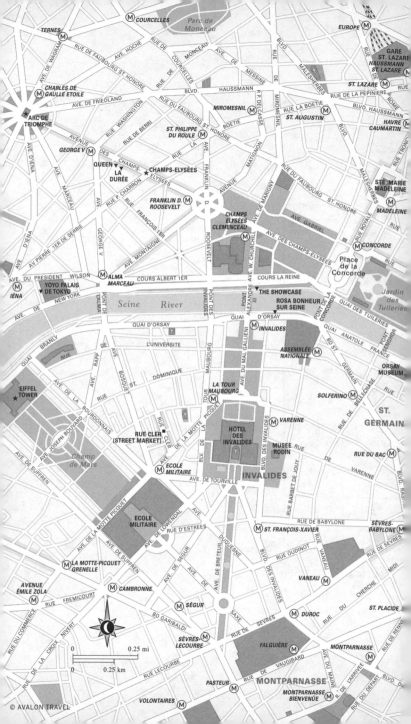

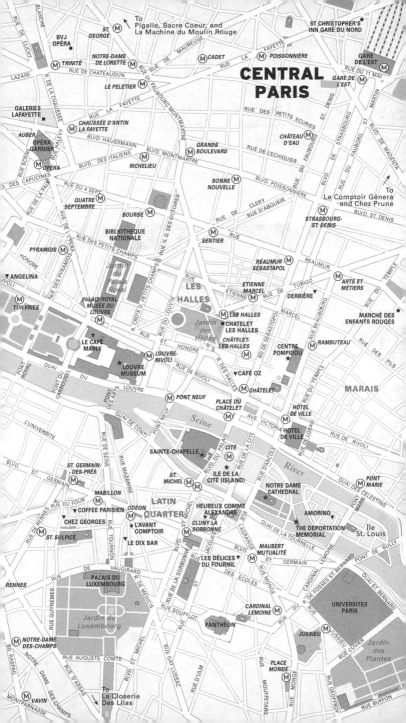

Paris is a treasure trove of art, cathedrals, and magnificent architecture. From the Eiffel Tower to Sacre Coeur, from *Mona Lisa*'s coy smile to the gargoyles that guard Notre Dame, Paris is full of sophisticated beauty. But—like a deliciously flaky *pain au chocolat*—the city's real treat lies beneath its surface. Even if you don't fall in love *in* Paris, you will fall in love *with* Paris. Dig deep into the city to discover the people, sights, sounds, tastes, and smells to understand the Parisian joie de vivre.

PARIS 101

Paris's location on a couple of islands in the Seine River made the city, founded in 250 BC, a strategic stronghold. By 1200, Paris was one of the most powerful cities in Europe, with a massive castle, cathedrals, trade unions, and all the makings of a major capital. As the city evolved, the French royalty levied untenable taxes on their subjects to finance wars and opulent palaces like Versailles. Peasants were starving, and a groundswell of anger gave rise to the French Revolution in 1789. Over 10 long years, thousands of nobles were jailed or publicly beheaded by the guillotine.

The revolution was a success in terms of eliminating the ruling class. But it takes more than that. You've got to govern. By 1799, France was struggling to find a leader who could harness the country's nationalist fervor. A man rose through the ranks (and well beyond his short stature) to become self-proclaimed emperor of France. His name? Napoleon Bonaparte. After conquering much of Western Europe by 1812, Napoleon was exiled—twice. He escaped his first exile quickly, suffered tremendous losses at the Battle of Waterloo in 1815, was exiled again, and lived out his days in disgraced solitude on a small island between Brazil and Africa. But Napoleon did leave his mark on modern society. Our legal and public educational systems and even units of measurement today derive from the developments Napoleon undertook during his reign.

As France entered the modern age, Napoleon III, Napoleon's nephew, was elected president in 1848 in France's first democratic election; the French constitution forbade a second term, so he declared himself emperor in 1852 and reigned another 18 years. Napoleon III wanted to beautify his capital city, making it fit for an emperor. He commissioned his favorite architect and city planner, Georges-Eugène Haussmann, with the immense project of modernizing Paris. Thousands of Parisians were displaced to make room for new wide boulevards and the grand avenues that we see today.

Paris enjoyed a golden age around the turn of the 20th century. An engineer, Gustave Eiffel, completed his tower for the 1889 World's Fair, while an eclectic group of outcast artists flocked to the city and developed a new artistic style they called impressionism. The 20th century brought two world wars, but even through the difficult years, Paris continued to attract artists and bohemians. Paris was on its heels after World War II, but thanks to Allied support, the city began the process of reconstruction.

Today, France is liberal and progressive, and the Parisian joie de vivre is as palpable as ever.

PLAN AHEAD

RESERVATIONS
Reservations are recommended for the following sights, which can book out as much as a month in advance:
Eiffel Tower (toureiffel.paris/en)
Louvre (louvre.fr/en)

PASSES
Paris Museum Pass
The **Paris Museum Pass** (en.parismuseumpass.com) gives you free entry and line-skipping privileges at a number of Paris's major museums, including the Louvre, the Orsay, and Versailles. Choose from two-day (€48), four-day (€62), and six-day (€74) options. In peak tourism months, the line-skipping privileges can be more valuable than the savings—it'll take a herculean effort to see enough sights to actually save money. Purchase the pass online or at any participating museum.

LOCAL HAPPENINGS
Tour de France
The Tour de France, which loops more than 2,000 miles around France each July, is the best-known and most competitive professional cycling event. Cyclists from all over the world push themselves to the brink of exhaustion during this three-week-long stage race. The starting point changes yearly, but the race always ends with eight laps through central Paris, up and down the Champs-Élysées and under the Louvre in a grueling sprint to the finish. The festive atmosphere draws tens of thousands of visitors every year.

Bastille Day
France's national holiday, Bastille Day (July 14), commemorates the day when rebels stormed the Bastille prison in 1789, kicking off the French Revolution. Paris hosts a grand parade accompanied by fireworks, musical performances, dances, large communal meals, and, of course, wine and champagne. Expect the entire country—including sights and museums—to shut down. Don't fret; Bastille Day parties are much more fun than anything else you might have planned.

THREE DAY ITINERARY

It's important to be efficient when sightseeing in Paris. Three days isn't much time to see even the major highlights, so get ready to walk—a lot. You'll also be using the easy-to-navigate metro system to extend your tour into the outer edges of the city.

DAY 1: BIENVENUE Á LA GAUCHE

MORNING

Grab breakfast at the hostel or pop into your local *boulangerie* (bakery) to try your first heavenly croissant or *pain au chocolat*. The baguettes in Paris are so good that you can just take one of them with you and munch as you walk (no need for toppings or even butter).

Head into Île de la Cité and spend a few hours exploring Paris's quintessential sights: the stunningly beautiful royal chapel of Sainte-Chapelle, the epically Gothic Notre Dame Cathedral, and the compelling and thought-provoking Deportation Memorial.

Catch a free, 90-minute Latin Quarter walking tour with **Discover Walks**, meeting at 11:00 (daily May-Oct 15) at the unmissable equestrian statue of Charlemagne in front of Notre Dame. This casual, tip-based walking tour will take you to the Left Bank, Paris's student and bohemian quarter. You'll wander through some of the city's narrowest lanes while enjoying a fun narrative that brings the ancient streets to vibrant life.

AFTERNOON

After your walking tour ends (remember to tip your guide), mosey over to the quaint Place de la Contrescarpe, where options abound for cafés, *bistrots, boulangeries, creperies,* and more. You'll find thick burgers at Petit Gaston and elegant menu options at La Contrescarpe, both facing the square. Remember that mealtime is practically sacred for the Parisians, so relax, eat slowly, and drink in the scenery (and perhaps some wine). Continue south on Mouffetard, window-shopping until you reach Les Gobelins metro station.

Hop on line #7 heading in the direction of La Courneuve to get to **Palais Royal Musee du Louvre.** Enter the museum via the subterranean mall. If you have an EU student card or EU student visa in an American passport, bring it to get free entry. It'll take you about three hours to see the Louvre's destination masterpieces: *Winged Victory, Venus de Milo,* the French crown jewels, and of course, the *Mona Lisa.* The free museum map will help you navigate the seemingly endless halls. Afterward, grab a sandwich in the well-appointed cafeteria at the mezzanine level overlooking the ticket lines underneath the main glass pyramid. Or go for the posh **Café Marly** or **Angelina** nearby.

EVENING

Cap off the evening by heading over to the **Eiffel Tower** (via bus #69 or #72 from the north side of the museum, Rue de Rivoli) and taking in the City of Lights at its finest, just as her lights begin to twinkle. If the weather is warm, grab a bottle or two of wine afterward to enjoy on **Champ de Mars,** the park spreading out from the feet of the tower. *Bon nuit!*

DAY 2: THE ROYAL RIGHT

MORNING

Kick off your day at the **Arc de Triomphe** (Metro: Charles de Gaulle-Étoile). Climb the arch for a beautiful panorama of Paris's most exclusive districts. Watch the traffic snake around the busiest *rond-point* in France—also the only roundabout in France where incoming traffic has the right of way.

Walk down the past-its-prime **Champs-Élysées** without spending too much time on the overpriced shops. If you're into 20th-century and modern art, you've got two compelling options at the bottom of the boulevard, the **Grand Palais and Petit Palais**—at the latter, entrance to the permanent exhibits is free.

Get excited. Lunch and sightseeing in Paris's best neighborhood are up next.

AFTERNOON

Take metro line 12 from Concorde north toward Front Populaire. Hop off at Abbesses and spend the afternoon wandering up and down the picturesque boulevards in Montmartre, Paris's most bohemian district. Climb the hill to discover my favorite church in Paris, the **Sacre Coeur.** The beautiful steps—a famous backdrop to many a film—make an excellent place for an impromptu picnic (either on the steps or on the grassy hill) while taking in the view and enjoying the serenades of surrounding buskers.

Head back to your hostel for a rest and to get ready for tonight.

EVENING

Take the metro to Place de la République and kick off a crawl up the **Canal Saint-Martin** to experience Paris's trendy nightlife. The funky **Le Comptoir Général** (Metro: Goncourt) is just a couple of blocks north along the canal; by mid-evening the place is always bumping. For more nightlife options, the Belleville district isn't far away.

DAY 3: MARKETS, MINNIE MOUSE, PALAIS ROYALE?

If you've got another full day in Paris, consider a day trip to either **Disneyland Paris** or the palace of **Versailles.** Alternatively, Paris's markets await—as does a quiet afternoon among the tombstones at the city's most famous cemetery.

MORNING

Head to the trendy **Marché des Enfants Rouge** (Metro: Filles du Calvaire, closed Mon) to find some of my favorite breakfast or lunch spots. Grab a coffee upon arrival, then take a lap to acquaint yourself with the market and its many food options. Choose between Italian, Korean, Latin American, and, of course, French street food—if you haven't had crêpes yet, now's the time.

AFTERNOON

Following the market, head to **Parc des Buttes-Chaumont** (a 30-minute walk or a short metro ride), a beautifully manicured park embodying 19th-century French romanticism. Alternatively, take the metro to **Père Lachaise Cemetery** (Metro: Père-Lachaise) to view rows upon rows of ornate graves. While you're there, pay your respects to Jim Morrison, Chopin, and Oscar Wilde.

TOP NEIGHBORHOODS

Paris is divided into numbered neighborhoods, or *arrondissements*. Each *arrondissement* has its own personality, but it's not all that helpful for visitors to try to understand the nuances of each one on a short visit.

The Seine bisects the city east to west. Two small islands, **Île de la Cité** and **Île Saint-Louis**, rest in the heart of it all. These picturesque islands are home to Notre Dame Cathedral and Sainte-Chapelle. To the west of these islands on the north side of the Seine (the Right Bank) is the **Louvre.** The Right Bank is also home to the grand shopping boulevard **Champs-Élysées,** which sits at its western edge. Just north of the two islands, chic **Marais** (which contains Paris's Jewish neighborhood) caters mostly to yuppies but offers lively shopping and nightlife. It's also home to the Pompidou Center modern art museum and Paris's gay district. To the north and east, you'll find trendy nightlife, several recommended hostels, and the pleasant Parc des Buttes-Chaumont along **Canal Saint-Martin.** Finally, the bohemian district of **Montmartre** hovers just outside the historical city walls north of the city center. In the middle of the neighborhood you'll find Sacre Coeur, the iconic hilltop cathedral with sweeping views of the city. The Moulin Rouge is on the border of Montmartre and Pigalle, a district with dozens of music shops and seedy nightlife.

The south side of the Seine (the Left Bank) is traditionally the home of starving artists, students, and philosophers. You'll find the **Eiffel Tower** and the Rue Cler market here, as well as the touristy **Latin Quarter,** just south of the islands in the Seine. **Odéon,** west of the Latin Quarter and close to Luxembourg Gardens, offers fun nightlife.

TOP SIGHTS

I've listed the most important and classic sights of Paris below. Overachievers can try QueFaire.paris.fr and EnlargeYourParis.fr for last-minute event and temporary exhibition info. These sites will help you fill any holes in your itinerary.

Eiffel Tower

It's not until you stand at the feet of this iconic structure in person that you realize that the photos you've seen come nowhere close to doing it justice. Completed in 1889 by Gustave Eiffel just in time for the World's Fair, this 1,063-foot tower was the tallest artificial structure in the world for a time, and it utterly dominates otherwise height-capped Paris. There's no better place to view Paris, and, as de Maupassant famously noted, it's the only place in the city where the view isn't dominated by the structure (the writer ate his lunch there every day so he wouldn't have to look at it—not everybody, it turns out, is a fan). The building comprises three separate levels. The first two are accessible by an elevator and by stairs, the third by elevator only. To save yourself some money, hike up the stairs to the first two levels. If you want to go still higher, purchase the extra ticket for the ride to the top. I find the view is better from the first two levels—the city's landmarks can still be seen in detail (they become indistinct from 1,000 feet up). After sunset, the tower sparkles with 20,000 strobe lights for five minutes every hour on the hour. This display draws a fun crowd of nocturnal picnickers (and warm-beer hawkers) all up and down the Champ de Mars.

If you don't have reservations, consider taking the stairs or going later in the day. The lines dry up after 19:00, but the views are not as good in the dark.

Stairs to 2nd floor €5 for ages 12-24, €7 for 25+, elevator to all levels €14.50 ages 12-24, €17 for 25+; mid-June-early Sept daily 09:00-24:00, rest of the year daily 09:30-23:00, 5 Av Anatole France, Eiffel Tower Neighborhood, +33 (0)8 92 70 12 39, tour-eiffel.fr, Metro: Bir-Hakeim

The Louvre

What was once the French monarchy's decadent city-center palace was converted into a public museum in 1793, shortly after Louis XVI was guillotined. With 8.5 million annual visitors and hundreds upon hundreds of historically significant

EIFFEL TOWER STATS

The Eiffel Tower was built for the 1889 World's Fair. Though it was originally only meant to stand for a few years, this iron monument to modernity and industrialization is still breathtaking today. These stats will help you begin to comprehend its scale:

Time to build:
Two years, two months, and five days

Cost to build:
US$36 million in today's money

Original purpose:
Radio tower

Height:
1,063 feet

Mass:
7,300 tons

Area of base:
410 square feet

Shift potential:
7 inches at the top due to warming and expansion of iron in the sun

Metric tons of paint covering the tower:
60

Frequency of repainting:
Every seven years

Number of lights:
20,000 bulbs and 336 lamps

Steps to the top:
1,665

Average daily visitors:
25,000

Distance traveled by one Eiffel Tower elevator in one year:
64,001 miles (about 2.5 circuits of the globe at the equator)

Total number of visitors:
250 million, and counting

artworks and artifacts, the museum can claim without blushing to be the world's greatest. Built on the foundations of an old medieval fort, this Renaissance palace was once a symbol of the wide gulf separating France's aristocracy and its lower classes. It was one of the revolutionaries' first orders of business to make the king's and the church's collection of more than 500 paintings available to the public.

The collection has grown by leaps and bounds since then. They say that if you were to spend 30 seconds in front of each piece in the Louvre's collections, you'd spend the better part of a year in here. Pieces span the course of human history, from prehistoric artifacts like the Code of Hammurabi to cutting-edge modern art. Since you clearly can't see everything, pick your route through the museum, focusing on the areas of art or history you're most interested in. Don't miss the highlights:

Mona Lisa, Nike of Samothrace (Winged Victory), The Raft of the Medusa (my fave), *The Coronation of Napoleon, Psyche Revived by Cupid's Kiss,* and *Venus de Milo.* Each of these popular pieces is highlighted on the free map available at the information desk, directly underneath the largest glass pyramid.

For those of you retracing the steps of Robert Langdon, the fictional professor in Dan Brown's popular quasi-historical novel *The Da Vinci Code,* you'll find the inanimate stars of the book here. Keep your eyes peeled for the meridian rose on the steps leading up to the *Winged Victory.* Stop by Da Vinci's works on display in the Italian Renaissance wing, including the *Virgin of the Rocks, Virgin and Child with Saint Anne,* and of course, the lady herself, *Mona Lisa.* The inverted glass pyramid (where the book comes to a head) is just outside the security checkpoint in the main entrance wing (follow the hallway out past Starbucks).

Buy your ticket in advance online (ticketlouvre.fr), or enter through the less crowded metro stop (Palais Royal-Musée du Louvre), where the security line should be shorter.

Online timed-entry tickets €17, free with EU student card or EU student visa in American passport, free to all first Sun of the month, open Mon, Thurs, Sat, and Sun 09:00-18:00, Wed and Fri 09:00-21:45, closed Tues, Louvre Neighborhood, +33 (0)1 40 20 50 50, louvre.fr, Metro: Palais Royale

Île de la Cité & Île Saint-Louis

These two islands, home to Paris's first prehistoric settlers, are the heart of both ancient and modern Paris. This tiny patch of real estate in the middle of the Seine contains several of Paris's most famous sights, but even just strolling down their picturesque lanes is a quintessentially Parisian experience—every bit as important a part of a visit as a trip to Notre Dame.

Île de la Cité is bustling with tourists. On the north side, you'll find the grand **Palais du Justice,** the judicial center of Paris and former prison where Marie Antoinette was held before she was guillotined in 1793. Next to it, in the middle of the island, sits the beautiful stained glass private royal chapel, **Sainte-Chapelle,** and **Hotel-Dieu,** Paris's oldest and most prestigious hospital. On the south side, you can't miss the iconic bell towers of **Notre Dame.** The low profile of Paris's **Deportation Memorial,** behind the cathedral, is more discreet, commemorating the 200,000 people deported to concentration camps by the Nazis during World War II. The metro stop, Cité, is worth a mention for the art nouveau design and style of the signage. Fans of the *Bourne* series will recognize both the **Pont Neuf,** the

bridge on the northernmost point of the island, and the nearby Samaritaine department store (Bourne's vantage point).

Île Saint-Louis offers a special quiet zone smack-dab in the middle of the city. Cross the bridges here and the sounds of Paris's constant traffic die away almost immediately. This is one of Paris's most exclusive residential districts, where the rich and famous keep their second (or sixth) homes and where apartments frequently go for around €15,000-20,000 per square meter. You can find *boulangeries* here that make for a relaxing break, and the **Amorino** gelato shop at 47 Rue Saint-Louis en l'Île provides a welcome sugar stop.

Free, always open, Île de la Cité and Île Saint-Louis, Metro: Cité

Notre Dame Cathedral

Notre Dame de Paris (Our Lady of Paris) never ceases to amaze. Not only is it one of the world's oldest and most famous Gothic cathedrals, it's also one of the most visited churches of any kind. Construction began in 1163 and continued in fits and starts for 170 years—basically, they built whenever there was the money and the will to build. The centuries were unkind to Paris's Lady. Vandals hacked away at her stone walls and looters ransacked her treasures; in the midst of the Reign of Terror, even her statues were not safe (like the French nobility, they too were hauled down to street level and decapitated by the mob). At one point, the church even served as a stable for livestock, which only increased its steady slide into disrepair. She was on her last legs in 1831 when Victor Hugo, then a relatively obscure author, published *The Hunchback of Notre Dame,* which cast the neglected church as a central character in the story. The massive success of Hugo's book thrust

MEANDER THROUGH MONTMARTRE

Historically, the neighborhood of Montmartre existed outside Paris's ancient walls, placing it outside the city's authority and tax jurisdiction. Parisians would make the short journey to Montmartre in search of prostitutes, strip shows, and cheap alcohol. The neighborhood earned itself a reputation as a hotbed for hedonism, with absinthe flowing freely and dancers at the Moulin Rouge kicking far higher than modesty allowed. Some of Paris's poorer residents (especially students and artists) were drawn to the neighborhood by its cheap rents and its unbridled character, which soon gave the neighborhood a distinctly bohemian flavor. Some of the world's most famous artists have called Montmartre home: Van Gogh, Matisse, Degas, and Renoir all laid their heads down here amid the ruckus each night. There are even tales of cafés accepting sketches from not-yet-famous artists as payment for their dinners.

Today, Montmartre is a wonderful neighborhood for a hilly stroll. Starting from the Blanche metro stop (near Moulin Rouge and with Pigalle and its countless music shops to the south), head uphill toward Sacre Coeur. You'll pass through some of Paris's most fascinating streets, lined with cafés, restaurants, galleries, and textile shops. Be sure to stop in at **Le Grenier à Pain** (38 Rue des Abbesses) for what many of Paris's food critics agree is the best baguette in the city. Wind your way through the back streets for a taste of daily Parisian life not overshadowed by the thousands of tourists that pass through the neighborhood on their way to the hilltop every day.

the cathedral back into the realm of public interest. A series of renovations, including the addition of the prominent pointy spire, restored the cathedral to its former grandeur, which is enjoyed by all in the present.

Inside, observe the beautiful stained glass of the two rose windows on either side of the transept, the products of countless hours and untold patience by 13th-century craftsmen who dedicated themselves to the windows' completion. Almost all of the glass in these two windows is original—it has survived countless conflicts and conflagrations almost entirely intact. You won't find a finer example of rose windows *anywhere*. After exploring the great halls of the cathedral, climb the stairs to the top of the tower and step outside for a magnificent view of the city. You may not see Quasimodo up there, but his friends (the gargoyles and chimeras) still stand guard, watching over the city and protecting her stone lady.

Free, climb the towers for €8.50, cathedral open daily 07:45-18:45, Sat-Sun till 19:15, tower open Apr-Sept daily 10:00-18:30, July-Aug Fri-Sat 10:00-23:00,

Oct-Mar daily 10:00-17:30, 6 Parvis Notre-Dame-Place Jean-Paul II, Île de la Cité, +33 (0)1 42 34 56 10, notredamedeparis.fr, Metro: St-Michel

Sainte-Chapelle

Dating back to the 13th century, this private chapel was commissioned by Louis IX, who wanted a place to house his passion relics (including Christ's crown of thorns). Its striking, nearly floor-to-ceiling stained glass Gothic windows tell Bible stories, starting on the left side of the chapel with Genesis and progressing up the left and down the right side with further Old Testament stories. The apse in the center contains three beautiful windows illustrating the passion of Christ, his infancy, and the life of John the Evangelist. Not all of these have survived intact, but thanks to painstaking restorations and regular cleanings, stunning Sainte-Chapelle shines like new.

€10 adults, Apr-Sept daily 09:00-19:00, Oct-Mar daily 09:00-17:00, 8 Bd du Palais, Île de la Cité, +33 (0)1 53 40 60 80, sainte-chapelle.monuments-nationaux. fr, Metro: Cité

Champs-Élysées

In French, *champs* means "fields." This entire area used to be the open fields beyond the old walls of medieval Paris. Today, the grazing fields have been replaced by the world's most famous shopping street. You can find everything here, from Bugattis to brioche, Maseratis to McDonald's, and fashion superstores to nightclubs. To save on energy, start at the top, near the Arc de Triomphe, and enjoy your stroll downhill, popping into any store that suits your fancy. While it's highly recommended for shopping during the day, the boulevard and surrounding streets get touristy and a bit seedy at night.

Free, always open, Champs-Élysées Neighborhood, Metro: Charles de Gaulle-Étoile

Arc de Triomphe

Commissioned by Napoleon and finished in 1833, this 165-foot arch, situated at the top of the Champs-Élysées, honors those who died in the Revolutionary and Napoleonic Wars. When you stand under it, the purpose is clear: It's a pure power move by one of the greatest emperors Europe has ever seen. Standing toe to toe with the grandeur of the French Republic makes one feel miniscule.

Underneath the epic arch (a source of intense national pride), you'll find the eternal flame marking the grave of France's unknown soldier, interred here and guarded constantly since World War I. Climb the 284 stairs for a beautiful panorama of the entire city. Look down the Champs-Élysées towards the Place de la Concorde or in the opposite direction toward the skyscrapers of modern Paris.

€12, Apr-Sept daily 10:00-23:00, Oct-Mar daily 10:00-22:30, Champs-Élysées Neighborhood, +33 (0)1 55 37 73 77, arcdetriompheparis.com, Metro: Charles de Gaulle-Étoile

Orsay Museum

Built as a train station and converted into a museum in 1986 to showcase mostly French artwork from 1848 to 1914, the museum is notable for its impressionist and postimpressionist collections, including masterpieces by Monet, Manet, Renoir, and Van Gogh. The original idea was to close the gap between the Louvre's collections (which had very little from after the mid-19th century) and those of the Pompidou (with its focus on more recent modern art). A visit to each of the three museums will leave art lovers with a very clear overview of the trajectory of art from the ancient to the modern. Don't miss the art nouveau furniture upstairs—one of my favorite exhibits anywhere in Paris.

€9 ages 18-25, €12 over age 25, free first Sun of the month, Tues-Sun 09:30-18:00 (Thurs 09:30-21:45), closed Mon, last tickets sold at 17:00 (21:00 on Thurs), 5 Quai Anatole France, Louvre Neighborhood, +33 (0)1 40 49 48 14, musee-orsay.fr/en, Metro: Solferino

Sacre Coeur

Located in Montmartre, Paris's ultra-bohemian neighborhood, the Church of the Sacred Heart is a beautiful, chalky-white travertine stone cathedral. It was built between 1875 and 1919, during a time of religious resurgence, and after World War I it was dedicated to those who died during the conflict. During World War II, 13 bombs exploded near the church, but (so they say) miraculously, nobody was seriously hurt and the church remained intact except for a bit of the stained glass. It is, for believers, not just a sacred site, but a divinely protected one as well. It sits perched atop the highest hill in Paris and has spectacular views of the city. I make my way to this church—one of my favorite in Europe—every time I'm in town. The façade is unforgettable, as are the mosaics inside—and entry is free. Sit on the steps or join the crowds on the grass. Come back at night and bring a bottle or two to toast the glittering city. *Salut!*

Free, daily 06:00-22:30, 35 Rue du Chevalier de la Barre, Montmartre, +33 (0)1 53 41 89 00, sacre-coeur-montmartre.com, Metro: Abbesses

Pompidou Center

The Pompidou's eclectic exterior conceals Paris's (and, indeed, the world's) largest and most impressive collection of modern art. The building was an ambitious project by a trio of famous architects from Italy and England. The design puts the guts of the building (like HVAC, plumbing, and wiring) on the exterior rather than inside the walls. The museum itself takes you through a comprehensive 20th-century timeline of

THE MOST FAMOUS NON-SIGHT IN PARIS

The Bastille neighborhood is named after the notorious castle-turned-prison. Built in the 14th century, the castle was converted into a prison by the oppressive 17th-century monarchs. On July 14, 1789, peasant hordes swarmed the Bastille, thinking it contained hundreds of their imprisoned compatriots. The 600 rebels took over the defenses, but found only a small contingent of opposition, along with just seven degenerate prisoners. It was a glorious success to no real point. Shortly afterward, the Bastille was demolished, as it symbolized the oppression of the revolution's ideals: *liberté, égalité, fraternité* (liberty, equality, fraternity). July 14 is now observed as Bastille Day, an annual holiday.

Though the castle is long gone, you've got to swing through the Bastille neighborhood at some point during your visit. Yes, you may see clueless tourists trying to find the castle, but you'll find only a massive roundabout circling an obelisk (the July Column), with the Opéra Bastille anchoring one side. The canal leading away from the square makes for a wonderful afternoon stroll in good weather—there are boats to look at and baguettes to munch on. In the back streets surrounding the grand plaza, you'll find bohemian nightlife, student bars, and a tasteful array of restaurants. Trendy Parisians are now turning their collective nose up at this neighborhood, as it's been discovered by tourists, but you can find gems, especially on Rue de Lappe.

creative expression, with pieces from cubist Picassos to colorful Warhols and avant-garde Chagalls. Even if you don't pay to go in the museum (though you should), you can ride the escalators to the top of the building for a 360-degree panorama of Le Marais and its incredible architecture.

The streets surrounding the Pompidou Center are also interesting to explore. Local food options abound just to the east in the Jewish district. Otherwise, check out the rooftop restaurant for a mid-priced post-museum snack (sandwiches start around €6).

€14 museum entry, free first Sun of the month, Wed-Mon 11:00–22:00, closed Tues, no admissions sold after 20:00, 19 Rue Beaubourg, Le Marais and Vicinity, +33 (0)1 44 78 12 33, centrepompidou.fr/en, Metro: Rambuteau

Père Lachaise Cemetery

With cemetery plots packed up against each other like sardines, this cemetery contains some of the most iconic gravesites in the world. From poets and rock stars to political leaders and revolutionaries, you can pay your respects by making your way northeast of Le Marais. Memorials, tombs, and sculptures practically trip over each other throughout this peaceful park. Must-see graves: Jim Morrison, Georges Rodenbach, Frédéric Chopin, Colette, Oscar Wil-

de, and Victor Noir. The cemetery is quite large, and you'll have serious difficulties finding graves without a map. Download one ahead of time, or snap a pic of one of the maps posted at each of the entrances of the cemetery. It'll help you find your way in this city of the dead.

Free, Mon–Fri 08:00–18:00, Sat 08:30–18:00, Sun 09:00–18:00 (17:30 in winter), 16 Rue du Repos, Le Marais and Vicinity, +33 (0)1 55 25 82 10, pere-lachaise.com, Metro: Gambetta

Extra Credit

The unmistakable glass-domed buildings of the **Grand Palais and Petit Palais** (Large Palace and Small Palace, daily 10:00-18:00, ticket office closes one hour prior, 3 Avenue du Général Eisenhower, +33 (0)1 53 43 40 00, Metro: Champs-Élysées-Clemenceau) at the bottom of the Champs Élysées feature rotating exhibits and art from a wide range of periods. The Grand Palais (exhibits €14, grandpalais.fr), built in neoclassical style for the 1900 World's Fair, isn't Paris's cheapest museum, but with three separate rotating exhibits, art lovers will feel they've gotten more than their money's worth. The Petit Palais (free) houses the City Museum of Fine Arts (focusing on 18th- and 19th-century art) and is free to explore. The café in the atrium provides welcome refreshment.

TOP EATS

You can't talk about France without talking about its famous cuisine. The tastes of Paris should easily be the highlight of your visit, and my recommendations will fit the bill across all budgets and preferences. Stay away from the touristy areas like the Latin Quarter, where restaurants tend to be overpriced. Menus with a *prix fixe* sign used to be a good value, but now more often than not, these menus hide cover and service charges and I prefer to steer clear. Tipping is not as assumed as it is in the United States. Look over your restaurant bill to see if service is already included. If it is, you'll see the words "*service compris.*" Otherwise, round up to about 10 percent if you liked the service.

For a cheap and tasty way to dine, opt for a **crêpe** (rhymes with "prep"). They're ubiquitous throughout the city, with options found on nearly every street corner, with street stands to boot. Crêpes can be had sweet or savory. Nutella-and-banana is a favorite. For lunch, ham-and-cheese is a classic, and I'm a fan of the tuna with a fried egg option.

Latin Quarter Options

Skip the touristy zone (with the exception of Heureux Comme Alexandre) and head to Place de Contrescarpe, where you'll find countless picturesque cafés surrounding the square and in the streets leading away from it. Try **Petit Gaston** for delectable burgers, or **L'Essential Anthony Bosson** for a posh *boulanger*. Rue Mouffard leads south from the square and offers quaint *creperies*, international cuisine, cafés, and more.

Montmartre Options

Pain pain (from €2.50, Tues-Sat 07:00-20:00, Sun 07:30-19:30, closed Mon, 88 Rue des Martyrs, pain-pain.fr, +33 (0)1 42 236 281) is your best option for cheap takeaway sandwiches and personal treats like chocolate eclairs and strawberry pies. **Coquelicot** (lunches from €12, Tues-Sun 07:30-20:00, 24 Rue des Abbesses, coquelicot-montmartre.com, +33 (0)1 46 061 877) is a step up, with options for hot breakfasts and lunch dishes like pasta and salad. **Café Miroir** (Tues-Sat 08:00-22:00, 94 Rue des Martyrs, cafemiroir.com, +33 (0)1 46 065 073) is my choice for lunch in this district. With a limited, always rotating and always

fresh menu for €19.50, it's one of the better sit-down values in the entire area.

Heureux Comme Alexandre

This is my top choice in town for a fondue dinner. Come for the €16 unlimited salad and potatoes fondue dinner, and stick around for the fun atmosphere and easygoing service. Nestled deep in the Latin Quarter, the hordes of tourists pass this place by, leaving you, as the name of the place suggests, "happy as Alexander." Reservations recommended.

Dinner €16, daily 11:00-24:00, 24 Rue de la Parcheminerie, Latin Quarter, +33 (0)1 43 26 49 66, Metro: Cluny-La Sorbonne

Coffee Spoune

For those who need to catch up on a few emails while in town, Coffee Spoune offers ample seating and table space. They also have delicious coffee, snacks, and full, healthy meals to keep you energized. Their Wi-Fi speed doesn't ever let up, making this a freelancers' hotspot.

Sandwiches from €5, Mon-Fri 08:00-17:00, Sat-Sun 10:00-18:00, 36 Rue Saint-Sébastien, Le Marais and Vicinity, +33 (0)1 43 55 37 20, Facebook: Coffee Spoune, Metro: Saint-Sébastien Froissart

Coffee Parisien

Don't let the name fool you. Coffee Parisien is closer to a taste of home than to a taste of authentic Paris. This retro American-style diner serves up classics like three-layered club sandwiches, massive bacon cheeseburgers, eggs Benedict, thick pancakes, hash browns, and more (the placemats are even in on the action, with short descriptions of all the past US presidents). The food and coffee leave little to be desired in this fun, casual eatery, but the service does lag a bit. Make your orders clear, and don't come here if you're tight on time.

Mains from €8, daily 12:00-24:00, 4 Rue Princesse, Odéon, +33 (0)1 43 54 18 18, coffee-parisien.fr, Metro: Saint-Germain-des-Prés

Ladurée

Welcome to the world headquarters of macarons! Consider a stop at Ladurée as part of your Parisian pilgrimage. Stop in for a fancy afternoon tea break and sample some of these delightful meringue cookies—the quintessential French treat. There are several locations to choose from, but the shop on Rue Royale offers some of the best service.

Snacks from €5, Mon-Thurs 07:30-23:00, Fri 07:30-00:30, Sat-Sun 08:30-00:30, 16-18 Rue Royale, Louvre Neighborhood, +33 (0)1 42 60 21 79, laduree.com

Angelina

Step into this gilded, luxurious café and you'll be entering a place of obsession. While some restaurants may fixate on the perfect steak or salmon filet, Angelina's obsession is a little unusual: They aim to make the world's finest hot chocolate—no other version comes close. Add on pastries, macarons, and fudge-drowned, sugarcoated desserts, and Angelina will floor you (and empty your wallet). If you've got the budget, you'll also find the poshest salads, omelets, and eggs Benedicts you'll ever try. Find Angelina on the north side of the Tuileries gardens.

Artfully presented starters from €25, beverages from €7, Mon-Fri 07:30-19:00, Sat-Sun 08:30-19:30, 226 Rue de Rivoli, Louvre Neighborhood, +33 (0)1 42 60 82 00, Angelina-paris.fr, Metro: Palais Royal-Musée du Louvre

Le Café Marly

Find this decadent café in the arcade facing the glass pyramids at the Louvre. A meal here will break just about any budget, but it's a welcome place for a glass of white wine after a long day inside the museum. The chance to eat beneath the arched courtyard walkway proves just too tempting for many (myself included), but I limit my splurge to one of their many delectable desserts (from €14). You're paying for the setting and the ambience, and for the company of well-heeled tourists. They *might* be able to seat you without a reservation, but it's a gamble. Call ahead.

Meals from €30, daily 08:00-02:00, 93 Rue de Rivoli, Louvre Neighborhood, +33 (0)1 49 26 06 60, cafe-marly.com, Metro: Palais Royal-Musée du Louvre

Derrière

Derrière ("backside") is a trendy and eclectic spot tucked into a retrofitted Le Marais mansion. You unique dining experience begins the moment you are seated and open up your highly creative menu. Enjoy your meal at the foot of a bed, on a sofa, or even in the kitchen and bathrooms. It's as much about the experience as it is about the (delicious) meal itself—you might play a game of Ping-Pong, or you might find yourself sneaking through a wardrobe into a hidden room. The friendly—if French-paced—service is happy to talk at some length about their artisanal dishes, like salads made with multicolored carrots, beef filet, and tuna tartare. The €38 buffet brunch (Sun 12:00-16:00) is a winner. Reservations are required. After dinner, consider a drink at **Andy Wahloo,** the cool and cozy cocktail bar next door.

Mains from €30, daily 12:00-11:30, find the unmarked passageway leading to a courtyard at 69 Rue des Gravilliers, Le Marais and Vicinity, +33 (0)1 44 61 91 95, derriere-resto.com, Metro: Arts et Metiers

L'Avant Comptoir de la Terre

The helpful staff behind the counter at L'Avant Comptoir de la Terre will happily talk you through their hors d'oeuvre menu, which features 40-plus options for hot and cold bites from the southwest of France. Don't expect them to show you to a table, though. This is a standing-room-only bar, and it's often packed elbow to elbow. It's a jovial place to pick up a glass of wine (more than 250 to choose from) and strike up a conversation or just enjoy the French chatter around you. Check out their sister location next door: **L'Avant Comptoir de la Mer** has a wide selection of fruit of the sea like oysters, clams, prawns, and polpo. Look up to find the menu—pictures and prices of the various dishes and wine lists are suspended from the ceiling. Both spots feature reasonable prices and a sophisticated, in-the-know vibe.

€4–20, daily 12:00–23:00, 9 Carrefour de l'Odéon, Odéon, +33 (0)1 44 27 07 50, hotel-paris-relais-saint-germain.com/savourez-les-restaurants.html, Metro: Odéon

Chez Prune

The quays along Canal Saint-Martin are packed with people chilling and drinking all night, and Chez Prune is a great location to stop for a cappuccino or excellent cheese and meat plates during the day. This cool, artsy bar is popular with locals (especially young Parisian professionals), yet it seems to escape the tourist eye—perhaps because it does very little to try to catch that eye. Inside, it's a relatively nondescript restaurant, but outside you're sitting on a corner just across the street from the canal. When the sun is shining, Chez Prune is a wonderful place to enjoy reasonably priced drinks alfresco.

Dishes from €13, Mon–Sat 08:00–02:00, opens Sun at 10:00, 36 Rue Beaurepaire, Canal Saint-Martin, +33 (0)1 42 41 30 47, Facebook: Chez Prune, Metro: Gare de l'Est or Jacques Bonsergent

Marcel et Clementine

This tastefully decorated hipster restaurant and bar near Sacre Coeur makes for an ideal place to start off an evening in Montmartre with some great food and atmosphere. They claim to make the best hamburger in the world, and after my first bite, I wasn't remotely inclined to argue the point. Their happy hour specials go easy on the budget. The foosball table inside is always a popular spot, but the sidewalk tables are my favorite.

Burgers from €16, Mon–Sat 08:00–23:30, Sun 10:00–23:30, 74 Rue de Dunkerque, Montmartre, +33 (0)1 40 37 91 60, marcelclementine.fr, Metro: Anvers

Gelato

Amorino and **Grom,** both popular chains with locations all over Paris, offer consistently exceptional gelato and other sweets. Amorino offers the option to add frozen macarons (from €3). The locations in busier parts of town are often open until or past midnight, so they make for a great late-evening sugary treat on your way to the bars.

TOP NIGHTLIFE

On an average night out, Parisians may have only a couple of drinks, but they'll go through a pack or two of cigarettes. Parisians don't go out with the intention of getting falling-down drunk. Drink for the French is a social lubricant.

Going out in Paris is expensive, so young Parisians (especially students) prefer to drink with friends in cramped-yet-cozy apartments. They might go out late to dance in the clubs, but it's just as likely that they'll stay in and keep the wine and conversation flowing. If you are invited to a French party, bring a bottle or two of nice wine—something from a specialty shop, not the supermarket.

French students take their foosball seriously. If you've got skills, find the table and wait your turn. The competition will be fierce, but you'll be making friends.

Anytime you go out, be sure to bring valid **ID** (bars 16+, clubs 18+). Your best bet is to bring your driver's license and a photocopy of your passport; leave the real thing at your hostel. It really puts a major damper on the night when you're bounced from the bar because you can't prove you're of age.

NIGHTLIFE DISTRICTS

Each *arrondissement* has its own distinct personality. From seedy to posh, each neighborhood has bars that cater to all preferences and tastes. The student neighborhoods of Belleville and Oberkampf and the trendy Canal Saint-Martin tend to be the most easygoing and fun, so that's where I go when I'm in Paris.

Canal Saint-Martin

Formerly backwater neighborhoods in Paris are becoming the city's trendiest and most exciting districts. Low rents in Canal Saint-Martin attracted bohemian types, and cafés and bars have been popping up regularly in the streets running along the canal, leading north from Place de la République. On clear days, there's nothing better than going for a late-afternoon stroll along this 4.5-kilometer canal, stopping in for a pint or a glass of cheap wine at any of the hipster joints that pique your fancy. Start your canal crawl from the north side of Canal Saint-Martin near several recommended hostels, then work your way south. Continue north and east from the canal, and you'll find yourself in vibrant Belleville.

Canal Saint-Martin, Metro: République or Goncourt

Oberkampf

Three streets in this gritty neighborhood near Canal Saint-Martin have become popular among the in-the-know: Rue Oberkampf, Rue St-Maur, and Rue Jean-Pierre-Timbaud. These narrow, hilly streets are now a destination for those weary of the increasingly commercialized and pretentious nightlife elsewhere. The atmosphere here is unmistakably Parisian, and the food and drinks are as cheap as you'll find anywhere in the city.

Canal Saint-Martin and Vicinity, Metro: Parmentier or Oberkampf

Belleville

This part of Paris, just east of Canal Saint-Martin, was once a town outside of the city, but it was brought into the fold in the 19th century. The cosmopolitan nature of the neighborhood makes for relatively inexpensive and always interesting nights out with a healthy mixture of locals and visitors. Focus on Boulevard de Belleville to find the most vibrant nightlife. It's common to see prostitutes walking around this area, but they'll only approach you if you look lonely.

Canal Saint-Martin and Vicinity, Metro: Belleville, Goncourt, or Colonel Fabian

Le Marais

Bordered on the west by Rue du Renard and the Pompidou Center, and to the east by the grand Boulevard de Beaumarchais and the Bastille district, this is one of Paris's most passionately eclectic and irreverent neighborhoods. Chic and slightly yuppie, Le Marais is full of practically unaffordable boutique hotels and restaurants, and cafés and bars that strive to outdo each other in their meticulous attention to detail. Le Marais is also Paris's gay district, featuring a number of prominent LGBT-friendly clubs and establishments.

Le Marais, Metro: Saint-Paul

Bastille

East of Le Marais, the Bastille district draws a young, hip crowd. **Rue de Lappe** and **Rue de Charonne** retain their classic charm, but the district is becoming more discovered and touristy by the hour. Still, a pleasant time can be had here, with plenty of shopping and a zoo to explore.

Le Marais and Vicinity, Metro: Bastille

Odéon

Once the center of the city's intellectual life (especially in the years between World War I and World War II), this Left Bank neighborhood teemed with philosophers contemplating existentialism, artists toying with surrealism, and musicians exploring the depths of jazz. Its reputation as a center of counterculture may not be as strong

---

LGBT PARIS

Le Marais, which overlaps with the Jewish Quarter, is Paris's gay district. By day in this bustling tangle of medieval lanes you'll find art galleries, design shops, adult stores, haute couture boutiques, florists, cafés, bakeries, and cozy restaurants. By night, the fun runs the length of **Rue de la Verrerie**, leading into **Rue de Roi Sicile,** with crowds spilling out onto the surrounding streets. The bears feel at home in the burly **Bear's Den** (6 Rue des Lombards, +33 (0)1 42 71 08 20). If you like beer, stop into **La Caves a Bulles** (45 Rue Quincampoix, +33 (0)1 40 29 03 69), an artisanal brew shop where you get bottles to go and enjoy them on the square in front of the Pompidou Center.

as it once was, but the neighborhood is still awash with great restaurants and bars, like **Le Dix Bar,** a cozy sangria bar. The best establishments concentrate around a single street, **Rue Princesse**—just across from the Sorbonne, Paris's premier university. If it's a young crowd of students and revelers you're looking for, this is where to start.

Odéon, Metro: Odéon

Pigalle

The Moulin Rouge is the epicenter of Pigalle's bar scene, and it dictates the flavor of the nightlife, which features sex clubs and seedy discos. Do a bit of research before checking out the dive bars. **Dirty Dick** (10 Rue Frochot, +33 (0)1 48 78 74 58), a funky neo-tiki bar, is one of the good ones. The rum drinks here are tasty, but too many of them will leave you reeling. You'll want to keep your wits about you on the streets of Pigalle—if you have a few too many, call a cab or have the staff call one for you.

Montmartre, Metro: Pigalle or Abbesses

BARS
Bar Ourcq

Bar Ourcq is a great place to kick off your evening along Canal Saint-Martin. It's your standard comfortable corner bar where you can get cheap drinks, socialize, and enjoy some good music in comfortable no-nonsense surroundings. If you don't feel like socializing, or if you're looking for more intimate conversation, take your drinks to go and tip them back along the canal (a stone's throw from the door). During the day, you can watch or (if you're lucky) join in one of the games of *pétanque* the locals play on the sand in front of the bar. Organic snacks, €1 sandwiches, and the convenient location make for a great start to the night.

Drinks from €3, Wed–Thurs 15:00–24:00, Fri–Sat 15:00–01:45, Sun 15:00–22:00, 68 Quai de la Loire, Canal Saint-Martin, +33 (0)1 42 40 12 26, barourcq.free.fr, Metro: Lumière

La Mano

With a futuristic Latin vibe, this place is as hard to leave as it is to get in. Through an unmarked door you'll find picky bouncers and occasionally long lines, so dress the part if you want to make it past the velvet rope. This is a dance party, and the rhythms almost never veer into chilled territory, so wear something that breathes—the later it gets, the sweatier the room becomes. Drinks are on the expensive side, but the unpretentious vibe and the undulating bodies on the dance floor make any night here an unforgettable experience.

Drinks from €10, Tues–Sat 20:00–05:00, 10 Rue Papillon, Montmartre and Vicinity, +33 (0)9 67 50 50 37, Facebook: La Mano, Metro: Poissonnière

Le Dude

If you're a fan of the Coen brothers' masterpiece *The Big Lebowski*, make a pilgrimage to this bar near Canal Saint-Martin. Every inch of the décor references the film in some way, with bowling lanes on the ceiling leading to pins over the bar and stenciled portraits of the Dude and Walter on the walls. Even if you're not a fan, this is a great place to throw a few back. Order the White Russian.

White or Black Russian €4.50, Mon–Sat 18:00–01:45 (closed Sundays), 214 Rue Saint-Maur, Canal Saint-Martin, +33 (0)9 73 54 27 14, Facebook: Le Dude, Metro: Gare de l'Est, Goncourt, Jaures, or Louis Blanc

La Bellevilloise

La Bellevilloise was once an institution dedicated to providing Paris's poorer working classes with political and cultural education. Today, this combination bar, restaurant, and cultural space is as socially minded as ever, promoting freedom of expression and cross-culturalism. Check their event listings ahead of time, as you might catch political hip-hop, a jazz trio, or a tango show. The listings are as diverse as their clientele. Pop down here for brunch on Sundays (sittings at 11:30 and 14:00) or for drinks anytime.

Drinks from €4, Wed–Thurs 19:00–01:00, Fri 19:00–02:00, Sat 11:00–02:00, Sun 17:00–late, 19–21 Rue Boyer, Canal Saint-Martin and Vicinity, +33 (0)1 46 36 07 07, labellevilloise.com, Metro: Gambetta or Ménilmontant

Point Éphémère

Run by a nonprofit agency charged with converting Paris's neglected buildings into lively cultural and arts centers, this place has it all: great food, art studios and galleries, a concert venue, a terrace, cheap drinks that you can take to the canal, and a cool crowd completely free of the stereotypical Parisian snobbery. They keep

their art and live music shows fresh with a constantly updated calendar of events, and the world-class acts they attract draw a cool and eclectic crowd. Staying true to its name, the Point is never the same thing for long—each visit offers something entirely new. Check their website for upcoming events.

Drinks from €4, book concert tickets online, Mon-Sat 12:00-02:00, Sun 12:00-23:00, 200 Quai de Valmy, Canal Saint-Martin, +33 (0)1 40 34 02 48, pointephemere.org, Metro: Jaures or Louis Blanc

Le Comptoir Général

This multifaceted artistic space set back from the canal in former horse stables throws down with the world's best eclectic bars. Slip quietly into this secret garden and explore some of the many rooms in the complex. There's plenty to discover: a deadly serious coffee bar, an excellent mixed drink bar, pop-up spaces for designers to sell their concepts, hanging gardens, and much more. The live music acts drawn to this place dovetail perfectly with the refreshingly unpretentious crowd, who are thrilled to dance under funky lighting to R&B, house, and hip-hop when there isn't a live act. Get in by 23:30 to avoid the line.

Free entry, daily 11:00-02:00, 80 Quai de Jemmapes, Canal Saint-Martin, +33 (0)1 44 88 24 48, lecomptoirgeneral.com/en, Metro: Goncourt

Le Dix Bar (10 Bar)

Le Dix Bar is a musty sangria bar with a dark wood interior in Odéon, one of my favorite neighborhoods. Vintage posters hang on the crumbling walls; everything seems to be in an advanced state of decay here, but that's half the charm. Come out

with friends and round your pitcher size up. Enjoy your fruit-infused wine upstairs or head downstairs to join the social crowd of drinkers.

Pitchers from €14, Mon-Sat 17:00-02:00, 10 Rue de l'Odéon, Odéon, +33 (0)01 43 26 66 83, lebar10.com, Metro: Odéon

Chez Georges

For a truly Parisian experience, come to this classic bar with a twist and enjoy some wine with a group of friends. Or fly solo and sit down at one of the many communal tables to strike up a conversation with the wine lover next to you. It draws a slightly older crowd. Don't miss the cellar: The arched exposed brick makes it impossible to ignore that you're in a bar with ancient roots. Sweaty dancing kicks off early and ends late on weekends.

Glasses from €6, Mon-Fri 15:00-late, Sat 12:00-02:00, Sun 19:00-02:00, 11 Rue des Canettes, Odéon, +33 (0)1 43 26 79 15, Facebook: Chez Georges, Metro: Mabillon

Rosa Bonheur sur Seine

For a stationary experience on the Seine, enjoy a round or two at this glass-wrapped barge that's been turned into a bar, restaurant, and dance venue. The cool breeze on the always-busy patio provides a welcome respite during the hot summer months. The crowd leans more toward tourists than locals; to find the locals, stay close to the bright yellow foosball table.

Tapas and beer from €5.50, Wed-Sun 12:00-02:00, Port des Invalides, south side of the Seine between Pont Alexandre III and Pont de la Concorde, Eiffel Tower Neighborhood and Vicinity, +33 (0)1 47 53 66 92, rosabonheur.fr, Metro: Invalides

Café Oz

Unapologetically touristy and international, this large Aussie sports bar with an open layout fits the bill for downtown dancing. The dance floor can feel like a carousel at times. Pub crawls kick off here, so new groups file in regularly, only to disappear just as quickly as they arrived. The game (predominantly rugby) is always on the big screens, with the party becoming rowdier when the game's over and the DJ starts spinning Top 40 and hip-hop (this is when the student crowd starts to fill the place). Their Halloween and Christmas parties are legendary. Check the schedule online.

Drinks from €5, Mon-Fri 17:00-late, Sat-Sun 12:00-late, 18 Rue Saint-Denis, Louvre Neighborhood, +33 (0)1 40 39 00 18, cafe-oz.com, Metro: Châtelet

CLUBS

Remember to bring a copy of your passport with your birth date on it, and dress to impress to get past the often-picky bouncers. They want a healthy mix of tourists and locals inside, and they want everybody to have a good and relaxed time, but at the more popular clubs, the bouncers draw a sharp line between the come-as-you-are bars and the polished nightlife venues. Don't bother showing up until 23:00 or so.

YoYo Palais de Tokyo

If you like to dance and want something above and beyond the college-dorm party scene, plan to spend at least one of your evenings at YoYo. This large, fashionable venue (formerly a theater) has plenty of room, and the air-conditioning blasts all night so it's a far cry from the cramped hothouses that know all too well that sweaty patrons are thirsty patrons. Famous house and techno DJs and hip-hop acts visit YoYo often, so check their website for event listings—purchase tickets well ahead of time because they tend to sell out when big acts are in town. Theme nights, including a BIG (Beautiful is Gay) party night, liven up the scene. Brace yourself for long, slow lines outside and plenty of security. Pregame on the Champ de Mars with some wine before crossing the river. You'll find the club tucked underneath the Modern Art Museum of Paris.

Covers from €10, Wed-Sat 23:00-late, 13 Av du Président Wilson, Champs-Élysées Neighborhood, +33 (0)1 84 79 11 70, yoyo-paris.com, Metro: Iena or Alma Marceau

Badaboum

Boasting one of the best sound systems in Paris, Badaboum is the destination for thumping electro, house, and techno. The dozens of color-changing tubes over the dance floor combine with the stage lighting to create an effect unlike any other. Don't expect a ton of variety with the music, but, so long as bass lines are your thing, you'll have no problem dancing until dawn here. The bouncers are extremely picky, so prepare to wait in line.

Covers and drinks around €10, Wed-Thurs 19:00-02:00, Fri-Sat 19:00-06:15, Sun 23:00-05:00, 28 Rude des Taillandiers, Le Marais and Vicinity, +33 (0)1 48 06 50 70, badaboum.paris, Metro: Ledru-Rollin

Nuits Fauves

Named after one of France's most iconic films, this Berlin-esque club on the river is one of Paris's electro hot spots. With graffiti on the walls and a network of scaffolding overhead, it feels like a warehouse party. The patio outside makes for a wonderful spot to get away from the pounding bass for a bit. I've gone out there for a break and ended up sitting and chatting at the wooden picnic tables beneath the umbrellas for hours. This place isn't marred by the pretentiousness you'll find at many of Paris's other nightspots.

Covers and drinks around €10, Thurs-Sat 23:00-morning, 34 Quai d'Austerlitz, Latin Quarter and Vicinity, Facebook: Nuit Fauves, Metro: Gare d'Austerlitz

La Machine Du Moulin Rouge

This massive triple-level dance club with DJs spinning a blend of electronic music (house and dubstep predominantly) and Top 40 can be found right next to the famous Moulin Rouge windmill. It's a great place to meet animated backpackers. Famous acts come through often, so check ahead of time to see who is playing. Surrounded by Paris's red-light district (home to seedy bars and sex clubs), the area immediately around the Moulin Rouge is safe and clean, but don't stray too far late at night.

Cover €15, drinks €12, Fri-Sun 23:00-late, 90 Bd de Clichy, Montmartre, +33 (0)1 53 41 88 89, lamachinedumoulinrouge.com/en, Metro: Blanche

PUB CRAWLS
Sandeman's New Europe Pub Crawl

If you've gotta do a pub crawl, these guys have you covered. The €25 fee will get you free drinks for an hour at the meeting point. Your itinerary will include about three stops, with a final stop at a club with a free entry. It'll be up to you to get home, but somewhere between the opening bell and when "Piano Man" comes on to close the night, you're sure to accrue lots of stories to tell during the walk or cab ride home. On a slow night, you'll be crawling with 20 new international friends; on a busy night, with 120 of them.

€25, Thurs-Sat 20:00, meet at the Bastille metro stop, Le Marais and Vicinity, newparistours.com, Metro: Bastille

TOP SHOPPING & MARKETS

SHOPPING DISTRICTS
Le Marais

Paris's gay and Jewish district is also one of its trendiest shopping areas, boasting some of the city's best boutiques and delicious restaurants and cafés. Unique finds from fashion to trinkets may not be bargains (nor are the high-end designer brands you'll find here), but shopping in these winding medieval streets comes with a deserved premium. Mainstream **Rue de Rivoli** and **Rue Vieille du Temple** are the primary intersecting streets in this area, but some of the most interesting shops are on any of the dozens of lanes turning off from the main thoroughfares. On Sundays, when so much of Paris shutters its shops, Le Marais is far and away the best place to shop.

Le Marais, Metro: Saint Paul

Rue Montorgueil

One of my favorite pedestrian avenues in Paris, **Rue Montorgueil** by day boasts pastry shops, flower stalls, bistros, and an open-air market selling a wide variety of meats, cheeses, and other goodies. By night, you'll also find top-notch nightlife, with bars varied enough to appeal to just about anybody. Leading north from the Châtelet-Les Halles metro stop, all the way toward Montmartre, Rue Montorgueil offers a casual scene for those who like to spend an afternoon or an evening strolling and keeping it low-key, stopping for snacks, drinks, and gelato at the sidewalk cafés.

Louvre Neighborhood, Metro: Étienne Marcel or Sentier

Champs-Élysées

Paris's most famous shopping boulevard is now overly mainstream. It doesn't offer much for travelers on a budget other than the grand vistas up the street toward the Arc de Triomphe on the high side and down toward the Tuileries and Louvre on the downhill side. It's a nice place for a walk, but prepare for heart-stopping sticker shock if you go into any of the shops.

Champs-Élysées Neighborhood, Metro: Charles de Gaulle-Étoile

MARKETS

Paris's traditional culinary scene centered on the market. Fresh ingredients were purchased daily and then carried home, often with the trademark baguette sticking out of the bag. Many Parisians still do their grocery shopping in this way, so the city's markets are a great place to catch a glimpse of daily life, with grandmas picking out the freshest fruit and children running home with the baguette that will shortly grace the dinner table. Use meslieux.paris.fr to find the closest market to you.

Rue Cler

Cute and cliché, Rue Cler, a quaint street just east of the Eiffel Tower, is a local market that stubbornly retains its identity. Weave your way through the schoolchildren running about to pick up a crêpe to enjoy on the street or buy some fresh French produce. Though the prices at the restaurants have become a bit outrageous due to the street's popularity, Rue Cler offers a picturesque little three-block slice of Paris complete with cafés, corner markets, and food stands.

Eiffel Tower Neighborhood, Metro: École Militaire

Marché Bastille

On Thursdays and Sundays, head to Paris's largest outdoor food market for a

BEST SPOT FOR BOOKS

Bookstore first, café second, **Shakespeare and Company** (daily 10:00-23:00, 37 Rue de la Bûcherie, Latin Quarter, +33 (0)1 43 25 40 93, shakespeareandcompany. com, Metro: Saint-Michel Notre Dame) is the city's most iconic literary destination. Sometime after Sylvia Beach opened the shop in the 1920s, literary heavies like Ernest Hemingway, F. Scott Fitzgerald, and James Joyce began hanging out here.

Today, Shakespeare and Company still exists solely to serve readers—and it's light years apart from the mammoth online book retailers and their consumer-friendly brick-and-mortar counterparts. It might be tough to find this year's bestsellers on these carefully curated shelves and displays, but you could chance upon a title that will change the way you see the world or the people in it. The shop's outdoor tables bustle with bookish chatter all day. If you buy a book, ask them to stamp the title page—turning your book into a keepsake.

cheap and delicious takeaway lunch, or, if you prefer to assemble your meal yourself, pick up some superb picnic supplies here. This diverse street market offers everything from fish and seafood to fresh produce, baked goods, artisanal desserts, ethnic dishes, and more.

Thurs and Sun until 14:00, Boulevard Richard Lenoir, Le Marais and Vicinity, Metro: Bastille

Marché des Enfants Rouges

Marché des Enfants is a permanent, semi-covered food market in an old courtyard that has been around since 1628. It's quite popular among trendy Parisians. Pop in for a quick and tasty lunch, where options range from Japanese to African and everything in between. Food stalls are happy to let you take your tray to the communal benches and tables around the market.

Tues-Sun 08:30-13:00 and 16:00-19:30, closed Mon, 39 Rue de Bretagne 3e, Le Marais and Vicinity, Metro: Filles du Calvaire

Marche d'Aligre

This covered market offers fresh and delicious artisanal produce, meats, and more just a hop, skip, and jump from the Bastille roundabout. The market is open six days a week (closed on Mondays), and only in the morning (they start to close up around 12:30). Beauvau, the covered market next

to Aligre, is open later in the afternoon (16:00-19:30), and inside you'll find everything from craft beer to horsemeat (yes, horsemeat).

Tues-Sun 09:00-13:00, Place d'Aligre, Le Marais and Vicinity, Metro: Ledru-Rollin

SHOPPING CENTERS
Galeries Lafayette

Claiming to be one of the oldest shopping malls in the world, Galeries Lafayette has an enormous variety of well-known international shops and a spectacular four-level atrium interior under an ornately gilded glass dome. Stop by in December to see their famous 50-foot-tall Christmas tree; decorated with lights and baubles, it reaches upwards towards the dome, making for a fantastic photo op.

Mon-Sat 09:30-20:00, 40 Bd Haussmann, Louvre Neighborhood, Metro: Chaussée d'Antin-La Fayette

Forum des Halles

Located right in downtown Paris, Forum des Halles is a newly renovated shopping center dug deep into the ground (it sits just above the metro). Very popular for Parisians coming in from the *banlieue* (the suburbs), it's a top choice for brands like H&M and Jack Jones.

Daily 10:00-20:00, Louvre Neighborhood, forumdeshalles.com, Metro: Les Halles

TOP PARKS & RECREATION

Paris has numerous city parks to explore. They're a great option for a cheap picnic or, if Paris's hustle and bustle are getting a little too much, places to catch a breather.

Luxembourg Gardens

This beautiful 60-acre park, just a few blocks south of Notre Dame Cathedral, contains flower gardens, fountains, ponds, and statues. The icing on the cake is an enormous Florentine Renaissance-style palace overlooking all of it. The manicured lawns and paths make the park a favorite among Parisians who stroll here or stop by one of the ponds or fountains for a moment's quiet reflection. The best spot for the latter is the Fountaine de Medicis at the east end of the park. The tranquil pool at the base of the fountain—shaded by a row of trees, which gracefully drop their leaves into the pool every autumn—is one of the most serene and romantic spots in the city. You'll find green chairs lining the pool. Take a seat, but before you sit, check the chair for bird droppings (*de rien*). In the southwest part of the park, catch a game of *pétanque*, the extremely popular French version of field bowling played on dirt instead of grass.

Free, daily 07:00-dusk, Odéon, Metro: Odéon, RER: Luxembourg

The Tuileries

The Tuileries are Paris's oldest gardens. Be sure to walk through this sprawling park as you're making your way from the Louvre to the Champs-Élysées. Take a moment to relax in the reclining park chairs and enjoy watching little French kids sail model boats on the ponds. Fun fact: *Tuile* is the French word for "tile." Paris's tile and ceramics factories were located here until Queen Catherine of the Medici family moved them out in 1564 to make room for her royal gardens, which were meant to remind her of her hometown of Florence.

Free, always open, Louvre Neighborhood, Metro: Tuileries

Champ de Mars

The Champ de Mars, or "Field of War," stretches southwest from the Eiffel Tower. This large open space was the parade ground where officers drilled their troops. Today, it's a favorite spot for Parisians to picnic on nice summer evenings. After dark, the crowds swell as the top of the hour approaches—for five minutes each hour, the tower comes to sparkling life. When there are important events or sports matches in Paris, large Jumbotrons are brought in for the crowds to watch. If you're lucky enough to be in Paris for New Year's Eve, you'll have to be even luckier to get a seat here for the fireworks display that kicks off at midnight.

Free, always open, Eiffel Tower Neighborhood, Metro: École Militaire

Parc des Buttes-Chaumont

This beautiful wooded park in Paris's northeast (very close to several recommended hostels) features more than a mile of romantic paths, making it a wonderful place to take a break from the city. In a move typical of 19th-century ingenuity, this ambitious park project (complete with artificial lake and 150-foot-tall peak) was reclaimed from a garbage dump and stone quarry during Napoleon III's modernizing and beautifying of the city. There's a beautiful rope bridge that makes for a perfect photo op. Follow this up with a short climb to the temple capping the peak for stunning panoramic views.

Free, always open, Canal Saint-Martin, Metro: Botzaris

PARIS

71

TOP TOURS

Paris is massive, and, while many feel comfortable guiding themselves around the city, a knowledgeable guide takes your visit to the next level, helping you get a better grasp of Paris's complex history. There are excellent walking tours and bike tours to choose from.

Discover Walks

This walking tour company offers some great itineraries that will take you through the heart of Paris. Tours are led by fun and engaging locals who are paid only by your generosity (they'll politely ask for a tip at the end of the tour). You could fill up an entire visit with their tours, which are organized by theme or neighborhood. Their **Latin Quarter Walk,** which covers the oldest parts of Paris including Île de la Cité and Notre Dame, is a great place to start. If you like their style, graduate to their tours focusing on chocolate or fashion.

Free, 11:00 and 14:30 daily, meet at the Charlemagne statue in front of Notre Dame, Île de la Cité, discoverwalks.com/paris-walking-tours, Metro: Cité

Bateaux Mouches

You're sure to notice the open excursion boats floating up and down the Seine. Touristy these may be, but they give you a perspective of the city that you simply can't get otherwise. An hour-long cruise in one of the larger boats costs as little as €13.50 (there's a recorded audio tour included). There are brunch and lunch cruises, and for something really special, they offer a romantic dinner cruise complete with piano and violin accompaniment. Anything but the bare-bones tour starts to run you in the money, so don't let yourself get carried away.

Tours from €13.50 (prices escalate quickly from there), Apr-Sept daily departures every 20 minutes 10:00-22:30, board close to Pont de l'Alma, Champs-Élysées Neighborhood, bateaux-mouches.fr, Metro: Alma-Marceau

Vedettes du Pont Neuf

This boat cruise is perfect for lovers on a budget. You can bring a bottle of wine on board, and it's only €10 if you book ahead of time. Time it just right by catching the boat that leaves at a quarter to the hour and you'll get a view from the river while the Eiffel Tower does its hourly light display. Show up 15 minutes early to get a good seat.

Tours from €10, leaves from Pont Neuf on tip of island, daily departures every 45 minutes 10:30-22:45, Île de la Cité, vedettesdupontneuf.com, Metro: Pont Neuf

Blue Fox Bike Tours

You can't ask for much more out of a tour guide. The Blue Fox four-hour Best of Paris tour provides an excellent introduction to Paris and its history. Blue Fox separates itself from the pack with first-rate customer service and fair pricing. It's a relatively small company that feels like a family.

Student single €30, daily May-Oct, reserve in advance, meet at Saint-Michel fountain, Île de la Cité, bluefox.travel/paris, Metro: Saint-Michel—Notre-Dame

Fat Tire Bike & Boat Tours

Cruising around by bike in the evening is my absolute favorite way to experience the City of Lights. Go for the late tour and cap your bike adventure with an evening boat cruise. Highlights include Notre Dame, the Louvre, a stop for ice cream, and then a ride down the Seine. With free wine included during the boat tour, this is the perfect way to wind down an evening. While the rides are a good time, the prices are climbing to a prohibitive level.

Day tours €34, night rides €44, tours mid-Feb-Nov, daily mid-Mar-Oct, check website for times and off-season dates, 24 Rue Edgar Faure, Eiffel Tower Neighborhood, fattirebiketours.com/paris, Metro: Dupleix

Le Paris Noir

Your guide Kevi will lead you through the streets of Paris, giving insight into a little-discussed perspective: that of black Parisians. The tour covers their oral, musical, and artistic culture and how each intertwine with the city and some of its well-known neighborhoods. Recognized by French and international media, Kevi does an excellent job of researching and developing new content. His delivery is charming and fascinating, and it's an eye-opening experience—one that will help you better understand 20th- and 21st-century Paris.

Tour prices and details available upon request online, leparisnoir.com

Dress Like a Parisian

Parisian guide Alois Guinut will help you discover Paris as the global capital of fashion through her enjoyable and customizable shopping-oriented walking tour. The flat rates make her tours ideal for a group of friends—you'll all be able to take advantage of Alois's expert eye and intimate knowledge of local boutiques and their wares. Contact her online and design a shopping extravaganza tailored to your tastes.

Two-hour Marais fashion tour €100, personal shopping €235-300, dresslikeaparisian.com

TOP HOSTELS

Paris is woefully lacking in budget accommodations, but be assured that those I've listed provide good value. Use **hostelworld.com** to find the latest hostel ratings, and don't forget to check out **airbnb.com** for private apartment options.

Hotel Queen Mary

This three-star hotel is in the heart of everything but won't break the bank. For those who value privacy above all else, you'll find it here. It has clean rooms, modern bathrooms, and an elevator (this is a luxury in Paris—take my word for it). The staff is extremely friendly and happy to point you in the direction of whatever you want to see—chances are, it's not far from the front door. This will cost you a good deal more than a hostel, but you'll be sleeping in style, if not quite luxury.

Rooms from €149 (prices will vary depending on season), American buffet breakfast (€8), room service, concierge, air conditioned, bar/lounge, dry cleaning services, Wi-Fi, TV with international channels, 9 Rue Greffulhe, Champs-Élysées Neighborhood, +33 (0)1 42 66 40 50, hotelqueenmary.com, Metro: Madeleine

Generator Hostel Paris

The Generator Hostel chain continues to take the Continent by storm, and the new Paris location shows exactly why they're enjoying so much success. They know exactly what budget travelers are looking for, and they do an excellent job of providing a fun, chill place to crash after your long days out on the town. Besides the new, clean rooms, mod decor, ubiquitous free Wi-Fi, and plugs and reading lights for each bed, you've also got an impeccable location in the midst of the trendiest part of Canal Saint-Martin and only minutes from beautiful Parc des Buttes-Chaumont. Deluxe penthouse and private rooms offering views of the neighborhood are also available.

Beds from €22, 24-hour reception, mini grocer, vending machines, free Wi-Fi, terrace, travel options desk, on-site bar and restaurant, laundry facilities, lockers and adapters for rent, 9-11 Place du Colonel Fabien, Canal Saint-Martin, +33 (0)1 70 98 84 00, generatorhostels. com, Metro: Colonel Fabien

St. Christopher's Inn — Gare du Nord

This hostel on Paris's north side lives up to the standards of the St. Christopher's brand of large hostels, with clean rooms, loads of amenities, and a great location. Just steps from Paris's northern train station and a couple of blocks from the trendy, up-and-coming Canal Saint-Martin district, you're in the center of it all. With over 600 beds, this hostel brings in loads of travelers from all over the world, creating a fun and social atmosphere to meet and connect with other globetrotters.

€24, free breakfast, optional upgrade, free Wi-Fi, bar, café, 24-hour reception, 5 Rue de Dunkerque, Canal Saint-Martin, +33 (0)1 70 08 52 22, st-christophers.co.uk/paris-hostels/gare-du-nord, paris@st-christophers.co.uk, Metro: Gare du Nord

St. Christopher's Inn — Canal

This is the original location, but my second choice of the two St. Christopher's hostels in town (Gare du Nord's location gives it the edge). Here you've got a fun vibe and a music bar downstairs featuring acts good enough to bring in locals. While it's a half-hour metro ride to sights like the Louvre and the Notre Dame Cathedral, the comfy beds, helpful yet busy staff, free breakfast, and reliable Wi-Fi make this one of Paris's better budget choices. It's also about a 30-minute walk north of the fun Canal Saint-Martin nightlife district. You can't miss the funky exterior: It looks as though someone has wrapped a bunch of giant

rubber bands around all six levels of the building overlooking the canal.

€24, daily breakfast, free Wi-Fi, chill-out room, bag lockers, 24-hour reception, 159 Rue de Crimée, Canal Saint-Martin, +33 (0)1 40 34 34 40, st-christophers.co.uk/paris-hostels/canal, paris@st-christophers.co.uk, Metro: Crimée

The Loft Boutique Hostel

The Loft tries hard to be Paris's top boutique hostel, and in many ways it succeeds. Highlights include the fun, intimate atmosphere in the common rooms, its cleanliness, and the included continental breakfast. The outdoor patio make for a pleasant and distinctly social vibe, especially when combined with the nightly happy hour prices. The neighborhood feels a bit bohemian and off the beaten path, away from Paris's major tourist areas, but it's close to both the Parc des Buttes-Chaumont and Père Lachaise Cemetery.

Beds from €23, 24-hour reception, outdoor terrace, on-site bar, free Wi-Fi, included breakfast, kitchen and laundry facilities available, 70 Rue Julien Lacroix, Canal Saint-Martin, +33 (0)1 42 02 42 02, theloft-paris.com, Metro: Pyrénées

Les Piaules

Nicknamed "the Bunks," this large Belleville hostel offers a bar, breakfast lounge, and free Wi-Fi. The location puts you right in the center of one of Paris's best up-and-coming neighborhoods, which means you can turn in either direction and stumble upon great nightlife and food. Each bunk comes with its own private light, privacy screen, and charging station.

Beds from €29 (8-bed room), private rooms from €90, baggage storage, Wi-Fi, lounge, photo booth, arcade games, 59 Boulevard de Belleville, Canal Saint-Martin, +33 (0)1 43 55 09 97, lespiaules.com, Metro: Belleville

Trendy Hostel

While this hostel southeast of the city center (about 20 minutes away on the metro) suffers in location, backpackers love it for just about everything else: comfortable beds, fun staff, great nearby restaurants, and a long list of value-adding amenities. You'll have a bit of a trek (or an expensive cab ride) to get back to your hostel at night, but the solid night's sleep you'll get might be worth it.

Beds from €18 with female dorms available, 24-hour reception, free maps and Wi-Fi, laundry facilities available, breakfast included, 2B Rue Édouard Vasseur, Greater Paris, +33 (0)9 82 47 90 24, trendyhostel.com, Metro: Pierre et Marie Curie

MIJE Hostels Marais

If the other venues listed here are beyond your budget or full, opt for this no-frills accommodation in one of the best locations in town. While the Wi-Fi doesn't reach the room, and many complain about the noise, you just can't beat the location. With its proximity to Île de la Cité, Le Marais, and the Bastille, you'll have easy connections anywhere you need to go. The beds and bathrooms are spotless thanks to the 12:00-15:00 mandatory daily vacate of the building, which gives the cleaners time to work their magic.

Gender-separated dorms from €35, singles from €60, 11 Rue du Fauconnier, Le Marais, +33 (0)1 42 74 23 45, mije.com, Metro: Saint-Paul

TRANSPORTATION

GETTING THERE & AWAY
Plane

There are three major airports in Paris: **Charles de Gaulle** (CDG), **Orly** (ORY), and **Beauvais** (BVA). Find information for all three at aeroportsdeparis.com. All offer quick and reliable connections into the city.

From **Charles de Gaulle,** take Paris's regional train system, the **RER.** You find it by following the signs marked RER (they'll lead you to the ticketing area). A one-way ticket will cost you €9.10, with trains departing every 15 minutes between 05:00 and 00:15. Remember, you'll need your ticket to exit the RER system, so keep it handy. This is your cheapest and fastest option into the city, with opportunities to connect onto Paris's extensive metro system, including service to Gare du Nord (for St. Christopher's Hostels), Châtelet-Les Halles (central Paris), and Luxembourg (south side of Paris) stations. Traveling via the RER and the metro, it'll take you about an hour to get from Charles de Gaulle into the center of Paris.

Another option is the **Roissybus** express bus (€10). Find it by following the Roissybus signs. Purchase a ticket from the RATP (the name of Paris's public transportation system) vendor, which is clearly marked and located right by the bus stop. Roissybus takes about 1.5 hours to reach the city center.

Lastly, you can hail **taxis** outside the terminal. These will cost you €45 for the one-hour trip into the city.

From **Orly,** hop on the **Orlybus,** which will take you directly into the center of the city. The bus will drop you at Denfert Rochereau metro station, where you can connect to the metro and ride it to your desired stop. Buses depart every 15 minutes, running from 05:35 to 23:00. The one-way journey costs €7.70 and will take you about 25 minutes.

You can also use Air France's **shuttle service** (€9), departing every 15 minutes and running to Porte d'Orléans, Montparnasse, and Invalides metro stations. It runs from 06:00 to 23:00, with a journey length of 25 minutes. Or, you can also take a **taxi** into the center for about €25.

From **Beauvais**, catch the Beauvais Airport official **shuttle** (€16), which is a nonstop journey from the airport to the Porte Maillot metro stop in Paris. The journey takes about 75 minutes.

Train

Rates from London—on fast trains taking just under 2.5 hours—range from €50 to €150 and up, depending on student discount and how far in advance you book your ticket. For more information, visit the **Eurostar** website (eurostar.com). Trains to Amsterdam (about €75) run often and take about 3.5 hours.

Six major train stations operate in Paris, so it's important to confirm your departure station when the time comes for you to leave. **Gare du Nord** (in northern Paris) serves connections to London, Amsterdam, and Brussels. **Gare de l'Est** (just east of Gare du Nord) serves Munich, Frankfurt, Luxembourg, and beyond. **Gare de Lyon** (east of Le Marais) most likely has your night connections to Nice, Barcelona, and Milan. All train stations are well connected via metro, and it is possible to buy tickets for your departure at any train station (no matter where you're actually departing from).

Bus

Paris has numerous bus options for France, Germany, Spain, Italy, and even the UK. The prices are appealing, but remember, you're trading value for time and comfort (I've often arrived stiff and exhausted, wishing I'd forked over the extra €30-40 for a train ticket). **Eurolines** (eurolines.fr) is the dominant company. Check their prices and full list of destinations online.

Car

Thanks to Paris's excellent public transportation system, I advise against renting a car, and this includes for would-be road-trippers. It's not that it's dangerous or unpleasant, but trains, planes, and buses will all get you to your destination quicker, in more comfort, and most likely at a cheaper price. When budgeting for your trip, don't forget to account for gas (about $10/gallon), parking, and speeding tickets from pesky automated machines—all on top of the rental fees, insurance and any service you might require.

GETTING AROUND

Take advantage of Paris's fantastic public transportation. The train, bus, and metro lines are all very well integrated: A single **ticket** costs €1.70. A *carnet* of 10 tickets (€12.70) saves you about 25 percent, and the 10 rides can be shared between multiple people. Look for the under-26 weekend day pass, a great deal at about €5.

Metro

Paris's **metro system** (ratp.fr) is easily one of the best in the world. You'll definitely want to use it to get around. The metro operates Sunday-Thursday 05:30-00:30 and Friday-Saturday 05:30-02:00. You'll rarely walk two blocks without passing a metro stop, and all routes are color coded and numbered. The system is safe and easy to navigate with large maps presented before and after the turnstiles. Ask for help if necessary at the ticket office found in most stations. You can get nearly anywhere in Paris with only one or two transfers. Make sure that you double check which side of the platform you should be on (this is clearly marked). The **RATP Lite** app offers a full map of the metro. Be aware that **pickpockets** operate throughout Paris's metro system. Keep your valuables tight and safe.

RER

The RER system, Paris's express regional train, zips straight through the heart of town and to destinations outside the city. It's much speedier than the metro or bus. If you're going outside of the center, it's a good idea to check their routes and schedules. The network is lettered A through E. Tickets within the city cost the same as on the metro; remember to hold on to your validated ticket because you need it to exit the system. The RER system also provides fast connections to the airports as well as popular day-trip options outside the city center, like Versailles and Disneyland Paris. Those tickets are more expensive. Numerous easy to use ticket kiosks have options in English; you can purchase your tickets with cash or plastic.

Bus

Paris has an extensive bus system that offers great views of the city while you ride. The maps at each bus station are helpful both for bus riders and those who are lost and need to regain their bearings. While these maps are very skinny, oriented tightly around the bus routes, you can usually get an idea of where you are and how to get where you need to go. If you buy your ticket on board, you aren't allowed any transfers. If that's an issue for you, consider buying a *carnet* of 10 tickets from any metro station and using them in the integrated system, because each ticket gives you 90 minutes'

worth of travel with as many transfers as you need—much better value.

Taxi

Taxis are a great solution if you're splitting a ride home from the club late at night, but they dry up quickly if you linger past closing time. Thankfully, **Uber** works in Paris.

Taxi fares are reasonable (a crosstown ride from the Eiffel Tower to the recommended hostels near Gare du Nord, for example, should run about €25). Head to a taxi stand or flag a cab down where there's room to pull over.

Bicycle

Paris is home to **Vélib'** (en.velib.paris.fr), the world's most extensive public bike system. To use it, you need a chip and pin debit or credit card to purchase a 24-hour access pass (€1.70). Users have 30 minutes to return the bike without a fee; subsequent hours cost a euro each. The most popular way to get across town for free on longer rides is to simply stop at checkpoints along the way. Just check in your old bike and pull out a new one.

Before checking out a bike, make sure the tires are full of air, the brakes work, and you can move the seat to the right place; a backward saddle signals to the maintenance staff that a bike needs service. Now, with a fully functional bike, you're free to cruise the 400 kilometers of bike paths in the city. But remember to play it safe. There are many Vélib' accidents each year, and Parisian drivers don't necessarily yield to bike lanes. Helmets are not provided at the rental stations. If you want to bike with a knowledgeable guide and without the stress of trying to navigate, consider **Fat Tire Bike Tours** (24 Rue Edgar Faure, fattirebiketours.com/paris).

DAY TRIPS

The RER regional rail system provides easy access to two excellent day-trip options just outside of the city (both are reachable in an hour or two). With an early start (07:30), you should be able to beat the crowds on just about any day.

Versailles

If you have the time, a visit to Versailles is the perfect way to cap your time in Paris. Constructed under the rule of the Sun King, Louis XIV, this unbelievably extrav-

agant palace, along with its seemingly never-ending gardens, makes physical the immediate and absolute power of the French monarchy. It's tough to wrap your mind around the sheer scale of this palace, so here are some statistics: 67,000 square feet, 67 staircases, 700 royal rooms, and nearly 2,000 acres of gardens. Tour the palace to see the gilded room where the Sun King slept, the floor-to-ceiling mirrors in the grand Hall of Mirrors (from a time when hardly anyone could afford even a pocket mirror), and much more. After the angry hordes had taken Paris during the French Revolution, they came 24 kilometers to Versailles to drag Marie Antoinette and Louis XVI down from their ivory towers and to the Place de la Revolution (now the Place de la Concorde) for their date with the guillotine.

The trip from Paris takes 30 minutes to an hour on the RER-C, depending on the train you catch, and will cost you €8.20. You will arrive at the Versailles RER train station, with the palace and breathtaking gardens just a few steps away.

€20 for palace and gardens, €18 for palace, daily 09:00–17:30, Place d'Armes, +33 (0) 1 30 83 78 00, en.chateauversailles.fr

Disneyland Paris

The wonderful world of Disney is just a 32-kilometer train ride from Paris's city center. Head to this amusement park to live it up with Mickey and Minnie—it'll take a minute or two for you to get used to their French accents—and rides like Hyperspace Mountain, Phantom Manor, and the earworm that is It's a Small World. If Belle and Aladdin and the rest of the Disney cast are your thing, budget a full day to visit Europe's happiest kingdom, which has been putting smiles on the faces of young and old alike since 1992. For extra credit you can visit Walt Disney Studios, a theme park that focuses on recent movies like *Toy Story*. These rides, coasters, and experiences take you on interactive behind-the-scenes trips and are geared toward a slightly older audience.

Ticket prices vary, depending on season and day of week. I recommend purchasing tickets ahead of time online (from about €50 for a single-day, single-park ticket, and €80 for combo tickets for both parks). To get here, take RER A4 (€7.60) toward Marne-la-Vallee Chessy from Châtelet-Les Halles. The last train back to Paris leaves shortly after midnight. Trains run every 15 minutes and take about an hour.

Ticket prices vary, daily 09:00–20:00, +33 (0)8 25 30 05 00, disneylandparis.com

HELP!

Tourist Information Centers

Paris has a couple of tourist offices. They are great places to stop in and pick up a free map. Get information online at en.parisinfo.com, or find Paris's official tourism office (open daily 10:00-19:00) and info desk at:

25 Rue des Pyramides
+33 (0) 1 49 52 42 63

Pickpockets & Scams

As with most European cities, violent crime within the city of Paris is extremely rare; however, be on the lookout for pickpockets, who flock like gulls to Europe's most popular cities. Beware if someone approaches you holding an object and asking if you've dropped it. The same thing goes if somebody asks you to take a survey or sign a petition. A surprisingly large percentage of pickpockets are children under the age of 16, so be on your guard if a group of young'uns starts to crowd around you. Lastly, keep a close watch on handbags or purses; never set them down and walk away, even if only for a second.

Emergencies

Dial 112 for emergencies, 17 for English-speaking police, and 15 for an ambulance.

Hospital

Hôpital Américain de Paris
63 Bd Victor Hugo
+33 (0)1 46 41 25 25

US Embassy

4 Av Gabriel
+33 (0)1 43 12 22 22

AMSTERDAM

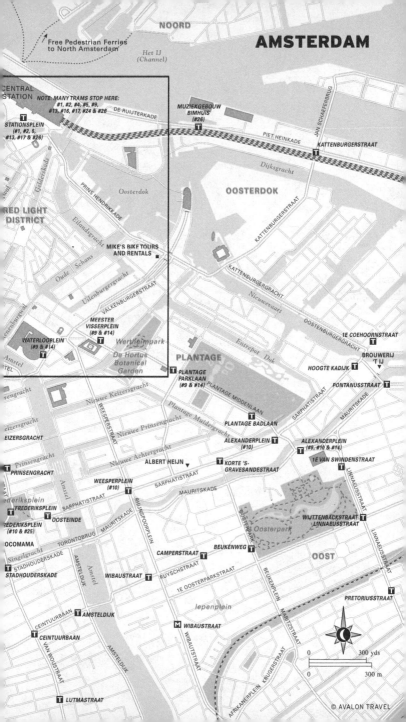

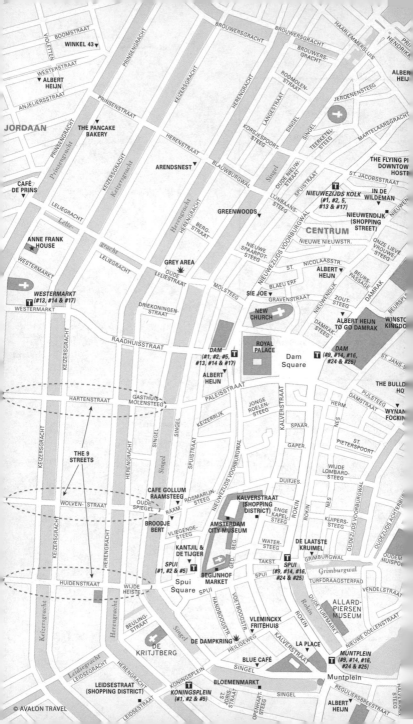

BOOMSTRAAT

VIOLETTEN

WINKEL 43 ▼

WESTERSTRAAT

▼ ALBERT HEIJN

ANJELIERSSTRAAT

JORDAAN

PRINSENSTRAAT

THE PANCAKE BAKERY

HERENSTRAAT

CAFÉ DE PRINS ▼

LELIEGRACHT

ANNE FRANK HOUSE ★

WESTERMARKT

WESTERMARKT (#13, #14 & #17)

WESTERMARKT

BROUWERSGRACHT

BROUWERSGRACHT

BROUWERS-GRACHT

HAARLEMMERSLUIS

PRI. HENDRIKA

ALBER HEIJ

ROOMOLEN-STRAAT

LANGESTRAAT

JEROENENSTEEG

MARTELAARSGRACHT

TEERKETEL STEEG

SINGEL

KORSJESPOORT-STEEG

THE FLYING PI DOWNTOW HOSTE

ST. JACOBSSTRAAT

OUDE NIEUW. STRAAT

NIEUWEZIJDS KOLK (#1, #2, 5, #13 & #17)

IN DE WILDEMAN

NIEUWEN.

ARENDSNEST ▼

BLAUWBURGWAL

LIJNBAANS-STEEG

GREENWOODS

BERG-STRAAT

NIEUWENDIJK (SHOPPING STREET)

CENTRUM

NIEUWE NIEUWSTR.

ONZE LIEVE VROUWE. STEEG

GREY AREA

OUDE LELIESTRAAT

NIEUWE SPAARPOT-STEEG

NIEUWEZIJDS VOORBURGWAL

ST. NICOLAASSTR.

ALBERT HEIJN

BEURS-PASSAGE

DAMRAK

DRIEKONINGEN-STRAAT

MOLSTEEG

BLAEU ERF

SIE JOE ▼

GRAVENSTRAAT

NIEUWENDIJK

ZOUT-STEEG

ONZE LIEVE VROUWE.

BEURSPL

NEW CHURCH ✚

ALBERT HEIJN TO GO DAMRAK

DAMRAK-STEEG

WINSTO KINGDO

DAM (#1, #2, #5, #13, #14 & #17)

ROYAL PALACE

Dam Square

DAM (#9, #14, #16, #24 & #25)

ST. JANS-S

ALBERT HEIJN

PALEISSTRAAT

JONGE ROELEN-STEEG

KALVERSTRAAT

HERM.

PIJLSTEEG

THE BULLD HO

DAMSTRAAT

WYNAN FOCKIN

HARTENSTRAAT

GASTHUIS MOLENSTEEG

SPAAR.

SPUISTRAAT

KEIZERRIJK

SPAAR.

GAPER.

ST. PIETERSPOORT

THE 9 STREETS

WOLVEN- STRAAT

CAFÉ GOLLUM RAAMSTEEG

OUDE SPIEGEL

ROSMARIJN-STEEG

RAAM.

NIEUWEZIJDS VOORBURGWAL

DUIFJES.

WIJDE LOMBARD-STEEG

KALVERSTRAAT (SHOPPING DISTRICT)

ENGE KAPEL STEEG

ROKIN

NES

KUIPERS-STEEG

OUDEZIJDS VOORBURGWAL

OUDEZIJDS ACHTERBU

BROODJE BERT

VLIEGENDE-STEEG

AMSTERDAM CITY MUSEUM

WATER-STEEG

DE LAATSTE KRUIMEL

HUIDENSTRAAT

KANTJIL & DE TIJGER

SPUI (#1, #2 & #5)

GED. BEG.

TAKST.

SPUI (#9, #14, #16, #24 & #25)

GRIMBURGWAL

OUDEM HUISPO

BEGIJNHOF MARKET

Spui Square

SPUI

Grimburgwal

TURFDRAAGSTERPAD

VENDELSTRAAT

HANDBOOGSTR.

VOETBOOGSTR.

ROKIN

Rokin

Oude Turfmarkt

ALLARD-PIERSEN MUSEUM

NIEUWE DOELENSTRAAT

BEULINGSTRAAT

DE KRITJTBERG ✚

VLEMINCKX FRITEHUIS

HEILIGEWEG

KALVERSTRAAT

LA PLACE

DE DAMPKRING

BLUE CAFÉ

MUNTPLEIN (#9, #14, #16, #24 & #25)

LEIDSEGRACHT

LEIDSESTRAAT (SHOPPING DISTRICT)

KONINGSPLEIN

KONINGSPLEIN (#1, #2 & #5)

ST. JORIS-STRAAT

OPENHART.STR.

BLOEMENMARKT

SINGEL

Muntplein

REGULIERSBREESTRAAT

HAME STEEG

ALBERT HEIJN ▼

© AVALON TRAVEL

LEIDSESTRAAT

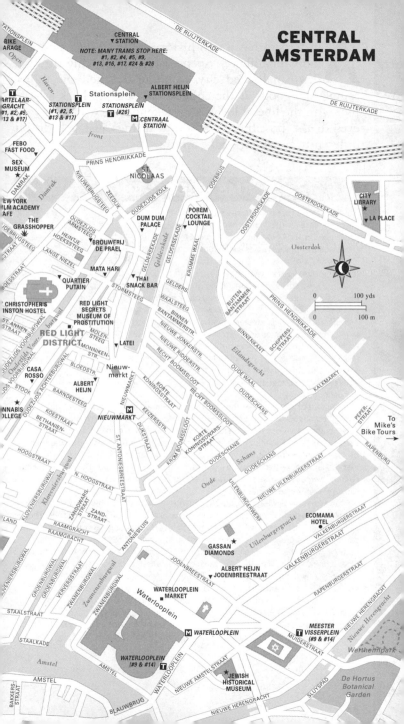

CENTRAL AMSTERDAM

DE RUIJTERKADE

CENTRAL ▼ STATION

NOTE: MANY TRAMS STOP HERE:
#1, #2, #4, #5, #9, #13, #16, #17, #24 & #26

ALBERT HEIJN STATIONSPLEIN

Stationsplein

STATIONSPLEIN
(#1, #2, 5, 13 & #17)

STATIONSPLEIN
(#26)

CENTRAAL STATION

DE RUIJTERKADE

Haven-

front

STATIONSPLEIN

BIKE GARAGE

Open

STATIONSPLEIN

ARTELAAR-GRACHT
#1, #2, #5, 13 & #17

FEBO FAST FOOD

SEX MUSEUM ★

DAMRAK

Damvak

PRINS HENDRIKKADE

ODEBRUG

ST. NICOLAAS

OOSTERDOKSKADE

CITY LIBRARY

■ LA PLACE

NEW YORK FILM ACADEMY CAFE

THE GRASSHOPPER

DEBRUGSTEEG

STRAAT

OESSTRAAT

LANGE NIEZEL

HEINTJE HOEKSSTEEG

OUDEZIJDS ARMSTEEG

NIEUWEBRUGSTEEG

ZEEDIJK

OUDEZIJDS KOLK

DUM DUM PALACE ▼

GELDERSEKADE

GELDERSEKADE

POREM COCKTAIL LOUNGE

OOSTERDOKSKADE

Oosterdok

Oosterdok

BROUWERIJ DE PRAEL

MATA HARI ★

THAI SNACK BAR ▼

STORMSTEEG

KROMME WAAL

GELDERS

PRINS HENDRIKKADE

0   100 yds
0   100 m

QUARTIER PUTAIN ▼

CHRISTOPHER'S WINSTON HOSTEL

RED LIGHT DISTRICT

RED LIGHT SECRETS MUSEUM OF PROSTITUTION

WAALSTEEG

BINNEN BANTAMMERSTR

BUITEN BANTAMMER-STRAAT

MOLEN-STEEG

ST. ANNEN-STRAAT

MONNIKEN-STR.

▼ LATEI

NIEUWE JONKERSTR.

NIEUWE RIDDERSTR.

RECHT BOOMSSLOOT

Eilandsgracht

SCHIPPERS-STRAAT

BINNENKANT

Oudezijds Voor-burgwal

Oudezijds Voor-burgwal

CASA ROSSO

BLOEDSTR.

Nieuw-markt

KORTE KONINGSSTRAAT

RECHT BOOMSSLOOT

Oude Waal

OUDESCHANS

KALKMARKT

PEPER-STRAAT

CANNABIS COLLEGE ★

ALBERT HEIJN

OUDEZIJDS ACHTERBURGWAL

BARNDESTEEG

KOESTRAAT

BETHANIEN-STRAAT

NIEUWMARKT

NIEUWMARKT

KEIZERSTR.

KORTE KONINGSDWARS-STRAAT

DIJKSTRAAT

KROM BOOMSSLOOT

Oude

OUDESCHANS

Schans

To Mike's Bike Tours →

RAPENBURG

HOOGSTRAAT

Kloveniersburgwal

N. HOOGSTRAAT

ST. ANTONIESBREESTRAAT

UILENBURGERWEG

NIEUWE UILENBURGERSTRAAT

ZANDDWARS-STRAAT

ZAND-STRAAT

ST. ANTONIESLUIS

RAAMGRACHT

RAAMGRACHT

ECOMAMA HOTEL ●

Uilenburgergracht

VALKENBURGERSTRAAT

VENIERSBURGWAL

GROENBURGWAL

GROENBURGWAL

VERVERSSTRAAT

ZWANENBURGWAL

Zwanenburgwal

GASSAN DIAMONDS ★

VALKENBURGERSTRAAT

LAND

STAALSTRAAT

JODENBREESTRAAT

ALBERT HEIJN JODENBREESTRAAT

RAPENBURGERSTRAAT

NIEUWE HERENGRACHT

STAALKADE

WATERLOOPLEIN MARKET

Waterlooplein

WATERLOOPLEIN

Nieuwe Herengracht

NIEUWE HERENGRACHT

Amstel

WATERLOOPLEIN (#9 & #14)

WATERLOOPLEIN

MUIDERSTRAAT

MEESTER VISSERPLEIN (#9 & #14)

Werthempark

BAKKERS-STRAAT

AMSTEL

AMSTEL

WATERLOOPLEIN (#9 & #14)

NIEUWE AMSTELSTRAAT

✡ JEWISH HISTORICAL MUSEUM

NIEUWE HERENGRACHT

SLUYSPAD

De Hortus Botanical Garden

BLAUWBRUG

Amsterdam has a rich history of social inclusion and individual liberty. Spend a few days biking through this canal-laced city, stopping to smell the tulips, sample the goods at the coffeeshops, and tip back a half-pint with the liberal locals. A weekend here will open your eyes to the possibilities of doing things just a little bit differently. So go on—take a taste!

AMSTERDAM 101

The Dutch are a proud lot. It was their ancestors who turned a small, marshy port into the home base for the world's first global corporation. The Dutch East India Company, established in 1602, was the largest company in its time to trade with Asia. It was so successful that private navies were employed to protect its interests around the globe.

The impact of these far-reaching companies made the Dutch language become the first internationally spoken language, and the Dutch guilder was the first internationally traded currency. A small town on the banks of a marshland quickly grew into one of the world's richest cities, sparking a golden age of arts, culture, innovation, and a wee bit of gluttony.

Along with its riches, Amsterdam also grew in physical size, but only through the labor-intensive process of driving millions of wooden pilings into the soft, marshy surroundings. As you stroll through this city, remember that every square inch has been reclaimed from the sea, placing quite a premium on real estate. That's the reason staircases are steep (so as to reduce their footprint) and buildings are built high and essentially stapled together (look for the metal brackets on the older, leaning buildings throughout the city).

In the face of any obstacle, the Dutch have been able to overcome, but not without painful lessons. One such lesson the Dutch learned occurred when speculation over flower bulbs led to the world's first stock market bubble and collapse. "Tulip Mania" saw these plants trading at the price of entire estates, and people were making money hand over fist...until the market realized tulip bulbs just weren't worth that much. Overnight, vast wealth disappeared, shaking the Dutch economy to its core. The small, sea-level country eventually recovered and made a triumphant comeback to become the vibrant capital of commerce that it is today.

As an economic powerhouse, the Netherlands welcomed migrants into its multicultural quilt. This history of integration and tolerance is also reflected in Dutch laws. They've seen few gains in trying to legislate morality. Rather, the business-savvy Dutch have taken a progressive approach in decriminalizing and taxing industries like cannabis and prostitution. Here's the Dutch rule of thumb for determining if an activity should be legal: Does it harm anyone? Is it good for business? Is it discreet?

As long as you answer these correctly, you can safely assume that whatever it is you want to do is legal, or at least decriminalized. This pragmatic approach has done a lot to show how legalization and regulation can undercut gangsters and pimps, and provide needed capital for support and recovery services for those who want out of their respective activities. What better way to experience this fascinating history and rich international culture than in the capital of the Netherlands itself, Amsterdam!

PLAN AHEAD

RESERVATIONS

Reservations are recommended (and often required) for the following sights:

Anne Frank House (annefrank.org)
Van Gogh Museum (vangoghmuseum.nl)
Rijksmuseum (rijksmuseum.nl)
Heineken Experience (heinekenexperience.com)

LOCAL HAPPENINGS

Keukenhof

Keukenhof (€24 combo ticket with transportation, 08:00-19:30, Stationsweg 166A, +31 (0)252 465 555, keukenhof.nl) is one of the largest flower gardens in the world and the Netherlands' most famous tulip field. It only reveals its true blooming splendor for a few weeks a year, from the last week of March through the second week of May. If you're in town then, make your visit to Keukenhof efficient by checking it out on your day of arrival or departure, as the only connection is on bus 58 via Schiphol Airport.

King's Day

April 27 is Amsterdam's biggest celebration of the year. The Dutch simply use it as an excuse to 1) sell their junk (the entire city turns into a yard sale) and 2) party hardy with free, world-class events and musical performances across Amsterdam. Make your hostel reservations long in advance and be prepared to pony up a bit more than usual for a bed.

Gay Pride Fest

The first Saturday of every August sees this historic world capital of tolerance and acceptance turn into one massive party. Club parties, canal parades, and street festivities draw hundreds of thousands, making this one of the most popular weekends of the year to be in Amsterdam.

Amsterdam Dance Event

Every mid-October, this five-day music festival and conference takes over Amsterdam with hundreds of events and concerts sprinkled throughout the city in a wide range of venues, creative spaces, and parks. Reserve your tickets and accommodation as far in advance as possible at amsterdam-dance-event.nl.

KNOW BEFORE YOU GO

KEY STATS & FIGURES

Currency:
The Netherlands uses the euro (€); 1 EUR = about 1.14 USD

Population:
820,000

Nationalities Represented:
177

Language:
Dutch

Bicycles:
880,000

Bike paths within the city:
250 miles

Bikes dredged from canals annually:
up to 15,000

Canals:
165

Bridges:
1,281

Houseboats:
2,500

CALIBRATE YOUR BUDGET

TYPICAL PRICES FOR:

Hostel dorm bed:
€35

Two-course dinner and drink:
€20

Pint of beer:
€6

Day bike rental:
€9

Single tram pass:
€2.90

MOVIES TO WATCH
Ocean's Twelve, The Diary of Anne Frank, The Fault in Our Stars

YOUTUBE VIDEOS TO WATCH
Holland: The Original Cool

THREE DAY ITINERARY

Amsterdam's touristy center is walkable, but consider renting a bike to get around in a jiffy. Make reservations for the Anne Frank House well ahead of time.

DAY 1: WELCOME TO AMSTERDAM
MORNING
Kick off your day at one of my recommended breakfast spots: **De Laatste Kruimel** or **La Place** in Central Amsterdam or **Bakers & Roasters** in De Pijp. All feature filling breakfasts and excellent coffee. Consider taking a sandwich to eat on the go later.

AFTERNOON
Take the better part of the day getting your bearings in the city on a bike tour. Three-hour rides with **Mike's Bike Tours** kick off daily at 11:00 (12:00 Nov-Feb) at Prins Hendrikkade 176, about a 10-minute walk east of the train station. You'll cover a great deal of ground on the bikes, with plenty of time to enjoy a pit stop at the windmill brewery, **Brouwerij 't Ij.** For a walking tour, catch up with the local guides toting orange umbrellas at **360 Walking Tours** on Dam Square, meeting daily at 11:00, 13:00, and 15:00.

After wrapping up back at the shop, consider keeping your bike for your stay at a discounted rate. If you're leaving on foot, hop on tram 2 or 5 south to Museumplein for either the **Van Gogh Museum** or the **Rijksmuseum.**

EVENING
Take tram 2 or 5 back north to rest up and refresh at your hostel. When you're ready, head towards the Red Light District. Right on its edge is where you'll find **Thai Bird Snack Bar.** After dinner, spend some time wandering about in the **Red Light District.** You'll be winding your way through some high-density raunch. In between the titillating window displays, there are plenty of touristy bars and coffeeshops (cannabis cafés). If you get the munchies, there are plenty of snacking options around.

LATE
If you're looking to experience Amsterdam's rollicking nightlife scene, drop south to the **Rembrandtplein** entertainment district. Parties there are loud, crowded, and sweaty—Dutch style. Bounce around until you find the venue that's right for you.

DAY 2: ANNE FRANK HOUSE & JORDAAN
MORNING
Snag breakfast at your hostel, or find classy English fare at **Greenwoods.** After breakfast, walk to the **Anne Frank House** (a 10-minute walk from Greenwoods). When you reserved your ticket online, you selected a time to visit, so be sure to arrive within 30 minutes of your time, or you'll forfeit your chance to visit. Without a reservation, you won't be able to enter until after 15:30, and you'll wait in a very long queue.

AFTERNOON
Grab lunch just down the street at the **Pancake Bakery** (worth calling ahead for

a reservation to guarantee a seat). Save some room for Amsterdam's best apple pie at **Winkel 43** in the **Noordermarkt** just across the canal. If it's Saturday or Monday, spend a while exploring the bustling farmers market, taking advantage of copious samples. Take this opportunity to wander deeper into the **Jordaan** district as well.

Walk about 30 minutes or use tram 14 (exit at Waterlooplein) to loop across town to **Gassan Diamonds** for a free diamond-cutting demonstration and factory tour. On the way, stop at the **Cannabis College** for an herbal education.

EVENING

Recharge at your hostel for a bit, then head to **Kantjil & de Tijger** for an Indonesian dinner that's easy on the wallet.

LATE

Head down Leidsestraat to Leidseplein and dive into any number of Amsterdam's relaxed watering holes, or dress to impress to get past the bouncers at clubs **Paradiso** or **Melkweg**. To party like a rock star, catch the **Amsterdam's Ultimate Party Pub Crawl**, kicking off nightly at Candela Bar with a power hour starting at 20:30.

DAY 3: MUSEUMPLEIN & MORE

MORNING

Starting in Dam Square, stroll down **Kalverstraat,** then **Leidsestraat.** Farther down Leidsestraat you'll find **B&B Lunchroom,** the best sandwich shop in the city. Take a sandwich to go, and for an appetizer sample a few of the local cheeses at **Henri Willig Cheeses.**

Resist the urge to eat while you walk and make your way to **Vondelpark,** a picturesque city park laced with gardens, running paths, and bike trails. Snag a bench and watch the bicyclists while you eat. If you've still got the munchies, enjoy a snack at **'t Blauwe Theehuis** in the middle of the park.

AFTERNOON

Exit the park through the south side toward Museumplein and pop into either the **Rijksmuseum** or the **Van Gogh Museum**—whichever you didn't visit on day one. Don't forget your photo op at the I Amsterdam sign on the square. (Insider tip: The front of the sign is always crowded with tourists. Instead, snap your shot from the back, then flip the sign around in Photoshop later).

After you get your fill of museums, walk about 15 minutes over to Europe's largest daily market, **Albert Cuyp Market.** Cute *bruin cafés* (brown cafés) line the street, perfect for an afternoon coffee or tea. If you're hungry, nearby **Bazar** has fresh and healthy Moroccan spreads to tide you over. Drop down to relax in **Sarphatipark,** a block south of Albert Cuyp Market. Stick around **De Pijp**—as the late afternoon turns into early evening, the neighborhood really comes to life.

EVENING

Take an hour-long evening canal cruise; they leave hourly from the **Lover's Canal Cruises** stand just across from the train station, opposite the Play In casino. Bring a discreet six-pack to drink while you take in the view of the city from the canals.

LATE

Take it easy on **Nieuwmarkt,** enjoying some half-pints with the locals at the cafés where the seating spills out onto the square.

TOP NEIGHBORHOODS

Amsterdam fans out south of the IJ River. At its heart, historic **Central Amsterdam** is home to the famous Red Light District and the Bloemenmarkt, as well as a nearly infinite variety of restaurants, coffeeshops, nightlife venues, and accommodations. No two nights in the center ever need to be the same.

Beyond the Singel Canal, **West Amsterdam** contains the Anne Frank House, the Nine Streets shopping district, and the beautiful (and largely residential) Jordaan neighborhood. Jordaan is unique in Amsterdam in that canals don't cut through the streets; with a constantly rotating carousel of cafés, boutiques, and one-off shops, it's one of my favorite neighborhoods to explore.

The ring of canals south of Central Amsterdam is home to the **Leidseplein** entertainment district, including quite a few of my recommended restaurants and coffeeshops. **Southeast Amsterdam** has a couple of noteworthy attractions (Gassan Diamonds, the Jewish Historical Museum), along with the Rembrandtplein nightlife district. The southwestern corner of the city is the **Museum District,** home to the Rijksmuseum and Van Gogh Museum (which cluster around the square called Museumplein) and Vondelpark, Amsterdam's city park. East of the Museum District is where you'll find the Heineken Experience, which is on the edge of trendy nightlife neighborhood **De Pijp.**

TOP SIGHTS

There are dozens of fascinating museums in this city—art and history buffs have more than enough to keep them occupied for weeks. If you're only working with a few days, here are the most worthwhile of the bunch.

Anne Frank House

The city's most famous historical landmark is where Anne Frank and her family hid for more than two years during the Nazi occupation of Amsterdam (during which the vast majority of Amsterdam's Jews were rounded up and sent to the concentration camps). It was in the secret annex of this house that Anne wrote her diary, sharing her deepest thoughts about growing up in the midst of an ongoing tragedy. The diary is one of the world's most translated books, second only to the Bible. Otto Frank, Anne's father, survived the war. He insisted that the apartment be kept exactly as it was left—opting for empty rooms instead of replica furniture. Your tour will take you through the house and the hidden bookcase, through which the family entered the secret annex. You'll see photos of the family, their concentration camp registration cards, and the original copy of Anne's diary. Make online reservations for a timed ticket well in advance of your visit—otherwise, you won't be admitted until 15:30 at the earliest, and you'll likely stand in line for hours.

€9, Apr-Oct daily 09:00-22:00, Nov-Mar daily 09:00-19:00, Sat until 21:00, Prinsengracht 267, West Amsterdam, +31 (0)20 556 7105, annefrank.org, Tram: Westermarkt

Rijksmuseum

Art from the last 800 years of Amsterdam and the Netherlands takes you from the city's humble beginnings through masterpieces of the Dutch Golden Age. The museum features artists such as Rembrandt, Goya, Van Gogh, Cuyp, and Vermeer. The museum is presented across three levels. You'll notice the exterior looks remarkably similar to that of the Centraal Station; the same architect, Pierre Cuypers, designed both buildings.

€17.50, daily 09:00-17:00, last entry 30 minutes before closing, Museumstraat 1, Museum District, +31 (0)900 0745, rijksmuseum.nl, Tram: Rijksmuseum

Van Gogh Museum

Containing some of the most recognizable works of the famously troubled Dutch artist, this museum is wonderfully compact, with the key pieces found on a single floor. Some highlights include: *The Potato Eat-*

ACT LIKE A LOCAL

Gezellig-What?

The Dutch have an expression, one word that is used for just about everything that makes you feel all warm and fuzzy on the inside: **gezellig** (pronounced GHE-zell-igh, with guttural-sounding Gs). Americans seek out the newest, the biggest, the best, but the Dutch seek comfort, warmth, and coziness. **Gezellig** is the goal. Tucked in front of the fire at Christmas is **gezellig**. A good brown pub in Amsterdam is just about always **gezellig**. Use your newfound cultural lingo to strike up a conversation. Nail the pronunciation and then ask locals what their favorite **gezellig** place is.

Make It a Half-Pint

The price for a half-pint in Amsterdam is usually exactly half the price of a pint. Since the value is the same, locals usually get half-pints; the smaller size can be finished while still cold, and drinking half-pints is more social, allowing for a do-si-do between drinks inside and cigs outside, grabbing a new half-pint each time.

ers, *Sunflowers*, *The Bedroom*, and *Wheatfield with Crows*, the last painting Van Gogh completed before his untimely death—many see in the painting a representation of the artist's long-simmering depression, which culminated in his suicide in 1890. Van Gogh only sold one painting in his lifetime: It wasn't until after his death that the world started to recognize him as a genius.

€17, daily 09:00-18:00, Fri until 22:00, Paulus Potterstraat 7, Museum District, +31 (0)20 570 5200, vangoghmuseum.nl/en, Tram: Rijksmuseum or Van Baerlestraat

Red Light District

Concentrating around the Old Church (Oude Kerk), this is where Amsterdam grew from a small fishing village into a world power. Docks used to line the north side of these streets, and this is where the ladies of the night used to catch sailors on their last night in town or help lighten their freshly lined pockets upon return. Today, you'll see the sex trade in action as you stroll by nearly nude prostitutes advertising themselves behind glass windows. For an in-depth look at the industry, consider popping into the **Red Light Secrets— Museum of Prostitution** (€10, €8 online, daily 11:00-24:00, Oudezijds Achterburgwal 60, +31 (0)20 846 7020, redlightsecrets. com), which is housed in rooms that were once hotbeds of activity. You'll also see touristy cafés and restaurants, coffeeshops, and souvenir stores. In recent years, the city council has made a point to reduce the number of red-light windows in this district, replacing them with art installations and boutiques. There's a lot to keep you busy, and unfortunately, many tourists don't venture beyond this district to experience the more authentic parts of town.

Free, always open, Central Amsterdam, Tram: Dam

Cannabis College

This venue in the Red Light District reveals the truth about cannabis and all of its potential uses. Pop in to learn about all things green, including information about the plant's many medical uses. They'll happily recommend places in town to pick up the best kush and the best places to smoke. They won't sell you any of the stuff themselves, but if you brought some with you, they've got an assortment of bongs and vaporizers they'll let you use. Pay a few euros to see the college's flowering cannabis garden, a handful of plants in various stages of growth from cute "babies" to flowering beauties.

Free, donations welcome, daily 11:00-19:00, Oudezijds Achterburgwal 124, Central Amsterdam, +31 (0)20 423 4420, cannabiscollege.com, Metro: Nieuwmarkt

Gassan Diamonds

Ever seen a two-carat diamond? Amsterdam has a long history with the diamond trade, and Gassan Diamonds is a great place to learn about the craft of diamond cutting from the best with an introductory tour of the factory. Watch as the craftspeople go about their business and get an education in the five Cs: cut, color, clarity, carat, and certification. Free entry and tours make Gassan a hidden gem.

Free guided tour leaves often, daily 09:00–17:00, Nieuwe Uilenburgerstraat 175, Southeast Amsterdam, +31 (0)20 622 5333, gassan.com, Tram: Mr. Visserplein

City Library

The last 150 years have seen a complete transformation of Amsterdam's harbor, starting with the construction of Amsterdam Centraal Station, completed in 1889. One of the most recent additions to the docklands is Amsterdam's City Library, a stunningly modern 10-story steel-and-glass structure just northeast of Central Amsterdam. The top floor offers magnificent views overlooking the city center. Stop in for lunch and enjoy a wonderfully colorful and affordable spread from a branch of **La Place**, a healthy Dutch self-service cafeteria brand.

Free, daily 10:00–22:00, Oosterdokskade 143, Central Amsterdam, +31 (0)20 523 0900, oba.nl, Tram: Centraal

EXTRA CREDIT

If you make short work of the essentials, here are a few more places to check out.

Heineken Experience

This is a top priority for many who come to Amsterdam. The tour provides endless Heineken propaganda and features a virtual reality "bottling experience," two half-pints, and long lines if you don't make reservations ahead of time. I prefer **Brouwerij 't IJ** for arguably better beer.

€18, €16 online, €25 Rock the Boat combo (includes canal tour), Mon–Thurs 10:30–17:30, Fri–Sun 10:30–19:00, longer hours July–Aug, Stadhouderskade 78, De Pijp, +31 (0)20 523 9222, heinekenexperience.com, Tram: Stadhouderskade

NEMO Science Museum

Situated in the bold building resembling a sinking ship in the middle of the IJ River, this interactive science and technology museum is designed for students, but enthralling and engaging for all ages. I get a particular kick out of the Dutch approach to sex ed in their "hands on" exhibit.

€16.50, Apr–Aug daily 10:00–17:30, Sept–Mar Tues–Sun 10:00–17:30, Oosterdok 2, Central Amsterdam, +31 (0)20 531 3233, nemosciencemuseum.nl, Tram: Artis

Jewish Historical Museum

Starting in the 16th century, Amsterdam was a haven for Jewish migrants, many of whom were wealthy merchants forced out of Spain and Portugal. The city's Jewish population was cut down to next to nothing during the Holocaust, but the resilient community has rebounded. This museum tells the long story of Jews in Amsterdam and of some of their more prominent synagogues.

€15, daily 11:00–17:00, Nieuwe Amstelstraat 1, Southeast Amsterdam, no phone, jhm.nl, Tram: Mr. Visserplein

ARTIS Amsterdam Royal Zoo

You can find one of the biggest zoos in Europe just to the east of the city center. A vis-

BE SMART: AMSTERDAM'S SMART SHOPS

"Smart shops" sell magic legumes and other "natural herbal mood enhancers." Selling psychedelic mushrooms is now illegal in the European Union, so producers sell truffles that have the same "magic" effect. The staff is normally happy to recommend doses based on your past and desired experience. If you choose to give this a try, pack something sweet like juice before you begin; it can help in case you have a bad trip.

Try **Kokopelli** (doses around €15, Fri-Wed 11:00-22:00, Warmoesstraat 12, Central Amsterdam, +31 (0)20 421 7000, kokopelli.nl), a nature shop and tripping lounge with friendly staff who will happily walk you through your options and tell you exactly what to expect. You can also start your psychedelic journey at **When Nature Calls** (doses around €14, daily 09:00-22:00, Keizersgracht 508, Leidseplein and Vicinity, +31 (0)20 330 0700, whennaturecalls.nl) on Leidsestraat—perfect for a trip in Vondelpark.

it to the zoo is a delightful way to spend an afternoon. You'll get up close and personal with lions, butterflies, gorillas, and even a family of elephants.

€21.50, daily 09:00-18:00, Plantage Kerklaan 38-40, Southeast Amsterdam, +31 (0)20 523 3694, artis.nl, Tram: Plantage

Bag & Purse Museum

Located east of Leidseplein, the Bag & Purse Museum features a collection of more than 4,000 different bags, trunks, pouches, and purses dating all the way to the Middle Ages. If you're a handbag fanatic or just have a casual interest in the history of fashion and design, you'll want to check this place out.

€12.50, daily 10:00-17:00, Herengracht 573, +31 (0)20 524 6452, tassenmuseum.nl, Leidseplein and Vicinity, Tram: Rembrandtplein

Sex Museum

This raunchy museum features erotic art and artifacts from early human civilizations through to modern sex toys and technologies. It's a kinky romp through the history of the carnal arts.

€5, daily 09:30-23:30, Damrak 18, Central Amsterdam, +31 (0)20 622 8376, sexmuseumamsterdam.nl, Tram: Centraal

Electric Ladyland

Made famous through Jimi Hendrix's third album, this experimental museum is a favorite among those who come to Amsterdam exclusively for the coffeeshops. It's a psychedelic experience filled with trippy, fluorescent mini displays and artwork.

€5, Tues-Sat 13:00-18:00, Tweede Leliedwarsstraat 5, West Amsterdam, electric-lady-land.com, Tram: Bloemgracht

North Amsterdam

Most tourists stay in or close to the center, but modern Amsterdam has expanded north beyond the IJ River. What used to be warehouses and industrial yards are now trendy modern studios, offices, and apartments. Free pedestrian ferries run nonstop throughout the day and are almost never full. Take a half day to see this very different side of the city. Come around lunchtime and stop in at **Ij Cantine** (lunch from €6.50, daily 09:00-24:00, Mt. Ondinaweg 15-17, +31 (0)20 633 7162, ijkantine.nl), accessible via the NDSM Ferry.

Have a funky afternoon and wild evening in a former boatyard with houseboats converted into bar, café, and creative spaces at **Café de Ceuvel** (healthy, organic lunches from €7.50, Tues-Thurs and Sun 11:00-24:00, Fri-Sat 11:00-02:00, Korte Papaverweg 4, +31 (0)20 229 6210, cafedeceuvel.nl) via the Buiksloterweg Ferry. Get a panorama across the entire city from a thrilling rooftop swing at gimmicky **A'dam Tower** (€12, daily 10:00-22:00, Overhoeksplein 1, +31 (0)20 242 0100, adamlookout.com).

If staying in this area sounds appealing, check out **Clink Noord** (beds from €18, Badhuiskade 3, +31 (0)20 214 9731, clinkhostels.com), the excellent budget hostel option, which comes with a full bar, clean modernist design, and an undeniably cool vibe.

Free ferries leave every 10 minutes 24 hours a day

TOP EATS

Amsterdam is undergoing a full-on foodie revolution that draws inspiration from around the globe but infuses it with characteristic Dutch innovation.

Dutch cuisine is very similar to what you'll find in other northern European countries: meat and potatoes. Their most famous dish is the filling *stamppot:* potatoes mashed together with your choice of veggies and a thick bratwurst-style sausage. *Bitterballen* are another mainstay. Think flash-fried balls of creamy, mushy...well, I don't really know (take it easy on the first bite—they're served piping hot). **Herring** (typically served raw with veggies) is also a popular lunch dish in this country with a long seafaring history.

Tipping is not expected, but most locals leave a euro or two.

The **Red Light District** is filled with plenty of places to grab a quick bite on the cheap (many of which are clearly tailored to people with the munchies). There are a number of surprisingly good cafés and sit-down options.

Dum Dum Palace

This spot serves Asian tapas amid mod fusion décor with cool interior lighting and decoration. The menu features numerous small plates with street food roots, such as dumplings, salads, and ceviche from places like Vietnam, Japan, Thailand, and Indonesia.

Meals from €12, daily 11:00–01:00 (open until 03:00 on weekends), Zeedijk 37, Central Amsterdam, +31 (0)20 304 4966, dumdum.nl, Metro: Nieuwmarkt

Thai Bird Snack Bar

Just steps from the Red Light District, in Amsterdam's Chinatown, is some of the best Thai food this side of Bangkok. This cheap eatery is almost always packed with in-the-know locals stopping by for a quick bite or some takeout. If the snack bar is full, consider its sister restaurant across the street (they have identical menus). I love the fast-moving service and bustling atmosphere, as well as the fresh pad thai and spicy curries.

Entrées €10, daily 14:00–21:00, Zeedijk 77, Central Amsterdam, +31 (0)20 420 6289, thai-bird.nl, Metro: Nieuwmarkt

Mata Hari

Named after a Dutch exotic dancer who spied for the Germans in WWII, this posh two-level restaurant and cocktail lounge with a dark wood interior dishes up rustic lunch and dinner options. For lunch, I love the overflowing charcuterie platter with burrata, ham, fennel salami, and olive tapenade. The real treats can be found on the dinner menu: braised lamb shank, ribeye, fresh filets of fish, oysters, and more. While pricier than the fast-food options in the neighborhood, it's a big step up in terms of quality, but still affordable. The Gatsby-style elegance is a welcome change from the tackiness that abounds in the RLD.

Innovative menu €16-24, reservations recommended, Oudezijds Achterburgwal 22, Central Amsterdam, +31 (0)20 205 0919, matahari-amsterdam.nl, Metro: Nieuwmarkt

Quartier Putain

This is my preferred coffee stop (and I do mean coffee) in the Red Light District. Squeezed between a day care center and a row of red lights, this is a surprisingly calm

BRUNCH IN DE PIJP

As we all know, hipsters love brunch, so it's probably no surprise that trendy De Pijp offers a bevy of tasty day-starting meals. My favorite is the uber-popular **Bakers & Roasters** (breakfasts €15, daily 08:30-18:00, Eerste Jacob van Campenstraat 54, De Pijp, +31 (0)20 772 2627, bakersandroasters.com), who do delicious breakfast in a long, bustling hall with common tables and friendly service. Brave the long line and choose from hearty fare like poached eggs, thick-sliced toast, American-style bacon, and smashed avocado. If the line is ridiculous, **La Boutique del Caffè Torrefazione** (€5, daily 08:00-18:00, from 09:00 on weekends, Eerste Jacob van Campenstraat 38, De Pijp, +31 (0)20 364 0500, boutiquedelcaffe.com) next door is an authentic Italian coffee roaster with excellent Arabica coffee and Roman-style breakfast panini.

café where you can sip on freshly brewed coffee and admire the back side of the Oude Kerk. This is just one of the many cafés and boutiques that have started to replace some of the prostitution windows.

From €2.50, Mon-Fri 08:30-16:00, Sat-Sun 10:00-18:00, Oudekerksplein 4, Central Amsterdam, +31 (0)20 895 0162, Facebook: Quartier Putain, Metro: Nieuwmarkt

Latei

Pop into Latei for a funky teahouse experience. Like what you see? From the furnishings to the decorations, everything in the place is for sale. The fresh pastries, homemade sandwiches, and steaming veggie soups hit the spot on a chilly day, and the teas and coffees are excellent.

Pastries from €2, Mon-Wed 08:00-18:00, Thurs-Fri 08:00-22:00, Sat 09:00-22:00, Sun 10:00-18:00, Oudekerksplein 4, Central Amsterdam, +31 (0)20 895 0162, latei.net, Metro: Nieuwmarkt

New York Film Academy Café

A warm and spacious bistro with a fully stocked bar and kitchen, this café is surprisingly easy to miss on the main drag from the train station to Dam Square, so keep your eyes peeled. Enjoy their bagel sandwiches, soups, and burgers under brick arches in the colossal Beurs van Berlage, the former stock exchange building.

Bites from €6.50, daily 10:00-24:00, Damrak 213, Central Amsterdam, +31 65 240 7900, nyfa-cafe.nl, Metro: Nieuwmarkt

Song Kwae Thai

Another great option for fresh and fast Thai is this spot just off Nieuwmarkt. The communal tables always seem to have a spot available, so this is prime option if you're with a group of friends.

Pad thai from €10, daily 15:00-22:30, Kloveniersburgwal 14a, Central Amsterdam, +31 (0)20 624 2568, songkwae.nl, Metro: Nieuwmarkt

Vleminckx Friteshuis

They only do one thing here, but they do it very well. This place is famous for its *frites* (fries). Crowds flock for a delicious hot snack served in a cone, which makes it portable (you'll see dozens of tourists walking with these cones in their hands). The line often wraps around the front of the building and down the street, but it moves quickly. The frites are definitely well worth the wait.

€3, daily 12:00-19:00, Voetboogstraat 33, Central Amsterdam, +31 (0)20 624 6075, vleminckxdesaus-meester.nl, Tram: Spui

De Laatste Kruimel

Find this gem just on the south side of the Red Light District, a stone's throw from the University of Amsterdam. The fresh scones, savory and sweet pies, delicious pastries, and hearty sandwiches will all help you start your day off on the right foot. The name means "The Last Crumb" in Dutch, and you'll know why when you're searching your pastry paper for every last morsel.

Pastries and coffee from €3, daily 08:00-20:00, Sun from 10:00, Langebrugsteeg 4, Central Amsterdam, +31 (0)20 423 0499, delaatstekruimel.nl, Tram: Spui Rokin

Febo Fast Food

There are quite a few of these hot-food vending machines sprinkled around town. No cashiers here—just a simple system of boxes that look a lot like transparent P.O. boxes. You'll have a hot burger or fries in your hands in no time at all. Burgermeisters are busy working behind the scenes to restock the popular selections. The food is about as good as you might expect, but you'll only drop a euro or two.

€3, daily 10:30-02:00, until 04:00 on weekends, Damrak 6, Central Amsterdam, +31 (0)20 638 5318, www.febo.nl, Tram: Centraal

Greenwoods

Craving more than the continental breakfast provided by your hostel? Come here for a classy but inexpensive English-style breakfast complete with tea or coffee. In nice weather, the canal-side seating makes for an ideal place to enjoy your eggs and toast. In addition to the one on Singel, you can find another branch at Keizergracht 465.

Breakfasts from €6, lunches from €8, Mon-Thurs 09:30-17:00, until 18:00 on weekends, Singel 103, Central Amsterdam, +31 (0)20 623 7071, greenwoods.eu, Tram: Nieuwezijds Kolk

Blue Café

In a glass box on the top floor of the Kalvortoren shopping center, this café offers excellent views across Central Amsterdam. I come here mostly for the coffee, as the food tends to be a bit overpriced.

Sandwiches from €7.50, Mon 11:00-18:30, Tues-Sat 10:00-18:30, Sun 12:00-18:30, Singel 457, Central Amsterdam, +31 (0)20 427 3901, blue-amsterdam.nl, Tram: Spui (Rokin)

La Place

This is one of those delicious self-service cafeterias where the employees are well paid and happy, the food is local and delicious, the ingredients are fresh and healthy, and the building is LEED-certified. Did I mention the free Wi-Fi? What else can you ask for? Pop into one of the several locations in town for an affordable casual lunch at communal tables with a nice mix of locals and tourists. Take your pick of fish and meats, curries and stir-fry, personal pizzas, salads, fresh-pressed juices, and more. This location is on the 7th floor of the City Library just northeast of Central Amsterdam; there's another city-center location at Kalverstraat 203.

Lunches €10-15, daily 09:00-20:00, Sat-Sun from 11:00, City Library, Oosterdokskade 143, Central Amsterdam, laplace.com, Tram: Centraal

Kantjil & de Tijger

Indonesian at its finest. Kantjil has the feel of a Southeast Asian fusion restaurant, but they are perhaps best known for Indonesia's most typical dish, *rijsttafel*. Think of it as a culinary smorgasbord, with small bowls of richly spiced rice, meats, and veggies. If you're on a budget, *nasi rames* is the best value; it includes many of the same great-tasting samplers as its bigger brother all piled on one plate. For even better value, take your meal to go from the much cheaper takeaway joint next door (pick your size, noodles, and meat, and you'll walk away for a third of the price of a sit-down meal).

Entrées from €15, takeaway €5-7, daily 12:00-23:00, Nieuwezijds Voorburgwal 342, Central Amsterdam, +31 (0)20 620 0994, kantjil.nl, Tram: Spui

Sie Joe Indonesian

For a less posh and possibly more authentic way to sample Indonesian, find this hidden gem just behind the Nieuwe Kerk off of Dam Square. Go for the *nasi rames*.

Plates from €10, Mon-Sat 12:00-20:00, Gravenstraat 24A, Central Amsterdam, +31 (0)20 624 1830, siejoe.com, Tram: Dam

Winkel 43

You haven't tried apple pie until you've indulged at Winkel 43. Their homemade, deep-dish apple pie is a steaming slice of heaven—by far the best I've ever had. Share a piece with a friend because the portions here are generous. (Who am I kidding? Keep it all for yourself!) Winkel also has a decent menu with sandwiches, salads, and appetizers if you don't ruin your appetite on pie.

Around €6, daily 08:00-01:00, Noordermarkt 43, West Amsterdam, +31 (0)20 623 0223, winkel43.com, Tram: Marnix-plein

Pancake Bakery

Hands down some of the best pancakes you'll ever have. Choose from a traditional variety or take a walk on the wild side with one of the bakery's international versions, ranging from Hungarian to Thai to Mexican. Sweet tooth? Try the *poffertjes*, mini pancakes layered in ice cream, chocolate, and powdered sugar. The staff seem a little overwhelmed with the steady stream of customers (most of them tourists), so don't expect beaming smiles.

Pancake plates €12-16, daily 09:00-21:30, Prinsengracht 191, West Amsterdam, +31 (0)20 625 1333, pancake.nl, Tram: Westermarkt

La Perla Pizzeria

You'll find some of the best wood-oven pizza in town in Jordaan. La Perla Pizzeria does pizza like the Neapolitans—fresh ingredients, never-frozen dough, and jovial Italian chefs in the back—and I, for one, am grateful. Go for quick stand-up service at the high-top bars in the oven shop, or take a seat across the street and enjoy sit-down service. My favorite: the Diavola (spicy pepperoni).

Personal pizzas from €8, daily 10:00-22:00, Sun from 12:00, Tweede Tuindwarsstraat 53, West Amsterdam, +31 (0)20 624 8828, pizzaperla.nl, Tram: Westermarkt

Broodje Bert

For a quick and affordable hot sandwich near the 9 Streets, Broodje Bert does just the trick. It's nothing fancy, but a hot sandwich and a canal-side coffee don't need to stray far from the ordinary. Throw in one of their delicious fresh salads and you've got all the makings of a filling lunch. Stop in at breakfast time for one of their omelets or a toasted ham-and-cheese sandwich.

€6 sandwiches, daily 08:30-18:00, Singel 321, West Amsterdam, +31 20 623 0382, Facebook: Broodje Bert, Tram: Spui

B&B Lunchroom

A convenient stop along the shopping drag, the made-to-order sandwiches here satisfy—to a surprising degree, considering the neighborhood and the price. The options are endless, and the staff couldn't be friendlier. While you're at it, snag one of their delicious freshly baked muffins for a snack (I always do, and I've never regretted it). In addition to the Leidseplein location, you'll find others around town.

Sandwiches €5, daily 08:00-18:00, Leidsestraat 44, Leidseplein and Vicinity, +31 (0)20 642 1816, onzecatering. nl, Tram: Prinsengracht

't Blauwe Theehuis

This idyllic teahouse with loads of outdoor seating is right in the middle of Vondelpark. Considering the picturesque location, prices aren't bad. If you're enjoying a day in the park or need a break from the hustle and bustle of the city center, pop in for a respite that won't hurt the wallet.

Simple sandwiches from €5.50, daily 09:00-18:00, Vondelpark 5, Museum District, +31 (0)20 662 0254, blauwetheehuis.nl, Tram: Van Baerlestraat

Bazar

Housed in a converted church, this Amsterdam institution is located right in the Albert Cuyp Market. Stepping in, you might feel as though you've been whisked away to another continent. The food matches the feelings, with fresh kebabs, falafel, sandwiches, and other dishes from Morocco and Turkey. The friendly staff will happily give you the lowdown on some of their more exotic dishes. There's an inscription high above in the rafters. Translated from Hebrew it reads, "Eating together is the oil of friendship." The wildly diverse crowd is a testament to the restaurant's successful attempt to harmonize cultures and religions.

Breakfasts and lunches from €6, dinners from €12, daily 10:00-24:00, kitchen closes at 23:00, Albert Cuypstraat 182, De Pijp and Vicinity, +31 (0)20 675 0544, bazaramsterdam.com, Tram: Albert Cuypstraat

Sir Hummus

This is my first choice for healthy vegetarian/vegan hummus and pita on the south side of town. Omnivores can get their protein fix with beans or they can add some slow-roasted beef to make the fuel even more potent.

Lunches €10, Tues-Fri 12:00-20:00, Sat-Sun 12:00-17:00, Van der Helstplein 2, De Pijp, +31 (0)20 664 7055, sirhummus.nl, Tram: Helststaat

Toko Kok Kita

For a picnic in Vondelpark, stop into this Indonesian deli for cheap, authentic spreads to go. A feast that would set you back €45 at my other Indonesion recommendations will cost less than €15 here. It makes for a great budget meal that will create wiggle room in your nightlife budget.

From €8, Tues-Sat 12:00-20:30, Amstelveenseweg 166, West Amsterdam, +31 (0)20 670 2933, kokkita.nl, Tram: Zeilstraat

Amsterdam Food Hall

What was once Amsterdam's tram terminal and warehouse is now the city's trendiest food hall, with cafés, dim sum, bars, healthy vegetarian, burgers, Vietnamese street food, and more. The place packs out with power lunchers in the hours around midday. After work is done, they return with a vengeance and the bars here remain packed until closing time (around midnight). Be sure to explore the entire complex: It has boutique shops, a cinema, a library, and common workspaces.

From €4.50, Sun-Thurs 11:00-23:30, Fri-Sat 11:00-01:00, Bellamyplein 51, West Amsterdam, foodhallen.nl, Tram: Bilderdijkstraat

Albert Heijn Grocery Stores

Albert Heijn is to Amsterdam as Starbucks is to Seattle: There's one on just about every corner. Those on a budget can dive into the aisles of this grocery store for a cheap lunch of anything from premade curries to sushi and sandwiches. Don't forget to pick up one of my favorite sweet treats: the *stroopwafel* (syrup-filled waffle). You'll find numerous locations throughout the city, including one inside the train station.

Daily 08:00-22:00, Nieuwezijds Voorburgwal 226, Central Amsterdam, +31 (0)20 421 8344, ah.nl, Tram: Dam

Dutch Cheese Shops

Widely recognized as one of the Netherlands' best cheese brands, **Reypenaer** (free samples, Singel 182, Central Amsterdam, +31 (0)20 320 6333, reypenaercheese. com, Tram: Dam) in West Amsterdam's 9 Streets offers visitors a chance to try a sample and see what has made the brand so famous among cheese connoisseurs. They proudly age their cheese in a warehouse without *any* of the bells and whistles of industrial production. This means a richer, more complex flavor (and an element of the unexpected, as each batch is slightly different). Cheese and wine go together like the Dutch and bicycles, so consider jumping in on their hour-long tasting experience (€16.50, book online, offered 5 times/day) with six different cheeses and three wines. Even if you're not an expert, you'll have a guide who'll help you make sense of what you're experiencing.

Thanks to numerous locations across town, you can't spend a few days in Amsterdam without stumbling into a **Henri Willig Cheese** (cheese rounds from €10, daily 09:00-19:00, Leidsestraat 52, Leidseplein and Vicinity, +31 (0)20 620 9030, henriwillig.com, Tram: Kaizergracht). Sample typical cheeses like Gouda, goat, sheep, smoked, and even spicy varieties, all made in the Netherlands. While it may feel a bit mass-produced and commercialized, a round of cheese makes for a great souvenir—provided you can get it home without devouring it.

TOP COFFEESHOPS

First off, if you're looking for coffee, you'll want to head to a café. As all Amsterdammers know, a coffeeshop is a place to buy and smoke the city's famous high-grade marijuana. There really isn't one best option in town. The recommended shops below are my favorites—they all have friendly staff, fair prices, and a welcoming atmosphere. Vibe is important, though, and that changes from hour to hour in these popular joints. If you're not sure about a spot, poke your head in and get a sense of it before ordering.

Dampkring

Made famous by the movie *Ocean's Twelve*, cozy Dampkring is a one-roomed, rose-colored coffeeshop with a cat named Bowie in permanent residence. The menu is on the pricey side, but the merchandise is top-shelf, featuring an array of award-winning strains. The edibles are also excellent, but be warned: They are potent. Order your greens in the back, drinks at the bar to the left.

Grams from €10, daily 10:00-01:00, Handboogstraat 29, Central Amsterdam, +31 (0)20 638 0705, dampkring-coffeeshop-amsterdam.nl, Tram: Spui

COFFEESHOPS & SMOKING ETIQUETTE

Amsterdam operates by a discreet code: You buy coffee in cafés, marijuana in coffeeshops, and psychedelic mushrooms in smart shops. Nothing is legal, just decriminalized. This is why you'll see no advertisements or signs. But they're not that hard to find (or smell): Just look for a numbered green and white license in the front window of each shop. Pop into a few shops on your first day to get a sense for your options. You're not obligated to buy anything outright, but don't expect courteous service if you're smoking something you bought elsewhere.

Find the menu at the weed bar. The staff will walk you through what they're offering. Weed has gone through generations of bioengineering, evolving over the past few decades into something way stronger than what people smoked back in the day. There's no shame in asking for a medium-strength strain. Take your time and don't be afraid to ask questions. If there are anxious-looking customers and you have a lot of questions, let them go ahead of you and watch how they behave. Most first-timers ask the same questions; eavesdrop and then make your order once you've figured out the lay of the land. If the staff is rude, walk out. There'll be another shop just around the corner. If you see fluorescent lights and posters of Bob Marley or toking aliens, you're in tourist territory. Keep moving.

If you're new to the party, don't mix marijuana with alcohol—many first-time mixers experience unpleasant side effects like sweating and nausea. (As it's illegal for coffeeshops to sell alcohol, this may not be an issue for you.) If you find yourself feeling unwell, some fresh air and some sugar will usually sort you out; go for a quick walk around the block and eat a chocolate bar or drink some soda or juice and you should be right as rain. Stick close to your friends, and let them know if you need to go back to the hostel.

Only a few bars have tobacco-smoking lounges. Remember, the Dutch treat "hard" and "soft" drugs very differently. Possession of cocaine, ecstasy, and other hard drugs will land you in hot water.

Here are some tips to get you started on your coffeeshop experience.

First, some terminology:

- weed/bud/herb/flower = marijuana
- hashish = a small brown brick you rub off into tobacco cigarettes or smoke out of pipes
- joint = weed in a paper wrapper
- blunt = weed in a cigar/cigarillo wrapper
- spliff = weed and tobacco (what the Dutch normally smoke—if they smoke)
- sativa = the "high" strain (think: high, happy, giggly)
- indica = the "stoned" strain (think: chill, relaxed, sleepy)

Here are some other things that are good to know:

- Prices tend to run €8.50-14 per gram. Don't pay more than €14 unless it's demonstrably the best weed on the planet.
- A good coffeeshop has a welcoming vibe, helpful staff, nice ambience, and comfy seating.
- After purchasing a gram, ask for a few papers for free. Purchase five grams and you should get a 5-10 percent discount and sleeve of papers included. Five grams should be plenty for a few friends over a weekend.
- Avoid pre-rolled joints, as they're filled with garbage. It's much better to purchase a gram or two of loose weed and buddy up with someone in the shop. People are usually happy to help you roll or otherwise prep your smoke, and it's a great way to strike up a conversation with new friends.
- Take it easy on edibles. Don't drink or smoke more after having them, and wait 1.5 hours before taking anything else or anything more. Make sure to ask how many doses are in the edible you're purchasing—some have one, some are good to split across four friends. They usually run €5-15.

Easy Times

Popular among tourists and locals alike for its space cakes and its clean and trendy atmosphere and friendly service, Easy Times is my pick for the Leidseplein district. Go easy on the space cakes and other edibles—they're potent. On nice days, the canal-side outdoor seating cannot be beat. The interior feels a bit more like a mod hookah lounge than a dark coffeeshop.

Grams from €8, daily 09:00–01:00, Prinsengracht 476, Leidseplein and Vicinity, +31 (0)20 626 5709, easytimes-amsterdam.com, Tram: Prisengracht

La Tertulia

In the midst of a chill neighborhood, La Tertulia welcomes first-time visitors with open arms. The ventilation system is humming all day, so the room doesn't get too smoky, and they've got a great selection of locally grown small-batch bud and all the gear you'll need to consume it (i.e., bongs, vaporizers, and pipes). They have a nice selection of drinks and edibles too. The corner location is discreet.

Grams from €8.50, Tues–Sat 11:00–19:00, Prinsengracht 312, Jordaan, coffeeshoptertulia.com, Tram: Elandsgracht

Boerejongens

Far and away the coolest, hippest coffeeshop in town. You pay a slight premium for the ambience, but the hipster vibe is off the charts. It's a far cry from the stoner culture (tie-dye, psychedelic art, etc.) that pervades so much of the smoking scene here. Find a cigar-style lounge upstairs with large leather armchairs and classical music and toke in *style*.

Daily 07:00–00:45, Baarsjesweg 239, West Amsterdam, +31 (0)20 412 2392, amsterdamgenetics.com, Tram: Corantijnstraat

Grey Area

An institution on Amsterdam's coffeeshop roster, this tiny café offers about six seats where you can roll up and meet fellow tokers. The staff is particularly welcoming, and they'll happily take beginners under their wing to explain the menu. If it's quiet, find a seat. If it's not, keep moving: The louder the room gets, the grungier the place starts to feel.

Grams from €9, daily 12:00–20:00, Oude Leliestraat 2, West Amsterdam, +31 (0)20 4204301, greyarea.nl, Tram: Dam

The Bulldog

Pop in here to calibrate the kind of scene you're looking for. This is a massively successful institution; it's also about as loud and touristy as they come. The Bulldog hotel next door to the coffeeshop has a lounge with a pool table that's one of my favorite spots in the city (and one of the few places you can drink and smoke in the same place).

Grams from €11, daily 09:00–01:00, until 03:00 on weekends, Leidseplein 15, Leidseplein and Vicinity, +31 (0)20 625 9864, thebulldog.com, Tram: Leidseplein

Amnesia

While the interior of this coffeeshop feels a little cheap, the canal-side seating (with boats lazily drifting by) is amazing on a sunny day. There are lots of options for toking: vaporize, blaze, smoke a bong, or even dab. Their dessert menu is the widest I've seen in a coffeeshop, offering tasty treats like milkshakes and pancakes with ice cream and chocolate syrup. Expect to pay a premium around 20 percent for the combination of location and reputation.

Grams from €13, daily 09:30–01:00, Herengracht 133I, Central Amsterdam, +31 (0)20 427 7874, Facebook: Amnesia, Tram: Dam

TOP NIGHTLIFE

The drinking culture among the Dutch is highly social. In the squares, young people mill about in the evening drinking beers and chain-smoking. Don't let Dutch cool intimidate you. Most of them will be happy to be drawn into conversation, and most of them speak excellent English (better even than some of the English-speaking tourists).

Bruin cafés ("brown cafés"—affectionately named thanks to their dark tobacco-stained interiors) are a mainstay of Amsterdam's drinking culture. The tobacco smoke is gone, so these picturesque spots are perfect for an afternoon tea or snack: coffee in the mornings, light lunches and snacks throughout the day, and half-pints toward the evening. **Café van**

Zuylen (snacks and coffee from €5, Torensteeg 8, +31 (0)20 639 1055, cafevanzuylen.nl) on Singel Canal is one supremely typical *bruin café* with copious canal-side seating in the summer. If you can't get enough of these cafés, **De Twee Zwaantjes** (Prinsengracht 114), **Café Nol** (Westerstraat 109), and **Café Lowietje** (Derde Goudsbloemdwarsstraat 2) are other noteworthy examples.

NIGHTLIFE DISTRICTS

Amsterdam's nightlife can be broken down by neighborhood. Each district has its own personality. Match your preferences to my descriptions and get ready for a wild ride!

Red Light District

The Red Light District boasts a rainbow of venues, bars, clubs, street food, peep shows, and more. And it's the densest, most touristy, and most overpriced part of town. While the RLD is worth an evening out, many tourists unfortunately never get beyond this district. Notice the window-shopping tourists change as the day turns to night. At night come obnoxious stag parties and creepers doing more than just window-shopping. Sprinkled with numerous police departments, the neighborhood is actually the safest in town, but keep a close hold on your valuables in the busy and crowded streets. Spend an evening wandering through the canals, bridges, and seductive windows. Some redeeming venues in this district are the recommended brewery **Brouwerij de Prael** and speakeasy cocktail lounge **Porem.**

Central Amsterdam, Tram: Dam

Nieuwmarkt

Just on the edge of the Red Light District, Nieuwmarkt was once a major gatehouse to enter the city. Now, the square is rimmed with bars of nearly every description. Amsterdam's gallows' nooses once swung here, but now you'll find a subdued, sophisticated vibe with locals sipping half-pints in the open air on the east side of the square.

Central Amsterdam, Tram: Dam

Leidseplein

The best entertainment district in Amsterdam is named after a town 20 miles down the road: Leiden. Farmers from Leiden would bring their milk to Amsterdam, sell it, and then blow all their money before going home. Today this area is known for its music venues, concert halls, comedy shows, and restaurants. It's where tourists and locals go out to club. Prices unfortunately reflect its popularity, and you'll often have to pay to use the bathrooms, even in bars where you're drinking. So don't break that seal! Beyond numerous dance bar options on the square, **Melkweg** and **Paradiso** are music venue institutions that have headliners like Lady Gaga and Beyoncé pass through often.

Leidseplein and Vicinity, Tram: Leidseplein

De Pijp

On the south side of town behind the Heineken brewery, you'll find Amsterdam's best-kept secret, where the locals hang out before heading to Leidseplein for the clubs. This is Amsterdam's trendiest and most up-and-coming district. Most of the action centers on Marien Heinekenplein, lined with half a dozen enjoyably social bars including the recommended **Kingfisher Cafe.**

De Pijp and Vicinity, Tram: Stadhouderskade

Rembrandtplein

This square, east of Leidseplein, and the surrounding streets tend to be packed with blue-collar Dutch party-seekers and tourists in the know. While a bit pricey, deals are easier to find here than in the touristy areas, and the parties get rowdy here on a nightly basis. You'll find cafés and brown pubs, restaurants, bars, and even Starbucks' flagship European location on this lively square named after one of the world's best-known painters. A rock star in life, I think Rembrandt would be happy with the scene that takes over his square on a nightly basis.

Southeast Amsterdam, Tram: Rembrandtplein

BREWERIES

Heineken isn't the only brewery with an Amsterdam connection. Try out these spots as well:

Brouwerij 't IJ

The city has given tax breaks to any company operating out of historic windmills in order to protect the heritage and keep these monuments to Dutch history alive. This local brewery offers a range of house brews as well as a fascinating and afford-able tour of the hoppy facilities. Brouwerij 't IJ is east of the city center, beyond the zoo; it's situated on the outline of Amster-dam's 17th-century expansion.

Pints from €4.50, pub open daily 14:00-20:00, €4.50 tours Fri-Sun at 15:30 and 16:00 (reservations recom-mended), Funenkade 7, Greater Amsterdam, +31 (0)20 622 8325, brouwerijhetij.nl, Tram: Hoogte Kadijk

Brouwerij de Prael

Real estate is so hard to come by in Am-sterdam that there are only a few breweries in the center. Step into the Prael brewery and you'll feel instantly at home in the cozy tasting room lined with mugs (these are owned by the regulars who frequent this place). If you want to more than wet your whistle, head to the back to see where the magic happens; you'll get a look at the massive fermentation vats and sample one of the brews (four-beer tasting tours also available). Tours leave on the hour.

Pints from €5, brewery tour (one beer included) €8.50, tour with 4-beer tasting €17.50, daily 12:00-01:00, Oudezijds Voorburgwal 30, Central Amsterdam, +31 (0)20 408 4470, deprael.nl, Tram: Centraal

BARS

If you love hops, you'll feel right at home in Amsterdam. There's an established ar-tisanal beer scene, and you'll find plenty of unique pubs bound to pique your fancy. For a low-key night of ale-sipping that will introduce you to a wide range of Dutch brews, follow my ale trail from In de Wildeman to Arendsnest, Café de Prins, and De Zotte.

In de Wildeman

Famous for its wide selection of beers both in bottles and on tap, this distill-ery-turned-bar is a great place to start an ale crawl, right in the old town. The cozy setting and helpful staff help you whittle down the hundreds of brew-tastic interna-tional choices.

Tastings from €2.40, Mon-Fri 12:00-01:00 (Sat until 02:00), Kolksteeg 3, Central Amsterdam, +31 (0)20 638 2348, indewildeman.nl, Tram: Nieuwezijds Kolk

Arendsnest

The second ale trail stop, pull up a seat at the bar and ask one of the bartenders to guide you to one of their beers (they proud-ly serve only Dutch beers here, so they're used to questions). There are a stunning 50 taps, so no matter what your preferenc-es, they've got you covered. Get started with the sampler tray of four beers for €6.

Daily 16:00-24:00, later on weekends, Herengracht 90, West Amsterdam, +31 (0)20 4212057, arendsnest.nl, Tram: Nieuwezijds Kolk

Café de Prins

For your typical little Dutch bar where you can enjoy everything from coffee and snacks to beer and music, this clean and bright spot checks all the boxes. Across the canal from the Anne Frank House, Café de Prins does a good job of staying under the radar and keeping all its cozy gezellig atmosphere.

LGBT AMSTERDAM

As one of the most inclusive and progressive cities in the world, Amsterdam has long been known to the members of the LGBT community as an excellent place to visit and live. Gay Pride dominates the city each year during the last week of July leading into August. There is no need to specifically seek out gay-friendly restaurants and bars in this town, as the city is broadly LGBT friendly. If you are at all uncertain, look for the rainbow flags in the windows. You'll find the gay, BDSM, and bear-focused scene on **Warmoestraat** (Central Amsterdam), just around the corner from Dam Square to the east. **Saarein** (Tues-Thurs and Sun 16:00-01:00, Fri 16:00-02:00, Sat 13:00-02:00, Elandsstraat 119, Jordaan, +31 (0)20 623 490, saarein2.nl) is a popular and long-standing lesbian bar towards the south end of the Jordaan district; it's worth checking out for the scene and the cozy setting.

For more information, find the **Pink Point LGBT information stand** (daily 10:30-18:00, Westermarkt, West Amsterdam, +31 (0)20 48 1070, facebook.com/PinkPointAmsterdam) on Westermarkt, in the shadow of Westerkerk, just steps from the Anne Frank House and the Homomonument.

Soups and sandwiches from €4.50, daily 10:00-01:00, Prinsengracht 124, West Amsterdam, +31 (0)20 624 9382, deprins.nl, Tram: Westermarkt

De Zotte

A constantly rotating menu offers an impressive lineup of Belgian brews. Watch out, the Trappists are coming! Hungry by now? De Zotte has some nice little cheese and meat plates to snack on.

Pints start around €4, daily 16:00-01:00, Raamstraat 29, Leidseplein and Vicinity, +31 (0)20 626 8694, dezotte. nl, Tram: Raamplein

Porem

If you like cocktails, this is a can't-miss—yet easy to walk by—speakeasy-style lounge. These bartenders take their profession seriously and are happy to craft the best drink of your life around your liquor of choice in a warm, low-key atmosphere. If upstairs is crowded, drop downstairs for some more room. Hungry? The team is happy to serve food from the Japanese restaurant out back, Geisha.

Sushi rolls €14, cocktails €12, Tues-Thurs 18:00-01:00, Fri-Sat 18:00-15:00, Geldersekade 17, Central Amsterdam, +31 62 261 4496, facebook.com/poremamsterdam

Wynand Fockink

Stumble into this quaint *genever* (Dutch gin) bar where the cup runneth over with history. You'll find it tucked into Pijlsteeg, an alley next to the NH Collection Hotel. Bartenders have been pouring Dutch gin here since the 17th century, so to say they

understand the territory is an understatement. They offer 45-minute guided tastings and distillery tours for €17.50 on Saturday and Sunday afternoons.

Drams from €3, daily 15:00-21:00, Pijlsteeg 31, Central Amsterdam, +31 (0)20 639 2695, wynand-fockink. nl, Tram: Dam

Winston Bar & Venue

Located on the ground floor of one of my favorite hostels, St. Christopher's Winston Hotel, this bar is popular with backpackers who come for the cheap prices, the open patio out back, and the smoking lounge. The in-house music venue frequently features rock bands. Check the website for an events calendar.

Drinks from €4.50, daily 10:00-01:00, until 03:00 on weekends, Warmoesstraat 129, Central Amsterdam, +31 (0)20 623 1380, winston.nl/bar, Tram: Dam

Kingfisher Café

At this comfortable, modern *bruin café*, you'll find locals sipping on beers and nibbling at cheese plates. Pull up a stool at the bar and strike up a conversation with the friendly bartenders. If you're looking to experience how locals spend a quiet and relaxed evening, look no further.

Pints from €6, Mon-Thurs 10:00-01:00, Fri-Sat 10:00-03:00, Sun 12:00-01:00, Ferdinand Bolstraat 24, De Pijp and Vicinity, +31 (0)20 671 2395, kingfisher-cafe.nl, Tram: Stadhouderskade

Café Gollem Raamsteeg

For beer aficionados, this cozy dark-wood bar specializing in Dutch and Belgian beers might as well be your mecca. For everyone else, it's a quaint and quiet refuge from the busy streets for a half-pint. What's better is that my favorite store in Amsterdam is across the street: the old book and print shop **Edward van Dishoeck** (Tues-Friday 11:30-17:00, Raamsteeg 1, Central Amsterdam,+31 (0)20 624 7190, eduardvandishoeck.nl).

Half-pints from €2.50, tastings from €10, Mon-Thurs 16:00-01:00, Fri-Sat 12:00-03:00, Sun 12:00-01:00, Raamsteeg 4, Central Amsterdam, no phone, cafegollem.nl, Tram: Spui

CLUBS

Amsterdam (like Paris and London) is on the small circuit of cities that the largest international acts *always* play when they come to Europe, so as soon as you know what nights you'll be in town, check the web to see who is playing at the big clubs and the huge concert venues like Melkweg, Paradiso, and AFAS Live (formerly the Heineken Music Hall).

Melkweg

Melkweg is one of Amsterdam's serious live-music institutions, regularly drawing crowds numbering in the thousands. Check out their program online and, if there are acts you can't miss, purchase tickets well before you arrive. The venue is expansive: the stage fronts a massive dance floor lined with two observation levels. International DJs, rock bands, rappers, and pop singers all come here to rock enthusiastic and young crowds. Plan on lines and cover.

Covers and show tickets from €7, shows generally start 20:00-23:00, Lijnbaansgracht 234A, Leidseplein, +31 (0)20 531 8181, melkweg.nl, Tram: Leidseplein

Paradiso

This famous nightlife venue, housed in an old church, has hosted some of music's biggest names since opening its doors in the 1960s. The list of past performers reads like a who's who of the music and entertainment industry: Amy Winehouse, Lenny Kravitz, The Rolling Stones, James Brown, Daft Punk, Lana del Rey, and plenty more spanning all genres.

Covers and show tickets from €10, the party picks up around 23:00 and goes until late every night of the week, Weteringschans 6-8, Leidseplein, +31 (0)20 626 4521, paradiso.nl, Tram: Leidseplein

PUB CRAWLS
Amsterdam's Ultimate Party

Take the guesswork out of a night out by joining Amsterdam's Ultimate Party pub crawl. You've got two choices: exploring the Red Light District's bars and clubs or hitting the clubbing district of Leidseplein. I'd personally opt for the latter—it's a broader cross-section of Amsterdam's nightlife scene, and it's easy to wander through the RLD and create your own adventure. Show this book for a discount.

Pricey at €20 (includes one drink and cover at each venue), kicks off nightly at 20:30, meets at Candela Bar (Korte Leidsedwarsstraat 85), Leidseplein and Vicinity, +31 (0)20 776 7888, joinultimateparty.com, info@joinultimateparty.com, Tram: Leidseplein

SEX SHOWS

Nothing is beyond the boundaries in this city, including the option to pay to witness bored-looking sex performers pound through a series of erotic acrobatics and naughty spectacles.

Casa Rosso

If you're in the market for a sex show, the city's most popular venue for this form of entertainment is your best option. Pay €45 for entrance (for €55 they'll throw in two drinks). Stay for as long or as little as you like. Eight erotic shows (some solo, some partnered up, some groups) are in the rotation, and each mini-performance lasts about 10 minutes, so after an hour you've basically seen it all and then some. For cheaper and instant gratification, drop two euros into the peep show at **Sex Palace** (#84) next door.

€45 entry, daily 19:00-02:00, until 03:00 on weekends, Oudezijds Achterburgwal 106-108, Central Amsterdam, +31 (0)20 627 8954, casarosso.nl, Tram: Dam

COMEDY SHOWS
Comedy Café

Catch the Thursday night international stand-up shows (in English) in this intimate venue in one of Amsterdam's newer expansions just west of the train station. Enjoy the canal views before and after the well-known guest comedians crack you up. Check the program online and purchase tickets ahead, as bigger names tend to sell out the venue.

€12.50, Thurs 20:30, 89 IJdok, Central Amsterdam, +31 (0)20 722 0827, comedycafe.nl, Tram: Centraal

Boom Chicago

This is your place for no-holds-barred English-language improvisational comedy that artfully blends the quirky Dutch sense of humor with a frank and politically incorrect attitude. Now a mainstay on Amsterdam's cultural scene, Boom Chicago has been putting on critically acclaimed shows since the early '90s.

Seats start at €14, shows run Wed-Sun, doors open at 20:00, showtime generally 20:30, Rozengracht 117, West Amsterdam, +31 (0)20 217 0400, boomchicago.nl, Tram: Rozengracht

TOP SHOPPING & MARKETS

SHOPPING DISTRICTS
Nieuwendijk, Kalverstraat, & Leidsestraat

This long, semi-unbroken chain of streets leads from the Centraal Station, through Dam Square, and all the way down to Leidseplein and Vondelpark. You'll have no problem spending an afternoon strolling these thoroughfares—start closer to Leidseplein (you'll notice that the streets, which are initially stylish and trendy, become first kitschier and then seedier as you get closer to the station). You'll find fashion boutiques, chocolate shops, grocery stores, souvenir shops, herring stands, and more.

Central Amsterdam and Leidseplein, Tram: Dam

The Nine Streets

The Nine Streets neighborhood (theninestreets.com), packed with cute, trendy, and independent shops and eateries, is really only three streets (Hartenstraat, Wolvenstraat, and Huidenstraat), but they cross over three canals (Herengracht, Keizersgracht, and Prinsengracht), cutting each of the streets into three sections (hence, nine streets). Find concept stores, boutiques, and vintage goods on every photogenic block. The district is just south of the Anne Frank House and Westerkerk, between the Singel and Prinsengracht canals.

West Amsterdam, Tram: Westermarkt

MARKETS
Albert Cuyp Market

Named after a famous Dutch author, the Albert Cuyp Market is Amsterdam's largest. It's also the epicenter of the recent cultural explosion in De Pijp. More than 300 vendors offer everything from chocolate-glazed waffles, fresh fruit, and fish to sparkly pants and leather goods. It's a cultural grab bag that speaks to Amsterdam's rich diversity.

Daily 09:00-17:00, Albert Cuypstraat, De Pijp and Vicinity, +31 (0)20 470 0888, albertcuypmarkt.com, Tram: Albert Cuypstraat

Bloemenmarkt

Flower stalls are parked permanently on houseboats at this touristy floating tulip market just south of the center near Muntplein. The crowd is on the older side here, but if you're a fan of tulips, this is your place to purchase a few bulbs to take home with you. Vendors are happy to package your bulbs to make sure they make it through customs intact.

Mon-Sat 09:00-14:30, Sun 11:00-17:30, Singel near the Mint Tower, Central Amsterdam, Tram: Koningsplein

Noordermarkt

On Saturdays and Mondays this square is packed with vendors hawking their fresh produce, meats, cheeses, and more. The outer stalls are mostly food, but dive into the heart of the market and you'll find a wide assortment of goods from antiques to clothes and jewelry (and anything else you can imagine).

Sat 09:00-16:00, Mon 09:00-14:00, Herenstraat 39, West Amsterdam, noordermarkt-amsterdam.nl, Tram: Marnixplein

Royal Delft Experience

Beyond the cliché windmill or phallic souvenirs, Delftware makes a great gift for loved ones back home. Named after a nearby town from where it originates, Delftware is classic blue on white and often depicts typical Dutch scenes. Splurge on hand-painted pieces or find much more affordable printed versions toward the

back of most stores. Find the Royal Delft Experience ceramics shop in the Munt Tower (Mint Tower) just on the south side of the city center. You can pay to tour the working factory, or just shop.

Experience: €5, Apr-Oct daily 10:00-20:00, Nov-Mar daily 10:00-17:30; shop: Apr-Oct daily 09:30-21:00, Nov-Mar daily 09:30-18:00, Muntplein 12, Central Amsterdam, Tram: Spui

TOP PARKS & RECREATION

Don't leave Amsterdam without exploring at least one of the city's beautiful parks, all of which offer a wonderful respite from the always-hectic city center.

PARKS
Vondelpark
New York's Central Park was modeled after Amsterdam's largest and most popular one, located south of Leidseplein. On a sunny day, it's hard to beat this picturesque setting for a relaxing picnic or bike ride. You can spend hours exploring the paths and discovering the small lakes that dot this 120-acre park.

Free, always open, Museum District, Tram: Emmastraat

Sarphatipark
Be sure to stop here while making your trek out to Albert Cuyp Market. This small, beautiful park is skipped by most tourists, so you'll easily find a great spot to picnic and take a load off after a long day of sightseeing. Manicured lawns and fanciful

bridges reflect the Romantic movement of the 19th century. The park is just south of the city center.

Free, always open, Albert Cuypstraat 2, De Pijp and Vicinity, Tram: Albert Cuypstraat

CANAL CRUISES
Lover's Canal Cruises
Amsterdam's most budget-friendly canal cruises offer day, evening, and dining cruises. Trips are narrated in multiple languages and often come with an entertaining captain. A canal cruise is a relaxing way to change your perspective on the city and take it in from the angle that it was built for. Find the kiosk just in front of Centraal Station.

Cruises from €15.50, Stationsplein 10, Central Amsterdam, +31 (0)20 330 1374, lovers.nl, Tram: Centraal

TOP TOURS

Mike's Bike Tours
Mike's small-group City Tour is a great intro to the city. They'll start you off with a potted history of Amsterdam with the aid of some beautiful historical maps, then saddle you up on cruisers to hit the town with a trusty guide. Along the way, you'll stop for a much-needed pit stop at a local brewery housed in a windmill. They also conduct Dutch countryside tours to get up close and personal with Netherlands' famous windmills, tulips, and happy Dutch cows. During the countryside tour, you'll take a 30-minute break at a local cheese farm, where you can sample some of their delicious Gouda and learn about how Dutch clogs are made.

€28, 11:00 daily Mar-Oct, 12:00 Nov-Feb, closed Jan 1 and April 27, 3.5-hour tour, Prins Hendrikkade 176, Southeast Amsterdam, +31 (0)20 233 0216, mikesbiketoursamsterdam.com, Tram: Mr. Visserplein

360 Amsterdam
Free Walking Tours
This ticket vendor and free walking tour hub offers visitors a great foot-powered intro to the city. Their passionate, local guides work hard to convey the ins and outs of Amsterdam's culture, focusing on the most compelling history and the insider stories that give this fascinating city so much character. If you like the guides and want to know more, go for one of their more in-depth tours (Anne Frank or Red Light District tours are about €20 each). Their office also sells skip-the-line entries for nearly all the key sights, and for not a penny more than the entry cost you'd pay at the door.

Free, tips accepted, departures 11:00, 13:00, and 15:00 daily from Dam Square, 2.5 hours, Dam 8, Central Amsterdam, +31 (0) 61 993 4503, 360amsterdamtours. com, Tram: Dam

TOP HOSTELS

All of these recommendations are clean and safe, and all have lockers, towels, and free Wi-Fi available. While staying in group dorm rooms, always lock up your valuables (whether you're in the room or not) just to play it safe. Real estate is at a premium in Amsterdam, so prices for bunks can climb upward of €30, €40, or even €60 during popular events and weekends. Many have their own drug policies, and some might be very strict (respect them to avoid being unceremoniously turfed). Generally, hostels have a designated smoking area. Amsterdam distinguishes between "hard" and "soft" drugs; the former are not allowed anywhere in the city, including even the most indulgent hostels.

St. Christopher's Winston Hotel

If you're looking for a hostel right in the middle of the action, look no further. Quentin Tarantino camped out here while writing the script for *Pulp Fiction*. Enjoy the fun bar, extensive free breakfast, music venue, smoking lounge, and patio out back, which backs up against the red lights.

Bunks from €35, 24-hour reception, free Wi-Fi, breakfast included, lockers available, full bar, Warmoesstraat 129, Central Amsterdam, +31 (0)20 623 1380, winston.nl, winston@winston.nl, Tram: Dam

Flying Pig Downtown

The downtown branch of the Flying Pig is in one of the oldest parts of town, just minutes from the Red Light District. It's known for its fun atmosphere, similar to the one you'll experience at the **Flying Pig Uptown** (bunks uptown from €16, same amenities, Vossiusstraat 46/47, +31 (0)20 400 4187, flyingpig.nl, uptown@flyingpig.nl, Tram: Van Baerlestraat), but this one puts you a little closer to Amsterdam's nightlife and attractions. You'll find the downtown location near the mouth of the sprawling Vondelpark, close to the Leidseplein entertainment and party district.

Bunks from €19, 24-hour reception, free Wi-Fi, breakfast included, lockers, café, bar, Nieuwendijk 100, Central Amsterdam, +31 (0)20 420 6822, flyingpig.nl, downtown@flyingpig.nl, Tram: Nieuwezijds Kolk

Bulldog Hotel & Hostel

Smack-dab in the center, the Bulldog is an excellent option to get the most out of your stay. It has a great atmosphere, as well as a fantastic breakfast and a pool table and bar to avail yourself of. Amsterdam is sprinkled with coffeeshops and bars of the same brand, but they tend to be rather touristy.

Bunks from €27, 24-hour reception, free Wi-Fi, laundry, lockers, breakfast included, Oudezijds Voorburgwal 220, Central Amsterdam, +31 (0)20 620 3822, hotel. thebulldog.com, info@bulldoghostel.nl, Tram: Dam

Cocomama

For those who shy away from grungy backpacker hostels, this boutique chain is redefining budget accommodations. While you'll pay a premium for it, you'll find a very different, much more chill vibe. You can relax in the lounge in the common room and sleep easy in comfortable, purpose-built bunks. This nonsmoking hostel, just across the Singel Canal from Albert Cuyp flea market, is run by fun and helpful staff. Its sister hostel, **Ecomama** (bunks from €32, 5-, 7-, 8-, and 12-bed dorms and small private doubles, free Wi-Fi, 24-hour reception, laundry, lockers, Valkenburgerstraat 124, Central Amsterdam, +31 (0)20 770 9529, ecomamahotel.com, hello@ecomamahotel.com, Tram: Mr. Visserplein), just east of Central Amsterdam, is equally environmentally and socially conscious and is also nonsmoking. Both hostels facilitate nightly activities like movie nights and pub crawls. Book ahead, as they sell out often.

Bunks from €35, 6-bed dorms, free breakfast and Wi-Fi, 24-hour reception, laundry, lockers, Westeinde 18, Leidseplein and Vicinity, +31 (0)20 627 2454, cocomamahostel.com, hello@cocomamahostel.com, Tram: Frederiksplein

Budget Hotel Tourist Inn

For clean, well-located private (though tiny) rooms, this is one of your best bets in town. Run as a budget hotel with options for a few shared dorms, Tourist Inn has welcoming staff who check you in quickly and are happy to recommend activities and sights. Rooms are split across two locations; the second location is just across the alley out back.

5- and 6-bed dorms €35, private single and double rooms €60-200, free breakfast, towels, and Wi-Fi, lockers, 24-hour reception, Spuistraat 52, Central Amsterdam, +31 (0)20 421 5841, tourist-inn.com, Tram: Nieuwezijds Kolk

Volkshotel
A trendy and posh hotel, bar, café, rooftop restaurant, and underground club have taken over this former newspaper building, and boy, have they done it right! The design of many of the hotel's comfortable rooms was outsourced to local artists and designers who were given the freedom to stretch their imaginations with far-out themes like Johnny Jukebox and Soixante Neuf.

Singles and doubles €119-189, special theme rooms are more expensive, free Wi-Fi, breakfast available, on-site bar, hot tub, sauna, and common workspaces, Wibautstraat 150, Southeast Amsterdam, +31 (0)20 261 2100, volkshotel.nl, Metro: Wibaustraat

TRANSPORTATION

GETTING THERE & AWAY
The excellent public transportation system in Amsterdam makes getting from the train station or airport to your accommodations easy.

Plane
From **Amsterdam Schiphol Airport** (AMS, schiphol.nl), trains leave for Amsterdam Centraal Station every 10 minutes from platforms one and two, and take about 15 minutes to get to the city center. Grab a snack from the grocery store so you'll have change on hand for the ticket machines. Purchase a ticket (€4.20) there or from the ticket desk. There is an express train called Fyra, but the time saved isn't worth the additional cost. Luggage storage is available in the basement of the airport.

If you're flying into **Eindhoven Airport** (EIN, eindhovenairport.nl), the bus (€25 each way) will take you straight to Amsterdam Centraal Station in about 90 minutes.

Train
Trains to Paris (about €75) run daily and take about 3.5 hours. For Berlin, trains cost about €50-60 and take 6.5 hours.

The **Amsterdam Centraal Station** is on the northern border of Central Amsterdam. If your hostel is anywhere in the center, it'll be no more than a half mile away from the train station, so consider walking if you're comfortable hauling your bags over the short distance. If your hostel is in the canal rings or farther, opt for the tram. There is a helpful **tourist information center** (look for the blue-and-white VVV logo) just out front of the train station across the tramway. Drop in there to get directions and pick up a map.

Bus
Buses from throughout Europe drop off at **Amsterdam Centraal Station.** Check eurolines.com for routes and prices.

Car
Amsterdam is about 500 kilometers (5 hours) north of Paris via the A1 highway. It's about 650 kilometers (6.5 hours) west of Berlin via the A2 highway.

GETTING AROUND
Most of the Dutch speak very good English. Don't be remotely afraid to ask for directions if you're lost or confused.

Amsterdam is small and highly walkable. You can get from one side of the historic district to the other in about 45 minutes.

The **Amsterdam Centraal Station** is the city's transportation hub. The public transit system is integrated so you can use the same passes across various methods of transportation. The rates are €2.90/single pass (good for one hour), €7.50/day, €12.50/two days, and €17/three days. If you're using the transit system at all, a day pass pays for itself pretty quickly.

Metro
While Amsterdam does sport a fast metro, you likely won't need to use it on your visit (though the Nieuwmarkt stop can be useful to access some sights in Central Amsterdam) unless you're staying at the recommended Volkshotel.

Tram

If walking and biking aren't your thing, trams will do just the trick. Purchase your ticket on board. Trams 2 and 5 are particularly useful to tourists. They run north to south, connecting Amsterdam Centraal Station with Leidseplein and Museumplein. Trams 13, 14, and 17 run east to west from Gassan Diamonds to the Anne Frank House.

Bus

Most visitors stick to the trams, but the buses are easy to use and utilize many of the same stops, so don't write them off.

Bicycle

Renting a bike for the entirety of your stay really opens the city up, and you can jet around like the locals. It's by far the most popular form of transportation in town, and there are more bikes within the city than human inhabitants. Heads up: Traffic can be intense and most bikes use pedal brakes, so I'd advise against renting if you're easily overwhelmed, or haven't ridden in a while. At any one intersection, you'll be negotiating pedestrians, other cyclists, cars, and delivery trucks and trams, with canal boats passing underneath; it's a lot to take in.

I recommend **StarBikes Rental** (€7/day, insurance €2.50/day, helmets €1/day, daily 08:00-19:00, +31 (0)20 620 3215, starbikes-rental.com) for their nondescript bikes that blend in rather than advertise they're rented with loud neon branding. Exit the station toward the water and turn right to continue a couple hundred yards until you find the shop at De Ruijterkade 143. Consider picking up a snack for the road from their fresh bistro or recharge with one of their healthy smoothies. Special-needs bikes are available on request.

DAY TRIPS

Haarlem

If you have an extra day and want to see what small-town Holland looks like, a visit to the quaint Dutch town of Haarlem is a great way to spend an afternoon. In Haarlem's city center, you'll find shopping, cafés, and a beautiful Gothic church right on the main square. Commuter trains to Haarlem depart every 10 minutes from Amsterdam Centraal Station and take about 30 minutes. The train station is on the edge of town, just a 10-minute walk from the center.

HELP!

Tourist Information

Stationsplein 10, Mon-Sat 09:00-17:00, +31 (0)20 702 6000

Pickpockets & Scams

Keep your wits about you, as pickpockets like to target overwhelmed, bewildered, and intoxicated tourists in the busy areas of the city. It's very unlikely you'll fall victim to violent crime during your visit, but if you're noticeably having an out-of-body experience, you're effectively painting a bullseye on your purse or back pocket. Stick with your friends and watch out for each other. Also, keep a map with your hostel circled on it. If you become disoriented *and* incoherent, just take out the map and point.

Emergencies

In an emergency, dial 112.

Hospital

VU University Medical Center
De Boelelaan 1118
+31 (0)20 444 4444

US Consulate

Museumplein 19
071 DJ Amsterdam
+31 (0)20 575 5309

ROME

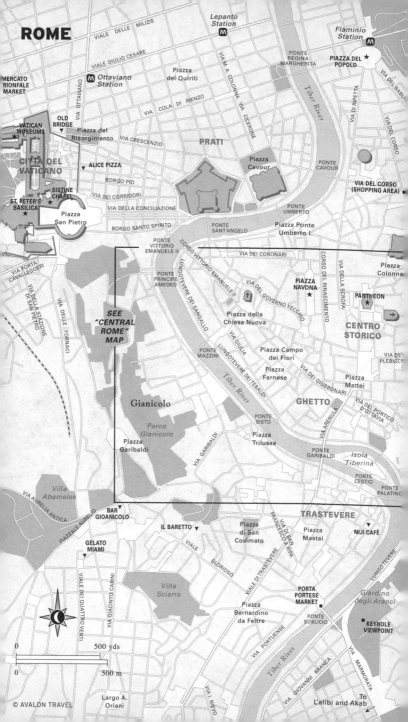

CENTRAL ROME

GELATERIA DEL TEATRO

VIA DEI CORONARI

CORSO VITTORIO EMANUELE II

VIA DI PANICO

VIA ACCIAIOLI

VIA DEI BANCHII NUOVI

VICOLO DELLE VAL

VIA DEL GIANICOLO

PONTE PRINCIPE AMEDEO

VIA DEL GOVERNO VECCHIO

BAR DEL FICO

SALITA DI SANT'ONOFRIO

VIA GIULIA

VIA DEI BANCHI VECCHI

ABI THEA

Piazza della Chiesa Nuova

LUNGOTEVERE DEI SANGALLO

CORSO VITTORIO EMANUEL

VIA DEL PELLEGRINO

VIA DEI CAPPELLA

LUNGOTEVERE GIANICOLENSE

VIA DI MONSERRATO

VIA DEGLI ORTI D'ALIBERT

CAFFÈ PERÙ

PONTE MAZZINI

VIA DELLE MANTELLATE

LUNGOTEVERE DEI TEBALDI

VIA IN CATERINA

Tiber River

VIA DEL FARNESI

VIA DI S. FRANCESCO DI SALES

VIA DELLA LUNGARA

VIA GIULIA

VIA DELLA PENITENZA

VIA DEI RIARI

LUNGOTEVERE FARNESINA

VIA CORSINI

PONTE SISTO

Q'S RUMMERIA

VICOLO MORONI

GIANICOLO HILL

Parco Gianicolo

VIA BENEDETTA

Piazza Trilussa

VIA DELLA SCALA

VIA DEL

FREN FRIZIC POLITE

0   200 yds

DAR POETA

VICOLO DEL BOLOGNA

LA RENELLA PANIFICIO

VICOLO DE CINQUE

0   200 m

ALMALU SHOT BAR

HOSTER DEL MON

VENDITA LIBRI, CIOCCOLATA E VINO

G BAR

VIA GARIBALDI

VIA GARIBALDI

TRASTEVERE

Piazza San Callisto

© AVALON TRAVEL

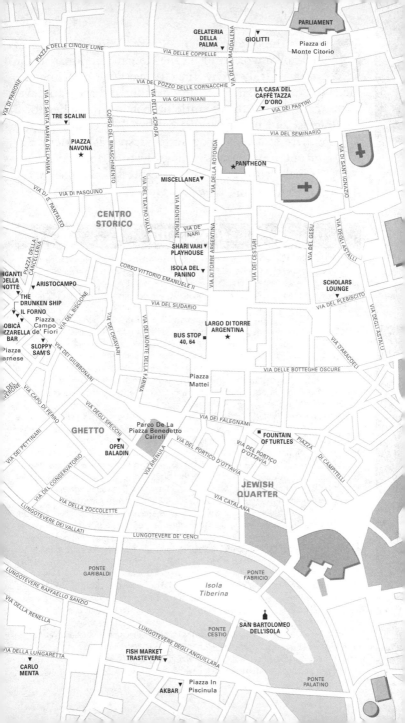

PARLIAMENT

Piazza di Monte Citorio

PIAZZA DELLE CINQUE LUNE

VIA DI PARIONE

VIA DELLE COPPELLE

GELATERIA DELLA PALMA ▼

GIOLITTI ▼

VIA DELLA MADDALENA

VIA DEL POZZO DELLE CORNACCHIE

VIA DELLA SCROFA

VIA GIUSTINIANI

LA CASA DEL CAFFÈ TAZZA D'ORO

VIA DEI PASTINI

VIA DI SANTA MARIA DELL'ANIMA

TRE SCALINI ▼

CORSO DEL RINASCIMENTO

VIA DEL SEMINARIO

PIAZZA NAVONA ★

PANTHEON ★

VIA DELLA ROTONDA

VIA DI SANT'IGNAZIO

VIA D. S. PANTALEO

VIA DI PASQUINO

MISCELLANEA ▼

VIA DEL TEATRO VALLE

VIA MONTERONE

VIA DE' NARI

VIA DI TORRE ARGENTINA

VIA DEL GESÙ

VIA DEGLI ASTALLI

CENTRO STORICO

SHARI VARI PLAYHOUSE ▼

ISOLA DEL PANINO ▼

VIA DEI CESTARI

PIAZZA DELLA CANCELLERIA

CORSO VITTORIO EMANUELE II

SCHOLARS LOUNGE ▼

NGANTI DELLA NOTTE ▼

ARISTOCAMPO ▼

VIA DEL SUDARIO

VIA DEL PLEBISCITO

VIA DEGLI ASTALLI

THE DRUNKEN SHIP

VIA DEL BISCIONE

IL FORNO

OBICÀ ZZARELLA BAR ▼

Piazza Campo de' Fiori

LARGO DI TORRE ARGENTINA ★

VIA D'ARACOELI

BUS STOP 40, 64 ■

Piazza arnese

SLOPPY SAM'S ▼

VIA DI GIUBBONARI

VIA DEI CHIAVARI

VIA DEI MONTE DELLA FARINA

VIA DELLE BOTTEGHE OSCURE

Piazza Mattei

VIA DEL TERONE

VIA CAPO DI FERRO

VIA DEI FALEGNAMI

FOUNTAIN OF TURTLES ■

PIAZZA

VIA DEGLI SPECCHI

GHETTO

Parco De La Piazza Benedetto Cairoli

VIA DEL PORTICO D'OTTAVIA

DI CAMPITELLI

VIA DEI PETTINARI

OPEN BALADIN ▼

VIA ARENULA

VIA DEL PORTICO D'OTTAVIA

VIA DEL CONSERVATORIO

JEWISH QUARTER

VIA DELLA ZOCCOLETTE

VIA CATALANA

LUNGOTEVERE DEI VALLATI

LUNGOTEVERE DE' CENCI

LUNGOTEVERE RAFFAELLO SANZIO

PONTE GARIBALDI

Isola Tiberina

PONTE FABRICIO

VIA DELLA RENELLA

PONTE CESTIO

SAN BARTOLOMEO DELL'ISOLA

VIA DELLA LUNGARETTA

LUNGOTEVERE DEGLI ANGUILLARA

FISH MARKET TRASTEVERE ▼

CARLO MENTA ▼

AKBAR ▼

Piazza In Piscinula

PONTE PALATINO

Rome is the city to which all roads lead, the center of the known world during the Roman Empire, and the capital of Italy today. The city overflows with ancient, medieval, and Renaissance architecture and art—and also comes complete with romantic little side streets, beautiful panoramas, and unforgettable cuisine. You could spend a lifetime here and still struggle to grasp this modern city with ancient foundations. Set aside time for the sights, but also make sure to pause for espresso, partake in the *passeggiata*, and drink in *la dolce vita*.

ROME 101

Legend has it that Rome was founded in 753 BC by a pair of orphans who were cast off by their human mother on the Tiber River. Their little raft landed in a bend of the river downstream, and they were taken in by a she-wolf and her pack. The fledgling city quickly grew into a regional, then continental powerhouse over the next 1,000 years thanks to technological innovations, incredible engineering feats, and a series of ambitious leaders with a well-organized military to back them up. Rome's population grew to over one million inhabitants and the city was the richest and largest the world had ever seen. Rome exerted its influence across an entire continent thanks to technological developments like the highway (many of today's European freeways follow the paths of Roman roads), arches, and water-delivery systems like aqueducts and plumbing. Today, you'll see evidence of ancient Rome's advanced technical prowess at sights like the Colosseum, brilliantly designed to allow tens of thousands of spectators to exit the venue in a mere 15 minutes, and the perfectly domed (and often-imitated) Pantheon.

Rome controlled its far-off territories by installing loyal governors enticed by land grants and plush appointments. Rome also let the inhabitants of newly conquered territories retain a good amount of autonomy—and even their pagan religions—as long as they paid their taxes to Rome. The Roman Empire's decline, which began around AD 300, was the result of overextension as well as weak and corrupt leadership. Leaders were struggling to hold together an empire that stretched across 6.5 million square kilometers without technologies like WhatsApp and Snapchat. Can you imagine?

Rome was finally sacked numerous times by barbarian hordes from the north, driving the entire continent into a period of lawlessness and violence called the Dark Ages, which lasted roughly 500 years. In medieval times, Rome was a dank backwater rife with crime and disease—not a place you'd want to hang out. With a population of only 15,000 after its peak of a million, Rome suffered from constant outside attacks and dealt with outbreaks of disease thanks to the mosquitos and pests that thrived in the warm, humid climate.

The Vatican City-State stepped into this vacuum of power to clean up the city, and inspired the entire continent to come out of the Dark Ages by financing artistic and technical innovations. The Catholic Church began commissioning artists, sculptors, and designers to deck out churches in a beauty and elegance meant to showcase the power of Christianity. The Renaissance sparked artistic and architectural innovations, leading to the design and building of ever-greater churches like St. Peter's Basilica.

Since then, Rome has been a hub of visual and culinary arts, with a contagious love of life and rich personalities to match their city's long history.

PLAN AHEAD

RESERVATIONS

Reservations are required for the **Galleria Borghese** (galleriaborghese.it) and the **papal audience** (papalaudience.org/tickets). The **Vatican Museums** are closed on Sundays (except for the last Sunday of every month. The worthwhile (and free) **Porta Portese** market is *only* open on Sunday. Reservations are recommended for the following sights:

Colosseum (etickets.coopculture.it)

Vatican Museums (biglietteriamusei.vatican.va)

Heads up: Many private ticket resellers show up higher in search engine results, so be sure to book your tickets through the cheaper, official booking sites listed with each recommendation.

PASSES

Roma Pass

The **Roma Pass** (€40, valid for three days upon validation, romapass.it) offers free entry and line-skipping privileges at two museums, discounted rates to a number of other sights (Vatican Museums not included), and a three-day metro pass. To get the most bang for your buck, use the free entries on the Colosseum and Galleria Borghese (reservations still required for the Galleria). Before you purchase, tally up the sights you want to see that are included to determine if it will be a good value. Pick up the pass at any participating sight (validate it when you enter your first sight).

LOCAL HAPPENINGS

Easter

Easter, is one of the biggest events in Rome, with millions of pilgrims coming from around the world. If you plan to be in Rome during this time, reserve long in advance, and be prepared to pay more for your stay.

HIGH AND LOW SEASON

June, July, and September are Rome's uber-busy months. August is when all of Italy shuts down for vacation. You can still experience all the tourist sites of course, but anyone who can afford to heads to the beach for a month.

Outside of this time, you'll find fewer crowds and cheaper prices.

KNOW BEFORE YOU GO

KEY STATS & FIGURES

Currency:
Italy uses the euro (€);
1 EUR = about 1.14 USD

Population:
2.7 million

National language:
Italian

National religion:
soccer (football)

Number of metro lines:
3 (with plans in the works for another)

Kilos of pasta consumed annually per capita:
28 kilos (over 50 pounds!)

Souvenir of choice:
Sexy Wine (try some at Miscellanea), limoncello liqueur, fashionable clothing

CALIBRATE YOUR BUDGET

TYPICAL PRICES FOR:

Hostel dorm bed:
€25

Two-course dinner:
€20

Glass of wine:
€6

Metro pass:
€1.50

MOVIES TO WATCH
The Talented Mr. Ripley, Gladiator, Angels & Demons, Eat Pray Love, EuroTrip, Ben Hur, To Rome with Love, Roman Holiday

THREE DAY ITINERARY

Rome's can't-miss attractions will easily fill three days. Start with Ancient Rome on day one and continue on to Renaissance Rome on day two. The Vatican Museums are closed on Sundays (except for the last Sunday of each month), so depending on your arrival date, you may need to switch days one and two to avoid missing them.

DAY 1: ANCIENT & MEDIEVAL ROME

MORNING

Catch breakfast at a neighborhood café close to your hostel in Termini. Once fortified, grab a bottle of water and take the metro (Line B) down to the **Colosseum**. I like to tackle the Colosseum before the sun (and the heat) is at its zenith, so make early reservations. Download Rick Steves' podcast/audio tour—for everything you need to know about the ancient ruins.

Spend at least an hour exploring the Colosseum, then head to the back of the site for a quick snack and coffee before your next Ancient Rome experience: the **Roman Forum.** Climb Palatine Hill for panoramas over the Circus Maximus and the rest of the Forum.

AFTERNOON

From the Roman Forum, climb the staircase to Capitoline Hill to look back over the Forum. To contrast old and new, continue to the **Campidoglio,** the square at the top of the hill—from there you'll be able to look out over modern Rome. Looking down the steps to the east, you'll see the **Vittorio Emanuele Monument**, which offers more spectacular views of the city and an excellent museum commemorating the unification of Italy.

Continue down the stairs and cross the busy street leading to Piazza Venezia. Weave your way through Rome's often-narrow back streets toward the **Largo di Torre Argentina**. When you arrive, look down onto the ruins of three temples dedicated to a few of the ancient Romans' many pagan gods.

Continue to the opposite corner of Largo Argentina and walk toward the Pantheon. When you come to the end of the first short block, my favorite sandwich shop in Rome, **Isola del Panino,** will be on your left. Pop in and order by pointing. No matter what time of the year you go, you'll always find my friend Fabio cranking out delicious sandwiches—tell him I say hello.

Take your sandwich and enjoy it in the shadow of the **Pantheon** before popping in (if it's Saturday, consider doubling back here later for mass at 17:00). Afterward, stop at the **Casa del Caffè Tazza d'Oro** coffee shop on the corner to the right as you leave the Pantheon for one of my favorite treats in all of Rome: *granita di caffè,* an icy espresso treat perfect for beating the heat. If you're in the mood for gelato instead, **Giolitti,** one of Rome's best *gelaterie,* is a short two-block walk to the north.

Continue north on the **Via del Corso,** a popular shopping street, toward the **Spanish Steps** and take in the always-bustling scene there. Relax on the steps or max your plastic in the city's top designer fashion stores. Whenever you're ready, catch the metro (Line A) from the Spanish Steps back to Termini and the hostel to rest.

EVENING

Take bus H from Termini into Trastevere. Get off at the first stop after the bridge over the river (the ride takes about 15 minutes) to explore Rome's medieval neighborhood. Enjoy a *passeggiata* (a mid-evening promenade) and take part in the Italian tradition of seeing and being seen (there's a reason the Italians are some of the largest producers and consumers of high fashion anywhere). You have some of Rome's best choices for dinner in Trastevere, including my favorite pizza in town at **Dar Poeta** or typical Roman dishes at **Carlo Menta**, an established local favorite.

LATE

Party it up with the locals at any of the trendy venues in **Trastevere.** Try **Niji Café** for classy cocktails or **Freni e Frizioni** for a more social vibe (and cheaper drinks). So much of Italian nightlife spills out into the streets and public squares, so get a drink and enjoy it alfresco.

DAY 2: RENAISSANCE & BAROQUE ROME
MORNING

Knock back an espresso both before and after your breakfast—you'll need the energy. The Vatican Museums contain one of the world's largest collections of art, sculptures, and priceless artifacts, and you'll want to be bright-eyed and bushy-tailed when you start your tour.

Catch the metro (Line A) to the Ottaviano stop for **Vatican City.** From the metro, follow the signs pointing toward Musei Vaticani (avoiding eye contact with the dozens of tour hawkers). You'll soon come to the walls, and from there you can just follow the crowds. If you've made reservations online, you can skip the often-long line and head straight to the entry gate. Flash your voucher and you're in. No reservations? Prepare to wait. Once inside, go with the flow through the **Sistine Chapel** and on to **St. Peter's Basilica.** If you're exploring on your own, the museum's twists and turns might spit you out a one-way exit—you'll have to go back through security to enter the basilica. If there's an option to leave from the back-right corner of the Sistine Chapel, take it and you'll find yourself in St. Peter's Basilica. If you find yourself outside, take the opportunity to grab a bite to eat before heading back to see the basilica.

AFTERNOON

Enjoy excellent pizza by the slice at **Alice Pizza** on Via delle Grazie. Before heading back to the basilica, reward yourself with a visit to **Old Bridge** *gelateria* just across the street from the Vatican City walls.

Head back towards the basilica through Piazza San Pietro, making sure to admire the Tuscan colonnade designed by Bernini. The line to get into the basilica may be long, but it moves quickly. As soon as you're inside, look to your right to see Michelangelo's famous **Pietà,** the pinnacle of Western sculpture. Once you've spent some time admiring the dome, you can go beneath the basilica into the free crypts, or you can climb the cupola for beautiful panoramic views.

If you're beat from the day of sightseeing, hop on bus 40 or 64 anytime—they'll take you back to Termini. If you're a superman or superwoman with energy to spare, I highly recommend the 30-minute walk/climb up **Gianicolo Hill** for another panorama across the entire city from above Trastevere. With your back to the front of St. Peter's Basilica, the hill is to your right beyond the buildings. You should be able to make out the trees behind church administrative buildings. This hill is where Rome's moped-riding young lovers take their squeezes after sundown—far from their parents' watchful eyes.

Spend the afternoon wandering back into the center of Rome (either from St. Peter's or Gianicolo Hill), exploring the old side streets. You'll find all sorts of boutique shops, *gelaterie,* cafés, and more beautiful baroque and Renaissance churches. Wend your way back to Largo di Torre Argentina and take a bus back to your hostel from there.

EVENING

Hop onto the metro (Line A) at Termini and take it to Piazza di Spagna, and enjoy an evening *passeggiata* past the **Trevi Fountain** and west toward the **Pantheon.** Grab dinner at **Miscellanea,** right outside the Pantheon. Mention my name and get unlimited house wine with dinner. You're welcome!

LATE

Rome offers a plethora of nightlife options. In the mood to party late into the night with Americans? Stroll over to **Campo de' Fiori,** a favorite of study-abroad students in Rome, with staples like **I Giganti della Notte** and **Drunken Ship.** More likely than not, you'll finish your night with a crowd of new friends heading to **Scholar's Lounge,** an Irish bar that's open late. Want to party with the locals? **Piazza Navona,** a short walk west of the Pantheon, is your gateway to many of the locals' favorite drinking haunts. Exit on the west side and you'll find an alleyway called Via di Sant'Agnese in Agone, right next to Tre Scalini. This alley will take you to some of my favorite nightlife venues in Rome, including **Bar del Fico** and **Abbey Theater.** If it's the club scene you're looking for, split a cab with your friends and head south to the clubs in **Testaccio.**

DAY 3: CHOICES, CHOICES, CHOICES

A *cornetto* pastry is the best way to start your day if you roll out of bed with a hangover. Day 3 is when you'll visit the Galleria Borghese (you'll need reservations). If you've had enough of museums and galleries, you can also make your way down to the wild Porta Portese market. For something completely different, you might want to consider a day trip to **Via Appia Antica.**

MORNING

If it's Sunday, lock up your valuables at the hostel and take bus H down to Trastevere and the **Porta Portese** market, which is notorious for its pickpockets. It's easy to fill a couple of hours strolling the length of the market.

Leaving the market, cross the river and climb Aventine Hill up to the **Giardino degli Aranci,** where you'll find the famous Aventine Keyhole—through this tiny aperture, St. Peter's dome is perfectly framed (possibly a considered design feature, but just as likely a lucky accident).

Wander across the nearby **Circo Massimo,** then north along the river into the **Jewish Quarter,** where you'll find dozens of restaurants—don't leave the quarter without trying the kosher gelato!

LATE AFTERNOON

If you're an art lover or even just a casual appreciator of beauty, visit the **Galleria Borghese** (reservations required). Miss the Borghese and you'll be missing some of the best examples of baroque art and sculpture Rome has to offer. No reservations? You can still bask in the splendor once enjoyed by the fabulously wealthy Borghese family with a visit to the **Villa Borghese,** where the garden is a perfect spot for a picnic. Four-wheeled bikes are available to rent, and pedaling them around the park on a warm day will give you a chance to explore every corner of the beautiful grounds—with no traffic to cut you off!

TOP NEIGHBORHOODS

Rome straddles a bend in the Tiber River. Most of the tourist sites are on the east side of the river, clustered around the neighborhoods surrounding Ancient Rome and the Pantheon. These areas (along with Vatican City) are sightseeing ground zero. **Ancient Rome** comprises the Colosseum and Roman Forum. Northwest from there is the **Pantheon neighborhood,** including that famous domed structure, the Trevi Fountain, and Largo di Torre Argentina (often shortened to Largo Argentina). The Pantheon neighborhood also offers romantic alleyways and some good (if touristy) options for food and nightlife, especially near Campo de' Fiori and Piazza Navona.

North of the Pantheon neighborhood, North Rome contains the Galleria Borghese, Via Veneto with the American embassy, the Spanish Steps, Piazza del Popolo, and Rome's most expensive shopping. Restaurants in this part of town are either upscale or mediocre tourist traps, so it's better to eat elsewhere.

On the west side of the river is **Vatican City** with the Vatican Museums, Sistine Chapel, and St. Peter's Basilica. South of Vatican City (and west of Ancient Rome) is **Trastevere**—fun to explore, but not as hip as it was seven or eight years ago. Still, no trip to Rome is complete without a visit. You'll find winding cobblestone streets, medieval churches, and quaint squares with ivy climbing the walls. Follow the locals as they make their way through the neighborhood each night (first dinner, then gelato, then drinks), and try to keep up.

Back on the east side of the river, East Rome is home to **Termini,** the city's main train station, which also gives its name to the surrounding neighborhood. All my recommended hostels are located here. You can find local university student nightlife in **San Lorenzo,** but keep your wits about you; the neighborhood has been on a steady decline for the last few years. It's always safer to move through this neighborhood in groups.

Monti, my favorite neighborhood, is sandwiched between Termini and the Colosseum and bordered by Via Cavour and Via Nazionale. Fresh produce markets, boutique shops, trendy restaurants, speakeasy cocktail bars, and much more line the streets. Missed by most tourists, Monti always makes for a fun night out with a mixture of hip travelers and locals—and, depending on where you go, a night that won't set you back too much.

Testaccio, directly south from Circo Massimo, feels in every way like a typical Roman neighborhood. You can find a daily produce and meat market here, but you're probably here looking for the other kind of meat market: Rome's happening club scene.

TOP SIGHTS

State-owned museums are free the first Sunday of every month, so anticipate crowds; during high season, it's definitely worth the price of entry to avoid them.

Colosseum

Commissioned in AD 70 by Emperor Vespasian, the Colosseum took a mere 10 years to build. This amphitheater packed in tens of thousands of jeering Romans (plebian and patrician alike). It was segregated, of course, with nobles and senators in the lower levels, merchants and soldiers in the middle levels, and slaves and women in the rafters. Entry was free with a numbered ceramic fragment. Emperors and campaigning local politicians curried favor with the mob by sponsoring events with exotic animal and gladiator fights, food, VIP seating, and more. Thanks to the design, all 50,000 spectators could exit the venue within 15 minutes, something most modern stadiums could only dream of.

Nearly 2,000 years after its construction, the Colosseum is Rome's most popular attraction. Queue along the outer walls, purchase tickets just inside, and continue directly up to the first floor, where you can complete a lap, looking down and imagining the battles that occurred here. Complete your visit with another lap on the ground

ACT LIKE A LOCAL

Go Take a *Passeggiata!*

Italian culture is all about seeing and being seen—and looking good at all times. There's even a term for it: keeping *la bella figura*, meaning keeping up appearances no matter what. That's why clothing labels are so prominent here: They know people are watching! If Romans go to the gym, they bring a change of clothes—it's not OK for people to see you sweat. If you see someone running outside, they're either a marathoner or, just as likely, they're not Italian.

What better way to display your labels (and the cute thing on your arm) than with a stroll through town before and after dinner? This aimless little neighborhood walk is called a *passeggiata*. It's a nightly ritual for many Romans, and something that you've got to try at least once. *Passeggiate* are also just a chance for Romans to get out of the house. Apartments in the city are small, with the paradoxical result that Italians often have to go out in public to get any sort of privacy from the family. Sunday afternoons are another popular time for *passeggiate*, as many of the city's streets become pedestrian-only for the day.

Breakfast, the Italian Way

You won't find bacon or hash browns anywhere in Rome (except at the Yellow Hostel breakfast). Italian breakfasts are simple—usually a corner café affair. Step in and observe the scene: career baristas who are passionate about coffee serving pastries to regulars who come in five days a week, always ordering the same thing. Everyone who comes in seems to be old friends with the proprietor. Depending on the café, you might pay for your order first, *then* deliver the receipt to the barista to redeem your coffee. Otherwise, order at the bar and pay before leaving—just watch what the locals do. Remember, sitting down at a table often comes with a small surcharge on each item ordered. The locals often have a single espresso at the bar to wash down a *cornetto*, a pastry very similar to—but not quite as good as—the French croissant.

Bread Basics

It's an American invention to dump olive oil and vinegar onto a side plate and sop it up with bread while you wait for your food. Italians would never do such a thing—it kills your appetite and fills you up with carbs. Italians use bread only during their meal to *fare la scarpetta*, an expression meaning "to make the little shoe" (i.e., scoop up) their leftover pasta sauce.

It's Pronounced "Broo-sketta"!

No matter what our friends at the Olive Garden say, anytime you see an *H* following a *C* in the Italian language, it turns that letter into a hard C. In other words, you pronounce the delicious tomato and garlic toast as broo-SKET-a, not broo-SHET-a. Conversely, *ciao* starts with a "ch" sound precisely because it lacks the H after the C.

Street Smarts

Rome is an urban jungle. Traffic will only stop when you boldly step out into the intersection, staring down oncoming drivers (they won't run you down if you hold eye contact). Be warned, this only works if you're within the zebra stripes. Outside of that, you're taking your life in your hands! The scooters might not slow down; instead, they'll pass by on either side as you walk so just keep your pace steady.

Here's the secret to crossing the road safely in Rome: Find a local and cross when they do.

floor, this time with a close-up view of the network of passageways used by gladiators, the cages and cells for animals, and trap-door loading areas that would have been covered by a wooden floor and sand (see a cross-section example on one side).

The Colosseum and Roman Forum share a single-entry ticket. If lines are long at the Colosseum, pick your ticket up at the gate to the Forum (on its broad side at the bottom of Via Cavour). Heads up: As soon as you arrive to the area, promoters will start hounding you, offering to let you skip the line with their private tour. On days when the line is long, taking an organized tour can be worth the extra cost, but, before you agree to anything, make sure you understand exactly what you're getting for your money. Ask them if you're one of the last to join the tour—many tour operators will take your money and then ask you to wait while they find other customers to fill out the tour, which might mean a wait just as long as the line.

€12 also covers Roman Forum, 48 hours of validity after first entrance, free first Sun of the month, daily 08:30 until one hour before sunset, last entry one hour before closing, Ancient Rome, +39 06 399 67 700, coopculture. it, Metro: Colosseo, Bus: Piazza Venezia

Roman Forum

The Roman Forum was the nerve center of the most impressive empire the world has ever seen. It was in this district that daily life went down, with toga-wearing politicians rushing between votes and making impassioned speeches, shopkeepers selling their wares, and triumphant military commanders parading back into town in victory processions lasting days on end as they touted their booty, new slaves, and plunder. Over the centuries, much of the Roman Forum disappeared due to urban cannibalism. (It was much easier to come here and take precut stones for your home rather than go to the quarry and cut them from the ground.) Floods carrying river silt and debris also covered the ruins over time.

Despite the site's decay, it is still possible to come here and see many remnants of Ancient Roman society, including the Temple of the Vestal Virgins, the arch of Septimius Severus, and the well-preserved Roman Senate House. When walking on the original Roman cobblestones, note how much lower in the ground you are than street level. This area was right in the floodplain of the Tiber River until the walls were built in the 20th century to prevent the floods.

€12 also covers Colosseum, 48 hours of validity after first entrance, free first Sun of the month, daily 08:30 until one hour before sunset, last entry one hour before closing, Ancient Rome, +39 06 399 67 700, coopculture.it, Metro: Colosseo, Bus: Piazza Venezia

Vatican Museums & Sistine Chapel

The Vatican, the spiritual and administrative home of the Catholic Church, has some of the best public museums anywhere in the world. Its awe-inspiring collection is the result of century upon century of amassed wealth and influence. You'll find the two most highly regarded ancient statues here (the Belvedere Torso

and the Laocoön Group) along with an endless parade of priceless Renaissance masterpieces. The pictures you've seen of Michelangelo's Sistine Chapel do not (I assure you) do it any justice. The Raphael Rooms (*Stanze di Raffaello*) with the famous *School of Athens* should not be missed. For some historical perspective, visit the Gallery of Maps, frescoes depicting each of the Papal States and their principal cities.

Make reservations well ahead of time to skip the often-long line to get into the Vatican Museums. Otherwise, beat the lines by getting up early or going late. Allow at least three hours inside to see everything; anything less than this and you're not really doing the place justice. Bring a bottle of water and snacks to keep the hangriness at bay. Download Rick Steves' audio tours and click through them at your own pace to get the inside take on what you're looking at.

On Fridays in high season, you can book a highly recommended evening entry to tour the museums. The price is the same, but the crowds are cut in half (19:00-23:00).

€16, additional €4 for online reservation, Mon-Sat 09:00-18:00, last entry at 16:00, closed Sun but open last Sun of the month 09:00-14:00 with free entry before 12:30, Vatican City Neighborhood, +39 06 6988 3332, confirm times at museivaticani.va, tickets at biglietteri-amusei.vatican.va, Metro: Ottaviano

St. Peter's Basilica

Catholicism's proudest church is dedicated to St. Peter, the first pope. It is said that Peter was crucified between chariot races at the racetrack that used to loop around this neighborhood. Peter's followers took him down and buried him clandestinely in a Christian grave in the hill behind the racetrack. The basilica's altar stands about 60 feet above this necropolis, with Bernini's swirly bronze baldachin rising high above. Designed by an ever-changing team of Renaissance master architects (including Michelangelo), St. Peter's was built to an otherworldly scale, one designed to makes visitors feel tiny and even insignificant. Take a look high above at the inscriptions that wrap the interior walls: Those letters are six feet tall. The images are not painted; they are mosaics, painstakingly pieced together by master craftsmen. Paintings fade, but tiles retain their luster for ages. The 10,000 square meters of intricate mosaics depict past popes, Bible stories, and all the characters you'd expect to see in Catholicism's most important place of worship.

As you enter, immediately to the right is Michelangelo's **Pietà.** In elongated and exaggerated features, Jesus's recently crucified body lies draped across Mary's lap. Michelangelo completed this piece—which many consider to be his masterpiece—when he was only 24 years old. He only returned later to sign it when he heard rumors that it was being attributed to someone else (it would be the only piece he ever signed). In 1972, a geologist attacked Mary's face and arm with a hammer, knocking chunks off the priceless sculpture, including Mary's nose. The Pietà has since been restored with marble taken from the back of the piece (raw marble is like a thumbprint—you'll never find two pieces the same coloring, hue, and pattern). Since the attack, it's only been possible to observe the Pietà from a distance (30 feet) and through two inches of bulletproof glass.

Consider visiting the basilica at 18:00, right before closing, for more dramatic lighting and a fraction of the crowds.

Visitors can go beneath the basilica into the free crypts or climb the cupola for a beautiful panorama of the entire city (€6 by stairs, €8 by elevator). Papal audiences with Pope Francis take place every Wednesday at 10:30 (arrival recommended at 08:30, free tickets required, papalaudience.org).

Free, daily Apr-Sept 07:00-19:00, Oct-Mar 07:00-18:30, dome open daily from 08:00, last entry to stairs 17:00 (16:00 Oct-Mar), to elevator 18:00 (17:00 Oct-Mar), Piazza San Pietro, Vatican City Neighborhood, +39 800 038 436, vatican.va, Metro: Ottaviano

Pantheon

A revolutionary feat of architecture and engineering, this domed temple has been studied and imitated, but never truly replicated. What was once a one-stop shop to worship all the gods of the Roman Empire (*pan* = all, *theon* = gods) is now an active Catholic church called the Church of St. Mary of the Martyrs. Raphael, the Renaissance master, is buried in the church, along

TREVI TRIVIA

Thanks to the tradition of tossing coins into the Trevi Fountain to guarantee a return trip back to Italy, the pool in front of the fountain collects thousands of euros daily. (Apparently, many tourists believe that the higher the value of coin, the higher the chance the superstition will work its magic.) Well, where does all this money go? For a number of years, it just disappeared. No one knew what was happening, until the police caught a homeless man swimming in the fountain late one night.

They caught him once, then again...and again...and again. He hadn't really committed a real crime, so he couldn't be detained for more than 24 hours. Each time he was caught, he was released. This went on until someone had the brilliant idea to create a waterproof fountain Roomba. The collected money (millions of euros!) is donated to the Red Cross each year. *Grazie,* tourists!

with the first two kings of Italy and one of their wives, Queen Margherita. (She's the one the popular pizza was named after. The three main ingredients—tomatoes, mozzarella, and basil—represent the three colors of the unified Italy's flag.)

Two wooden structures on this site burned down before Emperor Hadrian commissioned a stone version and completed it around AD 125. The Pantheon is the world's largest and oldest unreinforced concrete dome. At their base, the walls are nearly 30 feet thick, built with heavy brick and stone. As the walls climb higher and arch into the ceiling, the building materials become lighter. The uppermost portion is made of concrete mixed with light volcanic ash. The domed ceiling is only three feet thick and is recessed, a way to both to add decoration and to reduce mass overhead. It inspired the designs of some of the world's most famous domes, including the Duomo in Florence, St. Peter's Basilica, Thomas Jefferson's Monticello, and even the U.S. Capitol building.

You can catch mass here Saturday at 17:00 and Sunday at 10:30 and throughout the week each afternoon. It's a special experience—mostly because the noisy tourists are ushered out, leaving only the faithful and those content to remain in the building and observe a moment of quiet reflection.

Free, Mon-Sat 08:30-19:30, Sun 09:00-18:00, holidays 09:00-13:00, Pantheon Neighborhood, +39 06 6830 0230, Bus: Largo Argentina

Trevi Fountain

Rome's greatest fountain is dedicated to the Aqua Virgo, an aqueduct that once terminated at this spot (it brought fresh water to the ancient Romans, doing so steadily for 400 years). Running water was a luxury in the ancient world (and it still is, even in parts of modern-day Rome!). With aqueducts and sewage systems, the Romans harnessed technology to drive explosive population growth—crossing the one-million-inhabitants threshold wouldn't have been possible without these developments. The next Western city to cross that population benchmark would be London, nearly 2,000 years later.

The Trevi Fountain dates from the 18th century, when Pope Clement XII commissioned master architect Nicola Salvi to build a magnificent fountain (Salvi died before it was completed). In the center of the fountain stands Oceanus, flanked by two Tritons, each of which holds a horse—one rearing, the other docile. These opposing postures represent the two personalities of the sea: violent and calm. On the reliefs high above, a young girl (the virgo—or virgin—from whom the aqueduct took its name) leads parched Roman centurions to the headwaters of the aqueduct. Look to the right and you'll see a large stone vase that seems out of place. This is the Ace of Cups, and its placement was no accident. A local barber made a nuisance of himself by complaining about the fountain and offering unsolicited advice during its

123

construction. The vase served two purposes: It hid the fountain from the barber and the barber's shop from anybody admiring the fountain—a thank-you note for his constructive criticism.

Today, the Trevi Fountain overflows with tourists, drawing countless knickknack sellers and, every evening, eager (and sometimes pushy) Italian Casanovas looking for love or its approximation. At night there are far fewer tourists, making it an ideal place to sit, chat, canoodle, and perhaps share a bottle of prosecco. Thanks to a 2015 renovation, the Trevi is pristine—and guards are always standing by to keep it that way. Whatever you do, don't put your feet in the fountain. Instead, toss a coin with your right hand over your left shoulder. If it works, the fates will one day carry you back to Rome.

Free, always open, Pantheon Neighborhood, Metro: Barberini

Piazza Navona

Piazza Navona, another of the city's famous squares, used to be a track for athletic contests. The long square is still rounded at one end, the curve echoing the track where first-century Romans competed and trained. In the center of the plaza stands the only fountain that can possibly compete with the Trevi: Bernini's *Fountain of the Four Rivers*, with an Egyptian obelisk at its center, is a stunning example of baroque sculpture. The plaza fills with vendors selling all sorts of touristy garbage during the day, but they (and the crowds) thin out after dark, making it a prime spot for the *passeggiate* (strolls) that locals take every night. Don't miss the famous chocolate truffles at Tre Scalini and the excellent nightlife in the district just through the alleyway next to the church.

Free, always open, Pantheon Neighborhood, Bus: Largo Argentina

Largo di Torre Argentina

One of Rome's busiest squares for bus connections also looks down onto an open-air archeological dig. You'll see the foundations for three Roman temples (called, for simplicity's sake, Temple A, Temple B, and Temple C), the purposes of which are not known. Rome used to have a serious feral cat problem in the downtown area, but the city was able to solve the problem by relocating all stray cats to sunken ruins like this one. On the southwest corner of the square, descend a short staircase to visit Rome's **Cat Sanctuary** (hours vary). Largo Argentina today is more important to know as a reference point for public transportation than anything else, but there are a number of convenient shops nearby as well, including a bookstore, *tabacchi* (for bus tickets), and *gelateria*. You'll also find many recommended restaurants nearby.

Free, always open, Pantheon Neighborhood, Bus: Largo Argentina

Campidoglio

After climbing out of the Forum, you'll pass through this beautiful, perfectly balanced Renaissance square at the top of Capitoline Hill. Michelangelo was brought in to complete this half-finished square in the 16th century. The master had his work cut out for him. Pope Paul III wanted a square that connected Renaissance Rome with its ancient past; it had to reference the Roman Forum while also looking forward into Rome's bright future. Michelangelo's solution was ambitious—the existing medieval square was notoriously inharmonious, and his plans included a mirroring palace (the one closer to the Vittorio Emanuele Monument) that would make the square symmetrical. He completed the effect by overlaying the square with a geometric pattern, reflecting the age's stunning mathematical advances.

The equestrian statue of Marcus Aurelius in the middle of the square (a copy of the original, which can be found in a glorious setting in the Capitoline Museum) only exists today because it was thought to be a statue of Emperor Constantine, Rome's first Christian emperor. It is the only surviving bronze statue of Rome's pre-Christian emperors; the others were melted down and repurposed for either coins or statues. Aurelius saw himself as a bringer of peace, which explains why he is depicted without weapons or armor.

Free, always open, Ancient Rome, Metro: Colosseo, Bus: Piazza Venezia

Santa Maria in Aracoeli

As you descend from the Campidoglio down the Renaissance stairway, Santa Maria in Aracoeli is up and to your right. Sitting on the most holy and important hill in Rome, this church rests on ruins dating back to the early Roman Empire. In this single church, you can study a wide range of artistic and architectural styles, from Romanesque to Gothic and medieval to Renaissance and baroque. Thankfully, the church was not destroyed during the construction of the nearby Vittorio Emanuele Monument.

Free, daily 09:00-18:30, Ancient Rome, Metro: Colosseo, Bus: Piazza Venezia

Vittorio Emanuele Monument

The colossal Vittorio Emanuele Monument (aka Altare della Patria), commemorating Italy's first president, is located on Piazza Venezia and caps the head of Via del Corso. From the nicknames locals have given it—the Typewriter, Dentures, Wedding Cake—you can guess how Romans feel about this imposing neoclassical monument. The enthralling Museo Centrale del Risorgimento is worth a gander on your way up to the elevators zipping visitors to the roof of the monument. The €7 elevator ride to the top offers some of the best views of both ancient and modern Rome anywhere in the capital.

Free to visit the lower steps, daily 09:30-18:30; museum €5, daily 09:30-18:30, ticket offices close 45 minutes earlier; Piazza Venezia, Ancient Rome, +39 066 793 598, Metro: Colosseo, Bus: Piazza Venezia

Circo Massimo

This was Ancient Rome's largest stadium, seating more than 150,000 spectators at once—considerably more than the nearby Colosseum. The sheer scale of the stadium is mind-blowing. The entertainment that could fill the stands varied: there might be an afternoon of chariot racing, singing or musical events, gladiator combat, or athletic demonstrations. Located right in the downtown of Ancient Rome, with the Emperor's Palace overlooking the track, the Circo Massimo was near and dear to the empire's heart. Today, this empty field and long running track are great for a picnic or, if you want to stretch your legs, a few laps.

Free, always open, Ancient Rome, Metro: Circo Massimo

Galleria Borghese

This Baroque villa houses possibly my favorite museum on the planet, featuring some of the most incredible baroque paintings and sculptures ever completed. Even if they were the only pieces in the museum, Caravaggio's dramatically lit *David with the Head of Goliath* and Bernini's spectacular *Apollo and Daphne* would bring me back every time I pass through Rome. Reservations are required; get them at galleriaborghese.it. Find the museum deep inside the Villa Borghese gardens—bring snacks to enjoy afterwards in the grass.

€15, reservation fee €2, free first Sun of the month, Tues-Sun 08:30-19:00, Piazzale del Museo Borghese 5 (located inside the Villa Borghese gardens), North Rome, gebart.it, +39 06 841 3979, Metro: Barberini or Flaminio, Bus: Museo Borghese

Spanish Steps

This district just outside downtown Rome has been a hot spot for bohemians, wealthy tourists, and trendsetting artists for hundreds of years. The artists brought the ladies, and where the ladies went, the Italian men soon followed. The steps (the widest staircase in Europe) have been a popular meeting point ever since. Notice the range of international brands and cafés—Spanish Steps, English tea house, Café el Greco, and more. The steps were designed by an Italian, paid for by a Frenchman, and named for the Spanish Embassy to the Holy See at the bottom of the steps. To the right of the steps is a small house, now a modest museum, where English Romantic poet John Keats spent the last few months of his life (a must-visit for poetry lovers). Some of the best shopping in Rome is to be had in the streets surrounding this elegant square; the further you move towards Via del Corso, the high-fashion boutiques fade into mainstream outlets.

Free, always open, North Rome, Metro: Spagna

Piazza del Popolo

This piazza is an excellent example of *tridente*, a late-Renaissance urban-planning technique. See the three grand avenues leading south away from the square into central Rome? The central one is Via del Corso, which terminates at the Vittorio Emanuele Monument; to the left, Via del Babuino takes you to the Spanish Steps and Santa Maria Maggiore beyond; to the right, Via di Ripetta leads toward the old medieval center and the bridge that connects Rome and the Vatican. This design (resembling the three prongs of a trident) was the brainchild of an ambitious 16th-century pope—any homes in the way were unapologetically demolished in the goal of beautifying the church's capital city.

Today, Piazza del Popolo (the People's Square) is a great spot to people-watch and soak in some of the rich surrounding architecture without the overwhelming crowds that roar and jostle in the more popular squares. The obelisk in the center of the square is an obvious meeting point, and demonstrations often kick off here, proceeding south from the square to the center of town. Pop into the churches on the square to view some beautiful religious art, including two spectacular Caravaggios, the *Conversion of St Paul* and the *Crucifixion of St Peter*, which face each other inside the Basilica of Santa Maria del Popolo (Mon-Thurs 07:15-12:30 and 16:00-19:00, Fri-Sat 07:30-19:00).

Free, always open, North Rome, Metro: Flamino

Jewish Quarter

Rome has a rich Jewish history dating back millennia. Even though the Jewish community predates the Christian one in Rome, Christian Rome was not keen to recognize this history. Pope Paul IV relegated the Jews to this district just outside the bend of the Tiber River in a Papal Bull in 1555. This placed the Jewish community right in the path of the river that flooded numerous times each year. The community persevered through these horrid conditions, then enjoyed a short respite upon the unification of modern Italy toward the end of the 19th century—but when fascist fervor swept the continent in the 1930s, it was the Jews that bore the brunt of popular discontent.

Today, the Jewish Quarter is well worth a stroll. While many other parts of the city close down on Sunday, the Jewish Quarter is alive and bustling. Keep your eyes open to find inlaid stones with Hebrew inscriptions in buildings throughout the neighborhood. Don't forget to look down, either—you'll notice numerous small bronze cobblestones (aka "stumblestones") sprinkled throughout the area. Each stone marks a home from which Jewish victims of the Holocaust were deported. You'll see the name of each victim inscribed with their birth date, occupation, which camp they were deported to, and the last date they were known to be alive. Laying these stones started here in Rome, but you'll see them in a number of other Jewish quarters in Europe.

Before you leave this district, be sure to find the following three things: fried artichoke in the Jewish style (think Bloomin' Onion, *stile Romano*), kosher gelato, and Bernini's *Fountain of the Turtles*. The last of these is dedicated to the Jewish community: The turtles represent those who were forced to carry their earthly belongings on their backs until they could find a land to call their own.

Free, always open, Pantheon Neighborhood, Bus: Largo Argentina

EXTRA CREDIT
Churches, Churches, & More Churches

Historically, the church has been the richest patron around, so churches in Rome often house beautiful works of art. There are more churches in Rome than there are Starbucks in Seattle, so you can spend weeks on end exploring these solemn and beautifully decorated spaces. Breaking off on your own and exploring Rome's churches often leads you to some of the city's most memorable masterpieces. A few blocks from the Piazza della Repubblica is the quietly dignified Santa Maria della Vittoria. To the left of the altar, you'll find Bernini's celebrated masterpiece, *The Ecstasy of Saint Teresa*. Other churches worth exploring are the **Santa Maria Maggiore** (Termini, Bus: Equilino-Cavour, bus 70), with its beautiful ceiling and cavernous space; the science-oriented **Santa Maria degli Angeli e degli Martiri** (Termini, Bus: Repubblica, bus 64 or 70), and **San Bartolomeo dell'Isola** (Isola Tiberina, Bus: Sonnino, bus H), with a unique location on an island in the river. Remember that these are places of worship, and that flash photography or talking louder than a whisper will not be tolerated.

Free, most are open dawn-dusk

Monti District

If you're exhausted from marathoning through the Roman Forum and Vatican City, this quiet neighborhood just north of Ancient Rome might be a welcome change of pace. Monti offers a glimpse into Roman life and is a hive for up-and-coming artisan shops. Wander along **Via Leonina,** which runs parallel to the larger **Via Cavour,** to find some of Monti's gems. On Via Leonina are numerous excellent restaurants and **Finnegan's Irish Pub** (Via Leonina 66), a prime watering hole for Rome's many English-speaking guides. **Trieste Pizza** is great for a quick afternoon snack of fresh personal pizzas (from €2.50, Sun-Thurs 10:30-23:00, Fri-Sat 10:30-02:00, Via Urbane 112, +39 06 481 15319, Tonda. pizza, Metro: Cavour). **MercatoMonti** (Via Leonina 46) proffers handmade artisanal designer goods like jewelry and fashion pieces, and is a popular spot in the evening hours. And, as always, gelato is never far away in Rome; **Gelateria Fatamorgana** is the best around at Via degli Zingari 5.

Free, always open, Ancient Rome, Metro: Cavour

TOP EATS

Nobody should leave Rome hungry. The cuisine is an expected highlight, and it doesn't disappoint. There are choices to suit just about any budget. Breakfast is a cheap and simple affair, usually pastries and espresso. Your target price for each should be about a euro; if you're paying more for that, you're likely in a touristy café. For lunch, I love stopping into any little bakery (*paninoteca*) for delicious freshly made sandwiches. Some of my favorite Roman dishes are *cacio e pepe* (pasta with cheese and pepper), *carbonara* (egg, bacon, pecorino cheese, and pepper over spaghetti), and *amatriciana* (tomato-based sauce over buccatini—a thick spaghetti with a hole running through its center, reminiscent of a pool noodle). When looking at dinner menus, watch out for "false friends" as we called them in my language classes: *Pepperoni* are bell peppers, *acciughe* are anchovies (not artichokes), and *margherita* refers to the tomato, basil, and cheese pizza—not the tequila-laden drink.

And there's an Italian tradition that you just cannot miss: *aperitivo.* Many bars include an extensive yet simple buffet with the purchase of a drink. You'll find many young professionals heading to their favorite bar after work to take advantage of this incredible deal. The spread often comprises an assortment of simple carbs (like cold bean salads, tiny slices of pizza, and salty focaccia bread), so if you find a buffet with protein, it's a winner. Get your fill for the price of one €10 drink.

Tipping in Italy is not required, but, when you get good service, a 10 percent tip is appropriate and appreciated. Look at your receipt. If you see *"servizio incluso,"* a service charge (usually about 10 percent) has been added to the bill.

Miscellanea

Frisky Mikki runs this popular lunch and dinner spot located just at the back corner of the Pantheon. Pumping out pasta dishes, meat, salads, and delicious bruschetta, Miscellanea is a favorite of all who come here, from Italian senators and the Swiss Guard to cash-strapped study-abroad students and travelers. All are attracted to the quick service with a smile and the welcoming atmosphere. Immensely popular among students is a menu I designed with these guys a few years ago: For €15 you get bruschetta, pizza, two types of pasta, dolce, water, red and/or white wine, and of course, Mikki's famous Sexy Wine. Be sure to tell him *"ciao bello"* for me!

Pastas and sandwiches from €10, feast for €15, daily 10:00–03:00, Via Della Palombella 37, Pantheon Neighborhood, +39 06 6813 5318, miscellaneapub.com, Bus: Largo Argentina

Isola del Panino

Between Largo Argentina and the Pantheon, you'll find one of the best values in the heart of Rome. Fabio heads up the team at this panino factory, which attracts equal numbers of local lunchers and budget backpackers. Fill your sandwich with ingredients like grilled chicken, beef, ham, turkey, salads, cheeses, other toppings, and sauces, or go for a plate of pasta or salad. They'll toast the sandwich and wrap it in a way that makes it easy to eat on the go. There's no seating here, just a skinny bar along the wall.

From €3.50, Mon–Sat 05:00–18:00, Via di Torre Argentina 70, Pantheon Neighborhood, +39 06 944 14933, Bus: Largo Argentina

Obicà Mozzarella Bar

Obicà isn't just a meal; it's an experience. Tour Italy through the prism of the freshest mozzarella cheese you may have ever tasted. Your place mat is a map of Italy that shows exactly where your locally and regionally sourced ingredients are coming from. The restaurant has a mod, sophisticated decor, and the servers are clearly passionate about the restaurant's concept, particularly its intense focus on ingredients from close to home. Find a second Obicà location in the Piazza di Firenze.

Dinners from €12, daily 07:30–02:00, Piazza Campo de' Fiori 16, Pantheon Neighborhood, obica.com, Bus: Largo Argentina

Forno

This is not a sit-down restaurant, but an excellent spot to drop in and get a bready snack any time day or night (their salty focaccia bread is as good as any I've ever had). Forno (Italian for "oven") has an excellent location right on the corner of Campo de' Fiori, making it a convenient stop whenever the mood strikes. The excellent pizza won't fall apart on you when you're walking and eating at the same time.

Snacks from €1.50, Mon–Sat 07:30–14:30 and 16:40–20:00, Piazza Campo de' Fiori, Pantheon Neighborhood, +39 06 6880 2366, fornocampodefiori.com/storia.php, Bus: Largo Argentina

Tre Scalini

Tre Scalini, with outdoor seating spilling out onto Piazza Navona, is famous for its to-die-for chocolate gelato truffles. Imagine dark, white, and milk chocolate rolled into a ball and then dusted with chocolate powder and chocolate sprinkles and you're almost there. Try to have just one—I've never succeeded. When you're ready for nightlife, some of my favorite joints are just down the alley leading away from the square toward Piazza del Fico.

From €6, daily 12:30–15:50 and 19:00–24:00, Piazza Navona 30, Pantheon Neighborhood +39 06 687 9148, ristorante-3scalini.com, Bus: Largo Argentina

Casa del Caffè Tazza d'Oro

This café offers one of my favorite frozen treats in Rome: their famous *granita di caffè* (basically an espresso slushie). Pay at the counter in the back first, then bring your receipt to the front to claim your prize. To temper the sweetness, I like to ask for more granita, less whipped cream: *"Per favore, piu granita, meno crema."*

From €3, Mon–Sat 07:00–20:00, Sun 10:30–19:30, Via degli Orfani 84, Pantheon Neighborhood, +39 06 678 9792, tazzadorocoffeeshop.com, Bus: Largo Argentina

Alice Pizza

Alice Pizza near the Vatican offers my favorite pizza by the slice. You know it must be good when old nuns elbow you out of the way to order (quality, location, and lightning-fast service have made it the favorite spot of the Swiss Guard and other Vatican regulars). Head into either of the doors and get to the front of the hungry mass. Don't hesitate when it's your turn to order or you'll miss your chance, and don't be afraid to ask for more or less. The ladies at this place serve delicious pizza, but they're all business. Don't expect any smiles. More

THE ORDER—AND THE ORDERING—OF FOOD

In Italy, the dinner table is practically a religious altar: As with religion, there are rituals to be observed; you do things a certain way because that's the way it has always been done, and who are you to question it?

Aperitivo: Kick off your meal with a drink to toast with. This can often be a flute of prosecco or Spumante.

Antipasti: Begin your feast with *salumi* (cold cuts) and a selection of cheeses. Prosciutto, salami, and savory cheeses are typical.

Primo: This is typically a pasta or otherwise carb-focused course, like a risotto. Don't make the rookie mistake of filling up on this course—you've still got several more on the way!

Secondo: This is your meat course. Don't ask for chicken pesto pasta because Italians don't mix pasta and meat. It's sacrilege. So enjoy your pasta course, and then dig into something like pork chops, steak, or chicken breast with potatoes and veggies on the side.

Insalata: While we start with a salad, the Italians finish with it. Don't expect heavy, creamy dressings—they tend to keep their salads light and leafy.

Formaggi/frutta/dolce: What better way to finish your meal than with a selection of cheese or fruit? These will come before any sort of *dolce* (sweet), which may well be gelato, tiramisu, *pannecotta*, or cake.

Caffè/digestivo: To keep you going into the night, cap everything off with a single espresso. Many also pair their coffees with a round of whiskey, grappa, *limoncello* (lemon liqueur), or *sambuca* (Italian anise-flavored liqueur).

locations are sprinkled throughout town, including one by Largo di Torre Argentina (Corso Vittorio Emanuele II, 35).

Bites from €3.50, Mon-Sat 11:00-18:00, Via delle Grazie 9, Vatican City Neighborhood, +39 06 687 5746, alicepizza.it, Metro: Ottaviano

Dar Poeta

If you're in the mood for an entire pie, head to Rome's best pizzeria—tucked away in a small Trastevere alley. Run by three friends, this place pumps out wood-fired pizzas, all of them delicious, all of them affordably priced. Feeling spicy? Go for the *lingua del fuoco.* Hungry? Ask for *"pizza alto"* to get a double crust. Be sure to save some room for their famous *calzone cioccolatto* (chocolate calzone), more than big enough to split among friends (not that you have to share; keep it all to yourself—I won't tell). The word is out, so Dar Poeta fills up fast. Reservations are a must during peak season.

Pizzas from €8, daily 12:00-15:00 and 19:00-late, Vicolo del Bologna 45, Trastevere, +39 06 588 0516, darpoeta. com, Bus: Sonnino/Piazza Belli

La Renella Panificio

Pop into this industrial-chic bakery for some toasty focaccia or heavily laden sandwiches served through the outside window. The nearby steps of the Piazza Trilussa are a perfect place to sit and enjoy your meal in the sun. You can also head inside and enjoy a bite of fresh pizzettas at the bar. The restaurant is a community hot spot, and the staff do everything they can to make patrons feel welcome.

Bites from €2.50, Sun-Thurs 07:00-22:00, Fri-Sat 07:00-02:00, Via del Moro 15, Trastevere, +39 06 581 7265, panificiolarenella.com, Bus: Trilussa

Carlo Menta

Carlo Menta is a Trastevere institution that's often packed to the rafters with locals thanks to its fresh pasta, artichokes, and lasagna. Romans come here on Sunday afternoons and bring their entire multigenerational family along. Expect cheap prices (€1.50 cover charge but, with pizzas from €4, it doesn't get cheaper!), but don't expect any niceties from the busy staff. Split the liter of table wine with friends for a reasonable €8.

Dinners from €5, daily 12:00-24:00, Via della Lungarina 101, Trastevere, +39 06 580 3733, Facebook: Pizzeria Il Carlo Menta, Bus: Sonnino/Piazza Belli

ITALIAN COFFEE

Italians love their espresso almost as much as their Vespas. It can seem a bit intimidating to join in on the tradition, but you've got to do it at least once. Italians consider coffee a digestive, not to be consumed *with* food, only *after* food. Expect to pay about €1 per espresso, €2 per cappuccino, and double that if you'd like to sit down rather than take it at the bar. Here's a breakdown of your options at any normal Roman *caffè*:

Caffè: Your standard single shot of espresso, consumed in one toss back.

Doppio: A double espresso.

Macchiato: Espresso "stained" with just a touch of hot, steamed milk—my favorite.

Cappuccino: Your standard espresso-and-steamed milk mix, though it's smaller than the Starbucks counterpart you may be used to. *Never* to be ordered or consumed after the clock strikes noon. Italians believe that milk must not be consumed after breakfast, so keep this in mind if you want to blend in with the locals.

Caffè Latte: Glass of hot milk with a shot of coffee. *Latte* means milk in Italian, so you've got to include *"caffè"* in your order. Like the cappuccino, never order this after noon if you don't want them to snicker into their sleeves.

Caffè Americano: American-style coffee, as interpreted by Italians, meaning espresso diluted with hot water.

Caffè Corretto: An espresso "corrected" with a shot of liquor. Italians enjoy mixing coffee with grappa. I prefer mine with a splash of Baileys, the perfect blend of liquor and cream.

Caffè Ristretto: An even denser, more intense shot of espresso.

Fish Market Trastevere

For fresh seafood at a great price, head to Trastevere's best fast seafood joint, Fish Market. The jovial, welcoming staff will squeeze you (a little like sardines) into tables packed with locals, handing you a paper menu and a pencil. Order à la carte oysters, prawns, fish, salads, and more. They'll tally your items on the menu. Take your marked-up menu to the till and pay after your meal. With all the *frittura* (fried food), it can be a heavy meal, but it's oh so good! Don't forget a nice bottle of white wine to wash down your selections.

Plates from €5, Mon-Fri 19:30-01:00, Sat-Sun 13:00-16:00, Vicolo della Luce 2, Trastevere, +39 366 914 4157, fishmarket-roma.com, Bus: Sonnino/Piazza Belli

Pizzeria del Secolo

When I'm in the mood for a snack in the Termini neighborhood, I follow my nose to Pizzeria del Secolo. Friendly pizza maestros keep the ovens hot all day, creating steaming masterpieces like *caprese* (mozzarella, basil, and tomato), sausage with potato, and roasted eggplant. Order and pay by weight; you won't have to wait long while they cook up your selection. Dig in at one of their high-top tables.

From €3, daily 08:00-03:00, Via Palestro 62, Termini, +39 06 338 229 0001, Facebook: Antica Pizzeria del Secolo, Metro: Termini

Colosseum Area Options

It's not all that easy to find good food and value in the Colosseum area, but here are my two recommendations—perfect for when those gladiator sandals start feeling a little too heavy: **Il Bocconcino** (pastas from €10, Thurs-Tues 12:30-15:30 and 19:30-23:30, Via Ostilia 23, +39 06 7707 9175) offers *al dente* fresh pastas, beautifully presented salads, and tasty desserts like tiramisu and brownie à la mode, all in a casual, family-friendly atmosphere. I'd wager it's your best-value sit-down option in the district. If you prefer a quick, standing lunch, skip the pricier joints and head to **Goloseum** (*panini* from €3, Via S. Giovanni, Laterano 80/82, +39 339 249 7280), run by Dario, a charming local. He serves a wide array of cheap sandwiches and prefab pasta options in cozy, no-frills surroundings. Eat standing at the bar or take your sack lunch up the hill to enjoy in the Parco del Colle Oppio overlooking the Colosseum.

TOP GELATO

Gelato is not just a treat for tourists. At just about any time of year, you'll see locals of all ages filing in and out of popular *gelaterie* (ice cream shops). Your nose isn't your best guide to the best *gelateria*; use your ears instead. As you walk past an ice cream shop, listen. If all you can hear is Italian speakers, you've come to the right place. There are tons of knock-your-socks-off *gelaterie* across Rome—gelato crawl, anyone? For tips on finding the best, see page 159.

Giolitti

Step in the door, pay for your order, then take your receipt over to the overflowing flavors (all chilled to perfection). Just a three-minute walk from the Pantheon, Giolitti is your best classic *gelateria* in town. It's open late and is close to the Pantheon, the Spanish Steps, and Trevi, making this the perfect place to stop when enjoying a late-night sightseeing stroll.

From €2.50, seated bowls from €9, daily 07:00-01:00, Via degli Uffici del Vicario 40, Pantheon Neighborhood, +39 06 699 1243, giolitti.it, Bus: Largo Chigi

Gelateria della Palma

If you've got a hankering for obscure flavors, step into this sweet-tooth heaven. With more than 150 flavors, you'll find all the classics and a host of others—it's a taste extravaganza. Like chocolate? Choose from 20 different takes on the classic flavor. Only a few meters away from the Pantheon, make this your destination if you feel your energy sagging in the middle of the afternoon.

From €2.50, daily 08:30-00:30, Via della Maddalena, 19-23, Pantheon Neighborhood, +39 06 6880 6752, dellapalma.it, Bus: Largo Argentina

Gelateria del Teatro

Rather than just scooping it into a cone for you, this place actually makes its gelato right in front of your eyes. Ask the staff what is the freshest and experience gelato as you've never had it before. I highly rec-

ommend their coffee and pistachio flavors, but their classics are excellent as well.

From €2, daily 12:00-24:00, Via dei Coronari 65, Pantheon Neighborhood, +39 06 4547 4880, gelateriadelteatro.it, Bus: Largo Argentina

Old Bridge

This famous *gelateria* is perfectly situated to fortify you for (or help you recover from) the always-daunting Vatican experience. A busy location combined with a stellar reputation means there's always a line halfway around the block for Old Bridge, but don't let it deter you. Dive in. Get up to the front and place your order—pay first, then receive your gelato. There's another location in Trastevere (Via della Scala 70), which makes for yet another perfect post-dinner stop.

From €2.50, Mon-Sat 09:00-02:00, Sun 14:30-02:00, Viale Bastioni di Michelangelo 5, Vatican City Neighborhood, +39 06 4559 9961, gelateriaoldbridge.com, Metro: Ottaviano

Ice Cream Factory

I was skeptical at first, but was pleasantly surprised that this new entry into the gelato scene adheres wonderfully to the traditional processes. The name makes it clear that they've got a particular kind of customer in mind, but the product is every bit as authentic as what you'll find at the *gelaterie*. Don't be afraid to ask for a sample from the friendly staff: "*Posso assaggiare?*" (POSS-so assad-JAH-ray).

From €2, daily 10:00-24:00, Via Palestro 47, Facebook: Ice Cream Factory, Termini, Metro: Termini

Fatamorgana Monti

No, healthy gelato is not a mirage (as the name suggests in Italian). Fatamorgana Monti prides itself on its ingredients—all of them 100 percent natural. There is no artificial flavoring or coloring, so you can be sure that what you're tasting is the real

deal: 100 percent delicious scoops of tasty gelato (if not healthy, at least as good for you as gelato *can* be). They rotate through more than 300 recipes, and the cheery staff is happy to let you have a taste before you buy.

From €2.50, daily 12:00-24:00, until 01:00 on weekends, Via degli Zingari, 5, Monti, +39 06 4890 6955, gelateri-afatamorgana.com, Metro: Cavour

TOP NIGHTLIFE

If you've been elsewhere in Europe, you'll quickly notice that Italian nightlife has a distinct flavor. The Italians are a garrulous bunch, so the nightlife is highly conversational. Discussions are animated, with speakers gesticulating frequently and conversation volume rising and falling (more frequently rising). Get looped into one of these conversations and you might find yourself rooted to the spot until the early hours. Italian students tend to have tighter budgets, so they stretch their drinking dollars by enjoying beers or wine in the square (much cheaper than paying tourist prices for mixed drinks at the bar). This is why you'll find mostly internationals inside the bars and mostly locals outside. Amorous creepers abound at nightlife venues where tourists congregate, so ladies, stick close to your friends and keep a close eye on your drinks.

NIGHTLIFE DISTRICTS

Different neighborhoods host different kinds of nightlife (and attract very different crowds). The cheap student bars and the clubs tend to huddle together, but the glitzier clubs are sprinkled here and there throughout the city.

Trastevere

Local students like to drink beers on the steps of **Piazza Trilussa,** located right at the end of the Ponte Sisto bridge crossing the Tiber River. American study-abroad students love to hang out around **G Bar** and **Almalu Shot Bar.** With dozens of great hole-in-the-wall bars and cafés, Trastevere will reward you for ditching the map and just getting lost in its winding streets. You're sure to stumble upon something

utterly unique—something that will give you a better idea how the Roman nightlife is experienced by the Romans.

Trastevere, Bus: Sonnino/Piazza Belli

Campo de' Fiori

Shifting more towards quaint restaurants, this square is still a favorite for Rome's American students. When the sun dips behind the buildings, the "field of flowers" morphs from a daytime market to a happening nightspot. Do a lap of the square to pick out the vibe you like most. Its proximity to Largo Argentina bus stop makes it easy to find your way back to your hostel, and there are always taxis around if don't feel like taking the bus late at night. For a classy alternative to college nightlife, head down Via del Pellegrino to find

LGBT ROME

LGBT travelers will have no trouble experiencing Rome. **Via San Giovanni in Laterano** (Ancient Rome), directly behind the Colosseum, is the hub of Rome's gay scene. Here, you'll find great lunch spots, cafés, restaurants, and bars. **Coming Out** (Via di S. Giovanni in Laterano 8, Ancient Rome, +39 06 700 9871) is a favorite for its colorful drinks, welcoming scene, and rowdy parties. In Testaccio, **L'Alibi** (€10 cover, Via di Monte Testaccio 44, Testaccio, +39 06 574 3448) is one of Rome's most popular gay clubs. For more information and listings, head to **Arcigay** (Via Goito 35B, Termini, +39 06 645 011 02, arcigay.it), Italy's LGBT association.

Barnum Café (#87, +39 06 647 604 83) for a refreshing spritz and relaxed vibe. Nearby, you can enjoy extremely well-done cocktails at **Argot.**

Pantheon Neighborhood, Bus: Largo Argentina

Monti

The hottest scenes in Rome are in this up-and-coming neighborhood a far cry from the touristy areas surrounding the city's ancient attractions. With dozens of restaurants, cafés, and bars, your options are nearly unlimited. If you want to get a taste of local life, head to the square and strike up a conversation with the locals. To fit in, wear dark clothes and closed-toe shoes. Pick up a beer at the corner shop and take in the scene.

Monti, Metro: Cavour

Piazza Navona

Classy—if touristy—cafés line this square. Just off the square to the west you can find excellent and affordable local pubs, like **Bar del Fico,** offering great drinks and an extensive *aperitivo*. Head deep enough into the neighborhood and you'll stumble upon bars full of locals—you might just be the only tourist in the place.

Pantheon Neighborhood, Bus: Largo Argentina

San Lorenzo

With dark streets largely devoid of tourists but full of mingling Italians, this is central Rome's most authentic nightlife district. East of Termini, San Lorenzo bars offer €4 drinks and there is *pizza al taglio* (by the slice) on just about every corner. The action centers on two main streets, **Via Tiburtina** and **Via dei Sardi,** from which you can turn in just about any direction and discover yet another tangle of bars and cafés. Some travelers turn up their noses at the dark streets and the milling locals, associating the combination of unfamiliar crowds and dark alleys with a bad vibe, but this combination is precisely what keeps San Lorenzo authentic; it's where Romans can let their hair down, far away from the ubiquitous crowds of tourists. Start your night at the dependable **La Piazetta** (Largo Degli Osci 15-19) for cheap beers, *aperitivo*, and pizza by the slice.

San Lorenzo, Metro: Termini

Testaccio

Rome's ancient garbage dump for used clay containers has decomposed into a hill (look closely—the entire hill is made of layer upon layer of broken ceramics). Rome's trendiest clubs have made their nests in this clay hill. For the clubs, dress up and play the part. Pull that fancy suit or dress out of your bag; Testaccio is Rome's top see-and-be-seen neighborhood, so it draws a posh crowd. Start with a lap of the district. Take a look at the lineups and the patios to get a sense of the male/female ratio. The best times are had where this ratio is at least close to 1:1. Before heading out, ask at your hostel about transportation connections. Chances are you'll be cabbing it back to your lodgings at the end of the night.

Testaccio, Metro: Piramide

BARS

Niji Café

Easily my favorite cocktail bar in Rome, this speakeasy-style lounge has hipster cred for days. Aproned and tattooed staff members (most of them sporting beards, a few of them sporting impressive handlebar moustaches) expertly mix Prohibition-era cocktails. No matter how complex the recipe, these cocktail wizards know the territory like the back of their hands. Each drink is prepared with tender loving care and served with purpose—all in a refined and funky setting reminiscent of a sumptuous reading room. Order an old-fashioned and drink in the good life. Whiskey not your thing? Tell them to surprise you.

Drinks from €7, daily 18:00-02:00, Via dei Vascellari 35, Trastevere, +39 06 581 9520, Facebook: Niji Roma, Bus: Sonnino/Piazza Belli

Almalu Shot Bar

This teensy-tiny little bar deep in the back alleys of Trastevere is famous for its creative shots. Known for its nearly endless varieties (try their Harry Potter and their Blowjob), Almalu offers excellent drink specials throughout the week—they were the innovators responsible for bringing the €1 shot night onto the scene. Because so many of the bar's drinks are consumed in an instant, this isn't the place to sit and sip. This bar is often standing room only, with customers spilling out and socializing loudly on the nearby streets.

Shots from €1, Mon-Sat 18:00-late, Via Della Scala 77, Trastevere, +39 06 5833 3558, Facebook: Almalu Trastevere, Bus: Sonnino/Piazza Belli

Vendita Libri, Cioccolata e Vino

With dozens of establishments to choose from, operators know they need a gimmick for their bar to survive in Trastevere. Some pull it off quite well; others struggle. Vendita Libri, Cioccolata e Vino ("bookstore, chocolate, and wine") takes the cake with its chocolate shots and bookish atmosphere. Its shots are—get this—served in a shot glass made of chocolate. The atmosphere is better suited to a quiet glass of wine than round after round of shots, so if you're on a bit of a tear, it's best to just pop in for a quick one and move on.

Shots from €2, Mon-Fri 18:30-02:00, Sun 14:00-02:00, Vicolo del Cinque 11a, Trastevere, +39 065 830 1868, Facebook: Rivendita Libri Cioccolata e Vino, Bus: Sonnino/Piazza Belli

G Bar

Gilded ostentatiously, G Bar draws a crowd that loves rocking out to Top 40. Getting a drink upstairs takes patience, and you'll be lucky if you can breathe downstairs. They don't enforce a max capacity, so you'll be jostled by gyrating patrons on the always-packed dance floor. This doesn't seem to affect the bar's popularity, particularly among international students and local observers. You'll quickly learn why the bar is packed every night: drinks are cheap and strong!

Shots from €2, daily 15:00-late, Vicolo Dei Cinque 60, Trastevere, +39 347 994 1825, g-bar.it, Bus: Sonnino/Piazza Belli

Q's Rummeria Rum Bar Trastevere

This place takes sugar cane-derived alcohol seriously. Running along the wall are more shades of amber than you can shake a sugar stick at. The Rum Bar serves exactly what you'd think: shots and concoctions made with rum as the base ingredient. Be sure to give the freshly casked honey rum a try. Once you get your sipper, climb the stairs to get lost in their stash of games, like Connect Four and pick-up sticks. Don't miss the retro *Playboy* covers in the stairwell.

Drinks from €3, daily 19:30-02:00, Vicolo Moroni 53, Trastevere, +39 331 996 6996, qsrummeria.it, Bus: Sonnino/Piazza Belli

Akbar

Akbar is Roman shabby-chic on steroids. Come out to this bar for coffee in the morning, an extensive *aperitivo*, or drinks late into the night. The combination of excellent drinks, funky decoration (including drippy candles and low-slung chandeliers), and unique seating packs this place with cool locals every night, and the party always goes late.

Drinks from €7, daily 10:30-02:00, Piazza in Piscinula, Trastevere, +39 06 580 0681, alembic.it, Bus: Sonnino/Piazza Belli

Freni e Frizioni

This trendy *aperitivo* bar has taken over what used to be a garage with a name that fits: Brakes and Transmissions. Chow down on their extensive nightly buffet and get stuffed for the price of a drink. In warm weather, the trendy crowd spills out onto an adjacent intimate little square. Come here and party like a local; it's a great place to find yourself pulled into conversations.

Aperitivi from €6, daily 06:30-02:00, Via del Poloteama 4/6, Trastevere, +39 064 549 7499, Bus: Sonnino/Piazza Belli

Il Baretto

It takes a bit of effort to find this place, located about a 15-minute walk from the Sonnino/Piazza Belli bus stop, but you'll be glad you did: it's an oasis of Italian trendiness almost entirely unspoiled by the tourist hordes. The crowd and staff border on pretentious, so dress nice and act the part to enjoy an excellent happy hour and an *aperitivo* to suit any budget. At sunset, enjoy the outdoor patio overlooking the city and make note of the faces in the crowd: these are people who smugly know they are in the know.

Drinks from €8, Mon-Sat 07:00-02:00, Via G. Garibaldi 27, Trastevere +39 06 589 6055, Facebook: Il Baretto, Bus: Sonnino/Piazza Belli

Drunken Ship

Drunken Ship is a fave with the expat crew looking to down shots and play some beer pong. Don't come looking for especially cheap drinks or an authentic local experience. Instead, come for an enjoyable time getting drunk with fellow international backpackers. Somehow the guys at Drunken Ship have figured out how to do the impossible: convincing cheap students to buy expensive drinks every night of the week!

Drinks from €5.50, daily 15:00–03:00, Piazza Campo de' Fiori 20, Campo de' Fiori, +39 06 6830 0535, drunkenship.com, Campo de' Fiori, Bus: Navona

I Giganti della Notte

My fellow international students and I affectionately called this place "cheap bar," and the years have changed nothing. Every time I'm in Rome, I revisit my old stomping grounds and sit at one of the high-top tables outside and enjoy the scene on Campo de' Fiori with a beer or a cocktail. It's a great place for simple but inexpensive mixed drinks to get the night started.

Drinks from €4, daily 19:00–03:00, Piazza Campo de' Fiori 26, Campo de' Fiori, +39 06 6880 4095, Facebook: I Giganti Della Notte—Campo de' Fiori, Bus: Navona

Caffè Peru

Caffè Peru is possibly the cheapest pregame bar in Rome. With the robed Giordano Bruno statue in Campo de' Fiori at your back, turn left and exit the piazza; turn right after a block and continue up that street for a block. You'll see the brightly lit Caffè Peru long before you arrive. Don't come here for the décor, but do come for the unassuming atmosphere and the cheap drinks. Tucked away as it is, the bar is often empty, making it a perfect place for a quiet and cheap drink—a good opportunity to plan your evening's itinerary.

Drinks from €3, Mon-Sat 06:30–02:00, Sun 09:00–21:00, Via di Monserrato 46, Campo de' Fiori, +39 06 687 9548, caffeperu.it, Bus: Navona

Bar del Fico

Named after the piazza outside, Bar del Fico is a popular and casual spot to grab a drink and a bite with friends. It's best known for its extensive *aperitivo* buffet—I'll admit it, I've eaten my fill at the buffet many times (and all for the price of my rum and Coke) at the rustic wooden tables. A charming and simple bar, you might find yourself returning here more than once during your stay.

Drinks from €5, daily 08:00–02:00, Piazza del Fico 26, Piazza Navona, Pantheon Neighborhood, +39 066 880 8413, bardelfico.com, Bus: Largo Argentina

Abbey Theater

This Irish pub just around the corner from Piazza Navona is a great spot to catch a game (with 14 TVs, you're guaranteed a good seat). It also boasts free Wi-Fi, excellent happy hours, and live Irish music on the weekends. It's unlikely that you came to Rome for Irish music, €12 burgers, and pints of Guinness, but if you did, look no further.

Drinks from €5.50, daily 12:00–02:00, from 11:00 on weekends, Via del Governo Vecchio 51, Piazza Navona, Pantheon Neighborhood, +39 06 686 1341, abbey-rome.com, Bus: Largo Argentina

Scholar's Lounge

Located between Largo Argentina and Piazza Venezia, Scholar's is a cornerstone of Rome's student scene. Ask anybody who's spent a semester or more in Rome about Scholar's and they'll almost certainly have a number of stories to relate. They're open late, with karaoke nights twice a week and excellent cover bands on the weekends. Game on? They'll be playing it no matter what the hour. It's a great place to meet English-speaking students and to tip a glass or two of whiskey with friends new or old (they have an excellent selection of Irish and Scottish single malts).

Drinks from €5, daily 11:00–03:30, Via del Plebiscito 101, Pantheon Neighborhood, +39 06 6920 2208, scholarsloungerome.com, Bus: Largo Argentina or Piazza Venezia

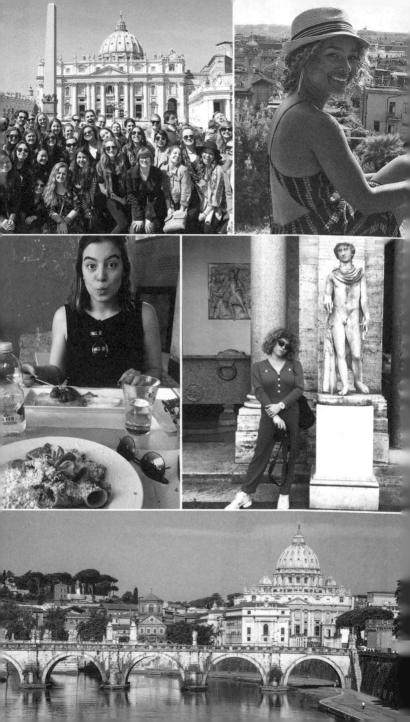

Open Baladin

Italy is a wine-drinking country. Beer buffs will be hard pressed to find the perfect pint in Rome (it's around, it's just not a specialty). A fan of IPAs? Good luck. Baladin's, with their wide selection of on-tap and bottled beer, will get you as close as you can get in the city. Along with their artisan beers, the bar serves a full menu of massive burgers, from the standard bacon cheeseburger to more creative versions topped with mozzarella and basil mayonnaise. Their hand-cut fries are delicious—salted perfectly, they'll have you reaching for that pint glass.

Pints from €5.50, daily 12:00-01:00, Via degli Specchi 6, Pantheon Neighborhood, +39 06 683 8989, openbaladinroma.it, Bus: Largo Argentina

BlackMarket Hall

If you're into cocktails and speakeasy-style lounges, this is a winner in the Monti nightlife scene. BlackMarket Hall is one of the only venues in Monti that offers outdoor garden seating. This makes it a popular spot, so I highly recommend reservations (via WhatsApp or email), especially on weekends when live jazz packs the place out. Come for the gastropub menu, stick around for the music, and get lost in the tangle of rooms while sipping elegant throwback cocktails that'll have you longing nostalgically for days that passed long before you were born. Its sister lounge, **BlackMarket Art Gallery** (Via Panisperna 101, +39 339 822 7541, blackmarketartgallery.it), offers classy cocktails in an intimate setting.

Via dè Ciancaleoni 31, +39 393 353 0498, facebook. com/blackmarkethall, blackmarkethall@gmail.com

CLUBS

If you want to go clubbing, Testaccio is the place. More than a dozen clubs and bars encircle this mound that rises up near the Piramide metro stop. To make the most of a night at the Roman clubs, dress to the nines (or at least the high eights) and pregame hard (drinking at the clubs is expensive). At the end of the night, plan to split a cab home with friends (try not to get separated from the group). Do your research and pick a few places to check out. Choose your favorite before midnight—when the clubs start to fill out around then, the lines can stretch for what feels like miles.

Akab

Akab, a two-story club with a massive dance floor, is Testaccio's best-known and longest-running dance club, spinning a wide mix of popular EDM, hip-hop, and R&B. You'll hear everything from house and club techno to "Straight Outta Compton" hip-hop throwbacks. Check the website for events—some events mean you won't get in without a ticket. Be sure to dress well to get through the door.

€10 cover, Thurs-Sat 23:30-05:00, Via di Monte Testaccio 69, Testaccio, +39 06 5725 0585, akabclub.com, Metro: Piramide

L'Alibi

L'Alibi is a popular gay-friendly club that is famous for its drag shows, which take place during breaks in the funky house and club techno. Check out the website for details and shows. Recently, they've taken to calling Friday night "Hetero Night," but that's more of a marketing ploy than anything (the club might not be overtly gay friendly on Friday nights, but all are welcome throughout the weekend). Rock out over two dark levels with low-slung arches, or, during the summer months, head outside to the open patio and terrace.

€10 cover, Thurs-Sun 23:30-05:00, Via di Monte Testaccio 44, Testaccio, +39 06 574 3448, lalibi.it, Metro: Piramide

Shari Vari Playhouse

Shari Vari, a posh and almost obscenely pretentious nightclub, comes with discerning doormen and velvet ropes to keep the riffraff out. If you can get past them, you'll be in the midst of Rome's sexiest bartenders and patrons. Excellent DJs keep the party moving all night. Shari Vari is popular among Rome's young professionals and the jet-set elite who are passing through; those who come here can afford the €12 drinks, and they dress to impress. If you want to avoid the pretentiousness of the late-night crowd, stop in here for coffee and breakfast and even *aperitivo* before the venue transforms into its trendy, swanky house and techno-spinning self.

No cover, drinks €10 during the week, €13 on the weekend, no T-shirts, shorts, or flip-flops, Mon 08:30-19:00, Tues-Sat 08:30-04:00, Sun 08:30-02:00, Via di Torre Argentina 78, Pantheon Neighborhood, +39 06 680 6936, sharivari.it, info@sharivari.it, Bus: Largo Argentina

TOP SHOPPING & MARKETS

Italy is one of the world's premier shopping destinations. Its reputation as purveyor of some of the trendiest and most elegant fashion has made Rome a destination city for the fashion forward. You can find everything in this city, from €1,200 purses and €5,000 suits all the way down to much cheaper clothes better suited to the traveling lifestyle (and budget). Even if you're not planning to max the plastic, enjoy the window-shopping. Time your visit to coincide with the July-August and January-February end-of-season *saladi* (sales) and you might just find some great deals. You can always find bargains at the outdoor markets.

SHOPPING DISTRICTS

Via del Corso

Translating directly to "Way of the Race," Via del Corso was once just that: a horse-racing course. Horse racing here was a popular spectator sport until a noblewoman saw a gruesome accident just beneath her window. The city council quickly moved to outlaw horse racing in Rome. Today, Via del Corso, extending south from Piazza del Popolo toward Piazza Venezia, is a bustling modern avenue with tons of recognizable Italian brands and, of course, plenty of international brands like Diesel, H&M, and Zara. It's cheaper than the ritzy shopping district closer to the Spanish Steps.

North Rome, Metro: Flaminio or Spagna, Bus: Piazza Venezia

Shopping Triangle of Death

Leave Via del Corso toward the Spanish Steps and you'll enter the area I've affectionately dubbed the Shopping Triangle of Death, home to haute couture brands like Zegna, Gucci, Prada, Yves Saint Laurent, and Louis Vuitton, and the graveyard of many a credit card. Near the Piazza di Spagna, the triangle comprises three streets: Via del Corso, Via del Babuino, and Via del Tritone. This is where fashion-conscious Italians come to spend their inheritance. The target market is shoppers with deep,

even bottomless, pockets—for the rest of us, it's diverting window-shopping.

North Rome, Metro: Spagna

MARKETS

Porta Portese

This Sunday-morning market is a fundamental part of the true Roman experience. Throughout history, vendors have sold their wares just outside of the city walls (inside the walls, the taxes cut into profits). While the ancient walls of Rome fell long ago, the tradition survives today. Go early on Sunday morning. Take only a bit of spending cash with you, and leave your valuables locked up in the hostel: Porta Portese is notoriously haunted by quick-fingered pickpockets who prey on bewildered tourists lost in the throngs of shoppers.

Sun 06:30-13:30, Trastevere, Bus: Sonnino/Piazza Belli

Mercato Trionfale

Rome's biggest and most central food market is just a couple of blocks from the entrance of the Vatican Museums. The market is well worth a detour just to check out the vast selection of meats, produce, and fresh breads and pastas. It's a great place to stock up for a picnic in any number of Rome's parks or squares.

Via la Goletta 1, Mon-Fri 07:00-14:00, until 19:00 on Tues and Fri, mercatotrionfale.it, Metro: Cipro

TOP PARKS & RECREATION

Giardino degli Aranci

Located on the south side of town, across the river from Trastevere and just north of Testaccio, this picturesque little garden of orange trees faces north and west. With Testaccio's daily farmers market nearby (always a hub of Roman activity and a great place to pick up some inexpensive pic-

nic-ready food), this is an excellent, quiet spot to sit on the grass and enjoy a meal alfresco. Take in the view from the square, and before descending back into Rome's screaming traffic, check out the nearby Aventine Keyhole (also called Il Buco di Roma or the Mouth of Rome). Through the keyhole you can see three sovereign states: the Order of the Knights of Malta in the foreground, Italy in the middle distance, and, perfectly framed by the garden, the Vatican's highest point, the dome of St. Peter's. The keyhole often has a line, but it's worth the wait. Pictures through the keyhole rarely turn out, so you'll have to commit the view to memory.

To get here, take the metro (Line B) to Circo Massimo and head north along the track of the Circo Massimo. From there, hang a left and go up the hill after about 300 meters.

Free, 07:00–sunset, Testaccio, Metro: Circo Massimo

Gianicolo Hill

Gianicolo (jah-KNEE-koh-lo), rising behind Trastevere and south of the Vatican, offers a beautiful panorama of the ancient parts of the city (and some of the modern ones as well). See if you can't pick out the domed roof of the Pantheon, green Palatine Hill, the crest of the Colosseum, and even Termini train station way off in the distance. The impressive building off to your left is the old Palace of Justice. For local teenagers and the *mammoni* (older men who still live at home with their mothers), this is the place to sneak away from parents' prying eyes for a bit of sun-

set smooching. This hike is a good way to cap a visit to the Vatican and St. Peter's Basilica.

Free, always open, Vatican City Neighborhood, Metro: Ottaviano

Villa Borghese

This picturesque, tree-lined park, just to the north and east of town above Piazza del Popolo, was once a noble family's private gardens. Today, it's Rome's most popular public playground, with manicured paths, a full-scale replica of Shakespeare's Globe Theatre, thousands of trees, a zoo, and a world-class art gallery (the Galleria Borghese). A favorite picnic spot for locals and tourists alike, this is the best place to enjoy the sun on a beautiful day. Its one-mile circumference makes it an ideal area to run at the beginning of the day. (A lap including the Borghese that starts from your hostel in Termini will probably be a little shy of four miles—a great way to jump-start your day if you're an early riser.) To add a bit of exercise and fun to your day here, rent a four-person **pedal cart** (€15/hour) or a **bike** (€6/hour) and explore the far corners of the park.

North Rome, Metro: Barberini

MAMMONI: DECONSTRUCTING THE MAMA'S BOY

We all know a mama's boy—the one who just can't live without mom's cooking (and often laundry services as well). Well, in Italy, you've got about 10 million of them. Italian mothers put their sons on pedestals, smothering them with love, food, clothes, and just about anything else a mother could do for her son. Weaning the men off of this steady stream of loving care has proved difficult. With life so good, why would you ever move out? Add that to the prohibitive costs of buying an apartment or condo in town and you've got the dilemma so typical for Italian men: Should I stay or should I go?

Though it feels a bit like the plot of *Step Brothers*, in Rome, it's not unusual for Italian men to live at home until they break the ripe age of 40. Even then, the economic prospects are difficult when it comes to buying property. They might make more than enough to live comfortably, but they don't have enough to purchase their own home. Where does all their expendable income go? Food, fashion, and nightlife. *La dolce vita*!

This also introduces a dilemma: Where do you take a hot date? You might notice Italian couples getting hot and heavy on the dance floor (or anywhere else for that matter). They're just being pragmatic; they really don't have anywhere to bring their partners that guarantees them privacy. Viewpoints like the one on Gianicolo Hill fill up with couples after dark—they've found the only kind of privacy that many of them are afforded (the public kind).

Villa Doria Pamphili

Dwarfing even the Villa Borghese, the Pamphili park is Rome's biggest. While the Villa Borghese is a site perfect for leisure, sprawling Pamphili is an ideal spot for exercise. There is much to see in the park, and to catch it all you'll need to keep up a brisk walking pace. Better yet, use the park and its trails (as so many of the locals do) as a running track. You'll see all there is to see in the park, and you'll definitely earn yourself a guilt-free night of food, cocktails, and gelato. If you've time to spare in Rome, it would be easy to spend almost an entire day exploring the park, wandering the manicured gardens, and getting away from the crowds in the extensive network of trails.

Free, Trastevere and Vicinity, Bus: Villa Pamphili

TOP TOURS

If you're on a tight budget, a high-quality tour in Rome may be beyond your means. For history buffs, though, a tour guide's inside knowledge is worth almost any price. If you've come to Rome to learn, choose the cheap watering holes and buffets over cocktails and dining out—spend the difference on an expert tour guide and your grand tour will be immensely rewarding.

Walks of Italy

Walks of Italy connects you with excellent local guides who bring the ancient, confusing, and overwhelming history of Rome to vivid life (like the archeological strata, Rome's history is piled layer upon layer, century upon century). Walks of Italy has highly experienced guides who can help you make sense of it all, and they tailor their mixture of dense history and comic relief to suit the tastes of each audience. Their attentive booking service makes arranging one of their tours a cinch.

Walking tours starting at €29, museum tours from €49, +39 069 480 4888, walksofitaly.com/rome-tours

Eating Italy Food Tours

Gastro tours, a relatively new concept, have taken the world by storm, and Kenny and his team are on the forefront of the movement. They have developed an excellent walking tour through Testaccio, one of Rome's richest neighborhoods. Sample the fruits, sweets, pastries, *salumi* (cold cuts, including but not limited to salami), cheeses, pastas, coffees, and gelati that weave their way through daily Roman life, all on this three-hour neighborhood walk. It'll be easy to see why there are now dozens of touring companies trying to replicate Eating Italy's successful model.

Testaccio Food Tour €75, +39 391 358 3117, eatingeuropetours.com

The Roman Guy Tours

High-end travelers should consider this passionate team of guides, headed by Sean Finelli, whom I'm proud to call a friend. He's designed all sorts of unique itineraries, from food tours in Trastevere to night tours of the Vatican and Colosseum. Sean gives the standard tours a twist with fun transportation methods around the city like pedal-assist bikes and golf carts, both of which save time and energy that's better spent at the attractions themselves.

Tours from $59 USD, +1 888 290 5595, theromanguy.com

Private Guides

Silvia Poggiani's (silviapoggiani@gmail.com, +39 3337371599) passion for Rome is immediately evident. Her small-group walks can be tailored to suit just about any itinerary or interest.

Francesca Pedulla (roma-tour.it, fmpedulla@libero.it, +39 3384389572) keeps visitors of any age fascinated with her encyclopedic knowledge of Italian art, history, architecture, and culture. Families and groups of friends traveling together in Rome can really maximize their time by reserving a day with either of these local and licensed guides. Figure about €60/hour plus entry fees—well worth the cost.

TOP HOSTELS

Hostels cluster around the Termini train station. Once a rougher part of town, this neighborhood has really cleaned up its act, and it gives you tremendous value for your money. Streets are brighter and cleaner than they once were, and quite a few inexpensive restaurants have opened—perfect for tucking in before heading into the pricier parts of town. If the hostels below are full, you can find more options at **hostelworld.com,** and there are always budget private apartments on **airbnb.com.** Trim your search to the Monti and Trastevere districts for the best combination of value and location.

The Yellow Hostel

With a 300-bed capacity, the Yellow is one of the most popular options in town. The owners have worked hard to develop a one-stop-shopping experience for backpackers coming to Rome. The result is a fun, social hostel with a bar, an on-site restaurant with substantial breakfasts, nightly DJs and parties, a micro subterranean disco, frequent walking tours, bike rentals, and even group yoga sessions. The rooms are washed down every day with industrial-strength bleach, so the smell can be overpowering for an hour or so after, but at least you know they're clean! Book through their website and save 20 percent at the bar throughout your stay.

Dorms from €35, private rooms €120, 24-hour reception, free (but slow) Wi-Fi, Via Palestro 44, Termini, +39 06 446 3554, the-yellow.com, Metro: Termini

Alessandro's Palace

Alessandro's Palace, near Termini, is fun, safe, clean, and bright, with an in-house bar downstairs. There's a rooftop terrace where you can take in the cool Roman air, and for those hotter nights they have air-conditioning in all of their otherwise spartan rooms. Alessandro Palace's sister location, **Alessandro Downtown** (Via Carlo Cattaneo 23), is another solid budget option; it's on the opposite side of Termini towards the Colosseum.

Dorms from €24, private rooms €90, free Wi-Fi, sheets included, showers, towels for rent, Via Vicenza 42, Termini, +39 06 4461 958, hostelsalessandro.com, Metro: Termini

The Beehive Hotel & Hostel

The Beehive has been helping budget travelers feel at home in Rome for years. With recent updates like an organic, on-site vegetarian café and a soul-soothing outdoor garden, it's now more popular than ever. Choose from either a handful of dorm beds or a private room (for a reasonable €40/night). Check out their website for current rates and more details. If these guys don't have availability, they have access to a broad network of budget options to fall back on—they'll sort you out.

Dorms from €25, private rooms from €40, check-in 07:00-23:00, check-ins outside this window for a fee, free Wi-Fi, sheets, showers, towels for rent, nonsmoking, Via Marghera 8, Termini, +39 064 470 4553, the-beehive.com, Metro: Termini

Ciak Hostel

This is a smaller, more intimate option near the Termini neighborhood. I like this place because it feels more like home than a big commercial hostel. With only about 35 beds in funkily decorated, comfortable rooms (one room has a Madonna picture frame set over classic-car wallpaper), Ciak is more like hanging out at a friend's house than a hostel. Deluxe private rooms with double beds are worth inquiring about.

Beds from €22, free Wi-Fi, sheets, showers, towels for rent, Viale Manzoni 55, Termini, +39 06 7707 6703, ciakhostel.com, Metro: Termini

M&J Hostel

This hostel is laid-back and staffed with helpful people at the reception desk, but, without a social room to speak of, it's clear that they're not trying to create the kind of atmosphere that powers so many of Europe's great hostels. It is, however, conveniently located just steps from Termini station. Consider yourself warned: The building seems to be in something of a downward spiral. The hot water cuts out at times, and the sewage system—if the smells that occasionally waft out of the open drains are any indication—might be as old as Rome's seven hills.

Dorms from €21, posh private rooms €90, free Wi-Fi, bar downstairs, Via Solferino 9, Termini, +39 06 446 2802, mejplacehostel.com, Metro: Termini

TRANSPORTATION

It's easy to get into the center from Rome's two airports. Once you've wrapped your mind around the public transportation system, the buses, metros, and trams are great resources for budget travelers. They'll help you cover ground quickly and make the most of your sightseeing time.

GETTING THERE & AWAY

Trains and buses arrive at Rome's main train station, **Termini,** located in its namesake neighborhood just east and uphill from the city center. From Termini you can catch local buses, metro connections, and taxis to anywhere in Rome. All of my recommended hostels are within walking distance of the train station. By the way, there's an excellent food court, **Mercato Centrale,** down the tracks a bit on the south side of the station (alongside the departure area for the Leonardo Express); it serves concept street food, Napolitano pizza, and other quick, typical bites like *brocoletti* and other bio-friendly options. The culinary delights start the moment you arrive in Rome with anything-but-typical train station fare.

Plane

Rome has two airports: **Da Vinci-Fiumicino** (FCO, adr.it) and **Ciampino** (CIA, adr.it). From both airports it's roughly the same amount of time and money to get to Termini.

The **Leonardo Express Train** departs every 30 minutes from Da Vinci-Fiumicino and will get you to Termini in 30 minutes (€15). This is the fastest and most comfortable option connecting to Termini, but it's also more expensive than the buses or the slower train.

Both airports are serviced by multiple bus lines including **Terravision** (terravision.eu) and **SITBus Shuttle** (sitbusshuttle.com). Competition has driven prices down to €7 one-way and €13 round-trip, and some of the buses offer free Wi-Fi. Buses depart frequently throughout the day and they take about one hour. Check timetables and prices online. On your departure day, give yourself a little extra time—the buses fill up during peak hours.

Taxis

Roman taxis now charge a flat rate from anywhere within Roman city walls to both airports (and vice versa). The rate to and from FCO is €48; to and from the closer CIA is €30.

Train

Though most trains arrive at **Termini** station, there are two other major train stations: **Trastevere** and **Tiburtina.** If your accommodations are not in Termini, it may make more sense to arrive and leave from one of these stations. From Florence, Rome is 1.5 hours via the fast train (from €25, reservation required) and 3.5 hours via the slow train (from €20). It's about 3.5 hours (€70) from Venice. You can find overnight options on slow trains as well.

Bus

All buses connect into Termini station, but most of the travel across Italy is done via train. You can find cheap domestic connections through **Eurolines** (eurolines.it) and its affiliates.

Car

I don't recommend driving in Italy. It comes with just too much headache: traffic, parking, hidden speed-trap cameras, and ZTLs (Zona Traffico Limitato) reserved only for cars with passes. To rent a car, you'll need a passport and an international driver's license (purchase one for US$20 from AAA before leaving home). Overall costs run high when you factor in everything that you'll be paying for: rental, insurance, gas, highway tolls, and any tickets you accidentally rack up along the way.

GETTING AROUND

Navigating the streets is your first mission, but with frequent *caffé* and gelato stops, even if you get lost you'll be doing just fine. The **bus, tram, and metro systems** use the same **ticket** (€1.50), which is valid for 100 minutes.

Metro

Rome's two metro lines intersect under the main train station, Termini. The red line, **Line A,** will get you to the Spanish

Steps (stop: Piazza di Spagna) and the Vatican (stop: Ottaviano). The blue line, **Line B,** zips you over to the Colosseum (stop: Colosseo) and the Testaccio neighborhood farther south (stop: Piramide). The newest line, Line C, opened recently, but it's not of much use to tourists (it's mostly used by commuters).

Bus

Buses in Rome work well but operate without timetables. Purchase a *biglietto* (ticket) at any *tabacchi* (tobacco shop). Once you're on the bus, be sure to validate your ticket in the yellow boxes. Non-validated tickets can earn you a €50 fine. If an inspector catches you without a validated ticket, he or she may insist on taking you to an ATM so you can pay the fine on the spot. Ask for the written mail-in ticket instead to ensure these inspectors are legitimate, and whatever you do, don't hand over your passport or ID because they may hold it ransom for cash.

Orient yourself by getting familiar with the main bus points in the city: **Termini** (near most hostels), **Largo Argentina** (Pantheon, historic center, nightlife), and **Piazza Venezia** (Vittorio Emanuele Monument, Via del Corso, Colosseum, and Scholar's Lounge). If you plan to use the buses frequently, you'll want to be familiar with a few routes. **Bus H** is the express bus from Termini to Trastevere, a neighborhood that doesn't yet have a metro station. For Trastevere, get off at **Sonnino/Piazza Belli,** just after you cross the river. **Buses 40** and **64** connect Termini and Vatican City, hitting the major Largo Argentina and Piazza Venezia bus stops along the way.

Tram

Rome has a limited but expanding tram network. **Tram 8** connects Piazza Venezia in central Rome with the Trastevere neighborhood all the way to Villa Pamphili. You may see other lines in town. As they don't intersect, riding them is really quite simple. Validate your ticket on the tram just as you would on the bus or metro.

Taxi

Taxis are a good way to get home at the end of the night, and they're affordable if you split the cost with friends. If you're riding in the center during the day, make sure that the meter reads Tariffa 1 and that it starts at no more than €5 when you get in. The Tariffa 1 zone covers all of Rome inside the old city walls. As soon as you go outside of that, you'll jump to Tariffa 2. At night, taxis start their meters at €6.50. This might seem steep, but I've found that the meters climb quite slowly, so it all comes out about the same as other European capitals. You won't find flat rates to anywhere other than the airport—if you're offered a flat rate, they're probably trying to take you for a ride. Turn them down. Uber operates here, but it will cost you significantly more than a taxi.

Bicycle

Rome's rough roads and devil-may-care attitude towards traffic laws translate to a city that isn't remotely bicycle friendly. Two-wheeled, human-powered transportation

is not recommended. There are rental options in Villa Borghese—where you'll find a few kilometers of trails without a car in sight. Outside of the park, riding is a harrowing experience. Via Appia Antica, the old Roman highway leading south to Naples and Sicily, is great to explore by bike—and there are tons of cafés and catacombs along the route.

DAY TRIPS

Touring Rome's major sights will easily fill three days and more. But if you've got time to spare, there are excellent options for day trips outside the city center.

Via Appia Antica

The Ancient Appian Way, which once connected all settlements and territories south of Rome to the capital, was one of the most important roads leading to Ancient Rome. It's still possible to walk a several-kilometer section just outside of the city. Along the way are a nearly endless string of crumbling churches, catacombs, tombs, and ancient ruins, making an Appian Way bike tour or walking tour highly worthwhile. It'll also give you a glimpse of the Italian countryside, something no amount of time in Rome can do.

Allow just about a full day for this excursion from the city center. Take bus 118 (leaves often) heading south toward the Via Appia Antica. Get off at Appia Pignatello—Erode Attico and follow the signs to the Via Appia Antica. From there, it's a three-kilometer walk back into the city center, where you can hop on the metro (Line B) at Circo Massimo. Rent bikes at **Appia Antica Café** (€10/2 hours, Via Appia Antica 175, daily 08:00-sunset, appiaanticacaffe.it, +39 06 8987 9575).

Free, always open, Greater Rome

HELP!

Tourist Information Centers

Many tourist information centers claim to be unbiased, but, in fact, they only promote a limited number of tours—inevitably those offered by their partners. Pop in for a quick rundown of the city and a free map, but think twice before biting at the lures they'll dangle in front of your nose. They're rarely the best-value options.

Pickpockets & Safety

Pickpockets take advantage of the commotion at train stations or public transit to snag tourists' wallets. On crowded trains, they'll slash your purse's straps so quickly that you won't even realize it's gone. Organize your bag in a way that will let you get at what you need throughout the day without flashing your cash, plastic, or valuables. Pickpockets dress fashionably (Roman camouflage) so they're not easy to spot. They often work with teams of young kids (as young as 8-12 years old—echoes of *Oliver Twist*) and hang out in the most touristy areas looking for easy marks. Be on

your guard in the following places: metros, bus 64, Spanish Steps, Termini train station, Campo de' Fiori, the Colosseum, and even inside the Vatican Museums.

Ladies should expect plenty of attention from locals. Keep your wits about you and try to ignore the catcalls. Be particularly wary when taking cabs late at night or wandering the streets (try not to be caught alone after midnight). Italian men can be persistent and handsy, sometimes even aggressive. If somebody is bothering you, seek safety in numbers or, if you're in an establishment, talk to the staff.

Emergencies
Dial 118 for an ambulance, or 113 for police.

Hospital
Policlinico Umberto I
Via del Policlinico 155
+39 06 499 71

US Embassy
Via Vittorio Veneto 119
+39 06 467 41

FLORENCE

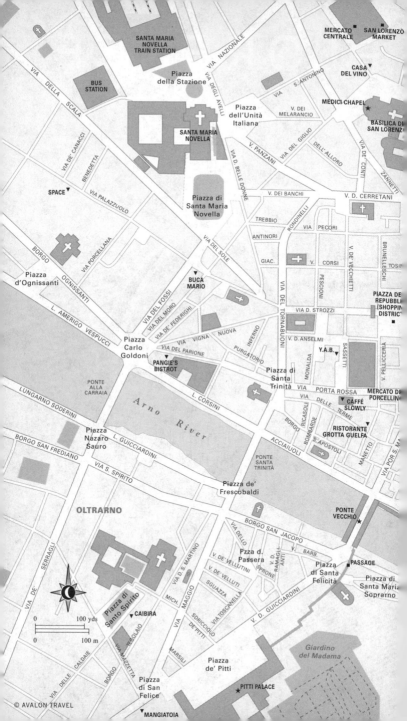

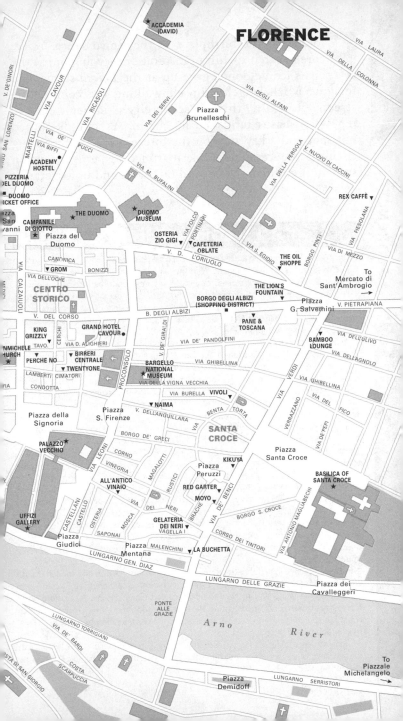

Florence is the birthplace of the Renaissance. You're sure to catch a whiff of inspiration as you glimpse the city's iconic dome, gaze up at the *David* statue, and imagine Michelangelo himself walking the cobblestone streets. Luckily, this Tuscan city's larger-than-life reputation hasn't tarnished its charm. As a study-abroad hot spot and a key stop on the international backpacking circuit, Florence offers modern attractions, too—from fun student nightlife to cheap and tasty eats and unforgettable gelato.

FLORENCE 101

Founded as a Roman outpost in AD 59, Florence sat on a crucial trade route connecting Rome with the rest of the continent. With the fall of the Roman Empire, all of Europe descended into chaos. Florence was one of the first regions to bounce back economically from the centuries-long turmoil of the Dark Ages. After being traded back and forth between warring rivals, Florence finally emerged as an independent city-state around AD 1100. The city used banking and trade to extend its influence around the subcontinent and beyond as it grew into the medieval age.

By the 14th century, a quarter of Florence's population was supported by the wool and textile industries. This trade allowed one family, the Medicis, to accrue immense riches and power—it didn't hurt that the Medicis were the bankers to the pope, either. Cosimo de Medici (1389-1464) was the first of the family to wield significant influence over the city from behind the scenes. The wealthy Florentines had the luxury of splurging on the finer things in life, like art and architecture, which helped Cosimo kick off a wave of artistic, literary, and architectural innovation.

Lorenzo de Medici (1449-1492), Cosimo's grandson, was the family's biggest patron of the arts and devoted vast sums to a handful of promising artists. Some of his friends (Michelangelo, Leonardo da Vinci, Botticelli) changed the course of history thanks to support from Lorenzo. This enlightenment of the human spirit and intellect—known as the Renaissance, or rebirth—accelerated social and economic development, slowly wrenching the rest of Europe from the grip of feudalism. During the Renaissance, buildings became taller, windows bigger, and decoration more exuberant. Paintings were brighter and more lifelike. Artists came to be paid in relation to their skill, not as a function of the costs of their raw art materials. Technical developments like sewage disposal allowed for population growth and healthier, longer lives. It may seem like a stretch, but one wealthy family's investment in the arts revolutionized the world and has a lasting impact today.

In 1862, Florence joined the Kingdom of Italy. Population growth and modernization efforts, like cutting new boulevards for traffic and commerce, continued into the 20th century. During World War II, Nazi troops occupied Florence for a year before Allied forces chased them out. The departing Nazis destroyed as many river crossings as they could but spared the Ponte Vecchio, thanks to a rare consideration by Hitler of the historic importance of the bridge.

Today, Florence's lifeblood is tourism, tourism, and more tourism. This historic city sees millions of visitors every year, but with my suggestions, you'll be able to find your own little corner of this fascinating Renaissance town.

PLAN AHEAD

RESERVATIONS

Most museums, including the Uffizi and Accademia, are closed on Mondays, creating a rush of tourists every Tuesday.

Reservations are highly recommended/required for the following sights:

Accademia (firenzemusei.it)

Uffizi Gallery (firenzemusei.it)

Duomo climb (Grande Musei del Duomo ticket required, book at museumflorence.com or at the ticket office)

Private sightseeing companies often masquerade as official websites for state-run museums, and they inflate their ticket prices dramatically. When purchasing tickets, only use the official websites listed in this book.

PASSES

Firenze Card

The **Firenze Card** (€72, valid for 72 hours, free public transportation included during validity, firenze-card.it) provides free entry and line-skipping privileges at most of Florence's major museums. Before purchasing the card, add up the entry fees for all the sights you plan to see. Your three days of exhaustive sightseeing kick off the moment you enter your first sight, so be sure to line up your visits within this window. If one of your three days falls on a Monday, when museums are closed, it'll be more difficult to justify the price (the same goes for Tuesdays, when crowds will slow your progress).

Duomo Sights

The Duomo itself is free and no ticket is needed to enter, though lines can get long. A single €15 ticket covers entry to all Duomo-related sights (Baptistry, bell tower climb, Duomo Museum, and the dome climb). The ticket, which you can buy online (museumflorence.com) or at the poorly signed ticket office from often-frustrated staff (7 Piazza San Giovanni), can be validated up to six days after purchase; once you validate it, you have 48 hours to see all the included sights. Reservations are required for the dome climb, and they are recommended for the bell tower and museum. Opening times frequently change, so check the website for up-to-date information.

FLORENCE

THREE DAY ITINERARY

As the de facto capital of the Renaissance, Florence is packed to the rafters with famous museums holding some of the world's most renowned artwork. People who spend less than three days here often spend their time madly dashing through the streets, racing from gallery to gallery. For the Uffizi and Accademia, I highly recommend making reservations well ahead of time. Skipping the lines means more time to enjoy the masterpieces.

DAY 1: BENVENUTO A FIRENZE!
MORNING
Today you'll be getting acquainted with the city. Grab a hearty breakfast at your hotel or a nearby café before striking out to join the walking tour. At 11:00, meet your local guide in front of Santa Maria Novella for a free and fun two-hour walking tour with **Florence Free Tour.** You'll cover the basics of local history and culture. You'll stroll past the **Duomo,** numerous famous piazze, and the **Uffizi,** and, close to the end of your walk, you'll learn about the history of the Ponte Vecchio.

AFTERNOON
Depending on where you end your tour, visit either **Oil Shoppe** or **All'Antico Vinaio** for fresh and cheap sandwiches to keep you going. Head back toward the iconic **Ponte Vecchio.** If you didn't get your fill of pictures during the tour, snap as many as you like now—the views up and down the river make incredible backgrounds for selfies.

Cross the bridge into the **Oltrarno** neighborhood and meander upriver and uphill, stopping to pick up a bottle of wine and, if you're planning a midafternoon snack, something perfect for a picnic at **Piazzale Michelangelo.** When you get to the top of the hill, take a seat on the steps and drink in the view (and your wine). You can see the Duomo and San Lorenzo, along with the spine of Santa Croce and the tower of the Palazzo Vecchio. Before you leave, get a few pictures of the replica of the world's most famous statue, Michelangelo's *David.*

EVENING
Did all that climbing make you hungry? Walk back down the hill, but hang a right on Via dei Benci and cross the Ponte alle Grazie to my favorite spot in the Santa Croce neighborhood for *aperitivi,* **Moyo.** Enjoy a drink and an impressive buffet of simple local dishes while listening to the cool grooves from the DJ.

It's probably still early, so go back to your hostel for a bit of a rest and perhaps a shower (walking in the Italian sun is sweaty work). Once you're refreshed, get ready for a crazy night out!

LATE
Head back to the Santa Croce neighborhood to kick your night off right. Try any (or all) of my favorite Santa Croce spots, including **Naima, The Lion's Fountain,** and **Kikuya.** Go to **Red Garter** last (it's great late).

DAY 2: UFFIZI & ACCADEMIA
MORNING
Overachiever? Get in line by 07:30 (yes, AM) at the **Uffizi** to avoid the lines that stretch out into the square by midmorning. Or better yet, sleep in, and as you walk past the long lineup, pat yourself on the back for making reservations ahead of time! You'll probably spend at least two hours exploring this world-class museum.

AFTERNOON
Walk north from the Uffizi about 10 minutes to the Piazza del Duomo for pizza by the slice at **Pizzeria del Duomo,** or stroll down Via dell'Oriuolo to the east of the Duomo to **Caffetteria delle Oblate** for a tasty lunch at a hidden gem housed in one of Florence's many beautiful libraries. If you saved room for dessert, two of my favorite *gelaterie,* **Grom** and **Perché No!,** are just a couple of blocks away.

Spend the rest of the afternoon **climbing the dome** (reservations required) of the Duomo to get a better grasp on the scale of the engineering feat (it was built without the use of scaffolding!) that represents the Renaissance's architectural high-water mark. Vasari's frescoes of the Last Judgment, completed near the end of the 16th century, are a marvel to behold.

If you're on your game, catch your afternoon **Accademia** reservations around 16:00 today. It's a one-floor museum, so it won't take too long, but you'll want to stand at *David*'s feet for quite a while—Michelangelo's gargantuan masterpiece (not a copy this time) deserves much, much more than a passing glance.

Reward yourself with a stop at **Casa del Vino** (open later Fri-Sat), near the **Mercato Centrale,** for wine tasting with my friend Gianni. Sample some of Tuscany's best vintages from among the hundreds of bottles neatly arranged on the beautifully carved wooden shelves.

EVENING
Walk back to the hostel to put your feet up for a bit (your dogs are probably barking). Choose between classic Florentine fare at some of my favorite restaurants, like **Osteria Zio Gigi's, Buca Mario,** or **Osteria Brincello,** or enjoy an evening out where the locals go, such as **Piazza Santo Spirito** in Oltrarno. Make sure you have reservations for dinner if you pick a popular spot like Buca Mario.

LATE
Get classy at **Hotel Cavour's rooftop bar.** Enjoy a beautiful night view of central Florence while you sip a cocktail. Afterward, join the party at my favorite downtown nightspot, **Club TwentyOne.**

DAY 3: DAY TRIP OR SHOPPING
If you have the whole day, consider a day trip to **Fiesole** or any of the other **Tuscan hill towns.** If you are cramped for time, spend the morning shopping for leather goods and delicious local produce at the **San Lorenzo Market.** Have the afternoon to work with? Walk over to the **Bargello,** another one of Florence's world-class museums—this one in one of the city's oldest buildings.

TOP NEIGHBORHOODS

Florence's compact medieval center is called the Centro Storico. You can trace the old walls, the tight medieval lanes, and the city's expansion beyond these walls on any municipal map. With the Duomo in the middle, the **Centro Storico** contains most of the sights short-stay tourists will want to see. It's here that you'll find the Accademia, the Uffizi Gallery, and the Ponte Vecchio, along with quite a few of the recommended restaurants, hostels, and nightlife venues.

Santa Croce, one of my favorite districts, is a few blocks east of the Duomo on the eastern edge of the historic center. This is where you'll find some of Florence's best nightlife, from trendy *aperitivo* bars to lounges and student favorites like Kikuya and Red Garter.

Crossing the Arno River, you enter **Oltrarno,** translating to "the other side of the Arno." This district is quieter, with more upscale restaurants and a fun local scene centered on Piazza Santo Spirito. It's also home to the Pitti Palace and the access point to the Piazzale Michelangelo viewpoint—the best place in Florence to catch a sunset.

TOP SIGHTS

Uffizi Gallery

This extensive art museum fills out what were once the offices of the astronomically wealthy Medici family. The galleries and corridors are crammed with priceless medieval and Renaissance works of art. As you walk through the Uffizi, you're walking forward in time, from flat, gold-encrusted medieval triptychs to the stunning Michelangelo masterpiece *Tondo Doni*. Other highlights include Botticelli's *Birth of Venus*, 10 Titians, and noteworthy works by da Vinci and Raphael, just to name a few. Lines can be long, so either make reservations or go early (07:30) or late (17:30) to avoid the crowds.

€12.50, €4 reservation, free first Sun of the month, Tues-Sun 08:15-18:35, closed Mon, Piazzale degli Uffizi, Centro Storico, +39 055 975 7007, uffizi.firenze.it

Accademia

Gracefully occupying a single floor, this museum is the permanent home of Michelangelo's colossal little squirt, *David*. This magnificent example of sculptural *contraposto* (a stance where the weight is placed on one foot, with the corresponding hip jutting out slightly, adding a suggestion of movement to an otherwise static pose) captures the moment just before the pint-sized underdog slew the giant in the biblical story of David and Goliath. Catch his gaze, and notice exaggerated features like furrowed eyebrows and veiny, oversized

hands, which add weight and tension to the piece. The posture and embellishments go a long way in bringing this stone to life.

As you walk down the corridor toward the larger-than-life sculpture, you'll be flanked by Michelangelo's "prisoners"—projects that the master could never quite bring himself to finish. The marble spoke to Michelangelo; he believed it was his job to free the shapes trapped within the stone. One afternoon in his workshop, the sculptor stood immobile, staring at a large block of marble for what seemed like ages. A man approached him and asked what he was doing. "Working," he replied.

€12.50 (cheaper when there are no required extra exhibits), additional €4 for reservation, expect 1-to 2.5-hour-long lines without reservations, free first Sun of the month, Tues-Sun 08:15-18:50, closed Mon, via Ricasoli 66, Centro Storico, +39 055 294 883, firenzemusei.it

The Duomo

Many say that the Cattedrale di Santa Maria del Fiore, or Duomo for short, is the building that kicked off the Renaissance. Brunelleschi, an engineer and architect, won the contract to dream up what was to be the greatest church around. He designed the floor plan and began construction on the cathedral before the technology to build a dome big enough to cap it even existed. A perfect example of form and function, the beautiful cathedral now dominates the Florentine skyline. Just about every large modern dome, from the Vatican to the U.S. Capitol in Washington DC, can point to this structure for its inspiration. Even today, the scale and beauty of the Duomo is captivating as you **climb the dome,** moving through the space between the double-domed structure to get to the top. The inside, lighter dome provides the ceiling to the church. The tiled outer dome supports the lantern at the top and protects the church from the elements, a design that greatly diminished the weight of this structure. You can also **climb the bell tower** for views over Florence. A heads up for the claustrophobic: Both hikes get tighter and darker the higher up you go.

Back in the day, you were not allowed to enter a Catholic church without having been baptized. As such, the **Baptistry** of the Duomo was separated, and new converts were baptized there so they could then enter the church holy and cleansed. This octagonal structure sports three sets of large bronze double doors. Designed by Lorenzo Ghiberti, these outward-opening doors were groundbreaking works of art, with vivid depictions of three-dimensional scenes on flat panels. The doors were a prime place to introduce the unbaptized and the illiterate to Christianity. The world-famous eastward-facing set recounts 10 stories from the Old Testament. The doors you see are replicas; to see the originals, head to the interesting and worthwhile Duomo Museum.

Free, €15 ticket covers dome climb, bell tower, Baptistry, and Duomo Museum (must enter all sights within 48 hours of first entry), Mon-Fri 10:00-17:00, May and Oct Thurs until 16:00, Nov-Apr Thurs until 16:30, Sat 10:00-16:45, Sun 13:30-16:45, Piazza del Duomo, Centro Storico, +39 055 230 2885

Duomo Museum

If you're anything like your dear author, you love geeking out about revolutionary structures like the Duomo. The Museo dell'Opera del Duomo is located just behind Brunelleschi's dome. This museum showcases Ghiberti's original Baptistry doors, along with historical drawings and images of Florence's main cathedral.

€15 ticket also covers Duomo dome climb, bell tower, and Baptistry (must enter all sights within 48 hours of first entry), Mon-Sat 09:00-19:00, Sun 09:00-13:45, last entry 45 minutes before closing, Piazza del Duomo 9, Centro Storico, +39 055 230 2885, museumflorence.com

Basilica di Santa Croce

The imposing facade of the main Franciscan church in Florence is a 19th-century veneer that covers a relatively modest 14th-century foundation. Famous for its permanently interred residents—Galileo Galilei, Lorenzo Ghiberti, Niccolo Machiavelli, and Michelangelo Buonarotti, are all buried here—the church charges €8 for admission, well worth it for those interested in more subdued Tuscan-style Renaissance churches. Just behind the church and through a garden you'll find the Leather School of Santa Croce (free, observe students' ongoing work Mon-Fri 10:00-17:30, entrance at Via San Giuseppe 5R, +39 055 244 533, scuoladelc-

uoio.com), a workshop that carries on Florence's long leatherworking tradition.

€8, Mon-Sat 09:30-17:30, Sun 14:00-17:30, Piazza Santa Croce 16, Santa Croce, +39 055 246 6105, santacroceopera.it

Bargello Museum

The Bargello deserves to be ranked among the greatest museums of Florence, but visitors tend to overlook it—more a result of museum overload than any fault of the Bargello. Its smaller crowds mean less jostling and more time to enjoy sculptures by Renaissance masters in relative silence. Donatello's *David*, with his jaunty cap and his lithe boyish figure, starkly contrasts with Michelangelo's thickly muscled and exuberant figure down the street. You'll also find Donatello's armored *St. George* statue (representing the Armorers guild), which was taken from its original exterior niche at the Orsanmichele Church and placed here to keep it out of the elements. The museum is housed in one of Florence's oldest and most regal buildings, a 13th-century palace that has, through the years, served as a prison, an execution courtyard, and police barracks. Each time I'm in Florence I make my way to the Bargello not only to see the statues, but also to admire the impressive inner courtyard, staircases, and halls.

€7, free first Sun of the month, mid-Apr-Oct daily 08:15-17:00, closed 1st, 3rd, and 5th Mon of the month; Nov-mid-Apr daily 08:15-14:00, Via del Proconsolo 4, Centro Storico, +39 055 238 8606, bargellomusei. beniculturali.it

Palazzo Vecchio

With foundations dating to the 14th century, this is Florence's old fortified town hall. It was built like a fortress because of the turmoil that frequently boiled over into outright conflict; Florence fought neighboring city-states and with itself (warring political factions made Florentine politics a bloody mess), making defensive features necessary. This didn't stop the fighting, but it did allow whomever was in power to keep challengers at arm's length. The rooms (more than 20 of them) are sumptuously decorated, many of them with Renaissance frescoes celebrating the Medicis. A tour should take about two hours, lon-

ger if you explore the temporary exhibits, which are often well worth the extra time. Climbing the tower costs extra, but the photo op from the top (with the Duomo in the frame) shouldn't be missed. In one of these rooms in 1527, a fight broke out between opposing political factions. In the melee, a chair was thrown; it smashed through a window and struck a statue in the Piazza della Signoria, breaking its arm into three pieces. That statue: Michelangelo's *David*. Oops.

Courtyard free, museum €10, tower climb €10, museum and tower €14, Apr-Sept Fri-Wed 09:00-23:00, Thurs 09:00-14:00, Oct-March Fri-Wed 09:00-19:00, Thurs 09:00-14:00, tower has shorter hours and closes when it rains, last entry to either one hour before closing, Piazza della Signoria, Centro Storico, +39 055 276 8325, commune.fi.it

Basilica di San Lorenzo & Medici Chapels

San Lorenzo was the parish church of the noble Medici family, and, if you've been following along, it won't surprise you to learn that it's one of the grandest and most elegantly decorated churches in town. The large and roughshod exterior might be dwarfed by the nearby Duomo, but you'll find the true treasure on the opposite side of the church: the Medici family tombs. Just about every important member of the noble family is buried here in ornate crypts. If you have any doubts about how big a deal these guys were, the tombs will clear up the confusion.

Basilica €6 (operamedicealaurenziana.org), Medici chapels €8 (firenzemusei.it), free on first Sun of the month, Basilica: Mon-Sat 10:00-17:00, Sun 13:30-17:00, Medici Chapels: Apr-Oct daily 08:15-16:20, Nov-March daily 08:15-13:20, Piazza di San Lorenzo, Centro Storico, +39 055 238 8602

Orsanmichele Church

Arguably more famous for its exterior than its interior, this church is a testament to the importance of the trades in Renaissance Florence. The church auctioned off niches around the facades of the building to the professional guilds of the city. Wanting to outdo each other (and fully utilize this billboard space), the guilds hired master sculptors to artfully represent their sponsors. See if you can pick out the

niches representing the Woodworkers and Stoneworkers, the Bankers, the Wool and Textile, the Shoemakers, and the Doctors guilds. Ghiberti, Donatello, and Brunelleschi all took their best shot at their respective guilds' patron saints. Donatello's *St. George* (with the large shield), designed and sculpted for the Armorers' guild, is my personal favorite. Making a statue out of bronze was ten times more expensive than using stone, so this will give you some idea of how wealthy the Armorers' guild was at the time. The Merchants and the Bankers, not to be outdone, also used bronze. Most of the statues are copies, with the originals having been placed in permanent protective custody.

Inside the church, check out the beautiful and ornate Gothic tabernacle (how they got it through the door is a mystery to me). The building, which used to be a grain market, also shows traces of its practical roots. Just inside the entrance to the left, you'll see a hole in the ceiling that was used to feed grain up to the aboveground storage—the hollow pillars would bring it back down. Notice the range of sloppy patches and cover-ups of the old frescoes all the way to the hyperrealistic modern reproductions in the Renaissance style around the left side of the interior.

Free, interior daily 10:00–17:00, upstairs open on Mondays, Via dell'Arte della Lana, Centro Storico, +39 055 23885

Ponte Vecchio

Right up there with the Duomo as an icon of the city, the oldest and most decadent bridge in town is also the primary crossing point of the Arno River in Florence. To avoid the common Florentine people, the Medici family constructed a long passageway connecting their private residences in Oltrarno to their offices at the Uffizi. A stretch of this passageway, called the Vasari Corridor, runs along the spine of the Ponte Vecchio. Originally, butchers and fishmongers had almost exclusive rights to sell on the bridge, but the Medici found the smell offensive, so they ordered them removed, replaced by goldsmiths and jewelers. Ahhh, much better.

Today, the bridge is still full of jewelers, shops, and tourists snapping selfies. My favorite photo op is not on the bridge itself, but from half a block north and west along the river. You can look back towards the bridge and see the shops stacked haphazardly like Jenga blocks along the length of the bridge.

Free, always open, Centro Storico

Piazzale Michelangelo

For those looking to get a workout in with their sightseeing, the almost 500 vertical steps to Piazzale Michelangelo are an efficient, blood-pumping way to do just that. Offering the best vistas of Florence, Piazzale Michelangelo is worth the sweaty hike—especially if you bring a bottle or two to reward yourself at the top. There is no better way or better place in the city to enjoy the sunset. The piazzale features a (vastly inferior) bronze replica of Michelangelo's *David*, dragged to the top of the hill in 1873 by nine pairs of oxen. at the square you'll sometimes find **TestDriveFirenze** (+39 331 20 55 888, testdrivefirenze.com, info@testdrivefirenze.com), a company that lets you drive a Ferrari with an instructor. Ten minutes in a roaring Italian pony will set you back €55. Bucket list, anyone?

Free, always open, Oltrarno

EXTRA CREDIT

Pitti Palace

It's impossible to miss the imposing façade of this palace. Inside you'll find dozens of richly decorated rooms and tens of thousands of pieces of art. Visit the palace to see late-Renaissance artwork bleed into baroque, with pieces by the likes of Caravaggio, Titian, and Raphael. The gardens in back provide a welcome respite from the crowds, heat, noise, and pollution of the city center.

€13, Tues-Sun 08:15-18:00, Piazza de Pitti 1, Oltrarno, +39 055 294 883

TOP EATS

Florence is more than the capital of the Italian Renaissance; it's also the heart of Tuscany, a region world famous for its rustic and delicious cuisine and wine. Florence's restaurants are an opportunity to indulge in some of the culinary delights for which Tuscany is famous: extra-virgin olive oil, fresh produce, and some of Italy's finest wines.

Pangie's Bistrot

Pangie's makes great focaccia sandwiches for €5 and also has a full menu of delicious *primi, secondo*, and platters with bruschetta, meats, and cheese. This casual, welcoming shop is small, with only a handful of tables. The sweet owners, Mario and Francesca, will happily make you a made-to-order sandwich that you can stow in your bag and bring out when waiting in line or moving from one attraction to another. They are open for lunch and dinner daily (except for the second and third Sundays each month).

Sandwiches from €5, daily 11:30-22:00 (closed on the second and third Sunday of each month), Via del Parione 43-45r, Centro Storico, +39 055 295 439, pangies.it

Osteria Brincello

Osteria Brincello offers what is easily some of the most solid-value and authentic Tuscan cuisine in town. Run by a jovial crew of friends and family, Brincello has a limited menu that is refreshed weekly. You can count on the freshest ingredients imaginable and simple and delicious Tuscan pastas, like *tagliatelle al ragu*, as well as Florentine steaks. Another plus: the location. You'll find this easygoing sit-down restaurant close to the train station and many of the city's best hostels.

Plates from €12, Wed-Mon 12:00-15:00 and 19:00-23:00, occasionally closed Sundays, Via Nazionale 10, Centro Storico, +39 055 282 645

Caffetteria delle Oblate

Stop by the historic Oblate library (which also serves as a peaceful study zone and community center) for a unique close-up view of the Duomo while enjoying a budget snack served cafeteria-style on the top floor. The open-air loggia is my favorite little getaway in the downtown area—it's free and has Wi-Fi too.

Free entry, lunch menu from €7, €10 *aperitivo* 18:30-22:00, library: Mon 14:00-19:00, Tues-Sat 09:00-24:00, Sun 11:00-18:00, Via dell'Oriuolo 26, Centro Storico, +39 055 263 9685, lospaziochespera-vi.it

Mercato Centrale

Florence's bustling main market is packed with everything from pigs' feet to fresh veggies and fruit. Find a vendor who has bread, meat, and cheese, and, pointing to what you want, ask *"Puo fare un panino?"* ("Will you make a sandwich?"). They'll make it for you right before your eyes. For quick, casual, and cheap eats, find **Nerbone** inside the market and sharpen your elbows to grab a plate of their delicious Tuscan fare. Pastas, sandwiches, pork, and other dishes all go for around €5 each. You can also head upstairs to the mod expansion for an artisanal foodie market hall experience with stands selling fresh fruit, delicious Napolitano pizza, gelato, beer, coffee, and even sushi.

Eats from €4, Mon-Sat 07:00-15:00, some sections open later, Piazza San Lorenzo, Centro Storico

Trattoria Mario

Trattoria Mario makes for an authentic escape close to Mercato Centrale in the middle of downtown Florence. These guys only do lunch, and they do it as well as anybody in town: There's plenty of the genuine Florentine article including pastas, steaks, salads, and even artichokes. Every

DINING TIPS

Keep these factors in mind when dining in touristy Florence:

Aperitivo: Like many northern Italian cities, Florence has a culture of *aperitivo*, an extensive buffet of pastas and salads all for the price of a glass of wine (or even better, the popular spritz, a refreshing cocktail made with sparkling prosecco and a dash of sweet Aperol or bitter Campari). *Aperitivo* hours are traditionally 18:00-21:00, with some places going later, until 22:30. With prices hovering around €10 for a drink and access to the buffet, this makes a great option for a budget dinner. If you find a spot serving protein (and not just carbs like pasta and couscous), it's a winner!

Coperto: Many restaurants charge a *coperto* ("cover fee") of €1-2 for sitting down at their tables. It's meant to cover the bread brought out to you and will be added to your final bill. You'll find *coperto* listed in fine print at the bottom of the menus out front of most restaurants. If the charge is any more than €2, keep looking.

Servizio: Check your bill closely to see whether service is included. If it is, you don't need to provide an additional tip. If service was not included in the bill, round up to the nearest round number (a general rule of thumb is 10 percent).

Tap water: Most restaurants do not offer free tap water, but you can try requesting *"acqua del rubinetto, per favore"* ("tap water, please"). If you just request water, your server will ask you "Still or sparkling?" and then deliver a nice bottle of water (which you'll pay for) to your table. Be sure to check the price of water before agreeing to anything. Bottles of water can run north of €6, so it's sometimes cheaper to drink table wine.

time I come to Florence, I head straight to Mario's.

Pastas from €6, Mon-Sat 12:00-15:30, Via Rosina 2r, +39 055 218 550

Pizzeria del Duomo

Imagine biting into a slice of thick-cut, freshly made pizza while taking in one of the best street-level views in Florence, where you can sit in the warm Tuscan sun and enjoy the beauty of the Duomo and Baptistry. This is my favorite *pizza al taglio* (pizza by the slice) spot in Florence. Mix and match your pizza slices with friends and grab a spot outside on the square or, if the sun is particularly hot, downstairs in the much cooler cellar. To find this place, look just behind the Baptistry in the Piazza di San Giovanni for the white Pizzeria a Taglio awning next to the pharmacy. The shop is immensely popular with the tourists who flood the square each day, but the owners haven't let this go to their heads.

Slices from €2.50, daily 11:00-24:00, Piazza di San Giovanni 21r, Centro Storico, +39 055 210 719

The Oil Shoppe

This fast and casual sandwich shop, a favorite among Florence's international students, is famous for its generously ap-

pointed sandwiches filled with local meats called *salumi* (prosciutto, ham, salami), veggies (eggplant, tomato), and cheeses (pecorino and mozzarella). Stop in for a bite to take away or eat in along the bar on the wall. Don't let the name of the place throw you off: Vegetarian and (relatively) healthy options are plentiful!

Overflowing sandwiches from €4, Mon-Fri 10:00-19:00, Via Sant-Egidio 22r, Centro Storico, +39 055 386 0091, paninoteca.firenze.it

Pane & Toscana

Another excellent choice for a fast and easy city-center lunch, Pane & Toscana packs its menu with two dozen kinds of typical Florentine sandwiches incorporating ingredients like artichokes, mushrooms, and smoked tuna, as well as a wide array of sauces. Select your fillings and have them on salty focaccia, a thick bun, or a healthy wrap. Tourists and locals alike enjoy the fast service and tasty sandwiches. You can grab a spot on the bench outside or *mangi in piedi* (eat while walking).

Sandwiches from €4, Mon-Thurs 11:00-22:00, Fri-Sat 11:00-23:00, closed Sundays, Borgo degli Albizi 31, Centro Storico, +39 345 123 5540, Facebook: Pane & Toscana

Osteria Zio Gigi's

Zio Gigi's offers surprising quality and value for a sit-down restaurant this close to the Duomo. I love the comfortable, welcoming atmosphere and the set menu for large portions without the large price tag. Pop in here for simple and hearty Tuscan fare, like pasta with meatballs, wild boar, and grilled veal. Uncle Gigi is a load of fun—he'll take good care of you no matter what time you stop in.

Lunches from €10, dinners from €14, daily 12:00–14:30 and 19:00–22:30, Via Portinari Folco 7r, Centro Storico, +39 055 215 584, Facebook: Osteria Zio Gigi

Moyo

Offering an extensive buffet with pecorino cheese slices, roasted ribs, salty focaccia, and more, Moyo is one of my favorite places in Florence to enjoy an *aperitivo*. Step in, order your drink at the bar, and get ready to run laps for seconds. Good food, well-poured drinks, and a trendy lounge atmosphere with a DJ spinning on the weekends all make this an excellent spot to sip cocktails around the dinner hour.

Aperitivo €10, daily 08:00–02:00, Via dei Benci 23r, Santa Croce, +39 055 247 9738, moyo.it

Buca Mario

If you like steaks, splurge at Buca Mario—Florence's best steakhouse. Wash down your meal with a local Chianti (allow your server to guide you towards the perfect bottle—they know their cellars). Reservations are highly recommended due to the restaurant's popularity; be sure to dress to the nines.

Steaks from €35, plus a €4 *coperto*, daily 19:00–23:30, Piazza degli Ottaviani 16r, Centro Storico, +39 055 214 179, bucamario.it

La Buchetta

A Florentine landmark thanks its authentic beef stew (*peposo*), the clean and refined La Buchetta does much more than stew. Its steaks, pastas (the Picci alla Buchetta—pasta mixed in a cheese rind before your eyes and topped with truffle shavings—is a real treat), and beautifully presented desserts never fail to satisfy. A meal here (usually around €50 a head) will take a bite out of your food budget and then some, but every time I'm in town, I turn my pockets inside out and head to La Buchetta for the superb steaks, crunchy bruschetta with mozzarella, and unforgettable cheese plates.

Peposo €15, daily 09:00–02:00, Via de Benci 3, Santa Croce, +39 055 217 833, labuchetta.com

All'Antico Vinaio

One of my favorite little holes-in-the-wall churns out meaty sandwiches and wine by the glass. You'll have to jostle a little bit to get to the front in this popular place, but it's a perfect protein pit stop to break up a long day of sightseeing. Eat your sandwich and drink your wine while standing or leaning up against the wall in the alley. When you're done, return your glass to the rack on the side of the door.

Sandwiches from €3, Tues-Sun 12:00–16:00 and Tues-Sat 19:00–24:00, Via dei Neri 74r, Centro Storico, +39 055 238 2723, allanticoVinaio.com

Ristorante Grotta Guelfa

I love this place for the varied menu, especially the bubbling pizzas, steaks, and perfectly sharable meat and cheese platters. Find this sit-down restaurant with white tablecloths and outdoor seating tucked under a classic Florentine portico.

Get your fill from €16, daily 12:00–22:30, Via Pellicceria 5r, Centro Storico, +39 055 210 042, grottaguelfa.it

TOP GELATO

Like it or love it, gelato will be a dietary staple during your visit to Florence. Challenge yourself to never try the same flavor, or *gusto*, twice. Many are tempted to get the extra-large after their first taste, but I always grab a small. There are so many flavors to try that it seems a waste to fill up on just one of them.

Perché No!

Italian for "why not?", this is considered by many to be the top *gelateria* in town, so you can't visit Florence without dropping in (it's just off the main shopping drag of Via del Calzaiuoli) and ordering a cone.

FINDING GREAT GELATO

Not all gelato is created the same. Here are my tips on what to look for when selecting your *gelateria:*

Look for natural colors. Check out the banana and pistachio flavors, and make sure they're the right color. What's the right color, you ask? The natural one, of course! Pistachio should be earthy green, not neon or lime green—and hopefully you'll even be able to see small chunks of nuts blended throughout the gelato. For banana, you're looking for a grayish-white color. If it's bright yellow, keep looking.

Walk away from artificial flavors. Don't ask me why, but some *gelaterie* stack their artificial flavoring in plain sight for all to see. If you see sacks of artificial flavoring behind the counter, beat a hasty retreat!

Say no to flair. Touristy places attract customers by piling their gelato high and stacking it with all sorts of flashy memorabilia. Although this is a treat for the eyes, it won't be a treat for the taste buds. The right temperature for gelato puts the mixture at a nearly liquid state that allows for the flavors to be pronounced and vivid. If the bins are piled high, that means there's a chemical stabilizer in the gelato.

Go for metal. Metal bins, which are reused, are a reliable indicator that the gelato has been made on-site. Plastic bins have likely been transported to the *gelateria* from somewhere else, so the gelato in your cone will not be as fresh. Half-full bins are usually a good sign that the owners keep their batches fresh, but look closely. Is there an icy crust on the top? If so, the gelato is far from fresh.

There are more delicious flavors than you can shake a stick at, and friendly staff that never seem to grow impatient with the long lines of tourists.

From €2.50, Wed-Mon 11:00-23:00, Tues 12:00-20:00, Via dei Tavolini 19, Centro Storico, +39 055 239 8969, perchno.firenze.it

Vivoli

A classic *gelateria* with an art nouveau-style wooden interior. By many accounts (including mine), Vivoli offers some of the best flavors around, like tiramisu, *fantasia*, and kiwi—all made from the freshest ingredients. Get your ticket at the cashier first, then redeem your prize at the bar.

From €2, Tues-Sat 07:30-24:00, Sun 09:00-21:00, Via dell'Isola delle Stinche 7, Centro Storico, +39 055 292 334, vivoli.it

Grom

This high-quality gelato chain is taking Italy by storm. With shops opening all over the country, you could plan a road trip around Italy popping from Grom to Grom. They pride themselves on their locally sourced ingredients and flavors that are updated regularly to suit the season. It may be a chain, but the quality and value are right on par with the independent options in town.

From €2, daily 10:30-24:00, corner of Via del Campanile and Via delle Oche, Centro Storico, +39 055 216 158, grom.it

Gelateria dei Neri

Gelateria dei Neri is another heavyweight in the Florentine gelato scene. Its colorful piles of goodness have me salivating just looking at them. Like many of Florence's *gelaterie*, it's open late, making it a great place to stop when moving from one nightspot to the next.

From €2, daily 10:00-24:00, Via dei Neri 9/11, Centro Storico, +39 055 210 034, Facebook: Gelateria del Neri

Gelateria La Carraia

Head to this sophisticated gelato shop if you find yourself on the south side of the Arno. This is definitely one of those places where it's hard to restrain yourself. It's in a neighborhood with far fewer *gelaterie*, so there's no need to hold yourself back. Dig in!

From €2.50, daily 11:00-24:00, Piazza Nazario Sauro 25-r, Oltrarno, +39 055 280695, Facebook: Gelateria la Carraia

NIGHTLIFE DISTRICTS

Centro Storico

Thanks to Florence's compactness, you'll find many nightlife venues popular with locals, students, and tourists all within walking distance of the hostels and each other in the Centro Storico. Prices generally climb higher and higher the closer you get to the Duomo.

Centro Storico

Santa Croce

This district may have once been a quietly cool spot, but the secret's out: Each night Santa Croce fills with students, locals, and tourists who want to party hardy and know that this is the best neighborhood in the city to do so. Especially in the Piazza Santa Croce, you'll find endless options for food, *aperitivo*, snacks, bars, lounges, clubs, and more. Many of my recommended venues are in this district.

Santa Croce

Piazza Santo Spirito

Head to the square in front of the Santo Spirito church in Oltrarno to sample the truly local nightlife. It's more subdued than Santa Croce, but that makes it just the ticket for people who want to avoid the crush. Savor a couple of beers alfresco on the steps, or enjoy a *passeggiata* (evening stroll) through the neighborhood or along the river. Many who do this make Santo Spirito their start and end point. **Caibira,** at #4 on the square, is an ideal spot for an evening spritz, especially if you find a space on their outdoor patio.

Oltrarno

BEER AND WINE

Vinophiles and hops lovers alike have plenty to look forward to when visiting Florence. Some of my favorite beer joints and *enotecas* are listed below—and almost all of them offer solid food menus as well.

Casa del Vino

If sampling wine is your thing, I highly recommend stopping in to say "ciao" to Gianni, who's the latest in a century-long family line of sommeliers. Admire the bar's beautifully carved wood shelves and the hundreds of bottles of regional wines (there's something for every budget). Gianni will happily tell you everything you wanted to know about Tuscan wines. If you want to make a picnic special or bring that perfect bottle up to the Piazzale Michelangelo for sunset, this is the place to start.

Tasting platters from €8, glasses from €4, Mon–Thurs 09:30–15:00, Fri–Sat 09:30–22:00, Via dell'Ariento 16r, Centro Storico, +39 055 215 609, casadelvino.it

Le Volpi e l'Uva

Le Volpi e l'Uva ("The Wolf and the Grape") is a classy little spot in Oltrarno with marble counters, a wine list that would make Bacchus get out of bed, and a selection of pâtés, cheeses, and cold cuts that go perfectly with your selection. With a focus on enlightened winemaking philosophies and practices, these merchants reward those growers and producers who break with tradition to produce distinctive wines that, once tasted, are never forgotten.

Glasses from €4.50, Mon–Sat 11:00–21:00, Piazza dei Rossi 1R, Oltrarno, +39 055 239 8132, levolpieluva.com

LGBT FLORENCE

Italians—especially younger ones—are progressive and welcoming, and in 2004 Tuscany became the first Italian state to pass legislation protecting gays from discrimination and providing rights for gay couples. Holding hands, sharing a room, or going out for food and drinks won't elicit a second glance, making Florence fun and enjoyable for everyone. **Piccolo Café** (Borgo Santa Croce 23r, Santa Croce, +39 055 241 704) in downtown Florence is a favorite for its welcoming atmosphere, friendly crowd, great music, and fun bartenders.

For more information and tips, check out Florence's two resource offices during normal business hours: **Service Center for the Queer Community** (IREOS, Via de Serragli 3, Oltrarno, ireos.org, +39 055 216 907) offers event schedules, maps, and information tailored for the LGBT community. **Arcigay** (60 Via del Leone, Oltrarno, +39 055 051 6574, Firenze@arcigay.it) is Italy's national gay association, and they frequently sponsor LGBT-friendly events in Florence.

Birreria Centrale

Pop in here for some delicious craft beer. The menu is surprisingly varied (and the food surprisingly delicious) for a beer hall, but this is Italy, after all. Enjoy steaks, pastas, gnocchi, and salads underneath brick cellar arches. Dine or sip away in an authentic and casual atmosphere decked out with tasteful old-fashioned touches. In nice weather, their outdoor patio is delightful.

Beers from €4.50, Mon-Sat 11:00-24:00, Piazza de Cimatori 1r, Centro Storico, +39 055 211 915, birreriacentrale.com

Mostodolce

Head here for a cold beer on a hot day. There are wonderfully quirky sketches and doodles that adorn the walls and the tables, and the beer was brewed just down the road in Prato. They offer surprisingly good burgers, pizza, and pasta for a beer hall, making this a great place for a pint and a bite before heading out.

Beers from €4.50, daily 11:30-02:00, Via Nazionale 114, Centro Storico, +39 055 230 2928, Facebook: Mosto Dolce

King Grizzly

For the beer drinker lost in a world of Tuscan wines, King Grizzly is a welcome refuge. The charming staff is happy to help you work through the extensive selection of hoppy remedies. Find some of the best local beers on tap in this centrally located bar between Piazza Signoria and Piazza del Duomo. The dark wood paneling inside and the friendly, unpretentious crowd create a fun atmosphere and guarantee a great time.

Beers from €4, daily 18:00-02:00, Piazza de Cimatori 5, Centro Storico, Facebook: King Grizzly

BARS

Hotel Cavour's Rooftop Bar

This bar occupies the rooftop terrace of the palatial Hotel Cavour. The quiet and classy spot pours great (if a little expensive) drinks, but more important is the view from atop the hotel. It's a rare vantage point from the center of Florence across the entire valley. Do a slow 360 while standing on the terrace, and you'll see Santa Croce, Piazza della Repubblica, the Bargello, Palazzo Vecchio, and one of the most spectacular views of the Duomo in the entire city.

Drinks from €10, daily 16:00-22:30, closed for private events and poor weather, Via del Proconsolo 3, Centro Storico, +39 055 266 271, albergocavour.it

REX Caffe

REX Caffe is one of the oldest jazz clubs in Tuscany. The intimate, standing-room-only space is a shade gaudy, but it's not the decorations that the well-dressed crowd come for—it's the scene (and the top-rate cocktails). When the jazz acts are playing, bearded bohemians bob their heads in time with the complex music. When it's not jazz, REX can be counted on for top-quality DJs spinning funky house that keeps the well-dressed crowd coming back for more.

Drinks from €5, daily 18:00-03:00, Via Fiesolana 25, Santa Croce, +39 055 248 0331, rexfirenze.com

Rari Ristoro sull'Acqua

The best things about Rari are the location and beautiful view across the river. While the service and food may leave a little to be desired, it's difficult to complain when you're sipping a spritz and watching the sun set over the Arno. They frequently host live music, and the bands have always been good enough to justify the 15-minute walk upriver.

Aperitivo from €10, daily 09:30–01:00, Lungarno Francesco Ferrucci 24, Oltrarno, +39 055 680 979

Naima

My friend Sergio heads up this fun sports bar, popular among students (thanks to their student discounts) and sports fans (locals and visitors alike). The game is always on, and the crowd is—as you might expect in an Italian pub—animated. This is a solid spot to begin your night, and, when the game is done, it's a hop, skip, and jump away from some of the best bars and clubs in town.

Beers from €2, daily 18:00–late, Via dell'Anguillara 54r, Centro Storico, +39 055 265 4098, Facebook: Naima

The Lion's Fountain Irish Pub

Every city in the world has to have an Irish pub, right? The Lion's Fountain is Florence's version, and it's everything you've come to expect from the classic Irish pub. You can count on a fun, casual scene focused on beer and shots and a steady stream of study-abroad students. If you've had it up to here with pasta and pizza, they serve savory pub grub and burgers throughout the day.

Drinks from €4, daily 10:00–03:00, Borgo degli Albizi 34, Santa Croce, +39 055 234 4412, thelionsfountain.com

Kikuya

This English-style pub is just steps away from Piazza Santa Croce, the focal point for so much of Santa Croce's world-famous nightlife. The relaxed atmosphere makes it a great place to unwind after a long day of sightseeing. Pull up a stool at the bar and ask the bartender to pull you a pint of draft beer from the UK. Polish the bar with your elbows while watching the local soccer game on the TV. The place is nothing special, but that's kind of the point.

Drinks from €5, daily 18:00–late, Via dei Benci 43, Santa Croce, +39 055 234 4879, Facebook: Kikuya Pub

Red Garter

Red Garter is a sports bar and steakhouse in the heart of Florence's best nightlife district. If you're avoiding the summertime swells by coming in the fall or winter, you can catch NFL games here every weekend—and gorge yourself on Florence's best greasy pub fare. No matter what time of year, there's always beer pong and karaoke and great live acts playing blues and rock. For obvious reasons, Americans studying abroad practically live at the Red Garter. There's no need to bone up on your Italian phrases before heading down to this watering hole.

Drinks from €5, daily 16:00–04:00, Via de' Benci 33, Santa Croce, +39 055 248 0909, redgarteritaly.com

Caffe Slowly

This café is famous for its *aperitivo* bar and cocktail lounge. If you've been munching all day on snack food or gelato, Slowly makes a great place for a light dinner and drink before going out to a bar or club. It's just a couple blocks from Piazza della Repubblica. Buy a drink and hit the buffet of appetizers and finger foods.

Aperitivo from €7, daily *aperitivo* 19:00–23:00, Via Porta Rossa 63, Centro Storico, +39 055 035 1335, slowlycafe.com

CLUBS

Florentines enjoy their nights out, and they have plenty of options. Before you head out, remember, Florence is a stylish city. Selective bouncers don't hesitate to turn away would-be partiers if they don't look or act the part (if you're intoxicated when you arrive, try to hold it together until you're past the velvet rope). Heads up: In several clubs around town, you'll receive a punch card upon entry. Each drink that you order will be logged on this card. At the end of the night, turn in your card to settle your bill based on the number of punches. Don't lose it, or you'll be charged for a full card (€100+!) before you're permitted to leave.

Otel Varieté

Otel, the gold standard for Florence clubbing, is 20 minutes outside the city center via taxi. Every weekend, this lavish club is flooded with the most stylish and high-profile locals. Dress your very best and arrive early to make sure you get in; the later it gets, the more difficult it becomes to get past the velvet rope. Expect incredible music, dancing, drinks, and, very possibly, the best night of your life partying with some of the most stylish and beautiful people in the world.

Cover varies by event, Fri-Sun 20:00-04:00, Viale Generale Dalla Chiesa 9, Greater Florence, +39 055 650 791, otelvariete.com

Bamboo Lounge

Bamboo is a great place to get down to Top 40, hip-hop, and R&B. Dress to impress, but don't expect to leave the club with your clothes looking fresh and pressed. You'll work up a sweat dancing and drinking the night away in this intimate venue popular with youngish locals and students. Check out their Facebook page for regular theme nights and upcoming events.

€10 cover usually includes a drink and *aperitivo*, Thurs-Sat 19:00-22:00, club Thurs-Sun 23:00-04:00, Via Giuseppe Verdi 57r, Santa Croce, +39 335 434 484, bambooloungeclub.com

Space

Space is a go-to nightclub for anyone visiting Florence. Popular with tourists and locals alike, this large, double-level club boasts an awesome sound system and light show. Bring some extra cash for the cover charge.

Cover from €10, daily 22:00-04:00, Via Palazzuolo 37, Centro Storico, +39 055 293 082, spaceclubfirenze.com

Y.A.B.

You Are Beautiful, a glamorous club in the heart of the city, is equal parts loved local

fixture and hated blight on the scene. Keep your drink card with you at all times to avoid the €60 exit fee. There's a €10 cover, but it includes a drink. If hip-hop and Top 40 are your thing, you'll spend most of the night on the dance floor. Because things get loose at this club, it can be a bit of a dangerous place for women to go on their own. Have fun, but stick close to your friends, and keep an eye on your drinks at all times just to be safe.

Cover €10, Mon and Wed-Sat 19:00-04:00, Via de' Sassetti 5, Centro Storico, +39 055 215 160, yab.it

Club TwentyOne

Small and rowdy, Club TwentyOne gets straight down to it: good club music, fun vibe, central location, and light-up disco floor. It's small, but this creates a party vibe that's positively infectious. Just by virtue of proximity, everybody is practically forced to join the party.

No cover on Wed, otherwise €5-10, shots from €3, Wed and Fri-Sat 23:30-04:00, Via Cimatori 13r, Centro Storico, +39 055 295 262, Facebook: Club 21 Firenze

Flo' Lounge Bar

This trendy and somewhat aloof *aperitivo* lounge and club is only open during the summer months (usually starting in May). Its proximity to the Piazzale Michelangelo means this bar boasts some of the best nighttime views anywhere. It's popular with locals and still coasting from the boost it got when the cast of *Jersey Shore* visited here a few years ago. Under the same ownership as Otel Varieté, this is one of those nice shoes, dark pants kind of places.

Aperitivo €12, summer daily 19:30-late, Viale Michelangiolo 82, Oltrarno, +30 055 650 791, flofirenze.com, check website for upcoming events and programs

TOP SHOPPING & MARKETS

SHOPPING DISTRICTS

Florence has shopping options just about everywhere in the historic center. Whatever you're looking for, don't spring for the first one you find. Shop around to calibrate your pricing and think long and hard about what it's worth to you (prices can be inflated to ridiculous levels in the center). When it

comes to things like leather goods (which Florence is known for), the shopkeepers expect you to haggle, so don't pay sticker price for anything. If they seem reluctant to bring the price down, start heading for the door—they won't let you leave without giving you a better offer.

Piazza della Repubblica

If Italy is the fashion center of the world, Florence and Milan share the title of the globe's fashion capital. Many of the world's top fashion houses are based here or in Milan. You'll find all the high-fashion brands in the streets surrounding Piazza della Repubblica, including Gucci, Fendi, Dolce & Gabbana, and Prada. Stop at either **Café Concerto Paszkowski** or **Café Gilli,** both on the north side of the square, to recharge with a high-class €5 coffee or lunch. Take your drink or food outside and enjoy the people watching. Be warned, this district is definitely not budget friendly.

Centro Storico

Borgo degli Albizi

I head to this street, which leads east from the Centro Storico, to find better prices without sacrificing quality. Storekeepers here need to work harder to keep the lights on, so they are eager to rope you into their shops. They'll haggle with you, so don't let the stickers shock you. If they don't have what you want or if they're not willing to meet you in the middle, step back out onto the street and keep looking.

Centro Storico

MARKETS

I love exploring Florence's markets. I make it a rule to judge the market on those who come there rather than those who sell there. If I'm surrounded by tourists, chances are I'll find the usual kitschy items. If all I hear is Italian, though, I'm on the right track.

San Lorenzo Market & Mercato Centrale

The daily open-air **San Lorenzo Market** is where you'll find rows upon rows of vendors selling leather goods, souvenirs, and some of the region's trademark food products. Many of the stalls are nothing more than outdoor versions of the stores behind them (these run all the way up and down Via dell'Ariento, Via Sant'Antonino, and Via del Canto dei Nelli). Show any interest in what they have displayed and the salespeople will coax you back into the store, where they have a wider selection. Haggle, and even if you think you've found a deal, do a full lap to make sure there's not someone just around the corner willing to make you a better offer.

San Lorenzo Market surrounds **Mercato Centrale,** the covered, permanent food market on Via dell'Ariento and Via Sant'Antonino. Inside, you'll find food stalls and tons of local produce, including olive oil, meats, veggies, and limoncello galore.

Free, Mon–Sat 09:00–18:00, Via dell'Ariento, next to the San Lorenzo church, Centro Storico

Mercato di Sant'Ambrogio

Just a 15-minute walk east of the Duomo, the Sant'Ambrogio market feels more distinctly local than other markets in town. Here you'll find covered and uncovered sections, permanent and less-permanent stalls selling everything from fresh produce and meats to clothes and shoes. If you're here around lunchtime, seek out a trattoria nearby that looks like it gets its food from the market.

Free, Mon–Sat 07:00–14:00, Piazza Ghiberti, Santa Croce, mercatosantambrogio.it

Mercato del Porcellino

This market, also known as **Mercato Nuovo,** is packed with touristy knickknacks and cliché leather purses and colorful scarves. Take a minute here to calibrate your prices, and then buy elsewhere.

Besides the touristy stalls, there are two minor sights in the Mercato Nuovo. The circular **Stone of Scandal** is where poor saps who ran up tabs they couldn't pay had to sit naked while being beaten with stones; don't tempt the locals to revive this practice by skipping out on a tab. There's also a **bronze boar** on the south side of the portico. Legend has it that if you take a coin, put it on the boar's tongue, and release it, and it falls into the grate below, you'll have good luck and a guaranteed return visit to Florence (similar to the ritual at the Trevi Fountain in Rome). It might be hooey, but it's worth a dime to play along.

Free, daily 09:00–18:30, Piazza del Mercato Nuovo, Centro Storico

CALCIO STORICO

Roughly translating to "old kicking game" or "historical soccer," *calcio storico* is a game that was created to keep Roman soldiers in fighting shape. Today, it's played on a sandy rectangular field in front of the Santa Croce church. Fifty-four players face off in what looks like mortal combat for 50 grueling minutes. In any given game, 10-15 players are carried off in stretchers. The brawl doesn't let up—when a player is removed from the match, play carries on, and the team that has lost a player must finish the game with no replacements. As such, players are incentivized to try to injure or otherwise incapacitate each other with flurries of kicks and punches. With elements of boxing, rugby, soccer, and American football combined into one open-field bare-knuckle gang fight, *calcio storico* seems a touch gruesome and medieval—barbaric even. The fact that there's a ball involved, and that the players are trying to get it into the net on either side of the field, somehow seems an afterthought amid the violence. The players identify by colors and come from four districts of the city; they practice all year for the annual competition on June 24, the feast day of St. John the Baptist, Florence's patron saint. Enjoy the fireworks from the Piazzale Michelangelo following the finals. If you aren't in town for the match, check out the HBO documentary *State of Play: Inherent Violence* to get a look at the game and its history.

TOP TOURS

Florence Free Tour

Florence Free Tour leads free daily walks around town. They're a fun and informative way to get oriented with Florence and its long and complex history. The morning walk focuses on the Renaissance history of the city; the afternoon walk digs deeper into Florence's most powerful family, the Medicis. Full of intrigue, secrets, and assassinations, the plot twists and thickens. To get a relatively complete picture of Florence's Renaissance history, take both tours; you'll have enough time between them to grab a quick snack or a gelato.

Free, tip-based, Renaissance Tour 11:00, Medici Tour 14:00, both tours start in front of Santa Maria Novella church (near the train station), Centro Storico, florencefreetour.com, info@florencefreetour.com

Italy on a Budget Day Tours

My friends at Italy on a Budget (IoaB) are the answer for those who can't quite afford private drivers and crates of limited-production wines. IoaB has a lineup of fun and wallet-friendly experiences to get you out of the city and into the countryside, including day trips for wine tasting, jaunts out to the Cinque Terre and Pisa, food tours hosted

by local farmhouses, and more. They also have longer weekend excursions for students and budget travelers to destinations like Naples and the Amalfi Coast. Check out their website for details and trip information. They're highly recommended if you have more than a few days and you've come to see the region, not just the city.

Experiences starting from €22, Via Nazionale 149R, Centro Storico, +39 055 05 03517, italyonabudget.com, info@italyonabudgettours.com

Tuscany Cycle

Tuscany Cycle will take you on a fun, casual ride in the countryside, which starts after a short car ride from their office in downtown Florence. Bilingual tour guides, bike rental, lunch, wine tasting, and round-trip transportation are included. Extend your bike rental for a discounted rate after the trip if you want. Lazy bums can opt for their Vespa tours—don't let slippery roads and a crash ruin the rest of your trip, though!

Day tours from €75, performance road bike rentals from €35/day, Via Ghibellina 133r, Centro Storico, +39 328 071 4849 or +39 055 289 681, tuscanycycle.com, tuscanycycle@gmail.com

TOP HOSTELS

Hostels in Florence are improving. Gone are the days when your only budget option was a convent with a strict curfew and long list of house rules—these are still available, by the way, and they are probably the last remaining €10 beds in town (sanctuarybbfirenze.com). Still, thanks to a relatively small center, the number of good hostels remains far more limited than in other parts of Europe. In addition to my recommendations, you can find more listings on hostelworld.com. Private rooms and apartments available on airbnb.com provide another excellent budget solution for short stays.

Plus Florence Hostel
Located just down the street from the main train station, Plus Florence is my favorite hostel in town. The dorm rooms are comfortable, and for those who prefer more solitude, private rooms are available. The hostel is roomy, there's a breezy rooftop terrace, and the property is exceptionally well managed, with brisk, efficient check-in and a fun, social atmosphere centered on a decent on-site bar downstairs. With six floors of dorms, there's almost always space. There are a few downsides: the opt-in breakfast is mediocre at best, and, though they advertise a pool, it never seems to be open.

Beds from €25, free Wi-Fi, breakfast optional, 24-hour reception, free lockers, Via Santa Caterina D'Alessandria 15, north of Stazione Santa Maria Novella, Greater Florence, +39 055 628 6347, plushostels.com

Academy Hostel
These are simple dorms (large open rooms with temporary dividers between beds for a semblance of privacy). The location—right between the Duomo and the Accademia, meaning it's stumbling distance from the bars—couldn't be better. The helpful staff is happy to recommend sights and activities. You'll also find common computers, a peaceful terrace, and limited kitchen facilities.

Dorms from €22, free Wi-Fi, free lockers and breakfast, 24-hour reception, Via Ricasoli 9, Centro Storico, +39 055 239 8665, book at academyhostel.eu for a 5 percent discount

Hotel Il Bargellino
Run by an expat Bostonian and her husband, this spot offers a quiet respite from the bustle of the city. Rooms are simple and comfortable. The rooftop terrace is a major plus for afternoon drinks, picnics, and great conversation with like-minded travelers.

Private rooms from €45, free Wi-Fi, no breakfast, Via Guelfa 87, near Stazione Santa Maria Novella, Centro Storico, +39 055 238 2658, ilbargellino.com, carmel@ilbargellino.com

GETTING THERE & AWAY

Plane

Six airports serve the region. Flight prices should help determine the right one for you. The most convenient airport is Florence's relatively small **Peretola Airport** (FLR, aeropor-to.firenze.it), just a 20-minute shuttle bus ride (running every 30 minutes) from the city center. Look for the **Vola in Bus** shuttle. You can purchase your ticket from the driver (€6 each way to connect into the main city-center train station).

It's a one-hour drive to Florence from Pisa's **Galileo Galilei Airport** (PSA, pisa-airport.com), the largest airport in Tuscany. A shuttle bus, **Autostradale,** offers 1.5-hour connections into Florence with departures throughout the day for €10 each way.

Budget airlines also use the **Bologna Airport** (BLQ, bologna-air.it). The **Appenino Shuttle Bus** service connects to Florence's main train station for €20. Follow signs at the airport and catch one of the frequent departures (takes about 1.5 hours).

It's also possible to fly into Rome's airports, **Da Vinci-Fiumicino** (FCO, adr.it) and **Ciampino** (CIA, adr.it), or into Milan's **Malpensa** (MXP, milanomalpensa-airport.com) and take a train into Florence (1.5+ hours, tickets €39+ each way).

Train

The main train station, **Santa Maria Novella,** is on the western edge of the historic center. It's about a 15-minute walk from each of my recommended accommodations. Train tickets from Rome run about €30 each way. From station to station takes about 1.5 hours. To Milan, it takes 1.5 hours on the fast train and costs €45+. Trains to Venice (about 3 hours away) run often and cost around €40.

When booking your tickets, be aware of the difference between the slow local trains and the faster regional trains—it can make the difference between a one-hour and a four-hour ride to the same destination. Also, if you're traveling with an open ticket (without a specific time and date of validity stamped on it), you must validate it before departure or immediately find a conductor to validate it. Non-validated tickets can result in €50+ fines.

Bus

Eurolines.com offers the best options for international bus connections into Florence. Connections from cities like Prague, Paris, and Barcelona push 15 hours each way, but at €50-100, they are usually your cheapest bet. Arrivals will drop you off at Florence's main train station, **Santa Maria Novella. Flixbus.com** is another international network with frequent connections to dozens of cities around Italy and Europe.

Car

Florence is about three hours north of Rome via the A1 highway and three hours south and west from Venice.

GETTING AROUND

Florence is a pedestrian city; just about all sights can be enjoyed on foot thanks to the compact size of the historic center. Buses and trams are the public transit options of choice. There is no metro.

Buses & Trams

Santa Maria Novella train station is also Florence's main bus station, serving as the hub for both local and regional bus connections. Validate your **ticket** (€1.20) once you step on the bus to avoid hefty fines. Unfortunately, playing the "stupid tourist" card just doesn't work here anymore. It is possible to purchase tickets on board, but they often run out, so it's best to pre-purchase tickets at any *tabacchi* (tobacco store) in town.

Car

Within Florence (especially in the center), parking can be quite difficult, and there are strict traffic restrictions. Watch for the **Zona a Traffico Limitato** (ZTL) sign, which you'll see throughout central Florence, meaning that traffic is restricted to buses, taxis, and local traffic. If you cross this sign, an automatic camera will snap a picture of your license plate and you'll be sent a nasty fine.

Renting a car opens the countryside to you. For those who want to explore the wider Tuscan region, a rented vehicle will give you a degree of freedom like nothing else. A GPS system is a must to navigate the confusing terrain outside of Florence.

Taxi

Catch registered white cabs at designated taxi stands. Taxis are normally parked outside of the Santa Maria Novella train station, Piazza Santa Croce, Piazza del Duomo, and Piazza della Repubblica. Once in the car, look over the rate information card and make sure the meter is set correctly. Daytime rates begin at €3.20, and evenings start at twice that (€6.40). Women traveling alone can ask for a 10 percent discount between 21:00 and 02:00, but you won't get it if you don't ask for it! Call taxis at +39 055 4242, +39 055 4390, or +39 055 4499.

Bicycle

Cycling is a great way to see more of Florence. Make sure you lock your bike up when you dismount (this goes for inside or outside of the city). When cycling, keep your head on a swivel. As if the pedestrians, other bikers, and vehicles aren't enough to worry about, there are horses and potholes just about everywhere. More relaxing rides can be done on the beautiful and well-maintained paths along the river. Rent bikes from tour company **Tuscany Cycle** (Via Ghibellina 133r, from €15/day) in the city center.

DAY TRIPS

Fiesole

Fiesole is only 30 minutes north of Florence via public bus. You can see it from high viewpoints in Florence like Piazzale Michelangelo—it's the town far off in the distance, on the opposite side of the valley up on the hill. This small town is your best shot at experiencing true Tuscany without the long and involved day trip to the farther-out hill towns. If you have four days in Florence, spend the fourth visiting Fiesole to get away from the city-center crowds. Explore the town's quaint little square, and don't miss the Roman amphitheater and relatively minor **ancient Roman ruins archeological site** (€7, generally daily 10:00-17:00, check website for current hours, +39 055 59118, museidifiesole.it) just behind the **Cathedral of Fiesole.** In summer, you'll also find a weekly **Sunday market**

selling souvenirs, handmade goods, and local produce (don't expect the prices to be much lower than what you'll find in the Florence markets, though).

Take in panoramic views of Florence and the surrounding valley while dining at my favorite restaurant in town, **La Reggia degli Etruschi** (Via S. Francesco 18, +39 055 59 385, lareggiadeglietruschi.com).

To get to Fiesole, take bus #7 from Piazza San Marco to the last stop at the top of the hill (about 30 minutes, €2 each way).

Tuscan Hill Towns

Florence is in the heart of Tuscany, a region famous for beautiful, isolated hilltop towns with medieval foundations. They sprang up along Roman trade routes and persevered through the challenging medieval ages. Today, these undeniably quaint and

irresistibly romantic hill towns are popular destinations for travelers. Trips to the Tuscan countryside never disappoint: You can throw a dart at a map of the region and the experience will be just about the same wherever it lands (provided it doesn't hit the Florence bullseye). Check out **Italy on a Budget Tours** (+39 055 0503 517, tuscanyonabudget.com) for their lineup of day trips to these towns. Siena, a couple of hours from Florence by train, is one of the more popular destinations.

HELP!

Tourist Information Centers

Get information online at firenzeturismo.it, or pick up maps and information on sights at Florence's two TI locations (open Mon-Sat 09:00-19:00, Sun 09:00-14:00). The first is near the train station, the second near the Duomo.

Piazza Stazione 4

+39 055 212 245

Piazza del Duomo (west corner of Via Calzaiuoli, inside the Bigallo Museum)

+39 055 288 496

Pickpockets & Scams

Though you'll find beggars on nearly every corner in Florence, pickpocketing isn't as much of a problem here as it is in cities such as Rome and Paris. That said, never leave your drink or belongings unattended, especially while out at the bars and clubs. Always keep your wits about you and, when preparing for a night out on the town, lock away your valuables at the hostel.

Emergencies

Dial 113 for English-speaking police, or 118 for an ambulance.

Hospital

Ospedale di S. Maria Nuova
Piazza S. Maria Nuova 1
+39 055 69 381

US Consulate General

38 Lung'arno Vespucci
+39 055 266 951

ENGLISH-LANGUAGE RESOURCES

The Florentine (theflorentine.net) is an English-language news magazine with news articles, culture reviews, an upcoming events calendar, classifieds, and more. The print edition is available for free around town and at the recommended Cafetteria Oblate.

Florence Is You (florenceisyou.com) is a multilingual newspaper, publishing arts and culture reviews, event listings, and articles about life in Florence. Free copies of the bimonthly paper can be found at various points around town.

VENICE

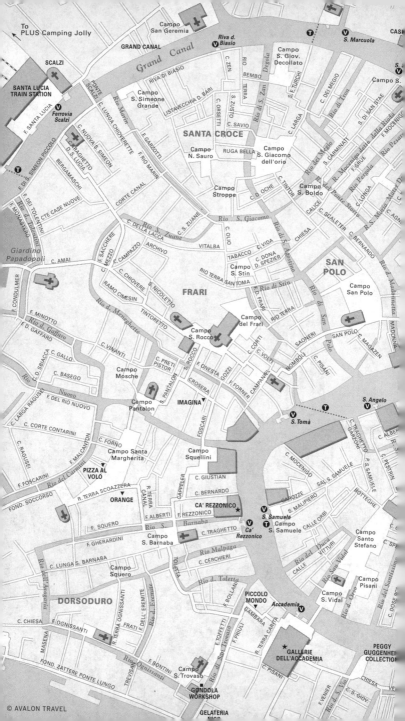

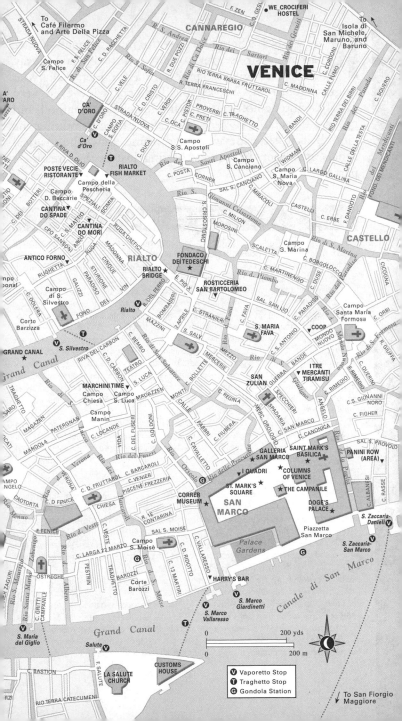

K nown as La Serenissima—the most serene—Venice famously sinks ever so slowly into elegant decay. Glide through the lagoon on a gondola, make your pilgrimage to St. Mark's Basilica, get wide-eyed at a glassblowing demonstration, sample delicious seafood, and go on a delectable *cicchetti* crawl. Save time to wander the city's backstreets, alleyways, and prime draw: the magical canals at sunset. In Venice, getting lost is the dreamiest part of the experience.

VENICE 101

Ingenuity, trade, and plundering hordes all contributed to the creation of one of the world's most distinctive cities: Venice. The name of the city derives from fishing tribes that lived on the shores of the marshy Venetian lagoon. With the decline of the Roman Empire, inhabitants of the surrounding area sought shelter in the difficult-to-navigate estuaries, creating small man-made islands for refuge. Venetians began pounding wooden pilings into the ground, reclaiming land from the sea inch by inch to expand their living space. They traded fish for basic needs like wood, wool, and grains while staying out of the way of the barbarian tribes roaming the Italian peninsula.

Before long, Venice grew into a powerhouse of trans-Mediterranean trade, sparking a golden period that lasted for nearly 1,000 years. Venice thrived as a hub of commerce, riches, and excess while the rest of Europe struggled through the Dark Ages. Immense treasures flowed through this port connecting East (Constantinople and the Silk Road) to West (massive consumer markets in Western Europe). Hybrid architectural styles demonstrate what a crossroads she really was, blending Western Gothic arches and colonnades with Byzantine domes and mosaics.

By AD 700, the leaders of Venice recognized that internal threats were just as much a hazard to the city as external ones. To protect against corruption and violent interfamilial feuds, Venice developed a process of electing its leader, or doge, so complex it just about guaranteed against the possibility of purchasing that seat of power. With this stable process of nonhereditary succession in place, Venice was free to direct all efforts in pursuing expansion of trade routes and further influence.

In 828, Venetian merchants made off with the bones of St. Mark from the coastal Egyptian city of Alexandria and brought them back to Venice. With these religious relics under "protection," Venice became not only an important economic destination but also a religious one. In fact, the doges decreed that it was every Venetian's obligation to go out into the world and bring back treasures to beautify their hometown. Venice was the jumping-off point for the crusaders, and the first port of entry upon their return, and the city benefited handsomely from this.

When Columbus put the New World on the map, attention gradually shifted from East to West, and Venice slid into decline after being battered by the plague. Contemporaries considered this to be God's punishment for Venice's excesses, having grown fat, lazy, and licentious from generations of wealth. The final debilitating straw was Napoleon's focus on quashing the island empire once and for all, to plunder her and to eliminate her as a threat to his power. Today, tourism is the city's strongest trade, with visitors flocking to take in the elegant buildings and architecture left over from Venice's heyday.

PLAN AHEAD

RESERVATIONS
Because the city is so compact, make hostel reservations well ahead of time.

PASSES
San Marco Square Museum Pass
If you're only visiting for two days, the **San Marco Square Museum Pass** (€20) will be of great value. It grants entry to both the Correr Museum and the Doge's Palace. Purchase the pass at the first site you visit and skip the line at the second. It also covers entry into the Archaeological Museum and the Biblioteca Marciana.

Venezia Museum Pass
The **Venezia Museum Pass** (€24 adults, €18 students, visitmuve.it), offers a single entry into each of 12 museums. If you're in town for three days or more, this is definitely worth it. The Doge's Palace, Correr Museum, Ca' Rezzonico, and the Glass Museum on Murano, are included. It pays for itself by your third entry.

LOCAL HAPPENINGS
Carnevale
Carnevale is Venice's Mardi Gras. It occurs annually during the two weeks leading up to Ash Wednesday (the start of Lent). Festivities are packed with people adorned in ornate, traditional costumes from throughout the ages. There are frequent parades and marches through St. Mark's Square, so you'll have to jockey with the crowds to get a good spot for viewing. The party reaches its climax in its second weekend with masquerade balls and face paint for as far as the eye can see. Remember: Early February is cold and damp in Venice. Bring layers, waterproof shoes, and wool socks!

Venice Biennale
This art festival (tickets €24, hours generally Tues-Sun 10:00-18:00, closed Mon, labiennale.org) now runs annually between April and September. The show alternates each year between contemporary art (with numerous exhibits and installations) and architecture and design showcases. It's like the Olympics of art: Each country has its own permanent exhibition space. The exhibits center on I Giardini and Arsenale, two areas tourists rarely venture into.

THREE DAY ITINERARY

Remember that a key part of the Venice experience is aimless wandering along the canals. Plan your route if there's somewhere you need to be, but save some time for exploring without a map. Use any number of Venice's dozens of museums and sights as orienting landmarks. Don't cross that long bridge back onto the mainland and you'll be just fine.

DAY 1: WELCOME TO VENICE
MORNING

Take the plunge into **St. Mark's Square** and brace yourself for your first Venetian breakfast. Take it standing at the classic **I Quadri** (don't sit unless you want to drop €20 on an espresso!).

After breakfast, stand in front of the flagpoles in front of **St. Mark's Basilica.** In a single clockwise-turning panorama, you can see the **Doge's Palace;** the island of **San Giorgio Maggiore** across the canal, through the famous **Columns of Venice** (with both the winged Lion of St. Mark and Venice's original patron saint, St. Theodore, on top), and the Venetian lagoon behind; the **Campanile** (if the line is short, go for it! The climb will cost you €8); thousands of pigeons; some of the most expensive cafés you'll ever see (you can find live music in many of them after sunset); the iconic colonnade, which lines three sides of the square with the Correr Museum at the far end; and finally, the **Torre dell'Orologio,** a clock tower with one of the world's oldest digital faces, on your right. If the line is short at the basilica, you're in luck. If the line is long and you have a backpack with you, find the free bag check in the alley leading away from the square on the left side of the building. For checking your bag you'll get a free skip-the-line pass.

AFTERNOON

It's time for lunch, so head to the streets a couple blocks behind the Doge's Palace to find **Panini Row.** Then double back for a free **glassblowing demonstration at Galleria San Marco.** If you attach yourself to a well-heeled tour group, you'll be treated to an extended demonstration and an aggressive sales pitch.

Follow the Per Rialto signs pointing the way to the **Rialto Bridge.** Enjoy the shops and the bustle along the way.

EVENING

The neighborhood just beyond the Rialto Bridge is a great place to begin a *cicchetti* crawl, snacking at the various bars all along the way. Pick from a wide variety of open-faced sandwiches, fresh seafood, and meatballs. For something to drink that won't swallow your budget in one gulp, ask your waiter for an *"ombra di vino rosso"* (a cheap glass of house wine). After dinner, stay on the north side of the bridge with the locals, who cluster around **Campo Cesare Battisti.**

DAY 2: THE DOGE'S VENICE
MORNING
If you're an early riser, start your day with an early-morning, jostling-free walk along the canals. Make your winding way towards one of Venice's less thronged areas: Cannaregio. You'll find some of the city's best hole-in-the-wall cafés, my favorite being the popular **Café Filermo.** Make your way back to the center (15 minutes or so) and catch your reservation at the **Doge's Palace.** Don't miss one of Venice's most iconic spans, the **Bridge of Sighs** (skip the line with the museum pass).

AFTERNOON
Hop over to **San Giorgio Maggiore Island** on *vaporetto* #2 and climb the bell tower there for a magnificent view of the entire lagoon. Heads up: When the bells toll at the top of the hour, it's deafening. Don't let it catch you off guard.

Head back to the San Marco neighborhood and enjoy a **gondola ride** with budget-traveler friends before 19:00 to avoid the price hike. First pick an area of town you like, then find a gondola in that area; your tour will be a 40-minute loop of the nearby canals. I like the area bordering the Grand Canal northwest of St. Mark's Square. If you're trying to save some cash, hop on a *traghetto* (a short gondola ride from one side of a canal to the other) for only €4.

EVENING
Catch dinner and spend a night out in **Campo Santa Margherita** enjoying a wide selection of excellent restaurants and bars.

DAY 3: CIAO VENEZIA, CIAO, CIAO!
MORNING
There are still plenty of things to see if you've got the time, but you'll have to prioritize. If you need some more art and history, the **Accademia** and **Peggy Guggenheim Venice** museums fit the bill. Endless shopping awaits you on the **Mercerie.** If you've had your fill of Venice, you've got the sleepy cemetery island, **San Michele; Murano,** the glassblowers' island; and **Burano,** the quieter lace-making island with cute little pastel houses. All are a short trip from the center.

AFTERNOON
Don't dillydally if you've got a late-afternoon or early-evening train or flight to catch. It's easy to miss a *vaporetto* departure or to get lost when trying to find your way out of the city. Give yourself some extra time just to be safe. *Buona fortuna!*

TOP NEIGHBORHOODS

The main island of Venice is shaped like a large fish. It's composed of six districts, and you'll be able to to navigate your way through these districts with the aid of the city's major landmarks. Most of the major sights are located in the body or the belly of the fish (the middle and the south end of town), with the main train station, bus terminal, and cruise ports in the northwest.

San Marco is the bull's-eye for most tourists, making it the most touristy district in an extremely touristy town. This is where you'll find the Campanile, St. Mark's Basilica, the Doge's Palace, the Correr Museum, and, between them, expensive cafés. The Accademia footbridge crosses from San Marco south to the district of **Dorsoduro,** where you'll find the Accademia and the Peggy Guggenheim Venice museum. Smack-dab in the middle of the main canal is the famous Rialto Bridge. In the surrounding neighborhood, also known as **Rialto,** you'll find a number of recommended restaurants as well as the famous fish market.

Chances are, a day or two of standing shoulder-to-shoulder with tourists will have you longing for a break from the crowds. Head to **Cannaregio**—Venetians live in this neighborhood, which was once a ghetto where Venice's Jews were crowded together. The deeper you penetrate this district, the more it will yield its off-the-beaten-path cafés and local hangouts. **Castello,** home to shipyards and the massive arsenal complex, was once Europe's biggest shipbuilding operation. Today, it's a quiet residential district with plenty of streets (a little wider than those you'll find in San Marco) and churches worth exploring. Quiet and residential **Giudecca,** across the Grand Canal and south of Dorsoduro, is a nice place to escape to when the crowds in the center start to get to you. It's also where you'll find my favorite hostel in town, Generator Venice.

If you want to get off the main island, you've got a number of nearby islands to choose from: **Murano,** famous for glassblowing, and **Burano,** known for its lacemaking, offer close-up views of their respective industries, both of which have deep roots in the area. The walled **San Michele Island** is a beautiful cemetery island that has been a popular burial site for more than two centuries. **Lido** is the long, skinny island with beaches, cars, and larger resort-like hotels. **San Giorgio Maggiore Island** offers the church bell tower to climb for beautiful panoramic views over St. Mark's Square.

TOP SIGHTS

St. Mark's Square

One of the most famous squares in all of Europe, Piazza San Marco embodies Venetian elegance—it will live up to all of your Venetian daydreams and then some. Laid out in the 9th century and built up in the 12th century, this square is named after Venice's patron saint, St. Mark, whose bones are interred in the basilica. Lined with Gothic colonnades and with live music (and thousands of pigeons) in the air, it's the epicenter of Venice's Disneyland-esque experience.

If you are so inclined, you can spend an entire day exploring the attractions that line the square. Three of Venice's biggest draws—**St. Mark's Basilica,** the **Campanile,** and the **Doge's Palace**—are here. The square also contains the **Torre dell'Orologio,** a clock tower that caps the high, arched gateway leading to Mercerie, Venice's merchant district. Dating back to the 15th century, the clock tower displays one of the world's oldest digital clocks. The roman numerals click away the hours in five-minute intervals, and two figures (probably shepherds) toll out the hours on the bell high above the square. On the ledge above the digital clock, the winged lion of St. Mark looks out over the crowd below.

Free, always open, San Marco

St. Mark's Basilica

By the 9th century, Venice had become a regional naval and mercantile power, but it lacked religious oomph. Venetians found what they needed when two merchants brought the bones of St. Mark to Venice from Egypt in 828. A local legend (probably fabricated long after the bones arrived) said that Venice was God's chosen home for St. Mark: The saint had been blown off course into the Venetian lagoon and was visited by an angel, who told him he would be laid to rest there. A more likely explanation: In the medieval world, relics brought substantial revenue from visiting pilgrims, and Venetians were keen to capture this market. So the Venetian merchants stole St. Mark's bones, hiding them under cuts of pork to deter the Muslim guards from searching their cargo too thoroughly. With St. Mark taking over patron saint duties from St. Theodore, the winged lion of St Mark quickly became the symbol of Venice.

The basilica we see today was completed in the 11th century as a replacement for the original St. Mark's basilica, which an angry mob accidentally torched in the 10th century. The church is one of the most richly decorated in Europe, with strong Byzantine influences clearly visible in the domes, decorated spires, and ornate, pointed arches. The sparkling golden mosaics on the facade illustrate the arrival of the relics of St. Mark into the Venetian lagoon. Inside, admire over 4,000 square meters of intricately detailed mosaics. In a nod to the power of the doge, you'll find two pulpits inside the basilica: one for the priest, the other for public announcements from the doge.

One of these announcements declared it the duty of all Venetians (merchants or crusaders) to capture and bring back treasures from overseas. Before long, St. Mark's Basilica was one massive robber's den, with a mountain of gold and jewels growing daily in the church's treasury; many of these looted treasures are still on display. Even the equestrian statues in the facade of the church over the entrance (now replicas) were stolen from what is now Istanbul.

If you have a backpack, find the free bag check on Calle S. Basso, just beyond and to the left of the façade when looking straight on the church. Check your bag here and you'll be given a ticket to skip the line—a rare win-win situation in a city overflowing with tourist traps.

Free general entry (€2 online reservation), free bag check, €5 to go upstairs to see the horses up close, €3 to go into the treasury (both highly recommended), general entry Mon-Sat 09:45-17:00, Sun 14:00-17:00 (until 16:00 Nov-Easter), St. Mark's Square, San Marco, group reservations +39 041 241 3817, basilicasanmarco.it

The Campanile

The Campanile, towering over St. Mark's Square, is Venice's most prominent bell tower (it's also far and away the tallest building in town). Unlike so many of Europe's high points, you can ride an elevator to the top of this one. Naturally, the 91-meter tower provides the best panoramic views of the city—and even a view of the

Alps in the distance on clear days. Originally built as a lighthouse to assist navigation through the lagoon, the golden spire and marble belfry were added in 1514. After a dramatic collapse in 1902 (fortunately, no one was hurt), it was rebuilt in time for the tower's 1,000-year anniversary. To avoid the crowds, visit as early as possible. (And remember that San Giorgio Maggiore Island, just across the canal, provides a much less crowded panorama—and a photo op that includes the iconic Campanile.)

€8, Easter–June and Oct daily 09:00–19:00, July–Sept daily 09:00–21:00, Nov–Easter daily 09:30–15:45, St. Mark's Square, San Marco

Columns of Venice

The first glimpse of home must have been a welcome sight for sailors returning from long voyages. As such, Venetian merchants became sentimentally attached to the Campanile and the two Columns of Venice. These marble columns with Doric caps stand more than 40 feet tall. **St. Theodore** (a Roman soldier who refused to conform to the state-sponsored pagan religion, and Venice's first patron saint) crowns one column. With his Byzantine origins, St. Theodore became politically inconvenient, and Venetians eventually bumped him in favor of **St. Mark.** His winged lion (cast in bronze), with one paw resting on a book, stands proudly on the second column.

Free, always open, St. Mark's Square, San Marco

Doge's Palace

This palace-turned-museum is an unforgettable example of Venice's marriage of Eastern and Western architecture. In a time when everyone else was hiding out in cold, dark castles, Venice's doge and government met and lived in this grand, beautifully decorated palace, continuously improved and embellished over the centuries. The first palace was built in 810, and it remained the center of political life in Venice throughout its golden age. Packed with spectacular Renaissance murals and gilded furniture, it was turned into the state-run museum in 1923. Your visit will take you through the governing cham-

SO YOU WANT TO BE A DOGE...

Being a doge—the elected ruler of ancient Venice—was a big deal. The office brought tremendous power and wealth with it. The Venetians wanted to ensure that the right people were elected in the right way. The resulting electoral process was about as convoluted as any in the world. Here are the 10 easy steps to the process of selecting a doge in the 13th century

1. A *ballottino*, a boy chosen at random, draws 30 names by plucking balls out of a vase, beginning the entire selection process by chance.
2. From the group of 30, 9 are randomly chosen.
3. These 9 vote up 40 names, each of which needs at least 7 of the 9 possible votes to be considered.
4. The 40 are then cut down to 12 by random draw.
5. Those 12 vote up another 25.
6. Those 25 are reduced to 9 again.
7. Those 9 choose 45, each of which needs at least 7 votes once more.
8. From those 45, 11 are randomly selected.
9. Those 11 choose 41, who must not have been included in any of the reduced groups that named candidates in earlier steps.
10. Those 41 then choose the doge by a vote.

The doge was carefully monitored by the nobles and not allowed to speak to foreign emissaries without direct supervision. All letters and communications coming in and out of the doge's palace were monitored, and appropriate gifts for the doge were limited to items of relatively low value, like flowers and herbs. All these seemingly overbearing precautions went a long way toward minimizing corruption at the pinnacle of Venice's power. Steering largely clearly of corruption, the city-state was able to spend its energy and capital expanding trade routes and the treasury, rather than funneling the city's vast wealth into the pockets of the powerful.

bers, the royal apartments, an impressive armory, and the once-rat-infested prisons where troublemakers were kept (including legendary lover Casanova for a time). While touring these vast halls, keep an eye out for the little mailboxes decorated with grotesque faces. These were slots in which you could submit letters accusing anyone of foul play or corruption.

Some of the people mentioned in these letters might have made the short journey from the palace's chambers to the prison across the **Bridge of Sighs,** so named because it was the last glimpse of the beautiful canals that prisoners would get for quite some time, perhaps ever. A shot of the bridge's exterior, best viewed from the next bridge over toward the lagoon, is an iconic image of Venice; during peak season, you'll have to elbow your way to the front of a crowd of shutterbugs.

Both the Doge's Palace and Correr Museum are covered by the San Marco Square Museum Pass (€20). Buy your ticket at the less crowded Correr Museum and you'll be able to skip the line at Doge's Palace simply by flashing the pass.

€20 adults, €18 students, ticket includes entry to Correr Museum, Museo Archeologico Nazionale, and Sale Monumentali della Biblioteca Nazionale Marciana, Apr-Oct daily 08:30-19:00, Nov-Mar daily 08:30-17:30, last entries an hour before closing, closed on Christmas and New Year's Day, St. Mark's Square, San Marco, +39 041 271 5911, palazzo-ducale.visitmuve.it

Correr Museum

I've always found the Correr Museum to be one of the most interesting in town. Bequeathed by a wealthy collector, the art went on display in 1836 and features paintings, sculptures, and artifacts, all of which combine to paint a detailed portrait of daily life in Venice from the 15th century onwards. Enter in the passageway on the far end of St. Mark's Square through the colonnade and turn right up the grand staircase. Plan to spend at least 90 minutes in this museum spanning the length of St. Mark's Square—longer if you're an ardent art or history lover.

€20 adults, €18 students, also includes entry to Doge's Palace, Museo Archeologico Nazionale, and Sale Monumentali della Biblioteca Nazionale Marciana, Apr-Oct daily 10:00-19:00, Nov-Mar 10:00-17:00, last entry

one hour before closing, St. Mark's Square, San Marco, +39 041 240 5211, correr.visitmuve.it

Glassblowing Demonstration at Galleria San Marco

Due to the fire hazard, glass factories are not permitted on the main island of Venice, but you can catch a professional glassblowing demonstration at **Galleria San Marco.** The welcoming team ushers you up the stairs and directly into the workshop. There, an artisan grabs a slag of molten glass and puffs their way through a series of pinches, rolling, reheating, kneading, and adding other pieces of glass for color and texture. A vase or a tiny horse statue takes shape before your eyes. An English-speaking guide narrates the artist's deft movements. Your 20-minute demonstration ends when your glassblower tosses the just-finished glass piece back into the oven, where it quickly melts—ready to be recycled for the next show. The team will then give you an enthusiastic 15-minute sales pitch, after which there'll be time for shopping. (Tip: Make use of the free restrooms while you're here—they're tough to find elsewhere.)

Find the passage between #140 and #141 on the main square and turn left at the T. Show this book and they'll give you a private demonstration and a 20 percent discount on any purchases.

Free, souvenirs from €15, daily 10:00-17:00, demonstrations running whenever there's an audience, 181A San Marco (see directions in listing), San Marco, +39 041 271 8671, galleriasanmarco.it

Grand Canal

If the canals of Venice are the city's arteries and veins, the Grand Canal is Venice's jugular. All of Venetian life passes through this man-made waterway, which cuts a bold z-shaped line through the center of the almost 200 islands that make up the city. You'll see everything pass through here that you'd see on a highway: taxis, buses, ambulances, private vessels, construction boats, grocery delivery services, police and firefighters, and more—all aquatic versions of their land-based counterparts. To make the most of Venice, you'll need to cross paths with this waterway at least once.

Free, always open, crossing points at Ponte degli Scalzi, Ponte Rialto, and Ponte dell'Accademia

Rialto Bridge

The Rialto Bridge (Ponte Rialto) is the grand, gleaming-white stone bridge you see in so many of the pictures of Venice that lure travelers from the world over. It's possibly the most famous stone bridge in the world. In the 12th century it was a pontoon bridge and then a timber bridge a century later, but, after a number of collapses, it was rebuilt in stone in the 16th century. Until the 19th century (when two more bridges were built) it was the only permanent bridge crossing the Grand Canal. Since, for centuries, so much of Venice's traffic crossed this bridge, it's perhaps no surprise that the Rialto district surrounding the span became and remained Venice's social and commercial heart. Today, the place is lined with shops where you can pick up touristy knickknacks, watches, and jewelry (don't expect any bargains).

Free, always open, Rialto

Gallerie dell'Accademia

Venice's most famous art museum, the Galleria dell'Accademia, features a wide range of pieces from the 14th to the 18th centuries. You'll find masterworks from greats like Tintoretto, Titian, Bellini, and Veronese. One exceptional highlight is Leonardo da Vinci's *Vitruvian Man*—that's the guy in a circle with his arms and legs outstretched that has been plastered on just about everything over the years. It's probably the great master's second-most-recognizable work of art.

€12, free first Sun of the month, Tues-Sun 08:15-19:15 (until 17:00 in winter), Mon 08:15-14:00, last entry 45 minutes before closing, Campo della Carita, Dorsoduro, +39 041 520 0345, gallerieaccademia.org

Peggy Guggenheim Venice

Housed in the palace overlooking the Grand Canal that was purchased by American heiress Peggy Guggenheim in 1949, this collection is the second-most popular attraction in Venice after the Doge's Palace, and for good reason—it's one of Italy's (and, indeed, the world's) premier modern art museums, housing an array of avant-garde American and Italian pieces from the 20th century. All the funky modern styles are represented including futurism, cubism, and surrealism, by greats like Picasso, Dalí, and Pollock. Free and informative background discussions are offered often.

€15, Wed-Mon 10:00-18:00, closed Tues, Dorsoduro 701, Dorsoduro, +39 041 240 5411, guggenheim-venice.it

Ca' Rezzonico

This collection of furniture and artwork from Venice's exuberant 17th and 18th centuries is housed in a merchant family's elaborate palace, built in Venetian baroque style with large windows and ornate balconies spread across three glamorous floors. The exterior's elegance matches that of the art inside, which includes masterpieces of Venetian baroque artwork from the likes of Canaletto, Longhi, and Tiepolo.

€10, covered by Venezia Museum Pass, Wed-Mon 10:00-18:00, Nov-March until 17:00, closed Tues, ticket office closes one hour before museum, Fondamenta Rezzonico, Dorsoduro, +39 041 241 0100, carezzonico.visitmuve.it

San Giorgio Maggiore Island

Directly across the Grand Canal from St. Mark's Square, through the Columns of Venice, proudly stands the island of San Giorgio Maggiore. A short *vaporetto* hop zips you to this tiny, one-sight island dominated by the grand, gleaming-white **San Giorgio church** (free, climb bell tower for €6, daily 09:00-19:00, Nov-Mar closes at dusk, +39 041 522 7827). Take the lift to the top for stunning views of the main islands of Venice and the entire lagoon. Note that the lift stops running 30 minutes before the church closes and is not accessible Sundays during services.

Connect to San Giorgio Maggiore aboard *vaporetto* #2 from a stand on St. Mark's Square.

Murano Island

As far back as the 7th century, this island was a commercial hub, but in the 13th century it became the center of an art form intimately associated with Venice: glassblowing. In 1291 the Venetian Republic ordered that all glassmaking operations be removed from Venice after a number of fires made the risks all too obvious. The industry moved across the water to Murano. Glassmaking grew into such an important industry there that artisans were afforded exceptional privileges: high social status,

immunity, the right to bear swords, and the privilege of marrying their daughters into noble families. However, there were costs as well; so valuable were their skills that glassmakers were not allowed to leave the republic under the penalty of death.

The dusty **Glass Museum** (Museo Vetrario, €8, covered by Venezia Museum Pass, daily 10:00-18:00, Nov-Mar until 17:00, Fondamenta Giustinian, +39 041 739 586, museiciviciveneziani.it) is a worthwhile visit to see samples of Venetian glass both ancient and modern. The dated displays take you all the way back to 1,900-year-old Roman glass, and continue through the techniques and artifacts from Venice's golden age. Time your visit for a live demonstration and tour (Tues and Thurs at 14:30), which provides an in-depth examination of the glassmaking process.

The operational factories are generally closed to the public, but there are a number of opportunities to watch artisans make a basic piece in front of your eyes (invariably followed by a sales pitch). Try **Vetreria Artistica Colleoni** (tours at 10:00, 11:00, 11:30, 14:00, 15:00, and 15:30 daily, Fondamente Colleoni 7, +39 041 527 4872, colleoni. com, vaporetto: Murano Faro), opposite the Glass Museum (just a 15-minute walk across the canal) for a 20-minute glassblowing demonstration by the team of artisans making custom and retail pieces. Your €10 ticket gives you credit for the same amount in the gift shop, and many of the smaller pieces start around this price point, so you'll walk away with a nice souvenir.

Otherwise, just follow the *Fornace Glass* signs—they'll take you to a workshop. They all tend to close around lunchtime (13:00-15:00), and the best time to visit them is in the morning.

Getting to Murano is easy enough. From the main train station, take the direct *vaporetto* #3. You'll be there in about 20 minutes. From San Marco take *vaporetto* #7.

Burano Island

Burano, known for its lace-making industry, is well worth the trip for some window-shopping. Burano's pastel-colored houses and quiet lanes make for an exceptionally peaceful afternoon just a short *vaporetto* ride away from the bustle of the main islands. On the main square, Piazza Galuppi, you'll find the small **Lace Museum** (€5, Apr-Oct daily 10:00-18:00, until 17:00 Nov-Mar, Piazza Galuppi 187, museomerlet-to.visitmuve.it, +39 041 730 034) demonstrating the island's stock in trade. Loads of items on display take you through more than five centuries of lace making. You can even catch local grannies carrying on the tradition in person—ask politely and they'll happily show you what they're working on.

Vaporetto #14 connects San Marco with Burano in about 50 minutes.

San Michele Island

San Michele Island has been Venice's cemetery for more than two centuries. With real estate on the main island at such a premium (and sanitation so crucial), it became necessary to transport the dead to somewhere far from population centers. The result is San Michele—an entire island of the dead and a unique sight to behold. It wasn't always a graveyard, so you'll also find Venice's first Renaissance church, **Chiesa di San Michele.**

Hop out here on a quick seven-minute ride. Take *vaporetti* #4.1 or #4.2 from Fondamente Nova B, on the north side of the main island, just north of Ospedale (Hospital) San Giovanni e Paolo.

Lido Island

Lido is the long and skinny island that separates the Venetian lagoon from the Adriatic Sea. As it's built on actual land, Lido feels more like a typical town—complete with buses and resorts—than Venice does. Come out here on a hot day to relax on the beaches and get away from the crowds.

Take the *rossa* (red) *vaporetto* from the San Marco Giardinetti stop for a fast-moving 12-minute ride across the lagoon. Buses take you up and down the island for €1.50. The best beaches are towards the very south end of the east side of the island.

TOP EATS

Like so many of Italy's coastal towns, Venice has a storied heritage of fresh seafood and delicious pasta. Not all restaurants are equal. You'll have to navigate your way through Venice's fair share of tourist traps. They're pretty easy to spot: menus in a dozen languages, neon lights, food out on display, recruiters who shove menus into the hands of passersby, and locations right on main tourist thoroughfares. The much better local places are usually a couple blocks off the busy streets. For the best food in Venice, take a *cicchetti* crawl of the restaurants lining the intimate **Campo Cesare Battisti** at some point during your visit.

Typical *coperto* is €3 per person for bread and service, with nice restaurants charging up to €5 or more. Any more and it better be a special spot!

Cantina Do Mori

This is your classic old-school Venetian wine and tapas bar. This place, with its wooden paneling and tin pots and pans hanging from the ceiling, harks back to a time long before neon lights and multi-language menus. Go for a mix plate of *cicchetti* from the bar and enjoy tasty regional wine in this social, tourist-friendly bar.

Finger food from €2, glasses of wine from €3.50, Mon-Sat 08:00-19:30, Sat 08:00-17:00, Sestiere San Polo 429, Rialto, +39 041 522 5401

Cantina Do Spade

This family-run cantina isn't so much about the smiles, but the typical Venetian food is lovely. Try their *cicchetti* at the front of the bar, or, if you're feeling adventurous, sit down in the back and order the *pasta al nero di seppia* (squid ink pasta). They have excellent *frittura* (fried fresh seafood). The meatballs in tomato sauce are also a classic highlight.

Dishes from €14, daily 10:00-15:00 and 18:00-22:00, closed Tuesday mornings, San Polo 859, Rialto, +39 041 521 0583, cantinadospade.com

Paradiso Perduto

Flanked by a series of popular choices along the Fondamenta Misericordia, Paradiso Perduto hums along with curt service dishing out fresh seafood options to locals and tourists alike. The good times spill onto the canal with outside seating. Inside, the communal tables create a jovial atmosphere, as guests chow down on overflowing *frutti di mare* pastas and filets of snapper caught earlier that day. On Mondays you'll find live piano music (reservations recommended), and during the rest of the week the music is piped through cheap speakers. The owner, Maurizio, often pushes these speakers well past their limits with corny Italian serenades and salsa music. He's just sharing his love of food and life (he may also be responsible for the nude sketches lining the walls).

€18 pastas, €25 *secondi*, €3 *coperto*, cash only, Thurs-Mon 10:00-24:00, closed Tues-Wed, Fondamenta della Misericordia, Cannaregio, +39 041 720 581, ilparadisoperduto.wordpress.com

Osteria Al Cicheto

Stop into this *osteria*, a quaint old-world bar popular with locals, just off the main drag when coming from the train station. Enjoy some of the most authentic *cicchetti* around in the wood-paneled bar, and wash it down with inexpensive but palatable Veneto wines. If you want to sit down, these guys specialize in beef tartare and *pasta al nero di seppia* (squid ink pasta).

Wines and *cicchetti* from €2.50, Mon-Sat 09:30-15:30 and 17:30-22:30, closed Sat mornings, Calle de la

CICHETTI CRAWL

Before embarking on a culinary tour of Venice's *cicchetti* bars, familiarize yourself with a few terms:

Cicchetti (pronounced "chee-khetti") are Venetian snacks similar to tapas. At bars across the city, you'll find displays of cod, anchovies, octopus, and other bite-sized morsels available to order. These make for a classy accompaniment to an *ombra* (glass of wine)—and also keep you from getting a little too lubricated. Many of these snacks come served like an open-faced sandwich on *crostini*: a slice of bread topped with a little olive oil and whatever the fishers caught that day. *Cicchetti* usually cost €1.50-3 each.

Tramezzini, a type of *cicchetti*, remind me of the sandwiches my grandma used to make for me. Made of soft white bread with the crust cut off and smothered in mayonnaise, these not-quite-filling sandwiches are typically Venetian—you'll spot locals downing them everywhere you go in Venice.

Places to Go:

Make a fun *cicchetti* crawl of the restaurants lining the intimate **Campo Cesare Battisti,** near the west side of the Rialto Bridge. Take some time to peek in at each of the listings to see which of them satisfies your taste buds without eating through your budget. Order your food and drinks one at a time to gauge service and value before going all in. There's no need to tip while on your *cicchetti* crawl.

Al Merca (Campo Bella Vienna 213): Very popular street bar with small bites and wine (€2.50) to take in the square.

Bussola Cocktail Lab (Campo Bella Vienna 222): Stop in for an expertly made spritz in a suave atmosphere that spills out onto the square.

Ancòra Venezia (Sestiere San Polo 120): An upscale sit-down piano bar with amazing seafood salads.

Al Pesador Osteria (Sestiere San Polo 125): Excellent food presentation with sophisticated service.

Osteria Bancogiro (Campo San Giacometto 122): Classy bar serving hearty Venetian fare—seafood, pastas, and bruschetta.

Naranzaria (Sestiere San Polo 130): Nice little tapas and wine bar; serves pizza on the terrace out back.

Misericordia and just a block from the Ponte degli Scalzi, +39 041 716037

Casa Bonita

This restaurant in the Jewish district of Cannaregio is a spot for tranquil canal-front drinks and bites and, most importantly, a chance to escape from the tourist crowds. Casa Bonita is known for its grilled fish and heaping plates of pasta with both seafood and meat options. The service is a bit on the slow side, but the presentation and funky atmosphere make it worth the wait. Take your meal outside on the canal or under the colorful chandelier inside. To get here, take a left just before Ponte delle Guglie (the first major bridge east of the train station) and continue to Fondamenta Savorgnan. For a drink nearby, try **Al Parlamento** (€3 spritz, daily 07:30-01:30, Fondamenta Savorgnan, +39 041 244 0214, alparlamento.it).

€30 dinners, Tues-Sun 12:00-23:00, Fondamenta Savorgnan, +39 041 524 6164, casabonita.it

I Tre Mercanti Tiramisu Bar

These guys are famous for their tiramisu, expertly made fresh each morning behind large windows in a wide range of flavors. If you've got a hankering for the typical Venetian treat, try it here in all shades of flavors, from classic to green tea and strawberry to mango.

Tiramisu cups from 3.50, daily 11:00-19:30, Campo della Guerra, +39 041 522 2901, itremercanti.it

Poste Vecie Ristorante

Cross the private wooden bridge into this classic splurge-worthy restaurant—supposedly one of the oldest in Venice. Converted from a 16th-century post office, the building was redone in the 1800s with beautiful frescoes and became popular among Venice's elite, including Casanova himself. You can indulge in some of Venice's finest dining surrounded by oil paintings and even two-hundred-year-old mail, which hangs next to a grand fireplace that roars all evening long in the fall and winter. It's a cozy, intimate place to take someone special.

Unforgettable meals (starter, entrée, dessert, and glass of wine) from €35, Wed-Mon 12:00-15:00 and 19:00-22:30, Rialto Pescheria, Rialto, +39 041 721 822, postevecie.com

Antico Forno
Step off the main drag and into this take-away joint cranking out steaming-hot slices of pizza all day long. The pizza is as good as the service is terrible. I usually get a slice (sometimes two) of their thick-crust spicy pepperoni and head immediately for the exit.

Marinara focaccia from €3.50, daily 11:30-21:30, Ruga Ravano 973, Rialto, +39 041 520 4110, anticofornovenezia.com

Rialto Fish Market
The Rialto Fish Market (*pescheria*) is a great place to come for lunch. Dozens of bars and stalls serve up seafood straight from the Mediterranean. A favorite of mine is **Muro,** a stall that serves heaping plates of calamari and seafood mixes (different every day) for €7-10, glass of wine included. The only way you can get fresher seafood is to eat it straight out of the net that caught it.

Free entry, Tues-Sat 07:00-14:00, Campo Bella Vienna 222, Rialto

Panini Row
The small street I call Panini Row is a great budget option close to St. Mark's Square. When standing in the square, walk towards the basilica and head down its left side. You'll come to a bridge on your right. Cross it, and after a block or so you'll find **Calle degli Albanesi** and **Calle le Rasse,** both of which have a good number of budget eating options (enjoy your meal alfresco). If you're in the mood to enjoy your food indoors, you'll find cozy wooden interiors at **Osteria Da Baco** (daily 08:15-01:00).

Calle degli Albanesi and Calle le Rasse, San Marco

Harry's Bar
Don't let the casual name fool you: This place is posh, with a price tag to match. Harry's is renowned for its famous clientele. Kings and queens, famous authors and film stars (Orson Welles and Charlie Chaplin just to name a few) have all bellied up to the bar here. Tourists like you and me might not be able to afford the food—the cheapest dish on the menu is the €19 bean soup—but we can afford a cocktail or two, and we'll be able to say that we've tipped a bottle in Ernest Hemingway's favorite watering hole in Venice—the ultimate seal of approval.

Drinks from €15, daily 10:30-23:00, Calle Vallaresso 1323, San Marco, +39 041 528 5777, harrysbarvenezia.com

I Quadri
Sample the elegance of St. Mark's Square at I Quadri, one of the square's institutional cafés. Be forewarned: A sit-down espresso here will run you in the neighborhood of €20. To save a little, take your breakfast and coffee at the bar inside. I Quadri, which has hosted the likes of Mikhail Gorbachev and Woody Allen, is a worthy splurge. If you're in after hours, try the typical *Vov* liqueur, made with egg whites, along with a Baicoli biscuit to dip in it. It doesn't get much more Venetian than that!

Meals easily climb past €50, daily 09:00-24:00, St. Mark's Square 121, San Marco, +39 041 522 2105, alajmo.it/en/sezione/ristorante-quadri/ristorante-quadri

Rosticceria San Bartolomeo
Come to this bright but comfortable cafeteria for some great comfort food at incredibly low prices. With dozens of tasty pasta dishes, seafood entrées, and meat options to choose from (all for €6-10), you're spoiled for choice—just point and smile to place your order. Eat your food on the lower level, or head upstairs for sit-down service.

Bites from €4, daily 09:00-21:30, Sottoportego della Bissa 5424/A, San Marco, +39 041 522 3569, Facebook: Rosticceria San Bartolomeo

Arte della Pizza
This is my favorite pizza by the slice in all of Venice. Grab a slice for €2, or get a whole pizza for €6. Order at the glass case and take it away or eat at the bar along the wall. Most get takeaway to eat along the nearby canal.

Pizza from €6, Tues-Sun 11:00-21:00, Calle Dell'Aseo 1861/A, Cannaregio, +39 041 524 6520, artedellapizzavenezia.com

Caffé Filermo

Owner Rafael sets the welcoming and fun tone in this bar with bites. It's an excellent place to start the day with real espresso and pastry, or to unwind with a glass of wine after conquering Venice's many sights. Café Filermo may be located on the main pedestrian circuit (it's between the Santa Lucia train station and St. Mark's), but it's managed to preserve an authentic feel and customers never leave feeling as though they've been overcharged—a rarity in this part of the world. Look for the Brazilian flag out front, pull up a stool or a chair, and strike up a conversation with Rafael or the often-social crowd.

Snacks from €3.50, daily 09:00-22:30, Strada Nova, around the corner and bridge from Campo della Magdalena church, Cannaregio, +39 041 524 4946

Marchini Time

Venetians stop in here for their caffeine and sugar power-ups. If you've got a long day of sightseeing ahead of you (and you probably do) stop in for a double espresso macchiato, a delicious cupcake, or one of their authentic pastries. Cannoli might not come from Venice, but it definitely hits the spot!

Coffee and pastries from €2.50, Calle de S. Luca, daily 07:30-20:30, +39 041 241 3087, Facebook: Pasticceria Marchini

Orange

A mainstay on the south end of Campo Santa Margherita, stop into Orange for a late-afternoon spritz and a range of pasta dishes, *tramezzini* sandwiches, fruit, and desserts. For a paltry €12, the two-course lunch menu is a steal. In the evening, it's a great place to enjoy a glass of champagne—pull up a chair in either the garden out back or on the new rooftop terrace overlooking the square, both of which are rare finds in Venice.

€1.50 surcharge for terrace, daily 09:00-02:00, Campo Santa Margherita 3054, Dorsoduro, +39 041 523 4740, orangebar.it

Pizzeria Al Volo

For quick and fresh pizza by the slice, drop into this spot on Campo Santa Margherita. There's no need to find a seat inside: The benches in the square make for great people-watching while you devour your slice of thin-crust pizza that comes piping-hot straight out of the oven.

Slices from €4, daily 11:00-24:00, Campo Santa Margherita, +39 041 522 5430, Facebook: Pizza Al Volo

Coop

Find this friendly neighborhood grocery store just toward St. Mark's Square from Campo Santa Maria Formosa. Pop in here and head to the deli counter to pick up heaping sandwiches (€3.50) and fresh pizza by the slice (€3)—and any other groceries you might need. The word is out, and travelers on a budget flock here at lunchtime. Keep an eye out for their six-plus locations around town; they're great for a cheap and easy snack anytime of day.

Daily 08:30-20:30, Salisada San Lio, San Marco, +39 041 241 2273

TOP NIGHTLIFE

Don't expect much of a late-night scene in this town unless you're here during Carnevale, when masquerade balls run to all hours. For the rest of the year, Venice's sparse nightlife tends to focus on a handful of squares around town. Your best grouping of spritz-serving bars is a stone's throw away from the Rialto Bridge. Just follow the noise off the north side of the bridge to **Campo Cesare Battisti**. Once there, it's easy to kick off a crawl down the line of pubs, trying each one's specialty drinks and dishes. If you want to party with Venice's younger crowd (mostly university students), **Campo Santa Margherita** is the most popular square for socializing. Generally, Venetians eat around 20:00 and head to the bars at 21:00.

BARS

Café Noir

For a chic cocktail lounge and wine bar that also serves food, try Café Noir in the Dorsoduro district, not far from Campo Santa Margherita. This mod bar, with its nondescript matte black exterior, may not make much of an aesthetic statement, but

LGBT VENICE

While Italy as a whole is generally conservative, members of the LGBT community will have no problems when visiting Venice. However, the nightlife scene in Venice is spotty to begin with, and the LGBT nightlife scene is even spottier. In fact, I can't recommend a single place on the main island for LGBT mingling. The city is full of friendly cafés, restaurants, and tapas bars, but you may just have to surf the mainstream wave for the duration of your stay.

they've built their reputation around their atmosphere, not their décor. Bartenders mix a wide array of ingredients and bitters, concocting delicious beverages that you can sip at the high-top tables. Their thick-cut panini hit the spot after a long day of sightseeing.

Cocktails from €6.50, sandwiches from €5, Mon–Sat 11:00–02:00, Sun 09:00–19:30, Calle dei Preti, Dorsoduro, +39 041 528 0956, Facebook: Café Noir

Imagina Cafe

This place is a triple threat, serving cappuccinos and pastries in the morning, tasty panini and salads at lunchtime, and cocktails at night. It even comes complete with a photography gallery with ever-changing exhibitions. As one of only a handful of Venice's pregame spots, this place packs out with partygoers getting ready to take on the night.

Drinks and snacks from €8, Sun–Thurs 07:00–21:00, Fri–Sat 07:00–01:00, Sun 08:00–21:00, Rio Tera Canal—Ponte dei Pugni, Dorsoduro +39 041 241 0625, imaginacafe.it

Piccolo Mondo

"This Little World" is the closest thing I've found to an actual club in Venice. It fills up with the only people on the island (mostly tourists) who are looking for a late-night party. Be prepared to pay €10 for a bottle of beer, and be sure to count your money both before and after you pay for your drinks (shortchanging seems to be a recurring issue here). Good luck finding your hostel at the end of the night!

Drinks from €10, daily 22:30–04:00, Dorsoduro 1056a, Dorsoduro, +39 329 167 1250, Facebook: Piccolo Mondo Disco Club

TOP SHOPPING & MARKETS

SHOPPING DISTRICTS

Rialto

There are dozens of shops on the Rialto Bridge itself, as well as in the surrounding area. You'll find the cliché touristy souvenirs: postcards, Venetian masks, snow globes, and little gondola figurines by the truckload. If you really want to bring a trinket home with you, come here to get ideas, but make your purchases farther off the tourist circuit—prices drop considerably the farther you get from the crowds.

Rialto

Fondaco dei Tedeschi

This renovated merchant house has morphed into an elegant, multilevel, high-end shopping mall with a colonnaded atrium and classy cafés. The highlight of

this shopping center, however, is the free terrace at the top with panoramic 360-degree views.

Daily 10:00–21:00, Rialto, dfs.com

Mercerie

The Mercerie (Merchants' Streets) is made up of a series of narrow streets—Mercerie dell'Orologio, Mercerie San Zulian, Mercerie del Capitello, and Mercerie San Salvador—linking the political and religious hub of Venice (San Marco) with the just-as-important commercial heart of the city (Rialto). Take your time strolling these tight lanes. Those looking for keepsakes will find something here—there's everything from glass trinkets to lingerie and, of course, Carnevale masks galore.

San Marco to Rialto

MARKETS
Rialto Market
This market just north of the Rialto Bridge is an excellent place to catch a glimpse of daily Venetian life. Vendors here sell fruit, fresh seafood, and vegetables. The produce is never locally grown, so read the origin information closely (some of it is imported from as far afield as Asia and South America). Whenever possible, opt for the produce originating in "Italia."

Free, produce and goods market daily 07:00–20:00, fish market Tues-Sat 07:00–14:00, Rialto

TOP PARKS & RECREATION

Gondola Rides
There's nothing more quintessentially Venetian than cruising down the canals in a gondola. In recent years, the *gondolieri* have unionized, picked up Paul & Shark as a sponsor, and standardized their prices, taking the stressful negotiation out of the experience. You can fit up to five people on one gondola, and the price doesn't change whether you've got one or the max load. Your best bet is to link up with fellow budget travelers and pool your euros. Note: With Venice in all its hypercommercialized glory, the romance of the experience sometimes gets lost. Temper your expectations. The canals are often packed with gondolas, and the *gondolieri* are often less than fully engaged—they might be texting for the duration of your ride, or they might even short you on cruising time. Some of them can border on lecherous, so try to ignore the catcalls and winks. If you're not willing to drop a wad on a full ride, hop on a ***traghetto*** (pedestrian ferry), which shuttles visitors across the Grand Canal at numerous points—there's one from the Rialto Fish Market. A ride on the poor man's gondola will be brief, but it only costs €4! Tipping *gondolieri* or *traghetto* drivers isn't expected.

Numerous starting points throughout the city, 30–40 minute ride €80 before 19:00, €100 after 19:00, last rides depart around 23:00, gondolavenezia.it

Palace Gardens
Located just around the corner from San Marco, toward the *vaporetti* stops, these small gardens are a welcome respite from the massive crowds, who seem to pass by this square without being enticed by its charms. I like to come here for a quiet moment to enjoy an icy *granita* or ice cream. If you've got picnic supplies, the benches are a nice place to tuck in.

Free, daily dawn-dusk

TOP TOURS

Touring Venice with a professional guide will help you make sense of the city's complex history and its equally confusing layout. Free tip-based tours are available, and for a more nuanced perspective, there are private and semiprivate options with the companies below.

GONDOLA TRIVIA

Venetian gondolas are a touristy cliché today, but the tradition evolved over hundreds of years, and the little boats are an undeniably important facet of Venetian culture. The highly coveted *gondolieri* licenses, of which there are only about 430, are often passed down from generation to generation, typically among men of the family; today, there is only one licensed female gondolier.

These are anything but simple rowboats, and to purchase one new costs around €25,000 (double that for a finely crafted one). Gondolas are slightly asymmetrical, allowing the boat to be steered and rowed from one side while still moving forward in a straight line. The prow is weighted in front so as to counterbalance the weight of the gondolier in back. The boats' 280 pieces (eight different kinds of wood) are assembled by hand. The curved metal prow of the gondola represents the S-shape of the Grand Canal, with the crest symbolic of the oddly shaped cap that the doge used to wear. The six forward-facing teeth represent the six *sestieri* (subdivisions) of Venice, and the one facing back represents Giudecca Island. You can take a peek at Squero San Trovaso (squerosantrovaso.com), a working gondola repair shop right next to San Trovaso church in Dorsoduro. Now all you've got to do is ride one! *Ciao Venezia, ciao ciao....*

Walks of Italy

My friends at Walks of Italy offer excellent guided walks with licensed guides, canal tours, *cicchetti* crawls, and private entries into the top sights of Venice all year long. Check out their website for tour itineraries and pricing.

Day tours from €70 per person, +39 069 380 4888, walksofitaly.com/venice-tours, info@walksofitaly.com

Discovering Venice

I love these small-group tours led by local, licensed guides, who take you through the most popular sights in Venice (and a few of the lesser-known ones). You'll learn enough about St. Mark's Square and the Rialto Bridge to start leading your own tours. You'll also go inside the basilica (free ticket included) and get into the backstreets and canals the ordinary tours often gloss over. Antonella, Eugenia, and Frederica also offer options beyond the standard walk in Venice, like boat tours out

into the canals and to the nearby islands. Find dates and schedules on their website. They meet between the marble columns on St. Mark's Square, Monday-Wednesday at 11:15 and Friday at 14:00.

€50 adults, €35 students under 25, discoveringvenice. com, info@discoveringvenice.com

Free Tour Venice

These daily tours follow the same format as other tip-based walking tours across Europe. They're broadly informative, fun, and casual, and they provide a good grounding in the city's history and its major landmarks. Tours cover the foundations of Venice, the city's rise as a trading power, its Napoleonic influences, World War II, and more recent history. Quality of guides varies, as might be expected with staff subsisting on tips.

Free and tip-based, daily departures at 10:45 and 16:30, meet at Campo Santa Stefano next to the statue, freetourvenice.com

TOP HOSTELS

When it comes to accommodations, Venice is definitely a seller's market. A room or a bed will cost you dearly. Options are limited, and the experience is more often disappointing than otherwise. Before making reservations, double-check your hostel's or hotel's location. Lido di Venezia is Venice's beach island, but you'll have to take a 20-minute ferry every time you want to go into the center. Same thing with Venice Mestre, the last town on the mainland before the bridge into Venice proper. It's not the end of the world if you're not in the center (it'll save you quite a bit), but you will have to transfer between your accommodations and the main island. Make reservations early—not just for hotels or hostels but also for Airbnb and other homesharing platforms, which are affordable alternatives to more costly traditional lodgings.

We_Crociferi Hostel

Housed in a renovated convent, this trendy 255-bed hostel offers some of the most comfortable budget beds around. It's a bit of a hike from the center, but at least they're on the main island. There's a decent on-site bar and the friendly staff will get your sightseeing and socializing needs sorted.

Dorm beds from €35, private rooms from €100, free Wi-Fi, €7 breakfast, female dorms available, lockers, canal-side terrace, Campo dei Gesuiti, Canareggio, +39 041 5286 103, we-gastameco.com, hello@we-crociferi.it

Generator Venice

Generator Venice is easily the best and most comfortable hostel in town. It's hard to even recommend any others, considering all that Generator has going for it: comfortable beds, new interior, friendly staff, and a slew of amenities. It's across the way in Giudecca, but worth the trek for the added comfort and socializing you'll find here.

Beds from €25, 24-hour reception, free Wi-Fi, on-site bar, hair dryers and lockers available, towels for rent, laundry facilities, breakfast options, Fondamenta Zitelle 86, Giudecca, +39 041 877 8288, generatorhostels.com/en/destinations/venice

Sunny Terrace Hostel

Also located on Giudecca, this institutional hostel seems to be converted student housing. It's an acceptable alternative if the Generator is full.

July-Sept only, beds from €22, terrace, spotty free Wi-Fi, Ramo della Palada, Giudecca, +39 347 026 8037, hostelvenezia.com

Venice Gold

Steel yourself for typically abrupt Venetian service and a long list of rules at this cozy B&B. Service aside, Venice Gold is a solid upgrade that won't break the bank. They've got five-bed dorms, single rooms, and double rooms. The location is great, just a few minutes from St. Mark's Square. This is the kind of place that insists on cash only for payment when you arrive, but they will not hesitate to charge the card you used for booking if you're a no-show or have to cancel within five days of your arrival time.

Dorm beds from €35.50, daily lockout for cleaning, reception 09:00-21:00, latest check-in at 21:00, free Wi-Fi when working, luggage storage for a fee, Castello, +39 328 209 4718, hostelbookers.com

PLUS Camping Jolly

This is the Italian version of "glamping." Opt for PLUS Camping Jolly for a fun stay in either rented tents, bungalows, or parked camper vans. I enjoy the on-site pool, bar, extensive optional breakfast, Wi-Fi, friendly staff, and genial backpacker scene. The commute into town, however, leaves much to be desired—it takes 45 minutes to an hour, with the last connections around 23:00. They organize shuttles frequently in high season, but the to and fro takes a bite out of sightseeing time and nightlife options.

Bungalows from €30, Via Giuseppe de Marchi 7, on the mainland, free Wi-Fi, optional breakfast, towels for rent, +39 041 920 312, plushostels.com/pluscampingjolly

TRANSPORTATION

GETTING THERE & AWAY

The Santa Croce district is dominated by infrastructure that facilitates tourists' arrival by train, cruise ship, ferry, bus, and car.

Plane

Two major airports serve the city. **Marco Polo** (VCE, veniceairport.it) is the closer option. **Treviso** (TSF, trevisoairport.it) is popular with budget airlines. From both, the bus will be your best connection into town.

From Marco Polo airport, the **ATVO shuttle bus** will get you into the center in about 20 minutes for €3. Purchase your ticket at the ATVO ticket window in the arrivals hall. If you're on a budget, you can take the local ACTV bus, which takes about 30 minutes, for €1.20. Both options drop you off at the same terminal, Piazzale Roma. As appealing as they might seem, skip the water taxi option, as it will easily run you €100+ unless you have a large group.

From Treviso, purchase your **ATVO bus** ticket (€5) in the arrivals hall at the ATVO ticket window. The journey into Venice takes about 70 minutes.

Train

Trains from Venice to Florence run often, cost €40, and take a little over two hours. Trains to Rome take almost four hours and cost €55 (you can find overnight options on slow trains for about €70).

Venezia-Santa Lucia, located in Santa Croce, is Venice's train station. Don't get off at Venezia-Mestre—this isn't Venice itself, but the last city on the mainland before crossing the bridge to the island. From Santa Lucia, you'll exit the train station directly toward the famous Grand Canal, always humming with *vaporetti*, gondolas, and private boats. From here, it's possible to walk anywhere you need to go, though it will take you about 30 minutes to reach San Marco. Two docks in front of the train station both have ferries that will get you to St. Mark's Square. Purchase your ticket (€7) from the clearly marked booth and hop on either the **vaporetto #1** (slow local ferry, excellent for your intro to the city) or

the **vaporetto #2** (express boat that makes fewer stops along the way).

Bus

Eurolines (eurolines.com) deposits international connections either at the **Venice Mestre Station** (on the mainland across from Venice Island) or at the main bus terminal, **Piazzale Roma,** in the Santa Croce district of Venice proper. Be sure to check which location is your final destination. Mestre is just a short connection into Venice proper via train. Your bus driver will be able to point the way.

Car

It is possible to drive into Venice, but you'll need to leave your car at the parking lot on Tronchetto Island on the edge of the city (about a 20-minute walk to the train station and beyond into the canals of Venice). Rates start around €21 per day. Cheaper options exist on the mainland in Mestre and Marghera, both of which are close to train connections.

GETTING AROUND

Walking is your primary way to get around town—so be sure to wear comfortable shoes! Even with orthopedic shoes, your feet will be dog-tired after long days navigating the crowds and canals. *Vaporetto* rides cost €7.50 a pop, so think twice before taking the option to put your feet up. Rather than trying to memorize districts

---

WHAT WAS THAT ADDRESS AGAIN?

The Venetian dialect (a distinct form of Italian) contains a number of intricacies that us landlubbers don't find all that intuitive. One thing you'll notice is the wide-ranging vocabulary just to designate whether something is a street, alleyway, or something else. A few examples:

sotoportego: small footway going under a building

canale: canals

rio: narrow canal

riva: footway along a canal (similar to a quay)

corte: dead-end courtyard

rio terra: paved-over canal that you can now walk on

ramo: small footway connecting two larger streets or a street to a canal (a *ramo* may take you to an alley that dead-ends onto a canal)

calle: Venice's closest equivalent to a standard street

fondamenta: footway leading along the side of a canal (think of it as a foundation for the buildings looking out over the canal)

ruga: store-lined walkway

salizzada: large pedestrian avenue

and the city plan, orient yourself by the major **landmarks** of the city; a map is a smart investment. Signs posted above eye level on just about every corner around town point the way to the major sights. Use them like breadcrumbs to find your way around:

Alla Ferrovia: To the train station
Piazzale Roma: To the bus terminal
Per Rialto: To the main and most famous bridge in town
Per S. Marco: To St. Mark's Square and Basilica

Heads up: It's not uncommon for proprietors to make counterfeit direction signs to siphon off the lucrative **Ferrovia—Rialto—San Marco** flow of tourists looking for these major sights. Look at direction signs closely to ensure they're legit.

Vaporetti

Vaporetti (bus-boats) give you a chance to see the city from the vantage point for which it was built: the canals. An extensive network of *vaporetti* connects stops around the island. Check signs to know where to catch the *vaporetto* you want. Boats going in opposite directions will stop near each other, but often not at the same dock. Look for diagrams and route numbers to know where to catch yours. A **single ride** costs €7.50, so **day and multi-day passes** (€16/12 hours, €18/24 hours, €23/36 hours, €28/48 hours, €33/72 hours, €50/7 days) quickly pay for themselves. Strategize to make a 12-hour pass worth the cost by consolidating all of your cross-lagoon sightseeing and *vaporetto* rides into one eventful day. Purchase tickets at the transport kiosks or at tobacco shops. Validate your ticket at the turnstiles before you step onto the loading platform. Service generally starts at 05:00 and ends around 23:30. See actv.it/en/hellovenezia for more information.

HELP!

Tourist Information Centers

Stop into one of Venice's information offices (both open daily 10:00-18:00, turis-mo-venezia.it) for information and directions to your accommodations:

Marco Polo Airport
+39 041 529 87 11
Santa Lucia Train Station
+39 041 529 87 11

Pickpockets & Scams

Be exceptionally wary when in the midst of crowds (which will be most of the time in Venice). Keep your hands on your wallets or other valuables in the bustling train station, aboard overcrowded *vaporetti*, and in crowded alleyways—these are the pickpockets' hunting grounds. A common trick groups of pickpockets will use is to have someone "accidentally" spill something on you—while the spiller is ostensibly helping you clean yourself off, his or her accomplices will be emptying your pockets. Also, be mindful of groups of children who encroach into your personal space. They aren't as innocent as they appear.

Venetian merchants are also notorious for taking your €50 note and claiming you only gave them a €20. To protect yourself, say the denomination loud and clear as you hand it over. This way, you'll remember it better, and they'll have a harder time trying to deny it.

Emergencies

Dial 118 for an ambulance, or 113 for English-speaking police.

Hospital

Ospedale San Giovanni e Paolo
Castello 6777
+39 041 529 4111

US Consulate

Venice Marco Polo Airport, General Aviation Terminal
Viale Galileo Galilei 30

MADRID

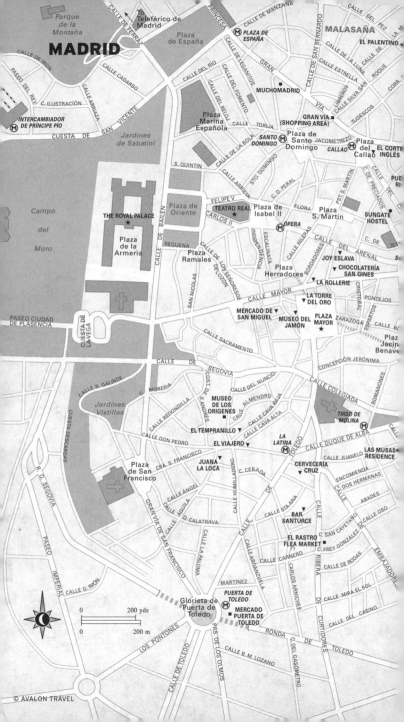

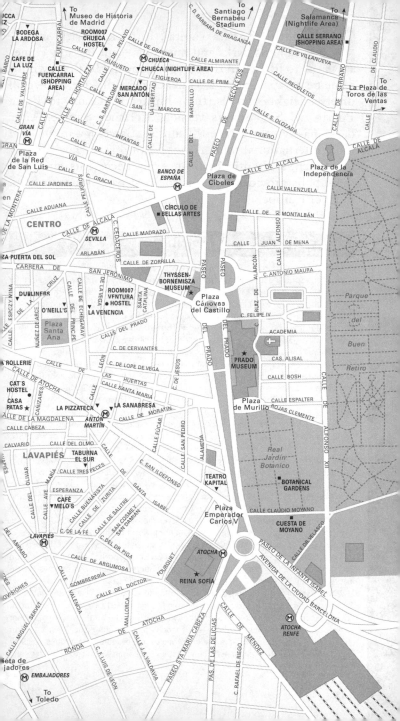

Madrid, Spain's capital, is packed with world-famous parks and museums—but it really comes to life when the sun goes down. Hit the town for some tasty tapas, catch a flamenco performance, and stroll diverse neighborhoods, from hipster Malasaña to Plaza Puerto del Sol, Spain's version of Times Square. After dark, massive clubs rage till sunrise. Barcelona might lure more international tourists, but Madrid is my favorite city for a rich, authentic Spanish experience. This energetic metropolis provides some of the best bang for your buck in all of Europe.

MADRID 101

Madrid was founded in the 9th century as a Muslim stronghold among a strategic network of forts sprinkled throughout Spain. Madrid's name stems from the Arabic word for "waterway," and its prime location was hotly contested between Christian and Muslim armies vying for control of the Iberian Peninsula. Eventually, Alfonso VI conquered Madrid in 1083, and the main mosque was converted into a Catholic church. As time went on, the Muslims who stayed in the city were isolated and eventually expelled.

By the 1700s, Madrid began taking shape into the city we know today through a series of ambitious construction projects that created the Royal Palace, Royal Theatre, the city gates of Puerto de Toledo, and the Botanical Gardens. In 1807, King Carlos IV and Napoleon signed a contract that allowed French forces entry through Spain to fight Portugal. Napoleon violated the treaty and began conquering and occupying Spanish cities along the way to Portugal. This led to a revolt on May 2, 1808, and a war that lasted for five years until the French forces were finally rebuffed.

Spain had a complex and bloody 20th century, replete with economic collapse in 1929. Political instability ensued, with a fascist military dictatorship headed by Francisco Franco taking control of the country. During the Spanish Civil War (1936-1939), German planes supporting Franco's regime bombed cities across Spain, including Madrid. They targeted the town of Guernica as practice for their intense blitzkrieg bombing runs and surveillance operations ahead of the outbreak of all-out world war. Picasso's infamous *Guernica*, now on display at the Reina Sofia museum, depicts the horrific strafing and bombing unleashed on the town on April 26, 1937, a busy market day. This bombing run killed nearly 1,000 people in two hours and leveled most of the town. After the conclusion of the civil war, Spain remained neutral during World War II.

Franco ruled an isolationist Spain for nearly 40 years until his death in 1975. Franco was convinced that things would remain status quo by returning power back to the king upon his death, but the king began setting up a constitutional monarchy as soon as Franco passed, ending the nearly four decades of oppressive military rule.

With the veil of fascism lifted, Spain burst onto the world stage as a nation that had a lot of living and celebration to catch up on, and Madrid is where it all went down. Today, while the economic situation in Spain remains challenging—with a nearly 50 percent unemployment rate for young adults—the mood is generally optimistic. Madrid's urban progress has accelerated, and it is one of Europe's most beautiful capital cities, pleasing for its intense animated spirit, welcoming people, and compelling blend of modern and proud classic culture.

PLAN AHEAD

RESERVATIONS

Reservations are recommended for the following sights and activities:

Prado Museum (entradasprado.com)
Real Madrid matches (realmadrid.com)

FREE ENTRY TIMES

A number of Madrid museums are free to enter on certain days or at certain times (evenings usually). For instance:

Prado Museum: free Mon-Sat 18:00-20:00, Sun 17:00-19:00, always free for those under 18 and students 18-25

Reina Sofia: free Mon and Wed-Sat 19:00-21:00, Sunday 15:00-19:00, always free for those under age 18 and students 25 and under with ID

Museo Thyssen-Bornemisza: free Mon

LOCAL HAPPENINGS

Holidays

Just like their siestas, Spaniards take their festivals seriously. If a public holiday falls on a Thursday (or even a Wednesday in some cases), people get their weekend started early. If you're in Madrid during one of these holidays, you'll be treated to some of the best and busiest nightlife of the year, but your shopping and eating options will be limited, often dramatically. Assume most businesses will be closed during the following national holidays:

January 1, New Year's Day
Holy Week and Good Friday
May 1-2, Labor Day and the Day of Madrid
August 15, the Assumption
October 12, National Holiday of Spain
November 1, All Saints' Day
December 6, Spanish Constitution Day
December 25, Christmas Day

KNOW BEFORE YOU GO

KEY STATS & FIGURES

Currency:
Spain uses the euro (€);
1 EUR = about 1.14 USD

Population:
3.2 million (double that of Barcelona, and 1 million more than Paris)

Language:
Spanish

Days of sun per year:
300+

Elevation:
650 meters (the highest capital city in Europe)

Dinner time for Madrileños:
21:00

Time to hit the clubs:
02:00

CALIBRATE YOUR BUDGET

TYPICAL PRICES FOR:

Hostel dorm bed:
€18

Two-course dinner:
€10

Pint of beer:
€2.50

Metro pass:
€1.50

MOVIES TO WATCH

Abre Los Ojos (Open Your Eyes), El Día de la Bestía (Day of the Beast), La Flor de Mi Secreto (The Flower of My Secret)

THREE DAY ITINERARY

Spain's capital is packed with beautiful architecture, sprawling parks, and photogenic boulevards. Madrid provides more than enough options for daytime sightseeing, and in the evening you'll experience the Madrileños' trademark love of life. This itinerary will help you balance the city's many sights with its dizzying party scene.

DAY 1: WELCOME TO MADRID

MORNING

Get your visit off to a sweet start with a breakfast of churros and chocolate at the famous **Chocolatería San Ginés,** just around the corner from **Plaza Puerta del Sol.**

At 10:00, join the three-hour walk with **Sandeman's New Europe Walking Tours** in **Plaza Mayor.** It's an excellent introduction to Madrid's top sights, including the **Royal Palace** and historic Moorish ruins dating back to Madrid's medieval roots.

AFTERNOON

Satisfy your appetite at **Taberna El Sur** on the way to Madrid's museum quarter. After refueling, continue downhill a few blocks to the **Reina Sofía.** Spend the siesta hours soaking in the museum's extensive collection of 20th-century artwork in nearly every media imaginable—from experimental film to sculpture. Elbow your way to the front of the crowd to get a good look at Picasso's *Guernica.*

Afterward, walk about a mile slightly uphill along the grand tree-lined boulevard of Paseo del Prado. Make your way past the Prado and the Apollo and Neptune fountains to the rooftop café at **Círculo de Bellas Artes** for a stunning panorama of downtown Madrid. Trace the thousands of steps you took today in one view and reward yourself with a cold beer or iced coffee.

EVENING

Rest up back at the hostel before heading out for dinner. Around 21:00, strike out for an authentic tapas crawl in the Malasaña district, one of Madrid's liveliest neighborhoods. **Bodega La Ardosa** is a good place to start your crawl. Explore this dense network of lanes and streets, and concentrate your imbibing efforts around **Plaza del 2 de Mayo** and the bars on **Plaza de Carlos Cambronero.**

LATE

In the mood for some clubbing? **Joy Eslava**—just around the corner from where your day began at the Chocolatería San Ginés—is just a 15-minute walk downhill from the Malasaña neighborhood, between the Teatro Real and Plaza Puerto del Sol. If you queue up before 01:30, the €10 cover will usually include a drink.

DAY 2: YOUR BIG MUSEUM DAY

MORNING

Get yourself up at an appropriate hour (this will vary depending on how "Madrileño" you really got last night). Splurge on breakfast and coffee at **La**

Rollerie, then walk a few minutes southeast to Madrid's top museum: the **Prado.** If you made reservations in advance online, you'll skip the line. The Prado is one of the world's best museums, so you'll want to spend at least a couple of hours exploring the collections.

AFTERNOON

After the museum, pick up some food to take to nearby **Retiro Park.** The park's name says it all: Rest your weary feet, sit in the shade, and enjoy a picnic. The park is large enough (350 acres) that you can escape the crowds. Make the escape complete by renting a rowboat and tooling around in front of the beautiful monument to Alfonso XII—if you're looking for romance, it doesn't get much better than this. You can also rent bikes and make your way around the park's many paths. For extra credit, find the fountain with the **Statue of the Fallen Angel,** widely accepted to be Europe's only statue dedicated to Lucifer.

Return the bikes or the rowboat, then cut across town on the metro from the Retiro stop on the north side of the park to the Ópera stop on the red line (line 2) to explore the **Royal Palace** (open daily until 20:00).

EVENING

Regroup at your hostel for a short siesta. After your nap, it's time to bond with other English-speaking backpackers at **O'Neill's** bar in Sol. The conversation can reach a fever pitch there, so for a quieter scene, grab a bottle of wine and people-watch at nearby **Plaza Santa Ana.**

Fancy catching a show? The nightly **Flamenco Show at Casa Patas,** just a few minutes' walk south of O'Neill's and Plaza Santa Ana, kicks off at 21:00 (there's a later show at 23:00). It features the best singers and dancers in town, and you can't leave Spain without witnessing the country's best-known cultural export.

LATE

Dressed to the nines? Wallet overflowing with euros? Make your way toward the Atocha train station (just east of the Lavapies district) to find seven floors of throbbing hedonism at **Teatro Kapital.** Your fancy duds will help you get past the velvet rope, and their expensive drinks will lighten your back pocket.

DAY 3: OPTIONS
MORNING

If it's Sunday, head straight to the bustling **El Rastro,** Madrid's largest flea market. You'll find everything from playing cards and antiques to electronic equipment and trading cards. Stop for lunch (sardines anyone?) along the way at my favorite spot in the neighborhood: **Bar Santurce.**

AFTERNOON

If the flea market didn't scratch your shopping itch, hop on the metro to **Calle Serrano,** Madrid's luxury shopping district.

If it's your mind that is itching, there are still plenty of museums to dive into. Just a 20-minute walk from El Rastro, you'll find masterpieces from Rembrandt, Klee, Dalí, Caravaggio, and Degas at the spectacular **Museo Thyssen-Bornemisza.**

If (like me) you love finding fresh air and views over the city, head west of Malasaña to the **Teleférico de Madrid** to catch a stunning panorama of Madrid. It will be a memorable exclamation point at the end of your visit.

Finally, if soccer is your thing, make a pilgrimage outside the city center to **Estadio Santiago Bernabéu,** the home of Real Madrid CF, for a multimedia experience and tour.

TOP NEIGHBORHOODS

Madrid is a sprawling modern metropolis. The **Sol** (Centro) district, with Plaza Puerta del Sol at its center, is the heart of the city—it's also far and away the most touristy part of town. This is where you'll find major sights like Plaza Mayor. There are dozens of excellent restaurants, bars, hotels, and nightlife spots here (Joy Eslava, a *discoteca* institution, being just one of them), but there are just as many tourist traps, so choose wisely.

The city fans out north and south from Sol. Beginning about five blocks north of Plaza Puerto del Sol you'll find two of my favorite districts: Chueca and Malasaña. **Chueca,** with its excellent shopping, food, and nightlife, is one of Madrid's up-and-coming neighborhoods and the hub of the city's LGBT community.

Bordered by Calle San Bernardo to the west and Calle Horteleza and Chueca to the east is **Malasaña**—for me, the most authentic neighborhood in Madrid's center. There's an unmistakable community pride here, along with unforgettable tapas, lively nightlife, and some of Madrid's best boutique shopping.

In the **Museum District,** sandwiched between Sol and Retiro Park (Madrid's 350-acre park), you'll find the world-famous Prado, the Reina Sofia, and Museo Thyssen-Bornemisza. North of Retiro and east of Chueca, **Salamanca** glitters night and day. This is the spot for high-end shopping and high-class nightlife—you'll see Madrid's glitterati on full display here, especially on weekends.

South of Sol, noteworthy neighborhoods huddle around La Latina and Lavapies metro stops. **La Latina** is where crowds of young, hip professionals fill bars and cafés, predominantly along two parallel streets: Calle Cava Baja and Calle Cava Alta, which offer a bevy of classy watering holes. **Lavapies,** just east of La Latina, is home to El Rastro market, Madrid's gritty underground district. It's too dark and run-down for many tourists, but the narrow lanes are the perfect place to find cheap *cañas* (half-pints of beer). The crowds and shops are far more ethnically diverse than the touristy parts of Madrid, so you'll find a wider range of delicious food (all of it cheap) and you'll be seeing a side of Madrid most tourists miss.

TOP SIGHTS

If you plan your visit right, you'll be able to see some of Europe's best museums without spending a cent on entrance fees. If you're a student (younger than 25) or if you're not yet 18, the museums are always free. Otherwise, they're free certain days of the week or month or at certain evening hours. Expect big crowds at these times. If you want the best museum experience, head over during the siesta hours and pay the entrance fee. You'll be able to get up close without jockeying for position, well worth the cost if there's a particular exhibit that interests you.

Prado Museum

One of Europe's finest art museums, the Prado houses Spanish masterpieces from the likes of Goya, El Greco, Ribera, and Velázquez, as well as works by international artists like Rembrandt, Raphael, and Orly. The museum is one of the largest in Europe, so either block out a significant portion of your day to see it all or study the floor plan and determine a route through the multiple levels that will take you through the periods and artists that most appeal to you. The ground floor dovetails medieval and early-Renaissance works from Spanish and continental masters. Climb the stairs to the second floor for High Renaissance and baroque masters starting from the early 17th century.

If you enter late, catch the following highlights before you're shuffled out the door at closing time: *Las Meninas* by Velázquez, *The Nobleman with His Hand on His Chest* by El Greco, *The Three Graces* by Rubens, and *Jacob's Dream* by Ribera. The museum is nicely air-conditioned, so it's a great way to cool down after a visit to nearby Retiro

Park. Free entry Monday-Saturday 18:00-20:00 and Sunday 17:00-19:00 make visits to the Prado easy on the budget, but you'll be swimming in a sea of visitors.

€15 adults, sometimes additional fee for temporary exhibits, free Mon-Sat 18:00-20:00 and Sun 17:00-19:00, always free under 18 and students 18-25, Mon-Sat 10:00-20:00, Sun and holidays 10:00-19:00, last entry 30 minutes before closing, closed Jan 1, May 1, and Dec 25, Calle Ruiz de Alarcón 23, Museum District, +34 913 302 800, museodelprado.es, Metro: Atocha, Banco de España

Reina Sofía

This imposing museum, housed in a former convent and hospital that has undergone a multimillion-dollar refurbishment, features Spain's biggest collection of 20th-century art, including iconic works from Spain's two most famous artists, Pablo Picasso and Salvador Dalí. It's here that you'll find what is perhaps Madrid's most iconic painting: Picasso's *Guernica*. The huge canvas in somber blacks and grays and jarring composition commemorates the abhorrent 1937 bombing of the small Spanish town. German warplanes utterly destroyed the village, killing hundreds of civilians; with almost all of the men fighting elsewhere in Spain, the dead were mostly women and children.

€8 adults, €3 under 18, free Mon and Wed-Sat 19:00-21:00, Sun 15:00-19:00, always free with valid student ID, Mon and Wed-Sat 10:00-21:00, Sun 10:00-19:00 (4th floor not accessible Sun after 15:00), closed Tues, Calle de Santa Isabel 52, Museum District, +34 917 741 000, museoreinasofia.es, Metro: Atocha

The Royal Palace (Palacio Real de Madrid)

It may be the official residence of the king of Spain, but you won't find King Felipe VI here except on special occasions—he lives in the Palacio de la Zarzuela just outside of the city. Madrid's Royal Palace is Western Europe's largest palace, bigger even than Versailles. It's also arguably Madrid's most beautiful building, constructed in the baroque style and bursting with ornate architectural accents in white stone, reminiscent of Buckingham Palace in London. The interior, done up in high baroque fashion, never fails to impress. You'll find intricate frescoes and gilded detailing, along with royal furnishings and paintings throughout the private apartments upstairs.

The palace is definitely worth the price of admission. The exterior is beautiful, but it's inside that you'll find priceless artifacts including a beautifully decorated Stradivarius string quartet (the only one of its kind in the world) and masterpieces from Velázquez, Goya, and Giordano. Also inside is the Royal Armory, featuring some of the most spectacular armor and weapons you'll see anywhere.

€11 adults, €5 ages 5-16 and students up to age 25 with ID, free under age 5, Oct-Mar daily 10:00-18:00, Apr-Sept daily 10:00-20:00, Calle Bailén, Sol, +34 914 548 700, patrimonionacional.es, Metro: Ópera

Plaza Mayor

Madrid's principal square sees thousands of visitors daily, making it one of the best places in the city for people-watching. Lining the square are tapas bars and cafés

galore. The food and drinks are better (and much cheaper) elsewhere, so just grab a coffee or a beer and enjoy the scenery. The square might not look particularly Spanish to you—that's because it's not. It was constructed during the Austrian rule of the Habsburgs in 1617, and is known in Madrid as "*Madrid de los Austrias.*"

Free, always open, Plaza Mayor, Sol, Metro: Ópera

Plaza Puerta del Sol

All of Madrid seems to converge on this large, sunny square in the very center of town. It's truly the heart of both the capital and the country as a whole—as evidenced by the KM 0 monument in the middle of the square. This is the point from which all the road signs in the country measure their distance to the capital. Bustling with activity and tourists in the day, the square is also lively at night. In the evening, you can follow your ears to the touristy bars just to the south of the square. During the day, the shops, cafés, and restaurants around the square are always busy. Sol is also a major metro station (with connections to the airport), so it'll probably be your first and last port of call in Madrid.

Free, always open, Puerta del Sol, Sol, Metro: Sol

Teatro Real

Madrid's majestic 1,750-seat neoclassical opera house was extensively remodeled in 1997 after being closed for nearly 75 years. It's come a long way since its time as a munitions dump during the Spanish Civil War. Today, you can enjoy a slice of high society at a show. The wraparound seating and first-rate acoustics mean that there isn't a poor seat in the house. Find tickets online from as low as €9.

Even if you're not interested in catching a show, the theater has a number of daily general, technical, and artistic-focused tours. The €8 general tours kick off every 30 minutes daily 10:30-13:00 and lasts about an hour. The artistic tour, a backstage look at operatic artistry, including costumes and performers, takes place once daily at 09:30, costs €12, and runs about 1.25 hours. The technical tour, with more of a focus on the stage logistics and the mechanics of production, also runs once daily at 10:00 and costs €16. All tickets can be purchased

on arrival at the box office, which opens at 09:15 daily.

Ticket prices vary, shows often, Plaza Isabel II, Sol, +34 915 160 660, teatro-real.com, Metro: Ópera

Flamenco Show at Casa Patas

Flamenco isn't native to Madrid—it comes from the southern cities like Seville and Granada—but that doesn't stop this cultural center and restaurant from putting on spectacular flamenco performances six nights a week featuring some of the best dancers and singers from all over the world. Grab a seat close to the stage of this intimate black-box venue, where the shows start late in the evening. Order a beverage and some food and drink in the passion of the Spanish soul—it's a deeply moving experience. There'll be vigorous stomping, and just as vigorous musicianship (box drums, violins, flutes, and, of course, plenty of guitars). The performers take their art deadly seriously, so photo flashers will be shunned and chatters will be hushed.

Tickets from €38, includes first drink, dinner options available, reservations recommended, shows nightly at 22:30, 20:00 additional show Fri-Sat (check online to confirm times and specials), Calle de los Cañizares 10, Sol, +34 913 690 496, casapatas.com, Metro: Antón Martín

Teleférico de Madrid

Take a ride in the *teleférico*, a cable car suspended high in the air, and get a bird's-eye perspective of some of Madrid's top sights. During your ride you'll fly by the Royal Palace and La Plaza de España, across the Manzanares River, and over the Casa de Campo, one of Madrid's most beautiful parks. Find the *teleférico* just west of Malasaña.

€4 one-way ticket, daily 12:00-21:00 (weekends only in winter), station just off of Paseo Pintor Rosales, just south of the intersection with Calle del Marqués de Urquijo, Greater Madrid, +34 902 345 002, teleferico.com, Metro: Argüelles

Museo Thyssen-Bornemisza

Much quieter than the Prado, which is always overrun by tourists (especially in the evenings when entry is free), the Museo Thyssen-Bornemisza offers a more subdued museum experience. This doesn't mean you have to sacrifice in the way of artwork. There are amazing impressionist and postimpressionist paintings here

that can keep even casual art lovers busy for hours. Come enjoy the works of greats like Van Gogh, Renoir, Monet, Manet, Gauguin, and many more. Check the museum website for the schedule of frequently rotating special exhibits.

€12 adults, €8 students, additional fees for special exhibits, free Mon 12:00-16:00, Tues-Sun 10:00-19:00, Sat until 22:00 (exhibits only), last entry 45 minutes before closing, Paseo Prado 8, Museum District, +34 902 760 511, museothyssen.org, Metro: Banco de España

Bullfights at Plaza de Toros de las Venta

Throughout the year, the Plaza de Toros de las Venta in Madrid packs out with tourists and locals alike to watch one of Spain's more controversial spectacles: the bullfight. The matadors disorient, tease, stab, and ultimately kill bulls one after another over a stretch of three-plus hours. Animal lovers will find the spectacle nauseating—I must admit to being taken aback by it myself. If you can stomach it, though, the bullfight is an undeniably integral part of Spanish culture. It's possible to purchase tickets from scalpers, but be warned: It is illegal, and if you get caught, they'll confiscate your ticket. It's best to purchase your tickets through official channels. Most major fights take place on Sundays, but times and days vary depending on the event—so keep your ears and eyes open for upcoming events.

€5-150, cheaper shows feature novice bullfighters and messier bullfights, days and times vary, Calle de Alcalá 237, Greater Madrid, +34 913 562 200, las-ventas.com, Metro: Ventas

EXTRA CREDIT
City History Museum (Museo de San Isidro)

If you're anything like your dear author, you get excited at the thought of learning about the history of any modern city with medieval foundations. In this modest and free museum you can check out a model of the old town—you'll be able to visualize how Madrid looked centuries ago, long before her streets were straightened out and cleaned up.

Free, Sept-July Tues-Sun 09:30-20:00, Aug Tues-Fri 09:30-14:30, Sat-Sun 09:30-20:00, Plaza de San Andrés 2, La Latina, +34 913 667 415, madrid.es, Metro: La Latina

Estadio Santiago Bernabéu

In Spain, soccer is a religion, and Estadio Santiago Bernabéu is one of its cathedrals. This gargantuan 80,000-seat stadium north of central Madrid is home to soccer's winningest team, Real Madrid. Like the New York Yankees of the soccer world, Real Madrid and its star players are household names the world over. It's also the richest team in Spain's La Liga, so it can afford the most expensive players—a winning formula if there ever was one. Visitors can tour the stadium throughout the week and until 3.5 hours before kickoff on game day. The 90-minute, multimedia experience takes you through a whirlwind of RM propaganda. You'll stand on the field and visit the changing rooms (there's a great selfie opportunity in front of Ronaldo's booth).

Game tickets can be hard to come by, with priority going to season ticket and pass holders—tourists bring up the rear. Purchase tickets online at realmadrid.com, call +34 902 324 324, or pick them up from the box office at the stadium or at most Caixa Bank branches in Madrid. You'll likely need to purchase tickets at least two weeks out.

Cheap seats from €50, self-guided tours €24, Concha Espina 1, Greater Madrid, +34 913 984 300, realmadrid.com, Metro: Santiago Bernabéu

TOP EATS

Madrileño cuisine consists of succulent meats like dried *jamón* (ham) served in paper-thin slices, salty cheeses like *manchego*, potato- and chickpea-based stews, lightly fried treats like churros, *patatas bravas* (fried potatoes with a spicy ketchup sauce), and *tortilla española* (potato omelet). The dishes can be a touch heavy, but they're well portioned, and the fresh ingredients Spanish chefs use mean you'll be burning clean fuel all night. Tapas, a favorite of locals and tourists alike, give you a chance to sample a number of dishes every time you sit down for a meal. Madrid is a magnet for people from all around the world, so your culinary options in the city are not at all limited to typical Spanish fare.

Malasaña is my favorite district in town for food. No matter where in the neighborhood you find yourself, there seems to always be a popular local spot just a stone's throw away. The action tends to center on three squares: **Plaza del 2 de Mayo, Plaza Juan Pujol,** and **Plaza de San Ildefonso,** but there are plenty of local favorites on the streets between them. For an authentic Madrileño feel, head to Malasaña's **Plaza de Carlos.** There are plenty of welcoming cafés and bars, such as Lamucca de Pez and El Palentino, with outdoor seating spilling out onto this cute little square.

The streets around **Lavapies** are home to Madrid's ethnic (especially Indian) population. The neighborhood has a gritty, underground feel, and you can find bargain food and drinks at every turn. The streets here are not as well lit as they are in the touristy areas, but the neighborhood isn't particularly prone to crime (no more than any major urban center in the United States). Still, play it safe—stick with your friends and keep your wits about you, and you're sure to have an awesome time. You can even find some fast-food gems in the streets around **El Rastro market** (Calle de Ribera de Curtidores).

In cafés and restaurants tipping is not expected, but rounding up to the next euro mark is appreciated. Before tipping, be sure to check whether or not your bill says *"servicio incluido."* Many of the touristy restaurants sneak this 10-15 percent charge onto the bill—they don't tell you unless you ask, hoping that unobservant customers will unwittingly tip them double.

Bodega La Ardosa

Bodega La Ardosa, in the Malasaña district, is one of my favorite old-time tapas restaurants in all of Madrid. Pop in for a cup of *salmorejo* and *patatas bravas*. Join the locals huddling around the tables, which have upended wine barrels as their base. A snack in here feels like a step into old-world Spain, and the dusty bottles of spirits and liquors lining the walls in single file add a historical presence to the place. When it gets full (which is often), it becomes standing-room only, making it even easier to meet the friendly locals and strike up conversation. Order only a dish or two to start, then wait to see what looks good coming out of the kitchen. La Ardosa is an excellent place to kick off a late-afternoon or early-evening wander through Malasaña.

€11-20, Mon-Fri 08:30-02:00, Sat-Sun 11:45-02:30, Calle Colón 13, Malasaña, +34 915 214 979, laardosa.es, Metro: Tribunal

Lamucca de Pez

On the uphill side of Plaza de Carlos is Lamucca de Pez, a bright, posh cocktail and tapas bar with friendly service, a trendy exposed-brick interior, and an extensive wine selection. They take well-deserved pride in their Italian-style pizzas and their expertly mixed alcoholic concoctions. The daily specials are excellent.

Bocadillos from €3, pizzas from €12, Tues-Sat 12:00-24:00, Sun 19:00-24:00, Plaza de Carlos Cambronero, Malasaña, +34 915 210 000, lamucca.es, Metro: Tribunal or Noviciado

El Palentino

Across from Lamucca de Pez is El Palentino, your classic nondescript neighborhood pub and bar that pumps out fresh *bocadillos* (sandwiches) all day and *cañas* (half-pints of beer) to wash them down. Come here to get a true glimpse into the jovial Madrileño lifestyle. This isn't as hip

EAT CHEAP IN MADRID

Here are some basic budget-friendly tips for eating in Madrid:

It's important to note the subtle differences between *pintxos* and tapas. **Tapas** are full plates of peppers, *jamón*, manchego cheese, octopus, and so on. *Pintxos* are little open-faced sandwiches topped with any number of meats, cheeses, or spreads. A *pintxo* or two will often come free with each drink order in local bars. So, for a few euros, you can get a glass of wine or a beer and a light snack. Triple that and you've got the makings of a nice meal and a buzz to boot.

Bocadillos are simple, made-to-order sandwiches on a small baguette. They're my top choice for budget eats just about anywhere in Spain, and you'll find them in virtually every Spanish café. Your only challenge will be deciding what you want on your sandwich: *chorizo, jamón, tortilla* (Spanish potato omelet), and even *calamares* (fried calamari rings) are just a few of the options. And the best part? Get your sandwich with *"pan con tomate"* (tomato puree ladled onto your bread to make it extra juicy). The Brits have butter, Americans use mayonnaise, Italians olive oil, but Spaniards—*tomate* (you'll long for it when you get back home). *Bocadillos* normally run about €3. They are filling enough to power most people until it's time for a characteristically late Spanish dinner.

Most restaurants will charge a **small cover** to sit down and get table service. Save money by standing and eating at the bar.

The **bread** at your table is often something you have to pay for, so before digging in, ask, *"gratis?"*

If you ask for water without specifying which kind, restaurant staff will always bring out a bottle, which will appear on your bill at the end of the meal. Ask for **tap water** by saying *"agua del grifo, por favor."*

Usually when restaurants post **pictures of their dishes** instead of menus in their windows, it's often a sign the restaurant caters to tourists, not locals. However, I find that the relationship is less linear in Madrid. Look around and listen as well to see if you hear mostly internationals or more locals.

Keep your eyes open for the ***menu del dia*** (menu of the day). These are often a great value. Make the most of lunch. For Madrileños it's the biggest meal of the day, just before siesta—no wonder they need to sleep it off!

a joint as Lamucca de Pez, but the vibe is more relaxed.

Bocadillos from €2.50, Mon-Sat 08:30-02:00, Plaza de Carlos Cambronero, Malasaña, +34 915 323 058, Metro: Tribunal or Noviciado

Bar Santurce

My favorite spot around El Rastro market is this popular little anchovy shop that cranks out platefuls of the salty snack. It's near the top of the hill on Calle de las Amazonas. An order of *pimientos de padrón* (fried peppers), fried anchovies, a bread bowl, and two *cañas* makes for an excellent afternoon stop if you're in the area. Step in and work your way to the front of the line.

Decide what you want before it's your turn to order. If you haven't had fresh anchovies before, Bar Santurce is the perfect place to do it! There's a pickle shop next door that hits the spot too.

Plates from €3, Tues-Sat 12:00-16:00, Sun 09:00-16:00, Plaza General Vara del Rey 14, La Latina, +34 646 238 303, barsanturce.com, Metro: La Latina

Cervecería Cruz

This is your classic come-as-you-are Madrileño beer hall: brightly lit, steel countertops, *abuelos* playing cards, and a food bar serving classics like *pimientos de padrón* and calamari made to order. Its location at the top of El Rastro market makes it extremely popular on Sundays.

Dishes from €3.50, daily 08:00-23:00, Calle de las Maldonadas 1, La Latina, +34 913 663 738, Metro: La Latina

Puerto Rico

Come out to Puerto Rico for simple, filling cuisine. You'll find typical Madrileño stews, roast chicken, and a tantalizing array of tapas. Thanks to its location and casual atmosphere, Puerto Rico fills up daily with power lunchers in the middle of the day and the after-work tapas-munching crowd in the evening. Their menu of the day, a three-course lunch for under €12, is a popular option, making this a great place to fuel up before a full afternoon of sightseeing. Don't miss their rice pudding and flan if you've got room for dessert!

Lunches and dinners under €10, daily 13:00-16:30 and 20:30-23:30, Calle de Chinchilla 2, Sol, +34 915 219 834, Metro: Callao or Gran Vía

Mercado San Antón

Step into this posh and polished multilevel food market for delectable treats galore. Find the baker for a fresh baguette, then pick up 100 grams each of *jamón serrano* and *queso manchego* (ham and cheese) from the butcher. The resulting sandwich will probably be enough for at least two lunches. Among the stalls, you can also find prepared food options like *salmorejo* and surprisingly tasty burgers.

Create your own adventure for around €5, daily 10:00-24:00, Calle de Augusto Figueroa 24, Chueca, +34 913 300 730, mercadosananton.com, Metro: Chueca

Museo del Jamón

This chain does one thing and it does it well: fresh slices of some of the world's best cured ham. Most of us Westerners lack a developed palate for *jamón*, but that's easy enough to fix. Pop into one of their downtown locations and order a smattering of different types to sample. Spring for a taste of *jamón ibérico de bellota* (pig raised on a diet of acorns)—widely regarded as the best thin-sliced ham in the world. Don't let them get carried away when slicing (you'll pay by the gram, and it's not cheap). Snap a selfie in front of the seemingly endless array of cured porcine legs hanging from the walls and ceiling.

Find other locations at Calle Gran Vía 72 and Calle de Atocha 54.

From €5, daily 09:00-24:00, Plaza Mayor 18, Sol, +34 913 692 204, museodeljamon.es, Metro: Ópera

Chocolatería San Ginés

Chocolate lovers can't pass through Spain without enjoying one of the country's top treats: churros (fried doughy sticks) dunked in hot chocolate (which is more like concentrated melted chocolate than something you could actually drink). Chocolatería San Ginés offers some of the best of both in the city. Enjoy your thick and rich cup of chocolate in a classic, green-and-white-tiled setting that is exactly what you'd think an old-school café should be: prominent espresso bar, outdoor seating, wooden interior with large mirrors, and local graybeards enjoying their favorite snack. The 24/7 café is tucked down a side street behind the Iglesia San Ginés de Arles, just a couple blocks west of Plaza Puerta del Sol.

Churros and chocolate from €4, daily 24 hours, Pasadizo San Ginés 5, Sol, +34 913 656 546, chocolateriasangines.com, Metro: Sol

Torre del Oro

Located right on Plaza Mayor, Torre del Oro is widely known as the main matador bar in town. As long as the bulls' heads mounted on the wall don't make you lose your appetite, you'll love their typical Madrileño dishes, particularly their fried anchovies and ham sandwiches. The food is great, but the restaurant itself is the main attraction, with dozens of framed pictures of bullfighters. In many of them, the matador clearly has the upper hand, but in quite a few, the bull is winning the contest (they must have taken their eye off the ball...or...bull).

Bites from €3, daily 11:00-02:00, Plaza Mayor 26, Sol, +34 913 665 016, torredeloro.sellsoc.org, Metro: Ópera

Café Melos

The party at Café Melos often spills out onto the street. This spot is famous for its inexpensive fare, making it popular among students and travelers on tight budgets. Besides the excellent tapas, try the *zapatilla*—a huge stuffed sandwich overflowing with ham and cheese, easily splittable between two people. If you've still got room, don't miss their flash-fried croquettes. The picture-based menu makes selection easy. Stop in for a late dinner or snack—it's on the way to some of the best bars in Lavapies.

Snacks from €3.50, Tues-Sun 08:00-02:00, Calle del Ave María 44, Lavapies, +34 915 275 054, Metro: Lavapies

El Corte Inglés

Find the Gran Via location of El Corte Inglés (there are many others in town), and head to the 9th floor for a high-end food court. There are tapas, oysters, pizza, pastries, gelato, and more. Pay for your order, and take it outside to enjoy the view of the city and the refreshingly cool evening breezes.

Meals from €5, daily 10:00-24:00, Plaza de Callao 2, Sol, +34 913 798 000, elcorteingles.es, Metro: Callao

La Sanabresa

La Sanabresa is your best choice near the Antón Martín metro stop for a high-value sit-down meal. Their lunch and dinner menus del día are astoundingly good value—a surprise considering the place's location in the heart of the touristy center. For €10-16 you will get three courses (starter, main, and dessert) with a drink, bread, and little taste of liquor to cap it all off. Mains range from grilled meats and fish (their pork and their salmon are both excellent) to stews and roast veggies. And it all goes down in a casual and inviting setting with white tablecloths and efficient but friendly service.

Mains from €8, Mon-Sat 13:00-16:30 and 20:30-23:30, Calle Amor de Dios 12, Lavapies, +34 914 290 338, Metro: Antón Martín

Taberna El Sur

El Sur's got the classic no-frills restaurant down pat. It's in a simple, dark-wood setting and has a diverse food menu ranging from Cobb salad to salmon frittura brochettes. Be sure to try the well-appointed sangria complete with cinnamon sticks. Whether you're stopping by for an afternoon or an evening meal, they'll sort you out nicely. You'll find it tucked just a couple blocks south of the Antón Martín metro stop.

Excellent-value meals from €10, Sun-Thurs 12:00-01:30, Fri-Sat 12:00-02:00, Calle de Torrevilla del Leal 12, Lavapies, +34 915 278 340, Facebook: Taberna El Sur, Metro: Antón Martín

Neapolitan Authentic Pizza

When in Madrid, do as the Romans do. You're sure to hear a few snatches of Italian conversation here, thanks in large part to the fact that this joint boasts the best pizza in Madrid. NAP does authentic, chewy Neapolitan crust to perfection, and their wood-fired ovens and fresh ingredients will make you think you can hear the Trevi Fountain in the background. It's all about the pizza here, though they also have leafy salads and authentic desserts. If you're looking for red checked tablecloths, though, you're out of luck. All you'll find here is steaming-hot old-fashioned pies.

Pies from €8, daily 13:00-16:00 and 20:00-24:00, Calle Ave María 19, Lavapies, +34 911 25 07 42, Facebook: NAP Neapolitan Authentic Pizza Madrid, Metro: Lavapies

Café de la Luz

A French teahouse through and through, everything here screams Parisian café. From the one-off furniture and warm, intimate lighting to the food (all fresh and healthy), every inch of this place is perfect for cozying up with a special somebody for some intimate conversation and broken bread. It's nice and quiet, so it's also a great place to catch up on some emails or do some quiet reading.

Coffee from €3, Sun 10:00-01:00, Mon-Thurs 10:00-02:00, Fri and Sat 10:00-02:30, Calle de la Puebla 8, Malasaña, +34 915 23 11 99, Facebook: Café de la Luz, Metro: Callao

La Rollerie

La Rollerie is my favorite breakfast choice in town. While Spaniards generally eat a light breakfast, La Rollerie breaks with tradition, offering everything from cinnamon rolls and pastries to bacon-and-egg bagel sandwiches. No matter how hungry you are when you arrive, you'll leave satisfied. They try a little too hard to mimic a French bakery, but, thankfully, they are on point when it comes to what matters: carrot cake, Andalusian breakfast (toast with tomato puree), and of course, coffee. It's a posher vibe, so they feel justified charging upwards of €10 for a breakfast. If breakfast is the most important meal of your day, you won't feel cheated.

Coffee from €3, daily 08:00-22:30, Calle de Atocha 20, Sol, +34 914 204 675, larollerie.com, Metro: Sol or Tirso de Molina

TOP NIGHTLIFE

Like all Mediterranean cultures, nightlife in Madrid starts late. Ask around your hostel to get a feel, but in most clubs the party doesn't really heat up until after 01:00; in some places it's after 03:00. Pace yourself, and plan to sleep late. (Make sure your hostel windows can block out the sun in the morning!)

Madrid's neighborhoods have distinct vibes, each with their own type of venue. Rather than picking a venue or a few of them, it's much more fun to pick a district that sounds like your kind of party. Bounce around to a few places—if the vibe isn't what you're looking for, it's probably not the bars that are the issue, it's the neighborhood. Many of Madrid's top eateries also double as fun nightlife venues, so if you love the place you're eating, ask the staff about what's going on after midnight.

NIGHTLIFE DISTRICTS

Malasaña

My favorite neighborhood in Madrid has a slightly hipsterish and trendy feel—like other such neighborhoods throughout the world, its hipster cred is only increased by the fact that it doesn't appear to be trying too hard (or at all) to be what it is. Locals meet for drinks in these narrow and tangled streets, and with dozens of bars and cafés to choose from, it's one of the best places in Madrid to just wander and see what you find. For a sure thing, stop by Plaza Juan Pujol, where popular bars spill out onto the streets with terrace seating.

Malasaña, Metro: Noviciado

Chueca

Chueca is Madrid's LGBT district; the Pride parade marches through this neighborhood every summer, and it's where the vast majority of the Pride celebrations throughout the week take place. The LGBT community helped save this once-run-down neighborhood from neglect, and the businesses show their appreciation,

proudly flying rainbow flags. You'll find the best bars and the tastiest food options around Chueca Square.

Chueca, Metro: Chueca

Sol

The area around Puerta del Sol is understandably touristy. Bars catering to international visitors crowd together just south of Madrid's central plaza. It's here you can find Irish bars and study-abroad students by the hundreds. If you keep your eyes open, you can still discover winners in the area, but it gets tougher with each passing year.

So much of Madrid's nightlife is pedal to the metal, so if you prefer a more low-key evening, grab a bottle of wine and head down to Plaza de Santa Ana, southeast of Puerta del Sol. The benches that line the square offer a quiet place to relax and people-watch, a great way to recharge the batteries after a long day of sightseeing. Refreshed and reinvigorated, you can hit the town after midnight.

Sol, Metro: Sol

LGBT MADRID

LGBT travelers will find Spain welcoming and progressive. Spain was the first country in the EU to legalize gay marriage, and has long been considered a liberal country in respect to equal rights for gay couples. Gay visitors should expect to enjoy safety and no unwanted attention during their time in Madrid.

All of my recommended nightlife venues are gay friendly. But Chueca and most of Malasaña are the places to go if you want to party in Madrid's broadly inclusive LGBT scene. Your best bet is to head to the main square and take a stroll around the neighborhood branching off from there. In the surrounding streets you'll find happy, accepting people, an excited buzz, and numerous cafés, restaurants, delis and grocery stores, bars, lounges, and dance bars and clubs (many of them flying the rainbow colors). Stores run the gamut of high street fashion to drag suits and more, for just about all tastes. **El Bulldog** (hours and cover vary by event, Calle de San Bartolome 16, +34 915 991 260, elbulldogbar.com) draws the bear crowd, **Griffin's** (events vary, Wed-Thurs and Sun-Mon 24:00-05:30, Fri-Sat 24:00-06:00, Calle Marqués de Valdeiglesias 6, +34 915 222 079, griffins.es) is the dominant drag spot, and **LaKama Bar** (events vary, daily 21:00-03:00, Calle de Gravina 4, +34 915 223 226, facebook.com/lakamabar) is a fun go-go bar serving cocktails in a lounge setting.

Madrid's **tourist information centers** (daily 09:30-20:30, Plaza Mayor 27, Sol) offer a free LGBT edition of *Time Out* for up-to-the-minute event info and ideas tailored to LGBT travelers.

Lavapies

In Madrid's grungy underground district (too gritty for some), you can find some hidden theaters and great music venues if that's your scene. You'll also find off-the-beaten-path (i.e., cheap) watering holes by the dozen. If you turn up your nose at clubbing, or if you want to wet your whistle for a song before you head out, Lavapies might be just the place you're looking for.

Lavapies, Metro: Lavapies

La Latina

La Latina, Madrid's trendiest upscale downtown neighborhood, boasts pricey tapas bars, classy restaurants, and an undeniably fun vibe. The action centers on two streets: **Calle Cava Baja** and **Calle Cava Alta,** which turns into Calle Grafal farther north. These parallel streets running just northwest of the La Latina metro stop are their own little world of classy bars, shops, cafés, and *jamón* shops. It's easy to make an evening starting at the top of one street and looping around, popping into any tapas bars that strike your fancy. The district is littered with tourist traps, so be prepared for wildly varying service and food quality. Rather than ordering a slew of dishes, I spring for one at a time; if the experience is up to par, I order more.

If you're doing a crawl in La Latina, start with two places: **El Tempranillo** (Calle Cava Baja 38, +34 913 64 15 32), which sports an impressive wine selection and *pintxo* menu, and **El Viajero** (Plaza de la Cebada 11, +34 913 66 90 64), a contemporary, simple-fare bar with a delightful terrace and offerings like beef sliders and ribs. Be warned: It's frighteningly easy to run up a monster tab at either of these places. In-the-know locals flock to **Juana la Loca** (Plaza Puerta de Moros 4, +34 913 640 525) on a nightly basis. Their excellent cocktails, delectable desserts, and a chill lounge vibe make this one of my favorite spots in town. When I'm in Madrid, you can find me here rubbing elbows with locals most evenings.

La Latina, Metro: La Latina

Salamanca

Celebrity spotters can head straight to Salamanca. The ritzy cocktail bars and ultra-posh clubs draw Madrid's glitterati nightly. With the hot vibes come the highest prices you'll find in town—not to mention the liberal dose of pretentiousness. Even with the high-end clientele, bars and clubs in this neighborhood seem to have trouble keeping their doors open. Hot spots appear seemingly overnight and are shuttered just as quickly. Jersey chaser?

ACT LIKE A LOCAL

Party Like a Madrileño

Madrileños eat around 20:00 or 21:00, enjoy time with friends and socializing for the next few hours, and then begin heading out around 01:00 or later. To draw revelers in earlier, many clubs have free cover or extra drinks included in the price of the cover fee before 01:30. While you'll get a little extra by showing up early, the venue will usually be dead until after 02:00.

Cervecerías (beer halls) are a great way to get some food to keep you going and enjoy the Spanish tradition of *cañas*—half-pints served cheap and easy from bright, steel-topped bars. Just sharpen your elbows and work your way up to the bar. If you're passive, you'll likely lose your place in line. Keep your ears open, take a look at what everyone else is ordering, and practice your order in your head while trying to make eye contact with the bartender. Ordering by pointing (and smiling) works too!

Come here for a chance to glimpse the Real Madrid crew, who show up in this neighborhood to celebrate a win (which is often).

Salamanca, Metro: Serrano or Velazquez

BARS & PUBS

La Venencia

Step into this classic Madrileño sherry bar for a vintage taste of Spain. First things first: if you're looking for a beer or cocktail, keep walking. They only serve sherry here. They've got more varieties of the stuff than you can count. The dusty bottles on the top shelf might have been there when Ernest Hemingway polished the well-worn bar with his elbows—this was one of his favorite places to drink in Madrid, and he drank at a *lot* of places in Madrid. If you're a sherry novice (like me), ask the bartenders for advice—they're on the gruffer side, so don't expect service with a smile. One very important rule: no photographs. This rule wasn't designed with tourists in mind; it was to keep the Fascist spies from photographing the Republican patrons. They've kept the rule since the civil war, so respect it. For best results, split a bottle at one of the tables in the back.

Glasses from €3, Mon–Thurs 12:30-15:30 and 19:00-01:00, Fri–Sat 12:30-16:00 and 19:00-01:30, Sun 12:30-16:00 and 19:00-01:00, Calle Echegaray 7, +34 914 29 73 13

Dubliners Pub

There are a few standard Irish pubs in the heart of Madrid, offering mediocre drinks and food, but they're dependable enough—if you've been to an Irish pub anywhere outside of the Emerald Isle, you know what to expect. You'll find the game on, and you'll find rowdy (and predominantly English-speaking) patrons. Don't expect locals or lightning-fast service at this touristy bar, but it's a good place to bond with fellow backpackers.

Glasses of wine from €2.50, Irish coffee from €6, daily 11:00-03:00, Calle de Espoz y Mina 7, Sol, +34 915 22 75 09, irishpubdubliners.com, Metro: Sol

O'Neill's

Visitors flock to O'Neill's nightly, drawn by its beer-hall feel, pool table, drink and shot specials, and comfortable living room-style ambience. You can count on a sloppy, sticky-floor good time here among friendly and boozy backpackers. You'll likely cross paths with American students living in Madrid on a study-abroad semester.

Beer from €4, Mon–Wed 17:00-01:00, Thurs 17:00-02:00, Fri 17:00-03:30, Sat 13:00-03:30, Sun 13:00-01:00, Calle del Príncipe 12, +34 915 212 030, Facebook: O'Neill's Irish Pub Madrid, Metro: Sol

CLUBS

New clubs seem to open up every week in Madrid, and they close just as quickly. It's a raging scene that continues till the sun comes up nearly every day of the week. I've listed the nightlife institutions of Madrid (none of these is at risk of going belly-up any time soon), but be sure to ask at your hostel about the city's hottest new venues.

Joy Eslava

A massive, horseshoe-shaped venue in central Madrid, Joy was converted into a nightclub from a 1950s theater, meaning this place was practically built for the impressive light shows and loud music that partiers drown in every night of the week. Music is heavily weighted towards club techno, but there's a healthy smattering of local and international hits. Drinks can be pricey, so pregame before showing up—not too hard, though, because the bouncers are notoriously picky.

Cover around €12 (sometimes negotiable), pricey drinks and beers from €10, Sun-Thurs 12:00-05:30, Sat-Sun 12:00-18:00, Calle Arenal 11, Sol, +34 913 663 733, joy-eslava.com, Metro: Ópera

Teatro Kapital

This is a club on steroids. Everything is jacked: the floor count (seven), the light system (spectacular and nearly blinding), and cover and drink charges (€20+ and €12+, respectively). They stack the stage with beautiful dancers, who never fail to inspire the crowd to shake their stuff for all they're worth. It's worth the money if nothing but the ultimate Euro-club experience will do. You should be able to get a free drink with your cover charge, but you'll often have to ask for it. Don't be pushy, though, and dress smart.

€20 cover with drink, Thurs-Sat 12:00-06:00, Calle de Atocha 125, Museum District, +34 914 202 906, grupo-kapital.com, Metro: Atocha

PUB CRAWLS
Sandeman's New Madrid Pub Crawl

Sandeman's New Madrid offers a nightly pub crawl that's far and away the best in town. If you want to pass off the responsibility for charting your night out, let them guide you to some of Madrid's best watering holes. Cheaper than their famous pub crawls elsewhere in Europe, this Sandeman's crawl is fun and social. You'll stop in three bars and finish in one of Madrid's famous clubs, where you can dance and drink until dawn and then some.

€12, nightly at 22:00, meet at Plaza Mayor, Sol, newmadrid-tours.com, Metro: Ópera

TOP SHOPPING & MARKETS

Madrid has the full range of shopping options, covering everything from cheap flea markets to high fashion.

SHOPPING DISTRICTS
Gran Vía

Gran Vía, Madrid's middle-of-the-road and middle-of-the-city shopping district, has just about everything. This slew of retail shops sells everything from touristy trinkets to shoes, hats, and clothes. This is your Champs-Élysées, Piccadilly Circus, and Piazza Venezia of Madrid. There are few surprises here, but it's perfect if your tastes don't stray too far outside of the mainstream.

Sol, Metro: Plaza de Santo Domingo, Plaza del Callao, or Gran Vía

Calle Fuencarral

This charming pedestrian boulevard runs north-south through the heart of Malasaña. It features pop-up fashion shops and hidden gems like boutique clothing and shoe shops. It's here that you'll uncover little treasures that'll make your friends back home green with envy. If you get tired of shopping, just pull up a pew at any of the cafés or restaurants. Get a seat outside—sit inside and you'll be missing the best people-watching in Madrid. There are some great options for food and brunch on Calle de Augusto Figueroa.

Malasaña, Metro: Chueca or Gran Vía

Calle Serrano

On Calle Serrano, a long street in the Salamanca district that runs north-south, you'll find haute couture shopping from the Plaza de la Independencia all the way north to Calle Juan Bravo. It's here you can find brands like D&G and Gucci.

Salamanca, Metro: Retiro, Serrano, or Ruben Dario

MARKETS
El Rastro

Bursting with stalls selling trinkets and antiques, this is the biggest flea market in Madrid. There's not much you can't find here—for the DIY fashion designer, you'll find bolts of fabric that'll have you eager to get home to your sewing machine. On Sunday during outdoor market hours, the atmosphere here gets a touch crazy. The avenue turns into one massive garage sale that's more *Antiques Roadshow* than *Storage Wars*. Each little side street has its own discrete focus: there's a street for birds, another for paintings, yet another for collectibles like trading cards and stamps. Cruise the main boulevard, but don't forget to wander off!

It's easy to get distracted with all the energy, but keep a hand on your wallet at all times (or put it in a zippered or buttoned pocket). If you're going to get pickpocketed in Madrid, it'll happen here.

Free, Sun 09:00-15:00, Plaza de Cascorro, La Latina, Metro: La Latina

Mercado San Miguel

Under classic architecture, you'll find a gastro-market with all sorts of delicious cuisine—seafood, *jamón* stalls, juice stands, paella, and more. The building, just around the corner from Plaza Mayor, dates to 1916, and it's got a lovely chic-mod vibe. Adventurous eaters should absolutely make sure to visit here at least once.

Free, Sun-Wed 10:00-24:00, Thurs-Sat 10:00-02:00, Plaza de San Miguel, Sol, Metro: Ópera

Cuesta de Moyano

If you're into old books, you'll spend hours on end poring over the thousands of books displayed in the 30-plus stalls that line this market. Book collectors come from all over the world to barter with the vendors and each other. A few of the stalls have decent English-language books to pick through, but the emphasis here is (as you might expect) Spanish literature.

Free, open daily (hours vary stall to stall), Calle Claudio Moyano, Museum District, Metro: Atocha

TOP PARKS & RECREATION

PARKS
Retiro Park

This park, directly east of the Museum District, is full of beautiful gardens, sculptures, buildings, and a man-made lake on which you can rent a rowboat and drift around in the sun. It's a great place to take a break during a busy day of sightseeing. A highlight is the Crystal Palace, a massive steel and glass greenhouse in the industrialist style so popular at the turn of the 20th century. Don't miss the dramatic Statue of the Fallen Angel either—it's the only public statue in Europe openly dedicated to Lucifer.

On the southwest side of the park are the delightful **Botanical Gardens** (€4, daily 10:00-21:00, earlier closing time in winter, Plaza de Murillo 2, Museum District, +34 914 203 017, rjb.csic.es, Metro: Atocha). The noise and stress of the city quickly fade away amid the more than 30,000 plants and 1,500 trees. You can find numerous prime locations for a little picnic to rest and recharge.

Free, daily 06:00-22:00, Plaza de la Independencia, Metro: Ibiza

Madrid Río

On the west side of town, Madrid's river walk is an excellent way to get away from the crowds—it doesn't seem to be on the tourist radar yet, and I can't for the life of me figure out why. Head over to the governmental and office district of Príncipe Pío, just behind the Royal Palace and Jardines de Sabatini. You'll find the path by the river, where it's quiet, idyllic, and revitalizing. You can also rent bikes and cruise farther up or down the river on the newly laid meandering paths, which stretch for miles in either direction.

Free, always open, Greater Madrid, Metro: Intercambiador de Príncipe Pío

VIEWPOINTS

In addition to the Teleférico de Madrid, a couple of other venues in Madrid offer sweeping views of the city.

El Corte Inglés

This large shopping center doubles as one of the best viewpoints in Madrid. Ride the escalators up to the 9th floor and relax in the café that overlooks the city skyline. It's a great place to watch the sun set over the city—in the right conditions, Madrid glows a golden orange.

Free, Mon-Sat 10:00–22:00 and 11:00–21:00, Sun Plaza de Callao 2, Sol, +34 913 79 80 00, elcorteingles.es, Metro: Santo Domingo or Gran Vía

Circulo de Bellas Artes Terraza

You'll find a classy terrace with a bar and café at the top of Madrid's Fine Arts Association building. The view from this city-center location is one of my favorites, and it doubles as a popular nightlife venue after the sun goes down, with DJs spinning late. The covered space isn't weatherproof, so give it a pass in bad weather.

€4 entry, Mon-Thurs 09:00–02:00, Fri 09:00–02:30, Sat-Sun 11:00–02:30, Alcalá 42, Sol, +34 913 892 500, circulobellasartes.com/azotea, Metro: Sol

TOP TOURS

Sandeman's New Europe Walking Tours

Sandeman's offers a number of free and fun tip-based walking tours. Sure, they're scripted, but they've honed these scripts to a fine point. It's a great introduction to Madrid and her history. Tours leave daily at 10:00, 11:00, and 14:00 from Plaza Mayor. You can count on an entertaining several-hour stroll picking up tons of fun facts and trivia—you can also expect a few plugs for their paid tours. They also do the best pub crawl in the city.

Free, daily, tours leave from Plaza Mayor, Sol, newmadrid-tours.com, info@neweuropetours.eu, Metro: Ópera

Spanish Cooking Classes: Paella, Gazpacho & Sangria

Here's my prescription for experiencing a new culture: take orally three times daily with drink on an empty stomach. If you enjoy hands-on cooking experiences, this crash course in some of Spain's favorite dishes is your top option in town. Choose from their selection of classes, from paella to tapas and even wine-tasting. Kick off your experience with a visit to the local market to pick up ingredients. Your friendly chef/teacher can help even the clumsiest kitchen novice feel right at home in the modern facilities, and they're more than happy to accommodate various diets and allergies. Classes take about four hours and start at 10:00. Book online ahead of time.

Options from €70, Mon-Sat, Calle de Moratin 11, Sol, +34 910 115 154, cookingpoint.es/classes, info@cookingpoint.es, Metro: Antón Martín

Letango Tours

Carlos and Jenn, a husband-and-wife team, run this upscale, custom tour outfit. While the price for one of their tours puts them a little out of range for budget-conscious backpackers, they're definitely worth a look for families or groups who want a memorable guided excursion that will take them outside of Madrid. Letango offers options for multiday excursions all around the Iberian Peninsula, with options focusing on a broad range of Iberian history, culture, and cuisine.

Multiday trips from €300, +34 661 752 458, letango.com, tours@letango.com

TOP HOSTELS

There's a wide selection of well-located budget accommodations around Madrid. It's good to search by the district you identify best with. Personally, I love to drill down to Malasaña for its proximity to the trendy, fun, and casual restaurants and nightlife. Others may prefer the hustle and bustle of Sol. Still others (especially LGBT travelers) may enjoy the extensive food and nightlife options in Chueca.

For more hostel choices, visit hostelworld.com to find the best deals. Many locals generate a little extra income by renting out their spaces on Airbnb, and the comfortable and well-located apartments listed there make a great option for those who know exactly what they want to see and where they want to go. Three-star hotels in Madrid range €80-120 per night.

Las Musas Residence

The simple and spartan Las Musas Residence is in the heart of Lavapies, where you'll find recommended restaurants, cafés, and nightlife. The hostel has big rooms for about €20 per night and sports all your basic amenities, including a communal kitchen. The free sangria and drinking-game nights turn the party up and draw backpackers like moths to light.

€18, 24-hour reception, laundry facilities, free Wi-Fi, common room, lockers, Calle Jesús y María 12, Lavapies, +34 915 394 984, lasmusasresidence.com, info@ lasmusasresidence.com, Metro: Tirso de Molina

Sungate One

All who stay at Sungate leave the hostel positively glowing. This is in large part thanks to the awesome atmosphere that the staff creates. They give this clean, centrally located hostel that extra little something that makes it feel like home away from home rather than just a place to crash. The 24-hour reception means you can check in any time of the day, and no matter what time you arrive, someone will greet you and give you the lowdown on the city, where to eat, and what to do. It's just up the hill from Plaza Puerta del Sol, so you're right in the thick of it whether you're looking for churros or *chupitos*.

Private twins from €30, 6-bed dorms from €18, Calle de Carmen 16, Sol, +34 910 236 806, sungateone.com, Metro: Sol

MuchoMadrid

Offering twins, triples, and quads, these budget rooms are ideal for those want to balance fun and sleep (you'll get both in good measure). Done up in a clean-yet-funky design, the bright rooms are comfortable and quiet. There's a well-appointed kitchen, but the hostel lacks a social area, so if meeting other cute backpackers without leaving the hostel is your goal, you may want to consider other options.

4-bed dorms from €20, Gran Vía 59, Malasaña, +34 915 592 350, muchomadrid.com, Metro: Santo Domingo

Cat's Hostel

A large hostel with marble pillars, ornate arches, colorful patterned walls, and 240 beds, Cat's Hostel is a uniquely vibrant place to stay. It also offers a party atmosphere with its own bar that's open late, along with a breakfast to help fuel you up for the day's activities. First on the docket: one of their free walking tours, which kick off daily.

€24, 24-hour reception, free Wi-Fi, laundry facilities, bar, €2 breakfast, lockers, computer access, Calle Cañizares 6, Sol, +34 913 692 807, catshostel.com, info@catshostel. com, Metro: Antón Martín

Room007 Hostel: Chueca

This is a large, social hostel with music nights, bar crawls, and a rooftop terrace (a boon on hot, sunny days that turn into cool evenings). The rooms are done up in a sort of shabby-chic decor that sometimes makes you feel like you're in a magazine shoot. This is one branch of a Madrid-based hostel chain that has it down to a science. You'll find Wi-Fi everywhere (though weaker in the rooms), good-value breakfast, great city-center locations, and helpful staff facilitating a social environment.

11-bed dorm from €22, Calle Hortaleza 74, Chueca, +34 913 688 111, room007.com/en, Metro: Chueca

Room007 Hostel: Ventura

This branch of Room007, centrally located directly between the Prado Museum and Plaza Puerta del Sol, shares many attributes with the chain's Chueca hostel. This location is smaller and more personal, with more than 100 beds split across four- and eight-bed dorms. Whoever is at reception will help you make the most of your time, and they'll offer you discounts at some of the very good partner restaurants nearby.

4- and 8-bed dorms from €24, female dorms available, 24-hour reception, Ventura de la Vega 5, Sol, +34 914 204 481, room007.com/en, Metro: Sol

GETTING THERE & AWAY

Luggage storage facilities are available at all major train stations and at the airport.

Plane

The massive **Madrid-Barajas Airport** (MAD, aeropuertomadrid-barajas.com) is the main international airport serving the city. It's your only option if you're arriving by air. (You may find cheaper options for Barcelona and Girona, but remember, those are more than four hours away by car.) You can connect into the center from the airport via metro, bus, or train.

Metro trains leave every five minutes (06:00-02:00) from Terminal T2 and Terminal T4. Take line 8, which you will probably want to ride to the end stop, Nuevos Ministerios. The approximately 15-minute trip will cost you €5. Consider purchasing a multiday metro pass at the machines just before you enter the metro (it'll cover your first trip into town).

The **Exprés Aeropuerto** (Airport Express) is a 24-hour bus service that has only three stops: O'Donnell, Plaza de Cibeles, and Atocha (this last stop only 06:00-23:30). Check the location of your hostel for your most practical hop-off point. The buses leave every 15 minutes from Terminals T1, T2, and T3, with a journey time of about 40 minutes. Purchase your ticket (€5) on board.

The C1 train line departs from Terminal T4 for a 10-minute journey into Madrid (€2.40). This line has connections to Chamartin, Nuevos Ministerios, Atocha, and Príncipe Pío stations.

Train

Trains between Barcelona and Madrid run often and take about three hours. If you purchase in advance through renfe.com, tickets can be as cheap as €50, but, as you get closer to the date of travel, they climb past €150. Avoid peak commute times (early morning and late afternoon) to avoid the steepest fares.

Madrid has two main train stations: **Atocha,** near the Reina Sofía, and **Chamartin,** about eight kilometers north of Puerta del Sol. Both are well connected with the local metro system, and you should have no trouble getting to your hostel. There are secondary stations as well, so always double-check your departure station before heading to catch your train. Other train stations that might be close to your lodgings include Nuevos Ministerios, Príncipe Pío, Delicias, Pirámides, and Méndez Alvaro. There is also the Recoletos station, though it is not connected with the metro. Trains usually run 06:00-23:00 and depart frequently for both national and international destinations. If you need to book in person, allow at least 1.5 hours—the lines can be long and painfully slow-moving.

Bus

Spain has an extensive network of bus lines that can get you across the country. Of the main bus companies, I recommend **Alsa** (alsa.es/en) and **Eurolines** (eurolines.es/en). Remember, though: it's a big country. You'll have to weigh cheaper prices against additional travel time. If arriving by bus, you will be dropped off at Méndez Alvaro (Estación del Sur) bus station, Madrid's main bus station, or Avenida de América bus station. Both are very well connected, making it easy to get to anywhere you need to go in the city.

Car

The drive from Barcelona to Madrid is no joke. You'll be driving for about six hours on the EU-funded and toll-supported E-90 freeway. Having a car does give you additional flexibility (you can stop at any of the Spanish towns along the way, which is a definite plus). Madrid itself is a car city, but it has some intense traffic. There isn't any sort of park-and-ride system, so your best bet is to park on the outskirts of the city within a few blocks of a metro stop and take the metro in to avoid hefty parking fees during your visit. Lock your doors, and leave nothing even remotely valuable in the car.

GETTING AROUND

Madrid's excellent public transportation network makes it easy to get around or across this sprawling city. Consider buying the great-value short-term day passes, which get you onto the integrated bus and metro network and can save you money if you plan on using the metro even just a few times a day. Spring for the one-day (€8.40), two-day (€14.20), three-day (€18.40), or five-day (€26.80) pass at the entrance to the metro from the airport. The local pass covers all of downtown Madrid and will include your first transfer into town.

Metro

Madrid's metro system (metromadrid.es/en) comprises more than 238 stations and 13 lines, making connections across town fast and easy. The metro runs 06:00-01:30, with trains coming every few minutes during rush hour (07:30-09:00) and every five minutes during regular hours. A single metro ticket costs €1.50.

Bus

Madrid has a new line of hydrogen-fueled (and air-conditioned!) buses. Buses run every 5-15 minutes 06:00-02:00. And for you late-nighters, night buses operate 23:45-06:00, with buses coming every 15 30 minutes.

Car

Consider renting a car only if you want to get farther out into the countryside, where the lack of bus and train connections dramatically limit your options.

Taxi

With more than 15,000 taxis serving the city, you won't have a problem flagging one down. Look for the white taxis with a diagonal red band on the side door with the city's emblem, featuring a bear, tree, and crown just above the stripe. With such a great public transportation system in place, only use these if you need to get across town in a jiffy or are coming back from the clubs before the next morning's rush hour.

Bicycle

With its big streets and fast-moving cars, Madrid is notoriously unfriendly for cycling. Biking around town is not recommended. The only exceptions are Retiro Park and the paths along the river, both great places to ride around and explore. You can find several bike shops on the east side of Retiro Park.

DAY TRIPS

Toledo

Toledo was Spain's capital for nearly 1,000 years. Today, it's a beautifully preserved stone town perched on top of a rocky outcropping. It's touristy and kitschy but also wonderful to explore for an afternoon. The **Cathedral of Toledo** (€8, Mon-Sat 10:00-18:00, Sun 14:00-18:00, Calle Cardenal Cisneros 1, +34 925 22 22 41, catedralprimada.es) will make the journey worthwhile. Stepping into this church, exquisitely executed in high Gothic style and dripping in golden accents with baroque embellishments, is a spiritual experience even for the nonbeliever. The **Mirador del Valle** is a breathtaking vista overlooking the horseshoe bend in the Tagus River. Time your visit for a clear day and hop the river via the bridge on the east side of town, then continue south to climb the hill to the viewpoint; you'll know it when you see it. For your museum fix, don't miss the **Alcázar of Toledo** (€5, Thurs-Tues 11:00-17:00, Calle Unión,

+34 925 23 88 00, museo.ejercito.es), the palace that dominates the city's skyline. Originally built in the 3rd century as a fort and Roman palace, the Alcázar of Toledo was the site of a siege during the Spanish Civil War. Today, this grand structure is a fascinating military history museum.

Trains and buses leave from Madrid's Atocha and Chamartin stations often and take about 40 minutes to get to Toledo. Fares start at €13 for one-way trips. Purchase tickets from the machines at the station.

Salamanca

Salamanca is home to a sizable population of Spanish and international students who drive the nightlife of this ancient city, once a Celtic settlement. The University of Salamanca is the oldest in Spain, but Salamanca's sights aren't merely academic. There's the famous Plaza Mayor and plenty of other diverting sights that are more than enough to fill a day.

Trains and buses leave from Madrid's Atocha and Chamartin stations often and take about 90 minutes to reach Salamanca. One-way fares begin at €13. Purchase tickets from the machines at the station.

Segovia

Segovia's has an eye-popping aqueduct (it's bigger than you think—much bigger) and a fairytale castle with great views over some of Spain's driest country. Spend a day meandering through its cobblestone streets. If you haven't had enough of cathedrals, you have a few to choose from here. Climbing the **Tower of Juan** in the **Alcázar de Segovia** castle to access the city's best viewpoint would definitely be the cherry on top of this day trip (€8 museum, palace and tower entry, €3 for tower only, daily 10:00-19:30, +34 921 46 07 59, alcazardesegovia.com).

Trains and busets leave often from Atocha and Chamartin stations in Madrid and take about two hours to reach Segovia. Fares are from €13 one-way. Purchase tickets from the machines at the station.

HELP!

Tourist Information Centers

Madrid's primary **tourist information center** (daily 09:30-20:30, Plaza Mayor 27) has a convenient location steps from Puerto del Sol. There are numerous other locations throughout town, all of them sporting signs with black text on a yellow background.

Pickpockets & Scams

Madrid has a relatively low crime rate; however, always keep a close watch over your bags and other items, as pickpocketing and street theft can and do occur. Be especially wary of crowded areas such as train stations and tourist attractions. In Spain, it's better to carry only what you need for the day rather than carrying all your cards and cash with you. Leave what you don't need in the safe at the hostel. The area just south of La Latina is known to have a higher density of pickpockets and thieves. Avoid going there alone at night, and keep your wits about you during the day, too.

Emergencies

In an emergency, dial 112. You can also dial 091 for police.

Hospital

Hospital Ruber Internacional
Calle de la Masó 38
+34 913 875 000

US Embassy

Calle Serrano 75
+34 915 872 240

BARCELONA

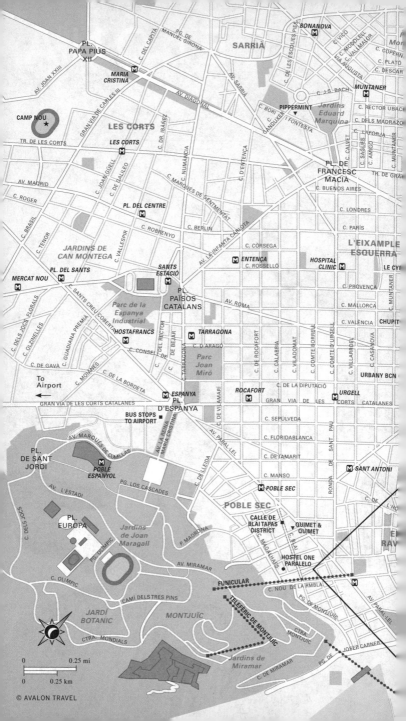

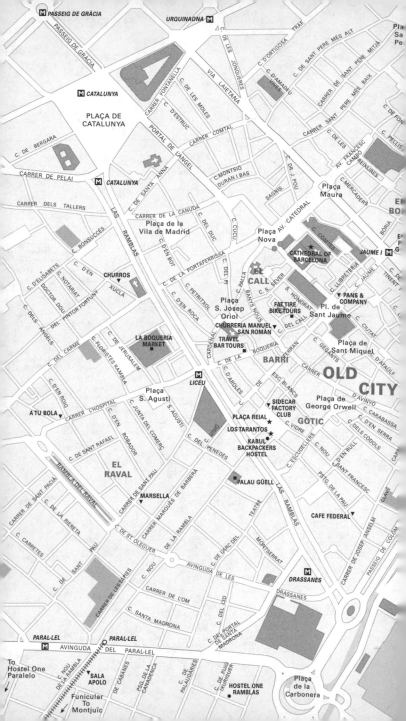

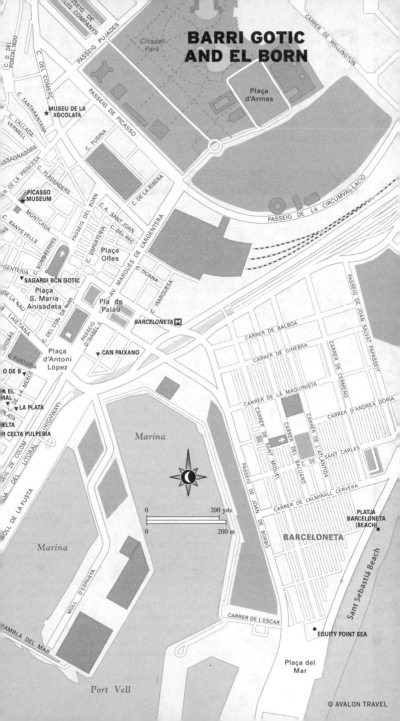

BARRI GOTIC
AND EL BORN

SEIG DE LLUIS COMPANYS

Citadel Park

Plaça d'Armes

PASSEIG PUJADES

C. D. DEL PORTAL NOU

C. D. DEL COMERÇ

C. TANTARANTANA

PASSEIG DE PICASSO

★ MUSEU DE LA XOCOLATA

C. L'ALLADA VERMELL

ISSAONADORS

C. FUSINA

C. DE LA RIBERA

CARRER DE WELLINGTON

R DE LA PRINCESA

C. FLASSADERS

PASSEIG DEL BORN

C.A. SANT JOAN

C. DEL REC

✦ PICASSO MUSEUM

MONTCADA

C. BANYS VELLS

C. SOMBRERERS

C. ESPARTERIA

Plaça Olles

AV. MARQUÈS DE L'ARGENTERA

GENTERIA

C. DUANA

PASSEIG DE LA CIRCUMVAL·LACIÓ

▼ SAGARDI BCN GOTIC

DE LA NAU

Plaça S. Maria Anisadeta

Pla de Palau

C. MARQUESA

PASSEIG DE JOAN SALVAT PAPASSEIT

LAIETANA

C. DEL CÓN

PASSEIG D'ISABEL II

BARCELONETA Ⓜ

CARRER DE BALBOA

CARRER DE GINEBRA

UGNAS

C. FUSTERIA

Plaça d'Antoni López

▼ CAN PAIXANO

CARRER DE CENMENO

CARRER DE LA MAQUINISTA

O DE B

A EL RAL

DE LA MERCÈ

CARRER DE SANT MIQUEL

CARRER DEL BALUARD

CARRER DE L'ATLANTIDA

CARRER D'ANDREA DORIA

▼ LA PLATA

PLATA

ELTA

R CELTA PULPERIA

SANT CARLES

DE COLOM

Marina

PASSEIG DE JOAN DE BORBÓ

CARRER DE L'ALMIRALL CERVERA

PLATJA BARCELONETA (BEACH)

MOLL DE LA FUSTA

0   200 yds

0   200 m

BARCELONETA

Marina

MOLL D'ESPANYA

Sant Sebastià Beach

AMBLA DEL MAR

CARRER DE L'ESCAR

● EQUITY POINT SEA

Plaça del Mar

Port Vell

© AVALON TRAVEL

Barcelona has it all: white-sand beaches, surreal modernist architecture, bustling markets with fresh local produce, and nightlife that pops till sunrise. It's the capital of Catalonia, Spain's northeasternmost territory, where the regional cultural pride is fierce. Get ready to soak in that culture and live like a local by finding your own perfect siesta-to-fiesta ratio.

BARCELONA 101

Founded as a military encampment and then an ancient Roman walled port town with—count 'em—72 towers, Barcino, as it was known, was handed back and forth between numerous conquering powers throughout the centuries. As a result, its citizens developed a unique cultural identity that blended the cultures that controlled the city over the years. Catalonia was consolidated under one crown in the 12th century and grew wealthy from its rich sea trade. When Ferdinand (king of Catalonia) and Isabella (queen of Castile, aka the rest of Spain), famous for establishing the Spanish Inquisition and for sponsoring Columbus, married in 1496, political power gradually shifted to Madrid. Buffeted by war and plagues over the next several hundred years, Barcelona endured a slow decline.

The 20th century kicked off with an ambitious city-planning project epitomized by a unique architectural style: Modernisme, also known as Catalan art nouveau. It left a significant mark on the city you see today. From palaces (Palau Güell) to private residences (Block of Discord), and light posts (Plaça Reial) to the grandest, most ambitious cathedral project in the world (Sagrada Familia), Barcelona was architect Antoni Gaudí's canvas, over which he enthusiastically spread his nationalist pride. During the bloody and tragic Spanish Civil War, many Catalan civilians fled to France after fascist dictator Francisco Franco came to power in 1939 and began actively suppressing the Catalan language, traditions, and culture. The only way to express regional patriotism was by cheering for the soccer club, FC Barcelona, which at least partly explains the passion of the team's modern fan base. For Catalans, *fútbol* was an opportunity to keep their muzzled culture alive. After 36 long years, Franco reinstated the Spanish monarchy, putting King Juan Carlos I, who promised to continue Franco's dictatorial style, on the throne. But upon Franco's death, the king returned the country to a democratic system.

In 1992, Barcelona hosted the Olympics and found itself back on the international stage. The city was revitalized with a brand-new metro system, beautiful parks, a cleaned-up medieval center, and four kilometers of brand-new white-sand beaches. (Fun facts: The sand was imported from Egypt, and the metro map mirrors the colors of the Olympic rings.)

Today, Barcelona is Spain's second-largest city after Madrid, and Catalonia is Spain's richest region. Children here learn Catalan first and Castilian Spanish second. The pride and identity of Catalonia is as strong as ever. This pride has fostered both energy and tension, as the people of Catalonia decide which future they want for their children: an independent state, or one that continues to pay into the system to support the rest of Spain.

Residents also feel the pressures of rising tourism to their city, due to high unemployment rates, heightened cost of living, and the increasing presence of tourism companies like Airbnb. Many young residents are being pushed out of the city center, resulting in an undercurrent of resentment toward tourists, which manifests itself in the form of graffiti and the occasional demonstration. Be mindful and do your part to plug into the local scene.

PLAN AHEAD

RESERVATIONS

Reservations are usually required for the following sights:

Sagrada Familia (sagradafamilia.cat)
Picasso Museum (museupicasso.bcn.cat/en, free Sun afternoon)
Parc Güell (parcguell.cat)

LOCAL HAPPENINGS

Gay Pride

Pride Barcelona festivities take place around the first or second weekend of July each year. Expect the surrounding weeks to be crammed full of music, parades, parties, debates, and lectures. Find the agenda and more at pridebarcelona.org. Book ahead for accommodations—the celebrations bring people flocking from all over Europe, and budget accommodations are the first ones to disappear.

Siestas

Siestas are real, people! Barcelona has four rush hour times every day: one in the morning and one in the evening, and another two bracketing siesta time. When temperatures are at their zenith, all the shops close and everyone runs home, where they enjoy a refreshing and heat-beating two- to four-hour nap after lunch. You'll notice shopkeepers locking their doors around 14:00 and usually reopening them around 18:30. If you can't bring yourself to waste the afternoon in this way, stock up on water and snacks before the shops close.

Holidays

If a public holiday falls on a Thursday—or sometimes, even a Wednesday—many Spaniards bridge the holiday into the weekend, giving themselves more days off. It's great for them, but not so great for tourists. All businesses will be closed on the following public national holidays:

January 1, New Year's Day
Holy Week and Good Friday
May 1, Labor Day
August 15, the Assumption
October 12, National Holiday of Spain
November 1, All Saints' Day
December 6, Spanish Constitution Day
December 25, Christmas Day

KNOW BEFORE YOU GO

KEY STATS & FIGURES

Currency:
Spain uses the euro (€);
1 EUR = about 1.14 USD

Population:
1.7 million

Languages:
Catalan and Spanish

Kilometers of beaches:
4.2

Nightclubs:
enough to keep you busy for years

CALIBRATE YOUR BUDGET

TYPICAL PRICES FOR:

Hostel dorm bed:
€24

Two-course dinner and drink:
€15

Pint of beer:
€5

Bicycle rental:
€10/day

Single metro pass:
€2

MOVIES TO WATCH

*Vicky Cristina Barcelona,
Barcelona, The Passenger,
Perfume*

THREE DAY ITINERARY

Organize your visit to Barcelona chronologically. On your first day, focus on the Old Town: the Barri Gotic and El Born. Then, on day two, you'll be exploring the Eixample, with its many beautiful examples of Modernisme. Save your third day for lounging on the beach or, for the adventurous, hiking in the hills or the nearby mountains.

DAY 1: WELCOME TO BARCINO
MORNING

Grab breakfast at your hostel or head to either of my favorite *churrerías* (churro bakeries): **Churreria Manuel San Román** or **Granja M. Viader,** both located right in the Old Town, near the starting point for your free walking tour.

After breakfast, walk over to **Travel Bar** to join up with the free three-hour walking tour—an excellent casual introduction to the layout and history of the city. The tour begins at 11:00. You'll explore the **Barri Gotic**, **La Rambla,** the **Cathedral of Barcelona,** and a number of other interesting spots. Two important reminders: Always watch your pockets in the tourist center, and remember to tip your guide!

Your guide will give you some free time inside **La Boqueria,** a famous market where you can grab a quick snack. Belly up to any one of the countertop bars inside the market. Instead of seeking out comfort foods (few and far between here), try something that looks strange and foreign—you might surprise yourself with what you like!

AFTERNOON

At the end point of your tour, you'll be about a 15-minute walk from the **Picasso Museum** in El Born. Spend a couple of hours exploring the exhibits. El Born is also home to the enticing **Chocolate Museum** and some tasty tapas at **Sagardi BCN Gotic.**

EVENING

Take a minute back at the hostel to freshen up (wipe that chocolate off your face), then head out to catch Travel Bar's three-hour **Paella & Sangria Cooking Class,** which meets daily at 17:45. Make your reservations earlier in the day to confirm your spot. Dress to stay out—the class lets out late, and you'll want to go straight to the bars.

LATE

Remember, Spaniards don't really kick off the night until the wee hours of the morning. Spend the time after your paella class in the nearby **Plaça Reial,** where you'll find some of my favorite nightlife attractions: **Los Tarantos Flamenco Show** becomes **Jamboree** when the show ends, or, on the opposite corner of the square, you'll find the indie rock temple **Sidecar Factory Club.**

DAY 2: THE EIXAMPLE & BEYOND
MORNING
Get ready for a day of Modernisme with a quick bite at **Pans and Company** or **el Fornet.** One of their tortilla sandwiches with a *café con leche* will make a filling and energizing start to your day.

After breakfast, take the **Discover Walks** Gaudi Tour (€19), which meets daily at 10:30 on the Passeig de Gràcia, in front of **Casa Batllo.** This 1.5-hour walk covers the **Block of Discord** and Casa Milá before ending at Gaudí's nearly finished masterpiece, the **Sagrada Familia.** Pop in to any café that looks good along the way and ask for a *bocadillo* (a Spanish sandwich). My go-to *bocadillo* is a *chorizo con queso* (sausage and cheese) or *jamón con queso* (ham and cheese).

AFTERNOON
After goggling the Sagrada Familia for a couple of hours, take bus 92 (from Carrer de la Indústria) up to **Parc Güell,** Gaudí's glorious failure—originally intended as a housing development, it is now a beautiful park. Alternatively, take bus V21 from the north side of the open square adjacent the Sagrada Familia downhill to the **beach** to soak up some rays! In the late afternoon, head back to your hostel for a reviving siesta—you'll probably need it.

EVENING
Leave your hostel to crawl along **Carrer de la Mercè,** the site of some of the best tapas bars in the city. Formerly a gritty street paced by Barcelona's prostitutes and sailors, it has changed its skin. You'll find some of the city's most authentic flavors here.

LATE
From Carrer de la Mercè, split a cab to Eixample with friends. Head straight to **Chupitos,** Barcelona's best-known shot bar, and **Dow Jones,** a stock market-themed bar, for a pair of fun and shamelessly touristy experiences.

Now fully loaded, head to the **Puerto Olimpico** for the glitzy nightlife that Barcelona is so famous for. Flag another cab back to the famous venues on the beach, including disco **Shoko** and its posher sister, **Opium Mar.** Rage until late to the sounds of world-class DJs, and then, as the party winds down, take you friends out onto the beach and watch the sun rise.

DAY 3: CHOICES, CHOICES, CHOICES
If it's Sunday, you're in luck: head to the **Cathedral of Barcelona** to catch the **Sardana dances.** If your day one or two lands on a Sunday, it's worth shuffling the itinerary to see this traditional Catalan dance. Tempted to join? You might get a chance, but wait to be invited—don't barge into the circle.

If you've got a late flight, you probably have time to pack a lunch and head out for a hike up **Montjuïc.** At the top, you'll enjoy panoramic views of the city and Mediterranean (and the air up there is much fresher). Or, if you've already worn your shoe leather thin, enjoy a lazy day soaking in the sun on **Platja Barceloneta** or **Platja Nova Mar Bella,** two of Barcelona's best beaches.

If you're staying for a fourth day, consider using your third day for a **day trip to Montserrat** for a strenuous and rewarding day of hiking outside the city.

TOP NEIGHBORHOODS

Barcelona's Old Town comprises two main districts: the Barri Gotic (Gothic Quarter) and El Born, a neighborhood of narrow, winding streets built on Barcelona's ancient Roman foundations. The **Barri Gotic,** with Plaça de Catalunya at the top and the famous street of La Rambla running through the middle, also boasts the Cathedral of Barcelona and the elegant Plaça Reial. **El Born,** with classy cafés and posh cocktail bars to suit the young professional set (and in-the-know tourists), is home to the Picasso Museum, some tasty tapas, and the Parc de la Ciutadella.

On the opposite side of the Gothic Quarter, you'll find **El Raval,** trendy and alternative as long as you stay above Carrer l'Hospital. Farther on, bordering Montjuïc, is **Poble-Sec,** with its excellent *pintxos* and unique local vibe.

Surrounding the Old Town up the slightly inclined landscape is the **Eixample,** or expansion, so named because it's the world's best-executed example of modern city planning, with an extensive grid layout. You'll find a number of key sights here, particularly Modernisme architecture, including the Sagrada Familia and the famous homes on the Block of Discord.

Barceloneta is on the east side of town, with El Born just inland, the marina to the south, and Barcelona's long stretch of beaches and boardwalk leading north along the waterline. Along the boardwalk, you'll find surf shops, local bars and cafés, and touristy restaurants. Along the north end is **Puerto Olimpico,** the town's port and the epicenter of Barcelona's energetic clubbing scene.

TOP SIGHTS

Sagrada Familia

This church, designed by Gaudí, is my favorite sight in all of Europe. If you see only one thing in Barcelona, make it the Sagrada Familia. We can count ourselves lucky that, within our lifetimes, we'll be able to see the architect's vision fully realized—those in charge say that the building will be completed by 2026, in time for the centenary of Gaudí's death. In 1883, when the project was only a year old, Gaudí took over as head architect, and the church has been

an ongoing construction site ever since (not counting the years during the Spanish Civil War, when construction was halted). The church has grown in fits and starts because, from the beginning, it has been entirely publicly funded: They build when they have money. When they run out, they pass the hat. Your entry fee will go towards the unimaginably large construction costs.

Both the exterior and interior are finally taking shape. Two completed facades dominate the east and the west sides—the Na-

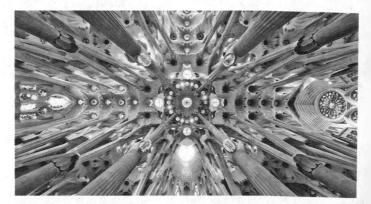

ACT LIKE A LOCAL

Getting on Barcelona Time

To fully enjoy Barcelona, it's important to adapt to the way that the Spaniards structure their time. If you try to follow the schedule you keep back home (swapping working hours for sightseeing ones), you'll likely only get frustrated and miss out on incredible experiences and opportunities. This is a typical timeline for a Friday in Barcelona:

08:30: Grab a light breakfast of a croissant and *café con leche* (coffee with milk).

09:00-12:30: Locals head to work. For visitors, this is a good time to hit the sights.

13:00-17:00: Some stores close down for lunch and siesta. A side effect: double the traffic in a major city where everyone commutes twice a day. You wouldn't be missing much in the streets if you decided to take a siesta after a large Spanish lunch.

19:00-21:00: Evening stroll time. The city is still wiping the sleep from its eyes. Stores are reopening.

21:00-23:00: Dinnertime (a time to savor and socialize; definitely not something to rush).

23:00-01:00: Pregaming with friends, either in parks or back at the flat.

01:00-02:30: Time for the bars. Energy drinks and simple cocktails to get ready for the club.

03:00 until morning (or until you can't keep your eyes open): Club like there's no tomorrow. Stumble out of the *discotecas* at Puerto Olimpico and watch the sunrise from the beach.

tivity and the Passion façades, respectively. The Glory façade is still in progress. Each of the exquisitely carved figures would be perfectly at home among the world's finest statues. Look closely at the Nativity façade (which faces the rising sun each morning), with the Holy Family in the center at the top of the door. Farm animals, magi, and a six-piece angel band surround the family in pious adoration. As with all of Gaudí's projects, look for the details, like the unhappy turtles that seem to be bearing the weight of the columns on their backs. This is the side Gaudí toiled on during his life.

Step into the church, and it feels like you've stepped into a giant rain forest complete with a canopy. The coloring is miraculous thanks to the detailed stained glasswork throughout. When Gaudí died, less than a quarter of the church was complete, so the view we get today is miles beyond what he ever saw—but we are, make no mistake, seeing his vision in stone, wood, and glass. The scale of this vision is almost as breathtaking as the building itself. When the final spire is raised, the tallest point in the building will be 170 meters (the nearby Montjuïc is 171 meters high—

Gaudí said he didn't want his creation to surpass God's).

Plan to spend at least 90 minutes exploring the cathedral. Ticket sales end 15 minutes before closing time. Don't miss the workshop to the side of the church and the small architectural museum downstairs in the crypt.

Reservations required, €15 adults, €13 students, entry to the towers €7 extra (must be purchased online simultaneously with entry ticket), Apr-Sept daily 09:00-20:00, Oct-Mar daily 09:00-18:00, Carrer de Mallorca 401, Eixample, +34 932 080 414, sagradafamilia.org, Metro: Sagrada Familia

La Rambla

Take a downhill stroll from Plaça de Catalunya (Barcelona's central square and the heart of Catalan pride) down La Rambla, the city's most popular and busiest series of contiguous streets. This experience is at the heart of any tourist's visit to Barcelona. Along this one-kilometer stretch are flower stalls, bird vendors, a world-famous market (La Boqueria), beautiful baroque churches, works by Gaudí and other famous architects, dozens of street performers, a square populated by the wealthiest traders from Barcelona's golden age, and churros galore—of course, with this many tourists, you can find the scam artists too. The street referred to as La Rambla actually comprises five streets, all following what used to be a spring coming from the surrounding hills: starting from Plaça Catalunya, they are Rambla de Canaletes, Rambla dels Estudis, Rambla de Sant Josep, Rambla dels Caputxins, and Rambla de Santa Mònica.

Explore the winding streets leading off from La Rambla on either side with a walking tour, or do it independently—it's a part of Barcelona that rewards aimless wandering. As you walk in the Barri Gotic, soak in the dense history beneath your feet and all around you.

Always keep your wits about you and watch out for scam games and pickpockets who rove the entire length of La Rambla day and night, preying on distracted or naïve tourists who think they can win anything in these slight-of-hand games (they'll fleece you faster than you can say "*olé*"). After dark, the drug dealers come out; after 03:00, things get seedy.

Free, always open, Barri Gotic, Metro: Catalunya

Picasso Museum

A museum dedicated to Spain's best-known revolutionary artist resides in Barcelona's trendy El Born district. Picasso spent many of his formative years here in Barcelona, and the impressive museum is juxtaposed against the backdrop of some of Barcelona's classical palaces. The museum features an extensive collection of works progressing through Picasso's various stages in chronological order. They say that Picasso, as a child, painted like a master in photo-realistic pieces, and as an adult, he painted like a child, with geometric shapes, disquieting coloring—in the opinion of contemporaries, at least—and stark outlines. A wander through the museum is a must for art fans and should take you about 90 minutes.

Prebook online, €11–14 depending on exhibits, students with ID card free, free all day first Sun of the month and all other Sun afternoons after 15:00 (reservations still required), Tues-Sun 09:00-19:00, till 21:30 on Thurs, closed Mon, Carrer Montcada 15-23, El Born, +34 93 256 30 00, museupicasso.bcn.cat/en, Metro: Jaume I

Block of Discord

This single block of ostentatious homes on Passeig de Gràcia, featuring **Casa Amatller, Casa Lleo Morera, Casa Batllo,** and, farther up, **Casa Milá,** is a perfect example of modernist architects attempting to outdo one another. Each house has a clear and distinct personality. The name of the city block reflects the jarring appearance of each of these homes when lined up next to each other. Paid entry into these modernist houses is possible, but casual observers are often content with admiring the exteriors for free. Some descriptions and details follow below.

Always open, Passeig de Gràcia, Eixample, Metro: Passeig de Gràcia

Casa Amatller

This home's namesake family made it rich off the chocolate trade. The ground-floor door is sometimes open for visitors to pop in and view the interior; go all the way in the back to find the chocolate shop in the building with the unmistakable Minecraft-style façade.

Free, €15 for guided tour, daily 11:00-18:00, English-language tours at 11:00 and 15:00, Passeig de Gràcia 41, fundacionamatller.org

Casa Lleo Morera

Bursting with modernist decoration, this building on the downhill corner of the block is really a collaboration between a number of artists and architects. Their various styles can be seen in the ornate balconies, numerous arches, and diverse architectural accents. See if you can't pick out some of the high-tech inventions that were just coming to light at the time this building was erected in 1906. And don't miss the trademark mulberry tree (*morera*), this family's namesake.

€15 for 70-minute English-language tour, €12 for 45-minute tour, Tues-Sun, check website for tour times, Passeig de Gràcia 35, casalleomorera.com

Casa Batllo

Colloquially known as the "dragon house," this fanciful house built for the Batllo family depicts the story of St. George and the Dragon, and it's loaded with symbolism. The columns on the exterior represent the past victims of the dragon, with the balco-

GAGA FOR GAUDÍ

St. George may be Barcelona's patron saint, but, if you proposed switching the old dragon slayer with Antoni Gaudí tomorrow, most of the people in the city would probably nod in approval. You'll see the architect's thumbprint on almost every block across the city—from street tiles, benches, and light posts all the way to churches, private palaces, and parks. As is clear in everything from the massive **Sagrada Familia** to the minute details on the furniture he designed, Gaudí was truly an architectural prodigy well ahead of his time. The **Block of Discord** (comprising **Casa Batllo** and **Casa Milá**) and **Parc Güell** are some of the most famous sights in the city. In Barri Gotic, don't miss his **lampposts in Plaça Reial** and, nearby, one of his early projects, **Palau Güell.**

nies made of skulls. The tiles of the roof are clearly the scales of the back of the dragon, with the spire of the turret representing the sword plunged into the serpent's back. The interior is just as detailed, with beautifully carved wooden door frames, styled light fixtures, and even an atrium paneled with darker tiles at the top, cooling to lighter tiles near the ground floor to help distribute natural light across all rooms evenly.

€21.50, €18.50 students, daily 09:00-21:00, Passeig de Gràcia 43, +34 932 16 03 06, casabatllo.es

Casa Milá

Casa Milá is also known as La Pedrera (the Stone Quarry) because of the striking appearance of its exterior. This, another masterpiece of Antoni Gaudí's unique and innovative modernist architecture, appears like a sculpted layer cake a couple of blocks uphill from the houses on Passeig de Gràcia. Peer up at the rooftop, where you'll notice a series of twisted chimneys, sculpted in such a way that they resemble the storm troopers from *Star Wars*.

€20.50, €16.50 students, Mar-Oct daily 09:00-20:00, Nov-Feb daily 09:00-18:30, last entry 30 minutes before closing, Provença 261-265, +34 902 20 21 38, lapedrera.com

Plaça Reial

This picturesque, Renaissance-style city-center square is one of Barcelona's many adornments that popped up during the explosive architectural period of the late 19th century. Barcelona's elite would come here for a stroll and to admire each other's palatial homes. Today, we peasants can

enjoy the scene, which is especially beautiful at night. During the day, enjoy *café con leche* at one of the many cafés that line the square, people-watch, and admire the lampposts that were designed by a young Gaudí. Each Sunday a stamp and coin market takes over the square. After sundown, you've got several bars, clubs, and shows lining the square to choose from.

Free, always open, Barri Gotic, Metro: Liceu

Los Tarantos Flamenco Show

A typical dance originating in the south of Spain, flamenco positively drips with fire and passion. Los Tarantos captures this mesmerizing Spanish tradition in a perfectly succinct yet varied show featuring tap dancers, box-drummers, guitarists, and guttural vocalists who belt out songs ranging from upbeat to morose. The music is infectious, the dance transportive; you'll be entertained, yes, but more than this, you'll gain a deeper understanding of the Spanish character. Even with three shows a night, the quality and syncopated energy of each show is impressively consistent, and the venue—intimate but casual—is anything but touristy. Come early and grab a drink, then post up as close to the stage as you can.

€15, 40-minute shows daily 20:30, 21:30, 22:30, and 19:30 in high season, Plaça Reial 17, Barri Gotic, +34 933 191 789, masimas.com/tarantos, Metro: Liceu

Cathedral of Barcelona

Not to be confused with the much more modern (and impressive) Sagrada Familia, the Cathedral of Barcelona is located right against what would have been the main entry gate into the old Roman town. Construction began in the 13th century and was completed in 1448 with the addition of a rather austere entryway. A much more boisterous façade and a set of stunning neo-Gothic towers were added in the latter half of the 19th century to make the picture complete. Take a lap around the exterior and check out the funky stone grasshopper and unicorn—these gargoyles ensure that water draining off the roof doesn't run down the walls.

The cathedral is dedicated to Barcelona's original patron saint, St. Eulalia, who met a famously gruesome end. The occupying Romans demanded that she recant her Christian faith. When she refused, the centurions rolled her downhill in a barrel stuffed with sharp objects and knives. As if this wasn't enough, they followed this with crucifixion and, finally, beheading. Much-suffering St. Eulalia is buried in the crypt underneath the cathedral.

Inside you'll find richly decorated chapels, the crypt of St. Eulalia, and a cloister with 13 white geese—one for each year of St. Eulalia's life at the moment she was martyred. Entry is usually free, but visits to the cloister and roof cost a few euros.

Free entry Mon–Fri 08:00-12:45 and 17:45-19:30, free entry Sat 08:00-12:45 and 17:45-20:00, free entry Sun and holidays 08:00-13:45 and 17:45-20:00; during free times museum is €3, terrace is €3, and choir is €3; entry with €7 donation Mon–Fri 13:00-17:00, Sat 13:00-17:30, and Sun 14:00-17:00, Pla de la Seu, Barri Gotic, +34 933 428 262, catedralbcn.org, Metro: Jaume I

Sardana Dances

Every Sunday (except in August), a traditional Catalan dance takes over the square in front of the Barcelona Cathedral. Participants put their belongings in the middle and hold hands while dancing in circles, leaping jauntily in time to music provided by a large band of traditional musicians. The arms raised up to the sky are a gesture of defiance, one that held special meaning when Franco forbade displays like these. If you show enthusiasm for the music and the dance, you may be asked to join one of the circles, but don't impose. The dancers tolerate tourists; don't push your luck, though.

Free, Sun 12:00, sometimes Sat at 18:00, no dances in Aug, in front of the Cathedral of Barcelona, Pla de la Seu, Barri Gotic, Metro: Jaume I

Chocolate Museum (Museu de la Xocolata)

A favorite of those with a sweet tooth, this small museum walks visitors through the history and process of chocolate making in Europe. Spanish conquistadors brought chocolate back with them when they returned from the New World. At first it was a little too bitter to catch on, but then some genius added sugar and the delicious treat quickly took Europe by storm. There are also extensive displays of artwork made of chocolate. Your €7 entry ticket is actually a chocolate bar—not bad! For a deeper and richer experience, book a wine and chocolate tasting online.

€7, Mon–Sat 10:00-19:00, summer till 20:00, Sun 10:00-15:00, Carrer del Comerc 36, El Born, +34 932 68 78 78, museuxocolata.cat, Metro: Arc de Triomf or Jaume I

EXTRA CREDIT
Palau Güell

Palau Güell, one of Antoni Gaudí's early projects, is worth going inside if you're a huge Modernisme buff. You can tell this is the work of a budding master, one who is still finding his way and maturing. For most, it's sufficient to peer in through the

entryway to get a glimpse into another Gaudí interior. This palace was designed for the same patron family as Parc Güell, built uphill and farther outside of town.

€12 adult, €8 students, Tues-Sun 10:15-17:30, Carrer Nou de la Rambla 3-5, Barri Gotic, +34 934 72 57 75, palauguell.cat, Metro: Liceu

Camp Nou Stadium

If soccer were a religion, the Camp Nou stadium would be one of the world's greatest cathedrals. Barcelona rooted for the home team, FC Barcelona, throughout Francisco Franco's oppressive dictatorship. When he banned everything Catalan, supporting the team became one of the only legal ways that one could openly wear Catalan colors and express Catalan pride. Fandom pervades every nook and cranny of the city, and Barcelona essentially shuts down every time its boys take the field (this includes away games, but it goes double for home games). You can take a self-led audio tour of the stadium and museum to see the vast amount of memorabilia and trophies amassed over the years by this dynasty.

€23, mid-Apr-early Oct Mon-Sat 10:00-20:00 (off-season until 18:30), Sun 10:00-14:30, shorter hours on and before game days, Carrer d'Aristides Maillol 12, Greater Barcelona, +34 902 18 99 00, fcbarcelona.com, Metro: L3 Palau Reial or Les Corts, L5 Collblanc or Badal

TOP EATS

I love the tradition of tapas and *pintxos* in Barcelona. When you order tapas, your food arrives hot on sharable platters; for *pintxos*, you pick and choose from a bar with preportioned bites of open-faced sandwiches.

You'll catch some of Barcelona's most authentic tapas on **Carrer de la Mercè** in the Barri Gotic. Do a tapas crawl down this street and end the night at the Plaça Reial for the incredible flamenco show at Tarantos, with drinks after on the square. For the best selection of *pintxos*, head over to **Carrer de Blai** in Poble-Sec. Here you'll find a series of cheap and tasty *pintxo* bars where bites start from as little as €1. It's an off-the-beaten path experience of Barcelona, making it popular with locals and the occasional in-the-know traveler. Snacks here are noticeably cheaper than the options in the Barri Gotic.

Tipping is not expected, but rounding up to the next euro mark is appreciated. Be sure to check whether or not your bill says *"servei inclòs,"* as many touristy restaurants sneak this 10-15 percent charge in there. If it's there, you won't be expected to tip anything.

Tasca el Corral

Pop in here for friendly service and some tasty dishes to kick off your crawl: fresh *manchego*, *chorizo al cidre* (or try *chorizo al diablo* for a plate of flaming-hot sausage), *pan amb tomaquet*, and a one-liter *jarro* of sangria.

Plates from €3.50, Sun-Thurs 13:00-02:00, Fri-Sat 13:00-03:00, Carrer de la Mercè 17, Barri Gotic, +34 93 315 20 59, Facebook: Tasca el Corral, Metro: Jaume I or Barceloneta

La Plata

If you like anchovies (and who doesn't?), this is your place to toss them back like popcorn. Balance out the savory snacks with a small plate of tomatoes. Get some *vino tinto* (red wine) or sweet red vermouth (a favorite with locals) to wash it all back, and enjoy the casual, standing social scene. The no-frills decor caters to locals who expect simplicity.

Plates from €3, Mon-Sat 10:00-15:30 and 18:30-23:00, Carrer de la Mercè 28, Barri Gotic, +34 933 15 10 09, barlaplata.com, Metro: Jaume I or Barceloneta

Bar Celta Pulperia

Celta is the anchor of any tapas crawl down Carrer de la Mercè. Stop in for a feast of fresh *polpo* (octopus), *patatas bravas* (fried potatoes with a spicy ketchup sauce), and even *gambas* (meaty jumbo prawns). This place and its waitstaff are always busy, so pop in, scope the dishes, and make note of what looks good to you. When you finally make eye contact with a member of the crew, they'll appreciate it that you have your order ready.

Plates from €5, daily 08:30-24:00, Carrer de Simó Oller 3, Barri Gotic, +34 933 15 00 06, barcelta.com, Metro: Jaume I or Barceloneta

TAPAS & *PINTXOS*

Major treats for any visitor coming to Barcelona are the tapas—snack-sized, finger-food dishes—and *pintxos,* open-faced mini sandwiches topped with a wide range of ingredients, from sausage and seafood to veggies to cheeses. The key to getting the most out of tapas and *pintxos* is sampling a couple of plates at one location and then moving on to the next—this is how the locals do it. Here are some can't-miss flavors that every first-time visitor to Barcelona must try at least once. Consider this your Catalan culinary hit list:

Pimientos de padrón: A plate of steaming, salted fried green peppers that's made to order.

Polpo: Freshly steamed and spiced octopus, usually presented on a wooden platter. If it's on the menu, look down the bar and find the heaping plate of tentacles that the chefs are slicing and dicing. Price alert: This is not a budget-friendly snack (oftentimes a serving costs around €18).

Tortilla de patatas: Spain's delicious potato and egg omelet. Additional ingredients are often tossed in, along with salt and pepper, but it's just as good plain for breakfast, lunch, or a quick bite on the run. Get it in a *bocadillo* (sandwich) for the best way to get full for around €3.

Patatas bravas: Hot, freshly fried potato wedges doused in a slightly spicy ketchup-mayonnaise sauce. If you're trying to add some starch to round out the meal, this one's a no-brainer.

Pa amb tomàquet: Toasted bread rubbed down with fresh garlic and tomato. This is my personal favorite side order, and with prices around €2, I never have to dig far into my pockets.

Escalivada: A stewed mix of grilled onions, eggplant, and peppers. You'll find this everywhere in the Catalan region and throughout Spain.

Anchoa: Fresh anchovies with nothing but a slice of lemon on the side. Get over your inhibitions and order a plate to share between friends—pop 'em like popcorn at the movies. Salty and crunchy, they're best washed down with a glass of *tinto* (red wine)—what more could you want?

Jamón ibérico: Spain has delicious cured ham, and this is your chance to try some of the best in the world. Hams come in different grades and prices based on the pigs they come from, how these swine were processed, their place of origin, and what their diet was. Plates run about €16 for the good stuff.

Queso manchego: Spain's dry, salty cheese goes well with the other options above. Order 100 grams at the supermarket along with some *jamón* and a baguette for a perfect afternoon meal. Don't be afraid to sample (say *"probar"*) a few different selections before purchasing.

Salmorejo: Creamy tomato soup topped with diced *jamón* and generally consumed for breakfast. (I'll take it any time of day, though.)

Gazpacho: A savory side dish to your lunch or dinner. Fresh tomatoes are tossed with garlic, salt, spices, and a little bit of vinegar for the perfect zing. You really can't go wrong. Gazpacho is served cold and is especially popular during the hot summer months.

Sagardi BCN Gotic

Not on Carrer de la Mercè, but nearby, this is an upscale *pintxos* bar welcoming tourists and locals alike for stand-up meals or sit-down finger-lickin'-good tapas. Get your empty plate and move down the line, picking whatever looks good on the bar. Go slow! Dishes are constantly refreshed, and when that tempting hot dish makes the rounds through the room, you'll be glad you didn't load your plate too high. Settle up your bill by turning in your toothpicks at the end of your meal. Their summer wine, *tinto de verano,* is delicious. Get a similar experience at any of Grupo Sagardi's other operations, including **Basca Irati** (Carrer del Cardenal Casanas 17) and **Euskal Etxea** (Placeta de Montcada 1).

€2.10 per *pintxo*, daily 13:00-24:00, Carrer de l'Argenteria 62, El Born, +34 933 199 993, sagardi.com, Metro: Jaume I

Can Paixano

Come out to this small, classic bar, also known as Xampaneria, for delicious Barcelona-style beef, chicken and pork burgers, and other simple tapas. One block from the Barceloneta metro stop, this eat-on-your-feet fast-food joint offers bottles of *cava* (Spanish champagne) for next to nothing. As soon as you have a good idea what you want, sharpen your elbows and make your way to the front—this place gets packed to the gills with hangry customers ready to chow down, so prepare for a bit of jostling. If you're a pacifist, pop in when the bar is slower late in the afternoon.

€4-12, Mon-Sat 09:30-22:30, Carrer de la Reina Cristina 7, Barceloneta, canpaixano.com, Metro: Barceloneta

Café Federal

Café Federal is my favorite spot in town to catch up on email. So many of Barcelona's freelancers use the café to work that they've had to ban laptops on weekends. You can stop in, enjoy a ham, egg, and cheese breakfast sandwich, breakfast skillet, or pancakes, and catch up on your work or correspondence. The service is curt. There's a second location in the city center at Passatge de la Pau 11.

Delicious breakfasts from €6.50, no laptops allowed on weekends, Mon-Thurs 08:00-24:00, Fri 08:00-01:00, Sat 09:00-01:00, Sun 09:00-18:00, Carrer del Parlament 39, +34 931 87 36 07

Ciudad Condao

Come for the classic and elegant dark-wood setting; stay for the tapas and *pintxos*. Posh locals and in-the-know visitors gather here nightly to share wine, conversation, and good times. They specialize in seafood, so be sure to try their prawns, fresh fish, or even lobster paella.

Options from €7, daily 08:00-01:30, Rambla de Catalunya 18, Eixample, +34 933 18 19 97, Facebook: Ciudad Condao, Metro: Passeig de Gràcia

Cera 23

If you've got a date to impress or if you're in the mood for some of the best food and atmosphere in Barcelona, come to this candlelit, subterranean hole-in-the-wall in El Raval. The tapas are spectacular, the service friendly, and the wine list extensive (they'll help you find a good local wine and pair it with your meal). This is a great place for quiet, intimate conversations.

Entrées €13-17, Thurs-Mon 13:30-16:00 and 19:00-23:30, Tues-Wed 19:00-23:30, Carrer de la Cera 23, El Raval, +34 934 240 808, cera23.com, Metro: Sant Antoni

A Tu Bola

For a cheap and fresh alternative to the typical heavy fried cuisine, check out the creative chicken, beef, pork, and falafel balls on order at A Tu Bola. Everything but the bread is processed in-house, resulting in healthy and energizing plates and wraps—a quick and easy lunch on your way to Montjuïc or if you're staying in El Raval or Poble-Sec.

Pita sandwiches and salads from €6, Wed-Mon 13:00-23:30, later on weekends, Carrer de l'Hospital 78, El Raval, atubolarest.com, +34 933 15 32 44

Quimet & Quimet

The steady stream of tourists hasn't yet driven the locals out of Quimet, so it still retains a distinctive neighborhood feel despite being discovered. Expect to share counter space (and personal space) with the diverse and international crowd. Their authentic, caviar-topped *pintxos* might be some of the best you'll try (they merited a mention on Anthony Bourdain's *No Reservations*). Indulge in the vermouth, and if you're a seafood lover, don't miss the scallops and prawns.

Pintxos from €3.50, Mon-Fri 12:00-16:00 and 19:00-23:00, Carrer del Poeta Cabanyes 25, Poble-Sec, +34 934 42 31 42, Facebook: Quimet y Quimet

La Esquinita de Blai

Fresh and hot *pintxos*, friendly service, affordable prices (pay by the toothpick), and bottles of *cava* bring me back to this spot time and again. Open throughout the day for breakfast, lunch, and late dinner, there's never a bad time to drop in for a sip or a bite.

Pintxos from €1.50, daily 09:00-01:00, Carrer de Blai 16, Poble-Sec, esquinitadeblai.com, +34 931 88 92 03

Blai 9

Decidedly the poshest *pintxo* option on Carrer de Blai, Blai 9 treats the senses. Flash-fried parmesan melted onto your *pintxo* toothpicks, quail eggs topping chorizo and caramelized onions, and tempting shot glasses full of delectable veggie-stuffed flautas with guacamole make this a foodie paradise. With beautiful presentation, they're doing everything they can to bring Spain's popular bar food into the world of haute cuisine.

Pintxos from €2, daily 09:00-24:00, later on weekends, Carrer de Blai 9, Poble-Sec, +34 933 29 73 65, blai9.com

Bó de B

Students with tight budgets flock to Bó de B for sandwiches overflowing with meats and cheeses (from only €3!). Grab one to go on your way to the beach—you'll find it right at the end of Carrer de la Fusteria, near the bottom of Via Laietana. Lines can be long (25 minutes around lunchtime), but the service is quick. Don't bother trying to find a place to eat inside—just take your sandwich to go and enjoy it on the beach nearby.

Sandwiches from €3, Mon-Fri 11:00-24:00, Sat-Sun 13:00-16:00, Carrer de la Fusteria 14, Barri Gotic, +34 936 674 945, Facebook: Bo de B Barcelona Official, Metro: Jaume I

Pans and Company

For another grab-and-go option, this Spanish-owned and -operated chain is a dependable choice for a quick and tasty lunch (there are a number of branches around the city). Pair your sandwich with a *café con leche* for a midafternoon caffeine bump.

Sandwiches from €4, generally daily 07:00-24:00, Plaça Sant Jaume 6, Barri Gotic, +34 933 15 16 06, pansandcompany.com, Metro: Jaume I

Churrerías

Granja M. Viader (€3, Mon-Sat 09:00-13:15, 17:00-21:15, Carrer d'en Xuclà, Barri Gotic, +34 933 183 486, granjaviader.cat, Metro: Liceu, Catalunya) is a classic sit-down option where you can participate in one of Spain's tastier traditions: churros. Find Granja M. Viader a block off La Rambla, near the Boqueria.

There's nothing fancy about **Churreria Manuel San Román** (€2.50, Mon-Fri 07:00-01:30, Sat-Sun 07:00-14:00 and 16:00-20:30, Carrer dels Banys Nous 8, Barri Gotic, +34 933 187 691, Metro: Liceu), one of my favorite spots in town for churros. There's no website and no frills—just delicious churros and chocolate. The chocolate is so rich that, depending how deep your love for chocolate runs, you'll either wish you could drown in it, or you'll need to split it with friends.

TOP NIGHTLIFE

Barcelona's nightlife rages until late every night of the week (on weekends, it's easy to party until the sun comes up). The most important thing is to adjust to the locals' nightlife schedule. The midafternoon siesta pushes dinner into late territory, usually 21:00-23:00 or so. Drinks start after dinner, typically with a few casual cocktails at a bar; after that, it's off to a nightclub. The bars start to get interesting around 01:00, and the clubs don't really warm up until 03:00, finally cooling off in the early-morning twilight. The locals' poisons of choice are usually fast and cheap (think two ingredients: rum and Coke, gin and tonic, vodka and lemon, etc.).

NIGHTLIFE DISTRICTS

Barri Gotic

This district has bars and cafés throughout, with many lining Plaça Reial. Expect crowds dominated by tourists and prices catered more to tourist budgets than local ones.

Barri Gotic, Metro: Liceu

El Born

El Born offers a series of classier, young professional-type trendy lounges and bars.

El Born, Metro: Jaume I

Eixample

This area has tons of choices for bars, lounges, and cafés, but because it's so big, it's best to have a definite plan before setting out.

Eixample

El Raval

Barcelona's alternative and counterculture zone has some of the city's best hipster cocktail and dive bars.

Eixample, Metro: Universitat

Puerto Olimpico

This area is home to beachfront clubs with dancers, fire shows, and electronic music. There's not much in the way of pregame bars here, so only head toward the beach when you're ready to throw yourself into the deep end of Barcelona's clubbing scene.

Puerto Olimpico, Metro: Ciutadella/Vila Olímpica

BARS

Dow Jones

Famous for its constantly inflating and "crashing" drink prices, this otherwise nondescript bar—a favorite among the American study-abroad crowd—makes drinking a game of speculation. Every time you order a drink, the price of that drink rises (they don't run low on supply, so it's demand that drives prices up or down here). As the night goes on, there are sporadic "crashes," sending drink prices tumbling and sparking a buying spree at the bar. All of the information is projected on screens, so you can keep your finger on the pulse of the booze market. This is a great place for people who don't care what they drink so long as it's cheap.

Mon-Thurs 19:30-02:30, Fri 19:30-03:00, Sat-Sun 12:00-03:00, Carrer del Bruc 97, +34 934 76 38 31, bardowjones.com, Metro: Girona

Coco Vail Beer Hall

For those in need of a brew, this is a great option just off the Block of Discord. Featuring exposed-brick decor, NFL, NBA, and NCAA games on large screens, and two dozen local and regional artisanal beers on tap, Coco Vail is a nice venue for backpack-

ers feeling a bit homesick. Conversations here are predominantly in English. They host 50-cent wing nights on Mondays and taco Tuesdays.

Beers from €4.50, daily 17:00-00:30, later on weekends, Carrer d'Aragó 284, cocovailbeerhall.com, +34 937 82 24 79

Chupitos

Chupitos is a fave among students abroad in Barcy due to its selection of shots (550+ varieties to choose from). Adventurous? Try the Boy Scout (perfect for pyromaniacs), the Monica Lewinsky (most often requested by groups of girls—you'll see why), or the Viking (you'll end up dizzy, but not from the alcohol). Chupitos is a relatively small place, and it's either dead or flush with shot-takers making a short stop before the clubs. Choose from any number of the locations around town; they're virtually identical.

Shots from €2.50, daily 22:30-02:30, Carrer d'Aribau 77, Eixample, +34 697 81 44 61, espitchupitos.com, Metro: Universitat

Pippermint

International students pregame here, where the bartenders pour massive cocktails into 1-liter, 5-liter, and even 10-liter cups—or should I say goblets? It's a cheap way to start the night—liberal pours mean you'll be well on your way to buzztown when you leave (hell, after a couple of drinks, you might just be the mayor). If it's an authentic Catalan experience you're after, keep looking.

Liters of cocktails from €12, Mon 08:15-01:30, Tues-Thurs 08:15-02:30, Fri 08:15-03:30, Sat 10:15-03:30, Sun 16:30-01:30, Carrer de Bori I Fontesta 20, Eixample, +34 932 010 008, pippermintbcn.com, Metro: Maria Cristina

Marsella

Two hundred absinthe-sodden years since it opened, this dusty bar is still at the top of the game. You can chase the green fairy here the proper way, complete with fancy spoon and sugar cube. If it's your first time trying absinthe—or if the night you tried it last is something of a blur—don't hesitate to ask for help. The service is friendly and they understand that their product is an exotic one for many visitors. Order your drinks at the bar, then take your supplies to

LGBT BARCELONA

Spain rates first in the Pew Research Center's most recent survey of acceptance of homosexuality, at 88 percent. The LGBT community is welcome in Barcelona, and you'll find numerous options for gay-friendly cafés, bars, restaurants, and clubs both in the Old Town and in the Eixample. Gay pride festivities in Barcelona take place around the first or second weekend of July each year. Book ahead for lodging—budget accommodations quickly disappear. Check out **Osbar** (Carrer de la Diputacio 225, Eixample, +34 934 53 46 42) for the bear scene. (*Os* means bear in Catalan.)

any of the cafeteria-style low-slung tables to get the party started just like Dalí did back in the day.

Daily 22:00–02:30, Carrer de Sant Pau 65, Barri Gotic, +34 934 42 72 63, Metro: Liceu

Le Cyrano

For quantity over quality, check out Le Cyrano, a self-service bar where you pay by the glass. How strong you choose to mix your drinks is entirely up to you. A precursor for nights that tip well into sloppy territory, the gimmick pulls in heavyweights and lightweights alike—all of them drinking up before heading off to the pricier clubs.

€5 per glass, Thurs–Sat 10:30–02:30, Aribau 154, +34 656 840 286, Facebook.com/lecyrano

CLUBS

If you've come to Barcelona in search of glitzy clubbing, the city has you covered like sea salt on *pimientos de padrón*. Covers generally run about €15, with your first drink included. Each drink after that will set you back €10+. Unless you've got euros burning a hole in your pocket, it's worthwhile to get your party started before heading to the club. Follow the four main promoters in town (Aashi Guest List, Michael Jordan, Kyke Navarro, and Kike Barcelona/De Lis Group) on Facebook—they throw parties at all the major clubs throughout the week. Drop their name at the door and you'll skip the line and enter for free. Otherwise, call ahead to the clubs or join events to get yourself on the list, saving you the time and hassle getting past the velvet rope.

The heart of Barcelona's clubbing scene is **Puerto Olimpico.** No matter which of the clubs you're going to, dress nicely (guys, this means long pants, dark clothes,

and nice shoes) to get past the picky bouncers. Close the clubs down, then stumble out onto the beach to watch the sun rise over the Mediterranean.

Opium Barcelona

Known as the strip's swankiest spot, this is a favorite among Barcelona's glitterati and celebrities (including members of FC Barcelona and their WAGs). It's a posh scene, so expect all the wonderful things that deep-pocketed clientele bring with them: pricey cover, expensive drinks, and picky bouncers. Of course, you also get an incredible clubbing atmosphere, world-class DJs, and some of the most beautiful people you'll see anywhere. Get your name on the guest list online ahead of time. This spot is best on Thursdays.

€20 cover including drink, drinks about €12, daily 24:00–06:00, Passeig Marítimo de la Barceloneta 34, Puerto Olimpico, opiumbarcelona.com, Metro: Ciutadella/Vila Olímpica

Shoko

This is a classy space filled with well-heeled locals and travelers, but without the exclusivity and pretentiousness you'll find at Opium. For my money, it's the most consistently good club on the strip. The music is well-balanced (mostly hip-hop, R&B, and commercial hits), and they pull off the Asian fusion concept without forcing it—this includes not only the décor and the flushed low lighting, but the food as well. Every time I've been here, I've danced the night away in the faux-bamboo forest. It's best on Tuesdays.

Drinks around €10, daily 12:00–06:00, Passeig Marítimo de la Barceloneta 36, Puerto Olimpico, +34 932 25 92 00, shoko.biz, Metro: Ciutadella/Vila Olímpica

WISHING YOU A CRAPPY CHRISTMAS!

Caga Tió, or "Crap Log," is a character in the unique Catalan Christmas tradition. Caga Tió is a small log with a smiley face painted on one end, with twigs for arms to support it. Oftentimes the *tió* sports a fun Santa hat. Beginning in early December, children give the *tió* little bites to eat (Americans do something similar when they leave cookies for Santa). They feed him every night over the span of a couple weeks and cover him with a blanket so that he will not be cold. On Christmas Eve, kids put the *tió* partly into the fireplace and order him to, well, dump out all the presents. To encourage him to take this generous defecation, the kids beat him with sticks while singing selections of typical Catalan Christmas songs. This fun little tradition originally symbolized the fertilization of the fields for an abundant crop in the upcoming year, but perhaps something has been lost in translation....

You'll see small *tió* figurines in souvenir shops across town, who appear to be caught in the middle of the act. They always make for a funny—if somewhat odd—gift for loved ones back home.

Razzmatazz

You're practically guaranteed a great time in this labyrinth of five rocking dance floors. It leans a little too far into the EDM spectrum for some, but in this massive complex (one of Europe's largest), there's always at least one room playing something funky and familiar. Check out the program online for upcoming events and DJs. If you're rolling deep, pick a rendezvous point for the end of the night. With this many rooms and free-flowing drinks, you're bound to get separated from your friends.

€10-12 cover including drink, drinks about €7, daily 23:00-05:00, Carrer Almogàvers 122, Greater Barcelona, +34 933 20 82 00, salarazzmatazz.com, Metro: Marina

Sala Apolo

Most famous for its Nasty Monday parties, when seemingly every punk and rocker in Barcelona comes out to rage, Sala Apolo is your alternative to the thumping techno and EDM that dominates so much of the club scene in Barcelona. Wear black to blend in with the young crowd, and if you've got tattoos, show them off. Come pregamed, as the drinks aren't cheap. There's live music throughout the week, and drum-and-bass DJs pack the house frequently. Check the website to find out who is playing when you're in town.

€8 cover and drinks, Mon 20:00-05:00, Thurs 20:00-05:00, Fri-Sat 19:00-06:00, Sun 21:00-05:00, Carrer Nou de la Rambla 113, Greater Barcelona, +34 934 41 40 01, sala-apolo.com, Metro: Parallel

Sidecar Factory Club

Sidecar is another very good alternative to the bass-and-bouncer scene. The music at this subterranean alternative rock bar varies wildly depending on who is playing or spinning. It might be rock or soul, or it might be funk or garage; check the website for listings. Thanks to its location right on Plaça Reial, the crowd can be a touch touristy (and so can the prices), but it's a scene in which everybody comes to let their hair down. Cocktails are colorful, and so are some of the regular characters.

€8-12 cover with drink, Mon-Sat 19:00-05:00, Plaça Reial 7, Barri Gòtic, +34 933 02 15 86, sidecarfactoryclub.com, Metro: Liceu

Jamboree Dance Club

When the flamenco show at Tarantos ends, the tables and chairs are quickly cleared away, making room for jazz musicians who jam under the medieval arches until midnight. When they wrap up, hip-hop and R&B quickly takes over. This means that, if you come for the flamenco show, you'll be able to enjoy three kinds of club all in the same night. It's a refreshing break for those who find electronic music tedious. Check out their show schedule online.

Jazz €5-35 depending on acts, hip-hop club cover from €10, drinks €8, Plaça Reial 17, Barri Gòtic, +34 933 04 12 10, masimas.com/en/jamboree

TOP SHOPPING & MARKETS

SHOPPING DISTRICTS
Avinguda del Porta de l'Angel
Plaça de Catalunya is the city's mainstream shopping drag. It starts with El Corte Inglés, Spain's largest department store retailer, and continues down the hill and past brands like Massimo Dutti, Zara, and H&M. Head uphill in the opposite direction to Passeig de Gràcia, which has upscale shopping like Hermès, Dolce & Gabbana, and Zegna.

Open daily, standard opening hours with afternoon closures generally 14:00-16:00, Barri Gotic, Metro: Passeig de Gràcia, Plaça Catalunya

MARKETS
La Boqueria
This characteristic public market, the best of its kind in Barcelona, is a must-see. You'll find everything from entire pig's heads to fresh smoothies, from half kilos of saffron to creative sushi. With so much variety, step out of your comfort zone; challenge yourself to try one thing you've never tried or never even dreamed of trying. Check price lists closely at any of the sit-down stalls—it's easy to run up a tab of €45 per person for a simple, quick lunch. The iced fruit drinks you'll find everywhere are a tasty, touristy treat. Public restrooms are in the back and downstairs.

Mon-Sat 08:00-20:30, La Rambla 91, Barri Gotic, boqueria.info, Metro: Liceu

TOP PARKS & RECREATION

Montjuïc and the boardwalk in front of Barcelona's beautiful beaches are my two favorite places to get a run in. Along the beach you'll find pull-up bars and workout stations about every half mile.

PARKS
Parc de la Ciutadella
Pack a picnic basket and head to Parc de la Ciutadella in the northeast part of Old Town, Barcelona's most easily accessible tract of green space. It's a picturesque example of a classic manicured European park, complete with artificial lakes and shimmering fountains. Some of the buildings you see today, like the Catalan Parliament building, are recycled from a 19th-century fort. You can also check out the **Barcelona Zoo** (€20, daily 10:00-18:00, zoobarcelona.cat, +34 902 45 75 45) while you're here.

Free, always open, Barri Gotic

Parc Güell
Gaudí's Parc Güell is a beautiful failure. It was one of the world's first gated, planned communities, built at the turn of the 20th century, but it never flourished in the way its designers hoped it would. Homes were supposed to populate the immaculately landscaped space, meshing perfectly with the surrounding environment. We can only wonder what this neighborhood could have been had the architect's vision been fully realized—but today we are all the poorer for its failure. Gaudí's fingerprints are absolutely everywhere in this whimsical park, from the benches to the walkways. You can visit much of the property, but the park's real drawing cards (the famous snaky bench, the columned would-be produce market, the photogenic *plaça*, and the breaking-surf passageway) are attractions with paid admission (reservations required). Bus #24 is your best bet for getting to and from this park built into the hill above Gracia.

Free entry for general park, required reservations €7 online for gated Parc Güell, daily 08:00-20:30, free and without reservations necessary daily 06:00-08:00, Carrer d'Olot, Greater Barcelona, +34 902 20 03 02, parkguell.cat, Metro: Lesseps

Bunkers del Carmel
The best sunset views in the city can be had from these Spanish Civil War bunkers. As day turns to night, Barcelona's broad thoroughfares (many of them a vivid green during the day) become columns of light, the tips of which touch the

sea. For those who make the journey, this unobstructed view of the city is often their most vivid memory of Barcelona. Many recommended hostels run a day trip up here as well. Bring a bottle of *cava* to enjoy at the top. To get here, take L3 up to Vallcara to transfer onto bus V17 and hop off at Gran Vista; the trip takes about 45 minutes from Plaça Catalunya.

Free, always open, Greater Barcelona, museuhistoria.bcn.cat

HIKING
Montjuïc

Montjuïc is the rocky outcropping south of town, to your right as you face the Mediterranean. It was home to a 19th-century fort and, later, the 1992 Olympics. Take the steep, hour-long hike up Montjuïc and soak in fantastic views of Barcelona and her coastline, or skip the hike and take the funicular and then the gondola straight to the top (starting from the integrated metro station, Parallel). Whether you walk or ride, bring a water bottle. Take your time exploring the star-fort castle (free, daily 10:00-20:00, €5 paid museums inside) while you're at it. For decades, this fortress stood as a symbol of Franco's regime and his oppression of Catalan culture. From this vantage point, Franco and members of his cabal had a bird's-eye view of the city. For those below, this felt as though Franco was always watching. Now, the hillside fort is a place where Catalan families come to picnic on weekend afternoons. It's easy to find the base of the hill from the marina or the back side of the Poble-Sec neighborhood. There's an impossible-to-miss path that'll take you up to the top.

Free, always open, Greater Barcelona,
Metro: Plaça Espanya

BEACHES
Platja Barceloneta

Due to its proximity to the tourist center, this is Barcelona's most popular stretch of sand for tourists, warm beer, and 10-minute massage hawkers. Everybody comes here to soak in the sun—the perfectly toned and bronzed, the leathery veterans of the Spanish sun, and, of course, the pasty tourists slathered in SPF 45. The people-watching is the best in Barcelona and easily fills an afternoon, but what makes it such a great place to watch also makes it crowded—sometimes even claustrophobically so. If you're looking for tranquil beaches where you can hear nothing but the crashing of the waves, you're in the wrong place.

Free, always open, Barceloneta, Metro: Ciutadella or Barceloneta

Platja Nova Mar Bella

This beach, a magnet for Barcelona's students and young locals, is quite a distance north from the center, making it dramatically less touristy then Platja Barceloneta. It is still, however, easily accessible on the metro, and I highly recommend the journey. It's the perfect combination of tourist-friendly amenities and authentic local experience—and the smaller crowds make it far less likely that you'll have sand kicked in your face or into your picnic basket.

Free, always open, Greater Barcelona, Metro: Selva del Mar or Poblenou

TOP TOURS

Fat Tire Bike Tours

Fat Tire's expert guides bring Europe's major cities to life with their two-wheeled tours. The Barcelona City Tour features a lineup of all the top sights, including the Cathedral of Barcelona and the Sagrada Familia. Cap your four-hour cruise around town with sangria on the beach before riding back to the shop.

€26, students €24, Jan-mid-Apr daily 11:00, mid-Apr-mid-Oct daily 11:00 and 16:00, mid-Oct-Dec daily 11:00, meets at Plaça Sant Jaume 15 minutes before tour—just look for the Fat Tire sign, office: Carrer Marlet 4, Barri Gotic, +34 933 429 275, fattirebiketours.com/Barcelona, Metro: Jaume I

Discover Walks
Modernisme Walk

Run by young, passionate local guides, Discover Walks is a fresh European re-

sponse to the craze for walking tours that is spreading across the Continent. Their tours never disappoint, and they give you a taste of each city's unique flavor. Their Modernisme Walk starts with Casa Batllo on the Block of Discord and finishes with Gaudí's unfinished masterpiece, the Sagrada Familia. They also have free, tip-based tours throughout the week, including a La Rambla and Barri Gotic Walk. Just watch for the guides' trademark bright pink vests, or check their website for details.

€19, daily 10:30, meets at Casa Batllo, Eixample, +34 649 60 99 41, discoverwalks.com/barcelona-walking-tours, Metro: Passeig de Gràcia

Travel Bar's Walking Tours & Sangria Classes

Travel Bar (daily 10:00-23:00, Carrer Boqueria 27, travelbar.com) has it all: coffee in the morning, €1 simple dinners from 19:30 to 21:00 (chili, curry, etc.), a bar at night, cooking classes throughout the week, and daily walking tours venturing out into the city. TB's introductory walk to Barcelona's Old Town (free, daily 11:00, 13:00, and 15:00, meets at Travel Bar Boqueria) is an excellent way for visitors to get acquainted with these streets. The walk traces the Roman foundations of the city, discussing the numerous high and low points of Barcelona history along the way, and then wraps up with a lunch just steps from the marina. The tour lasts about 2.5 hours.

Their **Paella and Sangria class** is a double winner too: Let a professional *paellador* walk you through the art of preparing the typical seafood-and-rice platter with perfectly spiced prawns, mussels, and calamari. You'll meet at the Travel Bar Boqueria and head to La Boqueria market for a guided walk through the dozens of stalls where you pick up fresh ingredients. From there, you'll head to the professional kitchens in Born, where you'll dive into your bags of seafood and spices. The class, which lasts about three hours, is capped off with a massive dinner and unlimited drinks. You can arrange to stay at the bar for a discounted after-party. It's hard to find better bang for your buck in the city (€32, meets daily 17:45 at Travel Bar Boqueria, day options at 14:00 during high season, Barri Gotic, reserve at travelbar.com, Metro: Liceu).

Bar daily 10:00-02:00, Travel Bar Boqueria, Carrer Boqueria 27, Barri Gotic, travelbar.com, Metro: Liceu

TOP HOSTELS

Hostels have done so well in this socially oriented city that many of the good ones have developed into competitive chains with locations all over town. The best ones manage to invoke the energy of their different locations through nightly pub crawls and meet-ups. If you're traveling alone or in a small group, these highly social evenings will plug you into the surprisingly broad network of hip travelers—deep friendships are formed in an instant. My favorite chains are **Hostel One** (hostelone.net), specializing in intimate, family-style, 40-bed hostels with free nightly dinners and day tours, and **Sant Jordi** (santjordihostels.com), with a fun, party-hostel atmosphere and great locations throughout town. Their baby dragon logo is a nod to the patron saint of Barcelona, St. George. Another great chain, **Urbany Hostels** (urbanyhostels.com), focuses on the mod backpacker who wants all the amenities at a great price. These are all included in my favorites listed here.

Kabul Backpackers Hostel

Kabul is a party hostel through and through, and its great location (smack-dab on the Plaça Reial at the bottom of La Rambla) makes it a great jumping-off point for club-hopping at night and visits to Barcelona's top sights and beaches during the day. Their free breakfast not only gives you a reason to get out of bed at a reasonable hour, it also allows you to start your day with a full stomach—meaning you don't need to start looking for a café or restaurant until after you've seen a few sights. Start your night right at their rooftop bar (open in high season).

Beds from €18, pub crawl options €5-12, 24-hour reception, laundry facilities, breakfast included, common room, Plaça Reial 17, Barri Gotic, +34 933 18 51 90, kabul.es, info@kabul.es, Metro: Liceu

Hostel One Paralelo

Located just around the corner from the best *pintxo* drag in town, Hostel One Paralelo offers full-privacy sleeping cabins, hiking options nearby, and a quiet terrace out back. Join one of the pub crawls and you'll be collapsing back into your bed early the next morning.

Beds aggressively priced from €20, breakfast €2.50, free dinners, different bar/club crawl each night, Wi-Fi, towels €2, padlocks €3, drinks €1, Carrer de Salvà 62, Poble-Sec, +34 934 439 885, hostelone.net, Metro: Poble-Sec

Hostel One Ramblas

This location with a family-friendly vibe welcomes guests by name on arrival day. Drop your bags and relax into their deep couches—and maybe try to strum out a few flamenco chords on their guitar.

Beds from €15 low season, from €25 high season, terrace for socializing, dinner, daily and nightly activities, Carrer d'Albareda 6-8, Poble-Sec, +34 934 431 310, hostelone. net, Metro: Drassanes

Sant Jordi Rock Palace

This immense hostel (150-plus beds), one of Sant Jordi's best new entries, features an on-site bar, a social room, bright reception area with helpful staff, large dorms, and a comfortable chilled-out vibe. The rooftop terrace and pool take hosteling in Barcelona to the next level.

Ten-bed dorms from €22, free Wi-Fi, 24-hour reception, breakfast extra, towels for rent, Balmes 75, Eixample, +34 934 53 32 81, santjordihostels.com, rockpalace@ santjordi.org, Metro: Passeig de Gràcia

Sant Jordi Alberg

This is one of the locations you'll want to reserve in advance. They do all the little things right here. The staff are shining examples of the best people that Barcelona produces, the value is great, and the free nightly pub crawls rage all night. All of this combines to pack out the place year-round.

Beds from €13, 24-hour reception, free lockers, laundry facilities, common room, Internet access, Calle de Roger de Llúria 40, first floor, apartment 2, Eixample, +34 933 42 41 61, santjordihostels.com, lluria@santjordi.org, Metro: Passeig de Gràcia

Sant Jordi Gràcia

For those who are returning to Barcelona, or for those who are willing to trade proximity to tourist attractions for a more community-oriented experience, Sant Jordi's location in the Gràcia district might be just the ticket. It's a welcome refuge far from the tourist hordes and a vastly more authentically Catalan experience. New

THE HUMAN TOWERS OF CATALUNYA

So you think you're tough? Let's see how you stack up against the *casteller* teams that put their strength, balance, coordination, and teamwork on full display in main squares across this region. *Castellers* erect freestanding, self-supporting human castles up to seven or eight levels high—these human towers are made entirely of people standing on each other's shoulders. *Casteller* teams come together and, in one massive orchestrated effort, lay the foundation (burly, large men), pile on the next layer (young, lean strongmen), and continue stacking humans as high as they can go. Groups of three scramble up the growing tower like monkeys up a banana tree. These towers often collapse before they are completed, leaving a doggy pile in the center of the square (the youngest *castellers* wear helmets for this reason). The tower isn't complete until the littlest *casteller* climbs to the top of the tower and raises one hand in the air to "cap" the castle. It's a beautiful Catalan tradition that fosters community spirit and teamwork, with a healthy salting of friendly competition between communities.

As if this weren't enough of a show, there's also a soundtrack. A small band playing traditional Catalan instruments, led by a wilting reed instrument, belts out a tune as if to narrate the whole operation. The music rises to a climax as the littlest *casteller* nears the top and continues at a fever pitch until each member of the tower has successfully scrambled their way down the (by now sweaty and wobbling) tower. In 2010, UNESCO declared the *castellers* an Intangible Heritage of Humanity. For dates and details of the next public events, visit castellersdebarcelona.cat. You can also find incredible feats of human castle-building on YouTube.

and modern, this hostel has a fun social room with beanbags, comfortable modern bunks, and clean rooms. The staff puts on events, tours, and nights out nearly every night of the week.

Eight-bed mixed dorm from €24, free Wi-Fi, 24-hour reception, laundry facilities, €3 breakfast, free maps and walking tours, frequent organized pub crawl, kitchen, €2 towels, Carrer de Terol 35, Greater Barcelona, +34 93 342 41 61, santjordihostels.com, gracia@santjordi.org, Metro: Fontana or Gràcia

Sant Jordi Sagrada Familia Apartments

Sagrada Familia Apartments offers single, double, triple, and quad rooms in a private apartment setting. The rooms are modestly decorated, clean, and modernly appointed. The slick design and smooth concrete is inspired by skateboard culture.

Basic singles from €30, free Wi-Fi, breakfast optional, towels included, laundry facilities, 24-hour reception, Carrer del Freser 5, Eixample, +34 934 46 05 17, santjordihostels.com, sagradafamilia@santjordi.org,

Metro: St Pau-Dos de Maig

Urbany BCN GO

Sporting a rooftop terrace, all-new facilities, a Jacuzzi, and comfortable, bright rooms, this isn't your papa's dingy hostel. They seem to have worked all the bugs out here. Enjoy a nearly perfect blend of comfort and social atmosphere at one of this chain's newest and most popular locations.

Beds from €22, 24-hour reception, laundry service, breakfast available, mini pool and Jacuzzi, free Wi-Fi, luggage storage, Corts Catalanes 563, Eixample, +34 937 37 96 18, urbanyhostels.com, info@urbanybcngo. com, Metro: Universitat

Urbany Barcelona

If BCN Go is full, try Urbany Barcelona nearby. The welcoming receptionists will greet you with a smile and they'll happily recommend activities or points of historical or cultural interest. The pool table, rooftop terrace, and social setting will be your favorite parts of the hostel. The beds are nothing to write home about, but (at least in the off-season) the price is right.

Dorms from €14, 24-hour reception, laundry facilities, breakfast extra, rooftop terrace, free Wi-Fi, luggage storage available, Avinguda Meridiana 97, Eixample, +34 932 45 84 14, urbanyhostels.com, Metro: Clot or Encants

Hostel Yeah!

Check out this massive, purpose-built 200-bed hostel. These guys have learned from some of the best hostel providers in the city, and they know their stuff. You'll enjoy walking tours, nightly €10 dinners, pub crawl and club options for €15, and double-paned windows that keep the sounds of the city from interrupting your beauty rest. There's a sweet terrace up top with a lounge pool and views toward Parc Güell. The central location puts you close to almost everything.

Dorms from €25, 24-hour reception, female dorms available, daily turndown cleaning, laundry and kitchen facilities, breakfast €3, free Wi-Fi, lockers, charging stations, Carrer de Girona 176, +34 935 310 135 or +34 636 711 346, yeahhostels.com, Metro: Verdaguer

TRANSPORTATION

GETTING THERE & AWAY

Barcelona has a well-thought-out transit system. No matter where you want to go, there are often a number of convenient and quick ways to get there. Most of the city's accommodations are easily accessible by public transit.

Plane

Two airports serve Barcelona. From **El Prat** (BCN, barcelona-airport.com), the **AeroBus** leaves every 20 minutes and goes directly into the center (40 minutes, €5.65 one-way, free Wi-Fi and charging plugs on board). Stay on until the end of the line, Plaça de Catalunya (Barcelona's main square). Your accommodations may be within walking distance of the square; if not, the metro station and bus stops are nearby.

If you're flying into **Girona** (GRO, girona-airport.net), simply hop on the **Barcelona Bus** into the city center (about 1.5 hours, €15 one-way). You'll get dropped off at **Estacio d'Autobus Barcelona Nord,** where you can connect into the metro system.

Train

The train system is excellent in Spain. Trains between Barcelona and Madrid take about three hours and run often throughout the day. If you purchase in advance through **Renfe** (renfe.com), tickets can be as cheap as €50, but prices climb past €150 closer to the date and during peak travel times. Since there's quite a bit of business traffic between these cities, avoid peak commuting times (early morning, late afternoon) to find the cheapest options. The rail trip to or from Paris takes about seven hours and costs around €130. Barcelona has two major train stations: **Estacio de Sants,** west of the Old Town, and **Estacio de Franca,** between El Born and Barceloneta. Both stations have integrated metro stops.

Bus

Barcelona has two major bus stations: **Estacio de Sants,** west of the Old Town, and **Estacio de Nord,** north of El Born. Check out **Eurolines** (eurolines.com) for your best national and international connections. While bus tickets may be cheaper than train tickets, time is money—don't sacrifice too much of your trip just to save 10 or 20 euros.

Car

By car, Barcelona is about six hours east of Madrid and about 10 hours south of Paris. The highways are relatively well maintained and well marked.

GETTING AROUND

Barcelona is a wonderful city to walk, but factor its large size into your planning. The heart of Barcelona, the medieval city called Barri Gotic, is a 20-minute walk from one side to the other. The Eixample, the city's more modern expansion beyond the Old Town, is much bigger, with block after block of traffic and modern buildings.

The **bus and metro systems** in Barcelona are integrated, meaning that you can use the same passes for both systems. Buy the **T10 pass** (€9.95), good for ten rides (this can be used by one person or ten—whichever you prefer). With this pass, you save more than 50 percent off the **individual ticket rate** (€2.15). Buy one of them for yourself and it's unlikely you'll need to pay anything more for public transportation. You can buy your T10 passes from the automated machines in the metro. Use change, as paying with a big bill will leave you with a pocket full of heavy change.

Metro

The metro is a fast and efficient way across town if you don't mind missing the views along the way. The metro was completely overhauled for the 1992 Olympics, and the metro-line colors reflect those of the Olympic rings. The metro closes at midnight during the week, at 02:00 on Friday, and goes all night on Saturday. Watch out: Pickpockets work the busy areas in the touristy metro stops like Plaça de Catalunya, so keep a tight hold on your belongings, and zip or button up valuables whenever possible.

Bus

Barcelona boasts an extensive network of buses. Routes and numbers are easy to read at each bus stop. Look for the arrow pointing toward the Mediterranean Sea to get yourself oriented, as the maps won't be oriented north-south but along the bus line

itself. Buy tickets before boarding or from the driver.

Taxi

Officially licensed Barcelona cabs are black with yellow doors. There are fleets of them across the city, and you can feel secure waving one of them down. Rest assured that the meter will be in the right setting. There are four tariff rates: T1 (€2.10 + €1.07/km) is weekdays 08:00-20:00, T2 (€2.10 + €1.30/km) is weekdays 20:00-08:00, T3 (€2.30 + €1.40/km) is weekends and holidays 20:00-06:00, and T4 is a fixed rate. My preferred networks are **Radio Taxi** (+34 933 033 033) and **Taxi Barcelona** (+34 933 300 300).

Bicycle

Barcelona has a **public bike rental** (bicing.cat) system for registered users. I recommend renting a bike through **One Car Less** (Calle Esparteria 3, +34 932 682 105, biketoursbarcelona.com) in El Born. For €10 per half day, you can hire a bike to ride the length of the beaches until you find that perfect and relatively quiet spot in the sand. There's not much of a reason to venture into the Eixample on a bike; I prefer to avoid the heavy traffic of the modern town, though there is a network of bike paths.

DAY TRIPS

Montserrat

For challenging hiking and beautiful views of the surrounding countryside and the Mediterranean coastline, look no further than Montserrat. Montserrat (Serrated Mountain) has a monastery, **Santa Maria de Montserrat** (free, daily 07:00-19:30 with masses often, +34 938 77 77 77, montserratvisita.com), tucked into the armpit of the rocky crag. Explore the gilded Gothic monastery and the ramparts looking out over Cataluña, then make a pit stop at the cafeteria and gift shop. To cap it off, take the funicular (€3.70, runs every 20 minutes until about 17:00 in the low season, 18:00 in summer months, cremallerademontserrat.cat) straight up the mountain to the peak.

Located on the R5 train line, in the direction of Manresa, the Montserrat station is just an hour away from downtown Barcelona. When you arrive, take the Aeri cable car for a beautiful view as you are carried up to the monastery. There are two more funiculars that can take you to different parts of the mountain, or you can just wander around the monastery.

Trains depart hourly from Plaça Espanya to Monistrol de Montserrat. Tickets will run you about €30. Allow a full day for the trip.

Other worthwhile multiday options are **Sitges,** a hub for Europe's LGBT community; **Figures** for Dalí sights; and **Girona** for medieval streets that have served as backdrops for the popular HBO series *Game of Thrones*. (Can't quite place it? Shame! Shame! Shame!)

HELP!

Tourist Information Centers

The **tourist information center** (Mon-Thurs 09:00-14:30 and 15:30-18:30, Fri 09:00-15:00), just beneath the Plaça Catalunya at the top of La Rambla, is easy to find. Pop in for sightseeing tips, sight reservations, maps, and help finding accommodations. You can also get plenty of helpful information at barcelonaturisme.com.

Plaça de Catalunya 17

+34 932 85 38 34

Pickpockets & Scams

Barcelona has a serious pickpocketing problem. Make it obvious that you're a tourist on any of the busy boulevards and you'll be painting a bull's-eye on your back pocket. Keep your wits about you. Busy metro stations are also prime pickpocketing zones. Wear your backpacks on your front, use a money belt, and keep your valuables close while in busy touristy areas. More often than not, you won't notice you've been pickpocketed until it's too late.

Gambling in public is illegal, and you should avoid the games on La Rambla, where gamblers work in teams to lure unsuspecting tourists. You'll win fast—then lose it all and then some in the blink of an eye.

Marijuana Clubs

Marijuana is being decriminalized at the time of publication, and discreet private clubs are popping up all over town. Search for "collectives" in your browser, and bring a passport to sign up. Some require a residence or Spanish ID number to join. No money exchanges hands save for "donations" required up front. The whole industry is operating in a legal gray area, so entrances to clubs will be discreet and unmarked. Find more information at marijuanabarcelona.com. .

Emergencies

For emergencies, dial 112. You can also reach the fire service (061) or city police (092), or dial 061 for medical emergencies.

Hospital

Hospital Clinic Barcelona
Emergency entrance: Casanova 143, 08036 Barcelona
+34 93 227 5400

US Consulate

Paseo Reina Elisenda de Montcada
+34 93 280 22 27

BERLIN

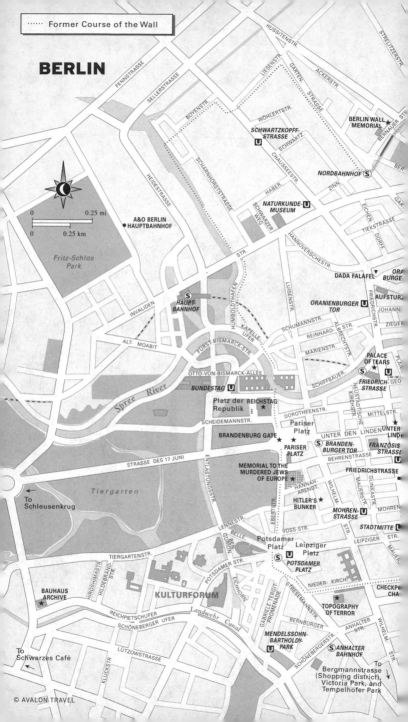

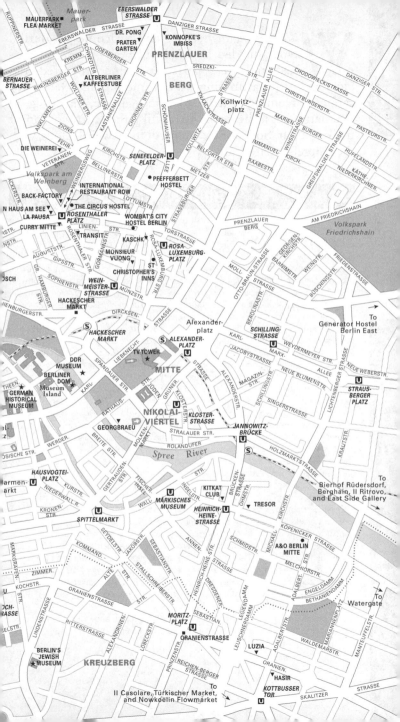

Willkommen, *bienvenue*, and welcome to Berlin! Once divided by the Cold War powers, Berlin's east and west parts have since reunited and blossomed into a thriving, vibrant metropolis. Germany's capital is teeming with history and culture, including an alternative nightlife scene that will either turn you on or freak you out. So embrace your will to be weird, along with the zeitgeist that awaits!

BERLIN 101

Berlin persevered through a difficult 20th century. Following Germany's defeat in World War I, inflation soared as a result of the reparations imposed by the Treaty of Versailles. By the early 1920s, four trillion German marks were equal to one US dollar, and it cost a wheelbarrow full of bills to purchase a single loaf of bread. This situation improved thanks to currency reform and a renegotiation with the Allied forces in 1924, and Berlin prospered during the latter half of the decade. With residents such as Albert Einstein breaking boundaries in science and artists like George Grosz making headway in the Dada movement, Berlin became the cultural haven of Europe. It also boasted the wildest cocaine-fueled nightlife the world had ever seen.

The good times ended as Hitler finagled his way into power. Hitler reenergized the country, but in a terrible direction, and embarked on a vicious genocide against Jews and other minorities, whom he blamed for problems like corruption and inflation. After systematic deportations and executions, only 1,200 of Berlin's 160,000 Jews were left in the city after the Holocaust. Approximately a third of the city was flattened by bombs during World War II, and parts of Berlin still bear the scars today.

Following the war, Germany was divided into East and West. The city of Berlin, located in the middle of East Germany, was divided into four allied zones: British, French, American, and Russian. The first three of those created an island of capitalism in the sea of communist East Germany. To maintain that foothold, the Western Allies put huge effort into sustaining the citizens of West Berlin. The quality of life was better in West Berlin and West Germany, so the East German population—including many intellectuals and professionals—slowly bled west.

Refusing to accept the exodus, the Soviets built a wall north-south through East Germany and bisecting East and West Berlin. In the middle of the night on August 13, 1961, the East German government laid the foundations for what they called the "anti-fascist protection wall." The existence of the Berlin Wall implicitly admitted that not everyone wanted to live in this supposed communist paradise. The Berlin Wall remained until 1989, when a miscommunication during a routine TV announcement kicked off a surge of East Berliners to the wall's checkpoints. Overwhelmed, bewildered guards permitted families to reunite across the wall, and the celebratory dismantling of the wall began as quickly as it went up almost 30 years before. The wall's collapse sparked the dissolution of the entire Soviet Union. East and West Germany were reunited, and the city of Berlin once again became the capital of Germany.

Today, East Berlin is the world's largest construction project, and is transforming once more to reflect the vibrant energy of the unmistakable Berliner culture.

PLAN AHEAD

RESERVATIONS
Reservations are required for the **Reichstag** (bundestag.de/htdocs_e/visits).

PASSES
WelcomeCard
Berlin's **WelcomeCard** (from €19.90, visitberlin.de) gets you discounts at a number of sights, but it rarely works out in the holder's favor. It's a far better value to pay for individual museum experiences and purchase metro passes for the days you'll be in town.

Berlin Metro Passes
Metro passes are €7 per day or €30 for a week. They can be purchased at any station. The day pass pays for itself by the third ride.

LOCAL HAPPENINGS
Gay Pride Festival
Germany's biggest gay pride festival, Berlin Pride (also known as CSD Berlin) takes place on the fourth Saturday in July each year. The week surrounding the event sees the city turned into a festive LGBT celebration. Each year, attendance inches closer to one million.

Unity Day
Unity Day commemorates October 3, 1990, when East and West Germany were officially reunited. Most shops will be closed.

Festival of Lights
Each year in October, the entire city lights up. Pick up a program (widely available around town) and put together a plan. The Brandenburg Gate, the Victory Column, the Berlin TV Tower, and countless other buildings and monuments are all bathed in colorful lights and moving displays.

Christmas Markets
Enjoy sausages and a mug of mulled wine at one of the many Christmas markets that pop up every year toward the end of November and run until the New Year. Security was tightened considerably in the wake of the Christmas market terror attack in 2016, so expect bag searches and increased vigilance.

THREE DAY ITINERARY

It's a tall order to soak in Berlin's history, experience its complex culture, and visit all its must-see sights in three days. But you'll cover a lot of ground if you stick to this itinerary and make advance reservations for the Reichstag.

DAY 1: WELCOME TO BERLIN
MORNING
Grab a quick breakfast at a corner bakery—**Back-Factory** and **Back Werk** are both great options—then embark on a six-hour walking tour with **Brewer's Walks** (leaving at 10:30am from outside the Freidrichstrasse S-Bahn station). If you prefer pedaling to walking, hop on the 4.5-hour bike tour with **Fat Tire Bike Tours** (meeting at 11:00 daily at Alexanderplatz on the north side of the TV Tower), a great way to orient yourself on your first day.

All introductory tours take you by sights like **Checkpoint Charlie,** the **Brandenburg Gate,** the **Memorial to the Murdered Jews of Europe, Hitler's Bunker,** and some of the intact remnants of the **Berlin Wall.** You'll be moving on quickly, so note any interesting sights you may want to revisit.

Or/and hop on city bus route 100, turn the bus ride into a guided tour by listening to **Jimbo's Cheap Man's Bus Tour** (free download). This route to West Berlin will give you a good grasp of the scale of the city. For a lunch stop at the turnaround point (Zoologischer Garten), try **Schwarzes Café,** just one long block down Kantstrasse from the stop.

AFTERNOON
If you're on a guided tour, you'll finish in the late afternoon. Consider renting a bike (from Fat Tire or another shop) for the rest of your stay—Berlin is a bike-friendly city. Get some **Mitte** shopping time in on **Unter den Linden** and on the streets surrounding the Weinmeisterstrasse U-Bahn stop.

Make a late-afternoon visit to the **Reichstag,** Germany's parliament building (advance online reservations required). Notice the glass dome and its striking architectural symbolism—it stands for Germany's promise of democratic transparency. Don't be late: Security operates on a strict timeline.

EVENING
Ease yourself into Berlin's nightlife in mainstream Mitte. The action tends to center on **Rosenthaler Platz.** For dinner, walk down **International Restaurant Row** or grab some authentic Italian pizza by the slice at **La Pausa.** After dinner, it's time for a round or two in the always-happening **Mein Haus am See**—as soon as you're feeling loose, head downstairs to the dance bar.

LATE
In a jazzy mood? You're not far from **Zosch,** a classic Berliner jazz bar. Descend into their World War II bomb shelter, order your beer by the liter, and enjoy the virtuosity on display.

DAY 2: IRON CURTAIN & MORE
MORNING
If your hostel is anywhere near the Rosa-Luxemburg-Platz U-Bahn stop, stop

for a caffeine fuel-up at **Kaschk**—my favorite coffee shop in Berlin, boasting some of the best fresh-roasted beans this side of the Alps. Then take a stroll through Mitte to the **Palace of Tears.** What was once the divided city's main border crossing is now a free and enlightening exhibit, illuminating the human pain caused by the wall.

AFTERNOON

Take S1, S2, or S25 to Nordbahnhof and transfer onto the M10 tram to the **Berlin Wall Memorial.** Climb the free observation tower nearby for views of a remnant wall and the entire city. Then, cross the street to the other side of the wall to get the East Berliner perspective. Afterward, your super-typical Berliner lunch is just a 10-minute walk away at **Altberliner Kaffeestube** on Arkonaplatz.

Loop on tram M10 toward Warschauer Strasse to the **East Side Gallery,** the Berlin Wall's oldest intact section and now the world's largest outdoor mural. Hundreds of famous artists used the wall as a canvas in the years following the collapse of communism; they recently returned to retouch their work, which is now more than 25 years old.

Being in this part of town puts you in perfect position to explore **Kreuzberg,** Berlin's most ethnically diverse neighborhood, centering on **Oranienstrasse.** Drop into the recommended **Hasir** to sample authentic Turkish cuisine.

EVENING

Return to the hostel for some R&R—you'll need to be energized before your night out in **Friedrichshain,** Berlin's famous entertainment district. Start with a kick-ass burger at **BurgerAMT** (consider splitting one of these massive burgers to avoid the risk of a food coma). Stop across the square for a digestif at **Szimpla,** the Berliner branch of the famous Budapest ruin bar. Ramp up the party at **Crack Bellmer** with Berlin's ultra-chill and sophisticated hipster set.

Don't miss the guys at **Big Stuff Smoked BBQ** in the **Markethalle 9** food hall for some of the best ribs this side of the pond. Their sister bar on the same aisle makes a mean old-fashioned.

LATE

Now it's time to weigh the many serious clubbing options in the neighborhood. There's lots to pick from, including **Raw Tempel**, **Watergate**, **Tresor**, **Berghain,** and the adventurous **KitKat Club.**

DAY 3: SHOPPING & DAY TRIP

MORNING

If it's Sunday, head north to the crowded, well-discovered yet highly worthwhile outdoor **Mauerpark Flea Market.** There are handmade crafts for days and street food that'll help you put the boozing of the night before firmly behind you.

AFTERNOON

An hour-long trip north will get you to **Sachsenhausen,** the Nazi concentration camp closest to Berlin's center; take the M10 tram to Nordbahnhof, connect onto the S1 north to Oranienburg station, and catch bus 804 to the camp. This is where the Nazis developed their concentration camp layout, to be used later at places like Auschwitz.

EVENING

Pröst to an amazing weekend in Berlin at a classic German beer hall like **Georgbraeu.** The beer has plenty of calories, but if you're still craving more, they have hearty meat-and-potatoes dishes galore.

TOP NEIGHBORHOODS

Massive Berlin might be a reunited city, but it's still divided into East and West sections, both of which contain neighborhoods worth visiting. Grab a coffee at any one of the amazing local cafés and review the following summary of the districts. Your experience of Berlin will vary significantly depending on which part of the city you focus on, so concentrate on the districts that sound like your cup of tea.

You'll spend the majority of your time in former East Berlin. At its center, **Mitte** contains most of the touristy sights, from the Reichstag, Brandenburg Gate, and Unter den Linden on one end to the TV Tower on the other, with a cluster of museums on Museum Island. Just north of the river is the Hackescher Markt and some excellent thrift store-like boutique shopping. While many tourists feel most at home in this central area, expensive and beaten-path zones like Rosenthaler Platz don't really provide any of the truly authentic flavors of Berlin.

The city is quickly gentrifying, and hotter spots have bled south and east from Mitte. East of Mitte on the north side of the river, **Friedrichshain** offers the impressive East Side Gallery and some of the city's most famous mega clubs like Berghain and Raw Tempel. Find **Kreuzberg** south of Spree, Berlin's most diverse district, with a sizable Turkish population. Come here to experience the Turkish flea market and enjoy rich and tasty kebabs by day and cheap drinks in super-cool dance bars by night. The action tends to gather between the two U-Bahn stations, Kotbusser Tor and Wauschauerstrasse. Neighboring **Neukölln,** bordering Templehof airport, was ignored for decades, but is now front and center. It's where Berlin's hottest new trends are emerging.

Northeast of Mitte, yuppie **Prenzlauer Berg** is where tattooed ex-punks with babies in tow have taken up peaceful residence. **Central Berlin,** dominated by Tiergarten Park, is a great place for outdoor recreation and a bit of sightseeing, but not much else. West and south of Tiergarten is **West Berlin,** generally more residential, yet there are hubs of activity in neighborhoods like Charlottenburg. Lacking the dense sightseeing punch that Mitte offers, most visitors don't get too deep into this side of town, so it's a good place to go if you want to avoid crowds and mingle with locals.

TOP SIGHTS

The Topography of Terror

On the site of the old Gestapo headquarters, this intense exhibit takes you chronologically through Germany's slide into fascism. This museum doesn't shy away from the country's difficult 20th-century history, detailing the early power grabs of the Nazis and the party's loathsome discrimination and scapegoating of Jews and other minorities. There is no attempt to shrug off the responsibility for the atrocities that followed. Outside the museum, you'll find a stretch of the Berlin Wall with exposed foundations just beneath. These were the cells where political prisoners were held, interrogated, and tortured by the Gestapo.

Free, daily 10:00-20:00, outdoor exhibit closes at dusk, Niederkirchnerstrasse 8, Mitte, +49 (0)30 254 50 90, topographie.de/en, U-Bahn: Kochstrasse

Checkpoint Charlie

The Berlin Wall's most famous checkpoint was controlled by the Americans during the Cold War. The third checkpoint after Alpha and Bravo, Checkpoint Charlie was the site of a tense 1961 showdown between American and Soviet tanks. You can snap selfies with the guards there, but *don't* get a stamp in your passport—the stamp technically invalidates it.

Nearby, the haphazard yet extremely thorough **Checkpoint Charlie Museum** (€12.50 adults/€9.50 students, daily 09:00-22:00, Friedrichstrasse 43-45, Mitte, +49 (0)30 253 72 50, mauermuseum. de, U-Bahn: Kochstrasse) focuses on the many escapes from East Berlin during the Cold War—many of them highly creative, featuring jerry-rigged hot-air balloons,

ACT LIKE A LOCAL

Embrace Your Inner Hipster

Berlin—with its younger-skewing population, its countless artists and musicians, its unmistakably bohemian lifestyle, and its cheap rent—has been a magnet for European counterculture types. It's one of the birthplaces of hipster culture (long before the term entered the common lexicon). While you're here, hit up a thrift market for some Berliner styles, revel in the alternative nightlife, and notice the quiet collective resistance to mass marketing, mass consumerism, and mass production. This is perhaps most evident in the city's many cafés and bars, so many of which have mismatched furniture gathered from god knows where—in Berlin, the lack of conformity is itself a kind of conformity.

Love the Ampelmann

Communist rule brought with it a host of miseries and privations: there were frequent and widespread food shortages; in East Berlin, oranges were only available at Christmastime; if you wanted a car, you might spend 10 years on a waiting list—at the end of your wait, you'd receive a car made from epoxy and heavy cardboard. But there was one aspect of East Berliner life that the East German comrades grew to love: the Ampelmann.

When walking the streets of Berlin, notice the cute little green walking man and red no-go man lights at each crosswalk. This is the Ampelmann. After the fall of the wall, all the crosswalk lights were standardized, which meant, at many intersections, the end of the Ampelmann. Locals protested the change. So vociferous were their objections that the city council replaced the Ampelmann crossings they had taken down. The Ampelmann has, since then, remained as an enduring and even endearing symbol of East Berliner pride. You'll find Ampelmann stores scattered throughout the east part of Berlin. You can take the Ampelmann home with you on everything from mugs to messenger bags.

hollowed-out surfboards, and more. The **Palace of Tears** is free and more professionally done.

Free, always open, Mitte, intersection of Zimmerstrasse and Friedrichstrasse, U-Bahn: U6 Kochstrasse

TV Tower

Standing about 1,200 feet, the TV Tower is the tallest structure in Germany. The tower was built by the communists in 1969 to show off their engineering prowess (they secretly imported Swedish engineers to finish the job). Hop on the speedy elevator for a spectacular 360-degree panorama over Mitte and the rest of the city.

€13, daily 09:00–24:00, Panoramastrasse 1A, Mitte, +49 (0)30 247 57 58 75, tv-turm.de, S+U-Bahn: Alexanderplatz

Brandenburg Gate & Pariser Platz

Built in 1791, when Berlin was the capital of Prussia, the Brandenburg Gate once served as the grand passageway to Unter den Linden, the beautiful tree-lined boulevard leading straight to the Berlin City Palace. Though the East German and West German governments worked together to restore the gate after World War II, the erection of the Berlin Wall meant vehicles and pedestrians were no longer allowed to travel freely through the gate. It was effectively isolated in no-man's-land, transforming from a symbol of passage and unity to one of separation. When the Wall fell in 1989, the gate was reopened.

The pristine white Brandenburg Gate stands today as a symbol of a unified Germany and is an iconic landmark of the city, crowning one of the most important squares in town: **Pariser Platz.** On this square, you'll find the famous Hotel Adlon (the five-star hotel from which Michael Jackson notoriously dangled his baby), the French Embassy, and the US Embassy with its unattractive (but apparently necessary) security wall that winds all the way around the building. Thousands of tourists visit the square each day, so it'll be difficult to get photos of anything without a sea of people in the shot.

Free, always open, Pariser Platz, Mitte, S-Bahn: Brandenburger Tor

Palace of Tears

The Palace of Tears occupies a Cold War checkpoint where East Berliners were permitted to cross into West Berlin, but only after serious interrogation by famously intimidating border guards. Those leaving East Berlin often did so not knowing whether they'd ever see their families and loved ones again. Today multimedia and interactive displays reveal what life was like behind the Iron Curtain, including examinations of some of the cleverer ways that East Berliners coped with life under communism. There are also exhibits covering the fall of the Wall and the long process of reunification that followed. You'll come away with a much clearer picture of the time, the people, and the forces that shaped the long-simmering conflict.

Free, Tues-Fri 09:00-19:00, Sat-Sun 10:00-18:00, Reichstagufer 17, Mitte, +49 (0)30 46777790, hdg.de/berlin/traenenpalast, S+U-Bahn: Friedrichstrasse

Reichstag

The Reichstag, built in 1894 and remodeled in the 1990s, is the traditional seat of Germany's parliament. Its magnificent glass dome represents the government's commitment to transparency. From inside the building there are stunning views of the Berlin skyline. Visitors can also peer over the shoulders of elected officials below. Take your time here and be sure to listen to the well-done audio guide, which will loop you up and down the spiraling track inside the glass dome. Enter the building through a security checkpoint to the right of the main entrance. Entry is free, but online reservations are required (you'll need to provide your passport information to make a reservation). Be early for your appointment and be sure to remember your ID. When you're done with your tour, take a break for a coffee or a meal in the roof-level restaurant. They serve breakfast, lunch, and dinner—on the pricey side, but considering your surroundings...

Free, reservations required, daily 08:00-24:00, last entry at 22:00, Platz der Republik 1, Mitte, +49 (0)30 227 32152, bundestag.de, S-Bahn: Brandenburger Tor, U-Bahn: Bundestag

Berlin Wall Memorial

Head up to Bernauer Strasse on the northern edge of Mitte to see a small, fully preserved section of the Berlin Wall. You'll see the double layer of defense, the combed and mine-strewn sand in no-man's-land, and the trespassing detection systems—any government that has to work this hard to keep its citizens from fleeing might be advised to go back to the drawing board. This stretch of wall was the only one to incorporate existing buildings, done so to save on building materials. People lived in these buildings, and several escaped through the westward-facing windows. One such instance led to a tug-of-war between East German police on one side and

"I AM A JELLY DONUT"

In 1963, during a speech in West Berlin, delivered to a crowd of 450,000, President John F. Kennedy announced to the world that the United States would stand shoulder to shoulder with West Berlin as it attempted to preserve freedom and democracy in the midst of tyranny and oppression. *"Ich bin ein Berliner,"* Kennedy repeated twice during his speech. While the phrase literally translates to "I am a Berliner," in German, the indefinite article *ein* is superfluous. The seemingly inconsequential syllable gives the phrase an unintended meaning: "I am a jelly donut." Needless to say, cartoonists had a field day, scattering jokes about talking pastries all over the press. Though he may have regretted this grammatical blunder, Kennedy's attempt to speak the Berliners' language only further endeared him to the German people.

Allied police on the other, with an escaping old lady hanging half in and half out of the window. Following the incident, the East Germans bricked up all the west-facing windows.

Visit the free museum on the ground floor, and then climb the stairs in the tower across the street for a panorama of the neighborhood and an overhead view of the Wall and no-man's-land. I recommend going to the far side as well to see what the wall looked like from the east.

Free, memorial grounds open daily 08:00-22:00, museum open Tues-Sun 10:00-18:00, Mitte, +49 (0)30 467 98 66 66, berliner-mauer-gedenkstaette.de, S-Bahn: Nordbahnhof

Memorial to the Murdered Jews of Europe

This bluntly named Holocaust memorial, completed in 2005, consists of 2,700 different-sized stone slabs positioned on a rolling plane. It powerfully evokes feelings of instability, claustrophobia, and disorientation—just a fraction of the emotions experienced by the Jewish people leading up to and during the Holocaust. As you delve deeper into this memorial, the sounds of the city fade away and are replaced by silence and an eerie sense of isolation, even in the midst of hundreds of fellow tourists. To prevent graffiti, the blocks were covered with a protective coating, which has actually worked quite well. Ironically, the company that provided this protective chemical was distantly affiliated with the company that developed Zyklon B, the chemical the Nazis used to gas millions in their extermination camps. When this came to light, the company provided the service and product free of charge. Visitors are politely asked to experience the site in respectful silence.

Free, always open, Cora-Berliner-Strasse 1, Mitte, +49 (0)30 2639 4336, holocaust-mahnmal.de/en, S-Bahn: Brandenburger Tor, U-Bahn: Potsdamer Platz

Hitler's Bunker

As Soviet and American forces tightened the net around Berlin in 1945, Hitler and his inner circle retreated to a subterranean command center with 10-foot-thick reinforced concrete walls and ceilings. Dark and damp, it was a suitably miserable place for history's most loathsome villain to spend his last days (in inglorious fashion, he took his own life in the bunker with either a gunshot to the head or a cyanide capsule—perhaps both). The bunker was destroyed after the war. What's left of it is buried beneath a nondescript parking lot. The parking lot is left deliberately empty to avoid providing any sort of pilgrimage site for extremists, but you can find a small signboard with information about what was below.

Free, always open, just southeast from the Memorial to the Murdered Jews of Europe at Wilhelmstrasse 77, Mitte, U-Bahn: Mohrenstrasse

East Side Gallery

The largest open-air art gallery in the world, the East Side Gallery is a preserved, mile-long section of the Berlin Wall that, following the collapse of communism, was painted over by hundreds of international artists. This once soulless piece of concrete is now a multicolored patchwork quilt of world-class street art bearing messages of peace and hope. Farther down the wall there are rotating exhibits on global conflicts.

Free, always open, Mühlenstrasse 45-80, Friedrichshain, +49 (0)172 391 87 26, eastsidegallery-berlin.com, U-Bahn: Schlesisches Tor

Museum Island

Right in the middle of historic Berlin is a concentration of the city's most famous museums. If your visit is a short one, two of these are worth your time: the **Pergamon Museum** (€12, daily 10:00-18:00, Bodestrasse 1-3, Mitte, +49 30 266424242, smb.museum, S-Bahn: Friedrichstrasse or Hackescher Markt), famous for its full-scale reconstructed city walls like the Ishtar Gates of Babylon and the Altar of Pergamon, along with thousands of other artifacts from the Islamic world; and the **Neues Museum** (€12, daily 10:00-18:00, Bodestrasse 1-3, Mitte, +49 30 266424242, smb.museum, S-Bahn: Friedrichstrasse or Hackescher Markt), which focuses on Egyptian architecture and artifacts (the Neues also rather elegantly integrates the ruins of the pre-WWII museum into the more modern building). With significant construction planned through 2021, it's important to check online ahead of time to verify that the museum you want to visit is open.

Climb to the top of the **Berliner Dom** (€7 adults, €5 students, Mon-Sat 09:00-20:00, Sun 12:00-20:00, until 19:00 Oct-Mar, closes around 17:30 on concert days, interior closed but dome open during services, Am Lustgarten, Mitte, +49 (0)30 20269119, berlinerdom.de, S-Bahn: Hackescher Markt), Berlin's most beautifully decorated Protestant church, for an amazing view of Museum Island and the rest of the city.

German History Museum

This extensive museum takes you from the early medieval ages of kings and serfs to the tumultuous 20th century through displays, paintings, artifacts, full suits of armor, weapons both ancient and modern, and much more. It's easy to spend several hours in just the permanent exhibition, which sprawls over two large floors. If you're on the fence on this one, check out their website; one of their innovative and edifying temporary exhibits might just move the needle.

Free up to 18 years, €8 adults, daily 10:00-18:00, Unter den Linden 2, Mitte, +49 (0)30 2030 4444, dhm.de, U-Bahn: Hausvogteiplatz

Unter den Linden

Take a stroll down Berlin's grand downtown boulevard that connects the Brandenburg Gate and Tiergarten with Alexanderplatz and the TV Tower. You'll pass historic buildings like the Berlin Opera, the State Library, the German History Museum, the Neue Wache (Memorial to the Victims of War), Humboldt University (where Einstein taught), and Bebelplatz, the site where, in 1933, the Nazis burned 20,000 books in a single evening. Into the flames went works by Albert Einstein, Karl Marx, and Heinrich Mann. There's a sunken memorial in the square—a glass panel that looks down onto empty bookcases with enough space for 20,000 volumes. The controversial $500 million reconstruction project of the City Palace (opposite the Berliner Dom) is also well underway and should be completed in 2019. Many Berliners feel the project to be a backwards-looking and therefore excessive expenditure, but you can stop at the visitors' office and decide for yourself.

Free, always open, Mitte, S-Bahn: Brandenburger Tor (Brandenburger Gate end) or S+U-Bahn: Alexanderplatz (TV Tower end)

DDR Museum

This unique museum with interactive exhibits gives visitors a chance to experience daily life as it was lived under the communist regime. Exhibits are fully hands-on. See what East Berliner denim looked and felt like, sit in a communist-era car, and wash your brain with some communist propaganda. Few people leave the museum with a burning desire to join their local branch of the Communist Party.

€9.50 adults/€7.50 online, €6 students/€4.50 online, daily 10:00-20:00 with crowds oppressive until 18:00 normally, Sat. open until 22:00, Karl-Liebknecht-Strasse 1, Mitte, +49 (0)30 847 12 37 32, ddr-museum.de, S-Bahn: Hackescher Markt or S+U-Bahn: Alexanderplatz

Berlin's Jewish Museum

This museum will send chills down your spine before you even step inside. The museum is housed in three separate building. The two more recent additions, both a flint-gray color, immediately strike the senses. The stark and jagged architecture (visually replicating the cold privations of the Holocaust) contrasts sharply the older, baroque building and the surrounding greenery. Designed by Daniel Libeskind, the unsettling design continues inside, with zigzag hallways, off-kilter windows, and unexpected voids, all of which combine to increase feelings of unease and apprehension. Plan on spending about half a day using the worthwhile audio tour as your guide through 1,000 years of the German-Jewish story. A significant renovation is on the horizon, so check the website for updates and information.

€8, Mon 10:00-22:00, Tues-Sun 10:00-20:00, last entry one hour before closing, closed on Jewish holidays, Lindenstrasse 9-14, Kreuzberg, +49 (0)30 2599 3300, jmberlin.de/en, U-Bahn: Hallesches Tor or Kochstrasse

TOP EATS

Berliner cuisine is diverse, thanks in large part to the influence of its multicultural—particularly Italian and Turkish—makeup. Traditional German cuisine (especially **schnitzel,** which is flattened, fried pork steak) can be found almost everywhere. **Currywurst** (a sausage with ketchup and curry) is a Berlin staple that's best eaten with a side of fries.

In restaurants, tips between 5 and 10 percent are appreciated—round up to the nearest round number and you'll usually be fine. In touristy areas (and sometimes elsewhere), you'll find bottled water, bread, and sometimes pretzels on the table when you take your seats. These are like hotel minibars—anything you touch will be added to your bill, so restrain yourself.

Back-Factory

Back-Factory is a simple cafeteria with mass-produced pastries and self-service coffee machines. The food isn't really noteworthy, but it's a super-convenient place to grab a quick breakfast pastry or sandwich on the go. There are multiple locations throughout town.

Pastries from €1.50, Mon-Fri 06:00-20:00, Sat 06:00-18:30, Sun 06:00-19:00, Rosenthaler Platz at Brunnenstrasse 1, +49 (0)30 40056105, back-factory. de, U-Bahn: Rosenthaler Platz

Georgbraeu

If you're looking for a beer hall with classic German fare and fine beer, look no further. Located in Berlin's old medieval town, this beer hall with brisk service whisks piping-hot racks of ribs, duck, and brats to your table, along with sizable salads and potatoes done just right. Their delicious house brews are presented under wreaths of hops. Just a few steps from Unter den Linden and the TV Tower, Georgbraeu is a great close-at-hand option if you find yourself in Mitte around dinnertime.

Mains from €14, beers €4, daily 12:00-24:00, Spreeufer 4, Mitte, +49 (0)30 242 42 44, brauhaus-georgbraeu. de, U-Bahn: Klosterstrasse

Kaschk Café & Bar

Kaschk (Norwegian owned and dripping in distinctly Scandi accents) gets my vote for best coffee in town, rounded out with a dozen rotating beer lines and a shuffle-board table. What more could you ask for? This is your quintessential hipster brewhouse—equally skilled with the grain and the bean—sporting bearded baristas and one long, common wooden table, minus the pretentious coffee snobbery. Ask the friendly staff about their latest beans. Tell them about your preferences and let them brew you up something unforgettable (it

works just as well with the beers). Check their website for a list of their rotating taps.

From €2.50, Mon–Thurs 08:00–02:00, Friday 08:00–03:00, Sat 10:00–03:00, Sun 10:00–02:00, Linienstrasse 40, Prenzlauer Berg, kaschk.de, U-Bahn: Rosenthaler Platz or Weinmeisterstrasse

Monsieur Vuong

For authentic Vietnamese street food, try some delicious pho at Mr. Vuong's. Loud colors are tempered with subtle decorations for a highly pleasing effect. Service is quick and friendly, and its location, only steps from recommended hostels and loads of boutique shops in Mitte, makes Monsieur Vuong a great place to stop in the middle of a busy day of combing through the thrift stores.

Dishes from €8, Mon–Thurs 12:00–23:00, Fri–Sun 12:00–24:00, Alte Schönhauser Str. 46, Mitte, +49 (0)30 99296924, monsieurvuong.de, U-Bahn: U Weinmeisterstrasse

Konnopke Imbiss

If you've never tasted currywurst before, put Konnopke Imbiss at the top of your list. Find this inconspicuous takeaway joint under the elevated U-Bahn rails. The steady stream of locals will let you know you're in the right place. Post up with everyday Berliners, who regularly come here to savor one of Germany's signature foods.

€4, Mon–Fri 10:00–20:00, Sat 11:30–20:00, Schönhauser Allee 44A, under U-Bahn tracks, Prenzlauer Berg, +49 (0)30 4427765, konnopke-imbiss.de, U-Bahn: Eberswalder Strasse

Transit

Try Transit for some quick and tasty Thai-Indonesian tapas. Mark your order on the ticket they provide and you won't have to wait long for fresh prawn tempura, spiced beef skewers, and healthy spring rolls. Come peckish or starving—no matter what your appetite, the servers will be happy to recommend something that fits the bill. The common tables and oversized light bulbs create an atmosphere perfect for starting off an unforgettable night out at the Rosenthaler Platz bars.

Dishes from €5, daily 11:00–24:00, Rosenthaler Strasse 68, Mitte, +49 (0)30 24781645, transit-restaurants. com, U-Bahn: Rosenthaler Platz

Altberliner Kaffeestube

The excellent Altberliner Kaffeestube has everything you'd expect from a typical Berliner meal, including meat-based dishes with heaping sides of sauerkraut, potatoes, and salads. While a staple for Prenzlauer Berg denizens, Altberliner does come with slightly inflated P'berg prices (as you'll probably notice, the people who live in the rapidly gentrifying neighborhood can afford it).

Mains from €12, daily 12:00–24:00, until 01:00 on weekends, Fürstenberger Strasse 1, Prenzlauer Berg, +49 (0)30 449 51 51, altberliner-restaurant.de, U-Bahn: Bernauer Strasse

Hasir

Thanks to its sizable Turkish population, Berlin has some of the best Turkish food this side of Istanbul. A world apart from the bar-adjacent kebab shops that cater largely to inebriated late-night patrons, Hasir might just serve the city's best Turkish cuisine. The recipe is simple: a classy, upscale interior and delicious kebabs with only the freshest ingredients. Their kofta (meatball) plates and their pita are superb. Make sure to try their fresh baklava before you leave. In addition to the Oranienburgerstrasse location, there's also a recommended location on Kreuzberg.

Dishes from €8.50, Oranienburgerstrasse 4, Mitte, daily 12:00–01:00, +49 (0)30 28041616, hasir.de, S-Bahn: Hackescher Markt and Adalbertstrasse 10

Il Ritrovo

After day one or two, you might be growing tired of sausage and curry. This family-owned restaurant gives you a healthy dose of Berlin punk and authentic Naples-style pizza, rolled and kneaded to perfection. Work your way to a free table and prepare yourself for what is probably the best pizza in town. Il Ritrovo is conveniently located if you're considering post-dinner drinks in the bumping district of Friedrichshain.

Pizzas from €7, daily 12:00–24:00, Gabriel-Max-Strasse 2, Friedrichshain, +49 (0)30 2936 4130, Facebook: Il Ritrovo, S-Bahn: Warschauer Strasse

Il Casolare

Stop into Il Casolare for some of the best Italian food in town, highlighted by al dente

tagliatelle and wood-oven pizza. They pride themselves on their authentic pastas (their carbonara, for instance, is *not* made with cream) and their pizza is excellent. Service isn't fantastic, but the food combined with the cozy interior and pleasant patio more than make up for it. Split a pitcher of their house wine with your friends.

Pizzas from €6, daily 12:00-24:00, Grimmstrasse 30, Kreuzberg, +49 (0)30 6950 6610, Facebook: Il Casolare, U-Bahn: Kottbusser Tor

BurgerAMT—Freidrichshain

Try this spot for juicy burgers with a hip-hop soul. Get the chicken barbecue or the bacon-jalapeño cheeseburgers with sweet potato fries on the side. The staff will help you navigate the menu at this joint right on Boxhagener Platz. You can even opt for a Mickey's 40 and enjoy the movies (hip-hop cult favorites) that are screened frequently. You might find a better burger if you look hard, but you won't find a better scenester burger joint.

Burgers from €6.50, Mon-Thurs 12:00-24:00, Fri-Sun 12:00-03:00, Krossener Str. 21-22, Freidrichshain, +49 (0)30 667 63453, burgeramt.com, S+U-Bahn: Warschauer Strasse

Markthalle 9

This is Berlin's pop-up culture at its finest. A daily food market, Markthalle 9 allows start-up restaurants to test their concepts, which translates to some of the best street food in town every Thursday evening. Options include Tex-Mex, Asian fusion, wine and cheese bars, and much more. There are frequent gastronomic and wine events, so be sure to check out the calendar online.

When you enter the market, hang a tight right for the best barbecue in town at **Big Stuff Smoked BBQ.** They cook up chick-

en, pork, beef, brisket, ribs, and more. Open for lunch and dinner (Tues-Wed 12:00-18:00, Thurs 12:00-22:00, Fri-Sat 12:00-21:30), it's best on Thursday nights. The bartenders mix a mean cocktail, so wash down your meal with your favorite; the old-fashioned was so good I had two more.

Mon-Sat 08:00-20:00, Sat market 10:00-18:00, Street Food Thursdays 17:00-22:00, Eisenbahnstrasse 42-43, +49 (0)30 61073473, markthalleneun.de, U-Bahn: Görlitzer

La Pausa

Take one step into this place and it feels like you've been transported to another country, with the smells of fresh pizza in the oven and the commotion of happy eaters to boot. Order pizza by the slice as you would in Italy, sprinkle with red pepper, and you've got a great late-night snack after a night out on Rosenthaler Platz.

Slices from €2.50, daily 11:00-02:30, Torstrasse 125, Mitte, +49 (0)30 2408 3108, U-Bahn: Rosenthaler Platz

Curry Mitte

You can't leave Berlin without sampling its most iconic (and filling) snack. If you are passing by Curry Mitte, jump on the opportunity. The currywurst and chips will sustain you—a late-afternoon snack there means you probably won't be hungry again until late in the evening.

Mon-Sat 11:00-24:00, till 06:00 on Fri and Sat, Torstrasse 122, Mitte, +49 (0)1520 106 95 59, currymitte.de, U-Bahn: Rosenthaler Platz

Schwarzes Café

This 24-hour café is a great option if you're orienting yourself with Berlin with the aid of Jimbo's Cheap Man's audio tour on bus 100. This historic and eclectic spot pulls off excellent brunches and coffee. Take your pick, from coffee to beer and tasty plates of fruit, omelets, and salads.

Plates from €8, daily 24 hours, Kantstrasse 148, West Berlin, +49 (0)30 313 80 38, schwarzescafe-berlin.de, S+U-Bahn: Zoologischer Garten

International Restaurant Row

Why some of the most interesting restaurants in town decided to huddle on a half block of Weinbergsweg, I can't tell you. What I can tell you is nobody is complaining. A lunch at these sit-down restaurants will run around €15, dinners €20-25; for travelers on a budget, bargains can be found at the takeaway shops or at **Back-Factory,** where you'll find cheap sandwiches, pastries, and coffee. International Restaurant Row has it all: from Moscow to Mexico, from Chinese pork dumplings to French pastries. Nearby is the recommended Circus Hostel and convenience shop (Weinbergsweg 26-27) that not only sells beer but also provides chairs outside where you can sip your brew (why the rest of the world's convenience store operators haven't caught on to this is a mystery to me).

Some of my favorite spots include **Gorki Park** (Weinbergsweg 25), serving excellent burgers and Russian staples like goulash; **Yumcha Heroes** (Weinbergsweg 8) for tasty but slightly overpriced dim sum; **Café Fleury** (Weinbergsweg 20), a classic, cozy French bakery and café with pastries, salads, sandwiches, and limited outdoor seating; **Soup 'n' Roll** (Torstrasse 117, around the corner from Weinbergsweg), which serves cheap and quick noodles; and **Bagel Company Berlin** (Rosenthaler Strasse 69) for breakfast bagels and sandwiches. Also check out **St. Oberholz Bar and Cafe** (Rosenthaler Strasse 72), a classic Berliner hipster café and bar with yuppies on laptops and a classy drinking crowd at night. If they're open, spring for the lifeguard high chairs outside to get a bird's-eye view of the crowd.

Prenzlauer Berg, U-Bahn: Rosenthaler Platz

TOP BEER GARDENS

Prater Garten

Established in 1837, Prater Garten is Berlin's oldest beer garden. It seats over 600 in a beautiful outdoor area shaded by chestnut trees. If the weather isn't cooperating, step inside to the spacious indoor beer hall, where you can enjoy not only liters of beer but also some of Berlin's best sausages and wiener schnitzel.

Pints from €4, Kastanienallee 7-9, Prenzlauer Berg, +49 (0)30 448 56 88, pratergarten.de, U-Bahn: Eberswalder Strasse

Schleusenkrug

You can find Berlin's most idyllic beer garden in Tiergarten Park, just on the north side of the zoo. On a sunny day, there's nothing better than the combination of crisp German lager and a cool breeze that makes its lazy way through the trees and to your table. This popular spot overcharges patrons for middle-of-the-road food, so show up fed or drink your lunch (German beer = liquid bread) out of a stein. The recommended Fat Tire Bike Tour refuels here.

Pints from €3.50, daily 10:00-24:00, Müller-Breslau-Strasse, Central Berlin, schleusenkrug.de, +49 30 3139909, S+U-Bahn: Berlin Zoologischer Garten

Bierhof Rüdersdorf

I stumbled across this unique, mod beer garden on my way out to Friedrichshain. With a crowd of locals milling around, I popped in and quickly saw why Berliners flock here. Tucked behind the famous and ultra-exclusive techno club Berghain, this small beer garden and posh, one-floor patio bar devours sunny afternoons whole. One beer quickly turns into three or four, and suddenly the sun has disappeared. If you're here late, you can keep your eye on the long line next door and decide when to make your move. Opening hours change frequently during the year, so check their website to make sure that, when you get thirsty, they'll be open.

Snacks from €2, burgers from €6, closed in winter months, Rüdersdorfer Strasse 70, Friedrichshain, +49 (0)30 2936 0215, bierhof.berlin, S-Bahn: Ostbahnhof

NIGHTLIFE DISTRICTS

In this sprawling city, nightlife thrives in several districts. Be warned, Berlin's trademark nightlife is gritty enough to rub first-timers raw. It has a well-deserved reputation as one of Europe's roughest club scenes—the differences between Berlin and, say, London or Paris are stark. However, what the best spots lack in cleanliness they more than make up for in attitude. People come out in Berlin to party in a thriving alternative scene—they're not remotely interested in elegance or luxury, and it shows.

Rosenthaler Platz

This five-point intersection caters to tourists and has all the essentials for an entry-level night on the town—proximity to good eats at the recommended **La Pausa** and **Curry Mitte** and to some of my favorite bars like **Mein Haus am See.** The wider district of Mitte has everything you'd expect in a standard European downtown district (i.e., good chain restaurants and tourist-friendly bars). There will be no surprises, and you'll pay a premium for this dependability.

Mitte, U-Bahn: Rosenthaler Platz

Friedrichshain

Friedrichshain, a dense tangle of nightlife complexes, bars, and restaurants, showcases edgy Berlin at its best. Though the district is beginning to show the wear of gentrification and mass tourism, it's still where you'll find the best nightlife, and everyone knows it. Start your night at **Hops & Barley** (Wühlischstrasse 22/23) or **Szimpla** (Gärtnerstrasse 15), two of the neighbor-hood's best bars. As the evening wears on, wander south toward **Watergate** and **Tresor,** two of the major clubs straddling the Spree River.

Friedrichshain, S+U-Bahn: Warschauer Strasse

Kreuzberg & Neukölln

Spreading south and east of central Berlin, Kreuzberg and Neukölln see constantly changing scenes of Berlin's living culture play out nightly. The streets are diverse, offering a never-ending array of creative stores, cafés, eateries, markets, bars, lounges and more. The streets are also darker, which attracts those buying and selling drugs, so you'll almost certainly be offered drugs around the transit stations. A night in these neighborhoods can be challenging, but if you're good with direction and open to exploring the unusual, this is where you need to be. Action in Neukölln tends to center on **Oranienstrasse;** in Kreuzberg, it's **Bergmannstrasse.**

Kreuzberg or Neukölln, U-Bahn: Hermannplatz

Prenzlauer Berg

The district has chilled out quite a bit in recent years, but it built its reputation on its edginess and you can still find some real gems. Focus your attention on **Kastanienallee** and **Schönhauser Allee,** leading uphill from Rosa-Luxemburg-Platz.

Prenzlauer Berg, U-Bahn: Rosenthaler Platz (Kastanienallee), U-Bahn: Rosa-Luxemburg-Platz (for Schönhauser Allee)

BARS

Bars in Berlin are always a bit alternative, and they'll keep you on your toes. Each featuring its own little twist, Berliner bars

LGBT BERLIN

Not just Berliners, but many of those around the world refer to Berlin as Europe's LGBT capital. With prominent public figures, celebrities, and local people unapologetically out of the closet, the LGBT scene hardly raises an eyebrow in the city that's seen it all. Germany's progressive bona fides are displayed in the country's extensive and strictly enforced antidiscrimination laws. Check out the website of **Out In Berlin** (out-in-berlin.com) for recommendations on cafés, restaurants, clubs, bars, nightlife districts, hotels, and more. Europe's biggest **Pride Parade** (every year at the end of July) draws nearly one million revelers (the lines at KitKat and Berghain look like parades in their own right).

reflect the city's eclectic makeup: There is everything from edgy cocktail lounges to Ping-Pong bars to authentic jazz cafés to keep the masses entertained.

Mein Haus am See

This is a quintessential Berlin bar: warm atmosphere, hipster clientele, and full service, with a few seating options: a smoking room, stadium seating in the back, and a bumping club downstairs with a rotating dance floor and other quirky features. It's open 24/7, so you can get your drink or coffee on any time of day. A night at Mein Haus am See ("my house at the lake") feels more like hanging out at a friend's place than a bar. As they put it, "It's not a bar, it's not a club... it's something sexier in between."

Drinks from €4.50, daily 24 hours, Torstrasse 125, Mitte, +49 (0)163 555 80 33, mein-haus-am-see.club, U-Bahn: Rosenthaler Platz

St. Oberholz Bar & Café

A smugly cool place to co-work by day transforms into the perfect place to kick off your night with beers and cocktails. This high-ceilinged, large-tabled, two-floor venue is bright, comfortable, and social. The knowledgeable bartenders will happily help you choose a beverage suited to your tastes. After a few drinks, you're ready to step outside and into one of the city's nightlife hot spots.

Beers from €5, Mon-Thurs 08:00-24:00, Fri-Sat 09:00-03:00, Sun 09:00-24:00, Rosenthaler Str. 72A, Mitte, +49 30 55578595, sanktoberholz.de, U-Bahn: Rosenthaler Platz

Dr. Pong

This bar is all about two things: Ping-Pong and beer. Slap down your five-euro deposit (for the paddle) and buy a few beer tickets at the door. You're now ready for a Ping-Pong battle royale. It's a massive multiplayer game, with a circling crowd of players alternating. It's an elimination game, so if you miss your shot, move aside and let the crowd winnow down to two competitors. Win one of these games and you'll be the toast of the room.

Drinks from €5, Mon-Sat 19:00-06:00, Sun 18:00-06:00, Eberswalder Strasse 21, Prenzlauer Berg, drpong.net, U-Bahn: Eberswalder Strasse

YAAM

For your reggaeton and dubstep fix, drop into YAAM (Young African Art Market), a community-powered creative space with yoga sessions and street art workshops by day and reggae and dance music by night. The partially covered location backing onto the river makes YAAM a popular summertime nightlife destination. Check the website for their diverse event listings.

Shows and drinks from €4, daily 11:00-24:00, later on weekends and for shows, An der Schillingbrücke 3, Friedrichshain, +49 (0)30 615 1354, yaam.de, U-Bahn: Ostbahnhof

Die Weinerei

This innovative bar relies on the kindness and honesty of strangers. It's the only bar I've ever been to that is based entirely on the honor system: Rent a glass for €2 and drink as much wine as you want. When you're ready to leave, put as much as you

think you owe in the tip jar. According to the owners, only a small percentage of their patrons pay less than what they owe.

€2 to get started, Mon-Fri 13:00-20:00, Sat 11:00-20:00, Veteranenstrasse 14, Mitte, +49 (0)30 440 69 83, weinerei.com, U-Bahn: Rosenthaler Platz

Café Luzia

Complete with an outdoor terrace that is always full in the summer, Luzia is one of the most popular bars in the Kreuzberg area. Inside you'll find old velvet armchairs, vintage wallpaper peeling away to reveal chipped red bricks, mismatched tables, and dim lamps that create a warm, laid-back atmosphere. It's Berlin hipster chic, but with the hard edge filed down considerably.

Coffee and beers from €4, daily 12:00-05:00, Oranienstrasse 34, Kreuzberg, +49 (0)30 8179 9958, luzia.tc, U-Bahn: Moritzplatz

Zosch

This bar churns out mediocre food and excellent beer all week. More importantly, it hosts jazz sessions every Wednesday that have been known to change lives. Magic for non-initiates and jazz heads alike, the crew jams away in the space's World War II bunker, delighting regulars and the lucky-to-be-in-the-know tourists in the room. Grab a stein and join the communal tables. Show respect to those who are there for the music by keeping your conversations hushed.

Liters from €7.50, daily 16:00-late, Tucholskystrasse 30, Mitte, +49 (0)30 280 76 64, zosch-berlin.de, S-Bahn: Oranienburger Strasse, U-Bahn: Oranienburger Tor

Crack Bellmer Bar

This cool lounge/dance bar in the Raw Tempel complex, with its high ceilings and creative lighting, is a great power-up stop—a prelude to an evening of partying in the even bigger clubs on the river. Considering how undeniably cool the crowd is, the drinks are surprisingly cheap. For just a euro, get Berlin's favorite shot, the Mexicaner—equivalent to a spicy slug of a Bloody Mary. It's the Berliner thing to do!

Drinks from €3.50, daily 19:00-very late, Revaler Strasse 99, Friedrichshain, +49 (0)30 64435860, crackbellmer. de, S+U-Bahn: Warschauer Strasse

Clash

A discreet entrance leads you to Clash, tucked into the back of a quiet courtyard. You'd never know this is one of the most popular rock bars in Kreuzberg. Cheap drinks (with prices posted on the chalkboard above the bar) and short lines at the long and well-staffed bar combine with loud music and frequent live acts to create an irresistible cocktail for rock fans. If you're on the south side of town, a round or three here is definitely worth the detour, no matter what time of day.

Beers from under €3, Mon-Fri 12:00-late, Sat 18:30-later, closed Sundays, Gneisenaustrasse 2A, Kreuzberg, clash-berlin.de, +49 30 32526387, U-Bahn: Mehringdamm

CLUBS
Raw Tempel

For a classic eclectic Berliner experience, drop into the Raw Tempel creative complex. There's a skate park, a pool, a soothing urban garden, a rock climbing wall, beer gardens, cafés, and more—enough to keep you busy for a full day. There's also an industrial electronic club venue, **Astra Kulturhaus** (excellent live shows often, astra-berlin.de, +49 (0)30 20056767), where EDM fans dance until the sun comes up.

Entry prices to various venues vary, Revaler Str. 99, Friedrichshain, raw-kultur-l.de, S+U-Bahn: Warschauer Strasse

Berghain

Once a working power plant, Berghain is massive, and so is its reputation. Its known mainly for two things: techno and explorations of the zones of experience where fantasy and reality merge. Ravers (their pupils often dilated) make the pilgrimage to Berghain's cavernous main room every weekend, arriving on Friday and stumbling out on Monday afternoon. Its global reputation as the reigning capital of the techno world means that more people come to the club than get in; the bouncers turn so many people away at the door that there are dozens of articles online that give tips on what to wear (and what not to wear/do/say) if you want to get in the door. As for the second part of the club's reputation, Berghain is not a place for voyeurs. It's a place for people who come prepared to party, so, if you take out your phone and

start taking pictures when you're in line, good luck getting in. Dress the part (dark clothes and edgy looks), and prepare yourself mentally. You'll see absolutely everything (and I do mean *everything*) when/if you get past the velvet rope. In Berghain, nothing is forbidden, so if you're easily offended, stay far, far away.

€15 cover, open 24 hours Fri-Mon, Am Wriezener Bahnhof, Friedrichshain, +49 (0)30 2936 0210, berghain.de, S-Bahn: Ostbahnhof, U-Bahn: Weberweise

Tresor

Tresor is hailed as the godfather of Berlin's techno scene. Occupying a massive, abandoned power plant across the river in the alternative neighborhood of Kreuzberg, it was one of the first to take driving techno beats to an industrial scale. This labyrinthine club includes three dance floors with long, dark graffitied hallways, dimly lit corners, and an abundance of pulsing strobe lights. Every inch of Tresor's 230,000 square feet is sonically stuffed—the world-class sound system (with top-tier DJs driving it) cranks out stomach-turning bass and ear-shattering treble. The crowd can't get enough, dancing well past midmorning. Berlin's longstanding nightlife staple draws a friendly, mixed crowd, and you'll find it much easier to get in than at Berghain. Get your dark, buttoned-up hipster mode on for your best chances at the door.

€10-15 cover, parties rock out every Mon, Wed, Thurs, Fri, and Sat, Köpenicker Strasse 70, Kreuzberg, +49 (0)30 6953 7721, tresorberlin.com, U-Bahn: Heinrich-Heine Strasse

Kater Blau

In a once-abandoned riverside complex underneath the U-Bahn tracks is one of Berlin's hottest underground party scenes. If it weren't for the long lines and extremely selective bouncers at the front of them, you'd be forgiven for thinking you'd stumbled into a squatter's rave. Everything feels derelict, but that's part of the draw. Entry is easiest around midnight, becoming more exclusive as the party kicks into high gear closer to 02:00. Check their website for upcoming events and DJs.

Cover €10, Find the "Kater" arrow and long line under the bridge, Holzmarktstrasse 25, Friedrichshain, katerblau.de

Watergate

Dance the night away at this medium-sized, double-floor nightclub that makes a perennial appearance on *DJ Mag*'s Top 100 Clubs list. Spinning a solid blend of house music and techno, Watergate is loved for its riverfront location, its open-air, glass-bottomed patio that seems to float on the water (a great place to catch your breath between beat drops) and its innovative LED-lighted ceiling that throbs in time with the music upstairs. Partygoers are happy to wait in the often long but always quickly moving line. It's more casual than some of the more exclusive clubs, but dress smart to avoid any hassle from the bouncers.

€15 cover, 21+ age policy, opens Wed at 11:30 and doesn't close until Sun at 12:00, Falckensteinstrasse 49, just east of Oberbaumbrucke bridge, Kreuzberg, +49 (0)30 6128 0394, water-gate.de, U-Bahn: Schlesisches Tor

KitKat Club

KitKat Club is a legendary Berlin nightclub and the home of the city's fetish community. Each weekend, the club is the place for wild, sweaty debauches with plenty of hedonism and role play. Inspired by the free-love beach parties of Goa in the '80s, this is where Berlin's freaks and geeks step out of their shells and into their studded leather costumes. Friday, Saturday, and Sunday are their big nights, with CarneBall (Saturday nights) being their trademark event; the bartenders perform their own cabaret show to the delight of patrons. The music in this LGBT-friendly club is mostly EDM and house. Doors usually open at 23:00, but the party reaches its zenith around 03:00, and it doesn't come down from that peak until the sun comes up. If you're going to make a night of it and really dive in headfirst, don't wear too much clothing— you'll just end up leaving it at coat check or losing it when you want to hit the sweaty dance floor sans shirt.

While the club is safe, friendly, and welcoming, it's much better to party with friends than solo on a first visit to KitKat Club. It's crucial to check the website both for dress code guidelines—you won't be allowed in with street clothes—and also to really understand what you're getting yourself into. Find the entrance to the club inside the U-Bahn station.

Cover €10+, parties run Fri-Mon usually but vary according to the program on the website, Köpenicker Strasse 76, Kreuzberg, kitkatclub.org, U-Bahn: Heinrich-Heine Strasse

PUB CRAWLS
New Berlin Pub Crawl
Sandeman's, the folks who run daily walking tours of Berlin, also organize nightly pub crawls—a great way to introduce yourself to some of Berlin's best nightlife. The €12 cost gets you a juicy welcome shot, entrance to a handful of bars, a fun crowd, and drink deals throughout the night. Picking up at the old post office on Oranienburger Strasse, this crawl shows you the best of the central Mitte district, ranging from grungy bars to hipster lounges. Wherever you end up, you'll be within walking distance of all the centrally located hostels. The pub crawls are popular and promoted all over town, so numbers often climb north of 80 members, which practically guarantees a wild and rowdy night.

€12, nightly 20:00, meet in front of the old post office at the corner of the Oranienburger Strasse S-Bahn station, Mitte, newberlintours.com, S-Bahn: Oranienburger Strasse

666 Anti Pubcrawl by Alternative Berlin
If a wild and rowdy night is exactly what you want to avoid, Berlin has an attractive alternative to your standard, boisterous pub crawl—appropriately called the Anti Pubcrawl. The group is much more conversational, and the bars they choose are less crowded. There are loads of interesting stories, classy drinks, and unique spots—everything from goth/horror rock bars to burlesque clubs. The crawl includes free entry to five bars and clubs and is capped at 15 or so people, so the experience is much more intimate than the Sandeman's crawl.

€12, nightly 21:00, meet at Tati Goes Underground Bar at Metzer Strasse 2, Prenzlauerberg, alternativeberlin.com, U-Bahn: Senefelderplatz

TOP SHOPPING & MARKETS

SHOPPING DISTRICTS
Friedrichstrasse
Comparable to Oxford Street in London, Friedrichstrasse lies in the area between its namesake station and Checkpoint Charlie. It's your standard downtown commercial zone with clothing brands like All Saints, Gucci, and Gap.

Friedrichstrasse, Mitte, S+U-Bahn: Friedrichstrasse

Hackescher Höfe Courtyards & Hackescher Markt
The trendy little downtown neighborhood surrounding Hackescher Markt offers an impressively wide selection of boutiques, designer shops, and big international brands like Urban Outfitters and American Apparel. Find Rosenthaler Strasse to discover the courtyards and wander through the maze of shops, cafés, and boutiques to get your retail fix. Originally a housing project, the area transformed over time into a quirky shopper's paradise, where unique finds wait around every corner. Keep your eyes peeled for deals! On Thursday and Saturday 09:00-18:00, there's a funky outdoor market selling handmade goods, snacks, and trinkets.

Rosenthaler Strasse 40-41, Mitte, +49 (0)30 2809 8010, S-Bahn: Hackescher Markt, U-Bahn: U Weinmeisterstrasse

Oranienstrasse & Bergmannstrasse
These two shopping streets in the district of Kreuzberg are geared toward people interested in vintage clothing, old records, books, and secondhand shops. These streets have a vibrant café culture, which makes them ideal for pleasant afternoons of window-shopping and people-watching. Oranienstrasse is most engaging between Oranienplatz and the Gorlitzer Bahnhof U-Bahn station. On Bergmannstrasse are charming cafés, shops, and restaurants running from Mehringdamm Strasse to the Marheineke Markthalle. Bergmannstrasse is a 20-minute bike ride south from Mitte, so time your visit here to overlap with a casual cruise through

the nearby and recommended Tempelhofer and Victoria parks.

Kreuzberg, U-Bahn: Gorlitzer Bahnhof
(for Oranienstrasse), U-Bahn: Gneisenaustrasse
(for Bergmannstrasse)

MARKETS

Berlin is a paradise for flea market hounds.
Macklemore would think he died and went
to thrift-shop heaven. Even the permanent
stores have a unique vintage edge to them,
so, whether you're buying new or used
items, you're sure to find tastefully eccentric styles and whatever else you may be
looking for.

Neukölln Flowmarkt

One of Berlin's newest and trendiest flea
markets, Neukölln Flowmarkt caters to hip
Berliners and in-the-know tourists. Located
alongside the Landwehrkanal canal, the
market sells funky, vintage clothing and
home wares, and there is a cornucopia of
top-notch food stalls. The market tends
to run every other Sunday, but check the
website to confirm dates, as they can vary
during winter break.

10:00-17:30 every other Sun, Neukölln Flowmarkt,
Maybachufer 31, Kreuzberg, nowkoelln.de,
U-Bahn: Schönleinstrasse

Türkischer Markt

The Türkischer Markt is the closest you'll
get to Istanbul's Grand Bazaar in Germany. This market serves the needs of the
Berlin's sizable Turkish community, so,
unsurprisingly, you can find some of the
best Turkish food around. The market also
sells clothes and a wide array of fabrics,
which has made it a popular spot with
Berlin's younger, DIY demographic who
like to design, sell, and wear their self-
made clothes.

Tues and Fri 11:30-18:30, Türkischer Markt, located
around Maybachufer 7, Kreuzberg, tuerkenmarkt.de,
U-Bahn: Schönleinstrasse

Mauerpark Flea Market

What was once a part of the Berlin Wall's
"death strip" (the no-man's-land between
the double walls) is now one of my favorite
outdoor markets in Europe. Brace yourself:
The throngs flocking to this popular flea
market can be overwhelming. Follow the
smell of fresh sauerkraut, currywurst, and
waffles until you find some enticing street
food—this should provide you enough energy to get you through a day of perusing
the stalls. Bands and magicians gather in
the amphitheater-like bowl, creating a jovial atmosphere. Many people who come
here (myself included) say they never want
to leave.

Sun 09:00-18:00, Bernauer Strasse 63-64, Prenzlauer
Berg, U-Bahn: Eberswalderstrasse

TOP PARKS & RECREATION

Tiergarten

When Berlin was still Prussian territory,
Tiergarten was the official hunting ground
of the king. It was converted into a public
park in the late 18th century. Spend an afternoon enjoying the many ponds, trees,
and open-air cafés this sprawling piece
of land has to offer. This leafy park takes
about 45 minutes to walk across, or you
can explore it more completely on a bike.

Climb 285 steps up the **Victory Column**
(€3 adults, Apr-Oct Mon-Fri 09:30-18:30
and Sat-Sun 09:30-19:00, Nov-Mar Mon-
Fri 10:00-17:00 and Sat-Sun 10:00-17:30,
Grosser Stern) in the middle of the park
for a beautiful panorama. The column
represents Prussia's victory over the Dan-
ish in 1864; by the time it was inaugurated
in 1873, Prussia had also been victorious
in conflicts with Austria and France. This
led the designers to further beautify the
monument, adding the golden statue of
the goddess Victoria (often referred to
by locals as Goldelse) to the top of the
column, where she stands with one arm
outstretched.

Thirsty? Head to **Tiergartenquelle** beer
garden (Bachstrasse, Mon-Fri 16:00-
24:00, Sat and Sun 12:00-24:00, S-Bahn:
Tiergarten) on the far west side of the park
for a pint. Hungry? Split any of the massive
meat-and-potatoes dishes with friends.

Free, always open, Central Berlin, S-Bahn: Tiergarten,
U-Bahn: Hansaplatz

SPREEPARK

What do a communist theme park, a cocaine smuggling bust, and unbelievable family drama have in common? Answer: Spreepark, Berlin's abandoned amusement park. In 1969, the communists opened Kulturpark Plänterwald in East Berlin and operated the amusement park continuously until the Wall fell. At that point, a family business headed up by Norbert Witte took over, changing the name to Spreepark. Spreepark's first few years went well. The owners added new rides, and visitors to the park climbed to 1.5 million per year. But the Witte family soon found themselves in hot water. The forest surrounding the park was rezoned, and Spreepark was not granted the permits it needed to add enough parking spaces to keep up with the growing number of customers. Ticket sales plateaued and then declined, and Witte slid deeper and deeper into debt.

At this point, Mr. Witte desperately searched for ways to move the park, sell the rides, and wash his hands of this whole ordeal. In 2002 he found an opportunity in Peru. He relocated his family (and six of the park's attractions), but he still couldn't get his head above water. With debts topping 10 million euros, he sought the help of "friends"—they were willing to help, but they wanted something in return. With his back against the wall, Witte arranged to ship his rides back to Germany—with over 400 pounds of cocaine hidden inside one of them! Witte, along with his son, was busted before he could leave Peru. Based on the amount of drugs found on Witte, the judge gave him eight years; even worse, because his son technically had more drugs on him when he was caught, the younger Witte was sentenced to 20 years (both father and son insist that the younger Witte knew nothing about his father's plans).

Nearly 15 years since Spreepark officially closed its gates, the park seems frozen in time. Adventurers often slip under or over the fence to get a peek of the park and its overgrown rides and the eerily empty grounds. Ferris wheels blow slowly in the wind, playhouses lean sideways, and swan boats float listlessly in scummy pond water. The site was taken over by the city in 2014 and remains closed to the public. Hopping the fence is certainly illegal, but many still get through and leave with pictures straight out of our worst fantasies about a postapocalyptic future. Check out a video I made about the park on my Facebook page (facebook. com/AndyStevesTravel). And if you decide to see for yourself, take the S-Bahn to Treptower Park or Plänterwald and look for a hole in the fence into Spreepark (there are a few of them).

Tempelhofer Field

The old Templehof airport was used by the Americans during the Berlin Airlift (June 24, 1948-May 12, 1949). When communists shut down land-access routes to West Germany, the Americans flew tons of food and supplies into the city—planes were landing as little as 2 minutes apart around the clock for 46 weeks. West Germans could not have survived without this help. Seeing the futility of the situation, the East Germans finally relented, allowing land-access routes to reopen. The field where the airport once stood is today an expansive park where Berliners come to relax. Cyclists, joggers, and kiteboarders run the airstrips rather than planes. The fascist-built terminal now has several sections that have been converted into temporary housing for thousands of refugees fleeing the conflict in Syria. From Mitte, Tempelhofer is about a 20-minute bike ride to the south.

Kreuzberg, M: Platz der Luftbrücke

Treptower Park

This park is home to the massive **Soviet War Memorial,** dedicated to the thousands who fell attempting to finish off the Nazis in the Battle of Berlin. Many of the

Red Army soldiers who died in the battle are buried here in Treptower. The monuments, heavy handed and at odds with the natural surroundings, are unmistakably Soviet.

Free, always open, S-Bahn: Treptower Park

TOP TOURS

Tours in this city are a must for those who want to make sense of a historical minefield (literally and figuratively). Each monument, each bullet-riddled façade, each public square has its own complex history, and, without a guide, this can be overwhelming. Guides will help you switch between the numerous lenses (medieval, Roaring '20s, Nazi Berlin, postwar Berlin, communist Berlin, and trendy modern Berlin) through which each space should be viewed. The best tours combine all of these lenses in a casual and introductory format that's perfect for first-time visitors. For history buffs who want to delve deeper, expert operators are available to provide more in-depth examinations of Berlin's history.

Brewer's Walks Berlin

The Brewer's team takes professional tour guiding to the next level. Come out for a history buff's enthralling all-day walking tour of the highlights of central Berlin or enjoy the free 3.5-hour walking tour each afternoon. Local experts, off-script and passionate about their hometown, delve deep into the historical events that put Berlin on the world stage. Choose from the **Free Berlin Tour** (free, tip-based, daily 13:00, 3.5 hours), the **Best of Berlin Tour** (€15, daily 10:30, 6 hours), or the **Local Beer & Breweries Tour** for serious aficionados (€35, tastings included, Thurs, Fri, and Sat 19:00, 3 hours).

All tours meet in front of Friedrichstrasse station at the corner of Friedrichstrasse and Georgenstrasse, Mitte, brewersberlintours.com, S+U-Bahn: Friedrichstrasse

Fat Tire Bike Tours

Fat Tire's enthusiastic guides help visitors grasp Berliner culture and history on two wheels over about 4.5 hours. Highlights along the route include the Berlin Wall, Hitler's Bunker, Museum Island, Checkpoint Charlie, Brandenburg Gate, the Victory Column, and the compelling Holocaust Memorial. Smart travelers make notes along the way so that they know where they've been and if/when they want to return. Tours meet on the north side of the TV Tower throughout the year at varying hours and days. You can extend your bike rental for an extra couple of days from €10 per day. Check out their website for tour details, prices, and meeting points.

€28 adults/€26 students, meet in front of the Starbucks under the TV Tower, Panoramastrasse 1a, Mitte, +49 (0)30 2404 7991, fattirebiketours.com/berlin, S+U-Bahn: Alexanderplatz

Alternative Berlin

Focusing on the fascinating subcultures that make up this diverse city, Alternative Berlin is a great choice for those interested in the street art and hidden neighborhoods that most tourists pass by without a second glance. Choose between their **free tour** (daily 11:00 and 13:00, 3 hours), the **Street Art Workshop** (€20, Mon, Wed, and Fri-Sat 12:00, 4.5 hours), and the **Real Berlin Experience** (€12, Tues, Thurs, and Fri-Sat 12:00, 4.5 hours), and their innovative and intimate small-group **666 Anti Pubcrawl** (€10, daily 21:00, free entry to five bars and clubs).

Walking tours meet outside Starbucks at the TV Tower, Mitte, alternativeberlin.com, S+U-Bahn: Alexanderplatz

Jimbo's Cheap Man's Bus Tour

Public bus 100 cuts straight through the center of Berlin, taking you on a double-decker ride past most of the city's major tourist sights. Create your very own hop-on, hop-off bus tour by listening to this free audio tour. Just google "Jimbo's Cheap Man's Bus Tour" and follow the link to the download. Thanks, Jimbo!

At the turnaround point, you'll be near the **Emperor William Memorial Church,** which dates back to the late 19th century. It was mostly destroyed in World War II, but one last tower remains standing (with a starkly modern extension nearby). It's a perfect example of Berlin's attempt to move forward without effacing the past. Inside the modern chapel, look for the architect's initials (EE) in the beautiful colored glass. There's a free ground-level exhibit with scale models of what the old church would have looked like before and after the war. You might notice some flowers strewn on the ground close the church. These are memorializing those who were run down when a terrorist plowed his vehicle through a Christmas market in 2016.

Audio tour free, bus ticket €2.40, bus runs every few minutes throughout the day, bus 100 running between Alexanderplatz (Mitte) and Zoologischer Garten, S+U-Bahn: Alexanderplatz

Sandeman's New Europe Walking Tours

Sandeman's came to Europe and shook up the tourism industry by offering mass-produced, scripted, tip-based walking tours led by expats and English speakers. Each day crowds gather to go on these entertaining 2.5-hour introductory tours of Berlin's center. During the tour you'll be given a tactfully short pitch about the company's other paid tours, including a day trip to **Sachsenhausen Concentration Camp** (€16, daily 11:00, 5+ hours), a **Red (Communist) Berlin** tour (€14, Tues, Thurs, and Sat 14:00, 3.5 hours), a day trip to **Potsdam** (€15, Wed, Fri, and Sun 11:00, 5+ hours), and, of course, the backpacker **pub crawl.**

Free tours daily at 11:00 and 14:00, meet at the Starbucks in front of Brandenburg Gate, Mitte, newberlintours.com, S-Bahn: Brandenburger Tor

TOP HOSTELS

You've got a plenty of options for a lively and social stay in Berlin. At one point, real estate was cheap, so owners collected properties and converted old buildings into fresh new hostels. Since then, real estate prices have skyrocketed, but prices for hostel beds have remained relatively flat—for now, at least.

Plus Berlin

One of the top-rated hostels in Berlin, this property is stumbling distance from the hottest nightlife venues in town and public transportation connections that will take you wherever else you need to go. The team at Plus does a great job checking you in, getting you oriented, and hooking you up with all sorts of activities and tours. Did I mention there's an indoor pool and sauna?

Beds from €14, 24-hour reception and security, free Wi-Fi throughout, laundry facilities, optional breakfast, on-site bar and restaurant, common areas, Warschauerplatz 6, Freidrichshain, +49 30 311698820, plushostels.com, U-Bahn: Warschauer Strasse

St. Christopher's Inns

Another solid addition to the St. Christopher's hostel chain, this place has it all: bar, lounge room, free showers, great location near Rosa-Luxemburg-Platz, and welcoming staff. Free walking tours depart from the hostel daily, and the drinks are cheap. Take advantage of their happy hour for added pregame value.

Beds from €16, 24-hour reception, free Wi-Fi, bar with happy hour, continental breakfast included, restaurant, Rosa-Luxemburg-Strasse 41, Mitte, +49 (0)30 8145 3960, st-christophers.co.uk/berlin-hostels, U-Bahn: Rosa-Luxemburg-Platz

Wombat's City Hostel Berlin

Wombat's Berlin location situates you right in the middle of Mitte, where you're virtually surrounded by endless restaurants, cafés, bars, and shopping. The on-site bar (with frequent happy hours) and rooftop patio (offering panoramic views of downtown) are solid places to kick off your night. At the end of the night, you'll return to spacious, modern, and clean rooms. Anything you might need lies within a 10-minute walking radius from Alexanderplatz, Rosenthaler Platz, and the Hackescher Hof.

Beds from €10, 24-hour reception, free Wi-Fi, bar, breakfast, rooftop patio, kitchen access, Alte Schonhauser Strasse 2, Mitte, +49 (0)30 8471 0820, wombats-hostels.com/berlin, U-Bahn: Rosa-Luxemburg-Platz

Circus Hostel

This classic Berliner hostel has a personal touch that makes it feel very different from its competitors. Enjoy the brewery downstairs and the tasty breakfast served each morning. Since the hostel is on the same street as International Restaurant Row, there are oodles of food and entertainment options only minutes away. Staff members lead free daily tours to far-flung corners of the city. If you're interested in private accommodations, check out their hotel and apartment listings online.

Beds from €18, 24-hour reception, free Wi-Fi, bar, breakfast, Weinbergsweg 1A, Prenzlauer Berg, +49 (0)30 2000 3939, circus-berlin.de, U-Bahn: Rosenthaler Platz

Generator Hostel Berlin East

Generator Hostel Berlin East offers clean facilities, loads of amenities, and all the pregame entertainment you could ask for. The Generator has its own bar and lounge, prime for mingling with other travelers, and is located in trendy Prenzlauer Berg, a hub of good shopping, convenient trains, and sophisticated nightlife.

From €14, 24-hour reception, free Wi-Fi, bar, restaurant, lockers, laundry facilities, mini market, Storkower Strasse 160, Prenzlauer Berg, +49 (0)30 417 24 00, generatorhostels.com, berlin@generatorhostels.com, S-Bahn: Landsberger Allee

Pfefferbett Hostels

This hostel in a massive former brewery is an affordable option for larger groups. Guests appreciate the clean rooms and retro-chic vibe. I like to relax in the backyard patio when the weather is nice, and the proximity to the Schönhauser Allee and Rosenthaler Platz nightlife makes for an easy stumble home. The team is working hard to install routers to get Wi-Fi to reach all rooms, but for now the signal only reaches the common room (they've got the thick brick walls to thank for that).

Beds from €15, 24-hour reception and bar, free Wi-Fi in lounge, breakfast, Christinenstrasse 18-19, Prenzlauer Berg, +49 (0)30 9393 5858, pfefferbett.de/en, U-Bahn: Senefelderplatz

TRANSPORTATION

GETTING THERE & AWAY
Plane

Berlin is served by two airports: **Schoenfeld** (SXF, popular with budget airlines) and **Tegel** (TXL). Find information on both at berlin-airport.de. A third airport, the Berlin Brandenburg Airport (BER), is scheduled to be completed in the spring of 2018.

Schoenfeld is about 15 miles south of the city center. From the airport, take Airport Express train RE7 or RB14 into the center and connect to the city's S- and U-Bahn systems. Connections leave every 30 minutes, cost €3.30, and take about 40 minutes.

If you're flying with major airlines, you'll likely arrive at the Tegel airport. Take bus

TXL into the city center. It stops at all three key transportation hubs: Zoologischer Garten, Hauptbahnhof, and Alexanderplatz. This bus takes about 30 minutes, costs €2.70, and leaves every 10 minutes.

Train

Trains from Prague reach Berlin in 4.5 hours. They run eight times daily and cost €40. Trains to Munich take about 6 hours and cost €90.

Just about all international arrivals show up at the massive, four-level Hauptbahnhof, on the western edge of Mitte. Berlin's other major stations are Ostbahnhof, in Friedrichshain; Spandau, on the far western edge of the city; and Zoologischer Garten, in the center, bordering Tiergarten Park. All stations have transfer connections with the S-Bahn public transportation network, so it's not difficult to get wherever you need to go.

Bus

The main bus station is Zentraler Omnibus-Bahnhof in West Berlin. From here you have easy connections with both the S-Bahn and the U-Bahn that simplify your trip into the center. When connecting out of town, leave at least an hour to get to the bus station (45 minutes in transit from Mitte and 15 minutes to hit the bathroom, grab a snack, and find your bus).

Car

Berlin is about 650 kilometers (6.5 hours) east of Amsterdam via the A2 highway. It's about 350 kilometers (3.5 hours) north of Prague via the A13 highway. It's about 600 kilometers (6 hours) to Munich via the A9 highway through Leipzig and Nuremburg.

GETTING AROUND

Walking is a great way to explore Berlin, but this colossal city would take hours to traverse end-to-end on foot. Try to gauge the distance ahead of time and organize your strolls by neighborhood, hopping on trams or the metro to save time and energy.

Berlin has an excellent **public transportation system**, but, as with other transportation systems in major European capitals, the first day or two of using it can be overwhelming. Study the transit maps and, once you get adjusted, you'll be zipping around Berlin on its trams, buses, and underground in no time. Once you can associate a few of the stations with the landmarks close to them, you'll be well on your way.

S-Bahn, U-Bahn, buses, and trams all use the same ticket. A single ticket costs €2.80 for zones A and B (which cover the city of Berlin itself but not Schoenfeld airport or outlying cities) and allows as many transfers as you wish for a total of two hours. The **day ticket** (€7) pays for itself by the third ride in one day, and a **weekly pass** will cost you €30. The **Small Group Day Ticket** (€20) is valid for unlimited group travel (up to 5 people) until 03:00 the following morning—easily the best deal in town.

S-Bahn & U-Bahn

The city is crisscrossed by Berlin's integrated metro system, which includes both U-Bahn and S-Bahn lines. Purchase your

ticket from one of the machines at each station. You must validate it before your journey by sticking one end into any of the validation machines located on platforms and station entry areas. Ticket control comes through often checking for validated tickets and fining those who can't present one (to avoid these fines, watch the locals and do as they do). While the S- and U-Bahns close down around 01:00 during the week, they run all night on Fridays and Saturdays.

Bus

When riding the bus, follow the same rules as you would for the metro. For a time- and wallet-efficient introduction to the city's layout, jump on bus 100. It's a double-decker bus cutting through the center of Berlin, connecting most major tourist sights, including the Reichstag and Brandenburg Gate, and ending at Alexanderplatz. Bus 100 departs from Zoo Station on the west side of town about every five minutes. Visit bvg.de for information on night bus schedules.

Tram

More than 20 new and comfortable tram lines make up Berlin's tram network, extending the reach of the S- and U-Bahns to the street level. Clear signage at each stop helps you know when your tram is coming and where it's going.

Bike

Renting a bike for the weekend makes this sprawling city accessible. Berlin, not wanting to be left behind by cities like Copenhagen and Amsterdam, has spent considerable amounts of capital and energy to make itself more bike friendly. Designated bike paths nearly everywhere are the fruits of these labors. Heads-up: Many intersections in Berlin's Mitte don't have street signs or lights, so it's up to cars, bikes, and pedestrians to yield to each other. Consider a tour with Fat Tire Bike Tours to see Berlin's traditional highlights and a number of more alternative neighborhoods as well.

Taxi

Taxis charge a flat rate of €3.20 plus €1.65 for each kilometer. They definitely aren't the cheapest option, so they're best split between friends when coming home after late-night partying on the far side of town. I've found **Taxi Berlin** (+49 (0)3020 2020, taxi-berlin.de) a reliable operator. If you're traveling in groups, ask for a *"Grossraumtaxi,"* a van with space for up to six people for the same price as a sedan.

DAY TRIPS

Sachsenhausen Concentration Camp

Sachsenhausen is the best option near Berlin for those who want to experience the remnants of a concentration camp or commemorate the victims of the Holocaust. It's located in the suburbs, a frightening proximity to the capital that demonstrates the brazenness of the Nazis. This was one of the first such facilities, a place where the Nazis tested the concentration camp model on human subjects—mostly Jews and political prisoners. As World War II progressed, their program of mass murder became chillingly systematic, and executions were commonplace. By the end the conflict some 200,000 souls had passed through these gates; 10,000 of them would die in the camp, either starved or tortured to death or executed.

A visit to Sachsenhausen provides a good overview of this machinery of death. The history is discussed in the on-site museum, which includes exhibits in the barracks and near the blood-curdling execution trench. The camp is free to enter, and there are tours (some for a fee, others based on donation) that run throughout the day. The paid tours are well worth the cost—they'll help you understand (as much as it is possible to understand) the horrors that unfolded in Sachsenhausen's living quarters and cells. **Official tours** (€14) of the camp are offered on Tuesday, Thursday, and Saturday at 11:45 and 14:30 at the visitors center in the south corner of the camp. The first tour has an optional meeting time in Berlin in Mitte (Potsdamer Platz by the historic traffic light tower at 10:20). Transportation is not included in the price. **Sandeman's New Berlin Tours** also provides day trips to Sachsenhausen from Berlin (€16, daily 11:00, 5+ hours).

To get there on your own from central Berlin, take the S1 or regional trains RE5 or RB12 to the end of the line (Oranienburg). From the station, it's a one-mile walk north following the signs to Gedenkstatte Sachsenhausen, or bus 821 takes visitors to the camp hourly in four stops. You can also opt for a short taxi ride from Oranienburg station to the camp; it should cost no more than €8. The whole journey takes about an hour each way via public transport.

Free, mid-Mar-mid-Oct daily 08:30-18:00, mid-Oct-mid-Mar daily 08:30-16:30, Strasse der Nationen 22, Oranienburg, +49 (0)3301 200 0, stiftung-bg.de/gums/en

Potsdam & Frederick the Great's Palaces

Forty kilometers southwest of Berlin is the town of Potsdam, where you'll find a gigantic park sprinkled with awe-inspiring 18th-century palaces built by Prussian ruler Frederick the Great. Germany's equivalent to Versailles, these ostentatiously opulent palaces are in dialogue with their French, English, and Austrian counterparts—each successive monarch tried to outdo the grandeur of his rivals. The palace's gardens seem to stretch forever, and so do the palaces. You'll find yourself leaving one palace and its hundreds of rooms behind you, and you'll gaze down a corridor of carefully manicured hedges and trees. What's that at the end of the pathway? It's yet another rococo palace, just as magnificent as the one you've just seen

The most famous and popular palaces to see are **Sanssouci** (€12, Nov-Mar Tues-Sun 10:00-17:00, Apr-Oct Tues-Sun 10:00-18:00, closed Mon) and the **New Palace** (€8, Apr-Oct Wed-Mon 10:00-18:00, Nov-Mar Wed-Mon 10:00-17:00, closed Tues). If you plan to visit both, buy the **Sanssouci+ ticket** (€19), which covers a single visit to all the Potsdam palaces (seeing them all in one day is quite the feat). Find more information on the palaces at spsg.de/en or by calling +49 (0)331 96 94 200. **Sandeman's New Berlin Tours** also offers day trips to Potsdam from Berlin (€14, Wed, Fri, and Sun 11:00, 5+ hours).

Connections to Potsdam are easy. Simply connect to the S7 in central Berlin or the RE1 regional train and take it out to Potsdam Hauptbahnhof. The trip is less than an hour each way.

HELP!

Tourist Information Centers

Berlin's tourist information centers earn commissions from hotels and sightseeing tours, so be wary of the products you're being offered. Find information centers at Hauptbahnhof train station and at Brandenburg Gate.

Pickpockets & Scams

Violent crime against tourists is virtually nonexistent in Berlin. Still, keep a close eye on your valuables while in train stations and other crowded areas. Always be on your guard if someone approaches you with questions, especially when they come within arm's length or closer. Do not accept any discount train tickets from street sellers—they are counterfeit, and they'll do you as much good with the ticket control as a chewing gum wrapper.

Emergencies

In an emergency, dial 112.

Hospital

Campus Mitte, Humboldt-Universität Faculty
Charitéplatz 1
+49 (0)30 450 50

US Embassy

Clayallee 170
14159 Berlin
+49 (0)30 830 50

PRAGUE

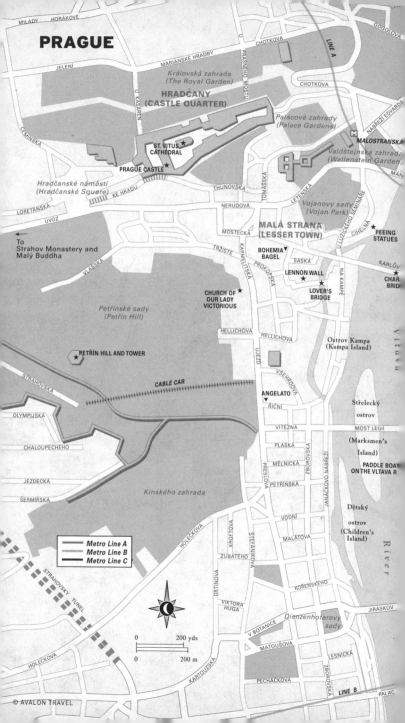

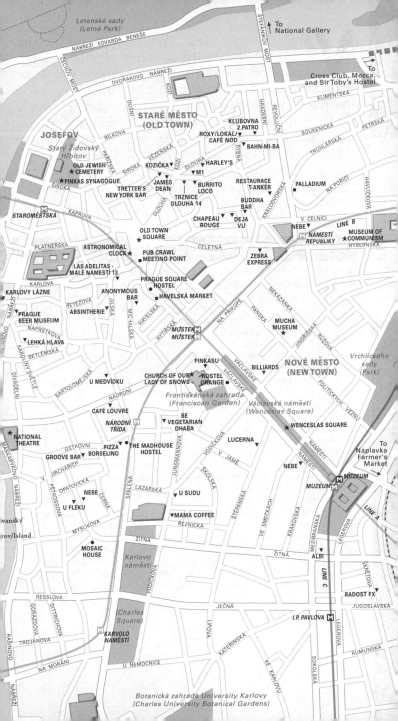

Visiting Prague feels like stepping into a time machine. The "City of One Hundred Spires" escaped widespread bombing in World War II and often provides an old-world backdrop in movies. Today, the traces of Czech-Soviet history are fading away as modern capitalism integrates itself into daily life. Wander the cobblestone streets, sip cheap beers in cozy pubs, and explore the timeless castle on the hill. You'll love Prague for its bohemian and baroque architecture, raucous nightlife, and picturesque setting, tucked into a bend in the Vltava River.

PRAGUE 101

The Prague and the Czech Republic we know today were very different places until the late 1980s. Because the Russians were the ones to liberate Czechoslovakia from Nazi Germany in 1945, the majority of Czech people were pro-Russia. Strong ties were formed with the USSR and its ideals of a communist state. In 1948, the Communist Party won control of the Czech government, and Czechoslovakia joined the ranks of other Central European countries in the Soviet Bloc.

With the support of Moscow and a highly oppressive government, the Czech economy saw a dramatic improvement. Yet with this growth also came the price of pursuing that "improved" communist state: mass imprisonment, corruption, and rigged trials. Once the boundaries and laws became clear to the people, the government eased up a bit, and a new way of thinking began to emerge. Greater freedom was granted in the media, the arts, and citizens' right to travel during this period, which became known as the Prague Spring.

These reforms were seen as a threat to communism, as they resembled the West and its "bourgeois" approach to life. Soviet troops, along with those from other Warsaw Pact nations, invaded Czechoslovakia on August 21, 1968, forcibly ending this progressive trend. Over the next 20 years, a period of "normalization" ensued that emphasized censorship, spying, and police brutality. This led to the stagnation of the Czech economy, as well as the arrests and abductions of more than 250,000 people who were seen as threats to the communist state.

By the late 1980s, the people had reached their limits. From November 17 to December 29, 1989, hundreds of thousands of Prague's citizens gathered in Wenceslas Square in the peaceful protest known as the Velvet Revolution. These protests led to the end of the single-party communist state and played a large role in the collapse of the Soviet sphere of influence as a whole in Central Europe. Czechoslovakia's first president, Václav Havel, was voted into office on December 29, 1989. A few years later, on January 1, 1993, Czechoslovakia peacefully dissolved into two different countries, forming what we now know as the Czech Republic and Slovakia.

PLAN AHEAD

RESERVATIONS

Additional security and crowds in the high season make reservations a smart idea for **Prague Castle** (hrad.cz/en/prague-castle).

The locals know that the best way to beat the crowds is to call ahead. They make reservations for food and nights out—everything from dinner and drinks to coffee and tea. The best spots in Prague are almost always brimming with tourists, so think like a local and skip the lines by reserving a ticket or a table a day or two ahead of time. This is a must if you want a table at one of the many popular local bars or clubs.

LOCAL HAPPENINGS

One World Film Festival

Movie lovers often time their visit to coincide with the **One World Film Festival** (Lucerna Cinema, Štepánská 61, oneworld. cz), which takes place in Prague around mid-March. It's the largest human rights film festival in the world, so don't go expecting light fare. Instead, you'll find sobering and thought-provoking documentaries that shine a light into some of the world's darkest corners.

Velvet Revolution Anniversary

A public holiday on November 17 commemorates the 1989 Velvet Revolution, a series of peaceful protests held in Wenceslas Square that saw the Czechs throw off the shackles of communism. Revelers take to the streets with a mix of pride and a bit of nostalgia of the stress-free (if freedom-free) times. Time has healed most of the wounds left behind by brutal communist rule, so the feeling is more festive than it is somber. Massive stages set up across town turn the entire city into one big no-holds-barred party.

KNOW BEFORE YOU GO

KEY STATS & FIGURES

Currency:
The Czech Republic uses the Czech koruna (Kč); 25Kč = about 1 USD

Population:
1,250,000

Language:
Czech

Number of metro lines:
3

Amount of beer consumed annually per capita:
143 liters

National drinks:
slivovice (a moonshine liquor made from plums) *becherovka* (an herbal bitters), and pilsner

Souvenir of choice:
puppets, Bohemian crystal

Favorite TV shows among Czechs:
The Simpsons, Friends, and *How I Met Your Mother*

CALIBRATE YOUR BUDGET

TYPICAL PRICES FOR:

Hostel dorm bed:
400Kč

Two-course dinner:
250Kč

Pint of beer:
39Kč

Metro pass:
24Kč

MOVIES TO WATCH
EuroTrip, Amadeus, Hellboy, Mission: Impossible, Kafka, A Knight's Tale, Anthropoid

PRAGUE

THREE DAY ITINERARY

It's easy to experience Prague entirely on foot. Wear comfortable walking shoes for this tour of the city.

DAY 1: OLD TOWN
MORNING

Kick off your visit with a hearty, breakfast at **Café Louvre,** the most classic of Prague's many Old Town cafés. After breakfast, make your way toward **Old Town Square.** Keep your eyes up to admire the baroque architecture above. On the southwest corner of the square is the 600-year-old **Astronomical Clock.** Time your arrival to coincide with the chiming of the hours, when the clock springs to life.

Join a free three-hour walking tour with **Sandeman's New Europe Walking Tours,** which meets daily at 10:45 at the Astronomical Clock. Your guide will take you through the **Jewish Quarter** and **Wenceslas Square** and over the **Charles Bridge** for some great selfie ops.

AFTERNOON

For a quick and healthy lunch, stop just outside the Jewish Quarter at the posh grocery store **Tržnice Dlouhá 14.** Return to the river to soak up the sun. Find a vantage point upriver from the Charles Bridge to take in the view or go for a paddleboat ride on the Vltava and take a picture from the middle of the river. The paddleboats can be rented from friendly vendors on **Slovanský Island.**

Next, head back into town for a pre-party drink at **AnonymouS Bar,** a fun speakeasy-style cocktail lounge with a mod sinister twist. If you like cocktails, stop in the nearby **Hemingway Bar** (reservations recommended) for a more classic setting.

EVENING

To experience Prague's bars properly, you'll need a guide. My favorite is the stress-free **Drunken Monkey Pub Crawl.** Look for the team in blue underneath the Astronomical Clock in the Old Town Square, nightly 21:00-23:00. If you're more interested in culture than nightlife, catch a live concert in one of the Prague's many theaters or concert venues or a baroque church or opera house. For more information, check the **ticket office** in the Týn Church passage just off Old Town Square.

LATE

For a late-night snack, the *klobasa* sausages sold at the street stands on Wenceslas Square are tasty. To really hit the spot, try one of the burritos rolling out of **Burrito Loco.**

DAY 2: LESSER QUARTER & CASTLE DISTRICT
MORNING

Shake off that hangover with a hefty breakfast sandwich at **Bohemia Bagel** across Charles Bridge in the **Lesser Quarter.** Loop around the corner for the **Church of Our Lady Victorious,** the **John Lennon Wall,** the **Lover's Bridge,** and the **peeing statues,** all within a 20-minute walking radius.

Once you've taken in the sights in the lower-lying areas, begin your hike uphill to the **Prague Castle** and **St. Vitus Cathedral.** It's free to visit the front

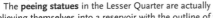

SPIRALLY, SUGARY GOODNESS: THE *TRDELNÍK*

The *trdelník* (pronounced tdr-DEL-neek) is a sugary, doughy treat that has nothing to do with the Czech Republic, but it's a favorite of tourists who don't seem to care. The bakers take a roll of dough and wrap it around a wooden cylinder to cook and toast the dough into a chewy, golden-brown dessert. When they're ready, the doughy spirals are tapped off the log and rolled in sugar, spice, and everything nice. Prices climb to 60Kč each, but it's worth it to keep your blood sugar up on those long days of sightseeing. Enterprising vendors have popped up all over town, several of them now offering to fill the treat with Nutella and soft-serve ice cream. A cold, stale *trdelník* is a complete waste of money, though this doesn't prevent vendors from selling them to hungry tourists lured by the smell of fresh ones; only buy *trdelníks* if they are steaming hot.

Dishes from 100Kč, daily 10:00-22:00, Strahovské Nádvoří 1/132, Castle District, +420 233 107 704, strahovskyklaster.cz, Tram: Pohořelec

Malý Buddha

For vegetarian food, Malý Buddha ("Little Buddha") is among the best in the city. Inside, it feels a little like you've stumbled into a hodgepodge of all the world's Asian restaurants (there's a large painting of Buddha on one of the walls and bamboo everywhere). Enjoy stir-fried and roasted veggie and tofu dishes in the quiet, warm ambience. There's a good mixture of healthy options and meat dishes—the former may come as a welcome respite for vegetarians or those who have grown weary of heavier Czech cuisine.

Dishes around 120-240Kč, Tues-Sun 12:00-22:30, Úvoz 46, Castle District, +420 220 513 894, malybuddha.cz, Tram: Pohořelec

Bahn Mi-Ba

The Czech Republic welcomed many refugees from the Vietnam War, many of whom settled in Prague and opened either convenience stores or sandwich shops such as this one. Simple, healthy, and filling, fresh Vietnamese baguette sandwiches (bahn mi) are a great snack when you just need a quick bite before moving on to the next museum or church. You'll find multiple locations around town. This location just off Dlouha is one of my favorites; another is near Wenceslas Square (daily 10:30-22:00,

Panská 1308/9, New Town, +420 607 777 354).

Sandwiches from 100Kč, daily 11:00-22:00, Rybná 26, Old Town, +420 734 487 324, facebook.com/banhmibacz, Tram: Dlouhá třída

Pizza Borsalino

The slices from Pizza Borsalino are an excellent late-night snack. Open nearly 24 hours, this pizza shop is a great place to stop in for something that can be wolfed down in the midst of a busy day of shopping or seeing the sights. The shop is a popular one and the pies disappear remarkably quickly, meaning that the slice you get will be hot and fresh. The service leaves much to be desired, but it's not a deterrent.

30Kč slices, daily 11:00-05:00, Ostrovní 102/34, New Town, +420 777 940 079, borsalinopizza.cz, Tram: Národní třída

Buddha Bar

Buddha Bar is an Asian fusion chain restaurant with locations around the world. It features a creative menu with fresh salads, innovative sushi rolls, numerous other main options, an extensive wine menu, and delicious, expertly mixed cocktails. The service is impeccable, and the ambience is breathtaking. Start upstairs with a cocktail at the bar. When you're ready, descend for a quasi-spiritual culinary experience at the foot of a giant statue of Buddha. Stay late

part of the cathedral, but you'll be missing a great deal if you don't go inside. A ticket will give you full access to the cathedral and three other locations in the castle. The longest queues are between 10:00 and 13:00, and the shortest of the three security lines tends to be the one at the top of the staircase entry on the east side of the castle.

AFTERNOON
In summer months, you'll find a bustling beer and wine garden just outside the castle's downhill exit, to the left as you look down the long staircase. Or you can double back through the castle to the uphill end to find the **Strahov Monastery Brewery,** my favorite place for a filling afternoon meal in a classic beer hall setting (reservations are strongly advised during high season).

If you opt for the brewery, consider visiting the tiny museum in the courtyard, **Prague's Miniature Museum. Petřín Hill** is also just south of the monastery. Descend through the steeply sloping park into the city, stopping at the **Memorial to the Victims of Communism.** Emaciated statues—representing the many liberties that atrophied during Soviet rule—haunt the staircase. Cross the street at the bottom of the steps for the best gelato in town at **Angelato.**

EVENING
Head out to Prague's most famous party street, **Dlouhá,** where you can start the night at the **Prague Beer Museum.** The beer is sure to stimulate your appetite. Head to **Lokál** for some hearty Czech cuisine. Also nearby are: **Klubovna 2. Patro, M1, James Dean, Steampunk, Tretter's, Harley's, Café Nod,** and **Roxy.**

DAY 3: DELVE DEEPER
MORNING
Whether you need a detox or just want to start your day with a healthy kick, stop in at my favorite coffee shop and vegetarian café: **Mama Coffee.** When you're ready to start exploring, you've got a few options: If you're a history buff or you're particularly interested in Prague's Jewish roots, visit the **Jewish Quarter,** especially the **Pinkas Synagogue** and the **Old Jewish Cemetery.** The **Museum of Communism** will give you a nuanced understanding of the Soviet period and its important figures. If you're an art lover, stop by the **Mucha Museum** to learn why Prague is a mecca of art nouveau. The museums are close to each other (find them both just north of Wenceslas Square) and wonderfully compact. You can tackle the pair of them in about 90 minutes.

AFTERNOON
For lunch, stay in the center. **Kozička** boasts excellent food and an inviting atmosphere. If you haven't already tried one, get a *trdelník* (spiraled pastry) from a street vendor and stroll south along the Vltava. As the afternoon winds to a close, climb the steps to the **Vyšehrad Castle.** In summer, you'll find outdoor bars and grills vending hot brats and cold beer.

EVENING
All Czeched out? Grab some margaritas and some tacos at **Las Adelitas,** my favorite Mexican spot in Prague. It's just steps from the Old Town Square.

LATE
If you went bar-hopping on your first and second nights, hit the clubs on your last night. Get low at **Radost** (their hip-hop night is great for those who have grown weary of Euro-techno). For top-notch pregaming, start your evening with excellent cocktails and great music at **Alibi.**

TOP NEIGHBORHOODS

The city of Prague straddles a bend in the Vltava River. The river makes for a great navigational aid, as long as you remember that it turns around the Old Town at nearly 90 degrees near Prague Castle and Letná Park. The **Old Town** (Staré Město) is where you'll find the famous **Old Town Square** and **Astronomical Clock,** as well as the **Jewish Quarter** (Josefov), which houses arguably the best collection of Jewish sights in Europe. The Jewish Quarter is also Prague's poshest district, with fine dining, fancy cafés, and high-fashion stores like Dolce & Gabbana and Prada. On the east side of the river, south of the Old Town, is the **New Town** (Nové Město), which includes Wenceslas Square.

From Old Town, cross the iconic Charles Bridge to discover the relatively quiet and ritzier **Lesser Quarter** (Malá Strana, with sights like the Lennon Wall and the peeing statues), tucked between the **Castle District** (Hradčany), **Petřín Hill** (capped by the Petřín Tower), **Letná Park** (with the giant, ticking red metronome) and the Vltava River.

Just north of Letná Park you'll find Prague's trendy up-and-coming district, **Prague 7** (Holešovice), home to some of the city's hottest clubs and backpacker hostels.

TOP SIGHTS

Old Town Square (Staroměstské náměstí)

Dating to the late 12th century, the Old Town Square was the central marketplace and hub of commerce in medieval Prague. As the centuries ticked by, Romanesque, baroque, and Gothic buildings rose around the square's edges.

While you're waiting for the Astronomical Clock to do its mechanical dance at the top of the hour, check out all the sights in Old Town Square. Step inside the ornate **St. Nicholas Church** or the Gothic **Týn Church** (Church of Our Lady Before Týn), accessed through a narrow passage in the building extending from the church's facade. Be sure to pop in to the **concert ticket vendor** right next to the front door of the church, where you can book cheap tickets to beautiful (and succinct) string and symphony concerts held in stunning and often historic venues around town. The vendors mark up these tickets considerably, so don't be afraid to haggle—they'll often shave a little off the top. Go for the cheap seats; almost all the venues boast excellent acoustics. Make one of these concerts the center of your evening and you'll be leaving Prague a touch more cultured than when you arrived.

The proud **Jan Hus statue** in the center of the square is a testament to the man who stood up against the Vatican in the 15th century. The 27 crosses in the cobblestones next to the tower are a tribute to the 27 leaders who were executed in 1621 as a result of the failed Protestant rebellion against Ferdinand II and the Holy Roman Empire.

Free, square always open, churches open generally dawn to dusk, Old Town, Metro: Staroměstská

Astronomical Clock

Take a moment and try to decipher this complex time-telling machine. Find it difficult? Imagine gazing upon this marvel of clock-making engineering back when it was constructed in the early 1400s. Designed by Mikulus of Kadan in 1410, the two outer circles of the clock show us Bohemian time (represented by the numbers 1-24) and modern time (represented by two sets of Roman numerals I-XII). The blue area of the clockface represents daylight hours, the orange and brown represent dawn and dusk, and the black represents night. The sun attached to the big hand signifies the its position in the sky (it'll be over the black at night), and the small hand represents the moon's position. The inner offset circle displays the signs of the zodiac.

The smaller circle beneath the clock was added in the late 19th century, depicting the date, zodiac sign, and pictures of everyday peasant life. If you look closely, you will also notice that every day of the year is inscribed around the circle with its patron saint, with an indicator showing the current date.

The four statuettes on either side of the clock represent the four despised traits of the day, manifested through a series of unapologetic, politically incorrect stereotypes: Vanity looking into the mirror, Greed represented through the caricature of a Jew holding moneybags, a guilty Turk succumbing to pleasures of the flesh, and a skeleton warning these hedonists of the imminent arrival of their final judgment day.

At the top of each hour, tourists and pickpockets alike gather to watch the 12 apostles parade through the two window openings. Though it's a show without 3-D glasses and special effects, you can't help but smile at this charming performance, which has been happening hourly for over 600 years. The performance is capped by a caped trumpeter beckoning you to climb the stairs of the **Old Town Hall Tower** (250Kč adults, 150Kč students, Mon 11:00-22:00, Tues-Sun 09:00-22:00) for spectacular views of the city.

Free, Old Town Square, Old Town, +420 236 002 629, staromestskaradnicepraha.cz, Metro: Staroměstská

Jewish Quarter

The Jewish Quarter (Josefov) takes up a full district of downtown Prague. Pariska Street, its primary boulevard, leads from the north end of Old Town Square and bisects the district. In a turn-of-the-20th-century attempt to modernize the city, much of Josefov was leveled, leaving only six synagogues where there were once dozens. Countless Jewish artifacts were collected with the aim of creating a museum tracing the history of European Jews—chillingly, Hitler approved of this, planning to call it the Museum of an Extinct Race.

Buy the Jewish Museum of Prague's **Ticket B** to gain access to the six main attractions in the Jewish Quarter: Maisel Synagogue, Pinkas Synagogue, Old Jewish Cemetery, Klausen Synagogue, Ceremonial Hall, and Spanish Synagogue. To avoid the often-long queue at the sights, pop into any of the neighborhood corner shops that have the Ticket B picture in the window. Buying a Ticket B from a corner shop will save you 30 minutes of standing in line.

Ticket B 330Kč, Jewish Quarter attractions Nov-Mar Sun-Fri 09:00-16:30, Apr-Oct Sun-Fri 09:00-18:00, closed Sat and Jewish holidays, Jewish Quarter, +420 222 749 211, jewishmuseum.cz, Metro: Staroměstská

Pinkas Synagogue

This synagogue in the Jewish Quarter has been converted into a memorial to the 80,000 Jewish victims of the Holocaust from this region. On its walls are inscribed the names of all the victims, delineated by family name and the known dates of birth and death. In a room upstairs, you can also find chilling crayon drawings by young children sequestered into Prague's Jewish ghetto before their deportation by the occupying Nazis.

Ticket B 330Kč, Nov-Mar Sun-Fri 09:00-16:30, Apr-Oct Sun-Fri 09:00-18:00, closed Sat and Jewish holidays, Široká 23/3, Jewish Quarter, +420 222 749 211, jewishmuseum.cz, Metro: Staroměstská

Old Jewish Cemetery

In this graveyard—the oldest surviving Jewish cemetery in Europe—the dead had to be buried on top of each other due to lack

of space. There are approximately 12 burial layers, more than 12,000 gravestones, and an estimated 100,000 souls buried here. A walk through this cemetery feels like stepping onto the set of a Tim Burton movie. The tombstones echo the haphazard arrangement of the Jewish Quarter as it looked before its demolition. Passages between the stones are narrow in places, nonexistent in others. The moss-covered headstones, some of them dating to the fifteenth century, lean their heads together, seeming to seek solace in community.

Ticket B 330Kč, Nov–Mar Sun–Fri 09:00–16:30, Apr–Oct Sun–Fri 09:00–18:00, closed Sat and Jewish holidays, next to Pinkas Synagogue, Široká, Jewish Quarter, +420 222 749 211, jewishmuseum.cz, Metro: Staroměstská

Charles Bridge (Karlův most)

Named after King Charles IV, who reigned during Prague's golden age, this wide stone bridge connects Old Town Prague with the Castle Quarter and Lesser Quarter. Legend has it that the keystone was laid in 1357 on 9 July at 5:31—a numerical palindrome (1357.9.7.531) that the town's astrologers and numerologists deemed auspicious. They might have been on to something: The bridge has stood stone-faced and steadfast for more than 700 years, withstanding countless wars, floods, and political upheavals. It's sustained heavy damage a number of times, but it'll take more than a few fallen arches to knock old Charles off his feet.

Day and night the bridge is packed with pedestrian traffic, trinket vendors, and caricature artists. At sunrise, though, it's practically deserted, allowing you to have it all to yourself. Notice how the twin towers on the Lesser Quarter side of the bridge are fraternal twins, not identical ones: One of them was recycled from a bridge that predates the Charles Bridge by a few centuries. You'll see deep gashes in the gateway between these two towers that might look as though Godzilla passed through, sharpening his talons on the way. These are the whetting-marks of mercenaries, who honed their weapons on these stones before battle.

Free, always open, Metro: Staroměstská

Prague Castle (Pražský hrad) & St. Vitus Cathedral

Prague Castle, with its medieval crenellations and turrets, stands tall like a proudly popped collar riding the high ridge that overlooks and defends Prague. This has always been the seat of Czech power as well as the official residence of the country's rulers. Constructed in the 9th century, the castle began as a wooden fortress surrounded by earthen bulwarks, slowly transforming into the imposing stone fortress it is today. Each ruler expanded the castle and its fortifications to some degree, so there's a potpourri of styles on display. Neoclassical additions obscure parts of the medieval castle from view, but only partly; the castle's stolid and martial roots run deep and are impossible to conceal.

Don't miss the breathtaking **St. Vitus Cathedral** (Apr–Oct Mon–Sat 09:00–17:00, Nov–Mar 09:00–16:00, Sun from 12:00, last entrance at 15:40 in winter, 14:40 in summer). You can enter for free and take a peek from the narthex. Go all the way up to the corner of the roped-off area and peer left for an often-overlooked masterpiece, a work of stained glass by Alfons Mucha. The piece—a richly colored depiction of Czech's patron saint and the saints who brought Christianity to the Slavs—is unlike any other piece of stained glass in Europe; this is partly because it's painted glass, which gave Mucha more freedom to shade and blend his palette.

Spring for a **Prague Castle Circuit B ticket** (250Kč) from any of the numerous ticket offices within the castle complex. It will give you access to **St. George's Basilica** and the grand **Old Royal Palace.** You'll also get to check out the **Golden Lane** (accessed by turning left on Zlatá Ulička u Daliborky), a cutesy street with dwarf-sized houses (free for visitors once the shops close down, included in your Circuit B ticket, Apr–Oct daily after 16:00, Nov–Mar daily after 15:00).

Adults from 250Kč, students from 125Kč to go inside the castle, churches, and Golden Lane; castle open daily 05:00–24:00, historic buildings open Apr–Oct daily 09:00–17:00, until 16:00 Nov–Mar, last entrance at 15:40, Pražský Hrad, Castle District, +420 224 37 3368, hrad.cz/en/prague-castle, Tram: Pražský Hrad, Metro: Malostranská

DAVID ČERNÝ'S CHARMING LOVE OF THE ABSURD

The Czechs have developed a unique and intriguing sense of self-deprecating humor, evidenced in various forms throughout the city. Nobody demonstrates this so well as Prague's own David Černý, the artist who is responsible for just about all of the slightly subversive statues and installations around the city. Černý takes an irreverent approach to today's hot-button geopolitical issues, using his controversial statues as a form of pointed political commentary.

The **peeing statues** in the Lesser Quarter are actually relieving themselves into a reservoir with the outline of the Czech Republic. Inside the Lucerna building just off Wenceslas Square, there's a statue of Czech's patron saint, St. Wenceslas, riding bare...belly (the piece is in flippant dialogue with the more conventional clothed statue at the top of the square outside).

Just off of Betlémské Square, you'll spot a man hanging by one arm high above the street with his eyes trained on the ground below, a reminder that Big Brother 's always watching. The massive TV tower in the Žižkov neighborhood has **giant baby statues** crawling up and down its vertical tubular walls.

Finally, tucked behind the shopping center at Národní třída, you'll see a large metal sculpture in the shape of **Franz Kafka's head.** The kinetic sculpture is one of Prague's most stunning public works of art. As the sculpture goes through its churning patterns, oscillating between fast and slow, Kafka's face appears, and then just as quickly disappears. The effect is breathtaking.

David Černý also owns a club about 20 minutes south of town called **Meet Factory** (meetfactory.cz), where DJs and artists come out to spin the night away.

Lennon Wall

After John Lennon's assassination in 1980, young Czechs created an unofficial memorial in the Lesser Quarter. The spontaneous outpouring of love and sorrow left behind a wall nearly entirely covered in graffiti messages speaking of the hope for freedom, peace, and unity. The communist government considered phrases like "Imagine" and "All You Need Is Love" subversive and had them painted over immediately, but the rebellious teens didn't give up. Night after night, they would replace what the daytime authorities had effaced. Their persistence outlasted the communist regime, and, eventually, the owner of the wall (the monastery behind it) announced that it would be leaving the portrait of Lennon and the scrawled lyrics as a monument to peace and freedom. Today, there isn't an inch of the wall that isn't covered in messages—many of them scrawled on paper and stuck to the wall with chewing gum.

The nearby **Lovers' Bridge,** which crosses into what is affectionately called Little Venice, is worth a gander. Lovers flock to the bridge and attach a lock to the grate as a symbol of the steadfastness of the heart. Together, they kiss the key and then throw it into the water below. Clichéd though it may have become, it's undeniably romantic.

Free, always open, Velkopřevorské Náměstí, Lesser Quarter, Tram: Malostranské Náměstí, Metro: Malostranská

Peeing Statues

Check out these two urinating gentlemen while you're wandering through the Lesser Quarter. The work of homegrown artist David Černý, whose hand is behind a number of Prague's best-known works of public art, these mechanical statues urinate into a pool shaped like the Czech Republic. Look carefully and you'll see that they're actually writing—they're spelling out lines from popular Czech literary works. The figures represent Nazi and communist invaders, one angling from the west and the other from the east.

Free, always open, Cihelná 2b, Lesser Quarter, Tram: Malostranské Náměstí, Metro: Malostranská

Church of Our Lady Victorious (Chrám Panny Marie Vítězné)

This baroque church is not famous for its architecture or its organ. Rather, its chief draw is its wax figurine of the infant Jesus. The icon, just over a 1.5 feet tall, is resplendent in finely tailored vestments, many of them donated. It might just be the best-dressed doll you'll ever see. The church is free to enter, and you can climb the stairs in the back right of the building to see a sample of the outfits that have been donated over the years. A crew of nuns is tasked with changing the baby into a new outfit about ten times a year.

Services often, open to the public in daylight hours, Karmelitská 9, Lesser Quarter, +420 257 533 646, pragjesu.info, Tram: Hellichova, Metro: Malostranská

Museum of Miniatures (Muzeum miniatur)

Step into this miniature world and check out two dozen sculptures, fully written-out poems, and pieces of art no bigger than a mustard seed. Peer into microscopes to discover trains perched on a single strand of hair or an Eiffel Tower placed into a grain of rice. It's somewhat gimmicky, but worth a stop if you are dining or drinking at the Strahov Monastery Brewery.

130Kč adults, 70Kč students, daily 9:00–17:00, Strahovské nádvoří 11, Castle District, +420 233 352 371, muzeumminiatur.cz, Tram: Pohořelec

Petřín Hill & Tower

Petřín Hill rises on the west side of the river, just south of the Castle District and Lesser Quarter. The observation tower atop the forested hill—clearly modeled after the Eiffel Tower in Paris—was built in 1891 as part of the Jubilee Exhibition, an event similar to the World's Fair that showcased national pride and achievements.

Climb the 299 steps to the vantage point for a panoramic view of the city. Add the height of the tower and that of the hill and you're at exactly the same elevation as the tower's sister structure in Paris.

At the bottom of the hill, you'll pass a lonely series of tall, gaunt human figures climbing a staircase. This is Prague's **Memorial to the Victims of Communism**, commemorating the thousands of men and women who died during the Soviet period, crushed beneath Moscow's heel.

Park free and always open, take the steps up the tower for 120Kč, tower open Apr–Sept daily 10:00–22:00, Oct and Mar daily 10:00–20:00, Nov–Feb daily 10:00–22:00, Petřín Hill, petrinska-rozhledna.cz, Tram: Újezd

Wenceslas Square

This long, narrow square has been an epicenter for Czech revolutions and protests. It served as the backdrop for the Velvet Revolution of 1989, which toppled the ruling Communist Party, and it was the site of fierce protests against the 1968 Soviet invasion of Czechoslovakia. At the protests' peak, Czech student Jan Palach immolated himself in the middle of the square in a dramatic gesture of resistance.

The buildings that line Wenceslas Square are like a visual encyclopedia of the Czech Republic's popular architectural styles: neoclassical, art nouveau, art deco, communist, and modern. The best place to take in the view is from the rooftop terrace at the recommended **Duplex** bar (daily from noon, closed in winter). The square is capped by the **National Museum** (free), which is rather dull—not really worth the time to see it unless you have more than a few days to spend in the city. The building's interior has played a supporting role in a number of feature films, most notably *Mission: Impossible*.

Keep your wits about you if you are in the square at night. Hustlers are on the lookout for easy marks, and the clubs, casinos, and seedier establishments in the surrounding area don't exactly showcase the best that Prague has to offer.

Free, always open, New Town, Metro: Můstek

Museum of Communism

This one-floor museum gives you a behind-the-Iron Curtain peek at life in the Soviet Bloc during the Cold War. Wide-ranging collections feature a vast assortment of propaganda posters and, as you'd expect, the ubiquitous Lenin and Stalin busts. There are also exhibits that detail the privations Czechs were subject to during the period. The majority of the people subsisted on spartan fare—usually little more than milk, canned beans, and lard.

190Kč adults, 150Kč students, daily 09:00-21:00, V Celnici 1031/4, New Town, +420 224 212 966, muzeumkomunismu.cz, Metro: Náměstí Republiky

Mucha Museum

An art nouveau extravaganza, this relatively small museum displays some of Alfons Mucha's best-known works, as well as many of his lesser-known (but no less spectacular) pieces. Mucha (1860-1939) pioneered art nouveau, a response to the rigid and inelegant physical world of the Industrial Revolution. There are dozens of paintings, photographs, and sketches by the master. Mucha's influence can be felt throughout the city, which prides itself on its art nouveau heritage. When you see organic shapes, vivid (but natural) colors, and a blending of a wide range of materials including ceramics, metal, glass, and wood—all shaped into a coherent whole that conveys the harmony of nature—it's art nouveau you're looking at. Keep your eyes peeled when passing by the **Municipal House** (náměstí Republiky 5) and **Hotel Europa** on Wenceslas Square; when you're passing through **Hlavní Nádraží,** the main train station, look up at the dome above.

240Kč adults, 160Kč students, daily 10:00-18:00, Panska 7, New Town, +420 224 216 415, mucha.cz, Metro: Můstek

National Theatre (Národní divadlo)

From the outside, it's easy to identify the National Theatre. The pattern on the tiled roof looks like it may have been the inspiration for Louis Vuitton's most easily recognizable pattern, the one found on the handbags and luggage of the ostentatiously wealthy. The palatial interior is where the real magic is, though. If you can, catch an opera. If you have a student ID card, you might be able to get as much as 50 percent off. Show up 30 minutes or so before the show and see if they have any available tickets.

Ticket prices and showtimes vary by performance, Ostrovní 1, New Town, +420 224 901 448, narodni-divadlo.cz, Tram: Národní divadlo, Metro: Národní třída

EXTRA CREDIT
Churches

As you wander, don't miss the opportunity to soak in the beauty of Prague's many baroque churches. There's decadent architecture inside and out, and some real gems in the form of religious paintings. You'll experience a kind of exuberance not felt in the more austere, Renaissance-style churches. Statues are draped in gold leaf, stained glass radiates in every archway, and pulpits capped with a dizzying array of statuary stretch the limits of the decorative arts. The permanently incomplete **Church of Our Lady of the Snows**—boasting one of the most spectacular vaults in Prague—and **St. Martin in the Wall,** a Gothic church that was built into what was the old Prague city ramparts, are both close to the center and highly worthwhile.

Vyšehrad Castle

Seldom visited but a beautiful sight, the Dracula-esque Vyšehrad Castle is a fun afternoon jaunt a 30-minute walk south of town along the river. This is the area where legends put the first settlements in the region—these early settlements expanded towards the bend in the river, where they took root and grew into the city of Prague as we know her today. The well-preserved modern star-fort's two-kilometer-long ramparts make for ideal vantage points, from which you can see the suburbs of Prague. Spend a moment reflecting as you walk through the ancient but extremely well-kept cemetery behind the church. The cemetery's centerpiece, the Slavin Pantheon, is the final resting place of Alfons Mucha and countless other Czech artists and geniuses.

Free, Apr-Oct daily 10:00–18:00, Nov-Mar daily 10:00–16:00, V Pevnosti 1n59, Greater Prague, praha-vysehrad.cz, Tram: Albertov, Metro: Vyšehrad

TOP EATS

With dishes generally consisting of some variation of meat, potatoes, dumplings, and gravy, classic Czech cuisine is not for the faint of heart (seriously—these dishes are artery-clogging monsters). A culinary renaissance has taken Prague by storm, multiplying the number of available healthy (or at least *healthier*) options, but not all of Czech's eateries got the memo. Most places do offer at least one vegetarian option.

Tipping isn't expected, but it's definitely appreciated. Note the subtleties: When settling a tab, hand cash to the waiter, who will make change right there at the table out of a large wallet. If your service and food were good, round up to the nearest 10 percent (tell your server how much change you want back). For example, if your meal was 350Kč (about US$14), hand the server 1000Kč and tell him or her you want 600Kč back. Saying "thank you" while handing over the cash effectively means "keep the change." To avoid awkward misunderstandings, wait until you have your change in hand before thanking the server for his or her service.

Lokál

For authentic Czech food that won't take a bite out of your budget, look no further than Lokál, a retro-communist beer cellar. The scribbles on the walls and raunchy bathrooms are a nod to what you can expect if you visit the authentic countryside beer halls. The menu is thankfully short and sweet, and the servers will happily provide an English menu upon request. Service is brisk, and the *svíčková* (beef sirloin in cream sauce) and goulash never disappoint.

About 120Kč, Mon-Fri 11:00–01:00, Sat 12:00–01:00, Sun 12:00–22:00, Dlouhá 33, Old Town, +420 222 316 265, ambi.cz, Metro: Staroměstská

Havelská Koruna

For a classic Czech-style cafeteria experience, try lunch at Havelská Koruna, just a few steps from Havelská Market and Old Town Square. The no-frills canteen serves all the classic dishes like *smažený sýr* (fried cheese), schnitzel, dumplings, and goulash—and all for less money than you might expect. Take a tray and fill up on anything that looks good before paying at the end of the counter.

There are many more **cheap canteens** throughout town, often tucked into public university buildings. Keep an eye out for *"Fakulta"* ("college") and you're bound to find an inexpensive and authentic place to eat or enjoy a coffee. One of the best

of these is the café in Prague's Film, TV & Performing Arts campus at Smetanovo nábřeží 1012/2.

Lunches from 100Kč, Havelská 501/23, Old Town, +420 224 239 331, havelska-koruna.cz

Kozička

This cozy brick hideaway serves tasty Czech food at lovely prices. It's also something of a double entendre: *Kozička* translates to "little goat," but it's also a slang term for a single breast. Because of its nondescript entrance, most tourists miss it, so it's a favorite among locals who are willing to overlook the brusque service for the cheap drinks, great atmosphere, and $10 steaks.

Dishes from 160Kč, Mon-Fri 12:00–04:00, Sat 18:00–04:00, Sun 19:00–03:00, Kozí 1, Old Town, +420 224 818 308, kozicka.cz, Metro: Staroměstská

Strahov Monastery Brewery (Klášterní pivovar Strahov)

This bright craft brewery boasts some of the best beer in town, and you can sip your brew in a building that has been producing beer since the 18th century (with a recent century-long hiatus). Part of the old Strahov Monastery compound on the top side of the Prague Castle, the brewery is a perfect pit stop for a pint and meal. Their seasonal brews never disappoint, and neither does their goulash (served in a bread bowl—a personal favorite). Their cheese plates and duck dishes are also excellent.

SPIRALLY, SUGARY GOODNESS: THE *TRDELNÍK*

The *trdelník* (pronounced tdr-DEL-neek) is a sugary, doughy treat that has nothing to do with the Czech Republic, but it's a favorite of tourists who don't seem to care. The bakers take a roll of dough and wrap it around a wooden cylinder to cook and toast the dough into a chewy, golden-brown dessert. When they're ready, the doughy spirals are tapped off the log and rolled in sugar, spice, and everything nice. Prices climb to 60Kč each, but it's worth it to keep your blood sugar up on those long days of sightseeing. Enterprising vendors have popped up all over town, several of them now offering to fill the treat with Nutella and soft-serve ice cream. A cold, stale *trdelník* is a complete waste of money, though this doesn't prevent vendors from selling them to hungry tourists lured by the smell of fresh ones; only buy *trdelníks* if they are steaming hot.

Dishes from 100Kč, daily 10.00–22.00, Strahovské Nádvoří 1/132, Castle District, +420 233 107 704, strahovskyklaster.cz, Tram: Pohořelec

Malý Buddha

For vegetarian food, Malý Buddha ("Little Buddha") is among the best in the city. Inside, it feels a little like you've stumbled into a hodgepodge of all the world's Asian restaurants (there's a large painting of Buddha on one of the walls and bamboo everywhere). Enjoy stir-fried and roasted veggie and tofu dishes in the quiet, warm ambience. There's a good mixture of healthy options and meat dishes—the former may come as a welcome respite for vegetarians or those who have grown weary of heavier Czech cuisine.

Dishes around 120–240Kč, Tues-Sun 12:00–22:30, Úvoz 46, Castle District, +420 220 513 894, malybuddha.cz, Tram: Pohořelec

Bahn Mi-Ba

The Czech Republic welcomed many refugees from the Vietnam War, many of whom settled in Prague and opened either convenience stores or sandwich shops such as this one. Simple, healthy, and filling, fresh Vietnamese baguette sandwiches (bahn mi) are a great snack when you just need a quick bite before moving on to the next museum or church. You'll find multiple locations around town. This location just off Dlouha is one of my favorites; another is near Wenceslas Square (daily 10:30-22:00,

Panská 1308/9, New Town, +420 607 777 354).

Sandwiches from 100Kč, daily 11:00-22:00, Rybná 26, Old Town, +420 734 487 324, facebook.com/banhmibacz, Tram: Dlouhá třída

Pizza Borsalino

The slices from Pizza Borsalino are an excellent late-night snack. Open nearly 24 hours, this pizza shop is a great place to stop in for something that can be wolfed down in the midst of a busy day of shopping or seeing the sights. The shop is a popular one and the pies disappear remarkably quickly, meaning that the slice you get will be hot and fresh. The service leaves much to be desired, but it's not a deterrent.

30Kč slices, daily 11:00-05:00, Ostrovní 102/34, New Town, +420 777 940 079, borsalinopizza.cz, Tram: Národní třída

Buddha Bar

Buddha Bar is an Asian fusion chain restaurant with locations around the world. It features a creative menu with fresh salads, innovative sushi rolls, numerous other main options, an extensive wine menu, and delicious, expertly mixed cocktails. The service is impeccable, and the ambience is breathtaking. Start upstairs with a cocktail at the bar. When you're ready, descend for a quasi-spiritual culinary experience at the foot of a giant statue of Buddha. Stay late for an after-party frequented by young and well-heeled Czech professionals.

Dishes from 350Kč, Tues-Sat 18:00-03:00, Jakubská 8, Old Town, +420 221 776 400, buddha-bar.cz, Metro: Náměstí Republiky

Zebra Express

If Buddha Bar doesn't fit into your budget, Zebra will—and it's close to almost everything (the main location is just inside the Powder Gate and around the corner from the Municipal House). Zebra offers excellent pad thai along with curries and sushi in a casual setting. Service is fast and friendly, and you can, if you're inclined, trade banter with the chefs, who'll beam at your compliments (they clearly enjoy their work). The second location in town, **Zebra Asian** (Melantrichova 5), is right on the corner of the Havelská Market, a block south from the Old Town Square.

Dishes from 150Kč, daily 11:00-24:00, Celetná 988/38, Old Town, +420 774 727 611, zebranoodlebar.cz, Metro: Náměstí Republiky

Burrito Loco

Cheap and quick Tex-Mex burritos, 24 hours a day—a solid business model almost anywhere in the world. When the late-night munchies strike in Prague, there's probably a Burrito Loco close at hand. Post up in the limited seating if there's space, or take your rolls to go and find a bench nearby. This location is in the midst of great nightlife venues near Dlouhá, but there are a number of other locations, including one at Spálená 104/43.

Burritos from 120Kč, daily 24 hours, Masná 620/2, Old Town, +420 606 039 333, burritoloco.cz, Metro: Staroměstská

Bohemia Bagel

If you're anything like me, you might be missing some of the familiar culinary comforts of home. Chief among these, at least for me, is the bagel sandwich. Head to Bohemia Bagel—a favorite among study-abroad students in Prague—for freshly made bagel sandwiches and a taste of home (they offer a bevy of Western dishes). This is a great place to stop for a quick breakfast (served all day), complete with coffee.

Bagels from 100Kč, daily 07:30-18:00, Lázeňská 19, Lesser Quarter, +420 257 218 192, bohemiabagel.cz, Tram: Malostranské Náměstí, Metro: Malostranská

Restaurace T-Anker

What's better than good food? Good food on a sunny terrace with a panoramic view of downtown Prague. Find T-Anker at the top of Kotva, the funky octagonal-shaped department store. Grilled options including duck, chicken, burgers, and fish, all of which pair well with their house-made brews on tap.

Mains from 180Kč, daily 11:00-20:00, till 18:00 Sun, Náměstí Republiky 656/8, 5th floor, Old Town, +420 722 445 474, t-anker.cz, Metro: Náměstí Republiky

Beas Vegetarian Dhaba

I'm a carnivore at heart, but there is something to be said for variety when it comes to protein sources. A light lunch or evening snack of Indian curries and salads is just what the doctor ordered after a night of binging on burritos and slabs of meat. This place is by far the quickest, easiest, and tastiest vegetarian option I've found in Prague. Just grab a tray (plastic, if you want it to go) and start filling it with all sorts of rice dishes, grilled veggies, and more. Their lassi isn't the best I've had, but it does the trick if you've got a hankering. There's another location in Old Town (Týnská 19).

Pay by weight (21.90Kč per 100 grams), Mon-Fri 11:00-21:00, Sat 12:00-20:00, Sun 12:00-18:00, Vladislavova 158/24, New Town, +420 777 551 256, beas-dhaba.cz, Metro: Národní třída

Lehká Hlava

Lehká Hlava is riding the wave of Prague's culinary revolution. Visitors leave this celestial little nook raving about its delicious vegetarian, vegan, and gluten-free dishes. Creative options like cucumber spaghetti and beetroot burger make this a popular spot for those seeking an alternative to the ubiquitous heavy fare. If you prefer cheap, fast, casual, and healthy food to the steaks and sausages, be sure to stop in. Also check out its sister location, **Maitrea,** just behind the Týn Church and a few steps from the Old Town Square.

Mains from 150Kč, daily 11:30-23:30, Boršov 180/2, Old Town, +420 222 220 665, lehkahlava.cz, Tram: Karlovy Lázně, Metro: Národní třída

Las Adelitas

Tucked inside a narrow passageway is the entrance to Las Adelitas, one of Prague's hidden gems. Descend the stairs to a Mexican restaurant quite a few steps above the burritos you'll find at street level. The atmosphere will have you half expecting to hear the waves of Puerto Vallarta. Grandma always told me, "No cheap margarita is worth drinking"—you might be spending a bit more, but the food (and the margaritas) will more than make up for the extra pesos. Enjoy the toasty, salted chips and the wide selection of appetizers and entrées (the soft tacos and tortilla soup are both excellent). If it's busy, sit at the bar.

100-200Kč, daily 11:00–01:00, Malé Náměstí 457/13, Old Town, +420 222 233 247, lasadelitas.cz, Metro: Staroměstská

Tržnice Dlouhá 14

This Whole Foods-with-a-twist-style grocery and deli makes an excellent stop for both breakfast and lunch, and one very close to Old Town Square. Their thick sandwiches with generous fillings and their deep-dish pizza are made from the same high-quality ingredients you'll find in the store. Come back around dinner time—throw together a charcuterie plate and a bottle of wine from their cellar downstairs and take it all to go for a classy and memorable picnic dinner.

Sandwiches from 80Kč, Mon-Fri 08:00–21:00, Dlouhá 14, Old Town, +420 224 815 719, dlouha14.cz, Tram: Dlouhá třída, Metro: Staroměstská

Angelato

Angelato whips up Prague's best authentic Italian gelato, with flavors that are a sugar-powered taste-teleporter that'll transport you directly to Italy. Gelato (and particularly *this* gelato) makes for a satiating reward after a long day of sightseeing in the Lesser Quarter. Find it close to the paddleboat rental location. There's also a second location between Old Town Square and Wenceslas Square, near the Havelská Market.

Cups of icy love from 75Kč, daily 11:00–20:00, Újezd 425/24, Lesser Quarter, +420 777 787 344, angelato.cz, Tram: Újezd

Café Louvre

Set one floor above street level, Café Louvre is Prague's most elegant Bohemian café. Having served some of the city's best brunches, lunches, and dinners for over 100 years, Café Louvre effortlessly reproduces the experience of Bohemian dining that its first customers enjoyed. They've always followed the lead of the coffee culture in nearby Vienna—doing everything that the Viennese do, and just as well. It's a must for anyone who, like my mother, says that breakfast is the most important meal of the day. The omelets are heavenly, and the high ceilings and smartly dressed waitstaff will make you feel steeped in luxury. Top it all off with a slice of the carrot cake.

Omelets from 140Kč, Mon-Fri 08:00–23:30, Sat-Sun 09:00–23:30, Národní 22 (upstairs), New Town, +420 224 930 949, cafelouvre.cz, Metro: Národní třída

Mama Coffee

Mama Coffee is a favorite among visiting coffee snobs (like me) and vegetarians. If you need to tackle a day of work while on vacation, this is your place for comfortable seating, Wi-Fi, and strong coffee. Every time I'm in Prague, I while away a few hours with a good book and a fresh ginger tea upstairs by the window. Toss in their tasty pastries and hummus lunch, and you'll be happy all day without racking up much of a tab. If you're here to work, bring earplugs.

Coffee and tea from 60Kč, daily 08:00–22:00, Vodičkova 674/6, New Town, +420 773 337 309, mamacoffee.cz, Tram: Vodičkova, Metro: Národní třída

EXTRA CREDIT

Honorable mentions include **Kaverna Adria** (Mon-Fri 08:00-23:00, Sat-Sun 09:00-23:00, Národní 40/36, New Town, +420 777 626 003, caffeadria.cz, Metro: Národní třída), a supremely elegant café with a pleasant outdoor terrace featuring striking art deco architecture and interior design—highly recommended if you're in Prague during the warm summer months.

Check out **Grand Café Orient** (Mon-Fri 08:00-23:00, Sat-Sun 09:00-23:00, Ovocný trh 19, Old Town, +420 224 224 240, grandcafeorient.cz, Tram: Náměstí Republiky), a striking Bohemian café that's not nearly as expensive as Café Louvre. It's located in the famous House of the Black Madonna, a unique building that is one of the best example of cubist architecture in the city, between Old Town Square and the Powder Tower on Celetna.

TOP NIGHTLIFE

Thanks to its popularity as an international student destination, Prague is notorious for having some of the best nightlife in Europe. The classrooms of local universities are sprinkled throughout town, which means students are not all crowded into a small handful of neighborhoods. No matter where you are in the city, you probably aren't far from a dark dive bar, a grungy dubstep club, a classy lounge, or a cocktail bar.

Pay attention to flyers and posters around the city, and ask at your hostel about what's on while you're in town—there'll be something every night of the week, but there might be something special on the calendar that only the locals are hip to. The pubs are cheap, the clubs are nuts, and the dance bars (my favorite) are sites of wild abandon. When there's a dance floor, there's usually a cover as well. Expect to pay 100-200Kč (less than US$10) to get past the bouncer.

NIGHTLIFE DISTRICTS

The Old Town of Prague is where to find hopping nightlife with a good mixture of tourists and locals. Once you get out of the dense streets of the Old Town and into the New Town (especially around Wenceslas Square and Prague 7), the clubs get bigger and the party more intense. The balance tips more towards the locals in these areas, but tourists are definitely welcome. Because there's so much variety, the best way to see what Prague has to offer in terms of nightlife is to jump on an organized pub crawl your first night in town. You'll probably find a few places you'll want to return to the next night and the one after that.

Dlouhá & V Kolkovně

You'll find nightlife throughout Prague's Old Town, especially on Dlouhá and V Kolkovně, the streets bordering the Jewish Quarter. These are the city's best-known party streets, and they're where you'll find me most nights when I'm in Prague.

Old Town, Tram: Dlouhá třída

Vinohrady & Žižkov

These neighboring districts, located east of the main train station, couldn't be easier to find—just look for the 700-foot-high TV tower. Both neighborhoods are popular among Prague's growing number of young professionals, so there are loads of cafés, restaurants, and nightlife venues, and very few of them leave you with empty pockets. If you've got the time, spend a night bouncing from hot spot to hot spot in these neighborhoods—especially the dance clubs like **Radost FX** (hip-hop) and **Retro Music Hall** (Top 40).

LGBT PRAGUE

When it comes to entertainment for the LGBT community, Prague has plenty to offer, including clubs with go-go dancers, such as **Factory** (Vinohradská 63, factory-club.cz) or **Escape Club** (V Jámě 1371/8, escapeclub.xxx). **Střelec Pub** (Anglická 2, facebook.com/clubstrelec) is for those who prefer good beer. **Club Termix** (Třebízského 1514/4a, club-termix.cz) is a smaller, more intimate dance club that packs out throughout the week, and its big brother, **Club Termax** (Vinohradská 1789/40, club-max.cz), is the largest gay venue in Prague—so big, in fact, that even when it's relatively busy, the cavernous rooms can feel rather empty. Both clubs have the same owner, and prices are similar (and reasonable) between the two. These clubs attract bigger DJs, so in case of special events, there is often a cover. **Friends Club** (Bartolomějská 11, friendsclub.cz) is open seven days a week and is very popular among the tourist crowd thanks to its nightly programs featuring karaoke, partying, meeting, talking, chilling, and even cabaret. Check their website to see what's on while you're in town.

Greater Prague, Tram: I. P. Pavlova, Náměstí Míru, Jiřího z Poděbrad, Metro: I. P. Pavlova, Náměstí Míru, Jiřího z Poděbrad

New Town

Beer halls, chic lounges, dance bars, and recommended hostels like Madhouse and Mosaic House make the north side of New Town (near Národní-Dancing House and Národní třída) one of the best places to meet people and dance until sunrise. There's a palpable party vibe, but it's a touch less reckless and a touch more dignified than some of the areas listed above.

New Town, Tram: Národní třída, Metro: Můstek

Náplavka

Two bridges south of Charles Bridge is the Jiráskův Bridge. Beginning just south of the bridge and extending for about five blocks along the east side of the river is Náplavka, a strip of street bars and pubs that only open in the summer. Because it's not open all year round, most tourists never hear about it, so it's something of a hipster haven (go here to see Prague's trendiest denizens). Word has begun to spread, though, and it's often packed to the gills on weekends and sunny summer afternoons. Make plans with your mates to head there after a paddleboat ride on the river. Beers start around 30Kč. Most of the beer gardens stay open as long as it's warm enough to enjoy a pint outside.

Greater Prague, Tram: Paleckého Náměstí, Metro: Karlovo Náměstí

BARS & PUBS
U Sudu

U Sudu is a Prague institution. Upon entry, it seems to be just another ordinary Czech pub, but head to the back and down the stairs and you'll find a labyrinth of exposed medieval brick cellars and lounge rooms.

Foosball tables are sprinkled around the place, and there seem to be new bars around every corner. The mood is convivial—the sound of jovial conversation bubbles out of each room. Drink, chill, and be merry, but try not to get lost on the way back to your table!

Daily 09:00–05:00, Vodičkova 677/10, Old Town, +420 222 232 207, usudu.cz, Tram: Lazarská, Metro: Národní třída

AnonymouS Bar

Head to the back of a quiet, dimly lit courtyard and step into this classy, low-key speakeasy themed bar. The Guy Fawkes mask is painted on nearly every surface here, and bar staff and patrons often don the masks as well, which can lead to a somewhat unsettling (but always memorable) experience. As you might expect from a concept bar (inspired by the film and graphic novel V for Vendetta), the cocktails are unique and cleverly named. They are, they say, starting a cocktail revolution. The staff will be happy to make suggestions for you based on your preferences.

Daily 17:00–02:00, till 03:00 on weekends, Michalská 432/12, Old Town, +420 608 280 069, Metro: Můstek

Prague Beer Museum

Located on Dlouhá, Prague's party street, this beer museum is more bar than it is museum—but who's complaining? Pick up a menu in this seductively lit bar and peruse the exhaustive library of tasty beers from around the world. No matter how obscure your tastes, I challenge you to find a beer that's not on the list! If you can't choose, go for the sampler paddle to taste a number of different beers on tap. Take your tray out to the patio in the back if the weather is good. The servers are sometimes in the mood to make recommenda-

ACT LIKE A LOCAL

Pivo, Prosím?

Thanks to its clean water, fresh hops and barley, and historic monastic brewing culture, the Czech Republic has some of the best beer in the world. The beer coming from the Bohemia-Moravian region has been imitated many times, yet nobody does it quite like the Czechs. Order one by saying to the waiter *"pivo, prosím"* or "beer, please." Even just holding up a finger will land a pint of frothy goodness on your table in short order.

Today, beer culture is alive and well in Prague. Bars and restaurants generally have two taps—light and dark—of the same beer brand. "Light" refers to the color (not to the beer's caloric content). The lighter-colored beer is the crisp, pilsner-style beer—predecessor to the American perversion of Budweiser and Coors. The darker beers tend to be heavier and sweeter, with a slightly higher alcohol content. Toast to the brewers and knock back a few of what many consider the best brew around. Here are some common brands you'll see:

Pilsner Urquell: Deliciously crisp and bitter. Quenches a thirst at the end of a long day of sightseeing and widely recognized as one of the best (if not *the* best) beers in the world. You may be surprised to learn that the Japanese brand Asahi now owns Pilsner Urquell. If you see a **Kolkovna** restaurant, that's a chain closely associated with Pilsner Urquell.

Budweiser: The younger half-brother of the Budweiser brand we all know in the States, originating from the Czech town, Budvar.

Staropramen: The runner-up to the better brands of Urquell and Budvar is brewed right in Prague. Staropramen isn't winning any accolades, but it's a light, cheap beer that will quench your thirst. **Potrefena Husa** is a restaurant chain affiliated with Staropramen.

Prague's Most Famous Beer Halls

While most of these have verged into touristy territory in the last few years, I still enjoy (and recommend) **Strahov Monastery Brewery** (Strahovské Nádvoří 1/132), **U Medvídků** (Na Perštýně 344/5), **U Fleků** (Křemencova 1651/11), **U Vejvodů** (Jilská 4), and **U Pinkasů** (Jungmannovo náměstí 15/16). **Národní Pivovar** (Národní 8) is a new and popular entry. All are worth a visit to experience the classic Czech beer hall—without which no visit to Prague is complete.

Yeast Extract

You may notice the 10°, 11°, 12° listed next to your beer options during your stay. No, that doesn't indicate alcohol percentage—it refers to the percentage of yeast extract in the brew, which loosely corresponds to alcohol strength. For a good guess at alcohol percentage from the yeast rating, divide by two, and subtract two. So a 13° beer is about 4.5 percent ABV.

tions, sometimes not. If it's the latter, don't take it personally.

Daily 10:00–03:00, Smetanovo Nábřeží 205/22, Old Town, praguebeermuseum.cz, +420 732 330 912, Tram: Karlovy Lázně

Hangar Bar

This is a retro Pan-Am-inspired airline bar complete with uniformed bartenders, dancers, fuselage-like passageways, and plenty of genuine plane memorabilia. Prices are reasonable, the vibe is social, and you're only a few minutes away from Old Town Square. It's a novelty that might get old quickly, but it's also a great place to snap a few pictures. When you feel like disembarking, **Aloha Bar,** a tacky tiki bar next door, is another great photo op.

Drinks from 80Kč, Wed–Sat 17:00–06:00, Sun–Tues 17:00–04:00, + 420 724 004 305, Dušní 9/9, Josefov, hangarpraha.cz, Tram: Právnická fakulta, Metro: Staroměstská

Café Nod

Another classy spot on Dlouhá (right next to Lokál), Café Nod is the sister bar to the Roxy club, another of Prague's great nightlife spots. Climb the stairs to a spacious bar/café/lounge that's perfect for anything from afternoon tea to late-night drinks. The space in the back doubles as an art gallery with frequent exhibits. Nod draws the young professional set who work downtown (particularly those looking to unwind), creating a chill and unpretentious vibe.

Drinks from 60Kč, Mon–Fri 10.00–01:00, Sat Sun 14:00–04:00, Dlouhá 33, Old Town, nod.roxy.cz, +420 604 790 921, Tram: Dlouhá třída

Tretter's New York Bar

Tretter's is your classic Roaring '20s cocktail bar, complete with professional bartenders, an extensive wine list, short and long drinks, and cigars; there's even a gentleman's guide integrated into the menu. This place used to be one of the undiscovered pockets of Prague I loved to visit, but locals and tourists have caught the scent, so the bar packs out later in the evening. Last time I was there, I waited at the bar for 10 minutes before I was served, but the old-fashioned they slid across the tiled bar top was well worth the wait.

Daily 19:00–03:00, V Kolkovně 3, Jewish Quarter, +420 224 811 165, tretters.cz, Metro: Staroměstská

Hemingway Bar

As far as I know, Hemingway never stepped foot in Prague, but his reputation as a notorious boozehound has made him popular with bar owners looking for a theme. The people at this dual-level cocktail bar know their cocktails. It's often full thanks to the bartenders' pristine reputation; they set the bar high in Prague's mixology scene. It's a good idea to make reservations here, especially on the weekends, as it's often hard to find room even for a party of two.

Drinks from Kč 210, Karoliny Světlé 279/26, Old Town, +420 773 974 764, hemingwaybar.cz, Metro: Staroměstská

Popo Cafe

Dank and a little sticky, this subterranean bar with a small dance floor is the spot for good, old-fashioned, college-style drunk fun. It's a favorite among local students thanks to its dirt-cheap prices and unpretentious atmosphere, meaning you'll be extremely lucky if you find a seat (especially on weekends). The crowded, sweaty atmosphere is a little much for many first-time visitors—claustrophobics should stay far, far away.

Daily 16:00–04:00, Michalská 15, Old Town, +420 224 240 637, popoujezd.cz, Metro: Staroměstská or Mustek

Groove Bar

Prague's classy young professional set packs out Groove Bar just about every night of the week, drawn to the relatively inexpensive drinks enjoyed at high-top tables. A live DJ spins deep house lounge beats—the beat is steady and mellow all night, and the music isn't so loud that it drowns out conversation. It's not overly pretentious, but dress the part if you want to feel at home—that means no hoodies or tennis shoes. If you want one of the much-coveted high tops, you'll need a reservation (especially on weekends).

Daily 19:00–03:00, Voršilská 142/6, New Town, + 420 777 610 279, groovebar.cz, Tram: Národni třída

Billiard Centrum MSK

For an old-world billiards hall experience, look no further than a small door tucked in an alley behind Wenceslas Square. The unassuming door opens into a massive room with nearly every imaginable size of pool and billiards tables, which run all the way to the very back, all with low-slung green lamps suspended above them. On weekends, call ahead to reserve a table. Access is via the passage through H&M off Wenceslas Square, or find the tiny V Cipu street leading directly away from the Mucha Museum.

Beers 32Kč, daily 14:00–02:00, V Cipu 1, New Town, +420 725 857 458, bcksm.cz, Tram: Václavské náměstí, Metro: Můstek

DANCE BARS

Dance bars (the good ones at least) balance precariously between pubs and clubs. An inch to left and you're sitting at the bar downing pint after pint without ever leaving your seat; an inch to the right and you're bellowing at the top of your lungs if you want to be heard. Find that balance, though, and you're destined for an unforgettable evening—you'll be in the perfect place to sow the seeds of fascinating conversation. When your jam comes on, bring that dude or damsel to the floor and let the music do the rest.

Klubovna 2. Patro

This club is probably my favorite spot—and, for now, the best-kept secret—in Prague. The name translates to "second-floor club," and, frequented by the classy hipster set, it sits in the elusive zone where the speakeasy, lounge, bar, and club all meet. It's quite popular with young, friendly Czechs who love the throbbing (yet never tedious) techno put on nightly. I like the affordable drinks, open dance floor, large bar, and the back room where you can chill out and catch your breath a bit. The proximity to many other popular venues on the same block makes this the perfect place to keep the party going or to wind down the evening.

Cover 100-200Kč, Mon-Thurs 17:00-02:00, Fri-Sat 17:00-04:00, pass through the discreet entrance in the back of a parking lot at Dlouhá 729/37, Old Town, so hip they don't even have a phone or website, Tram: Dlouhá třída

M1

A small club that's popular with Erasmus students, M1 is chic but not too snobby. If you're familiar with clubs in Europe, you won't find any surprises here. It's your standard club (single room, large dance floor) that plays a good mix of popular hip-hop and R&B. It tends to please just about everybody who is prepared to let their hair down and have a good time. Dress smart casual (no sports clothes and no hats).

Occasional 100Kč cover, daily 21:00-late, Masná 1, Old Town, +420 227 195 235, m1lounge.com, Metro: Staroměstská

Chapeau Rouge

Chapeau Rouge is notorious for being a head-trip—the fun kind. While the upstairs is (relatively) quiet and straitlaced, descend the stairs into the low-ceilinged cavern and things get loose. If intense dubstep is your cup of tea, you'll quickly find

yourself among like-minded friends. Just about anything goes in Chapeau—and what happens in Chapeau, stays in Chapeau. It's not a good place for those who don't like being around drugs.

Mon-Fri 12:00-04:00, Sat-Sun 16:00-late, Jakubská 2, Old Town, +420 222 316 328, chapeaurouge.cz, Metro: Náměstí Republiky

KU Bar & Lounge

Come out to KU Bar & Lounge for a good time in downtown Prague. Moet and Chandon branding adorns the glittering walls in this plastic and postmodern space. Dancers and smart lighting pump up the party late throughout the week. It's also known as one of the best parties in town on Mondays thanks to its Mad Mad Monday events.

Drinks from 90Kč, Rytířská 534/13, Old Town, +420 724 695 910, kubar.cz, Metro: Můstek

Alibi

This is my favorite pregame spot before I head over to Radost (just a few blocks away) for their Thursday hip-hop night. I'm not the only one who pregames here: Locals come to Alibi early to take advantage of their drink specials and their always-liberal pours. Don't miss a visit to the entertaining bathrooms.

Drinks from 85Kč, no cover, Thurs-Sat 18:00-04:00, Sun-Wed 18:00-02:00, Žitná 1575/49, New Town, +420 725 987 987, alibi-bar.cz, Tram: Muzeum, Metro: I. P. Pavlova

Nebe

With three locations in town, Nebe has the clubbing vibe down to a science. The crowd here dresses well, but they're not out to see and be seen—rather, they're in search of a night that stretches into the morning. Each of the locations has a slightly different vibe, but there's a few things they all have in common: great music, drinks that go down easy, prices that won't break the bank, and a sexy crowd itching to get on the dance floor. In addition to the Wenceslas Square location below, find other locations at Náměstí Republiky (V Celnici 1036/4) and Karlovo náměstí (Křemencova 10). Dress to impress.

Cover on weekends 100Kč, Mon 16:00-03:00, Tues-Thurs 16:00-04:00, Fri-Sat 16:00-05:00, Sun 18:00-03:00, Václavské náměstí 802/56, Wenceslas Square, New Town, +420 608 644 784, nebepraha.cz, Metro: Muzeum

James Dean

Thanks to its '50s-diner theme, you wouldn't be blamed for assuming this is a tourist trap (and it very well may be one during the day), but at night it turns into a raging party that goes until six or seven in the morning. With the relatively lax door policy, the male-to-female ratio tends to get slightly unbalanced at times—whole groups of men will stand on the dance floor gawking at the girls dancing on the stage. Nearby, **Steampunk Prague** (open late, V Kolkovně 920/5, +420 734 202 505, steampunkprague.cz) offers a similar bar experience upstairs and dance party vibe downstairs, with surroundings adorned in shiny brass, gears, and other mechanical elements.

Daily 08:00-late, V Kolkovně 922/1, Old Town, +420 606 979 797, jamesdean.cz, Metro: Staroměstská

Harley's

Widely recognized as Prague's pickup joint, this dive bar and club is the after-party location of choice. The place is steadily busy most of the night, but at 03:00, when most of the other bars close, Harley's suddenly becomes a sea of flesh. Upstairs are rowdy (and sometimes unintelligible) conversations. Downstairs, the party quickly becomes raucous. There's a small stage, to which bachelors on their stag parties are drawn like flies.

Daily 19:00-late, Dlouhá 18, Old Town, +420 602 419 111, harleys.cz, Metro: Staroměstská

Deja Vu

Get your drink on upstairs and your dance on down below. Depending on the DJ, the music here is hit or miss, so head downstairs and make sure the groove is to your liking before throwing down some cabbage for a drink. Sharable oversized drinks are popular at the upstairs bar, where you can lounge around some mean-looking garden lion statues. Check the website for drink specials.

Daily 18:00-late, Jakubská 648/6, Old Town, +420 222 311 743, dejavuclub.cz, Metro: Náměstí Republiky

Zlaty Strom

Just steps from Charles Bridge and the famous club Karlovy Lázně, Zlaty Strom is in the basement of an old hotel, but features 3.5 levels of bars and clubs. There's even a mini strip club (20:00-05:00) with poles on the bar. Zlaty Strom frequently plays host to Erasmus and student parties, which means it's often lively. The restaurant on the ground level is open 24 hours, making it a convenient and popular refueling stop when the evening is drawing to a late close.

Beers 89Kč, fast drinks 98Kč, Sun-Thurs free, Fri-Sat 100Kč cover, daily 19:00-06:00, Karlova 187/6, Old Town, +420 603 804 126, zlatystrom.com, Tram: Karlovy Lázně

CLUBS

Because there is so much competition, many of the clubs in town focus on a niche market (house, R&B, hip-hop, club techno, pop, etc.). Most of them charge either a 100Kč or 200Kč cover. If you're more interested in dancing than socializing, head to the nightclubs, which boast some serious sound systems. Crowds will be larger, but the venues are big enough to accommodate them. Expect to pay a premium on your drinks. Dance bars are perfect for those who want a balance of socializing and dancing, with much more reasonable prices. Decide what kind of bar you want and then do a couple of minutes of research. Look at the programs online—they'll give you a good idea what kind of music and crowd you can expect.

Karlovy Lázně

This famous five-floor club is the largest in Central Europe, and most people already have it on their itinerary when they arrive (or they quickly pencil it in). There are two floors of techno, one pumping '80s beats, one for hip-hop, and a chill level at the top with mood lighting, couches, and giant beanbags (my advice: stay away from the top floor). The crowd here trends younger—some of them still in high school—and that attracts swarms of male creepers who congregate by the bar or watch the dance floor intently. I've had great evenings here, but only when I've shown up too intoxicated to really pay attention to what's going on around me.

Many people get their cheap-drinks fix next door at **Café Lavka** before heading to Karlovy Lázně. Their happy hour (10:00-

24:00) features 60Kč shots, wine, and beer.

Daily 21:00-06:00, Smetanovo nábřeží 198/1, Old Town, +420 222 220 502, karlovylazne.cz, Metro: Staroměstská

Retro Music Hall

Taking Vinorhady and the rest of the city by storm, Retro is one of the hottest clubs in town. It features a wide range of DJs and themed music nights every day of the week. It also hosts concerts—mostly DJs, but occasionally live acts as well. Check out their website for upcoming events. Pyrotechnics and light shows take the party to the next level.

Covers from 80Kč, Wed and Fri-Sat 22:00-05:00, Francouzská 75/4, Greater Prague, +420 222 510 592, retropraha.cz, Tram: Náměstí Míru

Radost FX

Locals and tourists alike highly recommend this spot close to the top end of Wenceslas Square. By day, it's the city's best vegetarian restaurant; by night, it's a bumping hip-hop and R&B club. Rihanna filmed her music video for "Don't Stop the Music" here, so you can watch the video for some idea what to expect. Here's a clue: bumpin' hip-hop and R&B until the early hours. If urban grooves are your thing, you might just never want to leave.

Daily 11:00-02:00, Bělehradská 234/120, New Town, +420 224 254 776, radostfx.cz, Metro: I. P. Pavlova

Roxy

Occupying a space that was once a massive subterranean concert hall, the recently renovated Roxy gives off a slightly alternative, grungy warehouse feel with music to match. You never quite know what you'll hear at Roxy: it could be techno; it could be reggae; it could be house; it could be hip-hop. It all depends on the mood of the DJ. The vibe is casual—yes, sneakers and jeans are absolutely fine—and entry is often free during the week, but they do charge cover on weekends (100Kč).

Daily 19:00-05:00, Dlouhá 33, +420 602 691 015, roxy. cz, Metro: Staroměstská, Tram: Dlouhá třída

Lucerna

This is one of my favorite unpretentious dance clubs in town. Enjoy the music of the '80s and '90s on weekends (with the music videos your mom never let you watch playing on enormous projector screens). When your favorite throwback jam comes on, don't be shy. Belt out the lyrics at the top of your lungs—you can be sure that there'll be somebody else (or everybody else) on the dance floor doing the same. The emphasis on yesterday's hits draws a crowd that trends a little older, so if it's the younger, sexier crowds that float your boat, you should probably look elsewhere. Lucerna, though, is always a safe bet for a popping good time.

Doors usually open around 20:00 or 21:00, the party heats up around 22:30, Štěpánská 61, Wenceslas Square, New Town, +420 224 225 440, lucerna.musicbar.cz, Metro: Muzeum

Cross Club

Primarily a dubstep club, Cross (formerly a nondescript house in Holešovice) features one of the funkiest and most futuristic interiors I've ever seen, with servos spinning on the walls and a half-level above the bar where you can bear-crawl to your own little cove overlooking the scene unfolding below. Cross Club is a favorite among those who love their electronic music on the more intense side—particularly fans of drum and bass in its many incarnations. Check their website to find a night when the eclectic lineup of performers and DJs aligns with your musical tastes.

Cover usually around 100Kč, daily 14:00 till way late, Plynární 1096/23, Prague 7, (Holešovice), +420 736 535 053, crossclub.cz, Tram: Ortenovo Náměstí, Metro: Nádraží Holešovice

Fashion Club

A favorite among Prague's hedonists, Fashion thumps out primarily house and other forms of EDM, though they do have R&B nights. Come out for the glamorous see-and-be-seen vibe. There's plenty of pretentiousness to go around, but it doesn't have to be contagious. If you like the Miami or LA club scene, the Fashion Club is worth a visit (even if only for comparison's sake). Don't be tempted to take the stairs. Wait for the elevator—the club is on the top floor of many at the hexagonal shopping center.

Cover from 200Kč, drinks from 120Kč, Náměstí Republiky 8, +420 224 815 733, f-club.cz/en, Tram: Náměstí Republiky, Metro: Náměstí Republiky

PUB CRAWLS
Drunken Monkey Pub Crawl
This team puts on a rowdy party every night of the week. Their standard nights kick off with a double power hour—two hours of unlimited sugary shooters, wine, and beer from 20:00 to 22:00. They then take you on a tour of 3-4 of the top nightlife venues across town. You can also opt for their second power hour (22:00-23:00) if you want to mingle with some of the local students and start your nightlife tour a little later. Crawls start at their own bar, Drunken Monkey, and are a great option on weekend nights. Pick up a flyer from their reps in blue in the Old Town Square for more info.

Pub crawl 600Kč, open bar 20:00-22:00, U Milosrdných 848/4, Jewish Quarter, +420 775 477 983, drunkenmonkey.cz, Metro: Staroměstská

TOP SHOPPING & MARKETS

SHOPPING DISTRICTS
Pařížská
Get your high-end shopping fix by strolling down Pařížská—"Paris Street." This is Prague's own Champs-Élysées, offering stores like Prada, Louis Vuitton, and Gucci.

Jewish Quarter, Metro: Staroměstská

Wenceslas Square
Check out the stores lining **Národní** and quarter-mile-long **Wenceslas Square,** which have just about all the mainstream brands.

New Town, Metro: Můstek or Muzeum

MARKETS
Náplavka Farmers Market
Every Saturday, this bustling farmers market takes over a stretch of the walkway along the Vltava River. You'll find foodstuffs ranging from baked goods and pastries to meat, dairy, and sandwiches. Vendors sell handmade goods, and lines of food trucks offer a wide range of greasy fare. The beautiful setting makes for a scenic spot for a lunch and (for many) a welcome break from a busy day or days of sightseeing.

Famers markets have become quite trendy in Prague, and, while you once had to wait until the weekend, you can now find a fresh market nearly any day of the week in these squares: Náměstí Jiřího z Poděbrad (Wed-Sat), Tylovo náměstí (Tues-Fri), and Karlínské náměstí (Sat).

Sat 08:00-14:00, Náplavka street, just south of Jiráskův most, Greater Prague, Tram: Paleckeho náměstí, Metro: Karlovo náměstí

SHOPPING CENTERS
Palladium
Palladium is Prague's best city-center mall, housing all the standard brands like Puma and H&M, along with Starbucks and a food court.

Daily 09:00-21:00, Náměstí Republiky 1, Old Town, Metro: Náměstí Republiky

A SORE BUTT ON EASTER
Your Easter traditions may comprise Easter egg hunts, a morning at church, pastel-colored decorations, and so on. But the Czechs have their own set of traditions—one of them that demands our attention. Every Easter Monday, the boys and men of the Czech Republic weave eight decorated willow branches into whips called *pomlázka* and take them door to door throughout the neighborhood. The women who live at each house open the door and submit to an enthusiastic bum whipping as the men recite a fairly wordy Czech poem. At the completion of their exercise, the men and boys are passed alcohol and candy, respectively, and a colored ribbon is tied to the ends of the boys' sticks. This naughty tradition is supposed to bring good luck, health, and fertility to both the whipper and the whippee. The jury's still out on the benefits of the ritual, but I've witnessed the less-than-salutary effects with my own eyes: the men get stumbling drunk by noon, and, for nearly the entire day, the women wince and suck their teeth as they gingerly lower themselves into their chairs. I'll stick to the chocolate eggs.

Letná Park offers beautiful views, and the Vltava islands, just minutes from Charles Bridge, provide a chance to escape the city's packed streets and attractions.

Letná Park (Letenské sady)

A stunning view of the entire city can be had by climbing the hill to Letná Park. The park used to contain a massive monument to Joseph Stalin, but it was destroyed in 1962. In its place was erected a giant ticking metronome, which symbolizes time ticking away until the end of all tyranny around the world. On nice days, this is where Prague citizens get their sweat on, either jogging or in-line skating around the large, flat park. There's a beer garden about a quarter mile north of the metronome.

Free, always open, Letná Park, Tram: Čechův most

Střelecký Island

Cross Most Legií to get over to this island. From the edges of the island, you'll have an unimpeded view of Charles Bridge. Bring a picnic lunch and sit on one of the benches; you're sure to remember the view. In the summer months, a beer boat pulls up to the island's edge, so you can enjoy a pint of cold pilsner with your picnic.

Free, usually closed after sundown, between Lesser Quarter and Old Town, south of Charles Bridge, Tram: Národní divadlo, Metro: Národní třída

Slovanský Island

Winter in Prague can be freezing, but in the summer it's great to get out on the river to cool down away from the crowds. From Slovanský Island, you can rent paddleboats for up to four people (from 200Kč an hour). Bring some snacks, beer, and wine and make an afternoon of it! To get to Slovanský Island, cross the short footbridge just south of Národní divadlo.

Daily, closes an hour before sunset, just south of the National Theater and Legií bridge, Tram: Národní divadlo, Metro: Národní třída

Žluté lázně

Consider Žluté lázně Prague's beach. With volleyball and tennis courts, numerous beer gardens, cafés and restaurants, pizzerias, and a generally chill and fun-loving atmosphere, this outdoor adult playground is where the city comes to make the most of the weather when the temperatures climb. Once the sun goes down, freshly tanned Czechs stick around for dinner and the party to follow at their on-site dance hall. To get here, take the 20-minute ride south on tram #17 from any stop along the east side of the river.

Cheap entrance fee of 80Kč, daily 09:00-02:00, Podolské nábřeží 3/1184, Greater Prague, +420 244 462 193, zlutelazne.cz, Tram: Dvorce

Personal Prague Guides

My friends at PPG offer numerous private itineraries great for families and groups of friends who want a tailored experience. Send in a request with any specific needs and the team will get back to you with recommendations on what to see and do. Guides specialize in areas like music, Jewish history, art, literature, architecture, genealogy, and more. Check out their website for more info and pricing.

Walking tour 700Kč/hour up to 3 people, 900Kč/hour 4-8 people, groups up to 15-20 reduce costs, day trips from 5,000Kč including car and driving guide, personal-pragueguide.com, sarka@personalpragueguide.com

Sandeman's New Europe Walking Tour

Sandeman took Europe by storm with these free tours a few years ago, and you can count on them for cheap, entertaining, entry-level tours that neatly summarize the city's history and culture. They leave daily from the Czech Tourism Office on the Old Town Square (near where Pařížská meets the square) at 10:00, 10:45, and 14:00. The Castle Quarter Tours depart from the same place at 14:00; these stop to pick up others on Jan Palach Square just in front of Rudolfinum at 14:30 before continuing across the river and up the hill to the castle.

Tip-based and paid tours, pub crawl option available, newpraguetours.com

Biko Prague Bike Tours

Filippo met his wife in the Czech Republic, quit his job in the soul-crushing corporate tobacco world, and moved here to start this adventurous bike tour company. You can choose between numerous offerings that can be tailored to suit almost any fitness or skill level. I love these tours because they let you see a completely different side of Prague in the hills beyond the city, all with friendly guiding and coaching throughout.

Tours including bikes from 1,300Kč, Vratislavova 58/3, +420 733 750 990, bikoadventures.com

TOP HOSTELS

Mosaic House

Consistently blowing away backpackers with its value and mod decor, Mosaic House is my favorite hostel in town. This hybrid boutique hotel and designer hostel is a 20-minute walk from the Old Town Square, putting you close to all the city's main attractions. The showers, with their rain forest drizzle, are a luxurious touch—something you'll rarely find in hostels. They keep it happening at the bar with frequent live acts, creating a fun and inviting atmosphere. The hostel runs two nightly pub crawls kicking off at 19:45 and 20:45.

Beds from 190Kč, free Wi-Fi, laundry facilities, 24-hour reception, breakfast a pricey 235Kč (optional), Odborů 4, New Town, +420 221 595 364, mosaichouse.com, Metro: Karlovo Náměstí

The Madhouse Hostel

If you, like me, are bemoaning the slow death of social atmospheres in hostels around Europe due to mobile tech and social networking, hit up the Madhouse for the party hostel with the absolute best social vibe in town. Great for solo travelers, this is Prague's most legit backpacker hostel, and these guys put on events every night of the week to ensure that they live up to their reputation. As the name suggests, the Madhouse is not a place for travelers looking to sleep a full eight hours a night. You might not leave the hostel feeling rested, but you will have experienced Prague's notorious nightlife at its absolute craziest.

Beds from 450Kč, free Wi-Fi, city maps, laundry facilities, parties and events organized throughout the week, Spalena 39, Old Town, +420 222 240 009, themadhouseprague.cz, Metro: Národní třída

Hostel Orange

This is a favorite among backpackers for the chill atmosphere and prime location on Wenceslas Square. They have a hard time keeping their locks functioning properly, so don't head here if you're carrying the crown jewels with you. Without a common room, the Orange isn't as social as my other recommendations, but the value and location make up for it.

Beds from 155Kč, free breakfast, laundry available, free Wi-Fi, towels included, hair dryers available, 24-hour check-in, Václavské Náměstí 781/20, New Town, +420 775 112 625, Metro: Můstek

Prague Square Hostel

This hostel is in the heart of it all—you just can't beat its accessibility, not only to sights, but to the nightlife as well. Places like Chapeau Rouge, Roxy, and James Dean are just a five-minute walk away, with Wenceslas Square not much farther in the opposite direction. The staff are welcoming and happy to help you make the most of your stay in town. Because the hostel is in an older building, don't expect too many modern amenities (when it's busy, available electrical outlets are scarce), but what it slightly lacks in features, it makes up for in location right on the Old Town Square.

Beds from 300Kč, free Wi-Fi, free towels, 24-hour reception, free breakfast, Melantrichova 10, Old Town, +420 224 240 859, praguesquarehostel.com, Metro: Můstek

Sir Toby's

Located in the trendy area of Holešovice (Prague 7), this hostel gives you the opportunity to escape the touristy streets of Old Town and see a more local flavor of Prague. This means that you'll be a ways from the hostel if you end your evening in the Old

Town, but Prague's wild nightlife isn't for everybody. You'll find an attractive pub downstairs with live music, a nice outdoor area, and a friendly staff.

Beds from 270Kč, free Wi-Fi, 24-hour reception, 150Kč buffet breakfast, Dělnická 24, Prague 7 (Holešovice), +420 246 032 610, sirtobys.com, Tram: Dělnická

Prague Penthouses
Full disclosure: I have a few apartments in Prague posted to Airbnb and other booking sites. Skip the extra fees and reach out via the email address below to stay in af-

fordable luxury. I've hand-selected these apartments for their characteristic charm, excellent location, and comfort. Accommodating small groups (2-6 people), these well-appointed and comfortable flats feature free and fast Wi-Fi, full kitchens, large flat-screen TVs, and even a hammock here and there. If you're looking for a place to raise hell, look elsewhere—there's a strict and enforced no-noise policy.

Entire apartments from 4,000Kč, free Wi-Fi, free towels, 24-hour check-in and concierge, all locations in Prague 1, +420 775 411 417, prgapartment@gmail.com

TRANSPORTATION

GETTING THERE & AWAY
Prague is well served by all modes of ground and air transportation.

Plane
All of the major and budget airlines serve Prague's main airport, **Václav Havel International Airport** (PRG, prg.aero/en). Getting from the airport to the city center is easy and cheap. Get cash from an ATM in the airport and break a few big bills at a convenience shop—you'll need smaller bills to purchase your local transportation connection into town.

You have two options that will take you to the center: The **Airport Express** bus stops at Náměstí Republiky and Hlavní Nádraží, the main train station. It'll set you back 120Kč and take about 25 minutes to get to central Prague. A cheaper option is taking bus 119 to Praha-Veleslavín (the last stop) and connecting to the metro. From the airport, stride confidently past the row of taxis (a moment of indecision and one of the cabbies will start loading your luggage into his trunk). Catch bus 119 waiting for you at the next row. Take it to the Veleslavín stop. Follow the crowds down the stairs to the metro. Don't worry about which direction to take the metro—you're boarding at the end point, so it only goes in one direction. Your 32Kč ticket is valid for a 90-minute window across metro, bus, and tram. The journey to the center will take about 45 minutes. From this metro line, you can connect to any others as well as exit for local trams.

Remember to validate your ticket by plugging it into any of the yellow boxes on board the bus and at the top of the escalators leading down to metro platforms. Uniformed ticket controllers throughout the system are quite common—don't get caught without a validated ticket.

Train
Prague's main train station, **Hlavní Nádraží,** has numerous daily connections for both national and international destinations. Its location just on the edge of the Old Town makes it simple to connect to your accommodations (presuming you're staying close to the center). The station contains a well-stocked grocery store and a number of fast-food joints, so you can grab something to eat whether you're coming or going. Connections run often to Budapest (7 hours), Krakow (8 hours), Vienna (4.5 hours), and Berlin (4.5 hours). Check timetables and prices and make reservations online (czech-transport.com).

Bus
International connections into Prague arrive at **Prague Florenc Station,** east of the Old Town. Central Europe has a wide range of bus options. My favorite sites to find connections are **Student Agency** (student-agencybus.com), **Flixbus** (flixbus.com), **Orange Ways** (orangeways.com), **Berlin Linien Bus** (berlinlinienbus.de), and **Eurolines** (eurolines.com). Florenc has both tram stops and a metro station nearby for local connections.

LOST IN TRANSLATION?

In the Czech Republic, American movies are not only dubbed, but their titles are also often changed drastically. The reasons for this vary. Sometimes, American movie titles just don't sound right in direct translation, or they may even have a completely different meaning when translated to Czech. Regardless of the reason, the results can range from confusing to hilarious. Here are some of my favorites translated back into English:

English	Czech Title Translated Back to English
The Hangover	Party in Las Vegas
Bad Santa	Santa Is a Pervert
Hurt Locker	Death Waits Everywhere
Cool Runnings	Coconuts in the Snow
Any Given Sunday	Winners and Losers
Van Wilder	Sexy Party

Car

The Czech Republic has an extensive freeway network. Drives to nearby cities like Budapest (5 hours), Berlin (4 hours), and Vienna (4 hours) are easy.

GETTING AROUND

Prague's relatively compact city center is easily walked across in about 30 minutes. Oftentimes, walking is faster than taking a car through the tight, one-way streets of the downtown.

While the communist system didn't work out in many ways, it did leave behind an excellent public transit system of trams, metro lines, and city buses. The public transportation system is completely integrated, and even applies to the Petřín Hill funicular and a couple of minor river ferry routes just outside the city center (connecting Holešovice with Karlin, and south of town, connecting Anděl with the Vyšehrad Castle neighborhood).

Purchase a **ticket** (24Kč valid for 30 min, 32Kč/90 min) at one of the machines inside any metro station or at almost any of the many convenience stores around town. Make sure to validate it at the top of each escalator. If you'll be zipping across town often, consider a day pass (110Kč) or a three-day pass (310Kč). Note that you'll need to use the system at least five times a day to save on those longer passes. Look up routes, delays, and more information at dpp.cz/en.

The public transportation system operates on the honor system, but beware, there are ticket checkers all over the place! Always buy a ticket and validate it. You may wonder why nobody else seems to be validating theirs: It's because locals have monthly passes that don't require the same validation for single-use tickets.

Metro

The three-line metro system will move you from point A to point B in a jiffy. Connections are clearly marked on every landing area with both simplified and full maps on display, making it easy to know where you need to go.

Tram

Trams are a convenient way to get across town while enjoying the views en route. Pick up tickets and validate them on the machines to avoid a hefty fine. Ticket checkers are quite active on the popular and touristy tramlines.

Tram 22 is a great line to take to get oriented. It'll take you from Královský Letohrádek (near Prague Castle) through Malostranské Náměstí (Lesser Town Square), across the Vltava River, past Národní divadlo (National Theatre), and down to Národní třída, depositing you right near the shopping district and Wenceslas Square.

Familiarize yourself with the major landmarks near your accommodations so you can recognize them in the destination list at each tram stop. Inside each tram are maps that highlight your route. Use these maps to orient yourself. The stops only have a list of stop names.

Bus

Unless you're trying to get outside of the city for the day, most tourists generally don't use buses. Thanks to a superior city-center tram and metro systems, the bus system mostly offers connections to the suburbs.

Taxi

Prague is definitely a city where you want to call your taxis ahead of time—don't hail them on the street. **Nejlevnější Taxi** (+420 226 000 226) is my favorite. Don't even try to pronounce the name; just call the number and be thankful they speak English. This is the cheapest and most reliable company in town. If they're full, try **Tick-Tack** (+420 721 300 300). They provide free water and accept credit cards. If you ever feel that a cabbie is taking advantage of you (which happens frequently to tourists), pay a maximum of 300Kč (for a city-center ride—a trip within downtown should never cost you more than that), get out of the cab, and, if the cabbie insists you owe him more, pop into your hostel to ask for help. Uber and a similar Czech company/ app called **HaloTaxi** (+420 244 114 411) are also active in Prague.

Car

Prague is easy enough to navigate with a trusty GPS navigation system. Do your best to steer clear of the Old Town center, which is always congested. Blue lines allow for restricted parking upon payment at machines nearby. There are numerous parking garages available. They get cheaper the farther out you stay, so find a parking lot near a far-off metro station for cheaper daily rates. The garage near the Chodov shopping center is right on the red metro line and is staffed, offering rates of around 200Kč per day. There are also various park-and-ride (P&R) lots on the outer metro stops that charge only about 20Kč per day plus 100Kč per overnight stay. These lots are unguarded, so don't leave anything inside the car.

Bicycle

With its cobblestones and crowds, I don't recommend cycling in downtown Prague. If you love staying active, a tour with Biko Prague Bike Tours takes you into hills around Prague for beautiful views of the surrounding countryside.

DAY TRIPS

If you've got the time, I highly recommend getting out to the quaint Bohemian countryside for another take on Czech culture.

Kutna Hora

Famous for its bone church, Kutna Hora first came to prominence as a silver-mining town and was once a hub for royalty, nobility, and monastic life. Its town center is a UNESCO World Heritage Site. Tour some of the city's top sights:

The **Museum of Silver** (70Kč, Tues-Sun 09:00-17:00, closed Mon, Barborská 28/9, +420 327 512 159) is a slightly outdated museum housed in a fortified 14th-century noble residence; it offers options to explore an actual silver mine (310Kč, tours every 30 minutes) nearby.

Also known as the bone church, the **Sedlec Ossuary** (90Kč, daily 09:00-16:00, Zamecka 279, +420 326 551 049, ossuary. eu) on Zámecká houses a breathtaking library of macabre skeletal creations like chandeliers and coats of arms.

The **Cathedral of St. Barbara** (daily 10:00-16:00, Barborská, +420 775 363 938, khfarnost.cz) took more than 500 years to build. It's considered to be the town center's primary building of importance.

Trains from Prague take just under an hour. They leave from Hlavní Nádraží frequently and daily. Head to Kutna Hora's **tourist information center** (Palackého námesti 377/5, Mon-Fri 09:00-17:00, Sat-Sun 10:00-16:00) on the main square for a free map and to get oriented.

Okoř Castle (Hrad Okoř)

To explore some serious medieval ruins, consider the half-day trip out to Okoř Castle, which has foundations dating to the 13th century. Abandoned 2.5 centuries ago, the castle long ago fell into disrepair, but its formidable fortifications have survived this long period of neglect and disuse. Be sure to check hours before taking the hike out.

Get to the castle via a 40-minute bus ride from Prague. Take the green metro A line to Dejvická and take bus 350 from the west side of the square. Be sure to check timetables for your return trip before embarking on the walk to the castle from the bus stop.

Apr-May and Oct-Dec Sat-Sun 10:00-16:00, June-Sept Tues-Sun 10:00-16:00, closed Jan-Mar, +420 233 900 675, hrad-okor.cz.

Český Krumlov

Český Krumlov is a picturesque medieval-Renaissance Czech town in southern Bohemia. If you see a postcard from the Czech Republic and Prague isn't on it, you're probably looking at Český Krumlov, famous for its quaint atmosphere and for the lazy river's hairpin turn, which makes for stunning vistas when viewed from the castle high up on a ridge. This town is well

worth the 3.5-hour bus trip from Prague. Stay overnight and take your time exploring the castle and tiny old town—it may be only four blocks across, but the sights and the views should be enjoyed at a leisurely pace. The experience is especially pleasant when the weather is cooperative.

To get there, opt for **Student Agency buses** (studentagencybus.com), which leave from Florenc station. Tickets (200Kč one way) do sell out in advance, so reserve ahead of time. Trains take about 4.5 hours (around 550Kč) including a transfer in České Budějovice. While more comfortable, this option does take more time, and the train station is a ways from the center of Český Krumlov, so pack light or hail a taxi on arrival.

HELP!

Travel Tips

Having identification on you at all times is required. Avoid drinking alcohol on the streets in the city center, especially on public transportation.

While not absolutely necessary, it's definitely a comfort to have a bit of data—to avoid exorbitant roaming charges, pick up a local prepaid SIM card. This will make it much easier to navigate the city, update your itinerary on the fly, phone in reservations, and find food and drink when hunger and thirst beckon.

If you are a victim of any crime or have lost any of your travel documents (passport, etc.), contact the US Embassy and they will sort you out. Respect local authorities, and don't draw negative attention to yourself. Police are often happy to offer directions and, if you're in a bind, they'll help you find your way out. When talking to locals, don't misinterpret their reticence to communicate. They're not being rude; it's far more likely that they're just frustrated (they want to help, but the language barrier is making that difficult for them). Prague is a very safe city, but you can quickly find yourself in trouble if you seek out brothels and drugs.

Tourist Information Center

Find Prague's official tourist information center next to the Astronomical Clock. Pop in here for help on everything from finding

accommodations to booking concerts, bus tours, or local guides, or even renting cars.

Daily 09:00-19:00, Staroměstské námesti 1, Old Town, +420 221 714 714, praguecitytourism.cz

Pickpockets & Scams

Prague is an extremely safe city with a low violent crime rate. However, there are still scams and situations to be mindful of when touring the city. Pickpockets frequent the areas that tourists are known to congregate—and especially places where they are distracted, like the Astronomical Clock. If wandering the streets late at night, be mindful of strangers who seem drunk and try to get close. A high percentage of thefts occur at night in bars and nightclubs. Beware of anybody who tries to lure you into one of the many strip clubs off of Wenceslas Square. Most of these clubs are rip-offs, selling watery cocktails and leaving you broke by the end of the night.

Emergencies

In an emergency, dial 112. Dial 158 for police.

Hospital

Nemocnice Na Františku
Na Františku 8
+420 224 810 502

US Embassy

Tržiště 15
+420 257 022 000

BUDAPEST

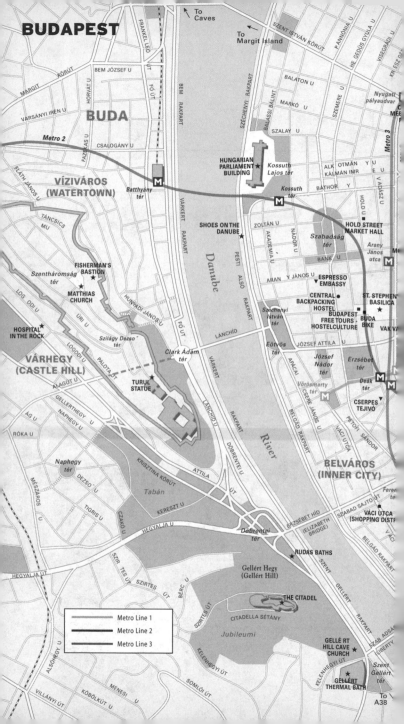

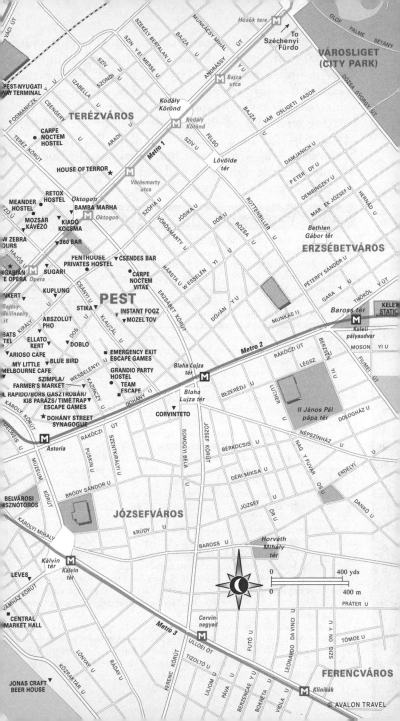

Budapest, with stunning baroque architecture, magnificent bathhouses, and rocking ruin pubs, is unlike any other city you'll visit. Rather than traditional sightseeing, offbeat experiences—from subterranean caving expeditions to escape games to partying on a boat on the Danube—will be the highlight of your trip. But there's plenty to see along Budapest's wide boulevards. And with lots of fun, social hostels, Budapest fits into even the tightest of budgets.

BUDAPEST 101

The Carpathian Basin was settled by Celtic tribes, who were attracted to the area's fertile land and abundant thermal hot springs. Around AD 100, the Romans arrived and established a military encampment, calling it Aquincum in a nod to the region's healing springs. The Romans built roads, baths, and amphitheaters, the foundations of which are still sprinkled around town today.

In 896, the legendary Hungarian—or Magyar—tribes arrived from the east and found the place to their liking. The fabled seven tribes and their brave leader, Arpad, followed their legendary *turul* bird, who carried the sword of the Hungarian people. The bird dropped the sword, and the tribes settled where it landed.

By the early 19th century, Hungary had become a part of the Habsburg Empire, which was centered in Vienna. In 1848, revolution burned through the continent and Hungary followed suit. The Habsburgs made an example of crushing this revolt. Curiously enough, the Hungarians were granted semiautonomy about 20 years later when the Austrians realized they needed a friendly capital in Hungary. This deal was cemented in the Austro-Hungarian Compromise of 1867, laying the foundations of the Austro-Hungarian Empire, a complicated powder keg of clandestine transcontinental alliances. The 1914 assassination of Archduke Franz Ferdinand, heir to the Austro-Hungarian throne, triggered a violent domino effect that ignited World War I.

After being on the losing side of World War I, Hungary was sliced up and lost 70 percent of its territories and two-thirds of its population. A couple of decades later, World War II brought widespread destruction along with executions and deportations of Budapest's Jews. Hungary was "liberated" by the Russians, but the Soviets hung around for the next few decades. Hungarians rebelled against communist rule by 1956. Thousands fled the country, and it took a massive effort to put down the rebellion.

Hungary, considered the "breadbasket" of the Soviet Empire because it produced food that was distributed across the Eastern Bloc, enjoyed a rather privileged position and relatively high standard of living under Soviet rule. Hungarians were even able to leave the country occasionally. That's not to say the populace wasn't policed. The Hungarian secret police (the State Protection Authority, or AVH) were responsible for torture, detentions, and executions that recalled those of the Nazi SS. By the 1980s, communism was crumbling around the Eastern Bloc, and Hungary was among those celebrating the fall of the Berlin Wall.

In the last 25 years, Budapest has undergone a transformation, but it remains culturally distinct from every other European city. You'll see posh shopping boulevards like those in Paris, trendy nightlife like Berlin's, a city layout similar to that of Prague (with a river down the middle and a castle on a hill), and an alternative vibe like that of East London. There's no other city that rolls all of this into one!

PLAN AHEAD

RESERVATIONS

Reservations are required for the **Hungarian Parliament Building** (parlament.hu/en).

Reservations are highly recommended for the following activities:

Caving (barlangaszat.hu; purchase tickets first thing at your hostel)

Spa parties (bathsbudapest.com/budapest-bath-parties; most hostels will be able to sell you tickets)

Budapest Boat Party (facebook.com/Budapestpartyhostels)

LOCAL HAPPENINGS

Sziget Music Festival

The Sziget Music Festival (szigetfestival.com) takes over an entire island on the Danube around August 10 each year. This weeklong event features massive headliners from the worlds of pop, indie, rock, metal, hip-hop, and EDM, with the action spread out over an ever-growing number of stages. The island is just a 10-minute rail ride from downtown Budapest (HEV from Buda side of Margit Island), so the entire city gets in on the party. The atmosphere is otherworldly. Word is out that this is one of the hottest tickets in Europe, so buy yours well in advance.

St. Stephen's Day

Celebrated on August 20 each year, St. Stephen's day is named in honor of Hungary's first king, Stephen I, who was also responsible for Christianizing Hungary. Fireworks and general celebrations are widespread, making it a great time to visit the city.

Day of Revolution

October 23 marks two important events in Hungarian history: the Revolution of 1956 (the failed Hungarian uprising against the Soviet Union) and the Day of the Republic (the day when communism officially fell and Hungary was declared a republic). The mood is jubilant yet pensive—many Hungarians can still remember the unhappy years when the country was a part of the Soviet Bloc.

KNOW BEFORE YOU GO

KEY STATS & FIGURES

Currency:
Hungary uses the forint (Ft);
285 Ft = about 1 USD

Population:
1,750,000

Language:
Hungarian

Size of Hungary:
93,000 square kilometers
(about the size of Michigan)

National dish:
goulash and anything spiced with paprika

Number of hot springs:
123 In greater Budapest

Famous Hungarian inventions:
Rubik's Cube, the ballpoint pen, binoculars, color TV, Microsoft Word and Microsoft Excel, the hydrogen bomb

CALIBRATE YOUR BUDGET

TYPICAL PRICES FOR:

Hostel dorm bed:
4,000Ft

Two-course dinner:
3,500Ft

Pint of beer:
600Ft

Bicycle rental:
3,500Ft

Metro pass:
350Ft

MOVIES TO WATCH
Mission: Impossible— Ghost Protocol, I Spy, 8MM 2, Transporter 3, Munich

MUSIC VIDEOS TO WATCH
Katy Perry's "Firework," Selena Gomez's "Round and Round," Jamie Woon's "Lady Luck"

THREE DAY ITINERARY

Budapest is one of my favorite cities, not just for the culture, affordable prices, food, and nightlife, but also because the sights are different from those in most other major cities. This three-day itinerary has you jumping from one unforgettable activity to the next.

DAY 1: TO THE BATHHOUSE!

MORNING

Before leaving your hostel, throw a swimsuit and a towel in your bag—you'll be visiting the baths later this afternoon. Pop into **Mozsár Kávézó** for breakfast. From there it's a five-minute walk to the **Yellow Zebra Bike Tour** office (behind the Hungarian State Opera House). Their guided bike tour (departing at 11:00 daily Apr-Oct) is an excellent four-hour introduction to the city.

AFTERNOON

You'll finish your tour back where you started, and you're just a few blocks away from **Bamba Marha** and its delicious burgers. You'll need the nourishment before the trip to **Széchenyi Fürdő**, the bathhouse located in **City Park**. From Oktogon, take the underground metro and get off at the Széchenyi Fürdő stop.

Spend the afternoon soaking in the mineral baths. You'll leave feeling rejuvenated (and probably a little sleepy).

EVENING

Head back to the hostel to freshen up. Once you're rested, it's time for a fun retro Hungarian dinner at one of my favorite spots in town, **Vak Varjú.**

LATE

You're in the perfect place to explore the **Gozsdu Court & Passage** and the dozens of bars in the surrounding Jewish Quarter. If it's Monday, Wednesday, Friday, or Saturday, you've got the option of a boat party—not to be missed!

DAY 2: CAVING & RUIN PUBS

MORNING

You'll be hitting the caves this afternoon, so dress comfortably and wear shoes that you can get dirty (very dirty). Purchase tickets from your hostel staff, and confirm the meeting place and time before setting out for the day.

Shake off your hangover with a bite at the **Great Market Hall.** There's all sorts of fresh food on the main level (a perfect place to stock up for afternoon snacks), while the upper level offers trinket shopping and a few hot food vendors. Also upstairs you'll find a stall selling *lángos*. Take yours outside and enjoy the view of Liberty Bridge and Liberty Statue atop **Gellért Hill.**

Walk north along **Váci Utca**, Budapest's main shopping boulevard until you reach Vörösmarty tér, Pest's central town square—you'll pass plenty of touristy and brand-name stores on the way. From here, catch tram 2 and ride it a couple of stops north toward the **Hungarian Parliament Building.** The five-minute ride will take you along the Danube River. Across the river you'll see the **Castle District** and **Fisherman's Bastion.** On the closer bank is the **Shoes on the Danube Memorial** (keep your eyes peeled; it's easy to miss).

To go inside the **Hungarian Parliament Building,** make an appointment online ahead of time. Tours take about 1.5 hours, so factor that in if you're planning to go caving.

AFTERNOON

Meet your group for the four-hour **Barlangászat Caving Tour** at Nyugati station, which is only a 10-minute walk from the Hungarian Parliament Building. Your shoes will get dirty with clay, but you'll have coveralls that'll keep everything else relatively clean. Enjoy your adventure!

If you're claustrophobic, give the caving a miss. Instead, enjoy the wide-open views from the **chairlift up to the Elizabeth Lookout,** Budapest's highest viewpoint.

EVENING

Refresh yourself with a shower at the hostel and then head for a classy bite at **Kiosk** overlooking the Danube. Your meal will include some spectacular views of the Citadel.

LATE

It's time to venture into the Jewish Quarter to experience the city's world-renowned ruin pubs. Start at **Kuplung,** continue on to **Szimpla** before it's too late (the crowds get intense close to midnight), and then pop over to **Instant/Fogas** to get your dance on. If you've still got the energy, hike or cab it over to **Corvintető** to finish your night strong.

DAY 3: JEWISH QUARTER SIGHTS & MARGIT ISLAND
MORNING

If it's Sunday, start at **Szimpla's farmers market.** More than a dozen vendors sell delicious organic cheeses, pastries, coffees, salami, greens, soups, and more. Don't miss the organic, vegan-friendly buffet (4,000Ft) upstairs. For something a little greasier, you'll find a food truck market just next door. If it's not Sunday, settle for **Sugar!** (one of their coffees and a sweet rice pudding will beat any hangover).

Make your way to the **Dohány Street Synagogue** and the Raoul Wallenberg Holocaust Memorial Park.

AFTERNOON

It's time to enjoy Budapest's best green space. Bring picnic supplies and head to **Margit Island.** Rent a bike if you want to stretch your legs a bit (the four-person bikes are a blast). On a nice day, there's no better place to picnic than alongside the river. Tram 6 will zip you there; get off at the stop at the middle of the bridge and take the path down towards the island.

Have energy to spare? Pick between a pair of museums (either the **House of Terror** or the **Hospital in the Rock**) or try one of Budapest's latest crazes: **escape games.**

EVENING

For dinner, head to **Belvárosi Disznótoros** on Király Utca for a cheap, filling meal.

LATE

For your last night in Budapest, start deep in the Jewish Quarter with a cocktail at **Hotsy Totsy,** or have a glass of wine at **Doblo.** If you've got an early-morning flight, you can finish your evening at **360.** If the evening is entirely your own, head over to nearby **Tesla** or hop in a cab and enjoy top-notch clubbing at **Ötkert.**

TOP NEIGHBORHOODS

Budapest is large but relatively easy to navigate. The majestic Danube River runs down its center. On the west side is hilly, residential Buda. Pest, on the east side, is flat and sprawling.

Just about all the action happens in Pest, within three major concentric ring roads. Inside the first ring (Karoly/Muzeum/Vámház Körút) is the **5th District,** also referred to as the Pest Town Center, which is home to the Hungarian Parliament Building and St. Stephen's Basilica. The second, larger ring (Szent Istvan/Terez/Josef/Ferenc Körút) encircles the **6th District,** including Andrássy út, a major boulevard where you'll find the Hungarian State Opera

House and House of Terror. Also inside this second ring is the **Jewish Quarter (7th District),** site of the Dohány Street Synagogue and the center of Budapest's raging nightlife scene. East of this second ring road, **City Park** houses the famous Széchenyi baths.

In Buda, the **Castle District** is home to the Fisherman's Bastion, the National Gallery, the Turul Bird statue, Matthias Church, and overlooking all of them, **Gellért Hill** capped by the Citadel. The castle in Buda is a hastily constructed Soviet copy of the genuine article that used to overlook the city, but this doesn't mean you should skip it.

TOP SIGHTS

PEST

Hungarian Parliament Building

Budapest's most iconic landmark, visible in nearly every photo of the city you'll find, is this spectacular building built between 1885 and 1904 to commemorate the millennial celebration of Hungary's 896 founding. Topped with 1,896 spires, this massive bicameral structure is a testament to Hungarian design and ingenuity—it was built entirely by Hungarian craftsmen using only Hungarian materials. To build it cost a staggering 38 million gold crowns, nearly $1.5 billion in today's money.

The building's basement has been renovated into a slick visitors center. Visitors must book tickets and reserve tours online ahead of time. They run at 10:00, 12:00, 13:00, 14:00, and 15:00 and take about 45 minutes.

6,000Ft, English tours at 10:00, 12:00, 13:00, 14:00, and 15:00 when Parliament is in session (usually Sept-May), Kossuth Lajos tér 1-3, 5th District, +36 1 441 4000, jegymester.hu, Metro: Kossuth tér

Shoes on the Danube Memorial

During the winter of 1944-1945, militia of the Arrow Cross, Hungary's fascist party, rounded up Jews from the city's ghetto, lined them up along the banks of the river, and shot them at close range. Sixty iron pairs of shoes mark the spot where

these murders occurred. This discreet but poignant memorial is a reminder of the importance of remaining vigilant against bigotry and ignorance.

Free, always open, two blocks south along the river from the Parliament Building (use caution when crossing the tram tracks and the busy road), 5th District, Metro: Kossuth tér

St. Stephen's Basilica

St. Stephen's bold, neoclassical architecture, with twin bell towers and prominent dome and spire, is recognizable from almost anywhere in town. On entry, you may be hassled by someone requesting donations, but the church is free to enter. You can find the famous mummified hand of St. Stephen in the back of the church toward the left of the altar. It is possible to climb the dome for less than US$2, but the views aren't particularly amazing.

900Ft, 1,200Ft for observation deck, Mon-Fri 10:00-13:00, Szent István tér 1, 5th District, +36 1 311 0839, bazilika.biz, Metro: Bajcsy-Zsilinszky út

Hungarian State Opera House

The Hungarian State Opera House was constructed during the height of the Austro-Hungarian Empire in 1884. As the second capital of the great Habsburg Empire, Budapest simply had to have an opera house, and license was granted to build one—with the condition that it not

THE NUMBERS GAME

The numbers **7** (the original number of Magyar tribes that settled in the C͟arpathian Basin), **896** and **1896** (the dates of Hungary's foundation and millennial cele͟bra͟tion), and (by extrapolation) **96** are basically all you need to know for just a͟bou͟t anything in town. How many points does the Fisherman's Bastion have? 7. H͟ow many spires on the Parliament Building? 1,896. How tall is St. Stephen's Ba͟silica? 96 meters. These numbers will come in handy during Budapest pub quiz nig͟hts.

be larger than the one in Vienna. Playing within the rules, the architects sought to make this opera house grander—but not bigger—than the one in their sister city. The hall they built has proud neo-Renaissance architecture and a gilded concert hall that comfortably seats over 1,400 patrons in three levels of balconies and a large main audience floor. I'd say they achieved their goal.

Free to pop in to the lobby, Mon-Sat 11:00 until showtime, usually 19:00, or until 17:00 if there's no performance, Sun open 3 hours before performance, usually 16:00-19:00, or 10:00-13:00 if there's a matinee, English tours daily at 15:00 during high season (June-Oct) for 2,900Ft, mini concerts often for the screaming deal of 600Ft, check show calendar and prices online, Andrássy út 22, 6th District, +36 1 814 7100, opera.hu, Metro: Opera

Dohány Street Synagogue

With capacity for nearly 3,000 worshippers, the Dohány Street Synagogue (also known as the Great Synagogue) is the second-largest synagogue in the world. While Budapest's Jewish population still hasn't recovered from the deportation of 600,000 Hungarian Jews during the Holocaust, the synagogue stands proud and

serves the 100,000 Jews living in B͟udapest today. Free tours in multiple la͟nguages leave every 30 minutes, ta͟king you through the **Hungarian Nation͟al Jewish Museum,** showcasing artifacts of d͟aily life and culture.

If you don't want to pay to ente͟r the collection, you can still ap͟preciate the stunning building from outsid͟e. The **R͟aoul Wallenberg Holocaust Memorial P͟ark** is in the back garden of the synago͟gue, but you can see it from the street (al͟beit through bars). It's designed in the sha͟pe of a weeping willow, or overt͟urned meno͟rah. Each of the thousands of shimmerin͟g leaves bears the name of a H͟ungarian vic͟tim of the Holocaust.

4,000Ft, Mar-Oct Sun-Thurs 10:00-17:30, Fri 10:00-16:30, closed Sat, closes at 15:30 Fri in Mar; Nov-Feb Sun-Thurs 10:00-15:30, Fri 10:00-13:30, closed Sat; refer to website for the annual list of days closed, knees and shoulders must be covered, Dohány Utca 2, Jewish Quarter, greatsynagogue.hu, Metro: Astoria

House of Terror

The House of Terror occupies the former headquarters of both the Nazi SS and the Arrow Cross, Hungary's fascist party. After the war, it was the home of the communist

ecret police. It's a sobering and even emotionally exhausting exhibit that highlights human cruelty. It takes at least 1.5 hours to make your way through the exhibits, featuring a look at daily life under communism. While visitors flock here, the museum has been widely criticized for its tendency to portray Hungarians as the victims of foreign occupiers, glossing over the role that Hungarians themselves played in the tragic events you'll learn about here.

2,000Ft, Tues-Sun 10:00-18:00, last entry 30 minutes before closing, Andrássy út 60, 6th District, +36 1 374 2600, terrorhaza.hu, Metro: Vörösmarty utca

Heroes' Square

At the end of Budapest's grandest Avenue, Andrássy út, you'll find Heroes' Square, a huge open space where Hungarians gather on special occasions. At the top of the square you'll see a colonnade and a row of statues commemorating 14 Hungarian heroes. In front of the columns is one of my favorite statues in Europe—the seven mounted leaders of the Magyar, fronted by the helmeted Árpad. The square is flanked by two museums: the **Museum of Fine Arts** (szepmuveszeti.hu) and the **Hall of Art** (mucsarnok.hu), both of which have rotating exhibits. The Hall of Art is the less impressive of the two, but both are worth a visit for ardent lovers of painting and sculpture who have time to spare. The Hall of Art contains far more modern collections than the Museum of Fine Arts.

Eastern end of Andrássy út, 6th District, Metro: Hősök tere

BUDA

Matthias Church

The majestic neo-Gothic Matthias Church is famous for its beautiful white stone architecture and colorful roof tiling typical of Hungary. Though its foundations date back to 1015, the church appears brand new thanks to recent renovations. Head inside and you'll be treated to a Technicolor kaleidoscope of holy decorations on nearly every square inch of the columns, arches, ribs, altar, stained glass, and pulpit. You can climb into the dome with a guided tour.

1,500Ft, Mon-Fri 09:00-17:00, Sat 09:00-13:00, Sun 13:00-17:00, sometimes open later in summer, Szentháromság tér 2, Castle District, +36 1 355 5657, Metro: Széll Kálmán tér

Fisherman's Bastion

With a name like Fisherman's Bastion, not many people know what to expect at this sight. Don't look for it on the river. Constructed to coincide with the country's millennial anniversary, the gleaming white ramparts with seven pointed turrets—one for each of the original Magyar tribes—are perched high on the hill and afford stunning panoramas across the Danube, over the Parliament Building, and into Pest. Climb the stairs for a small fee and slightly better view, or go for free after sunset.

800Ft, mid-Mar-mid-Oct daily 09:00-19:00, open and free to enter after closing time or off season, Szentháromság tér 5, Castle District, +36 1 458 3030, fishermansbastion.com, Metro: Széll Kálmán tér

National Gallery

The best collection of Hungarian art anywhere in the world, the National Gallery contains noteworthy works stretching back to Hungary's medieval period. You'll find beautiful sculptures, paintings, photographs from the 20th century, and a stunning set of 15th-century altars. If you're looking for recognizable names or canvases, you probably won't find them here.

1,800Ft (permanent collections), 2,000Ft (temporary exhibit), Tues-Sun 10:00-18:00 (last entry one hour before closing), Szent György tér 2, Castle District, +36 20 439 7325, mng.hu, Metro: Széll Kálmán tér

Hospital in the Rock

This cave network underneath the Budapest castle was used as a hospital during World War II. It was later used as a nuclear bunker during the Cold War. With some impressive engineering, the hospital was designed to withstand nuclear attack. Today, you can take a fascinating guided tour of these tunnels—well worth it for history buffs.

4,000Ft, daily 10:00-20:00, last tour departs at 19:00, Lovas Way 4/c, Castle District, +36 70 701 0101, sziklakorhaz.eu, Metro: Széll Kálmán tér

The Citadel

This decommissioned military fort, strategically located at the top of Gellért Hill and topped by one of Budapest's most iconic statues, offers amazing views. Start the climb after crossing either the Erzsébet Bridge or the Szabadság Bridge.

Whichever bridge you use, it's a pretty long hike to the top: Allow yourself about 2-2.5 hours to get up the hill, check out the views, enjoy some refreshments, and get back down again.

If you want to add a little more time to your descent, check out the **Church of the Rock** (sziklatemplom.hu/web/fooldal.html), a church that was carved into an existing cave on the side of the hill.

Free, daily 11:00-23:00, Citadella Sétány 1, Gellért Hill, Metro: Szent Gellért tér or Móricz Zsigmond körtér

TOP HUNGARIAN BATHHOUSES

You can't leave Budapest without taking a dunk in at least one of the city's invigorating aquatic wonderlands. This is one of the few activities (other than drinking) where locals and tourists mingle and mix. Water in this region comes out of the ground at 170 degrees Fahrenheit. This water is then cooled and channeled into the beautiful public bathhouses and pool complexes. Plaques by each pool will tell you about the temperature and mineral content. You'll find pools as cold as 16°C (18°C is as cold as I can stand) all the way up to 40°C (anything hotter and you'll start feeling and looking like a lobster on its way to the table).

Széchenyi Fürdő

This is the bathhouse that locals and tourists pack out pretty well every day of the year, and for good reason. For first-timers, this is the perfect introduction to Budapest bathing culture. Széchenyi (pronounced "say-jenny") is a delightful jumble of interior steam rooms, saunas, and outside pools encircled by grand baroque architecture. While away the hours in this labyrinth of pools, saunas, and steam baths one pool and room at a time. Spend some time lounging in the sun by the steps of the large warm pool outside and watch the old men play chess with plastic sets while half-submerged in the water. These men are fixtures here—every bit as permanent as the fountains.

4,900Ft for ticket and locker, more for personal changing cabin, cheaper after 19:00 and more expensive on weekends, daily 06:00-22:00, thermal bath open 06:00-19:00, may be open later on summer weekends, last entry one hour before closing, inside the City Park (across the bridge behind Heroes' Square), City Park, szechenyibath.com, Metro: Széchenyi Fürdő

Rudas

Built by the Ottomans centuries ago, Rudas is your legit Turkish bath, with low lights, burning-hot steam rooms, and *ice-cold* dunk baths. With no frills and only 6 pools (Széchenyi has 18), Rudas still manages to cover all the important bases,

with a temperature range (18-42°C) broad enough to make the experience authentic (and bracing). For a nominal fee, you can gain access to the new Jacuzzi on the roof of the bath—the view of the Budapest skyline combined with the heavenly soak more than make up for the added cost. This is the only bath in Budapest that is still gender-segregated during the week.

3,100Ft, men only Mon, Wed, Thurs, Fri 06:00-20:00; women only Tues 06:00-20:00; gender-mixed Fri 22:00-04:00, Sat 06:00-20:00 and 22:00-04:00, Sun 06:00-20:00, Rudas Gyógyfürdő és Uszoda, Gellért Hill, +36 1 356 1010, rudasbaths.com, Metro: Szent Gellért tér, Tram: Döbrentei tér

Gellért

The poshest bathhouse in Budapest, Gellért is the premier drawing card at the five-star hotel by the same name. Gellért features an outdoor wave pool (generally open in the summer) that toes the line between safe and dangerous fun. A handful of interior rooms are gender separated, so if you like, you can let it all hang out. Gellért is located at the base of the Gellért Hill, just across the Liberty Bridge.

5,300Ft for ticket and locker, 400Ft more for personal changing cabin, cheaper after 17:00, last entry one hour before closing, daily 06:00-20:00, Kelenhegyi Út 4, Gellért Hill, +36 1 466 6166, gellertbath.com, Metro: Szent Gellért tér

ACT LIKE A LOCAL

Splish, Splash: Hungarian Bathhouse Etiquette

As with any local cultural practice, there are a few rules you'll be expected to understand at Budapest's *fürdő* (baths). To avoid any unnecessary confusion or embarrassment, keep the following rules/guidelines in mind:

When changing, go for privacy or let it all hang out. Hungarians aren't shy when it comes to nudity in changing rooms. If you prefer privacy, book a private changing cabin (the added cost is negligible). If you're not shy, there's no need to hide behind a towel.

Consider a massage. You can make your spa experience even more heavenly with a massage. There are girls by the entrance with clipboards. The massages are reasonably priced, but you can definitely find better deals at any of the massage parlors around town (be advised, some of these places are selling more than just rubdowns).

Skip the medical treatments. Thermal and mineral spas are recognized in Hungary to have legitimate health benefits. Doctors actually prescribe a whole host of treatments, many of which are listed on the general price list you see when entering. Skip these and just ask for the basic entry.

Your wristband is your entry ticket, your locker access, and your exit ticket. When you pay your entrance fee, you'll be given a plastic wristband. You'll use it to get in and to access your locker for the duration of your stay. Drop it in the magnetic slot when you leave.

Bring your own suit and towels to save $$$. Towels and swimsuits are available for rent at the service counter in the basement (next to the men's changing room), but they're not cheap. Save money by bringing your own suit and towel.

Consider bringing flip-flops. They're nice to have in the showers and for getting around the various pools, but not required.

Don't be afraid to ask for help. Locker room attendants are there to help. If you have questions, just ask. They usually answer you in English.

Be aware of your surroundings. Remember that the baths are therapeutic and, for some, even medicinal. This is a place of relaxation, so calmness is the general rule. Horseplay or loud, obnoxious conversations will not be appreciated and might result in you being asked to leave. Public displays of affection, however, are perfectly acceptable.

TOP CAFÉS

Budapest has a legendary café culture, and it has blossomed into a full-blown hipster movement.

Sugar!

More than your typical sugar shack, this place amps the sweetness to the next level with handmade cupcakes and desserts to go with their wide assortment of candies and excellent coffee. My go-to is the sweet rice pudding with a dash of cinnamon sugar on top to split with friends—or, if you're fine with the impending sugar crash, you can hog it to yourself.

Sweets from 600Ft, Mon 12:00-22:00, Tues-Sun 10:30-22:00, Sat until 20:00, 48 Paulay Ede Utca, 6th District, +36 1 321 6672, sugarshop.hu, Metro: Opera

Arioso Flower Café

This tastefully decorated café has a wooden lattice on the roof that is constantly changing. When you're there it might have strings of light cascading down from the ceiling, or it might hold an assortment of flowers—blooms are the place's primary business, so the usual smells of the café mix pleasantly with the aroma of freshly cut flowers. The courtyard garden and patio is an ideal spot for a quiet conversation or a moment of reflection in the middle of a busy day.

Coffee from 500Ft, Mon-Fri 10:00-19:00, Sat 10:00-18:00, Király utca 9, 7th District, +36 30 299 0862, Facebook: Arioso Flower Café, Metro: Deák Ferenc tér

My Little Melbourne

This is some of Budapest's best coffee, and the baristas know it. Expect a self-confident hipster vibe here and at **BrewBar,** their sister café next door. It's a popular spot and seating inside is limited, so it's likely that you'll be taking your coffee to go. If you are lucky enough to find a pew, don't make yourself too comfortable—their Wi-Fi vouchers are only good for 45 minutes, which is their polite way of saying "keep it moving."

Coffee from 700Ft, Mon-Fri 07:00-19:00, Sat-Sun 08:30-19:00, Madách Imre út 3, 7th District, +36 70 394 7002, mylittlemelbourne.hu, Metro: Deák Ferenc tér

Stika

Stika seems to have late sleepers in mind. Their all-day breakfast and excellent coffee will give you that get-up-and-go no matter when you need it. The laid-back hipster vibe comes without the usual dose of pretentiousness—these guys seem genuinely eager to please. When the afternoon starts to turn into the evening, switch to one of their excellent beers or cocktails.

Coffee from 550Ft, all-day breakfast starting at 990Ft, Mon-Wed 8:00-23:00, Thurs Sat 8:00-23:45, Sun 8:00-17:00, Dob Utca 46, 7th District, +36 1 274 8044, Facebook: Stika Budapest, Tram: Wesselényi utca, Erzsébet körút

Csendes Létterem

Looking as though a garage sale exploded and covered every surface, this spot is a veritable wonderland of mismatched furniture and knickknacks. It's not a quiet spot, but there are tons of excellent mingling opportunities and great music. The full food and drink menu keeps patrons around well into the night.

Coffee from 500Ft, Mon-Wed 12:00-24:00, Thurs-Fri 12:00-02:00, Sat 16:00-02:00, Sun 16:00-24:00, Ferenczy István utca 5, 5th District, +36 30 727 2100, Facebook: Csendes Létterem, Metro: Astoria

Espresso Embassy

This place has probably the best espresso in town, and there are excellent fresh pastries and snacks to boot. The tables are more than big enough to set up a mobile office for a few hours, and the exposed-brick walls and arches give the place a hip vibe that is appreciated by the freelancers and in-the-know expats and tourists who pack this place out (especially on weekends). You'll find it just around the corner from Liberty Square and not far from the basilica, making it the perfect place to take a breather in the middle of sightseeing.

Espresso from 400Ft, Mon-Fri 07:30-19:00, Sat 09:00-18:00, Sun 09:00-17:00, Arany János u. 15, 5th District, +36 20 445 0063, espressoembassy.hu, Metro: Arany János utca.

Mozsár Kávézó

Mozsár Kávézó has all the necessities in a mod café: fresh pastries, good coffee, hot breakfasts, and fast Wi-Fi. What's not to love? Its location near a number of recommended hostels and the opera house makes it a convenient place to grab breakfast. On a hot day, the large windows turn the place into a stuffy greenhouse, so I take my breakfast outside on the patio.

Pastries from 400Ft, daily 09:00-23:00, Nagymező Utca 21, 6th District, +36 1 898 1115, Facebook: Mozsár Kávézó, Metro: Opera

Blue Bird

No frills, just excellent coffee. The tourists largely avoid this place, making it ideal for a quiet afternoon chat, and since they roast the beans on the premises, the smell can be intoxicating. Check out **Printa** (printa.hu) next door for cool prints and T-shirts. There's another Blue Bird a few blocks away in the Gozsdu Court & Passage that serves good breakfast and coffee, but this location is my favorite.

Coffee from 500Ft, daily 09:00-18:00, Rumbach Sebestyen 12, 7th District, +36 70 419 9025, Facebook: Blue Bird Roastery, Metro: Deák Ferenc tér

TOP EATS

Traditional Hungarian fare is simple, heavy, and filling. Classic dishes like **goulash** are as inexpensive as they are satiating. Budapest is, however, in the midst of a gastro revolution, which means an ever-increasing palette of options—from piping-hot Napolitano pizza and street food stands to mom-and-pop-style diners and haute cuisine. One street in particular overflows with all sorts of international cuisine: **Kazinczy Utca** in the Jewish Quarter (7th District). **Gozsdu Court & Passage,** a couple blocks west of Kazinczy Utca, is restaurant central. The offerings cater to the tourists who flood this area each evening, but they're still quite affordable. Closer to Oktogon you'll find Liszt Ferenc tér—another string of great restaurants, all of them with outdoor seating that packs out in the warmer months.

Hungarian service is notoriously hit and miss. Even top-shelf cafés and restaurants can feature brusque or downright rude service. If the service is good, tipping is appreciated. When you receive the bill, read it carefully and check whether they've included a "service" charge (usually 10-12 percent). If service isn't included, tip 10 percent or so.

Vak Varjú

If you're looking for a bit of traditional and affordably priced Hungarian grub, this is the place. Their goulash is superb and their duck entrées are a local favorite. The décor is playful yet elegant. Behind a railing on the second floor, waxwork dummies of a Hungarian grandmother and grandfather silently judge the diners below. There are also surprises in both bathrooms. If you're thirsty or sitting with friends, the 3.5-liter beer tower, with a tap that seals in the bubbles until you're ready to drink, makes for an excellent way to start the night.

900-3,000Ft, daily 12:00-24:00, live piano music often, Paulay Ede Utca 7, 6th District, +36 1 268 0888, vakvarju.com, Metro: Bajcsy-Zsilinszky út

Leves

Hungarians are a straightforward bunch, so it's no surprise that they appreciate this place for (among other things) its no-nonsense name: *leves* means soup in Hungarian. They don't mess about. It's delicious soup and not much else. Choose from four daily specials in either a large or a small bowl, top it off with some chunky croutons,

and you're ready to go. Take it out into the sun in any of the nearby squares.

Soups from 700Ft, daily 11:00-19:00, 14 Vámház Körút, 5th District, +36 30 241 7760, Facebook: Leves, Metro: Kálvin tér

Cserpes Tejivó Milk Bar

Milk bars—bars that sold subsidized milk, ensuring that comrades were universally fit and healthy—were a communist institution. In perfect Budapest hipster fashion, Cserpes Tejivó has turned this concept on its head, infusing it with a modern twist. With great sandwiches, fruit smoothies, and, of course, fresh milk (of the normal, chocolate, and butterscotch varieties), this is an excellent stop in the middle of the center for brunch or lunch.

Sandwiches from 700Ft, Mon–Fri 07:30-22:00, Sat 09:00-20:00, Sun 09:00-18:00, Sütő Utca 2, multiple locations, 5th District, cserpestejivo.hu, Metro: Deák Ferenc tér

Bors GasztroBár

A welcome player in the Kazinczy Utca restaurant lineup, Bors makes excellent sandwiches and innovative soups (try their

FOR THE LOVE OF *LÁNGOS*

Lángos (LON-gohsh) is a favorite local treat. Either savory or sweet, think of it as a deep-fried elephant ear from the carnival topped with almost anything you can imagine (sour cream, cheese, and garlic are local favorites). *Lángos* are sold from street stands and kiosks throughout the city. They're rich and heavy enough to be split by at least two, if not three or four, people. Get your taste in the Great Market Hall or at Lángos Papa on Andrássy út.

red cabbage and sour cherry). Day in, day out it packs out with locals. It's just a few doors down from Szimpla, so pop in here if you need a bite in between beers, or just a break from the loud and tourist-crowded ruin pub.

Sandwiches from 900Ft, Mon–Sat 11:30–21:00, Kazinczy Utca 10, 7th District, +36 70 935 3263, Facebook: Bors GasztroBár, Metro: Astoria

Masel Tov
Try deliciously fresh east Mediterranean cuisine in this informal yet undeniably trendy setting. There's a garden, cool ar-chitecture, and large-scale wall art. The crowd dresses fashionably, but it's not a place where a relaxed approach to fashion will get you snubbed at the door. Quite the contrary, it feels like a welcoming garden party. When you're done with your meal, Instant/Fogas is just up the road (you'll be able to hear it).

Hummus plates from 1,390Ft, Mon–Fri 18:00–02:00, Sat-Sun 12:00–02:00, Akácfa Utca 47, 7th District, +36 70 626 4280, mazeltov.hu, Tram: Király utca, Erzsébet körút

Iguana & Arriba!
These sister restaurants are famous for their delicious Mexican fare and margari-tas that might contain more tequila than anything else. You'll find quick-serve Arri-ba! a block from Oktogon on your way to Nyugati. Sit-down Iguana, just behind the Parliament Building, is a favorite among locals who book tables for everything from celebrations to dates, so call at least 24 hours before you plan to eat there. Start your meal with a pitcher of margaritas and their 5 Amigos sharing plate—the queso dipping sauce is out of this world.

5 Amigos for 2,330Ft, entrées starting around 2,000Ft, call ahead for reservations, daily 11:30–01:00, Zoltán

Utca 16, 5th District, +36 1 331 4352, iguana.hu, Metro: Kossuth Lajos tér

Café Vian
The healthy mix of tourists and locals should let you know that you're on to something good here. While most of the other nearby restaurants are good, Vian outdoes them all. Their chicken Caesar salad is the best in the city, and their lem-onade is pitch perfect (combine the two for a perfect heat-beating snack). It gets quite warm inside, so grab a seat outside. There are other locations in town, but the one on Liszt is the best.

Chicken Caesar for 2,000Ft, daily 09:00–01:00, Liszt Ferenc tér 9, 6th District, +36 1 268 1154, cafevian.com, Metro: Oktogon

Bamba Marha
Budapest's best burger joint, this quick-serve restaurant is riding the city's artisanal gastro wave. It serves perfectly spiced fries, creative dipping sauces, and, of course, mouth-watering burger patties (beef or chicken) cooked to absolute perfection. The double bacon burger (coated in ba-connaise—exactly what it sounds like) is all the savory nourishment you'll need for an afternoon or evening of Budapest's hard partying or soft leisure.

Burgers from 1,000–2,000Ft, daily 11:30–22:00 (last orders at 21:45), Andrássy út 46, 6th District, +36 20 216 2130, bambamarha.hu, Metro: Oktogon

Lángos Papa
Capitalizing on tourists' growing interest in the doughy Hungarian snack, Lángos Papa has built their entire menu around *lángos*, and they do them as well as anybody in the city. They offer a wide range of sweet and savory toppings. Choose from an authen-tic taste of Hungary by ordering the cream

cheese and garlic, or go for something else entirely. Aussies go crazy for the Nutella-topped *lángos*.

3,000Ft for a four-course *lángos* menu, daily 12:00-24:00, Andrássy út 38, 6th District, +36 20 950 2022, langospapa.hu, Metro: Oktogon

Goulash

You can't leave Budapest without sampling its best-known dish: goulash. Almost every restaurant in the city serves some version of the hearty stew, but there

a few standouts if you want to try the absolute best. **Zoska** (zoska.hu), close to Astoria, is very good, as is **Szendzsó** (Facebook: Szendzso Reggelizo Kávézó) on the Buda side of Margit Bridge. **Pöttyös Bögre** (Facebook: Pöttyös Bögre Bisztró), close to the bottom of Andrássy, has wonderful croissants to go with your goulash, and (I've saved my mother's favorite for last) **Anyám Szerint** (Facebook: Anyám szerint) is a quaint and unassuming little café in the Jewish Quarter.

TOP NIGHTLIFE

The Jewish Quarter, for decades a crumbling and almost abandoned commercial dead zone, is one of the best nightlife hot spots anywhere in the world. Drinks are cheap, and the experience is wildly eclectic, running the gamut from dive bars to swanky cocktail joints. Rest up: It's going to be a long, wild night.

NIGHTLIFE DISTRICTS

Király, Akácfa & Kazinczy Utca

Nightlife centers on a few primary streets in the Jewish Quarter. Here you'll find some of Budapest's best ruin bars, including **Fogas/Instant, Ellátó Kert, Kuplung,** and **Szimpla.** Along with nearby Gozsdu Court, these are the places that really define the vibe of the Jewish Quarter.

Jewish Quarter/7th District, Metro: Opera

Gozsdu Court & Passage

Gozsdu Court & Passage, located between Dob Utca (also great) and Király Utca, is an excellent way to introduce yourself to Budapest's nightlife. It's the point where the touristy and the quirky meet. In the passage itself, you'll find a dozen or so bars (many of them overflowing late at night), and in the surrounding area you'll find quirkier hipster joints. In the passage you've got **Epic Winebar,** a chill British-style pub called **The Pointer,** and **Spíler,** an upscale lounge and restaurant. In good weather, the **Gozsdu Sky Terrace** boasts a great rooftop view across downtown Budapest. Prices here skew "Western."

Jewish Quarter, Metro: Deák Ferenc tér

RUIN PUBS

After World War II, the 7th District was left to decay. It had been a Jewish ghetto for the last years of the war, and the misery

that was inflicted here made it a place to be avoided. Heavy fighting took place on these streets, and many of the buildings were strafed with machine gun fire, leaving pitted walls behind. Very slowly, businesses started to return to the district after decades of complete neglect. A few enterprising bar owners ventured into the 7th District with a novel idea: take a ramshackle tenement house and, rather than restoring it, leave it as is and convert it into a bar. These "ruin pubs" quickly became a cornerstone of BP nightlife. At first, they were a well-kept secret among locals, but word quickly spread and bars like Szimpla and Instant became globally recognized institutions. These pubs still look much the same as they did when they opened. Mismatched trinkets and knickknacks on every available surface only add to the peculiar ambience. I've listed some of my favorites below, but the 7th District hasn't stopped transforming. New bars are opening all of the time, so keep your eyes peeled.

You'll notice *kert* (garden) in the titles of most of these bars, meaning there's an outdoor space somewhere in the complex—great to enjoy the warm summer evenings. In winter, bars often cover the gardens with heavy tarps so you can still take in the fresh air without exposing yourself entirely to the elements.

LGBT BUDAPEST

The acceptance and status of the LGBT community have grown in leaps and bounds since Hungary gained its independence in 1990. As in most other European capitals, LGBT travelers should expect no issues while visiting Budapest, though same-sex couples tend to downplay public displays of affection. Gay Pride Budapest is held each year toward the end of June or early July. **Alter Ego** (Fri 10:00-05:00, Sat 10:00-06:00, Dessewffy utca 33, 6th District, +36 70 345 4302, alteregoclub.hu) is BP's oldest gay venue and has frequent drag nights. **Cirkusz** (Mon-Sat 09:00-18:00, Sun 09:00-17:00, Dob utca 25, 7th District, +36 1 786 49 59, cirkuszbp.hu), **Why Not?** (daily 10:00-17:00, Belgrád rkp. 3-4, 5th District, +36 1 780 4545, whynotcafe.hu), and **Anker't** are also LGBT friendly.

For the latest information on cafés, restaurants, nightlife, and accommodations, head to gay.hu/welcome-budapest, budapestgaycity.net, and budapest.com (clicking through to **Gay Budapest**).

Szimpla

Start one of your night's crawls through the 7th District here—it gets insanely busy anytime after 20:30 or so, so get there early. Before you leave, head upstairs to check out some of the rooms and nooks on the second floor. Immediately to your left as you enter is a hookah lounge. Renting one of the elaborate pipes is a great way to make friends, so put in your order and find a comfy place to chill. Don't be surprised if someone comes up to you selling carrots out of a basket—just embrace the eclectic vibe and make like a rabbit.

Beers for 550Ft, Mon-Sat 12:00-04:00, Sun 09:00-05:00 (farmer's market early), Kazinczy Utca 14, 7th District, +36 20 261 8669, szimpla.hu, Metro: Astoria

Instant/Fogas Kert

Two former competitors in the ruin pub game recently joined forces to create a massive ruin pub complex. Where Instant used to be is now (at least for the moment) a massive hole in the ground. Fogas has been expanded and is now a dizzying labyrinth of bars, gardens, and dance floors. There's a brand-new edgy rock bar downstairs, a welcome change for those who are tired of the usual Top 40 and club techno. A visit to Instant/Fogas is every bit as essential as a trek to Szimpla.

Beers for 600Ft, Sun-Thurs 16:00-01:00, Fri-Sat 16:00-03:00 Akácfa Utca 51, 7th District, +36 1 783 8820, fogashaz.hu, Metro: Opera

Kuplung

Kuplung, massively popular with locals and international students for its half-price Mondays (when the place becomes an orgy of drunkenness and frivolity), took over a former mechanic's shop and let its cheap drinks do the rest. It's a great place to chill out, drink up, play some Ping-Pong, and get your dance on all in one go. The music changes often, with skilled DJs spinning nightly and a dance floor just big enough to let loose with your friends. If chaos isn't your thing, go on any night other than Monday.

Daily 15:00-05:00, Király Utca 46, 7th District, +36 30 755 3527, kuplung.net, Metro: Opera

Ellátó Kert

This Mexican-themed, low-key ruin pub is a little off the beaten path, even though it's right around the corner from Gozsdu. There are foosball tables and plates of tacos to keep partygoers entertained and fed. One of the reasons Ellátó remains something of a hidden gem is it doesn't seem keen to pander to tourists' expectations, especially when it comes to cleanliness. It's dark, grungy, and authentic—a favorite with locals and those who want to dive into the 7th without encountering the tourist hordes.

Beers for 500Ft, Mon-Thurs 17:00-02:00, Fri-Sun 17:00-04:00, 48 Kazinczy Utca, 7th District, +36 20 527 3018, Metro: Opera

Anker't

Anker't feels more like a cutting-edge bar you'd find in NYC's Meatpacking District than what you might expect in Budapest's 7th District. There's exposed brick everywhere—the owners took over a run-down tenement and absolutely gutted the top levels, leaving nothing but the brick behind. Friday is the unofficial LGBT night, and the dance floor packs out with jubilant locals dancing to throbbing house. The only downside is the open sewer in the back corner of the main bar—if the conditions are just right, the place can have an acrid smell.

Beers for 600Ft, Sun–Tues 10:00–03:00, Wed–Sat 18:00–03:00, 33 Paulay Ede Utca, 6th District, +36 30 360 3389, ankerklub.hu, Metro: Opera

NON-RUIN BARS

Of course, Budapest isn't wall-to-wall ruin pubs. It's got a burgeoning cocktail scene, and a number of classy hipster joints that are anything but derelict. I've put together a very short list of some of my favorites, but every time I'm in town I discover something else—something new or some hole-in-the-wall I haven't yet peered into. In the 7th District especially, exploration can be extremely rewarding, so be sure to drop in anywhere the scene seems jumping.

Doblo

Nothing beats this award-winning wine bar when it comes to a place to spend an evening sharing a glass or two of excellent wine with close friends or someone special. The owners stripped the place down to bare brick and then brought in antique furniture. If you know your wines, you'll find tastings here to suit even the most discerning palate.

Glasses of wine starting at 950Ft, Sun–Wed 24:00–02:00, Thurs–Sat 14:00–04:00, Dob Utca 20, 7th District, +36 20 398 8863, budapestwine.com, Metro: Opera

Hotsy Totsy

Opening its doors in 2017, Hotsy Totsy is the brainchild of a pair of savvy bar managers-turned-owners. They've landed in the 7th District with a splash, immediately building a reputation for world-class cocktails and unbeatable atmosphere (they've even got a barbershop in the back). If you're on a tight budget, look elsewhere, but if you want to splurge on a few great cocktails in a belowground, Prohibition-era speakeasy, this is the spot. Their whiskey sour is next to unbeatable.

Cocktails starting around 1,500Ft, whiskey sour 1,680Ft, Mon–Wed 10:00–24:00, Thurs–Sat 10:00–02:00, Síp utca 24, 7th District, +36 1 614 5097, Facebook: Hotsy Totsy Budapest, Metro: Opera

360 Bar

Enjoy beers and cocktails with smart service at this posh rooftop club with a 360-degree panorama of downtown Budapest—spectacular at night when the castle, the Parliament Building, and the basilica are all lit up. Zip up the elevator to get a break from the street-level heat in the summer. They've usually got a DJ playing chill beats, and the well-dressed crowd knows what's up. Dress up to breeze past the doormen and join the see-and-be-seen crowd. The bar closes in cold and bad weather and for the entirety of the off-season (Oct–Apr, weather-dependent).

Reasonable cover for events 1,000Ft, otherwise no cover, cocktails from 1,750Ft, beer from 600Ft in 360ml pours, Mon–Wed 14:00–12:00, Thurs–Sat 14:00–02:00, Sun 00:00–12:00, Andrássy út 39, 6th District, 360bar.hu, Metro: Oktogon or Opera

Jonas Craft Beer House

Craft beer has swept across the entire continent, and Jonas is riding the wave. No matter what your beer preference, they've got you covered, and you can either enjoy it inside or take it out on the patio and enjoy the view over the Danube. It's not exactly a hop, skip, and jump from the center, but it's worth the tram ride or the brisk 20-minute walk. It's on the edge of a mall that looks very much like a half-submerged whale. The basement of the mall is full of quirky knickknacks and antiques.

Beers from 750Ft, Mon–Thurs 11:00–24:00, Fri–Sat 11:00–02:00, Sun 11:00–23:00, Fővám tér 11, 9th District (Greater Budapest), +36 70 930 1392, Facebook: Jónás Kézműves Sörház, Metro: Boráros tér

NIGHTCLUBS

A typical night out in Budapest starts early at the bars and ruin pubs and ends late at the clubs. Check out any of my favorites and it's likely that chirping birds will serenade you to your rest. The hangover you'll probably rise with will give you one more reason to hit the spa and soak the aches away.

Ötkert

They've got the formula down to an exact science here: one part gorgeous crowd to two parts incredible music; shake until dizzy. Get here on the earlier side to avoid the long lines. There's no need to dress to the nines to get in. Hip-hop and R&B blend with salsa and hits from the '90s. The DJs are less interested in sticking to a coherent theme than they are in making sure that the dance floor is constantly full. There's a great garden out back.

Occasional 1,000Ft cover, beers from 700Ft, Tues-Wed 11:00-24:00, Thurs-Sat 11:00-03:00, Sun 11:00-24:00, Zrínyi Utca 4, 5th District, +36 70 330 8652, otkert.hu, Metro: Bajcsy-Zsilinszky út

Corvintető

Corvintető feels like a '90s life-is-plastic rooftop dance bar. It all goes down in an old, gray communist-style building on the edge of the Jewish Quarter. Find the place down a side street and up a cargo elevator. The eardrum-shattering music in the main-floor bar, mostly dubstep, makes the guy-to-gal ratio gentleman-heavy, but the rooftop patio tips the scales in the other direction. They close late, so if you're not too bleary eyed, it's worth sticking around for the views of the sunrise from the roof.

Cover varies, beers from 500Ft, Wed-Sat 19:00-06:00, Blaha Lujza tér 1-2, 7th/8th District, +36 20 474 0831, corvinteto.hu, Metro: Blaha Lujza tér

A38

If you've ever wanted to party on a boat, this Soviet Ukrainian ship-turned-nightclub docked on the Danube is just the ticket. What makes the place so popular is its ability to attract the best concerts in the city. Check their website for upcoming events before you arrive, as shows often sell out. Even if there's not something to your liking, head down for a few drinks and dancing on their three dance floors.

Entry usually free, beers from 450Ft, Mon-Sat 07:30-11:00, Sun 12:30-00:00, Buda side of Petofi Bridge, 11th District (Greater Budapest), a38.hu, Tram: Petőfi híd

PARTIES YOU'LL ONLY FIND IN BUDAPEST
Spa Parties

Someone once had the brilliant idea of bringing strobe lights, lasers, a DJ, sound system, wet bar, and smoke machines into the bathhouses of Budapest for a massive, raging spa party, and "sparties" were born. They quickly took off in popularity, and each sparty is a guaranteed rager. To look past the rampant hooking up and floating

condoms, you'll need to be well lubricated yourself with as much Jägermeister as you can keep down. If you're already balking at the description, steer clear! Sparties happen often during high season and at different bathhouses, so be sure to ask at your hostel about where that week's sparties will be held. Book tickets through your hostel, online at sites like Széchenyispabaths.com/sparties, or at the ticket office on Szabadság tér. At the time of writing, ticket prices are running past €50, making many travelers (including myself) balk at the price and value. If only the wildest party will satisfy you, though, this is your ticket.

Danube River Parties

Competing party boat companies put on quite an experience throughout the week. Rock out on a two-hour cruise up and down the Danube with unlimited drinks and a full-on maritime dance floor as you float past the floodlit Hungarian Parliament Building and Fisherman's Bastion of the Castle District.

Budapest Party Hostels takes guests from all five of their locations on these parties, so if you're staying at one, just follow the hostel crowd. Book tickets online or at the hostel and get a sense for the various options available—depending on the night, there might be unlimited drinks or drink tickets. If it's an option, go for the bottle of champagne and pop the cork high into the night air.

5,000-7,500Ft (additional 1,500Ft for optional bottle of champagne—everyone does it), meeting points vary, confirm online or talk to your hostel staff, embarking at 22:30 on Mon, Wed, and Fri, 22:00 on Sat, 22:30 on Thurs, and 23:00 on Fri, +36 30 908 7598, budapestboatparty.com

PUB CRAWLS

Many hostels in Budapest organize their own pub crawls. The **Budapest Party Hostels** network isn't exactly known for quiet nights in, so they'll be sure to take you along when they hit the town (usually starting around 20:00). While organized pub crawls will help you get oriented in the maze of streets that make up the 7th District, getting a little lost in the neighborhood is part of the fun. If the pub-crawling crowd doesn't look like your scene, just find your way to the edge of the 7th (start-

ing with any of my recommended bars) and start opening doors.

HostelCulture Backpacker Pub Crawl

The team at HC put together a nightly party that takes you to some the hottest spots across town. Join their free daytime walking tour, get a free welcome beer and welcome shots along the way, and cap off the night in a club with their nightly backpacker pub crawl.

3750Ft (cheaper if you book online), every night 20:00-21:00 at the first bar, meets at Akvarium Club, Erzebet tér 12, 5th District, +36 70 424 05 69, backpackerpubcrawl. com/Budapest, Metro: Vörösmarty tér

TOP SHOPPING & MARKETS

Budapest is a paradise for those looking for retro clothes and nostalgic memorabilia. The Great Market Hall and the city-center shopping streets are can't-miss attractions for shopaholics. Typical Hungarian souvenirs are handmade woven goods, ceramics, woodcarving, lace, and pottery. Don't be afraid to haggle. Instead of letting the vendors guide you, decide as you're looking what the piece is worth to you. Negotiate from there.

SHOPPING DISTRICTS

Váci Utca

Starting at Pest's central square, Vörösmarty tér, and continuing down to the Great Market Hall, Váci Utca is medieval Budapest's main street and its kitschiest touristy drag. You'll pay higher prices for the location and the bright lights. Look for Hungary's famous herbal liqueur, **Unicum** (Hungary's answer to Jägermeister), as well as **pálinka** (clear spirits made with apricots and other fruit—male or female, it'll put hair on your chest). The beautiful handmade lace makes for an excellent and easily stowed present for loved ones back home.

5th District, Metro: Vörösmarty tér or Fővám tér

MARKETS

Szimpla Farmers Market

The Szimpla farmers market is one of the coolest Sunday-morning markets you'll ever see. It's a surreal experience to party late in the bars, then return the next morning and see farmers selling their harvest, probably arriving just moments after you called it a night. For an amazing Sunday brunch, head upstairs to the extensive buffet (4000Ft) of delicious vegan-friendly trayfuls of the day's produce from the farmers. For greasier fare, there's a parking lot full of food trucks just outside.

Free, Sun 09:00-14:00, Kazinczy Utca 14, 7th District, szimpla.hu, Metro: Astoria

Great Market Hall

Yet another beautiful building from the Hungarian millennial anniversary of 1896. Find produce and meat on the ground floor; souvenirs, a café, and cheap eats upstairs; and a large modern supermarket downstairs. The souvenirs upstairs are mostly mass-produced junk, but there are, if you look hard enough, diamonds in the rough.

Free, Mon-Fri 06:00-18:00, Sat 06:00-15:00, Vámház Körút 1-3, 5th District, Metro: Fővám tér or Kálvin tér

Belvárosi Piac

For a more off-the-beaten-path market experience, drop into the Hold Street Market. Located just behind the US Embassy, it was built in 1897 and has dozens of stalls for vendors selling everything from cheeses and breads to salami and paprika. The tourists haven't really discovered this place yet, so it's got a quiet and secret vibe to it. You'll find quick, varied lunch options (Russian, Hungarian, Mexican, Italian, and more) upstairs with a nice view over the quaint market hall. Grab an artisanal beer and watch the locals go about their work below.

Free, Mon 06:30-17:00, Tues-Fri 06:30-18:00, Sat 06:30-14:00, Hold Utca 13, 5th District, +36 1 353 1110, Metro: Arany János utca

TOP PARKS & RECREATION

For a butt buster, climb the Citadel hill. Otherwise, jog or bike around the City Park loop (3 km) or Margit Island (4.5 km) for a break from traffic. Budapest is also a gym-mad city, so chances are there's an air-conditioned gym near your hostel. Drop-in fees are usually reasonable.

City Park

The largest green space in the city is northeast of the center. In the park, you'll find the **Vajdahunyad Castle** (free, always open), built in—you guessed it—1896 to show off the various architectural styles found throughout the country. The original was built out of wood and canvas but was so popular that a permanent version soon took its place. You'll see styles reminiscent of Romanesque, Gothic, Renaissance, and baroque periods in this one funky structure. Deeper into the park are the **Széchenyi baths,** a zoo, and a circus. You'll find Heroes' Square at the entrance to the park, and during the winter, there's a massive sheet of maintained ice right next to the square—my favorite place in the world to go ice-skating. Get to City Park by hopping on the yellow (line 1) metro and riding it to the Széchenyi Fürdő stop.

Free, always open, City Park, Metro: Széchenyi Fürdő

Margit Island

This island in the middle of the Danube is long and skinny, shaped like a running oval. In the summertime and shoulder season, you'll find tons of bars, pools, and spas open to enjoy. Renting a four-seater pedal bike (about 2,500Ft/hour) is always my favorite way to explore the island. Toss

a liter or three of beer into your caddy and you're ready to cruise!

Margit Island is accessible via Margit Bridge on the south side and Arpad Bridge on the north side. Both bridges are open to pedestrians. But be careful—I've seen more than one bloody accident on the busy bridge and streets leading to the island.

Free, always open, Margit Island, Metro: Nyugati Pályaudvar

Chairlift to Elizabeth Lookout

Bar none, the views from the Elizabeth Lookout are the best in the city. It would be a hell of a sweaty climb to the top of János Hill, so save your shoe leather and take the chairlift instead. For 1,400Ft return, you'll be whisked to the top of the hill where the air is fresh and the views are breathtaking. Bring somebody along to share the ride to the top and the bottom.

1,400Ft return trip, May 15-Sept 15 daily 09:00-19:00, Sept 15-May 15 daily 10:00-15:00, Libegő, Greater Budapest, take the 291 bus from Nyugati to the last stop

Barlangászat Caving Tour

Under the hills of Buda lies a vast network of limestone caves. Get ready to get down and dirty as you explore some of them— you'll need to be flexible and able to crawl

through tight spaces. Your professional English-speaking guides will take you into several chambers deep in the earth, and you'll be crawling on your hands and knees in the passageways between each stop. The guides like to share stories and break down the geology of how caves occur. Since their options are vast, they select a route for you based on the relative skill level of the group. If you're feeling adventurous, let them know.

I highly recommend a caving expedition, but I can't stress this enough: If you or a member of your group has even a trace of claustrophobia, give it a miss. Wear comfortable shoes and clothes. Jeans get tight when crawling around, so stretchy shorts or athletic pants are your best bet. The provided coveralls protect your clothes, but your shoes will pick up a layer of Hungarian clay.

Barlangászat is currently the only operation licensed to take visitors down into the caves. Availability is limited and often sells out in advance. Reserve ahead via email or through your hostel on your arrival day. Tours run year-round no matter what the weather, and the caves are always around 55°F.

Tours meet at the bus 206 stop at Nyugati station, near the funky low-cover staircase leading up to the overpass. Guides will take you up to the caves via two buses, so you'll need four metro tickets per person. Or get there yourself by taking bus 65, which leaves from Kolosy square. Step off at the fifth bus stop, named Pál völgyi.

7,500Ft, four-hour tours Mon, Wed, Fri, and Sat afternoons, Tues and Thurs mornings, barlangaszat.hu, info@barlangaszat.hu, Metro: Nyugati Pályaudvar

Escape Games

Escape games have taken Budapest by storm. Here's how the games work: After a briefing laced with hints, you and your friends are locked into a room and charged with escaping. A "puzzle master," whom you can ask for tips if you run into a roadblock, monitors the room. You get about 60 minutes to solve a series of challenges and escape—the alternative is not a lifetime in the room, but it is a little embarrassing.

Go for the themes that intrigue you the most. Prices are generally set per game, getting cheaper for each person you add. The 7th District, where the run-down buildings add to the effect, is absolutely crawling with escape rooms. For the best results, embrace the challenge enthusiastically. Try every idea that comes up, communicate with your teammates, look everywhere in the room, watch out for time-wasting decoys, and, finally, don't take it all too seriously. Have fun and may the force be with you!

I picked my favorite based on friendliness of the staff, price, value, location, and theme success—these can get quite creative. In addition to the one described below, I also recommend **Mystique Room** (Egyptian and Cathedral themes, mystiqueroom.hu), **Escape Zone** (Labyrinth, Star Wars, and Back to the Future themes, escapezone.hu), **PANIQROOM** (Saw and Lost themes, paniqszoba.hu). The themes might be different when you come, and there might be an entirely new crop of competitors, so ask at your hostel to see if there's a new market entrant that's doing something unique.

E-Exit Escape Games

Descend a few steps into this nondescript little complex. The friendly staff sits you around a table and preps you for the challenge to come. Read the details of their hint sheet, and do your best to get out in 60 minutes. I found their themes—1984 Apocalypse, Heaven is Hell, and Scary Circus—fun and challenging.

Two people 8,000Ft/game, up to six people 11,000Ft/game, multiple time slots available daily, online reservations required ahead of time, Nyár Utca 27, Jewish Quarter, +36 30 889 3633, e-exit.hu, Metro: Blaha Lujza tér

TOP TOURS

Yellow Zebra Bike & Absolute Walking Tours

This is an entertaining and relaxing way to get oriented with the city and see all of Budapest's top sights. Pop into the office behind the opera house on one of your first days to hang out in their fun office/library/tourist zone. The friendly staff will happily hook you up with any of their 3.5-hour walks and rides, along with a slew of other activities (their Segway tours are a popular option). Take the day tour and they'll throw in a coffee and pastry break. Student and online discounts are available.

9,000Ft for bike tour, 10,000Ft for walking tours, Apr-Oct daily 11:00 daytime ride and daily 17:00 evening ride, Nov and Mar Fri-Sun daytime ride 11:00, Lázár Utca 16, 6th District, +36 20 929 7506, yellowzebrabikes.com, Metro: Opera

B Side Tours

My friend Bogi heads up this company that specializes in innovative and alternative walking, bus, and custom tours. Whether you're interested in history, seeing the main sights, gastro walks, pop culture, or enjoying the outdoor activities that Budapest has to offer, B Side tours will help you find that perfect balance between entertained and informed. Bogi's blog contains all sorts of free tips and info on her hometown.

Private tours for up to six people from 120 euro (36,000Ft), contact ahead of time for booking and info,

bsidetours.com, bsidetours@gmail.com, +36 70 775 2226

Buda Bike

I love the rides put together by the Buda Bike team. They have everything you might expect from a well-organized bike tour company, including an engaging highlights tour and more in-depth city rides. They also have more extensive rides that will take you into the Hungarian countryside.

6,500Ft, group discounts available, 10:30 and 14:00 in front of St. Stephen's Basilica (by the California Coffee Company), Szent István tér 1, 5th District, confirm season and availability ahead of time, budabike@gmail.com, budabike.com, Metro: Bajcsy-Zsilinszky út

HostelCulture

HostelCulture has put together some exciting itineraries designed specifically for backpackers, all of which will help you get familiar with the city. Their free city tour covers highlights like Matthias Church, the Hungarian State Opera House, and more. If you're looking to go a little deeper into a specific subject, their Communist History and Jewish Legacy tours are first rate. If it's Budapest's famous nightlife you're interested in, join their nightly pub crawl.

Free tip-based tour meets daily 10:30 and 14:00 in front of St. Stephen's Basilica, Szent István tér 1, 5th District, hostelculture.com/budapest-tours, Metro: Bajcsy-Zsilinszky út

TOP HOSTELS

Budapest is the most competitive hostel market in Europe. In the 6th and 7th Districts, you'll see hostels hanging their banners out on every street. A few providers have risen to the top, and by and large they've done so by capitalizing on the city's nightlife and all it has to offer. If you've come to Budapest seeking leisure and peace, the dorm-style rooms in the BPH hostels I recommend below might not be a good fit (a private room or an Airbnb are probably better choices). If you end up going with Airbnb, choose wisely—you should be able to find a place for around €35 (or 10,500Ft) per person per night. For the social scene and proximity to the action, the 6th, 7th, and 8th Districts are the neighborhoods to look into. The 5th District, home to the Parliament Building and the embassies, is on the pricier side, but the added cost doesn't mean a more thriving scene. The area gets rather quiet and boring at night.

Budapest Party Hostels is a collection of party-oriented accommodations (Grandio, Retox, Carpe Noctem VITAE, Carpe Noctem, Meander, and Penthouse Privates), each with a unique vibe and personality. Brace yourself for wild ride with these instigators—

the company actively seeks out party animals who have long since forgotten about moderation in any aspect of their lives.

Grandio Party Hostel

For serious partiers only! The most ramshackle of the BPH tribe, Grandio is the hostel to come to if you're looking for some "interesting" life experiences that you'll want to brag about to your friends but hide from mom and dad. The beds are upstairs, along with a social room. In the courtyard there's a social garden bar and in the cavern beneath is a sloppy late-night bar they call the Rave Cave. Legends are made here.

3,000–5,000Ft, free Wi-Fi, computers, 24-hour reception, common room, bar, bicycle rental, Nagy Diófa Utca 8, 7th District, +36 20 350 7441, grandiopartyhostel.com, info@grandiopartyhostel.com, Metro: Blaha Lujza tér

Retox Hostel

Retox is a solid all-around bet, but only if you've come prepared to party *very* late. The bar in the courtyard is one of the most raucous spots in Budapest (especially on Sunday nights), so there'll be no early bedtimes unless you bring industrial-strength earplugs. You'll get some rest here as long as your sleep schedule is on par with the other backpackers: passing out at 06:00 and waking up at 14:00. The other BPH hostels meet here for pregame most nights, making the bar's couches a great place to mingle. On Sunday nights they host the Jäger-train—they arrange glasses of energy drink on a table (sometimes 600+) and balance the Jäger on top. They tip one row and let gravity do the rest. Everybody drinks five of them, and the night gets messy

3,500–4,000Ft, free Wi-Fi, 24-hour reception, bar, hookah, computers, Ó Utca 41, 6th District, +36 70 6700 386, budapestpartyhostels.com, info@retoxpartyhostel.com, Metro: Oktogon

Carpe Noctem VITAE

For those who like to have a great time but also want the option to chill, this 130-bed hostel offers a lot of different common spaces with different vibes. The staff are friendly and helpful. There's a great (but small) rooftop patio and a comfortable living room area where party-weary travelers can play some video games, watch a mov-

ie, or catch the game. Comfortable private rooms with views are available for those who appreciate their own room but don't want to miss out on the party. It's quiet during the day, but they join the rest of the wild BPH crew at night.

3,500–5,000Ft, free Wi-Fi, computers, 24-hour reception, bar, hookah bar, free locker/lock, Erzsébet Körút 50, 7th District, +36 70 6700 382, carpenoctempenthouse.com, info@carpenoctemvitae.com, Metro: Oktogon

Carpe Noctem

The most low-key and comfy of the BPH bunch. By day, it feels like a good friend's living room. Backpackers lie slouched on the couches recovering from the night before. After dinner, which the staff cooks for the guests each night, the guests descend the stairs and join those from the other BPH hostels. At 22 beds, it's much smaller than its sister hostels, so guests appreciate the intimate ambience. They don't allow large groups to book here, which keeps the loud stag parties away. It also makes this the ideal place to meet people traveling alone or with only a companion or two.

4,000–6,0000Ft, free Wi-Fi, computers, 24-hour staffing, free lockers/locks, common room, Szobi Utca 5, 6th District, +36 70 6700 384, carpenoctemoriginal.com, info@carpenoctemoriginal.com, Metro: Nyugati Pályaudvar

Maverick City Lodge

With a wide range of options ranging from dorms (including female-only rooms) to double rooms and en suites, Maverick puts you right in the heart of the action in Budapest's 7th District. The newly built hostel/hotel aims to provide a predictable experience—one that is safe and clean, but still fun. This is Budapest with the rougher edges worn off, and all the comforts of home.

Beds from 6,000Ft, free Wi-Fi, fully equipped kitchen, daily room cleaning, free tea and coffee, air-conditioning, free lockers, Kazinczy Utca 24–26, 7th District, +36 1 793 1605, mavericklodges.com, reservation@mavericklodges.com, Metro: Astoria

Wombats Hostel

This Austrian chain has great hostels down to a science. They know *exactly* what the modern backpacker wants: bright rooms, free Wi-Fi throughout the hostel, break-fasts included, an on-site bar, and fre-quent free tours and pub crawls. The BP Wombats has an excellent location, just around the corner from Kazinczy Utca and across the street from the Gozsdu Court & Passage restaurants and bars, and they'll happily help you track down the scene that interests you.

Beds from 3,500Ft, 24-hour reception, free Wi-Fi, 20 Király Utca, 7th District, +36 1 883˚5005, wombats-hostels.com/Budapest, office@wombats-budapest.hu, Metro: Bajcsy-Zsilinszky út

Central Backpack King Hostel
Located just down the way from Espresso Embassy, the US Embassy, and the Parlia-ment Building, this 45-bed hostel brings together a casual mix of international backpackers. Budapest's raging nightlife is about a 20-minute walk away, so the hos-tel is as quiet as they come, but peace and quiet might not have been what you came for. If you end up at the bars in the 7th or 6th Districts, you'll have quite a hike (or a

short cab ride) at the end of the night. The place has a home-away-from-home vibe, welcoming staff, and comfortable rooms.

Beds from 5,000Ft, private rooms from 15,000Ft, 24-hour reception, Wi-Fi in all rooms, kitchen access, lockers and towels available for deposit, hair dryers available, 15 Oktober 6 Utca, 5th District, +36 30 200 7184, centralbackpackking.hostel.com, Metro: Bajcsy-Zsilinszky út

Penthouse Privates
Penthouse Privates is a collection of five private double rooms for travelers who prefer apartment-style accommodations. Relax in their comfortable common room, enjoy full access to a kitchen, and sleep well at the top of a six-floor building. There's no elevator, which means you'll be working off each meal and beer every time you go home.

8,500Ft, two-night minimum stay, free Wi-Fi, computer for use, on-site staff that comes and goes, Király Utca 56, 7th District, +36 70 671 2723, Facebook: Penthouse Privates, penthouseprivates@gmail.com, Metro: Opera or Oktogon

TRANSPORTATION

GETTING THERE & AWAY
Budget airlines make frequent connections into Budapest, making this city an attrac-tive stop on longer trips. Overnight bus and train options make for good connec-tions to Vienna and Prague. Train and bus connections from Krakow can be a little more involved, often connecting through Bratislava.

Plane
Plenty of budget airlines fly into Budapest's only airport, **Ferenc Liszt International Air-port** (BUD, bud.hu). Don't buy your tickets without checking WizzAir.com, a compet-itive Hungarian budget airline. It is im-portant to note that some budget airlines like Ryanair may label the Balaton regional airport as their main "Budapest" airport. Be sure to look closely to see if this is the case while researching your options. The train ride from Balaton will take you about two hours.

Connect from Ferenc Liszt International Airport into Budapest by taking **bus 200E**

to the Kobanya-Kispest metro stop. Take the metro into town to find your hostel from there, validating a new metro ticket each time you transfer. Change to the red or yellow metro line at Deák Ferenc tér if necessary. The whole journey will take about an hour and cost three metro tick-ets, running about 1050Ft total, or $3 USD.

Train
Budapest is served by two main train stations, both of them in Pest: **Nyugati** ("Western") and **Keleti** ("Eastern"). You'll be able to get to some of the hostels on foot from Nyugati, but it'll be a long, sweaty walk from Keleti. Best to take the metro, tram, or bus from the station. Connections run often between Prague and Budapest (via Keleti, 7 hours, €75 or 23,000Ft).

Bus
There are dirt-cheap bus options in Central and Eastern Europe. Begin your shopping by looking at timetables and prices at lux-express.eu, orangeways.com, and euro-lines.com. A ride to Prague may take up to

BUDAPEST

10 hours, but it'll only cost €20 (6,300Ft). There may be a required transfer for longer connections.

If leaving from Budapest by bus, triple check your bus station (there are several in town). The bus terminals are located on the southeast side of town at metro stops **Népliget** or **Pöttyös Utca.**

Car
Renting a car is not necessary to see the best sights of Budapest, but Budapest's center is car friendly. If you're touring from one city to the next, you'll almost certainly want to park your car for the duration of your stay—everything in the center is within walking distance. The closer to the center you park, the more expensive the hourly rates will be. When looking for parking, there are a number of park-and-ride (P+R) options near public transportation stations that will let you ditch the car for just a few euros a day. Erzebet tér P+R is your most central yet cost-effective option.

GETTING AROUND
Budapest is a big city with plenty of vehicles, pedestrians, and bikes. If the sun is shining and you plan on renting a bike, you'll only need a few metro tickets. If you're going to be on foot, you'll want to use the metro system to help you cover ground more quickly.

Budapest's trams, buses, and subways are all on the same integrated system. Buy an individual **ticket** (350Ft) from machines and vendors found in most stations. A booklet of **10 tickets** (2,800Ft) will save you about 15 percent. Tickets do not include transfers except inside the metro system. That means if you need to change to buses or trams, you need two tickets. Consider the 24-hour pass for 1,650Ft or the five-person 24-hour pass for 3,300Ft. Don't purchase tickets with large bills—the machines are unreliable.

I've seen more ticket controllers here than in any other city in Europe. Trying to play the "dumb tourist" card won't work. They'll demand 8,000Ft before they let you go.

Familiarize yourself with the primary stops and stations in the city in order to better know your way around. Start with:

Deák Ferenc tér, Oktogon, and **Blaha Lujza Tér.**

Metro
Budapest has a simple, four-line metro system. Visitors will most likely use the **yellow** (for the opera house, House of Terror, Széchenyi baths, Heroes' Square and City Park), **red** (connecting Buda with Keleti train station), and **blue** (coming in from the airport and Nyugati train station) lines.

Bus
Since the tram and metro networks are so easy to use, you can mostly get by without needing to board Budapest's buses, but they are the only option in some areas. The newer-looking buses are reliable—the 50-year-old tin cans less so.

Tram
Over 30 tram lines lace the city, but there are just a few lines you need to get familiar with. **Lines 46** and **47** originate at Deák Ferenc tér, running past Váci Utca and the Grand Market Hall across the river to Gellért and the Citadel. The newer trams (**Lines 4 and 6**) travel along Pest's middle ring road, connecting major sights like Andrássy út and Margit Island. **Line 2** runs north-south along the Pest side of the Danube, connecting the Grand Market Hall with the Parliament Building.

Taxi
Always call for a cab to get a fair rate. Never flag down a taxi or hop into a stationary cab in Budapest. The city has a serious problem with unlicensed taxis, and it's not unusual for them to charge tourists ten times the usual rate for a short ride. **Radio** (+36 377 77 77) and **City Taxi** (+36 211 11 11) are reliable.

Bicycle
Having a bike really opens up the city, making it a breeze to get around during a short visit. With plenty of bike lanes, you should feel comfortable getting around town. However, bike lanes are not always clearly marked. If the markings disappear, ride on the sidewalk until a clearly marked bike lane reemerges. If you're biking across town, wear a helmet. Rent bikes from **Yellow Zebra Bike Tours,** which offers discounts for its tour customers.

Eger & the Valley of the Sirens

The pretty little town of Eger is famous for its 16th-century castle, but the real draw is the Valley of Sirens, a back holler just outside of town. Eger's farmers and vintners have burrowed deep into the earth to create an elaborate network of wine cellars, each of which sells incredible wines. Pop in, strike up a conversation, have a snack, and toss back a few glasses; nobody returns from Eger clear-headed. Touring the cellars will take a full afternoon. Talk to the folks at your hostel about Eger if it sounds right for you.

Buses and trains leave often and take about two hours. Tourist bus connections to the Valley of Sirens leave from Eger's Dobo Square. Otherwise, it's about a 20-minute walk or 10-minute taxi ride (2,000Ft) from the square.

Castles & Local Touring

For a supremely ambitious day of exploring, check out three towns just northwest of Budapest. You'll see a famous basilica, take a luge ride, and explore castle ruins, returning back to your hostel richer for the experience and thoroughly exhausted. It's well worth it for adventurous travelers who are good with maps and aren't afraid to ask for help or directions.

Start your day with an early-morning bus out to the town of **Esztergom** (1.25 hours via bus, 850Ft, buses leave from Árpád híd autóbusz station). One of the first things you'll see is the beautiful basilica perched high on the hill overlooking the town. The basilica is free to visit. The crypts below are well worth the entry fee of 200Ft.

After this, take the bus to the village of **Visegrad** (bus 880, 850Ft). You'll have to ask your bus driver to let you know when you've arrived. Pop into the **Hotel Visegrad** and ask for help calling a taxi to take you up to some incredible ruins of a castle overlooking the bend in the Danube. Just beyond the castle is a fun summer luge with wheeled sleds that hurtle down the track at breakneck speeds (500 Ft/run, open in good weather, 11:00-16:00, +36 26 397 397, bobozas.hu).

After the castle, catch the bus (850Ft) to **Szentendre** and explore the beautiful baroque town center. Work your way from the bus stop to the river and catch dinner before continuing back to Budapest via light-rail from the station (850Ft). The train station is about a 15-minute walk south of the old town. When you get back into the city, get off at Margit Hid, near Margit Island, then connect back into the center across the bridge via tram 6.

HELP!

Tourist Information Centers

Find the official **Budapestinfo Point** (daily 08:00-20:00, +36 143 88 080) next door to the recommended Cserpes Tejivó Milk Bar (Sütő utca 2).

A good online resource is **WeLoveBudapest.com**.

Pickpockets & Scams

Don't take unmarked cabs. They prey on naïve tourists. Pickpocketing doesn't seem to be a major problem, but always keep your wits about you, especially at busy bars. Anticipate your change when purchasing goods, and step aside to count it before walking away. Watch out for counting "errors"—I've saved a good chunk of change by always counting it after paying.

Emergencies

In an emergency, dial 112.

Hospital

FirstMed Center
Hattyú St 14
+36 06 1 224 9090

US Embassy

Szabadság tér 12
+36 06 14 75 4164

DUBLIN

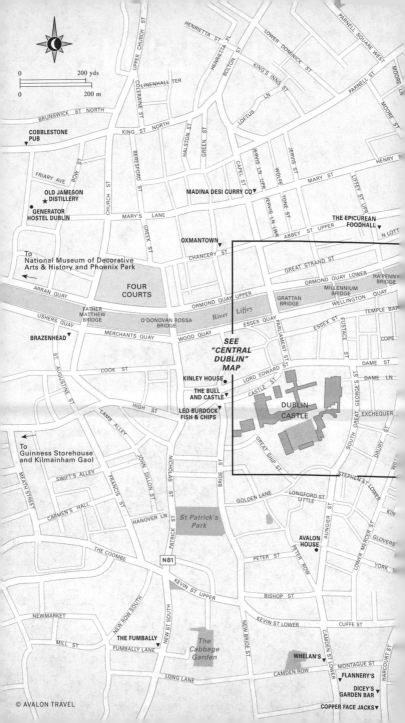

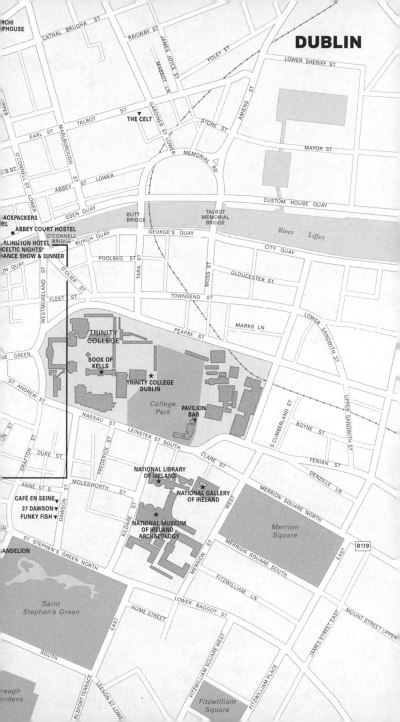

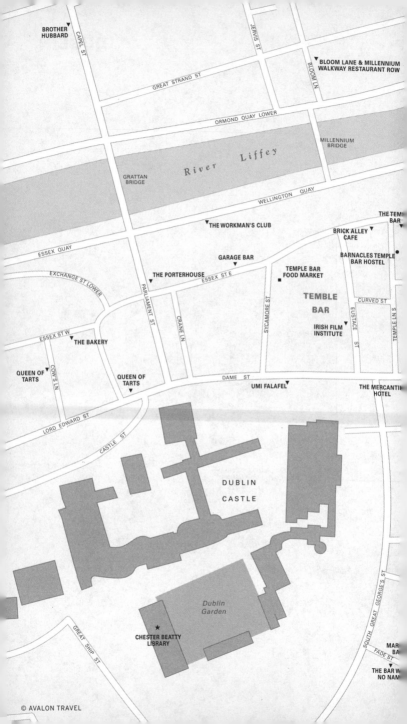

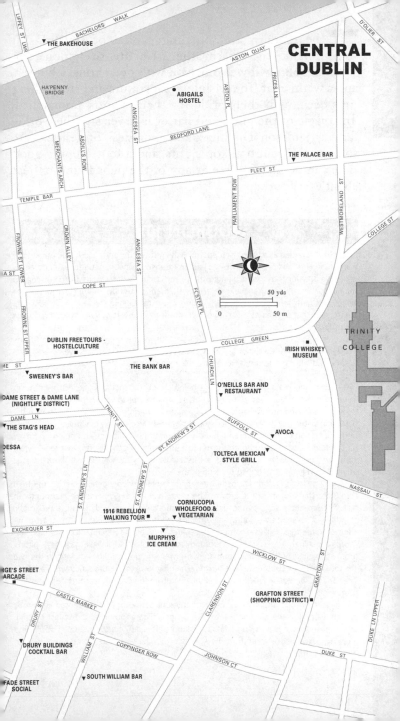

CENTRAL DUBLIN

LIFFEY ST LWR

BACHELORS WALK

D'OLIER ST

ASTON QUAY

▼ THE BAKEHOUSE

HA'PENNY BRIDGE

ANGLESEA ST

ASDILL'S ROW

MERCHANT'S ROW

• ABIGAILS HOSTEL

ASTON PL

PRICES LN

BEDFORD LANE

▼ THE PALACE BAR

FLEET ST

WESTMORELAND ST

TEMPLE BAR

MERCHANT'S ARCH

PARLIAMENT ROW

COLLEGE ST

CROWN ALLEY

ANGLESEA ST

FROWNE ST LOWER

A ST

COPE ST

FOSTER PL

0   50 yds
0   50 m

FROWNE ST UPPER

▼ DUBLIN FREE TOURS - HOSTELCULTURE

COLLEGE GREEN

• IRISH WHISKEY MUSEUM

TRINITY COLLEGE

ME ST

▼ SWEENEY'S BAR

▼ THE BANK BAR

CHURCH LN

O'NEILLS BAR AND RESTAURANT ▼

DAME STREET & DAME LANE (NIGHTLIFE DISTRICT)

TRINITY ST

DAME LN

ST ANDREW'S ST

SUFFOLK ST

▼ AVOCA

▼ THE STAG'S HEAD

TOLTECA MEXICAN STYLE GRILL ▼

ODESSA

NASSAU ST

ST ANDREW'S LN

ST ANDREW'S ST

▪ 1916 REBELLION WALKING TOUR

CORNUCOPIA WHOLEFOOD & VEGETARIAN

EXCHEQUER ST

MURPHYS ICE CREAM

WICKLOW ST

GRAFTON ST

GE'S STREET ARCADE

CASTLE MARKET

DRURY ST

CLARENDON ST

GRAFTON STREET (SHOPPING DISTRICT) ▪

DUKE LN UPPER

WILLIAM ST

COPPINGER ROW

JOHNSON CT

DUKE ST

▼ DRURY BUILDINGS COCKTAIL BAR

▼ SOUTH WILLIAM BAR

FADE STREET SOCIAL

The modern and bustling capital of Ireland still retains the charm the Irish are so famous for. Dublin will welcome you with open arms, a hot tea, and a warm chat. The Irish love for culture and storytelling runs deep, with their pride for their country unmatched. The magic of the grain and barley is never far: The world-famous Jameson Distillery and Guinness Storehouse are some of the country's top sights, and a foot-tapping good time can be had for free at any of the pubs found on just about every corner.

DUBLIN 101

Dublin was founded as a Viking settlement in the 9th century and called Baile Atha Cliath (City of the Hurtled Ford). The Vikings laid an extensive network of underwater defenses navigable only for those who planted them, preventing enemy ships from coming up the river to the city. After some time, this settlement picked up another name, the one we're most familiar with: Dublin. Just behind where the Dublin Castle stands today was a dark eddy that formed at the crux of two intersecting rivers (*dubh* means black, *linn* means pool).

Dublin eventually became the second-largest city of the British Empire in the 1600s and 1700s. After the devastating Great Hunger and London's oppressive colonial tactics, Ireland slid into decline throughout the 19th century, losing a full two-thirds of its population.

Decades later, in a glorious failure, a small band of students and intellectuals took up arms in 1916 and launched the Easter Rising, an attempt to win independence for the Republic of Ireland. In full battle mode, England brought in thousands of troops and a battleship all the way up the River Liffey and began shelling the city of Dublin. The leaders of the operation commandeered a handful of municipal buildings and holed up for six days before all were captured and taken to Kilmainham Gaol prison. Most rebels were summarily executed by firing squad, a miscalculation by the British that flipped public opinion from general apathy to the side of the rebels.

Seeking peace, London proposed a treaty of limited independence, making the Irish Free State still subject to the crown. The treaty divided the opinion of the country in half. The pro-treaty side, supported by England, was content with taking a pragmatic step *toward* sovereignty—and peace. And the anti-treaty side wouldn't stop at anything short of home rule, full autonomy, and a united Republic of Ireland. The two opposing camps began fighting, kicking off the bloody and tragic Irish Civil War (1922-1923), pitting brothers against brothers and ultimately drawing the political lines of Ireland that we see today, with six counties in the north remaining loyal to the British crown. *The Wind That Shakes the Barley* (2006) is an excellent movie to watch to learn more about this heartrending conflict.

During the 1990s and 2000s, Ireland entered a period of unprecedented economic growth, earning it the nickname the "Celtic Tiger." The good times didn't last though, as the economic crisis of 2008 hit the island particularly hard. But today, you'll find a city awakening once more from its slumber and charging into the 21st century with newfound confidence and optimism.

PLAN AHEAD

RESERVATIONS

Reserve hostel accommodations for **St. Paddy's Day** long, long in advance—at least three months ahead, perhaps longer if you're staying in an extremely popular hostel. Plan to make reservations for popular bars and restaurants you want to visit. It's also a good idea to plan ahead for at least one full day outside of Dublin at the Cliffs of Moher and Howth.

Dublin is a sport-mad city, so if there are rugby or football championships (the GAA finals or the Six Nations Championship, for example), budget accommodations quickly fill.

Reservations are recommended for the following sights:

Guinness Storehouse (guinness-store-house.com)

Jameson Experience (jamesonwhiskey.com)

Teeling Distillery (teelingwhiskey.com)

Kilmainham Gaol (kilmainhamgaolmuseum.ie)

STUDENT DISCOUNTS

Dublin's tourist attractions often offer student discounts. Keep your student ID on you at all times.

LOCAL HAPPENINGS

St. Patrick's Day

While traditionally more of a religious holiday, St. Patrick's Day has become a worldwide celebration of all things (stereotypically) Irish. The enterprising Irish have seized this massive economic opportunity. In Dublin, the festivities have grown from a boozy one-day celebration to a five-day festival filled with parades, street concerts, lectures, cultural events, and, of course, local drinking establishments packed to the rafters. St. Patrick's Day is March 17 every year, and most businesses are closed that day. On the morning of the holiday, the president, the archbishop, and the head of the Irish military attend St. Mary's Pro Cathedral in Dublin for high mass at 10:00. The mass is held in Irish, and visitors receive blessed shamrocks, which they then wear proudly at the parade.

THREE DAY ITINERARY

This itinerary takes advantage of Dublin's walkability. It hits all the must-see sights, but leaves plenty of time for you to explore the city's one-of-a-kind pub culture.

DAY 1: THANK GOODNESS FOR GUINNESS
MORNING
Start your day with the Irish scone and jam or scrambled eggs from the **Queen of Tarts** just off Temple Bar. After breakfast, walk a few blocks east down Dame Street to the Central Bank to catch a free **Next City** walking tour that will take you through the heart of Dublin (11:00 and 14:30 daily). The tour lasts about two hours and does an excellent job of orienting you to the city and introducing you to Irish history and culture.

AFTERNOON
Head west to the **Guinness Storehouse**—about a 20-minute walk from the city center. Or hop on one of the many city buses that run west along Dame Street (123, 13, 40). Spend the afternoon in the storehouse, climbing through this labyrinth of brewing science and enticing Guinness propaganda. Your ticket is also a voucher for a free pint, redeemable at numerous stations throughout the tour or at the top-floor Gravity Bar (last call at 17:00!), where you can enjoy a 360-degree panorama while imbibing the world's best-known stout.

EVENING
On your way back into town, stop for a traditional Irish dinner at **Brazenhead,** the city's oldest pub, or **The Bull & Castle,** one of my favorite gastropubs in the world. Both are on the Guinness Storehouse side of downtown, making either of them a convenient stop.

LATE
Create your own pub crawl from my recommended hot spots. Start at the famous **Temple Bar** and make your way to the nearby **Palace Pub, O'Neill's, and The Porterhouse,** where the party goes late every night.

DAY 2: TRINITY COLLEGE & HOWTH
MORNING
As soon as you can stand the daylight, grab a hearty breakfast at **The Bakehouse.** Their strong coffee is a rejuvenator. Fill your belly with pastries and grab a sandwich for later.

Cross the Liffey to meet at the front arch of **Trinity College** for a 30-minute tour, which includes entry to see the **Book of Kells.**

AFTERNOON
Hop on the DART train at Tara Street Station, just a block east from the O'Connell Street Bridge. The train will take you to the coastal town of **Howth.** Spend the afternoon hiking and exploring, then relax for a bit at the **Bloody Stream Pub.** The trip to Howth is about 40 minutes each way. This fishing village only takes 30 minutes to explore, and the semi-strenuous hike takes most people about 1.5 hours.

EVENING

Once you're back in Dublin, head out for dinner. Try succulent pulled pork sandwiches at **South William Bar** or the steaming tapas at **The Market Bar.** If neither of those options strike your fancy, you can find burritos, Thai, and sushi just north of the Millennium Bridge in Dublin's **Millennium Walkway Restaurant Row** (aka Dublin's Latin Quarter).

Alternatively, call ahead and reserve a table for the Celtic Nights Dance Show and Dinner at the **Arlington Hotel** (nightly at 20:30). Tap your feet along to the jigs as you sip a pint and enjoy a three-course dinner.

LATE

Head out for a night in the **Georgian Quarter,** where the locals rage and the party lasts till the wee hours. A 15-minute walk south from Dame Street on South Great George's Street will bring you to **Whelan's.** It's a great place for a pint or three, and if you're lucky, you'll catch some live music—acts usually start around 20:30, so get there before then if you want to see the stage. If there's no music, head to **Flannery's** for a few more pints. Close the night with some dancing and drinks at **Copper Face Jacks.** All three venues are within stumbling distance of each other, so if the vibe isn't right, just head on down the road.

DAY 3: FAREWELL TO DUBLIN

MORNING

Break your fast at **Brick Alley Café,** located right on Temple Bar, for some savory coffee and pastries. If you need something sweet, pair your coffee with an ice cream—a surprisingly great combo.

Spend whatever's left of your morning lazily meandering through the **Grafton Street** shopping zone. Rest your feet in **St. Stephen's Green** (bring a picnic lunch). There are a few top-class and free museums in the area: the **National Gallery,** the **National Museum of Archaeology,** and the **National Library** (all closed Mon). Of the three, the National Gallery, with its all-star cast of Van Gogh, Rembrandt, Caravaggio, and many more, is my favorite—for my money, it's the best art gallery in Ireland, which is no slouch in this department.

AFTERNOON

Take bus 37 or 39 from the southeast corner of the Trinity College campus toward the **Jameson Distillery,** and get off at Ushers Quay (pronounced "key").

EVENING

Fuel up for your last evening in town with some delicious beef and Guinness stew at the Irish Film Institute, just around the corner from Temple Bar. Pair it with a pint of Guinness to complete the effect.

LATE

For some nice cocktails and a fun night out, kick off at **37 Dawson Street.** Take one of the fringe-lined chairs by the bar and down an old-fashioned and a plateful of tapas in an atmosphere that fuses funky postmodern and vintage décor. Stumble out the back door and choose between burlesque-y **Funky Fish Cocktail Club** or the decidedly pretentious **Zozimus,** where the egos of the staff and patrons pair nicely with the inflated wine list. **No Name Bar** isn't far, and it's packed with the hipster set. There's also the sophisticated throwback bar **Odessa** and the mainstream **Mercantile Pub** for some no-nonsense drinks and dancing. Hats off to you if you can still read this after a tour of those fine establishments.

TOP NEIGHBORHOODS

The River Liffey runs east to the sea, bisecting Dublin. The **South Bank** is home to most of Dublin's cultural and tourist sights, including Trinity College, the Grafton Street shopping district, the national museums, the Guinness Storehouse, and **Temple Bar.** The Temple Bar neighborhood is bordered by the River Liffey to the north, Dame Street to the south, Fishamble Street to the west, and Westmoreland Street to the east. It's world famous for its dozens of top-shelf bars, with most offering live music nearly every night. It's the most touristy part of Dublin, and pints here are the most expensive, running up to €7.

Most of the worthwhile sights, restaurants, and accommodations on the **North Side** are within a few blocks of the river. You'll find a few recommended hostels, restaurants, and nightlife venues here, as well as the Jameson Distillery Tour and O'Connell Street, Dublin's grand boulevard.

South of Dame Street you'll find the **Georgian Quarter,** my favorite district for innovative restaurants and bars and nightlife. Many of my favorites are highlighted below.

TOP SIGHTS

Trinity College & Book of Kells

Ireland's oldest university was founded in 1592 by Queen Elizabeth I. It's still active today, and its claim to fame is the beautifully preserved "bog book," the Book of Kells, found inside the Trinity Old Library. This unique illuminated manuscript is one of the oldest in existence, and it illustrates each of the four gospels in beautiful, intricate Celtic weaves. A campus tour (€13, 30 minutes) includes entry into the library and viewing of the book. Tours meet at Front Arch and depart about every 30 minutes. Entry to see the book without the student tour is €10.

Free, tour €14, May-Sept daily 10:15-15:40, Feb-Apr and Oct-Nov Sat-Sun only, no tours Dec-Jan, Book of Kells without tour €10, June-Sept Mon-Sat 09:00-18:00, Sun 09:30-18:00, Oct-May Mon-Sat 09:30-17:00, Sun 12:00-16:30, College Green, South Bank, tcd.ie

Guinness Storehouse

Tour the Guinness Storehouse to learn about the history and brewing process behind one of the most recognizable brands of beer in the world. Follow an interactive virtual tour led by the grand master brewer himself, Fergal Murray. He first explains the four ingredients that go into the mix: water, hops, barley, and yeast. Continue upstairs to discover the tasting experience and a world of Guinness media and marketing materials (my favorites are the

"Guinness Is Good for You" posters). Your entry ticket is also a voucher for a free pint of the black stuff once you reach the Gravity Bar at the top level. Sip it while taking in Dublin's best 360-degree panorama. Alternatively, you can redeem your drink voucher at one of the pour-your-own-pint stations on the third and fourth levels. You can also redeem your voucher for a soda or juice.

The storehouse is south of the River Liffey, a 20-minute walk from Dublin's city center. You can also take bus 123, 13, or 40, all of which run to Guinness Storehouse from the city center, west along Dame Street.

€18 for students over 18, €20 adults, €14 online, daily 09:30-19:00, July-Aug until 20:00, St James Gate, Greater Dublin, +353 (0)1 408 4800, guinness-storehouse.com

Chester Beatty Library

Chester Beatty was born in the United States of Irish heritage and became a powerful mining magnate. He began collecting as a young man and developed an impressive assortment of everything from bottles to manuscripts, including pieces of New Testament manuscripts dating back to before AD 200. He moved to Dublin in 1950 and was made an honorary citizen of Ireland by 1957, and he donated his entire collection to the state when he died in 1968.

It's easy to spend two hours poring over the extensive collection, which features artifacts of all the major world religions.

Nearby, you'll see **Dublin Castle.** You can tour the staterooms, but I wouldn't say they're worth the time on a short visit. The castle stood as a sign of oppression throughout history, occupied by whoever was controlling the local people. Today, it's where important state functions are held.

Free, Mon-Fri 10:00-17:00, Sat 11:00-17:00, Sun 13:00-17:00, closed Mon Oct-Apr, just behind Dublin Castle, South Bank, +353 (0)1 407 0750, cbl.ie

National Library

This library caters to those interested in Ireland's long roster of literary greats. You'll find in-depth exhibits covering the works and lives of famous Irish authors like William Butler Yeats and James Joyce. If you have (or think you might have) any Irish roots, you can do a little amateur genealogical work using the searchable archive of Irish parish registries, which include records of births, baptisms, marriages, and deaths; ask the helpful librarians for assistance. The library's beautiful neoclassical interior makes even a short visit worthwhile.

Free, Mon-Wed 09:30-19:45, Thurs-Fri 09:30-16:45, Sat 09:30-12:45, Sun 13:00-16:45 (exhibits only), Kildare St, South Bank, +353 (0)1 603 0200, nli.ie

National Museum: Decorative Arts & History

Housed in old military barracks, this museum contains artifacts, art, historical pieces, and natural history from throughout the ages, with a fascinating military history exhibit to boot. The museum displays a selection of objects that tell the story of Ireland, from prehistoric coins to an AK-47. Find it just north of the River Liffey,

not far from the Jameson Distillery, Guinness Storehouse, and Phoenix Park. Start your day early and you'll have time to visit all four sights before dinner. To get here, take bus 25A or 25B to the Guinness Storehouse stop.

Free, Tues-Sat 10:00-17:00, Sun 14:00-17:00, closed Mondays, Blenburb St, Greater Dublin, +353 (0)1 677 7444, museum.ie, rotating exhibits, check online to see what's on

National Museum of Archaeology

This interesting state-run museum features an extensive history of Dublin's Nordic ancestry on one main ground floor and a smaller upper floor. Take an hour to check out all the gold jewelry and fearsome-looking Viking weapons. Don't miss the Viking ship and bog books and mummies that have been discovered in recent years—the damp, grassy bogs preserve anything that falls into them.

Free, Tues-Sat 10:00-17:00, Sun 14:00-17:00, closed Mon, Kildare St, South Bank, +353 (0)1 677 7444, museum.ie

The National Gallery

This recently renovated art museum features a plethora of Irish masterpieces, as well as works from international masters like Monet, Caravaggio, Van Gogh, Goya, Titian, Poussin, and Rembrandt. A large renovation that commenced in 2011 is finally nearing completion. The rejuvenated space, with a modernized entrance and much-improved galleries throughout the building, is poised in every way to compete with its English and continental rivals. The power lunch café on the ground floor makes for a convenient and economical pit stop.

Free, Mon-Sat 09:15-17:30, Thurs until 20:30, Sun 11:00-17:30, Merrion Square W, South Bank, +353 (0)1 661 5133, nationalgallery.ie

Little Museum of Dublin

This delightful and bite-sized museum, housed in a historic home that dates back to the Georgian era, packs just about every square inch of wall space with historical artifacts, posters, and memorabilia—all of it chronologically organized so, as you move down the walls, you move forward in time. A friendly interactive guide highlights points of interest or historical importance, including a special exhibit on U2 and the other musical greats who've called Dublin home over the years. The Little Museum is a great way to quickly soak up Ireland's colonial and revolutionary history. The €1 brochure neatly summarizes the pieces on display in the collection and makes for a nice memento. An expansion is on the horizon, supported by the optional donation of €2 on top of your entry.

€7 adults, €6 students, daily 09:30-17:00, Thurs until 20:00, included tours leave on the hour 10:00-16:00, 15 St. Stephen's Green, South Bank, +353 (0)1 661 1000, littlemuseum.ie

Kilmainham Gaol

Dublin's active jail from 1796 until 1924, Kilmainham Gaol, on the far west side of town, is well worth the hike. The site connects you like no other to the history of Irish rebellions—just about all of the leaders of the many uprisings entered these gates, a good number of them never to walk out again. The leaders of the Easter Rising in 1916 were summarily executed by firing squad here, with one exception: Éamon de Valera, who was spared thanks to his American citizenship. The jail itself was supposed to be an architectural model for modern prisons, featuring a layout that maximized the number of prisoners that could be "humanely" kept, and minimizing the number of guards required to monitor them. Explore the small museum while waiting for your tour to kick off at the top of each hour. To get here, take bus 25A or 25B to Con Colbert Road, doubling back around the corner to the jail once you get off.

€9 adults, €5 students (includes hour-long tour), July-early Sept daily 09:00-18:45, early Sept-June daily 09:30-17:30, last tour at 16:15, last admission an hour before closing, Inchicore Rd, Greater Dublin, +353 (0)1 453 5984, herit-ageireland.ie/en/kilmainhamgaol

Jameson Distillery

If you're a whiskey lover, this is the place for you. While they don't actually distill the whiskey here anymore, the guided tour is a great way to learn the trade and sample some traditional Irish whiskey. It walks you through the distilling process and sheds some light on those sneaky angels taking their share during the aging process. Be sure to raise your hand when asked for volunteers to get in on a taste test—you won't be disappointed! The distillery is north of the River Liffey, on the western side of Dublin near Smithfield and just behind the Generator Hostel. To get here, take any bus going west along the river, alighting at Ushers Quay.

€18, €15 for groups, online booking, Mon-Thurs 09:30-17:30, Fri-Sat 09:30-19:00, Sun 10:00-17:30, last tour at

17:30 Sun-Thurs and 19:00 Fri-Sat, Bow St, Smithfield Village, Greater Dublin, +353 (0)1 807 2355, tours. jamesonwhiskey.com

Celtic Nights Dance Show & Dinner

A Riverdance-style show that reflects Irish tradition and culture is a highlight for many visitors to Dublin. Fast-paced, costumed tap dancers (some of them world champions) stun audiences nightly at the famous Arlington Hotel dinner-and-dance show. The steep price of admission includes a three-course dinner no better or worse than you'd expect it to be (people come for the show, not the food). Numerous group and solo acts pound through a litany of traditional and modern Irish dance. Make—or avoid—eye contact with the dancers depending on whether or not you want to get dragged up on stage and taught the basics while everybody watches. If you're not shy, this can be an incredible photo op.

€34, hour-long show starts at 20:30, dinner seatings every 30 minutes from 18:30, reservations recommended online, 23 Bachelors Walk, North Side, +353 (0)1 687 5200, arlington.ie

TOP EATS

Dublin is in the midst of a transformative culinary renaissance, and this has changed the flavor of the city for the better. What used to be a country notorious for its bland and predictable meat and veg is now bursting with innovative restaurants, gastropubs, and cafés that take their trade seriously.

When it comes to traditional Irish food, you've got a few staples: fish-and-chips, of course, is a mainstay, and so are beef and Guinness stew (big cuts of meat and veggies in a thick, spiced stew), *boxty* dishes (savory potato pancakes usually wrapped around meat or veggies), and shepherd's pie (a filling of minced meat and veggies topped with mashed potatoes, usually served in a large ceramic bowl). The Irish do savory and filling comfort food very well. Look for any of these dishes on the menu at the sit-down restaurants listed here. Tip up to 10 percent on your dinner tab.

Queen of Tarts

Queen of Tarts is probably the cutest little place in the city. A breakfast here feels like a drop into Alice's rabbit hole, and you're guaranteed one of the best scones with thick cream you've ever had. They also have egg dishes if you've got a stronger appetite. Find another branch barely a block away (4 Dame St).

Scones from €4.50, Mon-Fri 08:00-19:00 (Thurs-Fri until 20:00), Sat 08:30-20:00, Sun 09:00-19:00, Cows Ln, Temple Bar, +353 (0)1 633 4681, queenoftarts.ie

Avoca

This housewares/fashion store sells an incredible range of products, and their hand-woven throws and blankets cry out to be touched. But the main attraction, at least for hungry locals and tourists, is down the staircase. Enjoy a wide array of fresh salads and sandwiches, and be sure to try the wraps—they're superb.

Plates and dishes from €6, Mon-Sat 09:30-17:30, Sun 11:00-17:00, 11-13 Suffolk St (just steps from the Molly Malone statue), South Bank, +353 (0)1 677 4215, avoca.ie/home

The Bakehouse

This funky 1960s-themed American-style diner frequently lures customers in off the street with the smell of fresh-baked bread and pastries. I always include a stop at the Bakehouse for one of their sandwiches on thickly sliced bread, but they've also got great pies, salads, baked potatoes, and a range of filling breakfast dishes.

Breakfasts from €5, Mon-Wed 10:00-18:00, Thurs-Fri 09:00-18:00, Sat 10:00-18:00, Sun brunch 10:00-15:00, 6 Bachelor's Walk, North Side, +353 (0)1 873 4279, the-bakehouse.ie

The Bakery

Situated at the west end of Temple Bar, this place is one of Dublin's most legit bakeries—it supplies many of the other pastry shops around town. Some of the freshest sandwiches and sausage rolls I've ever tasted come from here. Get a few to go and you'll have the workings of a great picnic on your day trip to Howth. Complete with a friendly staff, the Bakery is also friendly on your wallet.

Sandwiches from €4, Mon-Sat 08:00-17:00, Pudding Row 3, Temple Bar, +353 (0)1 672 9882

Bison Bar

Bison is the place to go for soul food on Wellington Quay. Their pulled barbecue pork and rib tips, accompanied by down-home sides like coleslaw and beans, never disappoint. Wooden accents and exposed brick give the place a sophisticated hipster vibe, but one without a trace of pretension.

Plates from €14, barbecue served 12:00-21:00 daily (or until the food runs out), 11 Wellington Quay, Temple Bar, +353 (0)1 056 3144, bisonbar.ie

Fade Street Social
Tapas & Restaurant

Select from a wide array of seafood and modern Irish dishes in this tradition-al-with-a-twist fusion restaurant. I love the tapas half of the space for the value. Energetic staff create a positive vibe in this bustling, exposed-kitchen café that is often packed with in-the-know locals. The adjoining restaurant, founded by Irish celebrity chef Dylan McGrath, features serious cuts of meat. If you're thirsty, head upstairs to the bold cocktail bar and its spacious and bustling patio.

Dinners from €14, 12:00-24:00 daily, 4-6 Fade St, Temple Bar, +353 (0)1 604 0066, fadestreetsocial.com

The Market Bar

This expansive Spanish fusion restaurant in what was once a downtown slaughter-house has some of the best tapas this side of the Irish Sea. The chorizo salad, *patatas bravas* (fried potatoes with a spicy ketchup sauce), and calamari all seem to disappear from the table the moment they arrive. Portions are small, so order a number of dishes and share them with friends. The industrial-chic décor (combined with taste-ful splashes of vibrant color) makes this a perfect spot for photos of food and drinks. Happy hour, with drink and food specials, starts at 19:00, so get there early.

Dinner from €15, Mon-Thurs 12:00-23:30, Fri-Sat 12:00-01:30, Sun 12:00-23:00, 14A Fade St, South Bank, +353 (0)1 613 9094, marketbar.ie

The Bull & Castle

This is my favorite spot in town for high-quality pub grub that's a cut above the greasy fare that you'll find in almost all Dublin pubs. Steak is the bar's special-ty, including steak sandwiches will have you pushing yourself away from the table quite satisfied. Staff members are happy to make suggestions for drinks to pair with your main. There's fine dining downstairs in this split-level restaurant, but upstairs is where you'll find me—especially when a game is on.

Dinners from €11, Mon-Tues 12:00-20:00, Wed-Thurs 12:00-20:30, Fri-Sat 12:00-23:00, Sun 12:30-20:00, 5-7 Lord Edward St, Temple Bar, +353 (0)1 475 1122, bull-and-castle.fxbuckley.ie

Leo Burdock Fish & Chips

There's no way around it: You just have to try Irish fish-and-chips while in Dublin, and Leo Burdock is the place to do so. No frills, great prices, and world-class fried good-ness. They've been serving Dubliners their battered and fried specialty for more than a century, and the lineups at lunch and din-nertime (along with a long list of celebrity clients) are a testament to their bang-on-the-money recipe.

Plates from €7.50, daily 12:00-24:00, 2 Werburgh St, South Bank, +353 (0)1 454 0306, leoburdock.com

The Fumbally

A perfect example of the relatively recent Irish food renaissance, the Fumbally ramps up the tastiness without gouging its customers. Located about a 15-minute walk south of Temple Bar, it's a favorite for pow-er lunchers or anybody who appreciates lean, fresh food like healthy sandwiches, freshly squeezed juices, and a wide array of salads and soups. Don't miss the pork sandwich, artfully assembled by bearded and aproned hipsters.

Sandwiches from €5, Tues-Fri 08:00-17:00, Sat 10:00-17:00 (kitchen closes at 16:00), closed Sun-Mon, Fumbally Ln, South Bank, +353 (0)1 529 8732, thefumbally.ie

South William Bar

This gastrobar offers a deceivingly simple menu of barbecue, with pork sandwiches, chicken wings, veggie nachos, and hot dogs that will make short work of your hunger. Crispy fries are served with a selection of seasonings, like curry, garlic, and cheese, flavored salts (lime, chili, or rosemary), and a wide range of mouthwatering dips. It's a dizzying array of choices and an intoxicating blend of aromas. South William is the nightly launching pad for locals, who leave the place with full bellies and head out to any of the trendy nearby bars and venues.

Dinners from €8.50, Mon-Wed 16:00-23:30, Thursday 16:00-late, Fri-Sat 13:00-late, Sun 14:00-23:00, 52 S William St, South Bank, +353 (0)1 677 7007, southwilliam.ie

Irish Film Institute
Most famous for its film festivals, the Irish Film Institute also contains a hidden gem of a restaurant. The food might not be a great value, but I've never left feeling I got less than what I paid for. It's a great spot to hit up when you don't feel like venturing too far from Temple Bar. The service is friendly and fast, and the menu features classics like beef and Guinness stew, fish-and-chips, and well-appointed burgers.

Dinner from €13, daily 12:30-21:30, 6 Eustace St, Temple Bar, +353 (0)1 679 3477, ifi.ie

Brick Alley Café
Just steps from Temple Bar, this café with wooden interior offers more value and quality than expected considering its humble appearance and touristy location. It's a cozy place to enjoy cup after cup of strong coffee, hearty breakfast sandwiches on fresh baguettes, pancakes with maple syrup, and sugary treats like artisan hot chocolate and rich chocolate cake. On nice days, grab one of the seats outside for some prime people-watching real estate. The service can be slow, especially when it's busy, but the central location and free Wi-Fi make for a clutch lunch stop. Full vegetarian and gluten-free options are available.

Pancakes from €4.90, Sun-Wed 09:00-22:00, Thurs 09:00-22:30, Fri-Sat 09:00-23:00, 25 Essex St E, Temple Bar, facebook.com/BrickAlleyCafe, +353 (0)1 679 3393

Indigo and Cloth
Just off Temple Bar, this popular café also doubles as a cutting-edge contemporary lifestyle and clothing brands shop. For my money, this is the best espresso shot you'll find in Dublin (served in locally made ceramics). The café only seats 6-8 people, but there's often a chair or two available. If there's not a seat, take your coffee to go and browse the boutique.

Espresso from €2, Mon-Sat 10:00-18:00, Sun 12:00-17:00, 9 Essex St, Temple Bar, +353 (0)1 670 6403, indigoandcloth.com

Tolteca Burritos
Chipotle wannabes are popping up all across Dublin, but I'm not complaining. Serving fresh and piping-hot shredded beef or pork burritos, Tolteca is packed out at lunchtime with Trinity College students who are drawn by the smell of quality ingredients and a wallet-friendly price list. The line can get long around lunch and dinnertime, but it moves quickly, and the large space offers ample seating for the hungry crowds.

Burritos from €7, daily 11:00-22:00 (closed 12:30-14:00), Sat-Sun 11.00-23.00, 21 Suffolk St, South Bank, +353 (0)1 677 9506, tolteca.ie

Murphy's Ice Cream
Hailing all the way from Dingle (350 kilometers west of Dublin on the Atlantic coast), Ireland's most famous creamery has taken the island by storm and has opened up locations all over the place. The Dublin Murphy's is a popular spot thanks to its innovative flavors and quality ingredients. It might just be the best ice cream you'll have in Europe. Go for the caramelized brown bread, sea salt, or spicy cinnamon—and there's always the Irish coffee. On hot days, I long for nothing more than a cup of Murphy's.

Cups €5.00, open daily from 12:00-22:00, 27 Wicklow St, South Bank, +353 (0)86 031 0726, murphysicecream.ie

Cornucopia Wholefood & Vegetarian
Vegetarians need look no further than Cornucopia's buffet. The vegetarian curries, enchiladas, salads, and bean-and-rice dishes make for healthy and clean-burning options—perfect not only for vegetarians but also for those (like me) who try to follow up indulgent experiences with more restrained ones. Heads up: The lines can get painfully long around lunch. The word is out, and young professionals flock to

cornucopia for the generous portions and fair prices.

Dishes starting at €9, Mon 08:30-21:00, Tues-Sat 08:30-22:00, Sun 12:00-21:00, 19-20 Wicklow St, South Bank, +353 (0)1 677 7583, cornucopia.ie

Umi Falafel

Whenever possible, I make it a point to avoid chains (this goes for recommending them as well). Umi Falafel is one of the few that managed to survive the cut, and you'll quickly see why. The service is lightning fast, and the food is fresh and (depending on your order) healthy. Head to the location on Dame Street and grab some fresh falafel (of course), tabouleh, or their delicious Moroccan or Lebanese salads. It's a smoothly run operation, so it's perfect if you want to strap on the feedbag and move on to the next sight in record time.

Lunches from €7.50, daily 12:00-22:00, 13 Dame St, Temple Bar, +353 (0)1 670 6866, umifalafel.ie

Brother Hubbard

If you're dieting, stay upwind of Brother Hubbard. The smells coming out of this Moroccan fusion restaurant around breakfast time have been known to make mincemeat of healthy-eating resolutions. If you aren't watching your waistline, pop in for cinnamon rolls, brownies, delicious hot chocolate and coffee, and amazing breakfast dishes like eggs over beans with chorizo. A local recommended that I try their pork sandwich, and I nearly fell off my chair—the meat was succulent, the bread perfectly toasted. I highly recommend their €30 set dinner menu, which takes you on a three-course culinary tour of Morocco, featuring kofta (meatballs), spicy tagine (stew), and couscous.

Brunch from €10, Mon-Tues 08:00-16:30, Wed-Fri 08:00-22:00, Sat 09:00-22:00, Sun 09:00-16:30, 153 Capel St, North Side, +353 (0)1 441 1112, brotherhubbard.ie

Kimchi Hophouse

Head to the north side of O'Connell Street for the friendly service and welcoming atmosphere of Dublin's oldest Korean restaurant. If you've never really experienced Korean cuisine, order the bulgogi (spiced and marinated beef grilled to perfection) or the bibimbap (a festival of veggies and a meat on a bed of rice or noo-

dles, all topped with an egg) and prepare to have your socks knocked off. There's plenty of delicious Japanese food on the menu as well.

Dinners from €13, Mon-Thurs 12:00-23:00, Fri-Sat 12:00-23:30, Sun 12:00-22:30, 160 Parnell St, North Side, +353 (0)1 872 8318, kimchihophouse.ie

Madina Desi Curry Co

This is my favorite spot in town for Indian food. Most people don't stick around to eat in the modestly appointed restaurant, opting instead to take their delicious, budget-friendly meal to go. Follow their lead. Get a plate of rice, tikka masala, and naan and you're good to go! Don't forget to stock up on napkins.

Curries from €8, daily 12:00-23:30, 60 Mary St, North Side, +353 (0)1 872 6007, madina.ie

Oxmantown

The best things in life are often the simplest as well. For lunch, what's better than the classically delicious combo of soup and sandwich? Loved by locals, this place feels like it's on the verge of exploding, but the crowds have yet to notice its quietly understated brilliance. I always go for the Ruby—thick pastrami and sauerkraut and a bit of spicy mustard—with a bowl of tomato soup that warms me up, especially on rainy days. Seating is limited inside, but there's plenty of room on the patio.

Sandwiches €5.50, Mon-Fri 08:0-16:00, 16 Mary's Abbey, North Side, +353 (0)1 804 7030, oxmantown.com

Millennium Walkway Restaurant Row

Near the north end of the Millennium Bridge is Bloom Lane, a narrow street jam-packed with some of Dublin's most popular restaurants. There are more than a dozen establishments that offer everything from quick bites on the go to fine dining. Consider the following options: **Bar Italia,** a mod Italian restaurant and wine bar; **Enoteca Delle Langhe,** another Italian choice with wine and standard fare; **Cactus Jack's,** a sit-down Mexican restaurant with tapas options; **Koh Restaurant & Cocktail Bar,** a classy Asian fusion restaurant with a carefully curated cocktail menu and surprisingly inexpensive takeaway options;

and **Boojum,** a favorite among students for its Tex-Mex burritos that are close to bursting at the seams. If you're in a group that can't seem to decide where to eat, head down to the Millennium Walkway—you'll soon find something everybody can agree on.

North Side

TOP NIGHTLIFE

Dublin is famous for its characteristic and upbeat nightlife, running the gamut from traditional pubs (often with live music) to rock bars and posh cocktail lounges. There are also a growing number of dance bars and clubs, many of them first-rate. The tourists flock to Temple Bar, where they party predominantly with other tourists—the locals avoid the crowds and expensive pints, preferring the bars in the district south of Dame Street. If you want to mingle with Dubliners, head there—or to any of the unassuming pubs that can be found almost anywhere.

NIGHTLIFE DISTRICTS

The thing about Dublin's nightlife is that you really can't go wrong no matter where you end up. There are so many pubs and bars around town that you'll often find the best parties simply by exploring on your own. If a trendy atmosphere is important to you, you'll find plenty of places to tip a pint listed below. If not, hop from pub to pub until you find the right mix of people and place. You can virtually ensure a great night by starting in one of the neighborhoods that are described below.

Temple Bar

Temple Bar, between Westmoreland Street and Fishamble Street on the south side of the Liffey, is both a Dublin neighborhood and a bar in that neighborhood. "Bar" refers to the riverbank that used to reach all the way to the street now called Temple Bar; Temple is the family name of the dynasty that once owned this stretch of riverbank. With a well-deserved reputation as the place to party in Dublin, Temple Bar draws young tourists and students, many of them in large groups. There are chanting bros, woo girls, and stag and hen parties galore—all of them stumbling over each other in one big sloppy mess. Pints

climb past €6, but if you want the wild party scene, this is its epicenter. Live music pours out of just about every bar on the street.

Temple Bar

Dame Street & Dame Lane

Dame Street marks the southern border of Temple Bar. Just south of Dame Street is Dame Lane, a small back alley with half a dozen bars and pubs that fill up with locals after quitting time. This has a much more authentic local flavor than anything you'll find in the heart of Temple Bar. The farther south you go (Drury Street and South Williams Street for example) the nicer (and more expensive) the bars and restaurants get. Here's where you'll find upscale dining, carefully crafted cocktails, and Dublin's well-heeled set.

South Bank

Georgian District

Locals in the know head to the Georgian District for Dublin's trendiest food and drink spots. You'll find restaurants with creative themes, speakeasies re-creating the nightlife of the Roaring '20s, pickup joints, and some of the best live music you'll hear anywhere in Dublin. It's no sur-

LGBT DUBLIN

While Ireland leans a bit socially conservative, the capital city of Dublin has a thriving gay scene with deep roots. You'll find Dublin's hostels to be extremely open and accepting. For a good time, head to **The George** (89 S George St, South Bank, +353 (0)1 478 2983), Dublin's oldest gay pub, which draws a young and rowdy crowd. Drag shows and great music keep the party going late just about every night of the week. **Gay Pride** (dublinpride.ie) is towards the end of June each year.

prise that the Georgian District is home to a number of my favorites—**No Name Bar, Copper Face Jacks, Whelan's,** and **Market Bar,** just to name a few.

Georgian District

IRISH PUBS

A popular local radio show once held a contest. The rules were simple: plan a route across Dublin that doesn't pass by a single pub. The winner was the man who called in and said, "Any route works—you just have to go into each one!" Authentic Irish pubs are warm, cozy affairs where amateur pickup bands play traditional Irish music nearly every night. Head to the bar and grab your pint. Pull up a stool and strike up a conversation with your fellow imbibers. In Dublin, this is a foolproof recipe for a great night.

The Temple Bar

If you're wondering which came first, the street or the bar, the answer is: the street. An enterprising entrepreneur started a bar named after the street in 1840, and when the street later rose in popularity as a destination for tourists from the world over, it catapulted this corner bar to the stars. Unless you arrive extremely early, there's no room to sit in the summer months. This is a bar you visit for the experience and the been-there-done-that story, so don't expect a bang-for-your-buck round of pints. There's live music and a smoker-friendly patio out back. Check the website for scheduled musical acts.

Pints €7.50, 48 Temple Bar, Temple Bar, +353 (0)1 672 5286, thetemplebarpub.com

The Celt

The Celt's claim to fame is its authenticity. There's no fancy packaging here—just a pub that feels and looks like so many of the countless pubs that dot the Irish countryside. A fireplace rages in the colder months, and there's live Irish singers and traditional players just about every day of the week. Look for the flag of the Irish Republic on the wall. Located a couple of blocks east of O'Connell Street, this gem is safely tucked away from the tourist hordes.

Pints from €4.50, 81 Talbot St, North Side, +353 (0)1 878 8655, thecelt.ie

The Palace

Located at the end of Temple Bar, the Palace has maintained its reputation as one of Dublin's foremost literary pubs. Its proximity to the *Irish Times* newspaper office made it a daily haunt of writers Patrick Kavanagh and Flann O'Brien—both household names in Ireland. However, they haven't gussied the place up just because the patrons have been known to scribble a line or two. Nondescript and full of old-time locals, this is one of your best options for an authentic Irish pub experience in Temple Bar.

Pints from €5, 21 Fleet St, Temple Bar, +353 (0)1 671 7388, thepalacebardub-lin.com

Brazenhead

With a list of former patrons including James Joyce and Jonathan Swift, this cozy pub with timeworn stone walls lays claim to the title of the oldest pub not just in Dublin, but in all of Ireland. Stop by the 800-year old establishment for the nightly live music—come early and enjoy a candlelit dinner. With a full dinner menu, the Brazenhead makes for a convenient stop on the way back from the Guinness Storehouse. The beef and Guinness stew will keep you full for days! Don't forget to check out the hundreds of badges tacked to the walls—all of them given to the bar by police officers and firefighters over the years (a testament to the fierce loyalty of Brazenhead's blue-collared patrons).

Pints from €5, 20 Lower Bridge St, South Bank, +353 (0)1 677 9549, brazenhead.com

The Stag's Head

Social and inviting, Stag's Head is nestled behind the Mercantile on Dame Lane. Sumptuous leather upholstery and dark wood paneling give the pub more than just a dash of masculine elegance. Head upstairs and find a spot on their comfy red leather couch.

Pints from €5, daily 11:00-01:30 (closes at midnight on Sunday), 1 Dame Court, South Bank, +353 (0)1 679 3687

Cobblestone Pub

Billing itself as a drinking pub with a music problem, the Cobblestone is a favorite among those who care about the quality of

ACT LIKE A LOCAL

The Trad

Traditional Irish music, or "trad," as it's called, is a mainstay of Irish culture. Locals grow up learning more than 150 traditional Irish songs in school, and they put this knowledge into practice with friends and family at the pub—which, in Ireland, really does mean "public house." Pubs are Ireland's "third space," where families enjoy spending time in a place that is neither home nor the workplace but something else entirely. Trad plays a significant part in this; it brings together voices and communities in a way that only music can. The better the party vibe and atmosphere, the better the *craic* (life of the party). Here's how to blend in with the locals and make the most of these Irish trad sessions.

Understand the trad. Traditional Irish music is kept alive by amateur musicians who aren't paid a thing besides a few pints of Guinness and the joy of playing the music of their forebears. Bands comprise any combination of the following instruments: the bodhran (pronounced BOW-ron), the penny flute, the Irish pipes if you're lucky, and maybe a fiddle or two. You may even get a vocalist, which really completes the ensemble. Songs can be upbeat and happy, or they can be melancholy—many of them wax nostalgic about the homeland (these songs can be heard any time that the Irish gather in lands other than their own) or about battles in which Irish forces played decisive (or tragic) roles. When these morose ballads, or "laments," come on, hold your tongue. It's gauche to speak loudly while the musicians are pouring their hearts out (this goes double if there's a vocalist). Trad sessions are comparable to a pickup game of basketball: They never quite end, and newcomers are always welcome, even if all they have is a pair of spoons to bang together. As a visitor, all you've got to do now is find your own little bar, pull up a stool, order a pint, and toast to the good life. *Slainte* ("To your health!"), my friends!

Sing along. Popular trad songs you'll hear at the pubs include "Galway Girl," "The Rocky Road to Dublin," "The Wild Rover," "Whiskey in the Jar," and "Molly Malone." Find the lyrics online and sing along! The melodies are as simple as they are infectious.

Tap your foot. Carried away by the enthusiasm and energy of a particular tune, you may be tempted to start clapping along with the music. If the musicians are on a fun riff, they'll continue; before you know, the song will have flowered into a 20-minute arrangement. After a while, your arms get tired, you get thirsty, and you stop clapping to pick up your pint glass to take a sip. The moment you stop clapping, you'll feel all the air go out of the room. Instead of clapping, tap your foot with the locals—or, if you're really impressed, let out a little whoop.

Buy a round. For the Irish, pints with friends at the pub is an almost religious observance. They've got the system down to a science: One person will set the machinery humming by buying a round. Buying the next round will be the responsibility of the person next to him or her—and so on and so forth. For the system to function properly, the circle, once started, must be completed. When it comes to your turn, don't be a skinflint, and don't dare run off to the loo hoping that nobody will notice! Any social credit you've built with the locals will quickly disappear.

There's nothing wrong with ordering Guinness. Order a glass or a half-pint. But whatever you do, don't order an Irish Car Bomb.

their music. Their trad sessions are widely regarded as the best in the city. They let the music do all the heavy lifting—there are no frills, no gimmicks, just a well-worn wooden interior and the kind of atmosphere that is the result of freely flowing booze and great music. The music usually starts around 20:00 or sometimes later. After a few pints, find a lad or a lass and take them out on the dance floor.

Pints €5, Mon-Thurs 16:00-23:30, Fri 16:00-00:30, Sat 13:30-00:30, Sun 13:30-23:00, 77 King St N, Greater Dublin, +353 (0)1 872 1799, cobblestonepub.ie

O'Neill's Bar and Restaurant

A few of the classic pubs in Dublin just feel like home as soon as you step inside. Close to Temple Bar, O'Neill's is one of these. It's been perfecting the pub experience for more than 300 years, so you can expect that when you come for a pint, some pub grub, or just some tea, you'll be treated to an authentic taste of old Ireland. Head upstairs to find one of O'Neill's many cozy snugs—historically, these were reserved for women to enjoy their glasses of Guinness in peace.

Pints from €5, Mon-Thurs 08:00-23:30, Fri-Sat 08:00-00:30, open till 23:00 on Sun, 2 Suffolk St, South Bank, +353 (0)1 679 3656, oneillspubdublin.com

BARS

The Mercantile

This hotel, restaurant, and bar is situated right on Dame Street, Dublin's main drag. This makes it a popular meeting point for nightly pub crawls that kick off after 20:00.

The interior is richly decorated with textured ceilings, ornate ironwork, and three full bars all done up in a posh, old-world style. Follow the beautiful staircase up to the top floor, which looks down onto the ground level. With quick and friendly service, the Mercantile is a great choice for an afternoon tea, or you can join the always boisterous after-work crowd. They've got several large screens, so you can also catch the game. The Mercantile's back door opens onto Dame Lane, where you'll find a whole slew of fun, casual bars—many of them great places to keep the party going late into the night.

Pints around €5, daily 08:00-late, 28 Dame St, +353 (0)1 670 7100, mercantile.ie

Drury Buildings Cocktail Bar

If your budget can handle €13 drinks, come out to the Drury Buildings Cocktail Bar, an elegant New York-style restaurant and cocktail bar that occupies what was once a six-story rag trade building. They flew in recycled timber, floors, and fixtures straight from New York and spared no expense in making the space into a harmonious whole. The leafy multilevel and balconied floor plan is complete with a budding urban garden. Their Prohibition-era cocktails (try the sidecar or the whiskey sour) might take awhile to arrive at your table, but they're proving that anything worth having is worth waiting for.

Cocktails from €13, Mon-Fri 12:00-23:30, Sat-Sun 12:00-00:30, 55 Drury St, South Bank, +353 (0)1 960 2095, drurybuildings.com

Garage Bar

Take a load off on one of the barrel stools here and knock back reasonably priced drinks with a crowd that doesn't really give a damn who you are or what you do. This is Temple Bar's alternative joint. They're more likely to be playing an indie film or a sci-fi classic on the televisions than the game, but that's part of the place's unique character. Don't come expecting an authentic taste of Ireland or old-world charm—it's just not that kind of place.

Drinks from €4.50, Mon-Tues 17:00-24:00, Wed-Fri 17:00-02:30, Sat-Sun 16:00-02:30, Essex St E, Temple Bar, +353 (0)1 679 6543, garagebar.ie

No Name Bar (Wooden Snail)

As with all things hipster, No Name Bar demands a little bit of digging—only those with their ear to the ground know how and where to find it. Look for the unassuming door on Fade Street with the wooden snail above it, and then climb the stairs into what is one of Dublin's best-kept secrets. The bar's interior is often jumping, but you'll find the heart of the party in the smoker-friendly garden out back.

Pints from €5, Sun-Wed 12:30-23:30, Thurs 12:30-01:00, Fri-Sat 12:30-02:30, 3 Fade St, South Bank, +353 (0)87 122 1064, nonamebardublin.com

The Bank

The Bank sports a spectacular interior in a renovated bank. I love this spot for the *craic*, especially when they've got a game on (which is often). Gazing up at the chandeliers and opulent golden architectural accents and visiting the vaulted loo, I have often wondered if this is what Gatsby's world looked like. Pints are priced reasonably enough, but, as you might expect, the cocktails will run you in the money.

Pints from €5.50, Mon-Wed 11:00-00:30, Thurs-Sat 11:00-01:30, Sun 11:00-24:00, 20 College Green, Temple Bar, +353 (0)1 677 0677, bankoncollegegreen.com

Whelan's

Made famous as a set in the tear-jerking film *P.S. I Love You*, Whelan's is a great spot that doesn't rest on its laurels. You've got several rooms and bars to choose from, including a midsize concert venue that plays host to resident and traveling bands seven days a week. It's one of those rare

"MOLLY MALONE"

You're sure to hear this popular song sharing the story of a 17th-century fishmonger who sold seafood by day and something else quite different by night. Learn the lyrics and you'll be able to join in when you hear the trad band strike up the tune:

Chorus:
Alive, alive oh,
Alive, alive oh,
Crying cockles and mussels,
Alive, alive oh.

Verse 1:
In Dublin's fair city,
Where the girls are so pretty,
I first set me eyes on sweet Molly Malone,
As she wheeled her wheelbarrow,
Through streets broad and narrow,
Cryin' "Cockles and mussels alive, alive oh!"

Chorus

Verse 2:
She was a fishmonger,
And sure it t'was no wonder,

As so was her Father and Mother before,
They each wheeled their barrows,
Through streets broad and narrow,
Crying "Cockles and mussels alive, alive oh!"

Chorus

Verse 3 (the sad verse):
She died of fever,
And no-one could save her,
And that was the end of sweet Molly Malone,
Now her ghost wheels her barrow,
Through streets broad and narrow,
Crying "Cockles and mussels alive, alive oh!"

Chorus

beasts: an excellent bar and an equally impressive musical venue wrapped into one. Check the website to find out what musical acts are playing while you're in town—some of the shows will require you to purchase tickets ahead of time.

Pints from €5, Mon-Fri 14:30–02:30, Sat 17:00–02:30, Sun 17:00–01:30, 25 Wexford St, South Bank, +353 (0)1 478 0766, whelanslive.com

The Porterhouse

With two locations in Dublin, this chain pours only what they brew, so you won't find any Guinness here. What you will find is a bar staff that can tell you everything you've ever wanted to know (and perhaps more) about the brewing arts. There are six Porterhouse bars spread over three countries, and the Temple Bar branch was the second to open. With the excellent lineup of live music throughout the week and the beautiful dark-wood interior, though, it just doesn't feel like it's part of a chain. There's a second (not as good) Dublin location next to Trinity College (45 Nassau St).

Pints from €5, Mon-Wed 11:30–24:00, Thurs 11:30–01:00, Fri-Sat 11:30–02:00, Sun 12:00–24:00, 16 Parliament St, Temple Bar, +353 (0)1 679 8847, theporterhouse.ie

The Workman's Club

Packed to the brim with local students, this is Temple Bar's best spot to party to loud rock 'n' roll. Come out for the prices, and, if you don't mind the sticky, sweaty, college-dorm-party vibe, stay awhile. As the name suggests, the bar stays true to its blue-collar roots. Dress casually to blend in with the locals. The venue is a favorite for traveling independent artists, so check the website for a full listing of upcoming gigs. If it all gets a bit much, head to the ground-floor Bison Bar for a wee dram of whiskey on full-on leather saddles.

Pints from €4, daily 17:00–03:00, 10 Wellington Quay, Temple Bar, +353 (0)1 670 6692, theworkmansclub. com

Flannery's

If I know I'm going to be clubbing at either Dicey's or Copper Face Jacks, this is an essential stop for drinks and a few laughs. Every time I look around the place, I'm struck by how everyone here seems to share my evening's agenda. Flannery's has built its brand around *craic* and a great mix of Irish hospitality and charm.

Drinks from €4, daily 11:00–02:30 (sometimes later), 6 Camden St Lower, South Bank, +353 (0)1 478 2238, flannerysdublin.com

The Pavilion

The student bar at Trinity College has cheap but passably good food and possibly the cheapest drinks in Dublin. Heads up: The place packs out during exam time, when students hit the bar coming and going—first for confidence, and then either to celebrate or to brace themselves for the next one. Depending on when you go and whom you talk to, the conversation in the Pavilion will vacillate between sharp, witty banter and incomprehensible nonsense.

Drinks from €3.50, Mon-Sat 12:00–23:00, Sun 12:00–18:00, inside Trinity College, South Bank, +353 (0)1 608 1279, ducac.tcdlife.ie/pavilion

DUBLIN'S POSH COCKTAIL CORNER

In a cramped back alley just off Grafton Street is an often-overlooked pocket of Dublin nightlife. The area is in the midst of a beautiful mixology renaissance, and Café en Seine, 37 Dawson Street, Zozimus, and Funky Fish Cocktail Club are leading the way, full steam ahead. The first two listed here are my favorites in that alleyway, and I've included another nearby cocktail bar for good measure.

37 Dawson Street

Eclectic vanity mirrors, mounted animals, framed anatomy posters, and an unmistakably hipster vibe make this place a must-see for people who like to drink in quirky places with oddball characters. Bartenders are more loquacious than you might expect for a place like this, and they seem to genuinely enjoy engaging with patrons and tailoring their suggestions to fit unique tastes. They don't have a cocktail menu, so I never drink the same thing twice here—sometimes it's an old favorite, others an on-the-nose recommendation from the staff.

Cocktails from €11, Mon 12:00–23:30, Tues-Wed 12:00–02:30, Thurs-Sat 12:00–03:00, Sun 12:00–24:00,

37 Dawson St, South Bank, +353 (0)1 902 2908,
37dawsonstreet.ie

Café en Seine

This is a strikingly beautiful, fully renovated, and tastefully decorated French-fusion café, bar, and restaurant with delicious brunch options early in the day, tea for the afternoon, and serious parties each night. The belle époque, art nouveau-inspired interior is the perfect backdrop for quiet drinks with a small group of friends new or old. DJs keep the dance floor packed on weekends. A rooftop patio is scheduled to be completed by the time this goes to press.

Drinks from €6, Mon-Tues 12:00-24:00, Wed-Sat 12:00-03:00, Sun 12:00-23:00, 40 Dawson St, South Bank, +353 (0)1 677 4567, cafeenseine.ie

Odessa

I love this little throwback (but not too far back) cocktail lounge on the 3rd and 4th floors of a building right behind Dame Lane. There's a deep-flowing '70s vibe to the place, and you can rub elbows with Dublin's socialites on the rooftop patio. By no means is it the cheapest place in town, but it's a reasonable value considering the elite clientele.

Drinks from €7, Thurs-Sat 18:00-03:00, Sun 18:00-23:30, closed Mon-Wed, 14 Dame Court, Temple Bar, +353 (0)1 670 3080, odessa.ie

CLUBS
Copper Face Jacks

Copper Face Jacks, aka Copper's, is a well-known sloppy meat market that draws Dublin's nurses, firefighters, and other night owls. That means their parties go hard and very late every night of the week in this large, double-floored dance venue. Dress to impress to give yourself a better chance at the door. Bouncers have been known to hold back the last person in a group to try to squeeze out an extra tenner.

Cover and drinks €10, Sun-Thurs doors open at 23:00, 29 Harcourt St, South Bank, +353 (0)1 425 5300, copperfacejacks.ie

Dicey's Garden Bar

Crowds favor Dicey's as a cheaper alternative to Copper's just down the street. You really can't complain about the €2 drinks every Sunday and Tuesday, but with them comes all the sloppiness of the crowd that this deal draws. The 23 large-screen TVs make this a great place to party with sports fans. DJs keep the crowd jumping seven days a week.

Drinks and cover usually around €5, daily 16:00-02:30, 21-25 Harcourt St, South Bank, +353 (0)1 478 4841, russellcourthotel.ie

Opium

This is a trusty and popular venue for thumping house and techno across several dance floors. This complex, which includes four different event venues under one capacious roof, is popular with both Dublin's socialites and the Brazilian expat crew, who pack the dance floor and keep the party going until the early hours. They also host live events, so check their website for upcoming events.

Covers from €10, daily 12:00-late, 26 Wexford St, South Bank, +353 (0)1 526 7711, opium.ie

PUB CRAWLS
Backpacker Pub Crawl

Next City, which runs daily walking tours through the city, also offers a fun way to check out the town after the sun goes down: an organized pub crawl. Don't worry about planning your evening's itinerary; just sit back and enjoy the ride. This reasonably priced crawl includes a free half-pint and shots at each stop along the way.

€12, kicking off nightly at 20:00 at the Mercantile Pub, 28 Dame St, Temple Bar

Traditional Irish Musical Pub Crawl

For an immensely entertaining evening, join this trad music pub crawl. Each stop gives you not only the opportunity for another tasty pint of Guinness or a bumper of Jameson's, but also one traditional Irish song after another. The guides are all trad musicians themselves, so they'll teach you a few of the songs and lead the entire group in a rousing sing-along. So long as you go easy on the whiskey, it'll be a night you won't soon forget.

€14, Apr-Oct 19:30 nightly, meets at Oliver St John Gogarty Hostel's pub, 58 Fleet St, Temple Bar, book at discoverdublin.ie/musical-pub-crawl

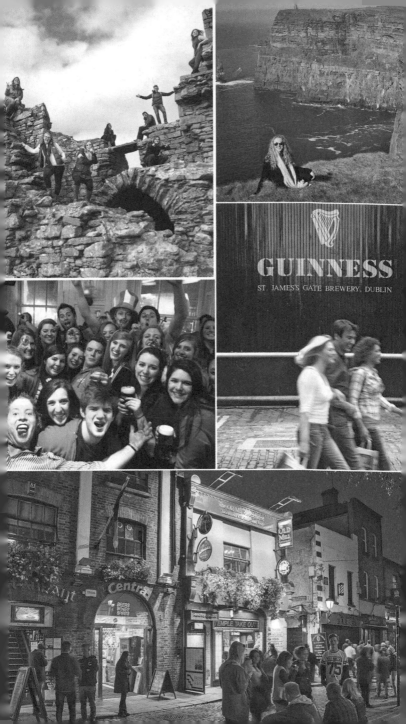

GUINNESS

ST. JAMES'S GATE BREWERY, DUBLIN

TOP SHOPPING & MARKETS

SHOPPING DISTRICTS

Grafton Street

The South Bank's Grafton Street, leading from the corner of Trinity College's campus several blocks up to St. Stephen's Green, is Dublin's main pedestrian shopping drag. You'll find everything from Diesel jeans to Starbucks coffee. While a bit mainstream, it's a one-stop shop for fashion, souvenirs, food, and coffee. Venture west on Wicklow Street and get lost in the lanes featuring a much broader range of options than you'll find on the main drag. Stephen's Green Shopping Centre at the top of the street has more of the same and a food court upstairs.

South Bank

MARKETS

Georges Street Arcade

Probably the most beloved market among locals and tourists alike, the Georges Street Arcade has it all. With over 50 shops and stalls inside an enclosed market, this place offers an array of vintage clothing and antiques. If you're looking for a chance to bring some of Dublin's music or art home with you, this is the place to find something far from ordinary.

Mon–Wed and Fri–Sat 09:00-18:30, Thurs 09:00-20:00, Sun 12:00-18:30, off of S Great Georges St, South Bank, georgesstreetarcade.ie

Temple Bar Food Market

Right in the center of Dublin's party district, this small outdoor market is a foodie's paradise, with vendors selling a wide variety of items from all over the world, including cakes, sushi, waffles, Spanish tapas, French bread, German sausages, and delicious homemade chocolates.

Sat 10:00-16:30, 12 Essex St E, Temple Bar, templebar.ie

TOP PARKS & RECREATION

St. Stephen's Green

St. Stephen's Green is a beautifully manicured park in the heart of Dublin. About two city blocks wide and two deep, it's studded with bridges, trees, and manicured shrubbery. Many of Dublin's most iconic Georgian buildings face out onto the park, so a walk along the perimeter will give you a good sense of what Dublin must have been like all her 18th-century glory. Just south of the green are the public, yet oft-overlooked **Iveagh Gardens.** Find the entry on Hatch Street Upper.

Free, daily dawn-dusk, South Bank

Phoenix Park

Spanning 1,750 acres, this is the biggest gated city park in all of Europe. The Irish president's mansion is on these grounds, and so is the US ambassador to Ireland's. Two herds of deer also call the park home—you might have more luck catching a glimpse of one of these than of either of the politicians. It's a great way to feel as though you've left the city far, far behind, even though you're only a few kilometers outside of the center. Pack a picnic and relax in nearly complete solitude surrounded by lush greenery. There are miles of trails and fields to explore, and, if you want to make a day of it, you can also see the **city zoo** (€16.80, daily 09:30-15:00, +353 (0)1 474 8900).

Free, always open, Greater Dublin

TOP TOURS

Next City Free Walking Tour

Next City offers free daily walking tours. I appreciate their engaging approach to touring, with knowledgeable guides who are eager to introduce you to their city. The tour takes about two hours, and it's an excellent way to get your bearings geographically and historically. Next City also offers a Fables and Folklore tour that delves into the spiritual past of Dublin; it's held on Mondays, Wednesdays, Fridays, and Saturdays. They also host the nightly Backpacker Pub Crawl (€12, nightly 20:00).

Free, daily 11:00 and 14:30, meet at the Central Bank, Temple Bar, +353 (0)83 117 1197, nextdublintours.com

1916 Rebellion Walking Tour

For those interested in Ireland's tumultuous and complicated 20th-century history, this Easter Rising tour retraces the steps of those who brought the world's attention to the plight of Ireland. Kicking off in a traditional Irish pub, the tour starts with a rundown of the main players and a broad overview of the timeline of events. Once you've got a good sense of who is who and what is what, the guides take you out to see the marks that the conflict left on the city (many of them still visible).

€12, meets Mon–Sat 11:30, Sun 13:00 at the International Bar, 23 Wicklow St, South Bank, +353 (0)868 583 847, 1916rising.com, lorcan@1916rising.com

TOP HOSTELS

Dublin has a wide selection of budget accommodations. They do fill up over popular periods like St. Patrick's week, New Year's, and Christmas, as well as during important sporting events. The 6 Nations, an international rugby tournament that keeps the Irish glued to their sets every year in February and March, brings rugby fans swarming into the city (and many of the Dublin fans into the bars). When Dublin plays at home, expect huge crowds. The same goes for important football matches. Hostels are the first accommodations to get booked up. Once you know the dates of your visit, reserve ahead through each hostel's online booking system.

Budget-friendly accommodations can be found on Airbnb, with the best properties huddling close together in **Rathmines** (3 kilometers south of the center) and the **Docklands,** which straddles the Liffey in the east part of Dublin.

Barnacles Temple Bar Hostel

Situated next door to the famous Temple Bar, this is the place to stay in Dublin. This hostel has grown organically over time, slowly taking over the building to add more dorms and common rooms. The chatty and eager-to-please staff will make sure that you have a wonderful time in the city, and they're happy to recommend sightseeing, activities, and nightlife options. Hang out in the common room to experience the relaxed, social backpacker vibe and make some friends. The stellar online reviews generate bookings fast and early, so if you want to join the party (and trust me, you do), make sure to reserve your spot ahead of time.

From €10, free Wi-Fi, free breakfast, common room, bunks and small private rooms available, 19 Temple Ln S, Temple Bar, +353 (0)1 671 6277, barnacles.ie, templebar@barnacles.ie

Abbey Court

Located on the north side of the River Liffey, Abbey Court combines inexpensive beds with a near-perfect location—a combination few of the competing hostels can match. The staff do their best to keep the place clean, but, with hundreds of guests each night, the housekeeping can get away from them at times. There's a solid communal kitchen, a social lounge, and a shebeen (speakeasy bar) out in the back in an old storage cellar. Each room in the place feels like it has just a couple too many beds, making space tight from the quad rooms on up to the large, 40-plus-bed snoring chambers.

From €15, 24-hour reception, free Wi-Fi, laundry, large bunk rooms, public kitchen, great storage, technology charging stations, private bar, food discounts at nearby restaurants, 29 Bachelors Walk, North Side, +353 (0)1 878 0700, abbey-court.com, info@abbey-court.com

Sky Backpackers Hostel

Guests here can look forward to a convenient location, welcoming staff, and newly refurbished facilities. The brightly colored common room has a very social atmosphere. The new paint job turned what had been a junky alley into a welcoming oasis—the perfect place to escape the always noisy Temple Bar.

Beds from €20, free Wi-Fi, common room, showers included, luggage storage available, activities and events organized often, deals offered for visiting musicians, 4 Litton Ln, North Side, +353 (0)1 872 8389, skybackpackers.com, liffey@skybackpackers.com

Abigail's Hostel

Abigail's, popular among backpackers and school groups, is another of Dublin's large, superbly located hostels. The location leaves nothing to be desired, and the free breakfast ensures that if you wake up hungry (and I always do), you won't stay that way for long. The slightly outdated rooms and overall cleanliness, however, lag behind some of the other popular hostels in town.

Beds from €14, free Wi-Fi, extensive free breakfast, showers included, 24-hour reception, adapters, towels and locks available for rent, common room, 7 Aston Quay, Temple Bar, +353 (0)1 677 9300, abigailshostel.com, stay@abigailshostel.com

Avalon House Hostel

A true backpacker hostel, Avalon has all the charm and social atmosphere you could ask for. The price is right, and the welcoming staff have put together free info sheets for you to grab upon arrival, with tips on food, sights, and nightlife. The hostel is stumbling distance from some of Dublin's best bars and clubs in the Georgian District, like Whelan's, Flannery's, and Copper Face Jacks. Avalon's sister property, **Kinlay House Hostel** (12 Lord Edward St, +353 (0)1 679 6644, kinlaydublin.ie, info@kinlaydublin.ie), is another good choice, offering similar experience and prices.

Beds from €12, free Wi-Fi, breakfast included, locks, towels, and adapters for hire, common rooms, free tours leaving daily from the lobby, free showers, 55 Aungier St (pronounced AN-jer), South Bank, +353 (0)1 475 0001, Avalon-house.ie, info@avalon-house.ie

Generator Hostel

The Generator chain has found the right formula across its many locations in Europe. This branch is popular among American students for its new, large, bright, and institutional interior and its fast, free Wi-Fi. I love the hostel's bar and restaurant, open just about any time I need food! The only drawback is its Smithfield location on the north side of River Liffey. The neighborhood is a 20-minute walk from central Dublin.

Beds from €18, free Wi-Fi, breakfast included, locks, towels, and adapters for hire, female-only dorms available, comfy new beds, Greater Dublin, +353 (0)1 901 0222, generatorhostels.com/en/destinations/Dublin, dublin@generatorhostels.com

TRANSPORTATION

GETTING THERE & AWAY

Since Ireland is an island, flying to Dublin is your best option if you're coming from outside the country. There are ferries from mainland Europe and the UK; however, they are slow, and are usually about the same price as a budget airline flight.

Plane

All major airlines and budget airlines fly into **Dublin Airport** (DUB, dublinairport.com). Aer Lingus flights arrive at the shiny new Terminal 2. All other flights use the older Terminal 1. Connections into the city center are quick and easy.

AirCoach, operating 24 hours a day, has buses running every 10 minutes during the day and less frequently at night. The connection into the center takes about 40 minutes (€7 one-way, €12 round-trip). There are numerous stops downtown, so, when purchasing your ticket, ask which stop is closest to your accommodations.

Dublin Bus's **Airlink, bus 747,** is convenient, and it's my usual choice at €6 each way. Monday-Saturday, the first bus is at 05:45, and then every 10 minutes until 19:40, when the buses start to come less frequently. On Sunday, the first bus is at 07:15.

You'll find the taxi stand just outside the arrivals hall. A cab from the airport to Temple Bar should be a flat rate of about €30. Cabbies will often offer to take you through the tunnel with the additional cost of the toll fee—generally the faster option except during peak hours (to airport: €10 Mon-Fri 16:00-19:00, €3 otherwise; from airport:

€10 Mon-Fri 06:00-10:00, €3 otherwise). You can also skip the hassle of negotiating a price with a cabbie by using the free Wi-Fi at the airport to ping an Uber.

If you're flying Ryanair and forgot to print out your boarding pass, there are computers and printers located in both terminals. You can also use them to print directions to your accommodations upon arrival.

Train

Ireland has a convenient domestic network of train connections around the island by the Iarnrod Eireann (irishrail.ie) service. Check the website for timetables and prices.

Dublin has two railway stations. If you're taking a train out of Dublin, double-check which of the two stations you're leaving from. **Dublin Heuston** serves all connections going west and south from Dublin (Galway, Cork, Dingle). It's on the west side of town, not far from the Guinness Storehouse and Phoenix Park. **Dublin Connolly** serves connections heading north (Belfast, Derry). The station is right next to the main bus station, north of the Customs House and the River Liffey.

Bus

Bus routes provide another layer of connections to most cities in Ireland. Do your research for timetables and prices on **getthere.ie** and book directly with the bus company offering the most convenient time and affordable price. Major bus lines include **GoBe** (gobe.ie), **Air Coach** (aircoach.ie), the national **Bus Eireann** (buseireann.ie), **CityLink** (citylink.ie), **Dublin Coach** (dublincoach.ie), and **Go Bus** (gobus.ie). All of these offer competitive pricing and free Wi-Fi on board.

Buses take 2.5+ hours to Galway, 3+ hours to Cork and 2.5+ hours to Belfast. Find the main bus terminal, **Bus Aras,** directly behind the Customs House in downtown Dublin, just north of the River Liffey and east of O'Connell Street.

Car

Think twice before renting a car in Ireland. While driving through the verdant countryside is an undeniably romantic notion, taking public transportation in the city is far easier than looking for parking and navigating Dublin's confusing streets. This goes double if you've never driven on the left-hand side of the road before. The experience can be downright terrifying for young drivers.

GETTING AROUND

Dublin's relatively compact center makes it an easy city to walk across. For this reason, I've only provided public transportation connection information for sights farther from the center. That said, hoofing it isn't a must. Dublin's integrated public transportation makes it a breeze to get around town via bus and trams. If you're around for a few days, consider picking up a **Leap Card** (leapcard.ie, refundable €5 deposit), equivalent to London's Oyster Card. Tap in and out with your Leap Card on both buses and trams to receive slightly discounted fares. Individual tickets are nontransferable, so you must purchase another ticket each time you transfer.

Bus

It's easy to get around Dublin on the buses, and the drivers are generally nice and happy to answer your questions. Purchase your ticket as you board with exact change, telling the driver where you want to go (the machine will keep the change if you overpay). Break your bills ahead of time so that you always have change on hand. Bus fare within greater Dublin is €2.70—remember to thank the driver when you disembark.

Look up routes on Google or through the nifty **Dublin Bus app** (available in the app store), which allows for dynamic route searches and shows you exactly where bus stops are located.

Tram

Dublin's tram system, **LUAS** (luas.ie), is highly convenient if your sightseeing or accommodations are near the tram tracks (and many of them are). Purchase your ticket at the easy-to-use machines located at any station. Ticket prices are determined based on the number of zones you intend to cross through. The **red line** connects the Connolly Train Station, the Busaras station, O'Connell Street, the Jameson Distillery, and Phoenix Park on the north side of town before looping south past Heuston train station and into

Rialto. The **green line** picks up at St. Stephen's Green and runs south.

Train

The **DART,** Dublin's regional commuter train service, is a convenient way to get outside the city for day trips to destinations like Dun Laoghaire and Howth. Connections for both leave from Tara Street Station, near O'Connell Bridge. Buy tickets online or at the station from one of the ticket booths. Find more information at irishrail.ie.

Taxi

Taxis in Dublin are safe and registered. **Uber** and its Irish equivalent, **Hailo,** are both safe and widely used options.

Bicycle

Dublin is rated as one of the top-10 bike-friendly cities in the world. A **public** **bike-rental service** (dublinbikes.ie) gives you access to over 1,500 bikes at 15 stations across the city. Annual users get their subscription for €20, while visitors can opt for a €5 three-day membership. Membership gets you unlimited 30-minute rides. If you don't manage to park the bike in one of the stations within 30 minutes, the service charges €0.50 for up to an hour, €1.50 for up to two hours, €3.50 for up to three hours, €6.50 for up to four hours, and €2 for each additional 30 minutes. Leapfrogging from one station to the next, plugging in your older bike and taking a new one, is a perfectly acceptable (even expected) way to make use of the system. Purchase your pass at any of the stations that take credit cards and follow the on-screen directions.

DAY TRIPS

Howth & Coastal Hike

Originally colonized by Vikings a millennium ago, Howth is a small coastal town that persevered as a fishing village and small port. The humble port gained notoriety in 1914, when 900 rifles were smuggled through it—rifles used a couple years later during the failed Easter Rising and subsequent Irish Civil War. Take a half day to explore the port and enjoy the local **farmers market** (Fri-Sun 09:00-18:00, better in the mornings), where you'll find blended juices and cutesy decorated muffins. You can also walk out on Howth's two piers, where locals like to feed the seals. One of the piers is capped by a 200-year-old lighthouse.

For lunch, head to the **Bloody Stream** (desserts from €4.50, Mon-Thurs 12:00-23:30, Fri-Sat 12:00-02:30, Sun 12:00-01:30, Howth Railway Station, +353 (0)1 839 5076, bloodystream.ie), located right under the train station. Relax in front of the fire at this bar and restaurant, which serves a delicious homemade apple crumble. They also have a nice selection of whiskeys and coffee; either will warm you from the inside out on a typical drizzly day on the coast.

If it's not raining, take the challenging 1.5-hour-long hike out around the head of the rock. The hike offers stunning views of the rugged coastline and Dublin Harbor. It's a perfect substitute for those who don't have time to make it all the way out to the Cliffs of Moher but still want to experience some of the natural beauty that Ireland is famous for. Be sure to walk up to the summit parking lot, where you'll get some amazing views across Dublin Bay. If you look south on a clear day, you'll see the Bailey Lighthouse and even the dramatic Wicklow Mountains out in the distance. Get started on the hike by following the street past the second pier and uphill along the coast. Before long, you'll find yourself at the trailhead. Pick up a free map at the train station, or look for signage of the hiking routes on the trail.

The suburban **DART** train from Dublin's Tara Street Station makes the 30-minute, €5 transfer to Howth easy and cheap. Trains in either direction depart every 30 minutes.

The Cliffs of Moher

Many people who come to Ireland put the Cliffs of Moher at the top of their to-see lists. Packing them into a single day trip from Dublin can be a challenge, but, even if you can only spare a day, you'll find even a rushed experience worthwhile—I haven't yet met anybody who regrets seeing the cliffs, which tower up to 700 feet above the water. Named after a fort once perched atop Hag's Head (the southernmost point of the cliffs), they're one of Ireland's top tourist destinations, with over a million visitors each year. While it used to be free, the park now charges €6 a head, using the steady trickle of small bills and coins to maintain the trails and park.

Start your experience at the visitors center, which will illuminate how the cliffs were formed and detail their more recent history. Multimedia displays and interactive screens will introduce you to some of the region's unique flora and fauna. A panoramic video mimics a bird's-eye view over the steep drop, which might give you a sinking feeling in the pit of your stomach. When you've absorbed as much information as you care to, strike out in either of two directions for a stroll along the cliff face. The rich, green lawns abruptly terminate at the cliff's edge, so there's a defensive wall that will keep you on the path. Thrill seekers can get closer, but don't push your luck. On a clear day the views will take your breath away. It's worth checking the forecast ahead of time, as limited visibility can really put a damper on the experience—and keep in mind that weather forecasting is still an imperfect art, especially on the west coast of Ireland.

Numerous tour operators will bring you directly from Dublin's city center to the cliffs. These tours leave early in the morning and deposit you back in the center around dinnertime. The drive from Dublin takes you all the way from one side of the country to the other—this takes about three hours with some stops in between. Consider a tour with **Wild Rover** (€50, daily 07:00 at Gresham Hotel, O'Connell St and 07:15 at Ulster Bank Bus Stop, 33 College Green/Dame St, next to Abercrombie & Fitch, wildrovertours.com), **PaddyWagon Tours** (€40, daily 08:00, meet on Suffolk St at the Molly Malone statue, paddywagontours.com), or **Day Tours Ireland** (€45, daily 06:50, meet on Suffolk St at the Molly Malone statue, daytours.ie/cliffs-of-moher).

HELP!

Tourist Information Centers

A word to the wise: Many enterprising companies have opened up storefronts on main tourist drags in Dublin like Grafton Street, Dame Street, and O'Connell. They've covered these storefronts with signs that say Tourist Information, and they pass themselves off as unbiased sources of information—they're anything but. They sell tours from only one company or suggest lodgings at hotels and hostels they've partnered with, enjoying a tidy commission for pointing you in their direction. The only official tourist information office is **Visit Dublin** (25 Suffolk St), which is super high-tech and staffed with helpful advisors.

Pickpockets & Scams

As in the rest of Western Europe, violent crime in Dublin is extremely low; however, purse snatching and pickpocketing do occur wherever tourists congregate, so always be on your guard in crowded areas such as train stations and sightseeing destinations. ATM fraud is on the rise in Dublin. Thieves use "skimmers"—small electronic devices that can be attached to the outside of an ATM—to steal card data. It's always important to check the ATM for any signs of tampering before using it.

Emergencies

In an emergency, dial 999 or 112.

Hospital

St. James's Hospital
James's St, Dublin 8
+353 (0)1 410 3000

US Embassy

42 Elgin Rd, Ballsbridge Dublin 4
+353 (0)1 668 8777

EDINBURGH

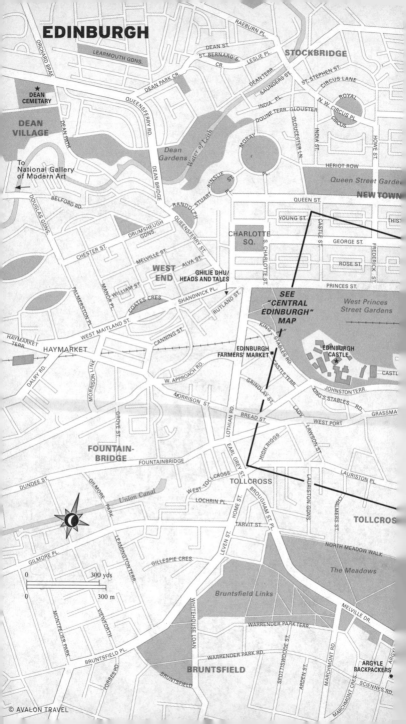

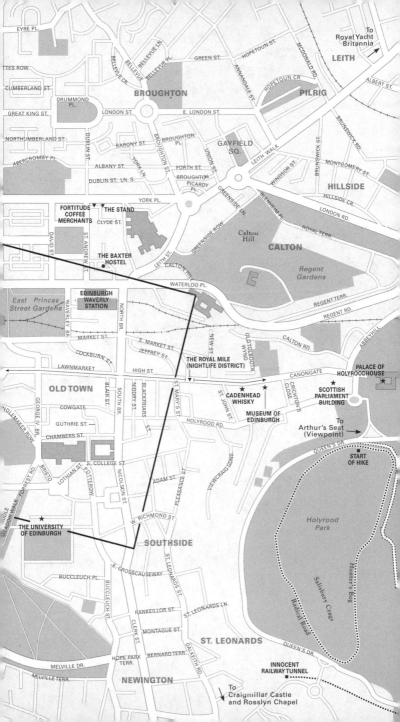

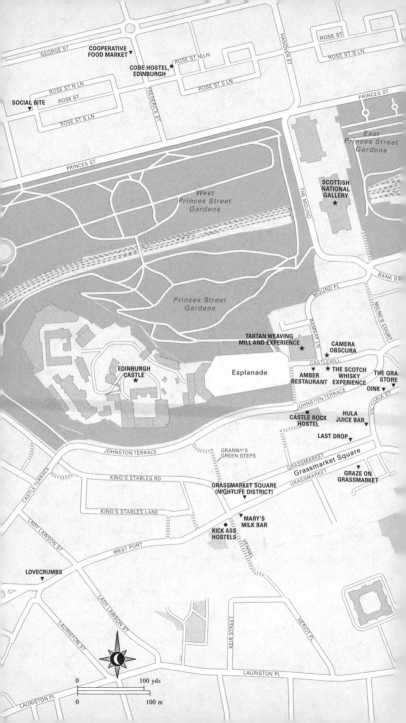

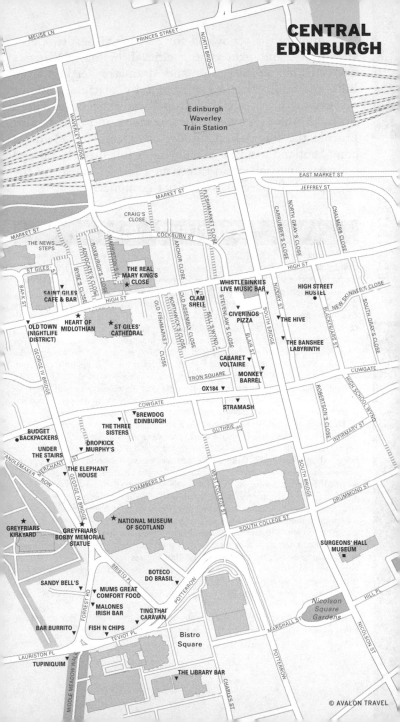

CENTRAL EDINBURGH

MEUSE LN
PRINCES STREET
NORTH BRIDGE

Edinburgh
Waverley
Train Station

WAVERLEY BRIDGE

EAST MARKET ST
JEFFREY ST

MARKET ST
FLESHMARKET CLOSE
NORTH GRAY'S CLOSE
CHALMERS CLOSE

CRAIG'S CLOSE
CARRUBBER'S CLOSE

MARKET ST
COCKBURN ST
HIGH ST

THE NEWS STEPS
WARRISTON'S CLOSE
ROXBURGH'S CLOSE
ANCHOR CLOSE
NEW SKINNER'S CLOSE

ST GILES
ADVOCATE'S CLOSE
★ THE REAL MARY KING'S CLOSE
SOUTH GRAY'S CLOSE

BYRNE'S CLOSE
WHISTLEBINKIES LIVE MUSIC BAR
★ HIGH STREET HOSTEL

★ SAINT GILES CAFE & BAR
BORTHWICK'S CLOSE
CLAM SHELL
NIDDRY ST
BLACKFRIARS ST

BACK ST
HIGH ST
OLD ASSEMBLY CLOSE
STEVENLAW'S CLOSE
CIVERINOS PIZZA
★ THE HIVE

★ OLD TOWN (NIGHTLIFE DISTRICT)
HEART OF MIDLOTHIAN
★ ST GILES' CATHEDRAL
BELL'S WYND
BLAIR ST
SOUTH BRIDGE
THE BANSHEE LABYRINTH

OLD FISHMARKET CLOSE
CABARET VOLTAIRE
COWGATE

GEORGE IV BRIDGE
TRON SQUARE
MONKEY BARREL
ROBERTSON'S CLOSE
HIGH SCHOOL WYND

OX184 ▼
STRAMASH
INFIRMARY ST

COWGATE
GUTHRIE ST

★ BREWDOG EDINBURGH
WEST COLLEGE ST

▼ THE THREE SISTERS
SOUTH BRIDGE

BUDGET BACKPACKERS ●
▼ DROPKICK MURPHY'S

UNDER THE STAIRS
CANDLEMAKER ROW
MERCHANT ST

▼ THE ELEPHANT HOUSE
CHAMBERS ST
DRUMMOND ST

GEORGE IV BRIDGE

★ NATIONAL MUSEUM OF SCOTLAND

★ GREYFRIARS KIRKYARD
SOUTH COLLEGE ST

GREYFRIARS BOBBY MEMORIAL STATUE

SURGEONS' HALL MUSEUM

SANDY BELL'S ●
BRISTO PL
BOTECO DO BRASIL

FORREST RD
▼ MUMS GREAT COMFORT FOOD
POTTERROW
Nicolson Square Gardens

▼ MALONES IRISH BAR
TING THAI CARAVAN
MARSHALL ST
NICOLSON ST

BAR BURRITO ●
● FISH N CHIPS
Bistro Square
HILL PL
POTTERROW

LAURISTON PL
TEVIOT PL

★ TUPINIQUIM
MIDDLE MEADOW WALK

▼ THE LIBRARY BAR
CHARLES ST

© AVALON TRAVEL

Edinburgh is renowned for its rugged beauty, Celtic roots, and gruesome medieval history. With its striking architecture and dramatic setting amid hills and cliffs that were carved by glaciers millions of years ago, it's one of Europe's most beautiful cities. Today, Edinburgh's solid volcanic stone and proud spirit provide the foundation for the city's compact medieval core. Scotland's capital is enjoying a full-on cultural and culinary renaissance. So throw on a kilt and bust out the bagpipes: Edinburgh is your city to conquer!

EDINBURGH 101

The foundations of modern Edinburgh were established with a fort atop Castle Rock built by an ancient Celtic tribe, the Gododdin, around AD 600, but evidence of settlement goes back much further than that, up to 3,000 years ago. Early settlers deliberately chose this easy-to-defend location. They named the fort Din Eidyn. In 638, the Angles, the ancestors of the English we know today, invaded the fort and claimed control over the area for the next three hundred years, naming it "Eiden's Burgh." It wasn't until the 10th century that the Scots finally reclaimed Edinburgh as their own.

Over the centuries, Scotland battled England for independence and sovereignty. The struggle is depicted in the film *Braveheart*, which follows young William Wallace in the late 13th century as he tries to unite the Scots and defeat the intruders from the south. Wallace led successful raids into England and battled English armies. Wallace's good fortune ran out in 1298, when he lost the Battle of Falkirk. Barely escaping with his life, he lay low until being captured seven years later. He was charged with treason against the British crown and punished by hanging, drawing, emasculation, and quartering.

Things only settled down between Scotland and England around 1706, when the Acts of Union were passed. This led to the unification of England and Scotland into the Kingdom of Great Britain. At this point, Edinburgh, the capital of Scotland, was infamous for being a dark, filthy city. Edinburgh is credited with having the world's first tenements, where numerous families lived in single rooms. Bordered to the north by a lake, the city walls to the east and south, with the castle to the west, the old medieval town could not expand outward, only upward. As the city grew taller and taller, the streets grew darker and were covered in whatever would have gone down the nonexistent sewage system.

With the advent of industrialization and trade, Scotland began its steady rise into prosperity, becoming known in the 18th century as the "Athens of the North" due to its classical architecture and its reputation for producing great minds, including Adam Smith, Joseph Black, and David Hume. Edinburgh came into its own as a center for intellectual and artistic thought. Also at this time, plans were drawn up for an expansion of the city just to the north of the Old Town. Once it was completed, anyone who could afford to move from the Old Town to this New Town did, leaving the filth and lower classes behind.

Today, Edinburgh is bustling with a renaissance of cuisine, culture, music, and live entertainment. It's a fascinating time to visit this vibrant northern capital.

PLAN AHEAD

RESERVATIONS
Reservations are required for **Real Mary King's Close** (realmarykingsclose.com). Reservations are recommended for the following sights:
Scottish Parliament (parliament.scot)
Edinburgh Castle (edinburghcastle.gov.uk)

LOCAL HAPPENINGS
Edinburgh Military Tattoo
Every August, more than 200,000 tourists and locals alike converge on the city of Edinburgh to observe the famous Military Tattoo. No, this isn't one giant inking session, but rather a massive concert repeated over about two weeks beginning in early August (Mon-Fri at 21:00, and twice on Sat, 19:30 and 22:30). Military bands perform in front of stadium seating erected in the Esplanade, the otherwise nondescript parking lot just in front of Edinburgh Castle. With the dramatic backdrop of the crenellations of the castle, dozens of performing military bands are followed by the lilting serenades of a lone bagpiper, bringing on more than a few goosebumps for the finale. If you plan to visit at this time, book accommodations and tickets as far in advance as possible, as prices skyrocket and availability quickly becomes scarce.

KNOW BEFORE YOU GO

KEY STATS & FIGURES

Currency:
British pound (£);
£1 = about 1.30 USD

Population:
495,360

Language:
English (with a brogue)

Top souvenirs:
Scotch whisky,
anything plaid,
a quaich (traditional drinking
cup with two handles)

Weather:
often chilly and damp
(layer up!)

Local dishes you've gotta try:
haggis and
Scotch eggs

CALIBRATE YOUR BUDGET

TYPICAL PRICES FOR:

Hostel dorm bed:
£14

Two-course dinner:
£12

Pint of beer:
£4

Daily bicycle rental:
£20

Bus pass:
£1.60 single, £4/day

MOVIES TO WATCH
*Braveheart, Trainspotting,
Harry Potter series,
Brave, The Illusionist,
Burke and Hare, One Day,
The Stone of Destiny*

TV SHOWS TO WATCH
*Game of Thrones,
Outlander*

THREE DAY ITINERARY

Edinburgh is a compact and walkable city, with most of the major sights concentrated on or around the Royal Mile. This itinerary hits the top sights while leaving enough time for a dram or two of Scotch whisky. If the forecast calls for rain you may need to rearrange this itinerary.

DAY 1: OLD TOWN & EDINBURGH CASTLE
MORNING
Break your fast at one of the many cafés on the way up to Edinburgh Castle. If you're a fan of smoothies, go for **Hula Juice Bar,** at the near corner of Grassmarket Square.

Hike the hill and explore the ramparts of **Edinburgh Castle** (opens at 09:30). Take advantage of the free guided walks that head out about every 15 minutes. Two hours will be ample for exploring and taking in the panoramic views.

AFTERNOON
After you've seen the castle, stroll down the Royal Mile, Edinburgh's most famous promenade. At the top of the Mile (just outside the castle) you'll find the **Camera Obscura** and the **Tartan Weaving Mill** immediately to your left. Camera Obscura is miss-able, but don't pass the weaving mill without going inside. You'll gain a new appreciation for all things plaid, but keep your hands off your wallet: There are lots of less touristy shops down the road overflowing with plaid goods. Consider the **Scotch Whisky Experience** opposite the mill. After a short tour, you'll be handed a nip of the amber stuff.

Continue your downhill stroll, hanging a tight right at the first roundabout. Snag a quick lunch on Victoria Street at **Oink,** where you'll find freshly made pork sandwiches for cheap. Other viable nearby options include the splurge-worthy **Grain Store** and **St. Giles' Café and Bar.**

Continue down the Royal Mile, dropping a little spittle on the **Heart of Midlothian** and popping into **St. Giles' Cathedral.** Along the way, enjoy the bustling shops, whisky tastings, and enough plaid to outfit you for a lifetime.

Toward the end of the Mile are several quick stops, all of them worthwhile. First, hit the whisky aficionado mecca, **Cadenhead's Whisky Shop,** then the free and interesting **Museum of Edinburgh,** then get a look at the **Scottish Parliament Building.**

LATE AFTERNOON
If it's a nice day, begin your climb up to Arthur's Seat for a beautiful sunset view of the town with the castle at its center. In one frame, you'll be able to capture the day's route—starting with the castle high on the hill down to the **Palace of Holyroodhouse** and the parliament building at the bottom.

EVENING
Regroup at your hostel before setting out for dinner and drinks on Cowgate. Don't miss **BrewDog** or the **Three Sisters,** which is always good for a social pint or dram. Just around the corner, **The Banshee Labyrinth** and **The Hive Nightclub** are packed out most evenings, and the party goes until 03:00.

EDINBURGH

DAY 2: NEW TOWN

MORNING

Grab some delicious breakfast and impeccable coffee at **Fortitude Coffee Merchants,** just beyond St. Andrew Square. Then double back to the south side of **Calton Hill** and begin your hike to the top—don't worry, the climb won't be as intense as the one to the castle. You'll be rewarded with a view back to the Old Town, across the New Town, and all the way out to the bay and North Sea. You'll also have a great view of the Parthenon-like National Monument of Scotland.

AFTERNOON

Take in the beautiful Georgian architecture and posh boulevards in the New Town. The two best shopping streets are **Princes Street** and **George Street.** Break for lunch and coffee at **Social Bite** on Rose Street. Stop at Cooperative Food Market on Frederick Street for picnic supplies and post up on Princes Street Gardens for a breathtaking broadside view of the castle and Old Town.

Continue west and a couple blocks north toward the **Dean Gardens** to wander along the Water of Leith. It's hard to believe you're in the heart of a capital city when you're wandering through this leafy park with a ravine and a river. If modern art turns your crank, leave the path after less than a mile to find the **Scottish National Gallery of Modern Art.**

EVENING

Head back to the hostel to rest for a bit before starting your night out on the town. This time head up to the student district by the University of Edinburgh to find some entertaining venues and spots to grab a bite to eat—I love the Brazilian food at **Boteco do Brasil.** On a budget? You'll find plentiful kebab and pizza-by-the-slice options in my **"University Triangle"** recommendations.

LATE

With over 30,000 students, the University of Edinburgh props up a nightlife scene in the surrounding neighborhoods every night of the week. Begin your night at **McSorley's** and follow that up with **Sandy Bell's** just across the street. Sandy Bell's has unforgettable traditional Scottish folk music seven nights a week.

DAY 3: DAY TRIP OPTIONS

Consider a full-day trip out to **Loch Ness** (tours leave quite early and get back late: 07:30-20:30), or follow the itinerary below if you want to stick closer to the city.

MORNING & AFTERNOON

Kill your hangover with a combination of lots of sleep and some hearty breakfast fare. With a full belly, start your tour of the regional whisky distilleries with **Haggis Adventures.** If whisky isn't your thing, make your way south to see the **Rosslyn Chapel** and **Craigmillar Castle,** both excellent examples of medieval Scottish architecture.

EVENING

Tonight's nightlife will be a touch classier than the student spots you hit last night. Spend your last evening getting started in **Grassmarket Square,** a plaza ringed by bars and restaurants located in the shadow of the castle's southern walls. Follow the nightlife toward Haymarket Station to explore the West End—full of bars more popular with locals than with tourists.

TOP NEIGHBORHOODS

The modern city of Edinburgh huddles around its medieval core. The crowds in the historic center, due to the proximity of the university and the concentrated tourist attractions, are predominantly tourists in the center and students on the margins. The **Royal Mile,** leading from the castle down to the Palace of Holyroodhouse, is the heart of the **Old Town** neighborhood, and it's where you'll find most of Edinburgh's noteworthy sights. Just below the castle is trendy nightlife and shopping in the **Grassmarket District,** centering on Grassmarket Square.

The **New Town,** just north of the Old Town across the North Bridge and Waverley train station, was the result of expansion during the latter half of the Georgian Age. It's a masterpiece of civic planning, conceived to give Edinburgh's wealthy a place to escape the fetid and overcrowded Old Town (the latter was essentially abandoned to the lower classes). Avenues here are much larger, and Edinburgh's money still concentrates here—there are posh galleries, museums, shops, bars, and restaurants everywhere.

On the other side of the castle and hill to the west is the **West End.** You'll find Haymarket Station here as well as stadiums, tons of student housing, lively bars, and a bustling blue-collar and student scene.

The University of Edinburgh lies south of the Royal Mile. In the **University District,** you can find exactly what you'd expect in any student neighborhood: cheap food, bars, entertainment venues, and bookshops. **Bruntsfield,** just south of the university across the meadows, is one of Edinburgh's trendier neighborhoods.

TOP SIGHTS

Many of the worthwhile sights, tours, and experiences in Edinburgh come with a price tag of £15-17, quickly burning through your sightseeing budget. Edinburgh Castle should be at the top of your list; just below this should be the tour of Edinburgh's underground. After that, everybody's list will be different. Use my recommendations to decide which of the sights are most up your alley. There are also a number of very good free or cheap sights and activities (e.g., Arthur's Seat, National Museums, and bars in Edinburgh's underground).

Edinburgh Castle

Think *Lord of the Rings* meets *Braveheart.* This proud castle sits atop volcanic rock carved out by glaciers long ago, giving it perfect natural defenses: sheer cliffs along three sides and a long uphill trek to the front door, er, gate. The foundations of the castle were laid in the 9th century with the construction of Edinburgh's oldest building, St. Margaret's Chapel, and primitive fortifications. Numerous additions were made during the tenuous centuries when England threatened the southern border of Scotland.

Frequent guided tours (included with admission) show you through numerous military museums and exhibits, the Scottish Crown Jewels (and a display demonstrating how they were found in the castle after being lost for nearly 200 years), the Scottish National War Memorial, and the ramparts of this fortress. Looking down the barrels of some serious cannons reminds visitors of the very functional defensive purpose of this castle, even while taking in the dramatic panoramas of the city.

£17, Apr-Sept daily 09:30-18:00, Oct-Mar daily 09:30-17:00, last entry one hour before closing, Castlehill, Royal Mile, +44 (0)131 225 9846, edinburghcastle.gov.uk

Scotch Whisky Experience

Just outside the castle, this motorized barrel ride takes you through a replica distillery, giving you a good overview of the history and process of the world-renowned distillate that is Scotch whisky. The experience is just this side of a tourist trap, but you'll walk away much better informed about Scotch—including the regions in which it is produced, each of them distinct. You'll also have a chance to sip from what is said to be the world's largest collection of Scotch. Go for the Silver package or upgrade to the Gold tour for an extra wee dram or two. Stopping in is worthwhile for both aficionados and those who have not yet developed a palate for Scotch. The restaurant downstairs, **Amber,** is surprisingly tasty—much better than anything you'd expect to find at such a touristy location.

From £15, nonalcoholic drinks provided for those under 18, Apr-Aug daily 10:00-18:00, Sept-Mar daily 10:00-17:00, tours leaving as often as every 10 minutes, 354 Castlehill, Royal Mile, +44 (0)131 220 0441, scotchwhiskyexperience.co.uk

Tartan Weaving Mill

Pop into this cheesy, dusty warehouse stuffed full of just about everything you can smack a plaid pattern on. Converted from the Old Town's water reservoir, it's now an obvious tourist trap, but it's a great place to learn a bit about tartans and get some idea of the range of plaid products you can expect to find in Edinburgh. There's a row of mannequins that form a life-sized timeline of old highland dress through the centuries. You might be tempted to drop a bundle on something, but prices are inflated here. Save your money for cheaper shops off the main drag.

Free, daily 09:00-17:30, 555 Castlehill, Royal Mile, +44 (0)131 220 2477

Camera Obscura

The Camera Obscura is an interactive museum with exhibits exploring optical illusions, mirrors, and visual tricks. Photography was pioneered here, so Edinburgh has a long history of optics, and Camera Obscura's main attraction is a live panorama of the city projected through a periscope downward through the museum's tower and onto a large viewing dish. Cool to see, but worth the 15 quid? That's your call.

£15.50 adults, £13 students, no elevator, six floors, Apr-Jun daily 09:30-19:00, July-Aug daily 09:00-21:00, Sept-Oct daily 09:30-19:00, Nov-Mar daily 10:00-18:00, 549 Castlehill, Royal Mile, +44 (0)131 226 3709, camera-obscura.co.uk

Heart of Midlothian

It may surprise you to see locals spitting on this simple heart-shaped pattern of cobblestones as they pass, but this tradition goes way back to the 1300s. Then, the heart lay just outside the door to the Old Tollhouse, where taxes were collected and prisoners were held, tortured, and even executed. While the tax building is gone, pedestrians today express their discontent with the machine by donating a little spittle. Go on, hawk a loogie yourself.

Free, always open, northwest corner of St. Giles' Cathedral, Royal Mile

St. Giles' Cathedral

Dating back to 1385, St. Giles' Cathedral is a fantastic display of high Gothic architecture. It was an ongoing project over the years, so you may notice the haphazard style from continuous improvements and additions. When entering, spend a few moments admiring the beautiful stained glass and painted ceilings of the main hall, then make your way to the spectacular Thistle Chapel in the back. Its ornately carved

wooden benches, bright stained glass windows, and heavenly network of ribbed vaults combine for a breathtaking effect.

Free (£2 fee for photography), £3 suggested donation, May-Sept Mon-Fri 09:00-19:00, Sat 09:00-17:00, Sun 13:00-17:00, Oct-Apr Mon-Sat 09:00-17:00, Sun 13:00-17:00, High St, Royal Mile, +44 (0)131 225 9442, stgilescathedral.org.uk

The Real Mary King's Close

Beneath the Royal Mile, you'll find The Real Mary King's Close, an underground labyrinth of the tight alleyways and dank tenements of 16th-century Edinburgh. As the modern city has grown, builders have chopped off the tops of the old tenements and reused the largely untouched foundations, simply covering them over and leaving the old streets and rooms still accessible underneath the stately Royal Exchange building. Taking a walk through these streets is like hopping in a fun time machine back to Old Edinburgh. Your entry ticket comes along with a tour led by a costumed and in-character guide spinning a funny and dry yarn to help you bring these empty streets to life. Must book in advance.

£15 adults, £13 w/student ID, Apr-Oct daily 10:00-21:00, Nov-Mar Sun-Thurs 10:00-17:00, Fri-Sat 10:00-21:00, 2 Warriston's Close, Royal Mile, +44 (0)845 070 6244, realmarykingsclose.com

Cadenhead's Whisky Shop

Learning about whisky is a requisite part of your visit to Scotland, and Cadenhead's Whisky Shop is your classroom. Pop by for an education in everything related to the grain-mashed goodness, and let them steer you towards a bottle that's perfectly suited to your tastes. While they don't produce their own liquor, these guys go straight to the source, bottling their spirits before the concoctions are watered down and colored to prepare them for mass distribution. This means their stuff is purer (read: higher proof) than what you'll find in any standard shop, and the decision about just how many drops to add to your dram is left to you. This small, intimate shop posts about new arrivals, classes, and tastings to their loyal followers throughout the week on their Facebook page. Tasty.

Free, 18+ only, tasting sessions £25 Mon-Fri 17:45, bottles from £28, Mon-Sat 10:30-17:30, closed Sun, 172 Canongate, Royal Mile, +44 (0)131 556 5864, updates and new arrivals on Facebook: Cadenhead's Whisky Shop Edinburgh

Museum of Edinburgh

If you want a good idea of exactly how Edinburgh was founded and grew through the ages, this free museum at the bottom of the Royal Mile will sort you out. Check out their extensive and somewhat eclectic collection of artifacts and displays—from a model of Edinburgh's medieval Old Town as it would have looked in the 16th century to weapons used in World War I and trench artwork created by soldiers tinkering away on spent shells and ration cans. You can even find an original 17th-century copy of the National Covenant—the foundational document that denounced the attempts of the Anglican church to incorporate the Scottish Presbyterian church—scrawled out and signed on a deer's hide. The location, displays, and the free bathroom make for a convenient and informative stop along the Royal Mile.

Free, generally open Wed-Mon 10:00-17:00, 142 Canongate, Royal Mile, +44 (0)131 529 4143, edinburghmuseums.org.uk

Palace of Holyroodhouse

Holyroodhouse is Queen Elizabeth II's "humble" country home and her official residence while on her annual visit to Edinburgh (it's been the principal residence of the kings and queens of Scotland since the 16th century). Walk its halls and visit the many royal audience and dining rooms and Mary, Queen of Scots' chambers in this fully functioning palace. As you might expect of a royal residence, the walls are decked out with priceless paintings, decorations, and tapestries. The palace

---

SCOT, SCOTTISH, SCOTCH, OR SCOTTS?

Scotch: type of whisky or tea
Scotts: Scottish language (Scottish Gaelic)
Scottish: nationality, dialect of English
Scot: someone from Scotland

A BRIEF HISTORY OF THE KILT

Kilts, which emerged in the 16th century, were originally more than 20 feet of fabric that was wrapped around the torso, secured with a belt, and then draped over the shoulders. In time, the kilt evolved to be more of the skirt that we see today (just don't call it that), with a separate piece for draping over the shoulders. The colors were a function of the dyes available in the region and the wealth of the person wearing it. Though we've been led to believe that nearly every family name has a "registered tartan" or plaid pattern, this was simply the marketing strategy of a cunning businessman to sell more plaid to tourists. Early sporters of the garb were simply glad to have something to wear—the color of the plaid mattered little. So, while it's fun to pick up some col-

ors, be skeptical of sales clerks telling you, "Gonzalez? Yeah, we've got a pattern for that clan!" See a life-size visual display of the evolution of styles in the recommended Tartan Weaving Mill at the top of the Royal Mile.

closes down for several weeks each year in preparation for the queen's stay early each summer. No need to ask the guards if Her Majesty's about—the Royal Standard of Her Majesty flies above the palace when she's in residence.

£13, students £12, Apr-Oct 09:30-18:00, last entry 16:30, Nov-Mar daily 09:30-16:30, last entry 15:15, check website for additional event closures, Canongate, Royal Mile, +44 (0) 303 123 7306, royalcollection.org.uk/visit/palaceofholyroodhouse

Scottish Parliament Building

Its modern steel-and-glass architecture makes the Scottish Parliament Building stand out from the stark backdrop of the Royal Mile and Holyroodhouse. After passing through some quick and friendly security, you'll come to a wonderful exhibit on the ground floor that covers the many ins and outs of the Scottish legislative system. You'll learn how Scottish politics weave culture and history into a modern framework of domestic government and allegiance to the British crown—an important ongoing discussion in 21st-century Scotland.

Free, reserve guided tours online ahead of time, Mon, Fri, Sat, when in recess 10:00-17:00, also Tues-Thurs 09:00-18:30, last entry 30 minutes before closing, closed Sun, bottom of the Royal Mile, +44 (0)131 348 5200, parliament.scot

University of Edinburgh

Medieval buildings sit side-by-side with modern glass-and-steel architecture on the campus of this university, one of the

oldest and most competitive in the world. It's located on the edge of Edinburgh's Old Town. Walking the grounds gives you a chance to enjoy some of the ancient architecture, but it also gives you an idea what UK college life is like. Just a couple hundred years ago, doctors of anatomy at the university were charging the public £5 each to attend live dissections, patronizing grave snatchers (and even serial killers) to keep the cadavers coming. Be sure to drop into the incredible double-level **Library Bar** (Sun-Thurs 09:00-23:30, Fri-Sat 09:00-03:00, +33 (0)131 650 4673) for cheap pints and pizzas, salads, and burgers surrounded by epic floor-to-ceiling bookshelves.

Free, campus grounds always open, University District, Old Town

Greyfriars Kirk & Kirkyard

Greyfriars Kirk ("church" in Scotch Gaelic) is a beautiful old church built in what were once fields just to the south of the Old Town. It's the main church for central Edinburgh and is part of the Church of Scotland. The kirkyard (or graveyard) around the church is supposedly the most haunted part of the city (some claiming it to be the most haunted graveyard in the world). It was a favorite hunting ground for body snatchers, and dozens of notable Scots are buried here. The most famous occupant, however, is a terrier named **Bobby,** who, after his owner's death, guarded his grave for 14 years before his own death in 1855. A statue and bar commemorating the world's most famously loyal dog sits just outside the entrance to the graveyard closest to the church. J. K. Rowling used to stroll through this graveyard, and one grave in particular may have been a source of inspiration: Thomas Riddel Esquire. You'll also find graves marked Moody and McGonagall. Potter fanatics have been known to leave affectionate notes on some of these graves, particularly Riddel's.

Free, daily 10:30-16:30 but may be closed for private events, Candlemaker Row, University District, +44 (0)131 664 4313, greyfriarskirk.com

National Museum of Scotland
This massive and recently renovated natural history museum takes up an entire block in Edinburgh's Old Town. Inside, find Dolly the Sheep (the world's first cloned animal, now mounted), a full-size T-Rex skeleton, and highly informative displays of artifacts (both ancient and modern) from Scotland and around the world. The diverse exhibits touch on Scotland's past and present, from the people who have called this land home through the ages to the forces (like the industrial transformation) that shaped Scotland and Edinburgh into the places they are today.

Rotating exhibits present more personal facets of the country. If you're lucky, you'll be able to get a look at the Lewis Chessmen, a hand-carved ivory chess set dating back 800 years, or, if maritime history is your cup of tea, you might be treated to an in-depth look at Scotland's countless lighthouses, which played surprisingly important roles in the country's history.

Free, daily 10:00-17:00, Chambers St, Old Town, +44 (0)300 123 6789, nms.ac.uk

Craigmillar Castle
One of the best-preserved medieval castles in Scotland, Craigmillar Castle boasts complete ramparts and chambers that were built around 1400 by Sir George Preston. This large stone castle is where a cabal of discontents planned the assassination of Lord Darnley, the unpopular husband of Mary, Queen of Scots. The noblemen stashed two kegs of gunpowder beneath the floor where Darnley slept at the nearby church, Kirk O' Field. The explosion leveled

the building, and Darnley's body—dressed in his nightshirt—was found in a nearby orchard. It is still not clear whether Darnley was killed by the blast or strangled after the fact. Either way, his last moments were anything but peaceful.

You'll find Craigmillar Castle south of town and well away from the crowds. It's reached by bus 3, 14, 29, or 30 from North Bridge, or a pleasant hour-long walk south via the (creepy) **Innocent Railway Tunnel** and path, a rail line leading south converted into a walking path starting on the south side of Arthur's Seat. If the hordes of tourists at Edinburgh Castle are more than you can bear, head south for a much more tranquil stroll through Scotland's medieval history.

£5.50, Apr-Sept daily 9:30-17:30, Oct-Mar Sat-Wed 09:30-16:00, closed Thurs-Fri, last entry 30 minutes before closing, Craigmillar Castle Rd, south of town, +44 (0)131 661 4445, visitscotland.com

EXTRA CREDIT
Surgeons' Hall
Many people are surprised to learn just how pivotal a role Edinburgh has played (and continues to play) in the development of modern medicine. This hall highlights just some of the many Scottish contributions to the healing arts over the centuries with eye-opening exhibits and displays that'll make you thankful to be living in the 21st century.

£6.50, students £4, daily 10:00-17:00, last admission 30 minutes before closing, 16-18 Nicolson St, University District, +44(0)131 527 1711, museum.rcsed.ac.uk

Royal Yacht *Britannia*
The royal family's floating home for 40 years has been converted into a 412-foot, 5-deck exhibit that gives you a stowaway's perspective of the vessel. Start your visit in the the bridge and follow a one-way track all the way into the sparkling-clean engine room (with a thorough audio guide as your captain). Experience the decadent, gold-encrusted interiors, including the dining hall and royal staterooms—with all of the landlubbers' comforts—and contrast them with the cramped crew's quarters. Make a pit stop for a snack and a hot cup in the Tea Room, where sandwiches start from £9. At 2.5 miles from the city center,

it's best to take a bus: 11, 22, or 35 from Waverley Bridge go here.

£16, students £14, Apr-Sept daily 09:30-16:30, Oct daily 09:30-16:00, Nov-Mar daily 10:00-15:30, Ocean Terminal, Port of Leith, Greater Edinburgh, +44 (0)131 555 5566, royalyachtbritannia.co.uk

National Gallery of Scotland

This classic art museum spans from the Gothic Age and the Renaissance to baroque, impressionism, and surrealism. You'll recognize names like Dalí, Duchamp, Rembrandt, and Titian, and you will see pieces by less famous but no less fascinating Scottish artists covering just about every medium and style imaginable. The Scottish landscapes will give you a particularly vivid perspective of how Scotland looks through the eyes of her greatest painters. The nearby Royal Scottish Academy has circulating modern art exhibitions that are often (but not always) free; schedules and details are at royalscottishacademy.org. With both museums perched on the mound between the Old Town and New Town, they make for a convenient visit—and a delightful one for art fans.

Free, daily 10:00-17:00, The Mound, New Town, +44 (0)131 624 6200, nationalgalleries.org

Scottish National Gallery of Modern Art

For a change, pop over to Edinburgh's modern art museum. Split across two neoclassical buildings, the exhibits are anything but classical. Highlights include Lichtenstein, Matisse, Magritte, and Picasso. "Modern One" is the permanent exhibition, and "Modern Two" is where you'll find temporary exhibits featuring any number of modern greats (when I was there, it was M. C. Escher). This is a great place to stir up some lively debate with your companions about the nature of art in its many forms.

Modern One free, Modern Two price varies, daily 10:00-17:00, 75 Belford Rd, New Town, +44 (0)131 624 6200, nationalgalleries.org

Rosslyn Chapel

The Rosslyn Chapel dates all the way back to the 15th century and features elegant examples of intricate medieval stonework, making the chapel a great side trip that will get you out of the city and into the picturesque Scottish countryside. Just beyond the church are the ruins of the 14th-century Rosslyn Castle. There's not much left of it, but there's a nice path that'll take you through some of the remaining walls. To get here, take bus 37 from North Bridge, which runs every 30 minutes and takes about half an hour.

£9, Mon-Sat 09:30-17:00, Sun 12:00-16:45, Chapel Loan, Roslin, +44 (0)131 440 2159, rosslynchapel.com

TOP EATS

Many of Edinburgh's most popular restaurants are clustered around Old Town's Royal Mile and New Town's Princes Street. If you'd rather avoid the crowds, it's quite pleasant to picnic at West Princes Street Gardens. You'll find all the food and picnic supplies you need at the nearby **Cooperative Food Market** (Mon-Sat 07:00-22:00, Sun until 21:00, 26-28 Frederick Street, +44 (0)131 220 0359).

The northern suburb of Leith has developed a reputation for excellent fresh seafood restaurants. South Edinburgh has a variety of cheaper cafés and restaurants for budget-minded travelers. The neighborhood surrounding the University of Edinburgh is also full of cheap and ethnic food options (i.e., kebabs and fish-and-chips), especially on Nicolson Street.

When sitting down, it's typical to tip by rounding up to the nearest even number. If service is exceptional, a tip of around 15 percent will be appropriate and appreciated.

Oink

This fast-casual food shop does one thing, and it does it well: steaming-hot and fresh pork sandwiches sourced from local farms in limited quantities. Get there early—latecomers often miss their chance to pig out on Oink's famously succulent roast suckling pig sandwiches.

Pop in here to sustain your energy on long days of sightseeing, and don't forget the applesauce and haggis (you'll see locals throwing the stuff back like mad). A second location at 82 Canongate on the Royal Mile means that, if you're in or close to the center, you're never too far from a great pork sandwich.

Sandwiches from £2.95, Mon-Sat 11:00-18:00, Sun 11:00-17:00, 34 Victoria St, +44 (0)189 076 1355, oinkhogroast.co.uk

Saint Giles Café & Bar

Saint Giles Café & Bar is one of the better options for a quick, simple, and affordable breakfast or lunch when you're near or on the Mile. You'll find it at the top of St. Giles Street, kitty-corner and slightly uphill from the cathedral. Pop in here to get your day off on the right foot with quiches, breakfast rolls, and fresh pastries. The charmingly rustic interior will make you want to come back for tea or wine later on.

Scones from £1.50, sandwiches from £7.50, daily 09:00-17:30, till 18:30 on weekends, 8-10 St. Giles St, Royal Mile, +44 (0)131 225 6267, saintgilescafebar.co.uk

The Grain Store

This splurge-worthy restaurant helps those who want to more than just check off their Scottish cuisine box—here, you'll do it in style. With impeccable decor, swift service, and some of the best entrées you'll find in Edinburgh, the Grain Store has established itself as the go-to restaurant for those who want to appreciate their saddle of lamb or venison and kale in a classy yet comfortable setting.

Mains from £20, Mon-Sat 12:00-14:30 and 18:00-21:45, Sun 18:00-21:30, 30 Victoria St, Royal Mile, +44 (0)131 225 7635, grain-store-restaurant.co.uk

Under the Stairs

This discreet and easy-to-miss little basement joint serves up solid-value lunch and dinner menus Mondays to Wednesdays, as well as expertly blended cocktails that are as good as those at any of the hipster bars in town. It feels more like a tastefully decorated living room with retro, mismatched furniture. I appreciate their limited menu, a far cry from the novels they drop on your table at most tourist traps. The food is expertly prepared and the ingredients are fresh. Every time I'm in town I head down the stairs for their burger with beetroot and horseradish relish and sweet potato wedges.

Menus from £12, cocktails from £7, daily 12:00-01:00, 3A Merchant St, Royal Mile, +44 (0)131 466 8550, underthestairs.org

Elephant House

Elephant House is a great place for reasonably priced panini, international foods, and hot drinks. This bright and cozy café overlooks Greyfriars Kirkyard and the Edinburgh Castle. On overcast days, the gloomy scene of stone piles makes it easy to imagine why J. K. Rowling found her seat by the window such an inspirational spot. She wrote much of the first few books of the Harry Potter series here—including, famously, the first paragraph of the first chapter on a napkin.

£11-16, Mon-Thurs 08:00-22:00, Fri 08:00-23:00, Sat 09:00-23:00, Sun 09:00-22:00, 21 George IV Bridge, Royal Mile, +44 (0)131 220 5355, elephanthouse.biz

ClamShell

They'll deep-fry almost anything at this no-nonsense fast-food joint, including pizza, ribs, haggis, and—my favorite— Mars bars! Deep-fried foods of almost

HUNGRY FOR HAGGIS?

Scotland's national dish, haggis, is one of the world's more interesting cuisines. It's made of—if you really want to know—sheep's heart, liver, and lungs minced together with onions, oatmeal, and some seasoning; this mixture is stuffed into a sleeve of stomach lining, which is then simmered until cooked. It's usually dished up with 'neeps and tatties, or mashed turnips and potatoes. Scots love it, and its bold flavor often catches brave tourists unawares (surprised at how much they enjoy it). It's definitely worth a try. **Bobby's Bar** (Mon-Sat 11:00-23:00, Sun 12:30-23:00, 30-34 Candlemaker Row, +44 (0)131 225 8328), just outside Greyfriars Kirkyard, is a great place to sample it. Bon appétit!

every imaginable variety may not be the healthiest options, but they have become as much a part of the Scottish food scene as hot dogs in America. Place your order, then post up at the high-top bar along the wall inside or on the outdoor seating under the sun (if there is any) and enjoy some guilt-free gooey goodness (what better time to indulge than when you're on vacation?).

£6, Sun-Thurs 11:00-01:00, Fri-Sat 11:00-02:00, 148 High St, Royal Mile, +44 (0)131 225 4338

Hula Juice Bar

Your dear author isn't usually a juice bar kind of guy, but Hula proudly breaks all the rules. Pop in any time of the day for delicious healthy smoothies with creative names like Whirling Dervish and Sunshine in a Cup, and if you're there around breakfast or lunch, fill your belly with their tasty bagels stuffed with bacon and cheddar. As you might expect at a juice bar, there are plenty of vegetarian options.

Juices from £3.50, Tues-Sun 08:00-18:00, 103-105 West Bow, Royal Mile, +44 (0)131 220 1121, hulajuicebar. co.uk

Graze on Grassmarket

Grassmarket Square is on a health kick, and this popular entry, which pumps out wraps, salads, and baked potatoes stuffed with locally sourced ingredients, is the best place to get your nutritious nosh on in Edinburgh. This vegetarian-friendly café is mostly a come-and-go spot, so it's stripped down and simplified, with only a few seats for those who choose to eat in.

Lunches from £3.50, Mon-Sat 07:30-18:00, Sun 11:00-16:00, 67 Grassmarket, Grassmarket District, +44 (0)131 629 4030, grazeongrassmarket.com

Mary's Milk Bar

At the far end of Grassmarket, the queue goes around the block for some of Edinburgh's best handmade ice cream. Go for any one of their cycling flavors, ranging from classic (like rich milk chocolate and salted caramel) to innovative (pumpkin, sweet potato, or even beetroot).

Cones from £2.50, cash only, Tues-Sat 11:00-19:00, Sun 12:00-19:00, 19 Grassmarket, Grassmarket District, no phone, marysmilkbar.com

Fortitude Coffee Merchants

When it comes to breakfast in the New Town, I head to Fortitude Coffee Merchants to start my day with some of the best coffee in Edinburgh. If, like me, you're a coffee snob at heart, you'll appreciate their quality beans and small-batch roasting—and you'll be in welcome company with the staff, who are happy to help you pick from their rotating roasts. While I wish they had a full kitchen, I'll settle for the locally sourced pastries and mini cakes. Fortitude offers just the right combination of caffeine and sugar to rev you up before you climb to the top of nearby Calton Hill.

Coffee from £1.50, Mon-Sat 07:30-17:00, Sun 09:00-16:00, 3C York Place, New Town, +44 (0)131 557 3063, fortitudecoffee.com

Social Bite

I love it when affordably priced good food made with local ingredients comes with a mission for social improvement. Social Bite makes excellent sandwiches, wraps, and soups in the New Town, offering both carnivorous and vegetarian options, making it an excellent stop for a quick lunch. What's more, a quarter of their employees have lived on Edinburgh's streets at some point. Social Bite is doing their part by helping people get their feet back under them.

If you feel like doing something yourself, you can buy an extra sandwich and drink that will be given to a local homeless person later that day—definitely something I can (and do) get behind.

Sandwiches from £3.95, Mon–Fri 07:00-15:00, 131 Rose St, New Town, +44 (0)131 220 8206, social-bite.co.uk

UNIVERSITY TRIANGLE

I've coined this term to describe a single city block, just across the street from the university, that comprises many (relatively) budget-friendly options that are extremely popular with students.

Bar Burrito

If you're missing Tex-Mex, this quick-serve burrito joint will hit the spot. They also offer takeaway and delivery.

Burritos from £6.50, Sun–Thurs 11:00-22:00, Fri-Sat 11:00-23:00, 55 Forrest Rd, University District, +44 (0)131 225 4779, barburrito.co.uk

Civerinos Slice

This hipster spot has wood-fired slices of pizza and whole pies—great for a quick lunch or a sit-down dinner with friends

Slices from £4, full pizzas from £18, daily 08:00 till late, 49 Forrest Rd, University District, +44 (0)131 225 4026, civerinosslice.com

Tupiniquim

The hours vary at this cute little Brazilian-style crêpe stand, though they tend to stay open as long as they're busy. Find savory meat, vegetarian, and vegan options for a quick lunch on the go or to enjoy in the hidden gardens behind the stand.

Crêpes from £4.50, Mon–Sat 10:00-18:00, opposite Bar Burrito, University District, +44 7 908 886 184

Ting Thai Caravan

Here you'll find Thai street food with common tables, brick and wood interiors, and quick service. This popular spot is always busy.

£8, Sun–Thurs 11:30-22:00, Fri-Sat 11:30-23:30, 8-9 Teviot Pl, University District, +44 (0)131 225 9801, Facebook: Ting Thai Caravan

Mums Great Comfort Food

The theme for this homey and slightly retro restaurant is "top nosh at half the cost," and it delivers just that (and in style to boot). Mums uses all local ingredients and they definitely don't hold back on the tasty calories, delivering all of the British classics we know and love—shepherd's pie, bangers and mash, fish-and-chips, and, of course, haggis.

Dishes from £7, Mon–Sat 09:00-22:00, Sun 10:00-22:00, 4a Forrest Rd, University District, +44 (0)131 225 7069, monstermashcafe.co.uk

Boteco do Brasil

Boteco do Brasil serves delicious plates heaping with black beans, pork, beef, and burgers in a casual atmosphere with funky furniture and exposed brick walls. The friendly servers take their cocktails seriously—the caipirinha is almost as good as the ones I've had on Ipanema beach. Six nights a week around 22:00, tables are cleared away to make space for the party to dial up a notch. Students are big fans of their disco and salsa nights, making this a great place to make new friends. There's nothing quite like this little slice of Rio across the street from Scotland's top educational institution.

Tapas from £5, burgers from £7, daily 11:30-03:00, 47 Lothian St, University District, +44 (0)131 220 4287, botecodobrasil.com

LGBT EDINBURGH

Edinburgh is a progressive and welcoming city. Members of the LGBT community will have no problems with the friendly locals, and there are numerous cafés, restaurants, and nightlife venues that cater to LGBT clientele. Most places center on what's known as the Pink Triangle, just north of Calton Hill on the eastern edge of the New Town. **The Street** (2 Picardy Pl, thestreetbaredinburgh.co.uk) is a popular bar with quite good food and a DJ that plays late. Same goes for **Café Habana** (22 Greenside Pl, facebook.com/habanaedinburgh). **Planet** (6 Baxter's Pl, New Town, facebook.com/Planet-Bar-Edinburgh) is a smaller dance bar with drink deals and a DJ spinning nightly; it's popular among all partiers, no matter what their persuasion. **CC Blooms** (23 Greenside Pl, New Town, ccbloomsedin-burgh.com) is a tasty restaurant by day and a classy nightclub by night.

Central Fish Bar

This is your classic fast-food joint for fish-and-chips, pizza, burgers, and kebabs. There's nothing flashy here, but that's kind of the point.

Kebabs from £4.50, daily 17:00–23:30, later on weekends, 15-16 Teviot Pl, +44 (0)131 226 6898, centralfishbaredinburgh.co.uk

TOP NIGHTLIFE

Thanks to Edinburgh's compact city center and the concentration of students in only a few neighborhoods surrounding the center, nightlife venues are never far apart.

NIGHTLIFE DISTRICTS
Grassmarket Square

The Grassmarket district is one of the best places to hang around at night, as it offers some of Edinburgh's most authentic, traditional bars, along with a bumping nightlife for later in the evening. If it's live music you're after, Dropkick Murphy's has what you're looking for, along with quintessential Irish pub atmosphere.

Grassmarket District

Royal Mile

Nightlife on and near the Royal Mile is better than what you'd expect for such a touristy area. While certain places can be a bit generic and overpriced, I've listed some of my favorites to keep you from falling into the tourist traps. There are some incredible finds sprinkled throughout the neighborhood. You'll even find bars and clubs, like **Whistlebinkies** and **The Banshee Labyrinth,** that are burrowed into old medieval cellars, making for a unique night underneath exposed brick arches dating back centuries.

Royal Mile

University District

This is where you'll find both the sloppy student hangouts and some notable exceptions—classy establishments with great food, fun vibes, and tasty drinks.

University District

Haymarket

The area surrounding the Haymarket train station has plenty of classic British-style pubs with heavy wooden interiors, bantering customers, numerous drafts on tap, and whiskies lined in row upon row behind the bar. This area is more low-key than the others, so it draws a higher ratio of locals than the touristy Royal Mile.

West End

BARS
Sandy Bell's

Sandy Bell's is an intimate bar that bursts at the seams most nights thanks to its deserved reputation as one of Edinburgh's best traditional Gaelic music—or "trad"—bars. They keep it fresh with nightly live folk music, 100-plus whiskies to sample, and a welcoming vibe. In such an intimate little spot, you'll find yourself part of the action before you know it. If you've never been to a Celtic jam session, Sandy Bell's is your best bet for this authentic and essential experience of Scottish culture.

Drams from £3, Mon-Sat 12:00–01:00, Sun 12:30–24:00, 25 Forrest Rd, University District, +44 (0)131 225 2751, sandybellsedinburgh.co.uk

The Banshee Labyrinth

The Banshee Labyrinth is aptly named: It's a veritable maze of cellars, bars, and chill-out areas, and if you only get lost once in here, count yourself lucky. Add a movie theater, a performance venue, funky lighting, a little alcohol, and an inexplicable otherworldly haze that just seems to float around this place and you might feel inclined to lose yourself permanently in the fog and join the ghosts of South Bridge. Bring an open mind and a readiness to embrace the unexpected; the evening will likely be one you'll be telling stories about for months. Check the website for upcoming events.

Drinks from £3.50, daily 19:00–03:00, 29 Niddry St, Royal Mile, +44 (0)131 558 8209, thebansheelabyrinth.com

Whistlebinkies Live Music Bar

This excellent pub right off the Royal Mile packs out the house with ales and a fully stocked bar. The whole venue is oriented toward the stage, with musicians playing most nights, and there's enough musical

ACT LIKE A LOCAL

Dreamin' o' the Dram

A visit to Edinburgh isn't complete without a sip of the good stuff: Scotch whisky. It takes a bit of time to develop a palate for it, but once you know some subtle features to watch for, the experience is much better.

Your first step is to get an education. There are five regions of whisky production in Scotland, all with different characteristics and personalities. Here are some key tips to get your liquid adventure off on the right foot with common brands to look for:

Lowlands: Creamy, soft, light; often referred to as "breakfast whisky" (Brands: Auchentoshan, Glenkinchie)

Highlands: More flowery; range of toffee and salt tones (Brands: Balblair, Clynelish, Aberfeldy, Drummer)

Speyside: The classic Scotch; citrus and zest, fruity, apple, fragrant (Brands: Glenlivet, Macallan)

Campbelltown: Light smokiness, spicy, oily; matured in sherry casks to add complexity (Brands: Springbank, Glengyle, Hazelburn)

Islay: Salty, very smoky, oily overtones; heavy peat, akin to a campfire (Brands: Lagavulin, Ardbeg)

Etiquette & Tasting

When you saddle up, your bartender will either pour your dram neat (no water, no ice) or ask how you like it. Take yours at room temperature with a few drops of water. Taking your whisky with a bit of water opens up its complexities. Tasting whisky is a multisensory experience:

Read the label to ensure there are no additives, and that the whisky was not chill-filtered, a process that removes a number of the complexities of the flavor profile.

Look at the color. Lighter or darker does not necessarily mean much in terms of taste or quality. What you're looking for are the legs that form after you gently swirl the glass. The thinner the legs, the more alcohol content you can expect. And the speed at which they form shows the viscosity of the whisky: more complex and intense flavors come with a higher viscosity, and more slowly forming legs.

Now, give your dram a "nose"—no swirl necessary. Leave your mouth slightly open as you take a whiff, and try to pick out some scents. Do you detect florals, fruits, and citrus? Or is it earthy, peaty, and smoky?

When you're ready to taste, take just a sip at a time, inhaling a little air as you go to continue waking up your olfactory senses. Swirl and "chew" the whisky in your mouth for up to five seconds and pay attention to the first sensations you detect, the ones you detect as you swallow, and then the finish. Now you're well on your way to becoming a Scotch whisky connoisseur in your own right. *Slanj!*

variety to keep everyone happy. The layout is such that you can rage up close with the band, dance in the middle, or keep a conversation going off to the side in the back.

Pricey drinks at £5, Mon-Thurs 17:00-03:00, Fri-Sat 13:00-03:00, Sun 17:00-24:00, 4-6 South Bridge, Royal Mile, +44 (0)131 557 5114, whistlebinkies.com

Three Sisters

When the weather's great, Three Sisters gets wild. The expansive outdoor seating area features large screens for the games, and afterward they roll out the karaoke machine, which keeps the stag and hen parties roaring all night. The venue's unique and funky vibe and its relatively inexpensive drinks have made it a favorite of university students throughout the week.

Drinks from £3.50, Mon-Fri 17:00-01:00, Sat-Sun 07:00-03:00, 139 Cowgate, Royal Mile, +44 (0)131 622 6802, thethreesistersbar.co.uk

McSorley's Irish Bar

Just like every other city on the planet, Edinburgh has its Irish pubs—but, while most Irish bars outside of Ireland shoot par at best, this one aces the hole. Their food and entertainment are both first-rate. Occupying what was once a medium-sized, horseshoe-shaped theater, the bar quite naturally draws focus towards the stage. If the footie is on, a massive screen gives everybody in the room front-row seats. The musical acts here keep the room jumping late into the evening. Hungry? The burgers and chips are unforgettable.

Beers from £4, daily 12:00-01:00, 14 Forrest Rd, University District, +44 (0)131 226 5954, mcsorleysbar.com

Dropkick Murphy's

Known for its late nights and rowdy atmosphere, Dropkick Murphy's is tucked underneath the George IV Bridge on Merchant Street. Find the bright green doors just a block off of Grassmarket Square and dive into the sloppy but always friendly crowd.

Drinks from £4, Thurs-Tues 20:00-03:00, 7 Merchant St, Grassmarket District, +44 (0)131 225 2002, Facebook: Dropkick Murphys Edinburgh

Ghillie Dhu

If you're into crowd participation, this venue will leave both sets of your cheeks sore from smiling and dancing the night away in an old converted church with high vaulted ceilings and bold chandeliers. Ghillie Dhu's weekend parties are much like an adult version of a middle school dance, with all the nervous excitement, but less of the awkwardness—thanks to the alcohol. Enjoy the full dinner starting at 19:00 for £30, or show up around 21:00 when the tables are pushed back and everyone is up to dance for just the cost of cover. Don't worry if you don't know what you're doing—the emcee will walk you through the basics and make sure you've got a partner to try them out on. If you've got your phone out, you're doing it wrong!

The cocktail bar next door, **Heads and Tales** (cocktails from £9, 1a Rutland Pl, +44 (0)131 656 2811, headsandtalesbar.com, info@headsandtalesbar.com) is an excellent option for a low-key old-fashioned mixed by bearded, aproned mixologists. I love the cozy atmosphere, low-slung ceilings, mismatched furniture, friendly service, and the unpretentious personal touch these guys are pouring out.

£30 dinner and show, £5 cover otherwise, Mon-Fri 11:00-03:00, Sat-Sun 10:00-03:00, live music kicks off at 21:30, 2 Rutland Pl, New Town, +44 131 222 9930, ghillie-dhu.co.uk

CLUBS

The clubs in town all seem to come with bouncers who like to dish out a hard time (arguing with any of them won't improve your night). Most of them will also expect a fiver for cover. Once in the door, though, good times await.

Cabaret Voltaire

Just off the Royal Mile, "Cab Vol" is one of Edinburgh's top clubs. Look forward to grungy, student-party night-infused atmosphere in this club. The place demands that you check any pretentiousness at the door; in exchange, you'll get raucous live music and DJ acts. Be prepared for feisty bouncers.

Cover around £6, Sun-Mon and Wed-Thurs 19:30-01:30, Tues and Fri 17:00-03:00, Sat 12:00-03:00, 36 Blair St, Royal Mile, +44 (0)131 247 4704, thecabaretvoltaire.com

The Hive Nightclub

This sweaty and cheap club packs out with a young crowd that appreciates the low prices and is willing to overlook the sticky floor. There's no cover Thursdays and Sundays, and student specials can be counted on to keep the bar jumping all night. The lines can get long on Fridays and Saturdays, so get on the guest list to skip to the front of the queue.

Cover around £3, drinks from £1, Sun-Thurs 22:00-03:00, Fri-Sat 21:00-03:00, 15 Niddry St, Royal Mile, +44 (0)131 556 0444, clubhive.co.uk

Stramash

This converted church is now one of the most consistent bets in town for excellent live music without a cover fee. Located right on Cowgate, you can count on nightly acts, pub grub until midnight, and free entry until 3am. Bands go on stage at 21:30 and 00:30 each night, offering a wide range, but tending toward rock.

£5 drinks, no cover, live music nightly and DJ, 207 Cowgate, Old Town, +44 (0)131 623 4353, stramashedinburgh.com

COMEDY SHOWS
The Stand

Known as Edinburgh's best comedy club, the subterranean Stand is so popular it often sells out, so it's best to book your tickets online ahead of time. On most nights the format's a rotating selection of five comedians over two hours, but on some nights they switch things up for improv and solo acts.

Tickets from £10, doors usually open at 19:30 and show starts at 21:00 but check schedule online, 5 York Place, New Town, +44 (0)131 558 7272, thestand.co.uk

Monkey Barrel Comedy Club

Edinburgh's newest option for comedy on the Royal Mile does not disappoint. Check out their website for descriptions of their creative nightly acts, ranging from standup to improv and spoken word. Shows generally kick off at 20:30 with doors opening at 19:00. I was particularly blown away by the accompanying pianist, adding just the right tension and comedic relief to the performers on stage.

Shows from £5, nightly shows 20:30, 9 Blair St, Old Town, +44 845 500 1056, monkeybarrelcomedy.com

PUB CRAWLS
New Edinburgh Pub Crawl

Hosted by the reliable crew at Sandeman's tours, the New Edinburgh Pub Crawl gives you a leg up in finding Edinburgh's tucked-away nightlife gems. You'll enjoy half-priced pints, three shooters, a dram of Scotch whisky, and drink deals in every pub you visit, ending with VIP entrance into Edinburgh's best nightclub. You'll also meet tons of travelers like yourself and make some great friends—if not lifelong friends, at least friends for the night.

£15, nightly 20:00 at the Inn on the Mile, Royal Mile, newedinburghtours.com

Edinburgh Pub Crawl

Each pub crawl tries to outdo the others on the quantifiables (number of bars, clubs, free shots, etc.), but sometimes you've just gotta go with the best vibe. These guys have been showing people a great night out for years, and they know how to get groups of partiers to bring out their wild side. Their crawls are always tons of fun.

£10, nightly at 20:30 in front of St. Giles' Cathedral, Royal Mile, edinburghpub-crawl.com

TOP SHOPPING & MARKETS

SHOPPING DISTRICTS
Royal Mile

Full of shops and street performers, the main tourist boulevard is a great place for souvenir shopping. You'll find just about every Scottish knickknack and touristy souvenir you can imagine (kilts anyone?). In addition, there are many tiny alleyways or "closes" that branch off High Street. These pockets are full of cafés, shops, and exhibits, so make sure to wander off the main drag and down Edinburgh's alleys.

Old Town

Princes & George Streets

Edinburgh's version of Oxford Street, come here to find all your top international name brands. While in the area, stop into

Edinburgh's famous **Jenner's**, a beautiful Victorian-style department store built in 1938 (Mon-Fri 09:30-18:30, Sat 09:00-19:00, Sun 11:00-18:00, 48 Princes St, +44 (0)131 225 2442, houseoffraser.co.uk).

New Town

Grassmarket Square

Grassmarket (27-31 W Port, grassmarket. net) is perfect for those whose tastes run a little deeper. They've got boutique fashion shops and vintage music and bookstores, interspersed with some of Edinburgh's trendiest cafés and bars. Check out the website to explore in advance the places to visit.

Grassmarket District

Stockbridge

Visit this neighborhood if you're into secondhand clothing, unique jewelry, glassware, and independent art galleries. Tea and coffee shops dot the area by the dozen on the north side of the New Town, on Kerr Street. Stockbridge is a great place to get your shop on, enjoy an afternoon tea, and watch the world go by. Head here in a hurry if your feet have had enough of the cobblestones and need a break.

New Town

Bruntsfield Place & Morningside Road

While a bit south of town, this area has a young vibe. Boutique and vintage clothing stores, chocolatiers, and cafés abound here. If the hordes of tourists near the center are getting to you, these places will give you the chance to hang out with mellow locals—the experience in the center and the experience here are like night and day.

South of University District (interesting until Cluny Ave)

MARKETS

Edinburgh Farmers' Market

Stock up on locally grown produce, organic beer, and fresh, seasonal fruits at the Edinburgh Farmers' Market. The market vendors assemble just off of Castle Terrace.

Sat 09:00–14:00, Castle Terrace, West End, edinburghfarmersmarket.com

TOP PARKS & RECREATION

Surrounded by dramatic geography, Edinburgh boasts some spectacular parks, hikes, and viewpoints. Since so much of the touristy center can be seen in a day or two, it's a good idea (even on short visits) to spend at least one day enjoying the city's natural splendor.

PARKS

Edinburgh has some beautiful, free, and open green spaces to explore and catch your breath.

Meadows Park

Because of its proximity to the University of Edinburgh, students make up the vast majority of visitors to this large, grassy, tree-filled park. It's a great place to sit with some lunch or perhaps a picnic and people-watch for an hour or two.

Free, always open, University District

Holyrood Park

Holyrood Park, in the heart of Edinburgh, has been a royal park since the 12th century. You'll stumble upon many great sights while wandering the footpaths and craggy cliffs in this pristine spot of local wilderness. See the Palace of Holyroodhouse, the ruins of Holyrood Abbey, and the extinct volcano Arthur's Seat (Edinburgh's highest peak at 251 meters) and you'll have made a good afternoon of it. The views are unbeatable, and the air is heavy with natural scents. There are few better places in Edinburgh to while away an afternoon.

Free, always open, end of Royal Mile

Dean Gardens & Water of Leith

Scotland's capital has beautiful parks and walkways by the dozen, and Dean Gardens is one of my favorites. With the Water of Leith (the river that borders the north side of the New Town) running alongside it,

Dean Gardens is one of the most beautiful stretches in the city. Make your way to the walkway along the river—just steps into the park, the noises from the city will fall away. You're immersed completely in Scotland's natural beauty.

Free, always open, New Town

West Princes Street Gardens

On a clear—and warm—day, one of my favorite things to do is to snag a sandwich or chips from one of the many eateries on the Princes Street strip and head to the nearby gardens, where there's always a bench free. I pull up a pew and, while I eat, I enjoy the view of the broad side of the Edinburgh Castle and the Royal Mile. Pick up your supplies at the **Cooperative Food Market** (daily 07:00-23:00, 26-28 Frederick St, +44 (0)131 220 0359).

Free, always open

VIEWPOINTS
Arthur's Seat

A sweaty 45-minute climb up this extinct volcano in Holyrood Park provides wonderful views of Edinburgh. It's a great place to snap a photo (or dozens of them) of Edinburgh Castle, the Palace of Holyroodhouse, the Scottish Parliament Building, and Calton Hill.

Free, visit during daylight hours for best views, Holyrood Park, just south of the Palace of Holyroodhouse

Calton Hill

A 15-minute climb to the top of Calton Hill, located in the northeast section of the city center, will bring you to a beautiful World War I memorial, accompanied by panoramic views of downtown Edinburgh, Edinburgh Castle, and all the way out to the coast. Put the memorial in the foreground of your photo for professional-looking shots of Edinburgh's skyline.

Free, visit during daylight hours for best views, 15 York Place, New Town

TOP TOURS

Little Fish Free Tours

For a fun and informative two-hour stroll through the Old Town and University District, meet up with the tight-knit team at Little Fish (meeting at the David Hume statue on the Royal Mile at 10:30 and 13:30). Stories range from heady Scottish enlightenment, literature, and architecture to pop-culture subjects like deep-fried Mars bars and Harry Potter sights.

Free, tips accepted, 10:30 and 13:30 daily, arrive 15 minutes early and wait at the David Hume statue in front of the High Court on Royal Mile, littlefishtours.co.uk

Mercat Tours

This group helps you dive into the history of Edinburgh's underground jumble of chambers, focusing on the day-to-day existence of those who lived in these spaces.

£13, tours daily at 14:00 and 16:00, meet at the Mercat Cross, office at 28 Blair St, +44 (0)131 225 5445, mercattours.com

Excursion Scotland

Colin Mairs heads up this small tour company. If you're looking for a deep dive into everything Scotland, Colin's your man. A

fun-loving, passionate Scot who sports a kilt more often than trousers, Colin offers everything from half-day tours of Edinburgh's best sights to weeklong, private custom tours of the entire country for small groups and families.

From £100, +44 (0)77 1623 2001, excursionscotland.com, excursionscotland@gmail.com

City of the Dead Ghost Tours

With Edinburgh's long history of resident body snatchers, serial killers, and crime, the ghost tour here is better than just about anywhere else in Europe. Dive into the grisly and macabre side of Edinburgh with this fascinating—and blood-drenched—walk. You'll pick up all sorts of ghoulish stories and freaky facts.

£10, tours nightly at 20:30 from Easter to Halloween, at 20:00 throughout winter, meet in front of St. Giles' Cathedral, +44 (0)131 225 9044, cityofthedeadtours.com, info@cityofthedeadtours.com

Rabbie's Small Group Tours

Rabbie's is a Scottish tourism institution, offering 1- to 17-day excursions with a wide range of focus all around the country. From castles to whisky distributors, and from highlands to lakes (lochs in Scottish), Rabbie's local guides know exactly where to take you to tickle your fancy.

Day trips from £42, +44 (0)131 226 3133, rabbies.com, info@rabbies.com

Haggis Adventures

This is your fun backpacker option for day trips (or for longer ones) to the areas around Edinburgh or around the country.

With their "mad sexy" guides, you're sure to have a great time learning about Scottish history, food, and culture while touring the jaw-dropping Scottish countryside. The groups these tours attract are one of the highlights of the adventure. Check out the full lineup of trips and dates online. Group and student discounts available.

Trips from £50, +44 (0)131 557 9393, haggisadventures.com

TOP HOSTELS

Edinburgh has a slew of fun, social, and affordable backpacker hostels in or nearby the Old Town. They do their best to work with (rather than against) the old buildings that they've taken over, giving them a uniquely Scottish character. My favorite ones do this exceptionally well.

The Baxter Hostel

A new 40-bed entry into the Edinburgh backpacking scene, the midsized Baxter is following the trend of boutique hostels with a focus on friendly service, great location, and solid value. The interior feels retro-chic with clean industrial lines, and their custom-fabricated steel bunks match perfectly with the exposed brick and wood-paneled walls—both go a long way toward creating a comfortable and low-key vibe. The enthusiastic staff will happily make sights and activities recommendations during your stay.

Dorms from £22, 24-hour reception, free Wi-Fi, full kitchen facilities, breakfast included, common room, 5 W Register St, New Town, +44 (0)131 503 1001, thebaxter.eu, info@thebaxter.eu

Code Hostel

This 30-bed hostel in the New Town prides itself on cleanliness and great value. The bunks are slotted like pods that you climb into (very much like the famous Japanese

airport cubby hotels). They're clearly economizing on space, but the cleanliness and value are there to compensate for the cramped quarters. Each pod is equipped with plugs, USB ports, and reading lights. I actually found myself enjoying the privacy, but it's definitely not for claustrophobics.

Pod beds from £20, daily 08:00–20:00 reception, free maps, free Wi-Fi, breakfast included, towels available for rent, common room, 50 Rose St N Ln, New Town, +44 (0)131 659 9883, codehostel.com, hello@codehostel.com

Budget Backpackers

Budget Backpackers sports bright, clean rooms, friendly staff, funky decor, and a great location just off Grassmarket Square, barely a block from the Royal Mile. Book early, as all 200 of their beds tend to fill up fast. En suite privates are also available if you'd prefer to skip the large dorms—the largest of which has 30 beds (some find the chorus of snores unbearable). The £5 nightly dinner is a great deal for those on a

budget. Numerous common areas and an excellent on-site bar make this one of the more social hostels in town.

From £14, 24-hour reception, Internet available on PC (no Wi-Fi), common room, kitchen access, optional breakfast, pool table, towels for rent, 37-39 Cowgate, Grassmarket District, +44 (0)131 226 6351, budgetbackpackers.com, hi@budgetbackpackers.com

Castle Rock Hostel

With its high ceilings, old-fashioned furniture, a fireplace, and a stone-brick exterior, this 300-bed hostel will make you feel as though you've truly experienced that "Scottish vibe." The rooms are clean, free walking tours of the city leave from the front door of the hostel every day, and they keep the evenings lively (crucial when the weather is uncooperative) with movie screenings and billiard tourneys.

From £14, female dorms available, free Wi-Fi, 24 hour reception, laundry (£4), breakfast (£2), bedside lockers, 15 Johnston Terrace, Royal Mile, +44 (0)131 225 9666, castlerocke-dinburgh.com, castlerock@macbackpackerstours.com

High Street Hostel

Some of the city's most welcoming staff and snug and secure rooms are at this gem of a hostel, just downhill from the Royal Mile on Blackfriars Street. Even though some of the city's best bars are only steps away from the hostel doors, you can almost hear a pin drop in the rooms. You'll wake up rested and refreshed. It's the best of both worlds.

Large dorms from £12, free Wi-Fi, 24-hour reception, breakfast (£2), luggage storage, lockers, 8 Blackfriars St, Royal Mile, +44 (0)131 557 3984, highstreethos-tel.com, reservations online

Kick Ass Hostel

New and brightly decorated, with a massive on-site bar and a social atmosphere, this is one of my favorite hostels in town. With a "Best New Hostel UK" award under their belt, the team at Kick Ass Hostel is off to a great start. Take in a view of the castle from the dorm windows, make a new friend or two over the Ping-Pong and pool tables, and charge up with plugs next to every bed in the house.

4-12 bed dorms from £15, free Wi-Fi, 24-hour reception, on-site bar and drink specials, Ping-Pong and pool tables, laundry facilities, 2 W Port, Old Town, +44 (0)131 226 6351, kickasshostels.co.uk, reservations online

TRANSPORTATION

GETTING THERE & AWAY
Plane
Edinburgh Airport (EDI, edinburghairport.com) is just 20 minutes from the center, and many of the budget airlines offer connections from most major airports in Europe. A cab from the airport to the city center will run you about £25-30. Otherwise, the frequently leaving **Airlink 100** bus connects you to the Waverley Bridge Station for £4.50 each way in about 30 minutes. A **tram** system also connects Edinburgh Airport with the city center (£5.50) in 30 minutes, stopping at a number of stations in the New Town along the way.

Don't forget to consider **Glasgow Airport** (GLA, glasgowairport.com) as a secondary option. While it is about an hour away (getting to Edinburgh takes two transfers on the train), there may be substantially cheaper flights into Scotland via Glasgow.

Train
Edinburgh has two primary train stations, **Haymarket Station** and **Edinburgh Waverley Station,** located on either end of central Edinburgh; before you arrive, confirm which of these stations will be your first stop in Edinburgh (same goes for when you're leaving).

To avoid the often-long lines at Waverley, the bigger of the two train stations, purchase your ticket in advance at virgintrainseastcoast.com. Direct express trains to London take about four hours and depart frequently.

Bus
National Express (nationalexpress.com) and **Megabus** (uk.megabus.com) offer dozens of national and international bus connections into Edinburgh, though the connection times, which can run over 10 hours from London, may bring many to

consider the budget airline options. Reclining seats and Wi-Fi en route make the ride more bearable, and ticket prices (from £10) make it an attractive option for those on a tight budget.

Car

From London, the M6 will take you through England's achingly beautiful lake districts to Edinburgh in about 7.5 hours, assuming minimal traffic. Otherwise, consider the smaller A1, which has significantly more detours and stops along the way.

GETTING AROUND

Thanks to the city's compactness, walking is definitely the best way to explore Edinburgh. It's only about a 20-minute walk across town. There are so many nooks and crannies to soak in, so many hidden treasures, that doing anything but walking will mean missing out on some of Edinburgh's jewels in the rough. Just keep in mind that the steep slopes up to the Old Town can leave some walkers huffing and puffing by the time they reach the top.

Edinburgh's public transportation system consists of buses and a limited tram system that connects the airport with the city center, stopping in New Town along the way. There is no train or metro transportation within the city.

Bus

Buses (£1.60 for a **single ride**) are a handy way to visit some of the city's farther-flung sights. If you plan to utilize public transportation three times in 24 hours, buy an unlimited **day ticket** for only £4. Have exact change handy and purchase tickets as you board, or stop into a Lothian Bus Travel Shop and get your tickets there.

Taxi

Edinburgh has classic black cabs, which you can flag down on the street or find at any of the city's numerous taxi stands. A downtown ride should run you no more than £15, but, even for that price, it's almost always worth walking rather than riding. **Uber** is also available in Edinburgh.

Car

Like just about every other medieval city of Europe, Edinburgh was built for pedestrians and horses and carts, not cars. Thanks to the public bus network, cars are not necessary to get around town, but they do provide some flexibility if you're considering heading into the Scottish countryside. If that's your plan, Edinburgh's **Park & Ride stations** (edinburgh.gov.uk/parkandride) let you park on the outskirts of the city for free and take public transportation into the city. You just need to pay for your bus ticket into town. Look up locations in Hermiston (open 24 hours), Ingliston (04:00-02:00), Sheriff-hal (24 hours), and Straiton (24 hours) for options. All are free and open seven days a week.

Bicycle

Edinburgh is a cycling-friendly city with tons of bike lanes and more being built every year. The city council is currently working to enact a public bike rental scheme similar to the ones in Paris and London. In the meantime, find one of the numerous shops where you can rent a bike for around £12 per half day. These include in the Old Town **Cycle Scotland** (£20/day, 29 Blackfriars St, +44 (0)131 556 5560, cyclescotland.co.uk) and **Bike Trax** (£17/day, 11-13 Lochrin Pl, +44 (0)131 228 6633, biketrax.co.uk) in the West End. Get ready to sweat it out on the steep hills! If it starts raining, the cobblestones get slippery; rather than risk injury, park the bike and hoof it.

DAY TRIPS

You've got a slew of day trips from Scotland's capital that will get you out into the rugged countryside and away from the big groups of tourists who make Edinburgh's center a crowded place. The best way to do it is with a local guide on a fun group tour. Check out my recommended tour companies for options for whisky tours, visits to castles, hikes out in the countryside, and more. Prices start around £50 for the day for a simple tour; for those who want to delve deeper, the bottomless loch is the limit. Tours can last for as long as weeks if you've got the time and money to spend.

Glasgow

Just a one-hour, £15 train ride away, Scotland's biggest (and most proudly patriotic) city is well within day-trip reach. With 100,000 more residents, Glasgow is Edinburgh's more industrial, grittier, hipster big sister, but it shares much of Edinburgh's refinement, with tons of museums and interesting sights. Attractions include the **University of Glasgow** (free, campus always open, about 1.5 miles west of the city center, gla.ac.uk), **Kelingrove Art Gallery and Museum** (free, Sun and Fri 11:00-17:00, Mon-Thurs and Sat 10:00-17:00, Argyle St, glasgowlife.org.uk), the **Gallery of Modern Art** (free, Sun and Fri 11:00-17:00, Mon-Thurs and Sat 10:00-17:00, Royal Exchange Square, glas-gowlife.org.uk), and a bustling city center. For those interested in art nouveau (like I am), Glasgow was the home of Charles Mackintosh, the leader of the northern art nouveau movement. Mackintosh dabbled in everything from design and architecture to watercolor and furniture. You'll see a number of his works as you walk the streets, including the Glasgow School of Art and the *Glasgow Herald* newspaper offices.

Glasgow also has a raging nightlife scene befitting the bigger, more modern-feeling city (Glasgow is aligned on a grid, so it doesn't feel medieval). **The West End,** around Byres Road and Ashton Lane, caters mostly to students thanks to its proximity to the university there. Otherwise, **Bell Street** and **Vincent Street** offer a string of great bars and clubs. Remember the early closing policies of Glasgow—midnight for bars, and 03:00 for clubs, so don't dillydally on your night out! If you've got a few extra days and prefer cities over natural beauty, Glasgow's definitely worth an overnight trip.

Loch Ness

Everyone's heard of the legend of Nessie, the aquatic monster of Loch Ness. Many make their way north of Edinburgh to the world's most famous loch to see if they can catch a glimpse of her. It's doable in a day, but it's best to leave early, otherwise you'll be getting back extremely late (it's 3.5 hours of straight driving). Your best bet is to link up with organized day trips that include fun guides and interesting stops along the way. I recommend **Haggis Adventures.** Their day trip starts at £65 for the 12-hour round-trip tour (haggisadventures.com).

HELP!

Tourist Information Centers

Find the main tourist information center just on the border of the New Town and Old Town at the top of the Princes Mall shopping center. Pop in here for pamphlets, maps, and souvenirs, but remember that local businesses pay for placement, so the recommendations are anything but unbiased.

Pickpockets & Scams

My best advice is to simply have your wits about you when walking the streets. Avoid sketchy neighborhoods, stay in well-lit, populated areas, keep your valuables close at hand, and never leave any belongings unattended. While extremely rare in Edinburgh, pickpocketing and mugging can still occur, but if you follow the guidelines above and lean on your good old-fashioned common sense, the only stuff that'll disappear out of your pockets will be the money you spend.

Emergency

In an emergency, dial 999.

Hospital

Royal Infirmary of Edinburgh
51 Little France Crescent
+44 (0)131 536 1000

US Consulate

3 Regent Terrace, Edinburgh EH7 5BW
+44 (0)131 556 8315

APPENDIX

FLYING TO EUROPE FROM THE UNITED STATES

Booking long-haul flights to Europe is a two-part process: First, find your longer flight to the Continent, then search for shorter flights into your chosen destination. If you're beginning your visit in Dublin or Venice, for example, search for direct flights to those cities, but also look into flights to **major transportation hubs** like London, Amsterdam, Frankfurt, and Paris. These airports offer many of the best connections to and from the States. If you're flying from the East Coast, you'll have a broader range of direct flight options to cities like Madrid and Rome.

If you only frame your search by your desired trip-starting point, search engines may get stuck on getting you to that destination on the same airline, skipping over good multi-airline options. The more creative and flexible you are in your search, the more likely it is that you'll find a budget-friendly option. To promote tourism, some airlines (e.g., Iceland Air) even offer free multiple-day layovers in certain destinations.

CITY-HOPPING

With planes, trains, and buses, getting around Europe is easy. Each mode of transportation comes with pros and cons. Buses, for example, are often the cheapest but most time-consuming option. Weigh the value of extra time in your destination against the money that you'll save.

FLYING

Budget airlines have opened up the Continent to backpackers on a budget. Before the advent of cheap flights, a budget trip from Paris to Madrid would have been an uncomfortable 14-hour overnight train ride. Now, airlines like Ryanair and EasyJet offer a stripped down service for those who value low prices over comfort. While the days of $5 flights are long gone, you can still find deals to get around the Continent for less than $100, as long as you know how to play the budget airline game.

Finding Cheap Flights

Let's help you get finding cheap flights down to a science. First, open up a series of browser windows and conduct the same search across all these different websites:

google.com/flights

skyscanner.net

cheapoair.com

kayak.com

momondo.com

Keep the search as flexible as possible across travel dates, travel times, and airports. Each search engine uses different algorithms to find results, so you may get back four different answers. Pay close attention to the following details:

- **Departure and arrival airports.** Many airlines use budget regional airports a couple of hours outside the city center. While this keeps costs down, it adds to your connection time and on-the-ground travel costs. Watch out for this in Paris and Barcelona in particular.

- **Baggage allowance.** Note how much it costs to check a bag. You are often given the choice between 15kg (33lb) and 20kg (44lb) for your checked bag. Pack according to the one you've picked—even if you're 1kg over, you'll have to pay extra.

- **Departure time.** Cheap airlines save money by running super-early and super-late flights. Some flights leave so early that public transportation to the airport is not even running yet. If that's the case, you'll need to factor in another €30-40 for a taxi.

Booking Cheap Flights

When you've selected your flight, book directly through the airline's website. This cuts out any middleman fees and potential system glitches, and puts you directly in touch with the airline.

The cheaper the airline, the more ads you'll have to click through and the more "options" you'll have to decline during the booking process. Ryanair offers you luggage, hotels, car rentals, airport transfers, and all sorts of other stuff you probably don't need or want. You'll have to scour each section to click the No Thank You box.

Be wary when it comes to the final checkout and payment. Before you click your final confirm, double-check the following elements:

- **Departure time.** It will be in 24-hour time. For reference: 09:00 = 9am, 19:00 = 7pm.
- **Departure date.** It will likely be in European format: February 7 is 07/02, not 02/07. Check the date visually with a drop-down calendar, or find it spelled out before purchasing.
- **Number of bags you'll need to check.** Pay to check a bag at the time of booking. It will cost you more to do so when checking in.
- **Departure and arrival airports.** Some cities have multiple airports, so always note the airport's full name. Also note necessary connection distances and costs, factoring these into your decision.
- **Final price.** Make sure the price hasn't risen exorbitantly since your first search. Tally the numbers and be sure you understand them. Always decline the option to be charged in US dollars—the "service" comes with a needless fee.

Avoiding Hidden Costs

Extra fees add up. It is important to read and abide by the fine print in all materials relating to your budget flight. Watch out for and avoid these hidden costs:

- **Airport check-in fee.** If you don't check in online ahead of time, some airlines now charge a €40+ penalty. To avoid this fee, pay attention to all emails you receive from your airline as your date of travel approaches.
- **Baggage checking and carry-on fees.** Checking a bag usually costs €35 for the first bag and €50 for a second. Certain airlines also charge for carry-on bags that are any larger than a medium-sized purse. If you're on a budget, pack light.
- **Boarding pass printing fee.** Print your boarding pass ahead of time, or keep it on your mobile device. Also note that some airports have printing stations that allow you to avoid this fee.
- **Heads up:** Ryanair requires all non-EU passport holders to get their visa and passport checked *before* going through security. You need a stamp on your boarding pass clearing you through to your gate. Be sure to do this ahead of time to avoid missing your flight.

Budget Airlines by City

There are many budget airlines based in cities throughout Europe. Pay attention to

DON'T BE PENNY-WISE & POUND-FOOLISH

I recently needed to get from Interlaken, Switzerland, to Prague for my next WSA tour. My options were a €210 direct flight to Prague on Swissair at a comfortable hour or an earlier €120 flight with EasyJet/Wizz Air that connected through Rome. I jumped on the cheaper option. Here's how the associated costs shook out:

€55 Interlaken-Basel train (about €20 more than the connection would have been to Swissair's airport)

€32 to check my extra bag at the gate

€15 to check in at airport in Rome

€17 on food throughout the course of the day

€38 to check my second bag again

This all resulted in additional costs to the tune of at least €20 more for a less convenient flight. The more expensive flight would have wound up saving me money! Learn from my mistakes and do the math before booking.

TRANSIT TIMES

		Amsterdam	Barcelona	Berlin	Budapest	Dublin
Amsterdam	Bus	x	24	8	21.5	N/A
	Train	x	11.5	6.5	17.5	16.5
	Plane	x	2	1.5	2	1.5
Barcelona	Bus	24	x	33	N/A	N/A
	Train	11.5	x	19	28.5	21.5
	Plane	2	x	2.5	2.5	2.5
Berlin	Bus	8	33	x	15	N/A
	Train	6.5	19	x	12	24
	Plane	1.5	2.5	x	1.5	2
Budapest	Bus	21.5	N/A	15	x	N/A
	Train	17.5	28.5	12	x	N/A
	Plane	2	2.5	1.5	x	3
Dublin	Bus	N/A	N/A	N/A	N/A	x
	Train	16.5	21.5	24	N/A	x
	Plane	1.5	2.5	2	3	x
Edinburgh	Bus	N/A	N/A	N/A	N/A	10
	Train	10	15.5	22.5	N/A	9
	Plane	1.5	3	2	3	1
Florence	Bus	26	17	18.5	15	N/A
	Train	17.5	21.5	16	14	27
	Plane	2	1.5	2	1.5	3
London	Bus	12	27.5	20	16	14.5
	Train	5	11	18.5	19	10
	Plane	1	2.5	2	3	1
Madrid	Bus	27	9	N/A	N/A	N/A
	Train	21	3	25.5	26	N/A
	Plane	2.5	1.5	3	3.5	2.5
Paris	Bus	5	15.5	16	31	25
	Train	3.5	7	8.5	16	18
	Plane	1	1.5	2	2.5	1.5
Prague	Bus	14	10	4.5	10	N/A
	Train	14	24	4.5	7	N/A
	Plane	1.5	2.5	1	1	2.5
Rome	Bus	30	21.5	22	22.5	N/A
	Train	18	22.5	18	16.5	N/A
	Plane	2.5	1.5	2	1.5	3
Venice	Bus	27	23	16	10.5	N/A
	Train	16	22	16	11	N/A
	Plane	2	2	1.5	1.5	2.5

Use this chart to plan the best mode of transit between cities. Travel time (given in hours) is approximate.

Edinburgh	Florence	London	Madrid	Paris	Prague	Rome	Venice
N/A	26	12	27	5	14	30	27
10	17.5	5	21	3.5	14	18	16
1.5	1.5	1	2.5	1	1.5	2.5	2
N/A	17	27.5	9	15.5	10	21.5	23
15.5	21.5	11	3	7	24	22.5	22
2.5	1.5	2.5	1.5	1.5	2.5	1.5	2
N/A	18.5	20	N/A	16	4.5	22	16
22.5	16	18.5	25.5	8.5	4.5	18	16
2	2	2	3	2	1	2	1.5
N/A	15	16	N/A	31	10	22.5	10.5
N/A	14	19	26	16	7	16.5	11
3	1.5	3	3.5	2.5	1	1.5	1.5
10	N/A	14.5	N/A	25	N/A	N/A	N/A
9	27	10	N/A	18	N/A	N/A	N/A
1	3	1	2.5	1.5	2.5	3	2.5
x	N/A	8	N/A	N/A	N/A	N/A	N/A
x	N/A	4.5	N/A	7.5	N/A	N/A	N/A
x	3	1	3	2	2.5	3	2.5
N/A	x	29	26	18	14	4	4
N/A	x	16	26	10	14	1.5	3
3	x	2.5	2.5	2	1.5	1	1
8	29	x	29.5	7	17.5	33	30
4.5	16	x	20.5	2.5	17.5	17.5	16.5
1	2.5	x	2	1	2	2.5	2
N/A	26	29.5	x	16.5	N/A	31	31.5
N/A	26	20.5	x	25	26	25	25
3	2.5	2	x	5	3	2.5	2.5
N/A	18	7	16.5	x	15	21.5	19.5
7.5	10	2.5	25	x	17	11.15	14
2	2	1	5	x	2	2	2
N/A	14	7.5	N/A	15	x	20.5	14
N/A	14	17.5	26	17	x	17.5	12
2.5	1.5	2	3	2	x	2	1.5
N/A	4	33	31	21.5	20.5	x	7
N/A	1.5	17.5	25	11.5	17.5	x	3.5
3	1	2.5	2.5	2	2	x	1
N/A	4	30	31.5	19.5	14	7	x
N/A	3	16.5	25	14	12	3.5	x
2.5	1	2	2.5	2	1.5	1	x

which city acts as a hub for which airline and you'll generally find cheaper flights.

Amsterdam: Transavia

Barcelona and Madrid: EasyJet, Vueling

Berlin: Air Berlin

Budapest: Wizz Air

Dublin: Aer Lingus, Ryanair

Edinburgh & London: EasyJet

Paris: Air France

Prague: SmartWings, Czech Airlines

Rome, Florence, and Venice: Alitalia

Not-So-Budget Airlines

If you prefer convenience, comfortable seats, and free luggage allowance, budget airlines may not be for you. With these conventional airlines, you'll pay more up front, but you'll generally forgo the sneaky hidden costs: **British Airways, Lufthansa, Turkish Airlines, KLM,** and **Swissair.**

TRAINS

Trains are the middle ground between planes and buses for both cost and time en route. Do your search at **sbb.ch,** and book your tickets at local train stations. All of Europe is on the same nifty system, so, for example, you can buy train tickets for travel within Italy while you're still in Paris.

Eurail Passes: Are They Worth It?

Eurail Passes are a good option for the organized traveler who knows when and where they want to go. They allow you to access as many train rides in as many countries as you decide for a flat rate (the rate covers a limited time period). Pass price depends on three factors:

- The number of countries in which it is valid

- The number of travel days (days in transit; not the duration of your stay) included (5, 10, 20, unlimited)

- The window of dates during which the pass is valid (3 weeks, 6 weeks, 2 months)

Minimize each of these factors to get the best rate. Consider how much time you'll be spending in each country. If, for example, you'll be traveling in Italy, Spain, and France, with a side trip to Amsterdam,

book the Eurail Pass for three countries only, paying retail for the short trip to Amsterdam from Paris.

Visit eurail.com to view the available options. I prefer to do my timetable research online and then book my train tickets in person at any train station. This ensures that I receive all applicable discounts and allows flexibility that I wouldn't get with the Eurail Pass.

BUSES

While buses are generally slower than trains and planes, they're often your cheapest option. I've found great bus connections to numerous cities departing daily across the Continent. If you sign up for an overnight bus trip, pack some hefty sleeping pills and eye covers. Keep your valuables in a money belt and wear it into the bus so you're not showing everyone your valuables before you go to sleep. Buses are generally safe, but thefts are not uncommon.

Some of my favorite bus line websites are **eurolines.com, orangeways.com, berlinlinienbus.de,** and **studentagencybus. com.** Buses are more popular in Central and Eastern Europe, and they provide a number of connections, some of which are as fast as rail travel.

RIDE-SHARING

The sharing economy has grown to include intercity drives across Europe. Luckily for us backpackers, there's a great website (carpooling.co.uk) where you can search for rides, post a needed ride, or jump on a trip last minute. This option has saved my hide more than once. Of course, there's always safety in numbers. If you have to travel alone, trust your gut—if something looks sketchy, don't get in the car.

CAR RENTAL

Renting a car can be expensive and frustrating. Planes, trains, and buses are often better choices. If you do want to rent a car, consider the following first:

- Most cars in Europe have manual transmissions.

- Parking is challenging and expensive and is regulated differently from one city to the next.

APPENDIX

- Historic city centers (where you're hopefully staying) are often restricted to special, licensed traffic.
- Signage may not be in English.
- Those under age 25 are obligated to purchase more expensive insurance.
- Gas runs US$8-10 per gallon.

- Most cars run on diesel. Fill up the tank with standard gas and you'll be springing for a new engine.
- Fine print in the rental contract. Get a good grasp of the accident insurance, when the car needs to be back, whether the tank needs to be full upon return, and whether or not there are additional costs if you take the car out of the country.

LOCAL TRANSPORTATION

Reading a bus or metro map in a foreign city can be confusing and frustrating, but technology has come to the rescue. Google Maps has integrated just about all public transportation systems and can recommend directions. I've included public transportation tips in each chapter.

TICKETS

Each city has its own system of ticket validation. I've outlined the exact process in each chapter, but the core concept is quite simple: After purchasing your ticket, you must validate it by time-stamping it. Tickets are generally time-based; validating starts the clock on your 30, 60, or 90 minutes of validity. You validate your ticket either on board or beforehand at one of the validation machines on the platform. There are hefty fines if you get caught with an unvalidated ticket—but don't let police officers take you to an ATM and force you to withdraw cash. Instead, insist on a paper ticket.

All cities offer multiday transportation tickets that pay for themselves after a couple of rides. Some sightseeing packages include local transportation as well. Do your research ahead of time, or speak to an attendant at a major station on arrival to see what multiday options are available.

METRO

As long as you know the name of your stop and can locate it on the metro map, you won't have any problems reaching your destination. As you enter into the metro, you will see signs for northbound, southbound, eastbound, or westbound platforms. Metro maps are oriented north-south-east-west. On the map, simply locate what station you're currently in and the station you wish to travel to, and go to the platform that gets you in the right direction. If there isn't a direct line between the two stations on the map, you'll need to transfer at the point where the two lines intersect.

BUS & TRAM

Bus and tram maps follow the same basic format. Locate where you are (usually printed in boldface) in the list of stops on the map. Buses (or trams) will go to every destination listed *below* the stop you're at. Everything above the stop has already been visited. If your desired stop isn't below your current station, you've got to find the stop for buses going in the opposite direction (usually but not always on the other side of the street).

UBER

Uber is active in a number of European cities, while in others, the taxi unions have blocked the company's access to the market. I mention whether Uber is active in each chapter.

I rely almost exclusively on two websites to find my accommodations: **hostelworld.com** and **airbnb.com.** Rather than searching by city, narrow your search to neighborhood. An inexpensive hostel might look great, but it might be well outside the city center. To make the most of your stay, pay a little bit more and stay in the thick of it rather than commute.

HOSTELS

I love hostels for their social scene, organized activities, and fun atmosphere. While you'll save money staying in a hostel, you may sacrifice quality sleep. In bigger dorms, people come and go throughout the night and day. If you're staying at hostels for the duration of your stay, invest in a good padlock—or, better yet, leave your valuables at home.

Hostel Booking Tips

- **Note the difference between professional photos and traveler shots.** The traveler shots show what the hostel is *really* like. The professional shots are the ones taken years ago when the hostel first opened.

- **See what amenities are included.** It may save you money to spring for the more expensive hostel if it includes towels, Wi-Fi, breakfast, and other amenities.

- **Read the reviews.** Watch out for fakes (good and bad). Some hostels review themselves favorably, and some review their competitors negatively.

AIRBNB

I use **airbnb.com** whenever I want peace and quiet. While this option lacks a social scene, I like having security and access to a kitchen, and the hosts are often keen to great bars, restaurants, and more. In cities like Paris, Airbnb can be an excellent value, while in cities like Prague and Budapest the value may be less: Hosts charge Western European rates when your money should go much further. Generally €50 will get you in a good double-occupancy room in most cities. Studio private apartments tend to go for €75 and up per night.

Airbnb Booking Tips

- Narrow your search by the type of accommodation you're comfortable with: entire apartment, private room, or shared room. A private room in a shared apartment will likely be cheaper than having an apartment to yourself. I stayed in a shared room once—only once, never again.

- Airbnb.com doesn't help you to organize search results by price. You'll have to click through several pages to ensure you're getting the best deal.

- There are hidden fees! At first, you define your budget, but Airbnb has devised a slick system that rounds up and shows you nice options for a few euros more than what you input. Fees include cleaning fees, service fees, and additional guest fees (displayed rates are often for one occupant only). Double-check the final price before booking and make sure it's still reasonable (some hosts charge as much as €80 for a cleaning fee!).

- Read between the lines and see if the apartment is just a moneymaker for the owner or if it's actually their home. Personally, I don't mind either way, but this is a factor for some travelers, depending on whether they want more or less interaction with their host. Read the reviews to anticipate whether the host's style will work for you.

- Pay attention to amenities like Wi-Fi and air-conditioning. Is the restroom private or shared?

- Look closely at the photos. Wide-angle lenses do wonders for the appearance of size of a room (look for the fish-eye effect).

- Don't hesitate to ask your host about special offers. It never hurts to inquire.

FOOD

Remember that not every meal of your stay needs to be French, Czech, Spanish, and so forth. Consider treating yourself to one or two local meals and filling the gaps with cheaper alternatives. In notoriously expensive London, Indian takeaway is an excellent budget option. Kebabs, sandwiches, and street food are cheap no matter where you go. Local supermarkets usually have

APPENDIX

everything you need for a relaxing picnic in the park.

Learn to recognize tourist traps. Don't eat at restaurants that are on the main square. If the restaurants have neon lights and menus in 10 languages in the windows, it's safe to assume the locals don't go there. Get off the main drags and find where the locals eat, and you'll pay the locals'—not the tourists'—price.

MOBILE DEVICES

With the rise in mobile technologies, travelers can stay better connected than ever.

A smartphone in your pocket—even if it's on Wi-Fi only mode—has really changed the backpacker experience. I usually purchase a local SIM card if I'm in any one country for more than a week. Otherwise, I rely on the free **Wi-Fi** at my hostel and in restaurants and bars.

I don't recommend purchasing **roaming plans** from your home provider for your entire time in Europe, as they're rarely a good deal. Many American providers are willing to temporarily suspend your account and drop the monthly price down to $10, effectively hibernating your plan until you return home.

Smartphones are a hot commodity, so keep them close. Consider finding a cheap phone to use while abroad. This way you stand to lose a lot less than your phone and everything on it while traveling.

European SIM Cards

You can purchase a European SIM card (the data chip within your phone) in the country you're visiting and top up as needed. With an unlocked smartphone, have the staff at the cell phone store plug in a SIM card. I've used **Vodafone** in most parts of Europe. SIM cards cost around €10 and come with €10 of credit. Opt for the pay-as-you-go plan, topping up by purchasing a scratch card from any convenience store. This method typically costs under €30 per month, whereas monthly plans can be upwards of €60 a month.

Apps

Your smartphone isn't just a camera for your trip abroad. Apps can go a long way toward enhancing your travel experience. **Skype** is a godsend for calling home easily and affordably. Pick a screen name for yourself and make a few practice calls before leaving home. **Facetime** is free while on Wi-Fi to others with an Apple device (and it works to and from anywhere in the world). See below for more of my favorite apps to use while traveling.

INTERNATIONAL CALLS

If dialing Europe from the United States, begin with the US international access code (011)—or, if you're dialing from a cell phone, replace the access code with a plus sign, which you get by holding down the 0. Next, dial the country code (each country has a specific one) of the country you're dialing. Next is a regional code, which is often a two-digit number, but sometimes is a single 0. Skip this when dialing internationally, but include it when dialing domestically. After the country code, the final phone number will be 9-10 digits.

CONVERTERS & ADAPTERS

Converters convert the electrical current so it doesn't blow out your electronics. Take a close look at whatever you're trying to plug in. If you see 110-220V, you *do not* need an electrical converter. If you only see 110V, you'll need a converter. In my experience, converters are not necessary for iPhones, MacBook Pros, and cameras (including SLRs).

Adapters adapt American plugs so that they can be plugged into European outlets. You'll need a continental adapter (with two round prongs) for continental Europe and a British adapter (with three rectangular prongs) in England, Scotland, Ireland, and Wales. Adapters are cheap. Purchase them before your trip for convenience.

TRANSPORTATION WEBSITES

Make use of helpful **flight search engines** (skyscanner.net, kayak.com, cheapoair.com, momondo.com), sites for booking **train travel** (sbb.ch) and **bus travel** (eurolines.com, orangeways.com, berlinlinienbus.de, and studentagencybus.com, renfe.com), and even a **ride-sharing** site (carpooling.co.uk).

TRANSPORTATION APPS

Airline apps like EasyJet are streamlined so you can book a flight on the fly with just a few taps. Similarly, **iRail** and **SBB Trains** let you search the Eurail database for train timetables. Much like a flight search engine, they let you prioritize by number of stops and also show the route on a map so you can make your journey as direct as possible.

Skyscanner

Global search engine that compares flights, though you can't use it to book directly.

Kayak

Impressively useful and cheap flight search engine. Use it for research, then book through the airline directly.

EasyJet

Book EasyJet flights directly.

Ryanair

Book Ryanair flights directly.

Aer Lingus

Book Aer Lingus flights directly.

iRail

Search the Eurail database for train timetables.

SBB Trains

Search the Eurail database for train timetables.

TripIt

Organize your flight travel, keeping confirmation numbers, rewards accounts, and other information handy.

ACCOMMODATIONS WEBSITES AND APPS

I rely on two websites for booking accommodations: **airbnb.com** and **hostelworld.com**, both of which have their own apps. **Booking.com** offers last-minute hotel options.

APPS FOR KEEPING IN TOUCH

WhatsApp

Free messages when connected to Wi-Fi. Set up an account and text away with any other friends who use the app.

Skype

Free and paid hybrid messaging and calling service that lets you video chat with fellow Skype users.

Facetime

Free video chatting while connected to Wi-Fi with other Apple device users.

Facebook Messenger

Dial or video call friends around the world for free.

Snapchat

Send short, self-deleting images and video updates.

WEBSITES AND APPS FOR MEETING PEOPLE

Meetup.com

Set up an account with Meetup and get the pulse on local events and gatherings tailored to your preferences. Whether you're looking to get involved in community service, sports, or hobbies, Meetup is a platform for broad and niche communities to get together and stay in touch.

Tinder/Bumble/Happn

Meeting new friends has never been easier. Thanks to the digital connection and dating platforms, you can swipe from the comfort of your hostel bunk, setting up dates with cute locals and fellow backpackers no matter where you find yourself (or for how long).

TRAVEL APPS

Weekend Student Adventures

My own freemium app provides a ton of on-the-go tips and tricks for more than a dozen of my favorite cities.

Rick Steves' Europe Audio Guides

Free, informative travel listening. Search and download all the subjects on your destinations before you leave on your trip.

XE Currency

Keep track of fluctuating conversion rates.

Mint

Balance your budget while abroad.

Venmo

A great app for paying friends back while on the road.

Duolingo

Learn basic and frequently used phrases in the local language while en route.

Hopper

Set up flight alerts before your trip.

Splittr

Bill-splitting app tailor-made for travel with small or large groups.

Google Translate

An excellent translation app you can speak or type into, helping to break down language barriers. Use the video feature to translate signs without any typing.

USEFUL PHRASES

CATALAN

English	Catalan	Pronunciation
Hello.	Hola.	**oh**-lah
Excuse me.	Perdó.	pehr-**doh**
Do you speak English?	¿Parles anglès?	**pahr**-lahs ahn-**glays**
Yes.	Sí.	see
No.	No.	noh
Please.	Si us plau.	see oos plow
Thank you.	Gràcies.	**grah**-see-ahs
Goodbye.	Adéu.	ah-**day**-ooh
How much does it cost?	¿Quant és?	kwahn es
Where are the toilets?	¿On estan els serveis?	ohn an-**stahn** ehls sehr-**vays**
I'd like...	Voldria.	vool-**dree**-ah
...a room	...una habitació	**ooh**-nah ah-bee-tah-see-**oh**
...a bed	...un llit	un yeet
...a ticket	...una entrada	oon-nah ahn-**trah**-dah
...a beer	...una cervesa	**ooh**-nah sahr-**veh**-sah
...wine	...vi	vee
Where is...	¿On està...	ohn ah-**stah**
...the train station?	...l'estació de tren?	lah-stah-see-**yo** dah tren
...the bus station?	...l'estació de bus?	las-stah-see-**yo** dah boos

CZECH

English	Czech	Pronunciation
Hello.	Dobrý den.	doh-**bree** den
Excuse me.	Promiňte.	**proh**-meen-tah
Do you speak English?	Mluvíte anglicky?	**mloo**-vee-teh **ahn**-glits-kee
Yes.	Ano.	**ah**-noh
No.	Ne.	neh
Please.	Prosím.	**pro**-seem
Thank you.	Děkuji.	**dyeh**-ku-yee
Goodbye.	Nashledanou.	**nah**-skleh-dah-now
How much does it cost?	Kolik to stojí?	**koh**-lek toh sto-**yee**
Where is the toilet?	Kde je záchod?	guh-**deh** yeh **zah-hod**
I'd like...	Rad(a) bych.	rahd bikh/**rah**-dah bikh
...a room	...pokoj	**po**-koy
...a bed	...postel	**pos**-tel
...a ticket	...lístek	**lees**-tek
...a beer	...pivo	**pee**-voh
...wine	...vína	**vee**-na
Where is...	Kde je...	guh-**deh** yeh
...the train station?	...nádraží?	**nah**-drah-zee
...the bus station?	...autobusové nádraží?	**ow**-toh-boo-soh-veh **nah**-drah-zee

DUTCH

English	Dutch	Pronunciation
Hello.	Hallo.	**ha**-low
Excuse me.	Pardon	**par**-don
Do you speak English?	Spreekt u Engels?	spreekt oo **en**-gels
Yes.	Ja.	ya
No.	Nee.	nay
Please.	Alsjeblieft.	alse-bleeft
Thank you.	Dank u wel.	dahnk oo vehl
Goodbye.	Doei.	doo-ie
How much does it cost?	Wat kost het?	vaht kost het
Where is the toilet?	Waar is het toilet?	var ees heht **twah**-leht
I'd like...	Ik wil graag...	eek vil ghraagh
...a room	...een kamer	ayn **kah**-mer
...a bed	...een bed	ayn bed
...a ticket	...een kaartje	ayn **kart**-yeh
...a beer	...een biertje	ayn biert-je
...wine	...wijn	vine
Where is...	Waar is...	var ees
...the train station?	...het station	het **stash**-yun
...the bus station?	...het bus station	het boos **stash**-yun

FRENCH

English	French	Pronunciation
Hello.	Bonjour.	bohn-**zhoor**
Excuse me.	Excusez-moi.	eggs-**cue**-say **mwah**
Do you speak English?	Parlez-vous anglais?	**par**-lay voo ahng-**lay**
Yes.	Oui.	wee
No.	Non.	nohn
Please.	S'il vous plait.	see voo play
Thank you.	Merci.	mehr-**see**
Goodbye.	Au revoir.	oh ruh-**vwah**
How much does it cost?	Combien?	cohm-bee-**ahn**
I'd like...	Je voudrais.	zhe **voo**-dray
...a room	...une chambre	oon **shahm**-bre
...a bed	...un lit	oon lee
...a ticket	...un billet	oon **bee**-yay
...a beer	...une bière	oone bee-**air**
...wine	...vin	van
Where is...	Ou est.	oo ay
...the train station?	...la gare	lah gar
...the bus station?	...la gare routière	lah gar root-**yehr**

GERMAN

English	German	Pronunciation
Hello.	Guten Tag.	**goo**-ten tahg
Excuse me.	Entschuldigung.	en-**shool**-di-gung
Do you speak English?	Sprechen Sie Englisch?	**spree**-ken-zee eng-lish
Yes.	Ja.	ya
No.	Nein.	nine
Please.	Bitte.	**bee**-ta
Thank you.	Danke.	**dahn**-ke
Goodbye.	Auf Wiedersehen.	auf **vee**-der-zay-ehn
How much does it cost?	Wie viel kostet es?	vee feel **kost**-et es
Where is the toilet?	Wo sind die Toiletten?	voh zint dee toy-**leh**-tehn
I'd like...	Ich möchte...	eekh **mukh**-te
...a room	...ein Zimmer	ain **zimm**-er
...a bed	...ein Bett	ain bett
...a ticket	...eine Karte	ain **kar**-teh
...a beer	...ein Bier	ain beer
...wine	...Wein	vine
Where is...	Wo ist...	voh eest
...the train station?	...der Bahnhof	der **bahn**-hof
...the bus station?	...der Busbahnhof	der **boos**-bahn-hof

HUNGARIAN

English	Hungarian	Pronunciation
Hello.	Szia.	**see**-yaw
Excuse me.	Bocsánat.	**boh**-chah-nawt
Do you speak English?	Beszész angolul?	**beh**-say-es **ahn**-go-lool
Yes.	Igen.	**ee**-gan
No.	Nem.	nem
Please.	Kérem.	**kay**-rehm
Thank you.	Köszönöm.	**koo**-sze-nem
Goodbye.	Viszlàt.	**vees**-lat
How much does it cost?	Mennyi?	**men**-yee
I'd like...	Kérnék/ Kérnénk.	**kayr**-nayk/**kayr**-naynk
...a room	...egy szobàt	eidge **so**-bot
...a bed	...egy àgyat	eidge adg-yacht
...a ticket	...egy jegyet	eidge **yeg**-yet
...a beer	...egy sör	eidge shohr
...wine	...bor	bor
Where is...	Hol van	hol van
...the train station?	...pàlyaudvar	**pah**-yood-var
...the bus station?	...buszpàlyaudvar	**boos**-pah-yood-var

ITALIAN

English	Italian	Pronunciation
Hello.	Buon giorno.	bwon **jor**-noh
Excuse me.	Permesso.	pear-**may**-soh
Do you speak English?	Lei parla inglese?	lay **par**-lah een-**gle**-zay
Yes.	Si.	see
No.	No.	noh
Please.	Per favore.	pear fah-**vor**-ay
Thank you.	Grazie.	**grah**-zee-ay
Goodbye.	Ciao ciao.	chow chow
How much does it cost?	Quanto costa?	**kwan**-toh **koh**-stah
Where is the toilet?	Dove la toilette?	doh-**veh** lah twah-**leh**-tay?
I'd like...	Vorrei...	voh-**ray**
...a room	...una camera	**oo**-nah **kam**-eh-rah
...a bed	...un letto	un let-toh
...a ticket	...un biglietto	oon bee-lee-**eh**-toh
...a beer	...una birra	**oo**-nah bee-rah
...wine	...vino	**vee**-noh
Where is...	Dove...	do-vay
...the train station?	... stazione	stah-zee-**oh**-nay
...the bus station?	...stazione autobus	stah-zee-**oh**-nay **ow**-toh-boos

SPANISH

English	Spanish	Pronunciation
Hello.	Hola.	**oh**-lah
Excuse me.	Perdone.	pehr-**doh**-nay
Do you speak English?	¿Habla usted inglés?	**ah**-blah oo-**sted** een-**glays**
Yes.	Sí.	see
No.	No.	noh
Please.	Por favor.	por fah-**bor**
Thank you.	Gracias.	**grah**-thee-ahs
Goodbye.	Adiós.	ah-dee-**ohs**
How much does it cost?	¿Cuánto cuesta?	**kwan**-toh **kwest**-ah
Where are the toilets?	Dónde están los servicios?	**dohn**-day ay-**stahn** lohs sehr-**bee**-thee-ohs
I'd like...	Me gustaría...	may goo-stah-**ree**-ah
...a room	...una habitación	**ooh**-nah ah-bee-tah-thee-**ohn**
...a bed	...una cama	**ooh**-nah **kah**-mah
...a ticket	...un billete	oon bee-**yeh**-tay
...a beer	...una cerveza	**ooh**-nah ther-**beh**-thah
...wine	...vino	**vee**-noh
Where is...	Dónde está.	**dohn**-day eh-**stah**
...the train station?	...estación de tren	eh-stah-thee-**ohn** day tren
...the bus station?	...estación de autobuses	eh-stah-thee-**ohn** day ow-tow-**boo**-sehs

INDEX

PHOTO CREDITS

Check out Andy's tour company

wsa WEEKEND STUDENT ADVENTURES
WSAEurope.com

KICK-ASS BUDGET TRIPS

✓ Guided & Unguided City Tour Options
✓ Amazing Hostels & Passionate Local Guides
✓ Skip-the-Line Sightseeing & Typical Cuisine
✓ Caving Expeditions, Cooking Classes & More!

3—10 Day Packages from €199 at WSAEurope.com

MSTERDAM **PARIS** BARCELONA **EDINBURGH** PRAGUE **ROME** BUDAPEST **KRAKOW**

= trips & tips at **wsaeurope.com!**

ANDY
STEVES
TRAVEL
PODCAST

TRAVEL • LIFESTYLE
ENTREPRENEURSHIP
— Subscribe, Like & Review on —
iTunes & Soundcloud

ANDY STEVES' EUROPE
Avalon Travel
A Hachette Book Group company
1700 Fourth Street
Berkeley, CA 94710, USA

Editor: Leah Gordon
Copy Editor: Brett Keener
Production and Graphics Coordinator: Lucie Ericksen
Graphics Assistant: Indi Ericksen
Interior Design: Hayden Foell
Cover Design: Faceout Studio, Lindy Martin
Map Editor: Mike Morgenfeld
Cartographer: Brian Shotwell
Proofreader: Ashley Benning
Indexer: Rachel Kuhn

ISBN-13: 978-1-63121-796-8

Printing History
1st Edition — 2016
2nd Edition — April 2018
5 4 3 2 1